LADY GREGORY'S JOURNALS

Volume 1

The Coole Edition
General Editors
T. R. Henn, C.B.E., Litt.D.
Colin Smythe, M.A.

The interior of Coole. Above: the drawing room. Below: the library.

LADY GREGORY'S JOURNALS

VOLUME ONE

BOOKS ONE TO TWENTY-NINE
10 October 1916–24 February 1925

edited by

Daniel J. Murphy

COLIN SMYTHE
GERRARDS CROSS
1978

The Complete Edition of the *Journals* first published in 1978 by Colin Smythe Ltd., Gerrards Cross, Buckinghamshire as the fourteenth and fifteenth volumes of the Coole Edition.

British Library Cataloguing in Publication Data

Gregory, Isabella Augusta, *Lady*
Lady Gregory's journals. – (The Coole edition; vol. 14).
Vol. 1: Books 1 to 29: 10 October 1916–24 February 1925
1. Gregory, Isabella Augusta, *Lady* – Biography
2. Women dramatists – Biography
I. Murphy, Daniel J
822'.8 PR4728.G5

ISBN 0-900675-91-8

Printed in Great Britain
by Redwood Burn Ltd.
Trowbridge and Esher

CONTENTS

FOREWORD

Lady Gregory, the youngest daughter of Dudley Persse, was born on 15 March 1852 in Roxborough, Co. Galway, a west of Ireland estate. Her father, born fifty years before in the same house, married as his first wife, Katherine, daughter of the First Viscount Guillamore in 1826. The Persses had three children before she died in 1829. In July 1833 Dudley Persse married Katherine's first cousin, Frances Barry, and had a further thirteen children, eight boys and five girls.

The Persses were a typical Irish landowning family—interested in the turf, the hunt, and their land, but with no interest at all in books, or the religion, poetry or language of the peasantry. It was a staunchly Protestant family—tradition has it that one of Lady Gregory's half-sisters was a "souper", who went from cottage to cottage trying to convert Catholics by offering them soup and food to become Protestant, a fact indicated by Lady Gregory in her autobiography.[1] However, this tradition resulted in the same charge being levelled at Lady Gregory, when she was defending Synge's *Playboy* in 1907, and later by George Moore, who had to retract this accusation. Wilfrid Scawen Blunt, writing of the Orangeism of the home, tells of the difficulty Lady Gregory had in persuading her mother to accept a visit from him. When he was reluctantly admitted to the house, Mrs. Persse talked only of Jesuit intrigue and of Popery; it was the first time she had had a Roman Catholic under her roof.[2]

There was so little family interest in creative writing that the house possessed neither a copy of Shakespeare nor a work on the literature of Ireland.[3] Had she been asked, as a young girl, to name an Irish poem, she would probably have said "Let Erin remember the days of old" or "Rich and rare were the gems she wore", poems she had heard some guest sing at the table, for there was no copy of Moore's works (other than *Lalla Rookh*) at Roxborough.[4] Reading was confined to the evenings when the family would gather in the drawing room to read the papers, and the children had works of an uplifting character.[5] What conversation there was the elders kept to themselves, and Augusta, "the youngest girl, was glad enough to be seen and not heard, to win what glimpses of literature I could from the few books that lay there".[6]

She was privately educated by an English governess who must have been pleased with her pupil's apt mind. But young Augusta's interests were fired by other sources than those referred to by her governess; the clandestine teaching of an old Catholic upstairs nurse, Mary Sheridan, who had lived in the family of the pardoned rebel, Hamilton Rowan, "tempered the strict Orangeism of the drawing room" and led her to read books never taught by her governess.[7]

By whatever means possible, Augusta augmented the interest in Ireland which the nurse had awakened in her. Thus when she earned sixpence for reciting from memory her Sunday Bible lesson, she would save the money until the children were taken, as a special treat, to Loughrea, a market town five miles from her home. There, she would go to a bookshop, and standing on tiptoe would hold up her sixpence "and the old stationer, looking down through his spectacles, would give me what I wanted, saying that I was his best customer for Fenian books".[8] Thus she came, by what few books she bought and by what information she could secure, to know poetry that was closer to the tradition of the country than Moore's sentimental verse. The "clandestine teaching" of her nurse, the nationalist sentiment of the Fenian books, and the physical beauty of the country around her home, all combined to awaken in her a romantic love of Ireland.[9] But this love of country, which remained with her all her long life and which was the source of all the attitudes expressed in her *Journals*, was difficult to sustain in a household which considered patriotism to be, in Dr. Johnson's words, "the last refuge of a scoundrel".[10]

Augusta's interest in the poetic tradition of the countryside was immensely stimulated when she learned that what she sought was the heritage of the country people all around her home. She searched among "farmers and potato diggers and old men in workhouses and beggars at our own door",[11] there she found a poetry which far surpassed any she had ever known. In an attempt to learn more of this poetry and tradition, she twice asked for permission to take Gaelic lessons. There was an old scripture-teacher who spent a part of his time near Roxborough teaching such pupils as he could find to read Gaelic, in the hope that they might turn to the Bible, the only book then printed in Irish. But her asking, "too timid with the fear of mockery", went unheeded.[12] She later attempted to learn Gaelic from her cousin, the Gaelic scholar Standish H. O'Grady, but she was frustrated on this occasion too, for her mother, thinking that O'Grady was interested in one of Augusta's elder sisters and disliking the marriage of cousins, forbade him the house.[13]

For a time it seemed that this life at Roxborough was to be all she would know of the world, but on 4 March 1880, she married, as his second wife, Sir William Gregory, a former Member of Parliament and Governor of Ceylon, and owner of Coole Park, one of the larger estates in Co. Galway. His first wife had died in Ceylon, and he had returned to Ireland and the family estate in 1877.

It would be difficult to overestimate the impact that the move from Roxborough to Coole had on Lady Gregory. She moved from a world of fox hunts and horse races into one of culture, learning and society. Sir William was a scholar, a sophisticated world traveller, and an intellectual with a life-long interest in books and art. At the time of his marriage he was a Director of the National Gallery in London, and most of his interests and friends were English. Blunt attributed Lady Gregory's anti-Home Rule opinions to her unionist, Protestant home and her husband's fright over the "no-rent" agitation. While it is certainly true that her husband's English attitudes reinforced the "Orangeism" Lady Gregory brought from Roxborough, his influence in other matters was liberalising.

Not all Sir William's acquaintances were Protestant and loyalist: through her marriage, she met Count Florimond de Basterot and Edward Martyn, who were both Roman Catholic and nationalist. Initially they provided a counterbalance to her family's and her husband's English orientation. The Count in particular, augmented the enlightened attitudes of such friends as Wilfrid Blunt by telling her about "French books, and French and Italian history and politics".[14] Thus her marriage brought about many liberalising influences: meeting influential friends in the world of politics and society, the visits to many parts of the world, and her charitable activities constituted the liberal education which she needed to counteract the narrow provincialism of her own home. Her marriage gave her the "quick enrichment" of travel and conversation.[15]

Lady Gregory spent the twelve years of her married life raising her son Robert, reading in the Coole Library, performing the duties of a mistress of a large Galway estate and a London house, helping the poor around Coole and in a South London parish, and travelling. She also tried, again unsuccessfully, to learn Gaelic, for she found the grammar difficult and her teacher languid, and she had to abandon the attempt.[16] After the death of

Sir William in 1892, her life continued in the same manner, though as society now interested her much less, she spent more of her time alone at Coole. She once more started to learn Gaelic, this time with the help of her son and a fine Irish Bible lent by Edward Martyn, and found the task "a light one in comparison with those first attempts".[17] To occupy herself in the long stretches of time which she spent alone at Coole, she first edited her husband's autobiography which went through two editions in 1894, the year of its publication, and then edited a selection of his grandfather's letters, *Mr. Gregory's Letter-Box, 1813–1830*. Her widowhood gave her "the leisure for observation necessary to give insight into character, to express and interpret it". Loneliness made her rich.[18]

In this manner Lady Gregory reorganised her life, spending more time at Coole; whatever English friends she retained were visited less frequently, and her home in London, which had been so much a part of her married life, was sold: thereafter she took rooms, or stayed with her nephew, Hugh Lane. This long residence at Coole, broken only by infrequent visits to London, enabled her to perfect her Gaelic, to renew her interest in folk traditions and folk poetry, and eventually to join the Gaelic League, which had been formed by Douglas Hyde to encourage its use as the native language of Ireland. She established a Gaelic class at the gate lodge, hoping to teach the local people the language of their forefathers.[19] She herself went to the Gaelic-speaking Aran Islands (at the same time as, but not meeting, J. M. Synge), increasing her knowledge and collecting folk-lore.

In addition to her work for the Gaelic League, she joined Sir Horace Plunkett's co-operative farm movement, the Irish Agricultural Organisation Society, which was designed to help Irish farmers combat their agricultural problems through a programme of "self-help by mutual help". She organised meetings for Plunkett in her district, hoping to ensure good management of the dairies, to raise the quality of the milk and butter, to lower prices of feed and manure, and to assure the members of firmer, better markets. Not only did she organise co-operative meetings, but she also personally appealed, in "Ireland Real and Ideal", to the English Government to supply organisers and experts and to aid the movement financially. The Government grant in answer to a former request, she wrote, was to supply two dairy inspectors and one dairymaid: "Thirty thousand farmers have learned that the Chief Secretary's fair words have neither buttered nor bettered their parsnips. They are quiet still, because growth takes place best in quiet, or because for the moment they have forgotten their power."[20]

These twin interests in the Gaelic League and the I.A.O.S., together with her continued interest in the folk traditions around her, gradually changed Lady Gregory from an anti-Home Ruler to a firm nationalist.

Her interests in Irish affairs changed in scope when she met the poet William Butler Yeats at Edward Martyn's home in August 1896. Yeats talked to her there, in the rooms she took in Queen Anne's Mansions, Westminster, and later at Duras, (Count de Basterot's home at Kinvara, on the Co. Galway coast, north of Coole), of his hopes for a theatre in London where he could produce verse plays. Lady Gregory persuaded him to give them in Dublin, and between them, they convinced Edward Martyn to give up a proposed German production of his *Heather Field*, and join Yeats in a Dublin performance.

Their plans for a national theatre in Ireland began to mature and in 1898, Yeats, Martyn and Lady Gregory sent out a formal letter asking for a guarantee of £300 to carry the theatre through its first three years. Lady Gregory put up the first guarantee of £25, but in the event, all the expenses were born by Edward Martyn.[21]

Yeats and the theatre soon filled more and more of Lady Gregory's "long spaces of time alone". Sometimes he would lack words for whatever play he was writing during his stays at Coole, and Lady Gregory would supply them. From such casual contributions, her share in Yeats's plays soon increased to the point where Yeats was giving her credit as co-author. Writing of the help that Lady Gregory gave him in *Cathleen ni Houlihan*, Yeats describes how he had conjured up the plot in a dream, but when he looked for words, found he "could not create peasant dialogue that would go nearer to peasant life than the dialogue in *The Land of Heart's Desire* or *The Countess Cathleen*". Although Lady Gregory had not yet written a play, her folk-lore collecting had given her a good feeling for the speech of the country people in the west of Ireland, and a greater understanding of their mind.

After the success of the short seasons of the first few years, a permanent company was established to provide plays throughout the year, at a theatre and with money supplied by Miss Annie Horniman: this was the Abbey Theatre. It opened on 27 December 1904, with Lady Gregory as its Patent holder. Throughout the rest of Lady Gregory's life the Theatre became one of her chief preoccupations, both in its day to day running, getting finance for it, writing plays for it, and in the general policy decisions and choice of plays. The Abbey Theatre is therefore one of the central concerns of her Journals, because through all those years, the problems and responsibilities fell chiefly on her shoulders. She had to cope too with the temperaments of the actors, actresses and fellow directors, planning performances, placating and encouraging playwrights—all these run through the Journals.

By the time the Journals begin in 1916, the Abbey had fallen on difficult times. By the terms of its Patent, it could only put on foreign classics and plays by native Irishmen, and they were always desperate for new plays to supplement those already in their repertory. That is why the arrival of Sean O'Casey was so important to the Abbey: his popular plays enabled it to recapture the audience lost through the constant repetition of old plays, and they provided the financial stability the Theatre so desperately needed.

One of the other concerns of Lady Gregory throughout the latter part of her life was the survival of Coole. Lady Gregory was not its owner, for it had been left to Robert by Sir William, and on his death in 1918 it became his widow's. Margaret Gregory was left it under the terms of the simple service Will that Robert had executed. However, under the terms of Sir William's Will, Lady Gregory had "so far as the rules of law will allow" the right to live at Coole for the rest of her life, a fact that Margaret Gregory appeared to forget. The Journals relate how Lady Gregory fought to retain Coole for her beloved grandchildren until they had grown up, and Richard, as son of the house, could choose what to do with it. So she was concerned about its finances, upkeep, and maintaining its cultural tradition. Eventually she bowed to the inevitable and the Estate was sold to the Forestry Commission, though she lived there until the end of her life.

Another major concern of the Journals is Margaret and the grandchildren, Richard, Anne and Catherine. She did everything in her power to make their stays at Coole as enjoyable as possible. She took them to the sea at Burren; bought everything her financial circumstances allowed her to that would make them happy, and ensured that Coole was always welcoming to them, as well as a place they could bring their friends to, so that it became more of a home to them than anywhere else.[22]

The Journals were begun, originally, to record her efforts to regain the Lane Pictures for Dublin. The Lane controversy, which is mentioned throughout the Journals, has a long and involved history. Hugh Lane, Lady Gregory's favourite nephew, began collecting a group of French impressionist paintings, which he originally offered to Dublin, on the condition that they built a gallery to house them. When the City failed to provide one, Sir Hugh Lane, in his Will of 1913, bequeathed them to the National Gallery in London. They were at that time on loan to the National Gallery, but were not on display, and were relegated to the Gallery's basement, which incensed Lane. He changed his mind and in an unwitnessed Codicil, dated 3 February 1915, he left the paintings to Dublin. This Codicil was written on the eve of a journey to the U.S.A., and he was returning on the *Lusitania* when it was torpedoed and sunk on 7 May 1915. All the evidence points to the fact that Lane believed that his Codicil was legally valid even though it was not witnessed: certainly all the comments he made while he was in the U.S. indicate this. Whatever the merits of the case, and Dublin's right to the pictures was overwhelming, the British Government and the National Gallery refused to let the pictures be returned. Lady Gregory tried cajolery, petitions, and persuasion of the most important influential people she knew, to have the Lane pictures returned to Dublin, but to no avail. (In 1959 a compromise solution was agreed whereby the pictures were divided into two groups which alternated between London and Dublin for five year periods. This arrangement is still in operation.)[23]

The Journals are important for a number of reasons; social, political and artistic. On a social level, they record, not only through Lady Gregory's eyes, but through those of her household staff, the most important events in the area round Gort, the nearest market town to Coole. These included cattle driving, and land disputes, which were frequently vocal and sometimes violent, with the parish priest often intervening to settle them. The most shocking parts of the Journals deal with the Black and Tans, British ex-soldiers who were used to terrify the country in an attempt to suppress the drive for an independent Ireland. They used burnings, beatings, maiming and killings, one of the most brutal of which was the murder of the two Loughnane boys whose bodies were so mutilated that they could not be recognised. Lady Gregory also records the house burnings that occurred if a complaint was made about the behaviour of any of the Black and Tans.

The Journals record Lady Gregory's friendship—one of the most important of her life—with W. B. Yeats. Coole was a place of tranquillity, and Yeats spent many summers there, writing, talking, and indulging in one of his few hobbies, fishing. Lady Gregory's chance meeting with Yeats at Tillyra Castle, as guests of Edward Martyn, brought about one of the most enduring literary relationships in modern literature, but as they were both concerned with the Abbey Theatre and the fight for the return of the Lane pictures, a great deal of the material in the Journals about the Yeats–Lady Gregory relationship deals more with the Abbey and the pictures than anything else.

Lady Gregory contemplated publishing the Journals several times when she believed that she needed additional financial aid to run Coole, but each time she rejected the idea, and it was only at the end of her life that they were handed over to Putnams. The following Journals are exactly what Lady Gregory then contemplated publishing.

DANIEL J. MURPHY

A NOTE ON THE TEXT

Lady Gregory's Journals exist in two major versions; one is a holograph and the other a typescript that Lady Gregory typed and retyped during the latter part of her life. The holograph version consists of forty four "books", actually "penny notebooks". None of these "books" deal with any definite time period: when the notebook was filled, Lady Gregory simply started a new one, often noting the time covered on the cover or first page. As the notebooks progressed, Lady Gregory began to pin material to the pages, so they became extremely unwieldy.

The Journals were purchased, as part of the Lady Gregory Archives, by the Berg Collection of The New York Public Library. On their receipt, the Curator of the Berg Collection decided to remove all the pinned material so that the notebooks could be used by scholars.

The typescript version, upon which this edition of the Journals is based, corresponds with the holograph version except in minor details, details that Lady Gregory either omitted because they might embarrass someone living, or added where the original had the letters XYZ. The typescript therefore, represents all that Lady Gregory wished to preserve of the Journals that she began in 1916.

It is interesting to note that there are additions to the typescript. There are some notes in W. B. Yeats's hand (which are identified as such in the text, or the notes) and some expansions of initials, or changes made by Lennox Robinson when he was preparing his selection in the early 1940s (marked by an asterisk in this edition). In the present edition mis-spellings of names have been corrected (for example, Lyle Donoughy to Donaghy), though one variant has been left as typed: Sean O'Casey is often referred to as Casey, just as Lady Gregory would do when talking of him. Where she has typed out the same passage twice, the shorter passage has been deleted, but in all other cases the text is as Lady Gregory typed it, except when punctuation needed tidying, where it has been made consistent. Spelling mistakes, caused mainly by typing errors that Lady Gregory rarely corrected – she expected whoever was going to edit the text to do that – have been rectified: to have used [sic] in all these cases would have been absurd.

ACKNOWLEDGEMENTS

To the memory of John Gordan, former Curator of the Berg Collection of The New York Public Library; my thanks to Lola Szladitz, present Curator, for her unfailing kindness; Kay Ryan, for her many kindnesses while she was with the F.R.A.P.; James Tobin, Chief of the Reference Room of the N.Y.P.L.; Joseph Mask, Book Delivery Division and Alf Mac Lochlainn and the staff of the National Library of Ireland.

My thanks to the following for permission to quote letters in this volume: to the Society of Authors for the Bernard Shaw Estate, The Fitzwilliam Museum for Wilfrid Scawen Blunt, to Mr. J. C. Medley for George Moore, to Mrs. Aileen Bodkin for Thomas Bodkin, to the Society of Authors on behalf of Mrs. Iris Wise for James Stephens, to Michael B. Yeats and Anne Yeats for W. B. Yeats.

I have not been able to trace the present copyright holders of a number of the letters in this volume, and I should be most grateful if those who have not been approached for permission to publish would get in touch with Colin Smythe Ltd.

I am especially grateful to Colin Smythe who filled in gaps in the notes, corrected others, and executed his duties as a publisher and saved me some embarrassing moments. To Colin, my profoundest gratitude.

Daniel J. Murphy

BOOK ONE

I wrote from Lindsey House, Cheyne Walk on 2 November, 1916: in a letter that later became a diary.

I have been here three weeks on this business of trying to get the pictures out of the National Gallery's hands here, for Ireland. A troublesome business, ups and downs, waiting on other people and so on.

A few days after the Codicil had been found I went, taking a copy of it, to see Lord Curzon,[1] the most active of the London Trustees and the one who appreciates most the French pictures. He would of course like to keep them, but said he thought Hugh's wishes so clearly expressed, ought to be respected, and he would say that, when the time came, to the other Trustees. He wrote to me on 1 June "mentioned today to the National Gallery Board the subject which you had been good enough to bring before me the evening before. I think the right thing would be for the executors to address them formally through solicitors and lay the whole case before them". And he repeated this in a letter in the autumn, on 17 September, 1915.

But in the autumn of 1916, having heard privately that the London Trustees had the full intention of keeping the pictures, I came over to London.

OCTOBER, 1916. Having arrived at Lindsey House I wrote a letter to Lord Curzon, asking if I could see him about the Lane pictures. I took my note first to the Air Board and saw X.Z.[2], who said I had better leave it at Curzon's house, as he wasn't there that day, had several important functions, a debate in the Lords and a committee on something else. He said Curzon thinks a great deal of his position as a trustee of the N.G. and will put off any war business if there is a meeting there. His account of Curzon is that he is really a clever man, he has never met anyone so quick at seeing the weak point in a case (my poor statement!). They don't like him in the Air Office however because he is very inconsiderate, very lazy, and very untruthful. "We don't mind his telling lies but we mind his thinking that we believe them."

He is also much taken up with a South American widow he is supposed to be engaged to (I heard of her elsewhere as asking people's opinion as to whether she ought to marry him). She has sailed for South America now, and there is a wireless everyday to the Air Board to say how the ship is faring!

So I left my letter at 1, Carlton House Terrace, and in spite of all his functions and engagements, I had an answer that evening.

10 OCTOBER, 1916. "Dear Lady Gregory, I am afraid it is useless my seeing you. For the matter is not in my hands, nor at this moment even in the hands of the Board. They are waiting to be advised by their legal advisers and in the interim it would not be right for any individual Trustee to intervene. Yours sincerely, Curzon."

(Waiting for) legal advice means that they stick to legality, so that is a fight!

I had gone to Mr. Bird the lawyer in whose hands the will is, before I went to Curzon, to find out when the pictures would legally become the property of the London N.G. He said I might assume they were now their property, although the business is not actually through the Courts.

First I wrote a statement of our case, that I might ask for signatures to support it in case of publication.

Very few—two writers, G. B. Shaw and Yeats, two politicians, Redmond[3] and Carson, one Irish artist, Orpen.[4]

It was hard to begin, Parliament was just opening, Birrel[5] who I had looked to for help was away. Still one must do something for a beginning so I went with Yeats to the House of Commons, asked for a Dublin member Alderman Byrne who Mrs. Duncan, present Manager of Dublin Modern Gallery had written about, saying he was most zealous about the pictures and anxious to help me. After a long search he was found. He was amiable but inattentive, jumping up to greet friends and interrupted me once to say a reporter of the *Irish Independent* was looking very hard at me (a paragraph appeared next day saying that Lady Gregory had been seen in the House of Commons in earnest conversation with Mr. Byrne accompanied by her secretary—Yeats!). Then he read the statement and said airily he would get Redmond's signature—and Carson's—*and* all the eight Dublin members'! A shock—but hard to refuse as it is so much a Dublin question—the building is anyhow. So I went off leaving the statement with him and like Ali Baba adding chalk marks in Bagdad I wrote off to A.E.[6] and H. Plunkett[7] for their names to help to swamp the Dublin M.P's. Both gave their name willingly.

Then I wrote to Bernard Shaw and he came to see me. He began by saying that when he had first heard of the matter that it was hard to get butter out of a dog's mouth. However when he read the statement he thought the case a very strong one and signed. I asked if he would write in support of it if it should come to a fight. He said he had nowhere to write now, that his quarrel with the *New Statesman* had taken his name off the list of directors. However he might write in the *Nation* if Massingham will take it but papers are very shy of him now. He had been asked to write an article for the *Manchester Guardian* American number, but it was returned with the editor's apologies and a cheque for ten guineas. This he sent back saying he was much obliged for the rejection as he could get a higher price from a New York paper. He recommended an amiable appeal to Lord Curzon but withdrew that when I told him of his mendacities. However he was cheering and as always kind. I asked if Kilsby his chauffeur had been conscripted, he says, no, he was written to but wrote to say he had put £50 into War Loan and would have to withdraw that if he was called up and has heard nothing since. Charlotte (Mrs. Shaw) has a bad knee and he is kept in the country to poultice it with a sort of putty every day.

On my way to dine at the Royal Hospital on Sunday evening I called on Orpen and got his signature. He looked pale and low, in khaki, has been working "as a third-class clerk" in the Office but has just heard he may be sent to Macedonia next week. (Birrell's first visit?)

I had written a note to Mr. Birrell and he came to see me and I set the case before him. He was entirely on our side, said he didn't see how the Trustees could think of keeping them—that the codicil would be valid in Scotland "and in most intelligent countries". He didn't think an Act of Parliament would be necessary, thought it would be enough for them to apply to the Courts for leave to transfer the bequest. He made some slight alterations in my statement, and advised me to send it myself with a letter to the Trustees, that I had an indisputable right to do this, having been named as Trustee by Hugh. He advised an amiable letter in the first place. I said it was good of him to take an interest in Ireland still, and he said he was so glad to do so on a subject that wasn't blood and bones! Madame Vandervelde at Yeats' suggestion asked me to lunch to meet Robert Ross,[8] and Adye, editor of the *Burlington*, and Clutton Brock[9] Art critic of *The Times*. There was general conversation at lunch. Brock had written the note in *The Times* saying John's exhibit at the Academy is the best piece of decorative work done by an Englishman. He thinks he will go far in that way but doesn't care for his portraits. [They talked of "Mr. Britling".[10] "Heinrich" had really been a tutor to Wells' children and is about the best thing in the book. Brock (supposed to be a great churchman) spoke of Bishops as all looking either vulgar or pathetic.] After lunch I spoke about the pictures and all were sympathetic. Brock said the London Trustees wouldn't mind parting with them because they don't know a good picture when they see it, and Ross said they would be afraid to put them up because they would show up the badness of the pictures they had been buying. All promised help if possible. Ross said he would see Treasury people about it.

A few days after this I had a letter from Robert Ross

40, Half Moon St.,
24 October, 1916.

Dear Lady Gregory,

I have seen a good many people in regard to Hugh's codicil. I have studied the constitution of the London National Gallery in regard to the functions of the Trustees and I have consulted two barristers. I trust you will not think I am a depressing friend but I do not believe it is possible *except by an Act of Parliament* for the Trustees to repudiate the bequest except on the ground that the pictures were forgeries and quite worthless. Amiable dispositions towards yourself or Hugh's memory or Ireland cannot, as far as I see, be of any avail. Supposing for the sake of argument that the Trustees and the Treasury were moved by your appeal, and illegally handed over the pictures to Ireland, it would be open to any tax-payer to bring an action against the Trustees for breach of trust, but I don't believe for a single moment that the Trustees will entertain the idea for a moment, however sympathetic they may feel towards yourself. They have been subjected to severe criticism both in Parliament and the Press and they would hardly subject themselves to such a risk of further and (from the English point of view) justifiable attack out of mere sentiment. I will try to come in on Thursday as you so kindly suggest. Unless my visit is postponed I am due to stay with the Asquiths next Saturday and I will speak to the P.M. on the subject if he is there, but I know he will express no opinion without consulting the permanent officials and Lord Curzon. Very sincerely yours,

Robert Ross.

This was a blow, he had evidently seen Witt. I was very cast down. I walked to Birrell's but he was out, and left a card saying I was still in trouble over the pictures. Next day I was just writing to Margaret telling her of this rebuff when Birrell walked in. I showed him the letter and he was very indignant and said "Ross has been got at". He still thinks it would be "a shameful transaction" and says "if they don't give way to politeness you must throw mud at them". I said we were well able to do that! I told him of McColl's visit and he said it was an extraordinary thing that a biographer should go against the wishes of the man whose life he was writing. He says an Act of Parliament, if it doesn't meet much opposition, wouldn't be very expensive as we needn't engage lawyers. Finally, seeing in Ross's letter that he was going to the Asquiths' he said "I'll write to the Prime Minister[11] himself before he gets there".

This cheered me up and later in the evening I went to see G.B.S. (about the theatre) and told him of ups and downs. He was amused at the refusal being put on the ground of the state of Ireland and London being safest and said that would be a reason for seizing all our possessions. And as to a tax-payer taking proceedings against the Trustees, that, he said, was pure humbug, that the tax-payer would have to come into Court and prove that the loss of the pictures was a personal loss and injury to him; and then the pictures would have to be investigated, to prove that they might have been of benefit to his moral nature. I think he will be very helpful in throwing mud. Altogether it was a more comforting day.

Having written a letter to the Trustees, I went to the National Gallery and saw Mr. Holmes the new Director, to ask who it should be sent to and if I should send a separate letter to each Trustee. He told me to address it to the Secretary and said he himself would guarantee that all the Trustees should see it before the Board Meeting. He was evidently sympathetic (doesn't like Witt I fancy) but said he couldn't give an opinion, it was not his place. I asked on what ground they were likely to refuse and he said they claimed that London was safer than Dublin for them. I said I didn't see that, for we are over our Rising[12] and London still has Zeppelins. "Well" he said, "it would be very much based on the state of Ireland". (In fact they are counting on our unpopularity for the moment to get sympathy).

McColl came to talk over Hugh's *Life* and stayed two and a half hours. I spoke of the pictures and he said the Trustees would, he believed, keep them. I said that was hard, that he would see in doing the book that Hugh had spent many years of his tragically shortened life in trying to serve Dublin in making this Gallery and it had been his wish at the end. He could only say that "Dublin has got a big bequest already". He didn't want to talk of it (he, Witt and Aitken[13] of the Tate are great friends) but I told him I hoped his book would end with a note that Hugh's wishes had been carried out.

A letter from Byrne M.P. via Dublin and Mrs. Duncan, saying he couldn't remember my address (given him on my card) but wished me to know that the copy of the statement signed by Redmond had been lost before it reached Sir E. Carson[14]. . . . T. Bodkin came here one day and said that Byrne was a low little publican and quite untrustworthy. But Bodkin, who wanted to be made Director of the Dublin National Gallery (quite incompetent), has a good many stones in his sling. He had brought one of the N.G. (Dublin) Trustees, fat Mr. Waldron who, when he saw the Titian portrait of Baldassare, asked if it was by Lancret (he, Bodkin, told me none of the Trustees know anything at all about pictures) and he spent his time telling Waldron little spiteful things about Langton Douglas the new Director, an unpopular man but a real expert. Bodkin has been supplied through the *Freeman's Journal* and Parliamentary party with a place instead of the N.G. at £100 a year more, £600, on the Charity Commission. It is necessary to have two Commissioners, one Protestant, one Catholic (and whoever leaves money in charity has the pleasure of knowing these salaries are the first charge on it). I showed him my statement and his only suggestion was that Dillon's[15] name should be asked for and that the paragraph about John Quinn[16] should be taken out on the double ground that "he has a very bad name over here because of having supported Casement" and that "no one in England has ever heard of him". I didn't think much of Mr. Bodkin.

Langton Douglas is indiscreet and Holmes told me he had written to the Trustees asking if they were getting a Continental Gallery as otherwise the pictures would come to us. They were indignant, said it wasn't his business to write or theirs to answer him. It was this I think that caused the idea of a Continental Gallery to consolidate. Yeats has been told as a secret that they had been given money for one. Douglas says Duveen told him they were going to build an addition to the Tate for it. Alec Martin thinks that Duveen has probably given the money himself.

Alec Martin is very sympathetic and doing his best. He wrote to Robert Ross proposing that English artists should sign a protest saying that honour should lead the Trustees to give up the pictures. Ross didn't answer but he met him later at lunch at Adye's and then he said "he couldn't as a beneficiary under the will write anything".

Hugh left him £100 and this is his gratitude. Martin told him that was the very reason he should write. Adye promised to write in our support in the *Burlington*. This was after Ross had seen Witt for his second letter was in a different tone.

I wrote 30 October to Sir E. Carson, stating the case and asking his help. He answered yesterday.

I was disappointed at this, he doesn't seem interested and I don't want to force myself upon him. So yesterday evening I telephoned from Kelly's studio, where I was for tea, to ask if Lady Leslie was at home and as she was, I went to see her—and in such pouring rain!—knowing she knew Carson and his wife. She was very nice and said she would do what she could, that she would send Sir John to see Carson at once as they are such friends. That she herself, though she is for Ulster, is also for Redmond, so wouldn't have so much influence but she will try the "terrain" and see Lady Carson. So when I got home I sent her off the statement she had asked for, and I hoped for the best. Meanwhile Yeats has seen Drey who promises to support us in *Manchester Guardian*, and I have asked A.E. to be ready with a letter for *The Times*, and Shaw for the *Nation*, and we must secure Garvin[17] of *The Observer*.

9 NOVEMBER. On Saturday evening, the day after I had been to the Leslies'; Mr. Bailey came in unexpectedly as we were at dinner and stayed to dine. He promised to go and see Carson whom he knows and thought I had done very well so far. We had a long theatre talk and we made an amicable arrangement that Shaw's plays are to be put off for the present and Miss O'Neill is to come over for December in Irish plays that we may get up the old repertory.

Bailey came again yesterday to look at the handsome tables I want him to keep for the gallery and said he had found Sir E. Carson very much interested about the pictures, and ready to help, especially about getting a private Bill through if necessary. So that is all right and all I can do for the present. I feel quite out of work.

Paul Harvey came to dine Friday and said their difficulty in the Air Board is that Curzon is so disliked by four men out of every five that it is almost impossible to get anything he takes up through. That may help us against him in the picture question. Curzon's Secretary showed him a letter in answer to one he (C) had written to his housekeeper, asking an explanation of more bacon having been used in the servant's hall that week than the week before! A good example to us, but we haven't Air Boards to look after!

[A. Martin said he had been having a correspondence with Curzon about the cleaning of a picture. Curzon said the cleaner,

Rayard, had charged too much as it was a small picture, £4. A. Martin answered that the size of the picture had nothing to do with it, but its condition. It had taken the cleaner a week, and had to be backlined as well. But he said the price to be given was a matter for Curzon, not for him. C. answered that he only gave his usual cleaner £1 and thought that enough.]

An article in *Irish Times*[18] today on the resolution passed by the Corporation asking for return of the pictures.

10TH. Steer came in yesterday evening. I didn't ask him what he had heard at McColl's, but he was not so sympathetic as before. He said "Well, I hope you'll get the pictures but if you don't I'll have great pleasure in looking at them here." I said "No friend of Hugh's could have pleasure in looking at them in London knowing they were kept against the wish of the owner". He said "If it was his real wish". I think the Witt group must be trying to get up a case against that. But Mrs. Duncan has written that just before he left Dublin for America he told her he intended to bring the pictures back and re-hang them there.

A rather depressing letter from Langton Douglas; he says "One thing I do know, there are certain Members of the Board of the English N.G. who have formed themselves into a kind of Committee and it is their intention to keep the Lane pictures and to put them into a new room at the Tate Gallery."

12TH. I felt low over this (or perhaps it was the knowledge of a new air battle that made me down-hearted). I went to call on Birrell and ask if there was anything more I could do before the Board Meeting. He was very cheerful, said he could not imagine the Trustees holding on to them. He had spoken to many people, among them John Morley and Lord Courtney and all said the same thing, that it was inconceivable. I stayed for an hour chatting with him. He said the engagement was off between Curzon's daughter and Benson's son. "She doesn't like him"; and knowing that they are perhaps the two most dangerous of the Trustees and a rift would be useful, I said "That's splendid" so heartily that he burst out laughing.

I lunched with the Shaws. Granville Barker there in khaki looking very well but saying he has given up the stage, that no one wants you to do anything but only to talk about it. He was amused when I told him of the ladies who said when I asked about one of his lectures "It doesn't matter what he said, he looked divine". Shaw had had letters from Keogh[19] begging him to press for his plays to be put on but had answered "Lady Gregory has me on a string and I can't do anything without her leave".

14TH. A letter from Robert. And in the evening a wire saying he was safely through Friday's big battle—a great relief. I had felt very downhearted and tried to persuade myself it was about the pictures. A fidgety day, about letting the house for Margaret. And I went to the National Gallery with some notes to add to my letter and Holmes was making up a lecture and only saw me for a minute but said the notes were worth sending in. Very tired at night. Lady Leslie had called to tell me she had been working up Lady Carson about the pictures and also that the Duchess of Connaught[20] was very anxious to meet me. She wants to settle a day.

16 NOVEMBER. I received today the Trustees' letter or their Secretary's . . . "The Trustees of the National Gallery are at present in consultation with His Majesty's Treasury as to their position in regard to the questions raised by you concerning the Will of the late Sir Hugh Lane and I am to add this, as soon as the conclusion of their consultation is attained, my Board will have the honour of communicating with you again".

What one wants to know is whether they have asked the Treasury to help them to keep the pictures or to help them to give them up. I went round to Birrell and he thought it good on the whole knowing that the Treasury is already "salted". He will go round and see McKenna to find out what is going on. If the Trustees are well inclined, well and good. I asked what it would be best to do if it is war, whether a letter in the Press or a question in Parliament. He said certainly a question in Parliament if we get some important person to ask it. I suggested Sir Edward Carson and he said "Yes, his forbidding and severe countenance would give it weight." I feel pretty hopeful on the whole and was able to go lightheartedly to buy toys for the children at the Disabled Soldiers' Workshop.

Yesterday I spent between Putnam's and Murray's, both wanting my *Visions and Beliefs*,[21] English rights. I inclined to Putnam, the Murray house is getting very sleepy.

19TH. Ayot St. Lawrence. A letter from Langton Douglas yesterday impatient to be at the Trustees.

I lunched with the Shaws at 10, Adelphi Terrace. Mr. and Mrs. Parry there, she was Miss Gertrude Bannister who had been turned out of a school for being Casement's cousin but this had led to her marriage so it was all for the best. There was some talk at lunch about spiritualism. G.B.S. said his mother had been very much given to table-turning and that the spirit used to come who gave his name as Matthew Heffigan, a name he has used later in *John Bull*, and who was a most awful liar. They tried to verify some of his statements and they were always false. His mother, however, went on quite happily. G.B.S. himself became an adept at cheating at séances and gave no belief to anything in them. He says his mother's real love was for gardens, that he used to say that if he were run over by a dray she would say "Oh poor fellow" but if a beautiful rose had been crushed she would go out of her mind with grief.

We came on here in snow but the house is warm and bright with fires in every room and pots of chrysanthemums. They told me of Clutton Brock's lecture on art. G.B.S. says that he is in the hands of a little Morris gang and says what he is told without understanding it. He was asked questions after his lecture and crumpled up. He had abused "machine-made ornament", and G.B.S. got up and asked whether he meant by that machine-made or machine-duplicated ornament. He said he didn't know and G.B.S. said that made all the difference because the machine is capable of making beautiful ornament (he interpolated a description of one which can form ornament by sand subjected to musical vibrations) but the duplication of ornament is a very different thing. And that the work of the Kelmscott Press is largely machine work, there is only one copy of each book, the Chaucer for instance, which is from the individual hand, all the rest are duplications. Then a lady at the back of the room stood up and asked Brock whether it was not a fact that what made the Kelmscott Chaucer[22] so great was its being the product of one single great man. Brock said he didn't quite know, perhaps Mr. Shaw would say. Shaw said that the type had been invented by Morris and the drawings were by Burne Jones, and that they had been reduced to proper size by Catterson Smith; and that perhaps Chaucer himself had had something to do with the book; and then the lady sat down. He says Morris began by trying to get dyes as pure and bright as on a pack of cards but that they were not so permanent as the intermediate tones which he had to adopt but it wasn't because he liked them best. He was indignant one day with a lady who came to look at things in his shop and said they were "too bright". He said "If you want dirt Ma'am, you must go and look for it in the mud". Manners were not his strong point. He was called from his work one day to see a Bishop who wanted to give an order for stained glass and insisted on seeing Mr. Morris himself, and he burst into the shop saying "Where's that bloody Bishop"? G.B.S. said once: "What do you want with wall-papers? The best thing to do with a wall is to whitewash it", and Morris said: "You are quite right". He was outgrowing his early ideas but his followers stuck to them.

[Clutton Brock had protested against the Victorian habit of bedding out and especially denounced lobelia saying people only grew it to show they had a greenhouse. "Well, lobelia doesn't need a greenhouse. It is an annual and is sowed from year to year in any little frame or shelter and it is in lovely shades of blue, the rarest colour in flowers."]

Last night G.B.S. read me a story he had written. He had been asked for one for a Gift Book to be sold for the Belgian Children's Milk Fund and had refused, saying the Society of Authors objected to these Gift Books. But the lady came again to say she had got leave from the Society of Authors to print it, if she gave them a percentage. He was quite taken aback and said he hadn't promised it, but in the end sat down and wrote it straight off. Then the lady brought it back in a few days to say she wouldn't put it in the Gift Book but Mrs. Whitelaw Reid had offered £400 for it to put in the *New York Tribune*. So the Belgian children will get plenty of milk for that.

He read it and it is beautiful and touching, about a child and the Kaiser.[23] He said that his idea was to show that the Kaiser is not quite a demon. I told him "Raymond" in Lodge's book[24] said there are books yet unwritten on earth stored up "on the other side" to put into some writer's mind, and I believe that was the origin of this story. He read also the first act of a play, very amusing, "The House in the Clouds" (afterwards *Heartbreak House*!) but says he doesn't know how to finish it, it is so wild, he thought bringing my "fresh mind" to bear on it might be a help.

He had been to Birmingham to see a new little play of his own, and has seen Masefield's *Chimney sweepers of '98*[25] not good; but at the end when someone says "At the next Rising I shall be too old" or some such words, he found his eyes full of tears.

21ST. I told G.B.S. it was the irony of fate that Sir Oliver Lodge who has painfully put his intimate story forward, will convince no one but those already believing, of the survival after death, whereas his own little story will go far to establish it, for people will say "Lodge is a dreamer but Bernard Shaw has so much common sense!" He said "I'd have burned it if I had known that", but I said "I wouldn't have told you if I hadn't known it was safe in America".

I came back to Lindsey House, expecting the letter from Birrell which was to tell me how things are at the Treasury—and Ruth had forwarded [it] to Ayot St. Lawrence and the dear knows when it will come back. So when Langton Douglas came in the evening I had no fresh news for him, but he was very good and offered £100 towards getting a Bill through. He says Witt,

Curzon and Edgar Vincent are the core of the Committee—Curzon!!

22ND. When Birrell's letter came it was discouraging.

I telephoned to Lady Leslie and was cut off in the middle of her answer so took a taxi—a rare extravagance—and went to Great Cumberland Place but she was out. She had tried to say on the telephone that she would be at home between 4.30 and 6. So I went off to Harrod's on Margaret's business and got back to Great Cumberland Place at 5.30. She was sympathetic but Sir John away—I thought he might have taken me to Carson. She had met Asquith at dinner the night before and spoken of the pictures, and he said: "Oh I know all about them" but said "they could have them in Dublin if they had made a building". He had agreed with her that I was "so wonderful for getting things through", I wish I were! She had also met Langton Douglas who told her he would give £200 or £300. She said she would try and see Lord Curzon to know what the Trustees' point of view is. The Duke of Connaught was coming at 6 and she made me stay to meet him. He looked very well in khaki and said: "I last met you at Montreal", and seemed very cheerful, but I made off as soon as I could, very tired.

This morning, after a bad night of head-ache, I wrote a letter to Sir E. Carson and went round to see Birrell, taking a newspaper extract about a National Gallery Bill now in the House of Lords enabling the Trustees to sell some Turners. I thought our Bill might be brought in as a clause. Birrell was doubtful but thought we might oppose it in the Commons if they are obdurate. He had met McKenna, Chancellor of the Exchequer, at dinner and talked to him, but he declared he would take no part in the matter one way or other. He had evidently been talked to by Curzon and said the codicil was written in "a moment of irritation", that the Will was the weighty and well-considered document. The Codicil "thrown unsigned among his papers". Balfour was there and said: "I would be against giving anything to Ireland". Rather hard on me with my child at the Front.

Birrell thinks Carson might draw up an Indemnity Bill and submit it to the Trustees, even to get them to show their hand, which they have not done yet. I asked about a question in the House but he says it is difficult to know to whom the question should be put; the Trustees have no one responsible for them, but one might raise a Debate on Supply. I lunched with Mrs. Jefferson, meeting a "Princess Caraggio", who talked occult things, and Lady Robert Manners, and as she took me in her car, I left my letter at Carson's.

No answer from Carson, and it is weary work waiting. I lunched with Lady Haliburton; her niece had been to see Bowen-Colthurst in prison, she says he is now quite mad, shrieking.

Evening. A very depressing morning, all seeming at a standstill, and at 1 o'clock I was going out when Birrell came and I ran out to meet him.

He had seen Carson yesterday in the House of Commons, said he was pettish and overcome with work, but had said he knows all about the pictures and will do his best if the Irish Party will support him. Birrell said they would, but he seemed doubtful, but of course they will as Redmond signed my statement. And Carson said the *Prime Minister* had suggested (as I did yesterday) that a clause might be added to the National Gallery Bill now before the House of Lords. Birrell had thought this would not be covered by its title, but the P.M. said the title could be changed. Birrell thinks we should publish the matter anyhow, for he can't imagine the Trustees being able to make any defence in the open. So I went out in high spirits to buy candies for the children and a hat for Margaret.

SATURDAY 25TH. To New Buildings. W.S.B.[26] looking ill and old, but has had a fit of influenza and his quarrel with Judith has upset him. He read me his ballad on Roger Casement, not very good. He had not known him but had been tremendously struck with his speech after trial "envies him his death". He is quite a Sinn Feiner now and is even down on Dillon for having sung "God save the King" on a platform. Mrs. Asquith had been to see him and said Asquith's plan for Ireland had failed because Redmond and Dillon had refused his offer to govern Ireland. He says Asquith and Margot get on very well, having the same root idea to keep in Office as long as they can and get as much as possible out of it. Margaret Sackville came and next day read her "Pageant of War",[27] very good indeed, and Belloc[28] came in the evening and after dinner he recited and sang most charmingly his own verses and some old French ones and French war songs. I asked if any new ones were being made and he said "No, and won't until there is a victory". I asked when that would be, and he said: "Between April and June". But his prophesies have failed so often, we shouldn't ask for any more. He says the Government can't find a Food Dictator it is such an unpopular office. They thought they had got Saltmarsh, but someone told him it was a booby trap and he withdrew. I sat up till 1 o'clock reading the privately printed volumes of George Wyndham's[29] letters and talked them over in the morning with W.S.B. I said the Irish part of his life was what would be remembered, he passed the Land Act, and had cared for the poor, but the rest of his life was too scattered and there was nothing likely to endure. He agreed; says he was asked to edit his poems but found them not worth it. He had, he says, an Irish nature, loved life and society and drank too much, was full of charm but was ready to play the fool, though, as he says of Belloc, he "played it well". I remember how he was missed a couple of years ago but now one never hears his name. W.S.B. says he was to a great extent responsible for the War. He had great influence with Arthur Balfour and persuaded him to the alliance with France that has done the mischief.

Came up to London Monday morning, 27th, and Yeats had just arrived from Ireland and we had a consultation about the pictures, and decided we must begin to work in the Press. We didn't know if *The Times* would print a letter, but I wrote a note to the Editor, Geoffrey Robinson, saying I had once been introduced to him by Hugh, and it was on Hugh's business I wanted to see him. Yeats took off the letter to Printing House Square, and was back in an hour, saying Robinson had heard he was there, and asked to see him, and had said he would like me to send a statement, and then would like to see me and talk it over, so I set to work to add to my old one. Then Langton Douglas came in, not very pleased with our "clause" plan, thinking a separate bill would be better; but we must take when [what] we can get.

The *Morning Post* and another paper had articles rather against the Trustees' own proposal.

28TH. Had to rewrite a bit of my statement to fit in with a question asked by Hazelton in the House; and then took it to Birrell. He was a little disappointed, having been with Sir John Simon at Oxford on Sunday, and having failed to impress him as much as he expected about the codicil. Simon thought if it had been found loose among papers (as Witt and Co. are giving out) it would not sound convincing, and that witnesses might have to be examined if a Bill was brought in. Birrell was pleased with my letter, and glad to find in it that the codicil had been in an envelope addressed to Ruth. He longs to see the defence of the Trustees.

Then on to the typist near British Museum to get it typed, and then to lunch with Yeats, and as we were at lunch Ruth arrived with a telegram from Mrs. Asquith asking me to lunch either today or tomorrow. It was too late for today, but I telephoned that I would go tomorrow. Then back to typist for the MS. and then to the House of Commons by appointment to see Redmond. Yeats came with me, and after a wait, R's secretary rushed out in excitement saying a seaplane had been over London and bomb had fallen in Eaton Square and one on the Palace Theatre, and at Victoria Station and in Brompton Road. When I told Redmond the Trustees gave as an excuse for wanting to keep our pictures that they would be safer here than in Dublin, he laughed and said: "And a bomb has just fallen within half a mile of us"! He had been talking to Carson, and they will work together. He says they are very good friends, were on the Leinster Circuit together in their young days. I said I thought the Trustees might probably give in if we promised to support their Bill in return but crush it otherwise. He wants me to see Northcliffe[30] and get his support.

29 NOVEMBER. A bad morning, for I had a headache, and post brought back my *Times* letter, with one from the Editor saying that, as I wished to see Lord Northcliffe, there was no use in my seeing him—Huffy! It was Redmond who urged my seeing Lord N. to get the support of all his papers, and I didn't like to do it without consulting Robinson, so mentioned it to him. It is a check.

I lunched at 10 Downing Street. Mrs. Asquith kept from lunch for a bit to talk the matter of the pictures over, but doesn't understand it very well, but is always cordial and affectionate. I was put in the place next the P.M. but he didn't come in till late, and then a French lady on his other side claimed him so I didn't have much talk. I told him Yeats was showing his confidence in the stability of Ireland by buying a castle[31] and he said he must be getting very rich, so I had to tell him it was only £80 lest he should stop the Civil list payment. He told me of a long journey to Biarritz he had to make on his appointment, to kneel and kiss the King's hand, and how cold it was, and how he had wandered on to the golf course and found there only two daughters of some friend in Scotland, and he felt he had gone a long way to meet neighbours. I said it was the same with me, I felt aggrieved when after the long journey through France I came to furze bushes and stone walls just the same as in Galway. After lunch, saying goodbye, I said "I'm so glad not to have to trouble you about our pictures as Mr. Birrell has done so already". "Oh yes, and I'm very much interested about them". I said I thought we had a good chance now the N.G. Bill is coming to the Commons as it is likely to be opposed, and we could give our help if they are nice to us. "Oh you would blackmail them", he said and laughed. I said "Well, I have suggested it, and I think Redmond and Carson will be able to carry it out". "Carson? Is he in it too?" and so we parted. Mrs. Asquith asked me to bring Yeats to lunch on Friday, and Elizabeth A, to see a rehearsal at the Savoy tomorrow.

1 DECEMBER. Yesterday morning as I was in my bath Kate came to the door with a wire from Lady Leslie "Duchess (of Connaught) calling at 3.15" so Ruth got her flowers earlier than usual for her "Thursday", and came with me to the Savoy for the rehearsal. Mrs. Asquith and Anthony and the Dulacs and the Laverys were sitting, a little group, in the stalls, and called to me. Mrs. A. very impatient at the rehearsal delays. I asked Lavery[32] if he would not help us about the pictures, and he said it would be shameful of the Trustees not to give them up, that it was the whole aim of Hugh's life to bring art to Dublin, to make a great collection there. He knows some of the Trustees very well, Lord Plymouth and D'Abernon and Brownlow and Mr. Heseltine, and asked for my statement to get himself up in the facts, and he will see or write to them. That may be a great help, so I didn't feel my morning wasted, and was able to enjoy the rehearsal of the tableaux, Mrs. Lavery was looking beautiful as a Madonna in cloth of gold sitting in a shrine, and Lady Chichester as a piece of Wedgewood, and Mrs. Sandys kneeling in an illuminated missal page, and a Chinaman squatting, were the best. It dawdled on till 2 o'c, and then we came home, and were ready to receive the Duchess and Lady Leslie. The Duchess spoke very warmly of Hugh, said they had liked him so much, and he was so amusing and kind. She said she had been so sorry to miss me at Montreal through her illness, and she seemed really interested in the pictures. Later G.B.S. came, and W.B.Y., and they and Mrs. Troubridge discussed psychic things, G.B.S. on the mocking side and talking of his cheating in old times.

6 DECEMBER. [1.12] On Friday* I went again to lunch at 10, Downing Street. I met Yeats in Whitehall and as we got to the door we saw Lloyd George driving away. We didn't know till next day that was the moment of the crisis. Asquith seemed very cheerful at lunch, had Lillah McCarthy on his other side and talked of the De Musset play she was going to act and I told him about Shaw's new play which amused him. He asked if Shaw was making much money and I said I supposed so, as he was groaning at having to pay £10,000 to the Exchequer between this and the New Year. He said "He has lost his social principles", but I said: "He lives very simply, a very small flat in town and a vicarage in the country; his motor his only luxury, as he is a vegetarian and

* The dating of the entries for the rest of Book I is complicated by the fact that not only does Lady Gregory enter the dates on which she wrote up her Journals but she was a week out in her memory. For clarification, the probable dates are placed in square brackets within the text e.g. [1.12] for 1 December. Her letter in the *Times* appeared on 6 December 1916, a Wednesday, not a Tuesday.

teetotaller and non-smoker". He said "He has none of the common vices then"; I said "He has none at all" and he said "Oh, yes he has, enough to swear by". I told him of the Ballylee Foundations having been built to withstand floods, and he said to Yeats after lunch: "I hear you have water both below and above, having no roof". Yeats said "I think I may manage with stilts below but I must put on a roof". He said "What about Lane's pictures? Are you in favour of getting them back to Ireland?" Yeats: "Certainly I am". Asquith: "But Dublin behaved very badly about them". Yeats: "Yes, but generations to come ought not to be punished for the sins of one generation". Yeats told him about the lectures we are starting at the Abbey on Sunday evenings and said he had given leave to the young men to discuss an Irish Republic, but that they were not to fix the date for it without consulting him or me. Asquith said "that is right, keep them out of time and space". I feel as if recording his last words, now he has resigned.[33] He parted from me with particular cordiality, hoping soon to see me again.

I sat for a while with Mrs. Asquith, she spoke with sympathy of Ireland and said "I went on my knees to Kitchener in that room (the outer drawing-room)—on my knees—I had known him all my life, to beg him to let the Irish have their own Divisions at the beginning of the War, but he would not. I had a liking for him but he was the stupidest man with a touch of genius I have ever known. He spoke the truth but he always kept back a part of it." She spoke again of the attacks being made in the papers, but I don't think she realised how serious things were. I said when we were attacked in Dublin over the theatre we comforted ourselves with the Eastern proverb: "It is not at the empty apple tree stones are thrown. They are thrown at the tree that bears the golden fruit".

I went on to *The Times* Office with my letter (this Thursday, 30th) and saw the Editor's Secretary and explained that it was through courtesy rather than discourtesy I had mentioned Northcliffe to him; that I would be quite content if *The Times* would publish my letter. She said it would be published if I shortened it, so I did that at once and left it.[34]

Saturday morning, 2 December, I had my answer from the Trustees refusing to give back the pictures and saying; [words missing].

I was very indignant and went off to Birrell to consult as to what to do next but he was away in the country. Then I thought I had better see Redmond but had to find out his address so walked to a Post Office in the Fulham Road but they had only a telephone book. Then to a chemist's—only a telephone book—but they said the undertaker a little lower down had a Directory he sometimes let them look at. I went there "funerals and cremations arranged," but I must have looked too healthy to be hopeful for I was churlishly refused the sight of the book "It took too much time". So then I tried Marven's furniture shop and they were quite civil and I found the address, Winstey Gardens, West Kensington, took a taxi there, and went upstairs, a dark uninviting set of flats. An Irish maid opened the door, I sent in my card but Redmond was in bed with a chill and at the moment asleep and Mrs. Redmond was out. So I left and thought to try Carson, made a long journey there, couldn't get a taxi and had to walk from Sloane Square to end of Eaton Place—and he was in the country. Then to Yeats' and luckily found him and he gave me lunch and we talked things over. We thought of going to *The Times* Office but telephoned and found no one would be there till between 4 and 5, Sunday afternoon.

GALWAY, 14 DECEMBER. Spent Sunday [3.12] morning re-writing my letter and then went to Birrell. He came down and read the answer and was very indignant—"Brutes, hypocrites". But when I told him I had offended Geoffrey Robinson by mentioning Northcliffe he was rather put out, thought it would shut *The Times* to me, thought I ought now to go ahead and see Lord N., [but didn't know how or where, couldn't help me though he used to know him and his brothers as little boys who didn't have a meat dinner every day of the week. Their mother was an excellent mother and they have always been devoted sons. He seemed less hopeful than before, a little cross even and I left him feeling depressed.] I had been to Una before about Northcliffe; she says he lives with his mother at Broadstairs, doesn't live with his wife, doesn't care for anyone but his mother. She couldn't tell me how to get at him, perhaps I might have to go to Broadstairs. Yeats came in the afternoon and we went later to *The Times* Office. Another Secretary of the Editor's came down, inclined to snub us, asked if we had an appointment. I explained that the Editor had accepted my letter and that I had had to change some things in it because of the Trustees' answer. I said I knew it was a crowded time but that it is just at a time like this that iniquitous deeds are done and that Art is long, Politics brief. He slightly relaxed, said he would speak to the Assistant Editor, and we left, rather dejected.

MONDAY, 27TH [4.12]. I had by post a note from *The Times* enclosing proof of my letter but saying "The Editor regrets he has not room for it". I thought this meant he would use it later but when

I took it to Yeats he was certain it was a refusal. I did not like to lose any chance and said I would go again to *The Times* Office and find out. Yeats was against this, thought it humiliating. I said I would bear any humiliation if I could save the pictures. So I set out, Yeats coming with me to Blackfriars but awaiting near the station while I went into the Office. I saw again the Secretary, Miss Mills, and asked whether the note was a refusal. She said she didn't know, she had been puzzled herself when she saw the copy of the note, she would ask the Editor when he came in and telephone to Yeats at the Royal Societies Club by 5 o'clock. So at 5 I went to the Club, but no answer. Yeats grew desperate and said we must do something, and telephoned to make an appointment for me with T. P. O'Connor[35] next day. Then after 6, I grew desperate at the behaviour of *The Times*, went to Lord Northcliffe's house in St. James' Place and left a card asking if I might see him on the matter of Hugh Lane's pictures "of great importance to us Irish" and which Sir E. Carson and Mr. Redmond were about to take up in the House of Commons.

TUESDAY MORNING, 28TH [5.12]. Nothing from *The Times*, nothing from Lord N. The Cabinet crisis on and not much chance of anything. I went to T. P. O'Connor to consult about working the Press. He said *The Times* is the only daily paper that matters; that I should get all letters into it. *The Observer* good also of the Weeklies. He knew of the matter, but not very accurately and was quite eager about it. He had changed a good deal since I had seen him, looked unhealthy, and like Redmond lived in an unlovely flat. I did a little shopping for the children and got tired and came back to Lindsey House at a quarter to five, found a telegram from Lord Northcliffe asking me to come and see him at St. James' Place about 5. So I ran off, got a bus to Sloane Square and a taxi from there and arrived not much after 5. He brought me to his library, a younger looking man than I expected, dark, with a square powerful face. He asked for my story and listened to my story and listened well. When I told him the superior safety of London was given as a reason for claiming the pictures, and that G.B.S. had said that would be an excellent excuse for seizing all our valuables, he laughed and said "They might seize this house, I am half Irish". He asked what help I wanted from him and I said "The support of your papers", and he said "That will be all right. Your letter will be in *The Times* though perhaps not tomorrow". He then asked when I would like comment on it and I said "Later, when the matter comes to Parliament". He asked me then what the state of Ireland is. I said "Bad". He said "Worse than you have ever known it?" I said "No, for there are no murders and outrages now as in the Land League days but profound discontent and dissatisfaction". He said Horace Plunkett had been to see him the day before "But he is always so vague". And so we parted, he taking me down to the hall door. He said he had lost my card and been trying all day to find me, I was not in the Directory and then he tried for Irish plays but they are not in London, and then telephoned to Sir E. Carson, remembering his name being mentioned, but he was "in the House of Lords with the Slingsby baby", and at the last he had found the card.

Next morning, [6.12] Tuesday, my letter was in *The Times*. And I had an apology from the Secretary.

So now the Press had to be attended to, and I went first to see E. Lawrence at Murray's to consult about Editors or Press men and he telephoned to a friend, Collins, who told him the best to go to and I said Yeats would go to some and I to others. Then I went on to Yeats but he was reluctant, said he didn't like going to Editors he didn't know, then I found he would like me to come. So we set off to *Westminster Gazette*, saw Spender, who was at first rather cold, then suggested Yeats should write a letter; anyhow he won't be against us and he wrote a friendly though feeble note in next day's issue. Then the *Observer*; Garvin out but Yeats went up and saw another editor and made an appointment for next day. Then a long walk to *Evening Standard*(?) and by the time we got there I was so tired I asked Yeats to do the talking this time. We saw a Mr. Johnson who took us to his room, and Yeats, refusing to sit down, explained the case with eloquence, till at last Johnson said: "Are you W. B. Yeats, the poet?" Then they made friends, and when we left Yeats said: "I'm afraid I've been like Gladstone with Queen Victoria and have addressed you like a public meeting". Then we had lunch and I got home and Yeats saw Howard Gray, the *Pall Mall* man who was very nice (praised *Golden Apple* very much) and gave us a nice note next day.[36]

THURSDAY, 30 NOVEMBER [7.12]. I saw Alec Martin at Christies, and had the Trustees letter typed, and home for the afternoon. Margaret Sackville came, and Yeats. We had theatre business and then went up. Margaret S. read her *Pageant of War*, and Yeats rather criticised her method, so I made him read his *Easter 1916* as an example. Mr. Adye and one or two others were there, and it was extraordinarily impressive. Then to lessen the tension I read Belloc's *Mrs Rhys* he had just sent me.

In the evening I had a letter from Ada, saying A.W. had had a slight stroke but was doing well.

FRIDAY, 1 DECEMBER [8.12]. A man from *The Observer* at 11 to interview me and Yeats. We showed him the house and pictures, and as he was leaving, Yeats found from something he said about the *Immortals* in the hall that he was a mystic, so prophesied friendliness.

Garvin had asked us to write a short article as well, as he hadn't time to do so, and we had begun it the evening before, so we finished that, and I took it to be typed, and then to *The Observer* office; and then went a long way off to see Lovaine (my nephew) in Gray's Inn Road Hospital. It was pitch dark when I came out, and I had to walk a long way till I came to a 'bus stand, but got home then with only one change, very tired, about 6. Then came a wire from Margaret that the Doctor thought A's case serious, so I decided to come to her Sunday evening as I could not get a train through if I went on Saturday.

Saturday morning I was going out to get Margaret's things at Harrods when I had a wire from her and one from Frank, saying I was urgently needed in Galway. So I scrambled the toys unsatisfactorily, and took a taxi to the Bank to get some money. Yeats in the afternoon.

Sunday. I went to Birrell's, but he was away, so I went to Lavery to propose his, as Garvin suggested, going to the King. Garvin had said: "Lavery can do anything with the Royal Family". He was very sympathetic but said the King would be of no use, had no ideas and would only send him to someone else; the Queen might possibly do something. But on the whole he thought it would be better to go to Lord Plymouth and if he was sympathetic they would both go to Lord D'Abernon. He was unluckily unwell and hadn't been able to do anything yet. He showed me the picture he is painting of Casement's trial, and a letter from Casement to a cousin asking who that man was who is taking sketches from the jury box "from the disfavour which he looks at the Judge I think he is in danger of being had up for high treason". He says he means in future to give as many pictures as he can afford to Ireland. I went on to Una Pope Hennessy, read her Yeats' "Easter" poem. She is low about Mesopotamia, and very depressed by Ashmead Bartlett's articles in *The Sunday Times*, demonstrating that we have already lost the war.

Yeats came in the afternoon and dined and was to take me to the train, but no taxi was to be had. I sat waiting, in hat and cloak, my luggage in the hall, but had to give it up at last and settle down for the night.

Monday. It was perhaps all for the best, I had thought it would be a free day, all my work done, and that I would go to the

National Gallery to look at pictures, and then to the New English, and then to Hamley's for Richard's steam yacht, and then have a quiet afternoon. But when I had dressed and was about to make the most of this leisurely day, I found an "inspired" (by Witt) paragraph in *The Times*, claiming that Hugh had intended his pictures for London, if a Continental Gallery were built, and as before offering to comfort us by an occasional loan. So first I got the bundle of Hugh's correspondence with the N.G. Trustees Yeats was to have gone through next day, and marked and copied extracts. Secondly rewrote Lavery's letter, third, dictated a letter for Ruth to sign, giving her evidence. Then sent her off to Lavery and composed a letter for Yeats. Then 2.30 to his club, and to lunch at Stewarts at 3, chocolate and a bun. Then to typist's with letter. Ruth joined us, from Lavery's; he had already written a new letter, and that also we had typed. Then 5 o'c Yeats went to *Times* office with the letters, and I, very tired, went on in the dark to Woburn Buildings. Ruth came there too, and we dined with him. He had a copy of A.E's fiery letter to *The Times*. He had impressed on the assistant Editor he saw that it and Ruth's were important. Then I went to Euston and off. Sat up all night in a third class carriage, couldn't get even a corner, but slept in the boat, and at Kingstown was cheered by a paragraph in the *Irish Times* giving summary of Ruth's letter and A.E's, which had both appeared in *The Times*.

31 DECEMBER [?21.12]. Since then I have been in the sick-room. But now we have a second nurse I can get out. And today at Yeats' bidding I wrote a letter to *The Observer*.[37]

23 DECEMBER. Went to Dublin and did business; helped in eviction of Keogh's two brothers from the Abbey, and engaged Millington as business manager. Made overtures of peace to the Sinclair Company, who had been badly treated without my knowledge, an injunction taken out against them when they were playing *Duty*.[38] Arranged programme for Spring; saw Miss Purser[39] and Mrs. Duncan about pictures. Gogarty[40] says: "The King sends for Lloyd George, but Northcliffe sends for the King!"

Back to Galway. A. much the same.

BOOK TWO

On 27 January, 1918, I wrote to my son, then on the Italian Front, from Dublin:

> "I only heard a few days ago that the Public Meeting I had been working for is to take place the day after tomorrow at the Mansion House, the Lord Mayor in the Chair, to ask the Government to return the Lane Pictures. So I had to write letters to our London helpers, and I sent a cable message to John Quinn. They have asked me to speak to the unpopular resolution asking for subscriptions. However, I am hopeful, a great thing getting a move on, and the Government is in a hole and anxious to create a 'favourable atmosphere' in Ireland. Yeats was invited to speak but he is 'settled in Oxford'. I wish he could have come, but like Mrs. Brer Tarrypin at the other end of the racecourse, he may help—go on deputation to the P.M. and write letters to editors of papers to remind them that they have taken our side. It will be wonderful if we get them back—I shall feel 'now lettest Thou thy servant depart in peace' if they come. Oh what a happy world it might be with you back and the war at an end!"
>
> (But that letter was sent back to me unopened.)

The published report of the meeting[1] tells of the help, by letter or presence, of Lords Granard, Decies, Middleton, Plunket, Mayo, Desart, Rossmore, Powerscourt; the Lord Mayor of Belfast; Dr. Bernard, Archbishop of Dublin; Rt. Rev. the Moderator of the Presbyterian Church, the Right Hon. Mr. Justice Madden, Lieut.-General Sir Bryan Mahon, and many others. The Members of Parliament present included Mr. (now President) Cosgrave, and the Lord Mayor presided. A resolution was passed "calling on the Government to take steps to ensure the restoration of these pictures which Sir Hugh Lane destined for the Dublin Municipal Gallery". There was an overflow meeting, among the speakers being Canon Hannay and Mr. Stephen Gwynn. Alderman S. T. O'Kelly, speaking as a representative of Sinn Féin, said from the platform that, "when he met Sir Hugh Lane in New York, shortly before he sailed in the *Lusitania*, he asked him when he was going to restore the pictures to Dublin?" and Sir Hugh Lane replied very decidedly, "They will all be in Dublin yet".

8 SEPTEMBER, 1918. On Saturday, 21 August, I went to Dublin on Abbey business. I was tired next morning, Sunday, but in the afternoon I went to the National Gallery to see Hugh's bequest, the pictures by old Masters from Lindsey House. I stayed there a long time, looking sadly at the Goya, and at the Rembrandt I used to look at so often when I came in late and tired to Lindsey House, there was such sunshine in the face—and the Titian *Courtier* and the rest. Hugh's portrait by Sargent was hanging in one of the rooms, lent by the Municipal Gallery. Sargent had told me how Hugh had gone to him for a drawing, but he had painted him instead, he was so interested in "the nobility of his face". It looked very sad and tragic. The eyes seemed to follow me, seemed to reproach me for not having carried out what he had trusted me to do, the bringing back of the French pictures to Dublin.

I had worked so hard in London, and after I left all seemed to be abandoned; and the papers, even *The Times*, all but the *Nation*, having rejected my protest made me very hopeless. I stayed there for a long time and prayed . . .

Then I went to ask if Mrs. Duncan could give me any news. I found her but just come back from the country. She asked me if I had seen the *Irish Times* of Saturday. I had not, for I had missed the papers at home and there were none to be had on the journey. There was a paragraph in its London correspondence saying that the yearly report of the National Gallery just published claims the pictures as its own.

This was another blow. And Mrs. Duncan said the Committee had ceased to sit; that it had wasted the effect of the Mansion House meeting by merely sending another request (as I had done long ago) to the Trustees; and that the answer (which they had not even told me of) was a refusal, saying that since their letter other facts had come to light which had strengthened their case.

Mrs. Duncan thought that John Dillon was in town, and as he had written a sympathetic answer to my letter I went to his house in Great Georges Street to consult him. But the house was closed and the bell not answered.

Next morning, Monday, or rather in the night time, I remembered that Mrs. Duncan had said the Corporation was having a meeting on Monday afternoon but it would probably be taken up with strike troubles. But at 1 o'clock I went to the Mansion House and asked to see Mr. Foley, the Lord Mayor's Secretary.

He was out, but I waited, and when he came I told him of the two new facts since the big meeting—the announcement that the English Government had given a site at Millbank for the new Gallery to be built, and the claim of the National Gallery to the pictures in their Report. I reminded him that he had come to a Committee meeting I was at, and had said, but not allowed us to report, that the Corporation had earmarked £10,000 towards the building of a new Gallery; that I had asked the Lord Mayor on the platform at the Meeting if he would announce this; that he had said it was impossible; and that if an announcement could be made that the Corporation had definitely promised the building it would checkmate the enemy's move. He said that as nothing was being done to get back the pictures the £10,000 had been used for other purposes; but that he would consult the Lord Mayor as to whether a resolution on the matter could be carried at that day's meeting. He said he would let me know in the evening, but I had no message and feared this was another disappointment.

The next morning the *Irish Times* had a report of the Meeting, and in a paragraph headed "The Lane Pictures" it said:

> "Mr. Foley drew attention to the fact that the annual report of the British National Gallery contained a List of the pictures of the late Sir Hugh Lane, which they intended to use as the nucleus of a new gallery. These pictures were those which Dublin felt it was entitled to receive under the codicil of Sir Hugh Lane's Will. In order that they should not be accused of letting that development go by default, he moved that the Corporation re-affirm its decision to provide a gallery for those pictures. Dublin's case had the sympathy of Lady Gregory, Mr. Asquith, the late Mr. John Redmond and Sir Edward Carson."

The Motion was seconded by Mr. Cole and Passed.

Oh such joy! It was the first time that intention had been published, and it takes away the enemy's claim that they were the first to promise a gallery.

I went to thank Mr. Foley. Then to tell Mrs. Duncan and ask her to write something for the *Nation* and stir up the *Irish Times*. She had been amazed at seeing the papers for she had never known a resolution brought up till it had been on the Agenda list for a fortnight. Then I was able to go to work at the Abbey, rehearsing *Sable and Gold*[2] with a good heart.

On Wednesday I felt that the Parliamentary Party ought to carry on the work, and Dillon being away I went to the Recruiting Offices to ask for Stephen Gwynn. But he was out, and after a long wait, a little Boy Scout taking messages and bringing no answer as to when he would be in, I went away.

On Thursday I tried again and found him (he had written asking me to come but I was at the Abbey and missed his note). He was very busy but kind, said he was just going to see the Chief Secretary (Mr. Shortt) and would put the matter before him though he is a man who doesn't know one picture from another and is only working at possible industries. Next morning I called again. He had seen Mr. Shortt who had promised to help. But as we talked he said: "If you could see Samuel, the Attorney General, he would be the best man to take it up". I didn't know Samuel, but said I would gladly see anyone who would be of use. So he took me to his Secretary, Miss Evans, and asked her to call up the Castle, and said if we would get an appointment with the Attorney General he would come with me.

For over an hour I sat there. First we couldn't get at the Castle, but at last we did, and Miss Evans had just asked Mr. Samuel when he would have time, when a trunk call—Belfast—cut us off. Later she was getting it again when a Sligo trunk call intervened with a message to a Lieut. Fox. In the end we got a promise of a quarter of an hour with him at 1.15, and I hurried on to go through the Abbey audits with Mr. Harris as arranged. But first I sent one of the little Boy Scouts to Mrs. Duncan begging for her copy of the Lane picture pamphlet, and Stephen Gwynn brought this on when he joined me at the Castle. He said, giving it, that it was lucky we had it, for almost the first questions were about dates and the exact wording of the Will and Codicil. He asked for my statement, and listened, and then said a Bill to release the Trustees from their obligation would be the only means of going to work. S. Gwynn said we would not be given time for a Bill, but Mr. Samuel said: "If your Party would give up a day granted them for some important discussion, the Government might make a deal and give it up for the purpose—Could you manage this?" Gwynn said he was not on very good terms with Dillon, but I said Dillon had written so sympathetically to me that I would ask him. Samuel said "but not yet, say nothing about it yet". I spoke of the Government having bought off the claim of the Layard heirs to the pictures left by Sir Henry to the National Gallery, and I thought some such bribe might be given in this case, but he said: "Oh no, we will go to work in another way. They can't give that Millbank site without leave from Parliament and we can block their Bill, until they agree to ours." There is a doubt, however, whether if it is a disputed Bill we can carry it through, but he said Carson should be able to do that and he will speak to him and to Bonar Law and he is sure Lord French and Shortt will both give their help. He kept the pamphlet and will get a copy of the National Gallery Report. So we left him, I much happier about the whole matter than I had been for many a long day. It is not I and a few Authors and Artists who are making the demand now, it is the City of Dublin and the entire Irish Party, Unionist and Nationalist. So I went back to rehearsals at the Abbey.

28 OCTOBER, 1918. About three weeks ago, I saw in the Irish papers that the Lane Picture Committee had gone on a deputation to the Chief Secretary, Mr. Shortt, and had a sympathetic reception. It had not given any sign of life for a long time, and I thought had probably been moved by my having gone to the Attorney General, and the Corporation having moved its resolution, re-affirming its decision to build a Gallery.

The week before last I had a postcard with announcement that a meeting of the Committee would be held Friday 18th. It was not mentioned if there was anything special to discuss, and I wrote to the Secretary, Mr. Atkinson, saying that I should not be in Dublin, but would be obliged if he would let me know if anything of interest should turn up. This I did not really expect, as the committee meetings had usually been languid.

On Monday 21st, I had a letter from Mr. Atkinson, saying that it had been stated at the meeting that Mr. Shortt had proposed they should submit the matter of the pictures to arbitration. That the Attorney General who was present had seemed to approve. That after some discussion the Committee had directed their Secretary to write to the National Gallery Trustees, proposing to leave the question to the arbitration of say, Mr. Asquith, Mr. Balfour and Lord Grey.

I was aghast and wrote to Atkinson, remonstrating.

I also wrote a vehement letter to Yeats, protesting against this sacrifice of all the work that had been done. For, I said, suppose the arbitrators gave it against us, that would be irrevocable, we could never ask for the pictures again.

I received next day, but not in answer to this, Yeats' account of the meeting, which alarmed me still more. But I hoped that when he received my letter of protest he would take some steps to have the mischief undone.

But on Thursday 24th, I heard from him: "Atkinson had called to show me your letter. He did not know what to do as he had been directed by the Committee to write to the National Gallery to propose arbitration. At my suggestion he is writing to

Sir Edward Carson, and if his advice is against the arbitration proposal will summon the Committee again".

I was at breakfast with the children when this came. I turned quite faint and sick . . .

This seemed to me even worse, for Carson might quite likely be glad to get out of his promised support of a Bill, a troublesome business for pictures which he doesn't care about. I had been wretched ever since the first letter, and would have gone to Dublin but didn't like leaving the children while there is influenza about. However, now I saw nothing to do but to pack up and leave by the 1.30 train. I wired to Yeats saying "Going to Gresham re pictures until Saturday".

I got there before 7 o'c and found no message, but went to the Abbey Theatre and after a while Yeats came in, and I got him to telephone to Atkinson who after some difficulty we got, at the School of Art, and asked him to come and see me at the Gresham.

Atkinson had written me a letter the day before which I had not received but which said "I would point out that the Committee do not propose to substitute arbitration for a Bill, and the terms of reference—'was the document intended . . . to be a codicil' seem to the Committee to be a safeguard".

I said that it did seem to me to exclude the idea of a Bill. It would in any case enormously increase our difficulties if this arbitration went against us. In my opinion a Bill would be impossible to carry through after it. He said the Committee were sure the N. G. Trustees would refuse, or that if they didn't refuse, no impartial Arbitrators could give it against us.

But he then became convinced I was right, and Yeats came to think so also. I pointed out that as to the arbitrators, Asquith would probably be ineligible, because in the Corporation debate, or rather Counsellor Foley's speech at it, published in the papers, it was mentioned that Asquith was on our side. And as to Balfour, I said that when Mr. Birrell had asked him to help in getting back the pictures his answer had been that he would not willingly give anything to Ireland. It was then the Rising that had put him out of temper, but the Conscription business is not likely to have sweetened him.

Atkinson, a good creature, was now sad, and I asked if the Committee would be got together next day. He said the sub-Committee could, so it was settled for 5 o'c the next afternoon.

I had again a sleepless night, this business seeming too hard, and no-one very helpful at hand, Yeats seemed to have lost his interest in it. But I just thought of telephoning to Foxrock,[3] where the Shaws were staying with Horace Plunkett, to ask if they would be in town during the day, as I should much like to see them before 4 o'c. The answer was that they would come between lunch time and 4.30. So I went and did business at the Abbey during the morning, and bought some sweets for the children, and sat down and waited, so tired that I had just dropped asleep in my chair in the reading room, when I heard a friendly laugh, and there was G. B. S., and Charlotte. I said I wanted to consult him, and he at once sat down and gave his attention to my story, and before I had gone far he exclaimed "Monstrous folly! Arbitration would be fatal!" Such a relief! However when I told him the terms of the question to be submitted, he said it was skilfully written and might not exclude legislation as far as equity went, but that in asking a question as carefully as you like you can't dictate the answer to be given, it might be so worded as to make a further opening of the matter impossible. I said "Oh! if you could come to the meeting!" and he said "I should have no excuse for meddling". I saw then that he would come, and said "Yeats is already coming, and if you do you will be like Aaron and Hur holding up the hands of Moses, and indeed I want that support". So he promised to come and a great burden fell from me, and I said "I had been so miserable and had prayed—now who says prayers are not answered?" And I had even sufficient detachment of mind to tell him how much I had enjoyed a *mot* of his I had heard that day "The Allies don't like Wilson's terms but are afraid to say so. They remember the old story of St Joseph coming to the gate of Heaven after an outing, and St. Peter refusing to let him in, and his saying 'If you don't, I'll take out my wife and child, and you'll have to shut Heaven'".

At 5 o'c we met at the School of Art. Sir Robert Woods,[4] who acted as Chairman, was there and said he would be very glad to hear anything Mr. Shaw had to say; and the few others, Mrs. Duncan and Cruise O'Brien and Atkinson were delighted to see him. We were getting on nicely till Mr. Bodkin appeared, in a thorny mood. He looked black, and when it was proposed that a new meeting of the General Committee should be summoned, he said he had a resolution to propose first. "That the Secretary, having been directed by a unanimous vote"—unanimous—here Yeats interrupted and said he had not been for it. Bodkin said he had not voted against it, and Yeats said there were so few against it that he thought it would be no use. Mrs. Duncan said she also had been against it, but hadn't voted so—"to write to the Trustees, ought to have done so at the first possible opportunity". "In fact, a vote of censure" said G. B. S. "I confess that Mr. Atkinson consulted me, and that when I had seen Lady

Gregory's letter I also was for postponement," said Sir Robert Woods. Mrs. Duncan broke in with many reasons against the arbitration proposal. I apologised for having taken so much upon myself, but gave my reasons, and said I considered it a grave discourtesy to all our helpers, Mr. Dillon, Mr. Boland, Captain Craig, Sir Edward Carson, in Parliament, and many other helpers. I especially reminded them of Mr. Quinn's telegram to the Mansion House meeting, on behalf of many Irish Americans. I said we had not exhausted our reserves, we had made no real effort in Parliament, or of our second line of defence in America, from which at the right time pressure could be brought. I said that in a matter like this it is not arguments that tell, it is forces. We have but to work on, never letting the question drop, and though I did not myself think a Bill possible in all the excitement of the moment, there will be the peace Conference, and offer of some measure of Home Rule to Ireland, and a new election, and possible new helpers. For instance, the English Labour Party had been against Ireland about Conscription, and has now most warmly supported the Irish resistance, making it a question of freedom, and having been given a hint that the real pressure for conscription comes from those who want to keep it up in order to keep Labour in its place. In the shifting of parties we must win, if we show no weakness, and a proposal for arbitration does show weakness. I could not let pass this proposal of irrevocably giving over our case into the hands of any three Englishmen. I also said Mr. Bodkin's name had been mentioned as well as mine in the Codicil, and that I looked to him for help.

It seemed to strike them then for the first time that I, as Trustee, should have been consulted; and the only trouble was to find a form of words for summoning the Committee again without offending them. But I happened to say that I should have come up for the meeting if I had known anything of importance was to be discussed, and Shaw said "That settles it easily. You have but to say the members of the Committee were not given full information". And that was done. And owing to G. B. S. everyone was in good humour. He had chaffed Bodkin a little, and been deferential to the Chairman. I said, in saying good bye, "When you're in doubt lead trumps say cardplayers, and when I'm in doubt I lead G.B.S.," and he laughed and said to the others "She always tells me what to do, and I just do as I'm told". And best of all, Bodkin, going out with Yeats said he was now quite convinced by the arguments. A card came on Tuesday with notice of Committee meeting to be held on the 1st, Friday at 8.30 p.m.

So on Thursday, I set out again for Dublin. Not a pleasant journey as I hadn't liked leaving the children, with so much influenza about. And at Athlone, where we waited a long time, there was a drunken soldier in a carriage near, bawling horrible language, calling the officials red-capped bastards, daring them to "come on". A crowd collected to listen to him but no one seemed to think of removing him. When we went on there was a loud dispute between two women who had got in, about a purse which one had lost and the other apparently had picked up, intending to keep. I could not hear very well with the noise of the train, but both were angry and it was an ugly sight. I read *Castle Richmond*[5] however, which is interesting for the Famine parts, and as always Trollope has enough story to carry on the interest.

I went to the Gresham, had tea, and then to the Abbey, a very small audience because of the influenza. All theatres are out of bounds now for Khaki, but the plays went well, *Sable and Gold* and *Spreading the News*,[6] though this is played rather too much as a farce, Donovan[7] as Bartley dressed as a stage Irishman, and a new policeman, very exaggerated. The patriotic parts of *Sable and Gold* were much applauded. It is said the authorities are getting suspicious of the Abbey, and say our actors say things on the stage that anyone else would be lodged in Gaol for. I went round and saw Donovan and settled to come and see *Grabber*[8] rehearsal next day which I did. In spite of all my cutting, the author has got at it again and restored or made a new feeble end, the old Grabber when at the point of death making moral reflections and insisting on having a settlement of his land drawn up in favour of his daughter, the author forgetting that when he first wrote this passage he had killed off the son, who he has now restored to life and would defraud. That had to be altered; and I had to tell them that "when I was tiny" as the children say, I had to walk about the schoolroom with a book on my head to keep it straight, and that the night before I had thought the next rehearsal should be with one, for they are almost all getting into an increased trick of nodding the head with every sentence. They took it good-humouredly. Then I saw Harris, about Income Tax, and then rushed off to the Hibernian where Ruth Shine had promised to ask Bodkin to meet me at lunch. He was there and very amiable. He is not now for arbitration, but said something else must be proposed, and I had already written notes, and one was that in case we can't get a Bill brought in we might try a deputation to the Prime Minister. He agreed and promised to write a draft letter for the Committee to consider, which would get things on more quickly than composing it in the crowd.

So I felt more at ease, and went in the rain to buy some toys for the chicks, and then to the Gresham, where it seemed a long wait till 8 o'c, for I began to get nervous again. But the papers are cheering now; the night before I had taken up the *Evening Herald*, and saw good accounts of the Italians' successes on the Piave, and all the Austrian prisoners taken. And then saw in such large letters across the top of the page that I had taken it for the title, "Capitulation of Turkey. Dardanelles open". I thought of poor Geoffrey, as in that Italian success I had thought of that other grave . . .

It was wet and when I was in the tram and had started, I found I had not my purse, and was afraid of being put out, but the conductor only took my name and address. But with that, and the darkness I went too far to the top of Stephens Green. However, I was before time at the Arts Club, and sat alone in the empty room for a while. Then Ruth came in, and Atkinson and some others, and Yeats. It was a small meeting, I was disappointed that Sir Robert Woods did not come; too busy probably with influenza.

When after the last meeting it had been arranged for Friday and Yeats had wanted my consent to altering it because he was going to give a dinner that night, I had said it should not be arranged for his convenience or mine, but for whatever day we were likely to get the best numbers, and that I hoped Atkinson would get the Lord Mayor or at least his secretary Foley. I heard no more of this, but when the meeting had gone on for a little time, Mr. Foley came in and I felt at once he was an element of strength, good humour and practical common sense. We wasted a lot of time over reading minutes &c, but a letter from Carson was read, rather vague but approving my view that there is a sign of weakness in proposing arbitration; and then I was asked to move a resolution to get rid of or defer the arbitration one, but I said I wished Mr. Bodkin to speak first. He did so, less on our side than I had hoped, but he read his letter proposing a deputation if a Bill failed, and that started discussion, and then I was asked for a statement, and made it as before, except that this time I quoted John Quinn's letter saying that since Gompers had declared for Home Rule, American Labour was taking it up, and that with this new help from America we should be able to get better terms. I said that if the pictures had not been restored by the time of the settlement, we might claim them as a part of it, just as Belgium is already claiming the return of her pillaged works of art.

This pleased Foley and some others, and anyhow the resolution deferring the carrying out of the arbitration resolution indefinitely was carried. Bernard Shaw's opinion, read from the notes of last meeting was a great help. Then it was decided Bodkin's letter was to be sent to Dillon, Carson &c. And as to a deputation, I said we could not decide on a date without knowing if the Lord Mayor is likely to be going to London on any other business, and we would arrange it to suit him, as he would give it great strength. Mr. Foley said he was not likely to be in London at any future time that he knew of. I was sad; but he added that in case a deputation was found feasible he would answer for it that the Lord Mayor, who had sent his apologies for not coming tonight, would make it his business to go over for it. This was splendid, and I asked if we might say that in the letter to the M.P.s and he said yes. So I went back to the hotel and slept till 4 o'c and got up at 6, and was so sleepy in the train that I slept from before Mullingar to Ballinasloe. And when I came home the chicks came running to meet me, and I gave them their presents, some beads and animal blocks to Catherine, and a book and draughts to Anne. And when they went up for their little sleep, I came to my typewriter and wrote to Dillon and Carson and Birrell and Boland and T. P. O'Connor, who I hadn't thought of, but found a letter from, asking me for a lecture to a Society he is forming at Liverpool. And now I can but say my prayers though if it were not for the care of the children I would go to London.

BOOK THREE

GRESHAM HOTEL, 3 FEBRUARY, 1919. Planting finished and the children in London. I was free to come to Dublin last Friday to try again what can be done about the pictures. I had written to Mr. Bodkin to come and see me on Saturday morning but he could not, and Yeats had never heard the pictures mentioned since I left, after getting rid of the arbitration proposal.

In the afternoon I found Mrs. Duncan at home, but neither had she any news. Then I wrote to Sir Robert Woods asking if he could see me on Sunday. He appointed midday, and I went to his house and had a satisfactory talk. He says Parliament does not really open until next week, nothing can be done there until then, he goes over next Sunday. He knows Sir Edward Carson quite well and believes he will work "to get anything for Ireland" (except Home Rule)! He will see him directly he goes over and here he will have a talk with the Attorney General, now his colleague in representing T.C.D., and let me know what he says. He asked for a copy of the pamphlet and of my new statement on causes of delay and I have sent him both. I am also to make a synopsis of our enemy's argument from Ruth's newscutting book. He is for just going on the justice of our case at present and not stirring up Sinn Fein or any National expression of opinion. I said I would keep that to fall on later if reason and justice failed. I came away much more cheerful and hopeful than I have been for a long time. I will go to London before the end of the week.

I went on to the Abbey to see a rehearsal of *Baile's Strand*,[1] very glad to hear poetry on the stage again. Yeats came on to lunch and then I read him my *Jester*.[2] He thought it good, made no criticisms except that the first act was perhaps too talky—he had not waked up till the second but he was in a hurry to get back to prepare notes for his evening talk on Psychic Research, and he found the drawing-room here cold and I don't think it was a very good time to read it.

As to the Abbey. Harris had written urging me to come up, there was something wrong, O'Donovan had talked of "interference" and Millington had written in the same way that there was a "strain". So on Friday evening after *Mixed Marriage*[3] I went up to the Office and saw Donovan. His grievance is that Mrs. Yeats looks on and criticises and, "not understanding the difficulties or business", makes suggestions and criticisms to Yeats who carries them on. However, I told him we mustn't grumble at anything. It is such a great matter getting a verse play on again. He is rather sulky at our taking Miss Magee[4] back at £5 a week for three months, but I was firm about that. We want some beauty on our stage for the eye as well as the ear.

Yesterday, Sunday afternoon, there was a sudden tumult and we in the reading room lifted the blinds and saw a surging, boohing mob threatening to break into the Hotel. I went to an open window upstairs to see better. There had been a meeting to protest against the seizure of St. Enda's School by the Military, and some Police Inspectors who were taking notes had been chased by the mob and had taken refuge in the Hall here. The mob boohed at them, the Management was afraid, I think, to let them out by a back entrance lest the Hotel should be broken into. The mob looked very threatening for a while.

Then, a man in black, I do not think he was a priest, stood up on something, I think on one of the tree standards in the middle of the street, and said in a very clear voice: "Fellow citizens, the Military seized without notice the house belonging to Mrs. Pearse at Rathmines. We have met to protest against it and some Police who came to interfere have taken shelter in the Gresham Hotel. The people of Dublin are not an undisciplined mob as they were in 1913. They are now organised. We make no war on private property. We are not going to attack the Gresham Hotel. I ask you to sing the Soldier's Song and to go home and leave the police to take care of themselves".

There was a little cheering, very little singing, and a great many went quietly away. The rest stayed, pressing near the door, and boohing whenever they caught sight of the policemen or boohing when another came. I was afraid the Military would arrive and there would be trouble, but after a while a young man in a sort of uniform got up just under the window where I was and said: "Fellow Republicans," (great cheering) "you know me as one of yourselves. I ask you to go home now and leave the police to themselves". And after that they went away quietly enough. (This was the first time I heard the word "Republican" used).

In the evening I was at the Abbey lecture or debate on the attitude of the Catholic Church to Psychical Research (Professor Howley). Yeats spoke very finely, saying that only the belief in the immortality of the soul could lead to that perfecting of the soul of the whole being, that perfect faith that brings us nearer to God. And he used my suggestion that the Research should be left to men of Science and of balanced mind just as medical research is, and not rushed into by unhappy people, unbalanced by grief, as one would not leave it to the suffering patient to experiment in drugs.

Though I had pressed and worked for these Sunday evening Abbey lectures for so long, this was the first I had been able to come to. It was a great happiness to me seeing that large keen audience, chiefly young men, having this Sunday evening intellectual excitement and listening to Yeats' fine closing sentences.

5TH, MONDAY. A dress rehearsal of *Baile's Strand*.

6TH. Abbey, and when I came back, Mr. Bodkin to talk about the Lane pictures, rather depressing as usual, thinks that if the Trustees begin to build their Gallery they will say that constitutes a Trust, and will increase our difficulties. But I must do my best.

17 FEBRUARY.—LONDON. Before leaving Dublin on the 10th I wrote to Sir Robert Woods to House of Commons, giving my address and asking him to let me know what he could do. I have been waiting for the answer at 13, Royal Hospital Road, not liking to take any steps till I heard. Yesterday he wrote from House of Commons:

> "I am very sorry your letter missed me. It was sent back to Dublin as I came here and I only got it yesterday.
>
> If you are still in London I am at your service though I see but little prospect of anything being done at present—the Government's hands are so full of really urgent business. I have spoken to Sir William Whitlaw who is with us. I have not yet met Sir E. Carson but shall speak to him the first opportunity. Yours faithfully, R. H. WOODS."

Discouraging. I am writing to say I will go to see him at House of Commons tomorrow.

MONDAY, 17TH. Birrell and his son came to tea. I didn't bother him much about the pictures, but he said Sir Robert Woods was the best to leave it to. He said he had meditated very much on the arbitration question when I wrote to him, but thought it would be a great risk. Of course he says, if the Trustees were gentlemen they would support a Bill to release them from holding the pictures, but then half of them are not. He says in arbitration, as in a Court of law, there are so many quibbles and possible objections to every course of action, that it is always doubtful if justice will be done. Then we went on to talk of juries and Trollope's novels and "Mr. Chaffanbrass". He is all for Trollope, admires his work immensely though he never met him. He particularly praises his description of the House of Commons in *Phineas Finn*[5] and especially Phineas trying to make his first speech. And when he went about Ireland he felt the truth of those first novels—Irish ones—which I haven't read yet. When I saw him for a moment last week I had asked him if he would like to read *The Education of Henry Adams.*[6] He hadn't heard of it, he was hurrying off to his publisher, Constable, and when he got there, he saw a copy of it lying on Constable's table, a specimen copy, it hasn't come to England yet. So he was very glad to borrow it. He told us how, when he was so ill two years ago, his doctor had told him he ought to settle his affairs, and though he answered: "You are speaking to a K.C., a Member of Doctor's Commons, etc., etc.," he had sent for a dealer and sold him, for £350, the first edition of "Gray's Elegy", which he had sometime ago bought at a book-stall for 2/6d. But when he got well he went to ask its fate, and the dealer told him he had sold it for £500, not to be paid at once. And then the man who had bought it died and he had put it up at a Sotheby auction which as Birrell says he ought to have done himself. It sold for £650. But the dealer wasn't happy, because after the auction an American had cabled ready to bid up to £800.

18 FEBRUARY. Yesterday afternoon I set out in fog and rain to the House of Commons. I sent in a card from the barrier but had to wait some time. There was quite a mob there such as I had never seen before, of common-looking people who had sent in their names, I suppose friends of the new Members. The policeman guarding the door called out to them several times not to press so close and block the entrance. I was standing aside a little way off and after a while Sir Robert Woods came. He had not been given my card but as it was 4 o'clock, the time I had fixed, had come to look for me and took me inside the lobby where we could sit down.

But he had done nothing. He said a Bill was impossible at present or until after March 31. He had not seen Carson, he saw nothing to do. I said the matter was urgent as the enemy are not idle. They will be laying the foundation-stone of their Gallery some day and getting more and more a vested interest in the pictures, and that we should give them some public warning. He said: "You had better put an advertisement in *The Times* doing that; saying a Bill is to be brought in". I said, "How can we do that without knowing there will be a Bill?" He said he was a stranger there and would not be much in the House, was going back to Dublin at the end of the week. Indeed he had a hunted, bewildered look. I had seen him a fortnight ago on his own drawing-room rug, triumphant at having been elected, certain we should get the pictures "on the justice of our case". Now he is restless, uneasy, a new boy at school and evidently wanting to be rid of the matter. However, he jumped up and introduced me to "Mr. Henry" who passed and who I didn't at first recognise as the Solicitor General. He was amiable, expressed sympathy, but "no private Bills possible". Then I sent in my card to Sir James Craig who Carson had referred me to when I was last here, but I had never seen him as I was just then called away. He came, very pompous and forbidding, Ulster accent. He began by saying that he had at the time Sir E. Carson turned us over to him, had several interviews "with your amiable friends, (Ruth Shine and Yeats) but none of them had made any effort to do anything". I said, "You have not met me before, and I am not amiable. And we have done something, we had an immense public meeting at the Dublin Mansion House, calling for the return of the pictures; and the Dublin Corporation has publicly reaffirmed its decision to build a Gallery for the pictures. Its not having done so was made the chief point against our claim. I myself saw Mr. Duke personally, and pressed for a Bill. He said private Bills were impossible, yet he promised to see the Prime Minister about it. The Lane Picture Committee went to Mr. Shortt, he put them off in the same way. Then he went out. Now I have come to know what Sir Edward Carson will do". He was a little more amiable then, but when I asked what he would advise us to do said: "You should draft a Bill". Sir R.—"How can that be done? I can't do it. I know nothing about it." Sir J.—"There are plenty of scriveners at the bottom of those steps who will do it for you." Sir R.—"But I don't know the technicalities. I am a stranger here." Sir J.—"Oh, they will lend you a hand." I said our preparing a Bill would not get us any farther. Sir E. Carson had promised to bring it in, and we must know if he held to that. He said of course it might be useless; that it could only be brought in by Government consent and that the Trustees' representative, Lord Curzon, being in the War Cabinet could prevent it. However, all he could say was that if we brought in a Bill he would do all he could to influence the Government to help it. He could not himself do it, being in the Government, and so he went.

Then we caught sight of Mr. Samuel, the Attorney General, talking to someone, and when he had finished we called him over. His suggestion was that a question should be asked in the House. I said Mr. Byrne asking a question had thrown us back, because he had been snubbed. He said Mr. Byrne was a bad one to put up (he had put himself up!) but that Sir Robert Woods might ask it. Sir Robert was pleased at the idea and asked how it could be done. However, Mr. Samuels, thinking more seriously, said if Sir Edward Carson would ask it he would be best, and that he would speak to him. Then I left, tired out, sad, yet feeling a beginning had been made.

20TH. This morning a letter from Sir Robert Woods:-

> "I have just seen Sir E. Carson. He hopes to be able to take the Lane picture matter up after tomorrow. He thinks we ought to be able to press the Government to take it up. I feel a little more sanguine now but we have a good deal of work still before us. If you have not already done so, it would I think be well to let him have a copy of the papers."

Such a mercy having some move made! I have sent off my statement, &c., to Sir Edward Carson and asked when I may see him.

For yesterday I heard from Harris that O'Donovan is leaving us, is supposed to be going to start a touring Company of his own, was dissatisfied at Miss Magee's engagement at £5 a week, and at Yeats having brought in Miss Molony[7] "a girl from Liberty Hall", and at not getting more pay. And so I must cut short my time here and go back to reorganise the Theatre for we have not one fine actor, not one of the old Company left.

Yesterday morning we went to the Memorial Service for Airmen at Westminster Abbey.

In the afternoon we took the children to tea with Birrell and they enjoyed climbing up the ladder in the library, and having a gramophone entertainment after tea. Birrell has read through and returned *Henry Adams,* thinks it "very remarkable, the first part; the last rather maundering". I asked if there was anything new to him in the account of the Civil War time. He said he had known pretty well how near Lord Russell[8] was to getting us into war with U.S.A., but he hadn't known how bad Gladstone's conduct had been, and has written to ask Lord Morley[9] what he thinks of it. He also is writing an autobiography "to leave something to pay for his funeral".

He has a Staffordshire bust of Wesley in the library, and says he wrote an essay on Wesley once, which gave great pleasure to Wesleyans, he has been constantly asked to open their chapels since then. I congratulated him on not being in Parliament now, and he says he would hate it, especially after the years in which he had the Chief Secretary's room in the House, a very comfortable one. When he was first shown it he remarked on its size but was rather taken aback by the porter saying: "It is large, Sir, because you will have to receive so many deputations". However, he didn't have many after all.

We didn't talk much of the pictures, though he much approved of my idea of a deputation of the Lord Mayor and one or two artists, Orpen and Lavery. The chicks were very good, and both Birrells very nice to them. He told them they should eat bread and butter before their cake; that as a clergyman's son he had been brought up to do so.

21.—Newbuildings. I came here yesterday and was taken up to W.S.B., and it was a shock to see him in bed, breathing badly and apparently very weak, and complaining of pain and not being able to keep warm. But I have been a good deal with him since then, and he has seemed much better, and talking as well as ever, though he says he wishes for death, and though he has had such a good life, would not begin it again on any account. His memoirs, 1889–1900 are in proof and I am reading them. He is much troubled by a lawsuit Judith has brought against him about some horses. Lady Anne had put all in the hands of the Public Trustee, and he says the Office is a nest of lawyers who try to keep up contentions as long as possible.[10]

He has read Gwynn's life of Dilke,[11] and says the attempt to whitewash him is absurd, that there was no doubt of his guilt in the case.[12] He was brought up very strictly but was demoralised by Gambetta,[13] with whom he spent a good deal of time in Paris. When he was appointed to the Foreign Office the young men there had heard he was a Puritan and were sad. But some of them said afterwards to W.S.B., "Dilke is not at all what we thought, he tells Austin Lee no end of improper stories".

Lillah McCarthy[14] came through the rain to call, motored from London by Professor ———— who has to do with food production for the Government. She has taken the Kingsway for her venture and is beginning with a play by Arnold Bennett. She was to have begun with *Heartbreak House* but G.B.S. wouldn't let her have it except for a short run, and she consulted Galsworthy and Masefield and others, and they wouldn't consent to have their plays put on in that way, so she gave up his. He doesn't want his to draggle out and be taken off.

W.S.B. has been talking of his life in diplomacy, about twelve years. An idle time but a good education, teaching one to understand foreign affairs and the methods of diplomacy and government. He began at Frankfurt and heard a great deal then of the struggle between Prussia and Austria. The Prussian Minister's wife, who was very indiscreet and used to tell all the diplomatic secrets, constantly asked him to dinner and told all that was going on. Bismarck hated her, and when he was in power later got rid of her ("Olympia" of his *Memoirs*).[15] He was also at Madrid for some time and liked it. There was not much intercourse with the Court, where there was but little entertaining going on. The Queen (Isabella) was very fat and ugly, with pale blue eyes and arms like lumps of raw meat. When there was a reception she would sit on a sort of throne with her little husband beside her and thousands of people would pass and kiss their hands. The Diplomatic Corps had to stand looking on at this, which was wearisome. But he got on very well with the Spaniards, as being a Catholic they called him a 'Christiano' as they did not all the rest of the English, and they hated the French even more. He used to go to a sort of entertainment they had where the only refreshments were sugar and water and each lady brought her "official" lover; and he liked the bull-fighting. Then at Buenos Ayres he used to make expeditions about the country and at Lisbon he was with Lord Lytton. When he married, he left diplomacy and lived in Paris for a while. It was there he began to keep a journal. He is publishing the part about 1870.[16]

Yesterday some sculptor (Williamson) wrote to ask for a photograph of the monument he had made to his brother that is in the Crawley Monks' Chapel. I had never seen it, but the photograph is beautiful. Mr. Williamson thinks it the finest thing done for a long time in England, and he is pleased and says he is prouder of it than of anything he has ever done. I quoted: "Raphael made a century of sonnets, etc.,". He said this morning "I know and have often said that you have done more than any other individual for Ireland". I remembered his saying in a speech that I had "focussed" and so greatly increased the value to Ireland of the work of others, of Hyde, Yeats and the rest.

23RD. He has been talking rather sadly about his poetry, having had as he thinks so little recognition. He says if he had been at a University he would have been in a literary set who would have written it up, but he has never been very intimate with writers. I said the recognition would come probably from some group of young men at Oxford or Cambridge, and he said yes, there is already at Cambridge a beginning of appreciation, begun he thinks by Cockerell. Shelley, he says, was the poet he cared most for in his youth, he did not care for Byron. And he admires Rossetti immensely, especially in his poems, and Swinburne, thinks these two the greatest of his contemporaries. He never met either of them. Towards the end of Swinburne's life he was to have been taken to see him, but Swinburne refused, "not approving of his opinions about Ireland". He has been telling me Mark Napier's account of Asquith's early days. They had chambers together but neither had much practice; Mark because he was idle and Asquith because he had no friend or influence. He lived chiefly by writing for the papers, especially the *Economist.* He used to live at Highgate with his "nice little bourgeois wife", and go to his chambers every day on an omnibus. He never went out or to the play, was a noncomformist and very serious. Mark Napier, living at Ranelagh House, asked him to tennis parties, which he refused, and one day pressed him to come and meet Margot Tennant. He said: "What, that butterfly! I don't want to meet her!" But sometime afterwards he did meet her and was much attracted to her. And when his wife died he became a suitor.

I read him last night my *Jester* and he liked it, especially the verse, and thought it amusing and original. But he is much worried by this bother about the horses, now in Chancery.

24TH. I finished reading the proofs and W.S.B. was pleased because I think they will have a greater success with general readers than any of his other memoirs. In talking of the war of 1870 and the Empress, he said that while Napoleon was still uncertain about marrying her she had gone to a reception at the Tuileries one night, and the official at the door didn't know her and was uncertain about letting her in, and another official told him to let her in: "c'est la maîtresse de l'Empereur", and she went to the Emperor in the ball-room and made a scene saying his attentions were leading to this insult, and so brought him to the point.

He read me some alphabetical sonnets he has written[17] and some of the others, and the Rossetti sonnet he thinks so fine "Lost Days". I did not agree about its high place; it is painful and I don't like "murderous" and other overcharged expressions. He says Rossetti never cared for any woman in an ideal way after his wife's death, but lived with models and felt angry with himself for it.

He admires Mrs. Browning's poems more than Browning's, her "Hellas" especially, though he confesses Browning is one of the most intellectual of poets. Oscar Wilde he says, overshadowed every other talker wherever he was. I asked if he was put out if not allowed to talk as much as he wished, but he says he never went to any house where he was not. I suggested Masefield as the next poet laureate (he had said it would lapse for want of acceptable candidates) and he thought that would be a good appointment.[18]

I left him this morning much better than when I had arrived, and he and Miss Lawrence and Dorothy Carleton[19] all said it was through my visit. It did me good also. I have had no news of the pictures but Donovan resigned last week, and I thought I must go over and reorganise the Company. Today Yeats writes saying Robinson[20] would like the post and wishing him to get it. I have rather reluctantly assented, saying that the Drama League, a vent for Robinson's morbidity, will be a help. He grew very slack before and very careless about keeping up the acting and lost us much money and our American tours. But I don't want to fight and will try and work with him. It will be easier than working the Company myself, but I would have tried to do it.

Back to R.H. Road and to Harrod's with Margaret and the chicks.

26TH. Out shopping yesterday, coats and a dress; and to see Alec Martin at Christie's, surrounded with pictures in the basement.

He has heard nothing of our enemies' doings; sees Witt often but doesn't speak of the matter, except that once he said: "I felt hurt when I went to the National Gallery to see those pictures that are exhibited labelled 'Lane Bequest', but Witt said nothing". I have heard nothing from Carson. It is disheartening waiting here. And last evening I found a letter from Harris saying both O'Donovan and Miss Delany[21] are laid up with "flu", so there may be no great hurry—but it is a worry.

In the evening W. G. Fay[22] came to see me, a friendly visit. I was so glad to see him. And it chanced a Mr. and Mrs. Matthias came in, who wanted to talk to me about a new Drama League that is being started, so we had a long discussion. But I am not hopeful or much interested in English projects. I have been pleased by Filmer, the Manager of the Birmingham Repertory Theatre, writing to ask me where he can get photos of Robert's scenic designs,[23] "one *Dervorgilla* scene I shall never forget. Is it possible to purchase anywhere his work for the theatre? . . . I always hoped to meet him and I learned of his death with that peculiar kind of regret one feels when an artist is taken".

28TH. Waiting, waiting and no word from Carson. I am sick at heart, but I was reading yesterday to the children Greatheart's saying in the Valley of Humiliation: "Some have wished that the next way to their father's house were here, that they might be troubled no more with either hills or mountains to go over, but the Way is the Way, and there is an end". So I must go on facing the Hill Difficulty. And I have resolved to try again at the House of Commons today.

2 MARCH—FRIDAY. After many wakeful night hours I determined to go to the House of Commons and try to see Sir Edward Carson. I took the children to their dancing class after lunch and was just leaving when I met Agnes Goldman coming in search of me. We went out and she, hearing where I was going, (and with a very sick heart), stopped a bus, and she and Hazel got in it also and I didn't find till they got out with me at Westminster and wanted to cross the road with me, that it was from pure kindness and out of their way they had come, and this cheered me and I went on more bravely, to be told at the door by the policeman that the House was not sitting. "Why?" "Don't know, I am sure, giving themselves a holiday I suppose". It was rather with relief I turned away, though it is only an operation postponed, and went on to buy chocolates to send to Richard to help to make up for the disappointment about half term—no parents or friends to visit them because Mrs. Marsham's brother is ill. A sad put off for the chicks. Then I went to the Royal Hospital for Hermione Lyttleton's wedding tea. She met me saying: "I adore your present" (the delph figure of the G.O.M.), and Mrs. Grenfell and Sir Neville also spoke of it with delight. It was in a very prominent place. Masses of silver, chiefly from the Cammell Laird Company, and a detective sitting between the loaded tables. Hermione looking very charming in white. I spent the evening alone, reading *China under the Empress Dowager*[24]—an amazing woman, an energy moving in the wrong direction.

SATURDAY. Awake again, late and early, fretting myself about the pictures. Then I resolved to telephone to Carson asking for an appointment. I asked Margaret to do it and she tried, but his name isn't in the Telephone Book except at King's Court (?) from which no answer came. I took the children to buy skippingrope and to skip in Royal Avenue, and then, having taken them home, I called on Miss O'Neill to ask about an Irish actor she had spoken of. I don't think he will be of any use, but presently she spoke of the pictures and said Mair would like to be of use. I said he could be of great use if he could arrange for me to see Carson on Tuesday or Wednesday for I must get back to the theatre after that, and she thought he would certainly do so. So there is hope.

To Ayot St. Lawrence. The Shaws in the train but didn't see me, I being third and they first-class. G.B.S. first attacked me about public schools (having been reading *Joan and Peter*[25] and *Loom of Youth*);[26] and denounced Harrow and wondered we could send Richard there, they learn nothing but to hate Classics and all knowledge, and their mind closes up. I said that had not been the case with two Harrovians, my husband and Robert, which left him rather weakened. Then he told me he had dropped into the National Gallery the other day and seen the Lane pictures surrounded with a crowd with catalogues, much interested in them, and had felt convinced it was the right place for them whereas the Dublin National Gallery is a silent desert.

3 MARCH. We lunched yesterday at Lamer with Mr. Cherry Garrard, Lady Scott and Nansen, and dined there also.

To continue about the pictures, G.B.S. was really very good, for Mr. Garrard asked me if we were going to get them, and I said I hoped so and I told him that G.B.S. said they were appreciated by more people in London. "But", I said, "George IV when very tipsy and entertaining a deputation from Cork, had news that the Italian Government was sending him some casts of statues, and in his good humour, made a present of them to the City of Cork. Probably very few people visited them there, but one poor boy did and was influenced by them, and so became our great sculptor, Foley;[27] and so it might be if we had the pictures in Dublin, even if many visitors do not visit the Gallery". "But, I", said G.B.S., "I am one whose whole life was influenced by the Dublin National Gallery for I spent many days of my boyhood wandering through it and so learned to care for Art". We have been talking of it this morning and he is sympathetic. I said to him: "I am more appreciated in London than in Dublin, but I spend more time in Dublin because I think I am more useful there".

Last night at Lamer, he gave an account of a wonderful and fantastic play he is writing beginning in the Garden of Eden, before Adam and Eve, with Lilith who finds a lonely immortality impossible to face and so gives herself up to be divided into Man and Woman. He had read me a scene in it (on the pier at Burren) about a thousand years in the future with the Irish coming back to kiss the earth of Ireland and not liking it when they see it.

Talking of Sir Hubert Gough having joined Stephen Gwynn's[28] middle Party he said: "A man who is a failure is always popular, because he always justifies all the other incompetents".

Nansen[29] talked of Irish folk tales, said Irish literature was the chief influence on Sweden in old days, and these tales on their stories. He had always been struck by their fantasy, the hero who was angry (Cuchulain) having to be cooled in five succeeding baths. I gave him *Gods and Fighting Men*,[30] finding a copy here I could borrow. (I sent another to replace it). I was telling him Mr. Blunt's experience of the Spanish Court, the standing for hours while the fat Queen had her hand kissed. He said: "It was just the same while I was Minister here in England. We had to stand and watch the ceremony for hours. The Dutch Minister all but fainted, and we were all tired out". We talked of forms of Government. He says "Kings will never come again and Parliamentary Government has become unworkable. In Sweden just now there are three equally balanced parties, and no one will join with another, so no legislation can be passed. Democracy seems the solution, yet America is not ideal and has a Constitution no one can make head or tail of". He spoke a little of an adventure at the North Pole when he saw all his belongings swept away, nothing left him but a chronometer and a penknife, and expected his death but was saved, and how well he had slept on the skins of three bears they had just killed, so thick and elastic with blubber, he had slept for 44 hours from 6 p.m., and was puzzled when he awoke to see the sun still in the West. Mr. Garrard made us laugh by telling us how he had asked Lady Cunard if she had ever seen Wagner conduct! Lady Scott wore in the evening a becoming Egyptian headdress. She had been at Clewer with Margaret, and remembered her with her hair in very long pigtails coming to be kissed Good-night. G.B.S. says he had given Nansen a "vivid account" of me, and had especially told him of *The Image*[31] as a play that would be appreciated in Norway.

At lunch Cherry Garrard was here. I told G.B.S. that I had heard the cheerful little ticking of his typewriter like chickens picking their way out of the egg, and had listened with joy as I used to do when I heard a purring from Yeats' room.

He composes on the typewriter from shorthand notes. I asked what he thought of the Pelman system. He says "simple humbug, people are paid to write it up". They had written asking him, offering him £50 to write on it. He had replied that they had offered a friend of his £100 and he was much hurt at their offer to him. They wrote back that they knew he did not care for money, and had merely offered this "as a sort of postage" as he paraphrases it, and offering him £200 or anything he liked to ask. He replied that he thought of asking them for a sum of money in return for *not* writing on it. But that he is already paying fees for two people (his Secretary and an Australian soldier who had written asking him to do so) and would wait till he saw what the effect is.

The Australian has given it up as he understands most people do after the first few lessons. His Secretary persevered for a while but it has not improved her in any way. I said that was not a fair trial, because he had already been acting on her as a sort of Pelman system. Some normal person should be taken. He says the exercises and counting are rubbish.

Last night talking of influences, Nansen said one of the chief influences on him had been reading *Brand*[32] when he was about 16. It taught him strength of will. We talked of Prohibition. G.B.S. says the wives of workingmen won't like it, because it is easier to housekeep so as to satisfy a drunken man on a smaller sum, than to satisfy a sober man on a larger sum; and women say their husbands come in morose and out of humour if they don't get something to drink.

G.B.S. read me his play beginning in the Garden of Eden. The first Act a fine thing, "a Resurrection play" I called it. The second, 200 years later, an argument between Cain, Adam and Eve, the soldier against the man of peace. I told him I thought it rather monotonous, an Ossianic dialogue, and he said he thought of introducing Cain's wife "the Modern Woman", or perhaps only speaking of her in the argument. I said even that would be an improvement, as Cain is unnecessarily disagreeable and one could forgive if he is put, by aspersions on his wife, in a passion, for one can forgive where there is passion. It is like drunkenness—"Ah, you can't blame him, he was drunk"—when a man has cut your head open. He laughed and agreed, or seemed to.

Back to R. H. Road and had tea with the children, and then Margaret and I got a taxi and came down to Walpole House and after dinner went on with Mr. Goldman and some others to the Theatre to see *Abraham Lincoln*,[33] a fine performance of a "chronicle play" in sequence of scenes, that gripped me through, I think, the personality of Rea who acted Lincoln with wonderful dignity, beauty of voice and variety of expression, giving Lincoln's words, taken from his speeches and recorded sayings. I came back to Walpole House, and am in a beautiful guest chamber. Agnes has been talking this morning of the public schools, a terrible indictment of them but it depends much on the houses and she, like me, shrinks from the responsibility of sending her boys elsewhere.

I had noticed a great look of the Speaker, Lord Peel, in Lincoln last night, and Agnes says an American lady had startled them when she had come to the Speaker's House by saying: "Well, if that ain't old Abe Lincoln sitting in the chair before me!"

6 MARCH. Yesterday, a pouring wet day, yet I thought of

making my attempt at the House of Commons. Miss O'Neill had rung up to say her husband had written to Carson but had had no answer, and I said then I must go and try for him. But later she rang up again and said she had spoken over the 'phone to Lady Carson who said he wouldn't be in the House, he was in Court, but would be there Wednesday. So I was saved a wet journey and I wrote to Lady C. saying I would go to the House this afternoon between 3 and 4 unless I heard from her that another hour would suit better. So I feel more hopeful.

Colonel or General Cockerell, M.P., from the War Office, and a lawyer who was standing for the County Council, came to dinner and talked a little politics—interesting—and the lawyer was an enthusiastic admirer of the Irish plays, which cheered me.

9 MARCH. Sad about pictures. On Thursday I set out for Westminster. I got there a quarter to 4 (having written to Lady C. that I would call to see Carson there unless another hour was fixed). I wrote a card and sent it in, waited an hour. Then I consulted the policeman and suggested sending in my own card, which he approved. No answer. At a quarter to 6, I wrote one to Sir James Craig and sent it in. No answer. At 7.30 people began to arrive dressed for dinner. I knew there was no further use in waiting, and I came away very tired and in want of tea, had had nothing since lunch at 1, and with great loss of self-respect, feeling disgraced in the eyes of the policeman. I was back here at 8.30, but found kindness greeting me, Agnes so sympathetic, had not been long in herself, and seeing my plight gave me champagne, wonderful champagne, from some great vintage, bought up chiefly by Mr. Goldman and Cecil Rhodes. He came in then very sympathetic, in his kindness too zealous, for he telephoned to the House, refusing to believe that Carson showed intentional discourtesy, and asked when I could see him next day and to that also there was no answer. So I am in that matter in the Valley of Humiliation still, and in absolute dread lest my importunity may have injured the cause of the pictures.

Next day I wrote to him saying I had, through an imperfectly understood telephone message (Miss O'Neill's) believed there was an appointment, but that no doubt there was a mistake, and asking his advice as to whether the deputation to the Prime Minister, of the Dublin Committee (artists and Lord Mayor) would be helpful or not. If there is no answer to that, anyhow the police won't know it!

Old Cobham Sanderson[34] of the Doves Press, and his wife, had come to lunch. They spoke much of Morris.[35] They had been to Paris with him and Mrs. Morris and one of the girls, all the women in aesthetic dress, and when they went out of the Hotel and called for a cab not one would take them and they were mocked at in the streets. In the Louvre among the pictures Morris had said: "I look on all this with the eyes of an upholsterer". He had a way of talking without looking at the person he was talking to, and yet he saw all that was going on. He had a hot temper. Once in Venice, when he was limping with a gouty bandaged foot, he went into a glass shop and ordered a great quantity of the commoner sort of glass for his works, such a quantity that the shop-keeper was incredulous, thought he was joking and followed him to the door talking and gesticulating. And at the door a crowd of boys gathered and began jeering at him, and at the ladies in strange attire, and Morris was angry and stamped his foot, forgetting it was the gouty one—and then was furious indeed. Another time he went to Burne Jones' studio, and found a suit of armour which Burne Jones had hired to paint a knight in, and not having a model had intended one of his maids to wear. Morris insisted on trying it on, and strutted up and down very much pleased with himself. But when he tried to take it off, it was too tight and he couldn't, and stamped about in a terrible fury for some time till exhausted. "He didn't care for anyone but was afraid of G.B.S.—used to ask anxiously, "What does Shaw say?", but W.S.B. thought he did perhaps care for the delicate daughter.

Fairfax Murray used to lunch sometimes with Burne Jones[36] who said: "Whenever he is here, the conversation is sure to turn on bow legs" for he was bowlegged.

ON FRIDAY 7TH, I went to Durrants and fitted; and called on Lawrence at Murrays'. The Glasgow publisher refuses to reprint his *Mrs. Bent*, its morals having been objected to.[37] Then buying a pad for A. and the maids and self (all this in pouring rain). To tea with the chicks at 13, R. H. Road. They were alone and Catherine with a cough, very glad to see me, and I had brought some sweets from Buzzards'.

Mr. and Mrs. Barron to dinner, he an "agreeable rattle", had known many people a little but it seems none well, and writes a daily column in the *Evening Standard*. A meeting going on in the dining room about Mr. Draper's candidature for the C.C.

SATURDAY. To Putnams, but no one there except Huntington's Secretary. I asked her to copy out for me the Gettysburg speech from a life of Lincoln in the house for Mr. Goldman, who had been so delighted with an address made by a Canadian officer—very good, but Lincoln's is inspired. Then back to Hammersmith, and to Lyric Theatre. I went to the stage door and asked for Mr. Filmer who had written asking for Robert's stage designs, but he hadn't come in, and as I sat waiting I recognised Rea coming in and said: "Is this Mr. Lincoln? I am Lady Gregory". He told me he had acted in *Workhouse Ward* at Birmingham. I asked him what part of Ireland he was born in, and he said: "I was born in Belfast, and my father was born in Belfast and lived to be 95, and my grandfather lived in Belfast and lived to be 105, and my great-grandfather was born there and lived to 107". I said: "If you go on acting as well as this I hope you will live to 110". He said he had very little to go on in his study of Lincoln but thought it out for himself. I said I was sorry he had not stayed on in Ireland and he said: "I don't say but I may be working with you some day". I don't think they will let him go, but seeing him so good has cheered me, there must be other fine actors to be found in Ireland.

Then I went to the Doves Press down little paved alleys and found Mrs. Sanderson full of excitement, having been asked to go and see Madame Markievicz[38] next day, she was just out of jail and was holding some receptions in London.

Upstairs the old man was sitting tranquilly in a quilted white dressing gown. He showed me with great pride his little rooms, the windows looking out different ways on the river, so that he can see sunrise and sunset. It is the old Doves Press house and there is a sloping ceiling in the small room, but there is noble work to be seen there, books of his own printing and his own bindings, his splendid Bible, and Poems of Shelley, and Swinburne's "Atalanta". One book, a not well printed one, by Karl Marx, is beautifully bound. Morris had asked him to put the loose leaves together, and he had put the most beautiful binding he could make and had given it back as a present. "It was sold at Morris' sale and at a price we could not reach, but it was bought and given to my wife by Bain the bookseller". He had tried in all the bindings to put something symbolic, but not too openly symbolic, of the contents—the brand in "Atalanta".

He showed me the only case he has kept of the type of the Doves Press. "I could not bear to think it should be used by the other man (Emery Walker), and although it was in my contract I would not let him have it—let him go to law with me if he will! I took these cases out night after night, for though it was tragic there was a comic element, and I had to avoid the water bailiffs and policemen. And one by one, for they are very heavy—feel them—I threw them over the bridge into the river. Once, instead of falling into the water, the case lodged in a mud bank and day after day I went and looked at it, fearing discovery, but it was still there. But one night a high tide came and carried it away". (When I told Yeats he said: "That must be the reason that Emery Walker can never bear to hear Sanderson's name mentioned"). It seemed to me a very tranquil sunset and that he had brought some noble beauty into the world.

Mr. Goldman had been all day dashing about in motors bringing in voters for the election to vote for Draper, but was not hopeful when he came back in the evening. Some other helpers came in after dinner, a Wesleyan clergyman, a Labour Representative, a Garage keeper, and other business men, eight I think. They came into the morning room where Agnes and I were having cocoa (looking very innocent, I said, after our glass of champagne at dinner). She made some for them and we talked, or at first I talked, seeing both host and hostess tired, telling of Gladstone's speech on Suffrage and Billy Sunday's meetings in U.S.A., and then they joined in. The Wesleyan said that Mrs. Booth was a saint—a Saint Catherine—you felt in the presence of sanctity when she came into a room, and if she put her hand on your arm you were conscious of it for days. He did not think much of General Booth except that he was a great organiser. (But Mr. Goldman told me next day that he had been in a ship going to the Cape with many emigrants on board and Church of England clergy going for some mission, and that the exhortations of these had left the poor anxious emigrants cold; but General Booth's address had comforted them and filled them with courage). One of the others, as we spoke of Gladstone, said what a help Mrs. Gladstone was to him. He had been at a great meeting at Glasgow and the G.O.M. wanting to read something he had brought could not find his eye-glass, and Mrs. G. had jumped up and tried the back of his neck, and at last, at the end of about five minutes had fished them up from under his coat, at which the whole assembly cheered, it had made a success of the meeting.

Then news of Mr. Draper's defeat came on the telephone. And then he himself came in, pale, but making the best of it, and the G's took him to the dining room to administer some champagne, leaving me in charge of the others. We got on very well, and Agnes had to take me away and thinks they would have stayed all night.

9TH—SUNDAY. Chiswick old Church, and lost my way in a high walled passage and found myself in a little village and passed Red Lion going home . . .

Rudyard Kipling came to lunch with his wife and daughter and I liked him, he was friendly and unaffected and we had

Roosevelt for a theme, he spoke of his truthfulness and courage. I had liked very much his "Greatheart" Ballad[39] on him and we went on to speak of *The Pilgrim's Progress*; he thinks " 'Greatheart' one of the finest characters in fiction". He loves also the Holy War. As we talked of America, I said *Queechy* and *The Wide Wide World* read in my childhood had given románce to common things—doughnuts and applepie and cheese—when I went there. He also had read these in his childhood, and also *Little Women* and *Little* ———. He had loved *Aunt Judy's Magazine*, but hated the *Sunday at Home* which I had loved, and where I had got my interest in Polar travel through Sir Leopold McClintock's voyage. (And years after, in my London life, I had found myself sitting at dinner beside Sir Leopold whom I had imagined of a bygone age!) He said one could not think too much of the influence of the books read in early years, and quoted someone saying: "Give me the first six years of a child's life". He did not talk of the Empire, but wondered why people who could live in those glorious countries Canada and South Africa ever wanted to come back to England. Mrs. Kipling, I think, used to feel exhausted after an hour of Roosevelt's society. She said Kipling had been to see Wilson but was not at all pleased with him, "All jaw and froth, thinks he knows everything".

They took me back to R.H. Road, Kipling enjoyed the motor drive like a boy, their first for a long time: "Oh, look at that dog—or that baby". "Am I ill, or is that the Brompton Oratory?" Mrs. K., "It is not". "Then I am ill". But it was after all. Anne was at the window and he took off his hat to her, which I tell her she must remember when she is reading *The Jungle Book*.

I had tea with the children, and packed, and off to Euston. A night journey and a rough crossing. To the Gresham, and at 11 saw Harris who was glad I had come; Yeats had not been to the Theatre but once to see one rehearsal. Donovan has taken with him the worst actors, but also Miss Hayden, and tried to get Miss Delany, and the remains of the Company were feeling uneasy, fearing we should come to an end. Yeats had wanted to close, which would have sent them all to O'Donovan. Lennox Robinson came, thin and languid, but anxious for the Management if he can arrange with Horace Plunkett to let him keep a part of the Carnegie Library work. We went on to the theatre to make out a possible programme, and settled on *Mineral Workers*[40] for next week. Robinson will rehearse it and then he will be away for a week and I will, if possible, get up *John Bull's Other Island.*[41] I have been there each morning since, wiring Miss Magee, trying to get a Broadbent on the telephone, rather hard, for Robinson is in feeble health from "flu" and Millington slow, though honest, and the telephone itself has broken down. But in the evening Millington roused himself to remember a Mr. Maddox, who had once played Broadbent for us. I asked where he lived and he said in his depressed way: "In St. Jerome's cemetery and I don't know if he can leave it". (He is Secretary there). But it is Thursday and we have not got him or another yet.

13TH. Yesterday Theatre, and coming in near 5 I found a letter from Miss Magee and wrote to her, and set out again to get a book of *John Bull* and post it—just in time.

I went in the evening to hear Stephens[42] read some of his new stories. I said: "What a fine house for him to live in" when we came to it (in Fitzwilliam Place)? But we had to go up, up, up to a flat in the very top. A nice room, simply furnished, Mrs. Stephens there, and T. Bodkin[43] and a young man "who had been in the Post Office" (at the Rising). I asked him if he had shed blood or had his been shed, and he said his had not been shed.

Stephens read the opening of his *Tain* stories, Tuan McCarrel, who is to tell the tales. I thought it extraordinarily fine, the changing from tired and decrepit man to stag, to hawk, to salmon, with their joy in earth, water, air. And he has made even the coming of Parthalon and the passing of his people living and fine, remembered by the lonely man who had outlived them. He sat, as A.E.[44] says, "quite like a little gnome, wetting his fingers at his mouth to turn each page, his face lighting up with the glory of his tale". He read "Becfola" also, but that is but a fairy tale and I cared less for it. Yeats repeated his Madame Markievicz poem, and a Pearse and Connolly one.

The Sinn Feiners are now coming back from jail by every boat. McCann,[45] who died in prison, had a great funeral the day before I came. He had been interned since May, all summer, autumn and winter, and died as the days lengthened. He had saved the life of a sailor once, had the Royal Humane Society's Medal, and their "thanks on parchment" for trying to save the life of a Kilkenny huntsman drowned whilst crossing a river.

14 MARCH. Theatre yesterday morning: no answer from Miss Magee or Breffni O'Rourke, for *John Bull* cast.

On Wednesday evening, 12th, I dined with Yeats at the United Arts, and Cruise O'Brien[46] gave imitations of Horace Plunkett at the telephone, talking to the Fingalls about an American guest that was sent to him, a cruel, though amusing exhibition; and also of Lyster hardly exaggerated in the fluffy and ineffective buzzing round the subject, for I had been with him that very day and recognised it. Then I went on to Stephens.

Yesterday afternoon, Stephens and his wife and Ruth. Yeats dropped in for a few minutes on his way to the Drama League, and Gogarty came then gave me George Wyndham's romantic essays.

Stephens asked me what had turned me to writing, and I asked what had chiefly influenced him. He said he had been brought up on Davis and *Young Irelanders*[46a], but when still in his teens he had read Blake—the edition edited by Yeats and Ellis—and it had swept him away. He had written fifteen poems within a few days. It had turned him to writing. Soon after that he had read and been influenced by Browning's "Men and Women" but Blake was the real inspiration. I gave him *Gods and Fighting Men* which he had asked me to lend him.

Gogarty says the apparent stupidity of the Government is "shamming to delay a settlement", and that when they do propose Home Rule it will be bound up with the system of secular education which they know will be resisted. He believes there will soon be a "demonstration rebellion", perhaps a dozen police barracks seized in one night, as a protest.

In the morning when I had seen him at the Abbey, he had talked of Mahaffy[47] "a treacherous friend with all his gifts. At Lady Ardilaun's[48] lunch he was sitting nine or ten from her where she couldn't hear him, and he said 'this beer business only began about 1776. There was a butler in our family, a very decent fellow who went into business. He was the first Guinness'".

I went to see the Wilson portrait[49]—a waste of £10,000—finely painted, a commonplace man sitting, as Gogarty says, "like a dentist" (I should say a doctor) ready to put his hand on the telephone. My suggestion had been Roosevelt, and now that he is gone I mourn the more that the chance was not given to Sargent to capture that marvellous rush of energy, that "perpetual delight". He might have been inspired to do it.

Gogarty said: "He ought to have been commissioned to paint James Stephens", and I say: "It would have been worth the £10,000 to see Mahaffy's face had that been proposed at the National Gallery Board." For Mahaffy has never forgiven that affront, Stephens' appointment instead of his nominee, and is even now working to get Stephens out because he neglected to answer two letters and some pictures were lost thereby.

15TH. My birthday.—A box of sweets from Ruth its only celebration.

Yesterday at the Abbey, and have got the *John Bull* cast. Miss Magee will come, and in the evening Robinson came with a wire from Breffni O'Rourke saying he will play "Broadbent". An immense relief. Maire Walker, whom I had got in for *Kathleen ni Houlihan*, said, "You have had another upset", and I said "Yes, another swarming of the bees but the hive goes on".

I met Yeats going to pay a bill at the butcher's which he had been given money for a fortnight ago and had forgotten. I bought towels and pillow-cases for Coole £20 worth, linen is so dear now. As Robinson was going (for the first time) to see *Rebellion in Ballycullen*,[50] I stayed at home and read Wyndham's *Essays*.

16 MARCH. Yesterday after a quiet morning writing letters and reading G. Wyndham's *Essays*, "The Poetry in Prison" interesting. The "Plutarch" I had already read with delight in my Tudor Edition.

I went to the almost empty matinée at The Abbey. The bills were there for Monday with *Kathleen ni Houlihan* and *Minerals*, but Millington said casually that Miss Walker has to go to Manchester after all and so can't play Kathleen till Wednesday, and *Rising* is to be played in its stead. A bad moment to make a change, when we are already weak with the loss of players. I left a card for Robinson asking him to come round, and told him I would rather myself play Kathleen than let it drop (after all what is wanted but a hag and a voice?). He said it was "splendid" of me, and we arranged a rehearsal for today but my heart sinks now; remembering the words will be the chief difficulty, and I could joyfully welcome Maire Walker should she return, yet if all goes well I shall be glad to have done it.

In the evening I set out again for the Abbey, but when the tram reached O'Connell Bridge, at about eight o'clock, there were immense crowds blocking the street and I went on to the pillar. I asked a newspaper seller what was going on and he said excitedly: "The Countess is coming back!" I got into another tram seeing it would be difficult to get to the Abbey and perhaps impossible to get anywhere, and we set out but very soon came to a stop.

Then a band was heard and then came a waggonette and pair and I saw Madame Markievicz standing and waving a bouquet, yellow, white and with long green sprays (I had noticed a man carrying it through the streets earlier and had thought regretfully that we have no actress now to whom it could possibly be on its way as a tribute). There was a large, long procession following the waggonette—we were still held up—and there was cheering when it came to the bridge. Madame Gonne[51] followed in another waggonette, but was not cheered. We must have been over half an hour there, the long procession moving all the time, and then a procession of helmetted police passed us but there was no disturbance or rioting.

17 MARCH. Yesterday morning to the Abbey and rehearsed *Kathleen ni Houlihan* feeling very nervous about it, and wishing Maire Walker would suddenly appear and do still wish it—though I think I would be disappointed afterwards if she did. At tea-time I called to see Sir Robert Woods, he came up to the drawing-room and said he was crossing in the evening. I said he would be able to see Sir E. Carson, but he seemed much put out that I had not seen him, and said he might not be able to do it—Westminster a large place, etc. I asked if there would be any use in supporting him with a letter from the Dublin Committee or the Corporation and he said "Oh no, you need not urge me". However, later he began: "I think it might be a good plan if the Committee would write me a letter. I could take it to Sir Edward and say 'I don't want to trouble you, but these fellows are at me'". But he said it should be written and posted on Monday as he may only stay in London till Thursday. So then I left and went to the Arts Club to try and find Atkinson or his address, but couldn't, and Yeats said he lived in Stephen's Green, but couldn't be sure if it was 75 or 7, and couldn't help me because he was giving tea to some ladies from Sligo, and expecting a young man who was an astrologer. I walked to 75, where Atkinson's name was on the door, but no answer to knock or ring. Then I went to Mrs. Duncan but there also knock and ring were in vain. So I came home and wrote to Atkinson and T. Bodkin telling them what Sir R. Woods said, and that I should be here till 11.15 tomorrow and then at the Abbey. Then I went to a lecture on Nationalism at the Abbey, Professor Magennis of the National University, dull, lengthy, but he waked up when there were questions, and declared the Peace Conference is certain to give Ireland independence and that Ulster must submit, like other minorities, to the laws, and if they won't, must be deported. Oldham spoke, saying that Parnell would not have done this having said: "We cannot spare one Irishman from Ireland" and that he himself had heard Ulstermen boast of a grandfather hanged in '98. But Professor Magennis would have none of it, said being born in Ulster didn't make them Irish, and that it may be their grandfathers had been hanged for sheep stealing—all this put the audience in great humour—and when the Professor, talking of hate, quoted "Gott strafe England", a man behind me shouted "Hear, hear!" Stephen Gwynn in the Chair didn't say much, but looked moody.

18TH. To the Abbey, and ran through *Kathleen* with

Shields, my heart sinking more and more at the thought of the stage. But in the morning Atkinson sent me in the copy of a letter he had written in the name of the Committee to Sir R. Woods, urging him to see Carson, very good. And then Bodkin called and approved of it, and this may really be a step forward. Bodkin thinks as I do, that Carson's influence is already waning, so we had better hurry him to action while it remains.

Tea with Lady Ardilaun. She looks very handsome, handsomer I think as an old woman than in her youth even, though she had then her flashing eyes. A Miss Maguire came in and the talk turned on dress, and Lady Ardilaun told how in her girlhood she had seen Lady Spencer when Lord S. was Lord Lieutenant, go on board a ship on some naval occasion in a long pink silk dress, a white burnouse and lemon gloves. She thought it the most lovely costume she had ever seen, and decided that when she married she would have a dress like that, and did have it when she was called upon to open a garden fete. 'After that Lord Spencer turned against the Irish landlords and was in disgrace for a long time, and they had to keep away and go to India. But at last I was at a party where I met Lady Spencer and I said: "After all, it is so long ago I don't want to keep up bad feeling", and I asked to be introduced to her. And I told her about my memory of that costume, and how I had copied it, and she said: "Not, I hope, the lemon gloves!" but I think I had!' (That was the bitter political time, I remember W.[52] telling me one evening he had been talking with Lord Spencer in St. James' Street, and he had asked him to come in and dine with them but he wouldn't because there wasn't time to go home and dress, and he was sorry afterwards because Lord S. had looked disappointed and might have thought the excuse was made for the political reason).

On to the Abbey, and my face was painted with grease paint—white with black under the eyes and red inside the lids—dreadful! Luckily my own hair is grey enough without a wig. And I had got a slight cold so I was a little hoarse and felt miserable. When I went on to the stage it was a shock to find the auditorium was black darkness, I thought for a moment the curtain was still down and hesitated. But I got through all right, only once Shields had to prompt me. He was kneeling beside me so it didn't matter. Seaghan was behind the fireplace, book in hand, but didn't have to use it. There were few stalls, but as I guessed from the applause and saw afterwards, the pit and gallery were full. Of course the patriotic bits were applauded, especially "They are gathering to meet me now", and I had two curtains all to myself. I wish tonight were over for all that. The actors seemed pleased, and Mrs. Martin (Charwoman) came and hugged me with enthusiasm. Home very tired and hungry, and the fire out, and had stale bread with butter and a glass of milk.

19TH. Working at *John Bull* at the Abbey under difficulties, not having all the cast, some at their work and some yet to find. Yeats came and took me to lunch and showed me a cutting from the *Morning Post* about his new book *Wild Swans at Coole*, saying the poem about R. was "certainly the most distinguished of the many proud laments for the fallen".[53]

At 7, I set out again for the theatre in pouring rain (as in the morning when I had a long wait and then had to go on top of tram till there was a place). I was even more nervous than the first night but got through without prompts and had my own two curtains. But the audience was not so large or so patriotic as the St. Patrick's night one, Millington thought there was "more thrill" in my performance then. And Yeats came up to the gallery afterwards and said coldly it was "very nice, but if I had rehearsed you it would have been much better". Ruth, however, said she had never known so much could be put into Kathleen's part. Madame Gonne—a former Kathleen—was there, and Isuelt and Mrs. Groen and Mrs. Stephens all together.

20TH. Off yesterday morning to rehearsal, no Broadbent turned up—he (Breffni O'Rourke) was touring in the North. But we got a "Spoilt priest", a young man called Farrell, a Gaelic enthusiast with long hair, a cloak, a green tie, and a saffron kilt, and saffron stockings (with a hole in them), an interesting youngster and I think will be very good. I rehearsed from 11 to 2 and had cocoa at Bewley's, and Yeats came in the afternoon and I read him a long play *The Sea-gull*, by a young man, F. H. O'Donnell, who had told me of it at the theatre. It was written in pencil and difficult to read, grammar shaky, dialogue poor but interesting, an idea in it, a hunchback conquering life. He himself, they say, is a draper's assistant.

Miss Walker was to be back to play Kathleen and I was glad to have that strain off, but knowing we should take no risks I got to the Abbey at a quarter to 8 and found consternation and a telegram from her to say that she had missed her boat, so I had to tumble into the cloak and skirt and get Miss Magee to grease paint me, and I played the part better and with more confidence than before, though it was a small audience.[54]

21ST. The rehearsal yesterday and two photographers came pressing for the photograph of me as Kathleen for the *Daily Mirror*. I refused, hating the idea, and wanted them to do a rehearsal instead as a help to the Abbey, showing it to be alive.

But at last we compromised, they did one of me and also of Farrell (in his gaelic costume), and Miss Magee, rehearsing in *John Bull*. No Hodson had been found and Broadbent won't be here till Monday. The rehearsals are like Alice in Wonderland's game of croquet. Lunched with Yeats who was leaving for Dundrum. Came home and found a note from Mrs. Stephens asking me to tea, and though I was tired and the rain heavy I didn't like to neglect it, having no means of sending an apology, so went and found several people, among them Nevinson. I asked him if he had come here as to a seat of war. He said yes, but he might have to return to London before his Sunday lecture as if the strike takes place that will be the real seat of war. He takes gloomy views, of England especially. Stephens proposed coming to tea, "I want to come and set you talking and listen to you". So they will come on Saturday. Then I had to go to the Abbey, not being sure if Miss Walker would be there, but happily she was, so no more Kathleen. Millington asked after her performance if she hadn't grown very poor and theatrical? I said she had so struck me, but I had thought it was perhaps professional jealousy. I stayed for a part of *Mineral Workers*; and we heard of a Hodson. Home very tired. *Times Supplement* with review of *The Wild Swans at Coole* and with verses from the poem on R., drove away sleep.

22ND. Rehearsal.—Farrell very shaky in his part and very self-confident. I settled to rehearse him alone next (Saturday) morning. But Hodson is good. I forget what I had done to make me so tired in the evening, when Ruth came in very excited having been suddenly told she could have a passage to Canada on the 2nd, and she had already begun packing which had brought back her aches and pains. When she left, about 7, a wire came from Margaret—"Children crossing tonight Friday. Would you meet them Kingstown or Broadstone tomorrow. Ellen has been wired for home".

Meet them in the morning! I asked for my landlady but she was out. I asked the maid at what hour they got up and she said not before 7. No chance of being called in time or of a cab, no chance of help from Ruth or anyone, and so tired! I nearly cried. But at last at 9 o'clock, having no telephone, I went to the Gresham and asked for a room and they were able to give it and undertook to call me in time. So I went to the Abbey with an easier mind. A Mr. Barry I had met at Clonodfoy introduced me to a Colonel Heseltene, who had been with Percy Trench in Mesopotamia and had "Gone over the top" with him the day he was killed. I sat with them and they enjoyed *The Mineral*

Workers and laughed aloud, a help with so small an audience. Then to the Gresham, not much sleep and up at 6 in the morning and off to the Broadstone in snow. And there, after a wait, the Kingstown train came in, and I saw Anne and Catherine very pale and draggled, and Ellen very sad, her brother being dead. I put her in a carriage and brought the little ones here to my lodging, and there was a fire and they soon had breakfast and they felt better, and I put them to bed. Then I went to the theatre and to see Harris, but couldn't wait to rehearse Farrell, had to leave him to Shields with the result that he announced he could not come to the Sunday rehearsal "having his correspondence to attend to", and I was anxious, he was so shaky in words. (He had been in the Civil Service but refused the oath of allegiance and was dismissed). Then back to the chicks, and after lunch the snow stopped and the sun shone out and we went to feed the ducks in Stephen's Green. I gave them their bath and put them to bed (my bed, taking an attic upstairs) and went for a while to the Abbey, a good pit but we have had hardly any stalls for the week. Home very tired.

23RD. A sound of weeping at 7.30, and down to the chicks; not much amiss, but stayed with them till maid and hot water came. Anne had that pain again and I went to consult Gogarty but he was out of town. We read and they said their hymns and then we got a tram to the Abbey for the rehearsal of the 'Sunday Men'. Anne stayed quietly listening, but Catherine was all over the theatre and made friends with everyone, and I finally found her in the Box Office having a telephone conversation with Millington in the Office upstairs. Rehearsal pretty good but no Broadbent or Farrell, and O'Kelly who has but a small part but who I hadn't seen before, dreadfully vulgar. I had to speak gently to him. Millington very good to the children. Home for late lunch and then reading to the children, and finally telling them stories which they then began to act as charades, and then Ruth came in. Then bath and bed for them (8.30).

A Miss Russell, reporter for *Chicago Daily News*, came in and asked about the theatre and we talked for a while and I invited her to Monday's dress rehearsal.

27 MARCH. (GALWAY). On Monday to rehearsal. Hodson had been ordered back to England to be demobilised, but had made appeals to be allowed to stay here for his part, and after wires to Headquarters and spending a night in the Union, he got leave to demobilise in Dublin. Paul Farrell shaky in his part and indignant because his portrait had only been in the *Daily Sketch*, "Not in the *Mirror* though I ordered three copies".

Back to lunch with the chicks and then to theatre again, and at last, after 3, Breffni O'Rourke arrived and began his rehearsal. He had acted the part eight years ago and didn't seem to know the words at all. Millington helped me very much by taking the children to the Zoo. They weren't back till 6, and then I took them home and when I put them to bed I had some tea and went off again to the dress rehearsal. We ran through the scenes with the tower in the background and Farrell sat wordless and motionless, having forgotten his part (I had to get that scene on again), and Miss Magee seemed to have forgotten hers, and all the performance was slow, and Broadbent wanted me to cut his last scene with Nora where she objects to visit the publican's wife, but I wouldn't—she is charming in it—and I told her not let him off. There were five priests (friends of "Aunt Judy") in the auditorium. She had asked me if they might come as they are not allowed to attend performances. They seemed to enjoy it all, Nolan had come on without dressing, having played the part before, and they were puzzled, and I sent him to put on his clerical coat and hat and then they were much amused at his part (Father Dempsey). They asked questions about G.B.S., whether he had not disapproved of the War; and said as the play went on "he gives harder hits at the English than at us", with great satisfaction. I told them of Paul Farrell's dismissal from the Civil Service because he would not take the oath of allegiance. And they said "Poor fellow"! The rehearsal was on the whole promising, they were only shaky in words. And Robinson was to have come but didn't till about 11 o'clock, but I felt justified in leaving without waiting for the first performance though I should have to see it after all my work. Home close on midnight, dead tired, could hardly crawl into bed.

Next morning, Tuesday, down in good time and when the chicks were dressed and fed, I did the packing, and after 11 o'clock we got out and off to the theatre for a last look. The actors were fresher and their words coming to them. The cab came for us and we went off to Broadstone and on to Galway, and were welcomed by "Godmother".

It was interesting work in Dublin though a strain, and I was glad to find I could still do good work; and the first performance went well and has good notices.

I met A.E. in the street. He feels just as when I saw him last, says Sinn Fein has no constructive policy and that he just works on at his co-operation.

Today I brought in the *Independent* and in reading it found a paragraph saying:

> "The Irish Unionist Party, at its meeting last evening, Sir E. Carson presiding, decided to ask the Chief Secretary to receive a deputation in order that it might lay before him a request that steps should be taken to secure for Dublin the pictures left by Sir Hugh Lane, which are now in custody of the English National Gallery, and which the Irish capital has so far failed to secure owing to the fact that the codicil bequeathing the pictures, though signed, was not witnessed. Sir Robert Woods has been taking a great interest in the movement for the recovery of the pictures for Dublin. A certain line of procedure will be suggested to the Chief Secretary by the deputation, assuming he receives it, but it is not thought desirable that it should at present be disclosed".

Thank God, that weight has now been taken on Parliamentary shoulders and my work for Hugh and Ireland has not been lost.

29TH. On Saturday 22nd, the evening the darlings had arrived, James Stephens came to tea and talked and played with them. I said it was strange that children now seemed to be born with a liking for tomatoes, which we had to acquire; and he said: "I have good cause to remember the first time I tasted one. I had come out of school and was walking with three other boys and at a fruit shop we saw for the first time a strange scarlet fruit. We looked and looked and—well—we each stole one, we could not resist it. The owner saw us and ran out, and we ran and ran, and then a big policeman joined in chasing us. The other lads were getting away but I had short legs and I saw I would be caught, so I determined that whatever happened I would taste the tomato, and I took a big bite. But at the queer horrible taste, I stood stock still and could not move, it was such a shock to me. So they caught me and cuffed me, but not very hard, for the shopkeeper knew who we were".

He sang charming little French songs, and gave the children rides on his back. He wants to do a big story of the wooing of Finn but is resting after the creation of Tuan MacCarell and is steeping himself in *Gods and Fighting Men*.

29 MARCH. Just looking after the chicks and taking them out and a good many letters have to be written re theatre.

Such a nice word about R. in the Review about Yeats' Poems in last Sunday's *Observer*. "All who remember Gregory, a man so much the artist that he was never at pains to seem one, so much a man that the unobservant might never guess he was an artist, will love the Epicide his friend has written".

COOLE, 6 APRIL. Richard home yesterday and Margaret. We got home safely and found all well. News-cuttings keep coming in explaining the "failure" of the Abbey as announced by Yeats and Robinson in their lecture. Yeats wants me to lecture now to undo the impression, but I think working at it will be better.

10 APRIL. Harris wrote yesterday that no contract has been made with the Drama League, yet they are announcing their performance of *The Liberators* for Thursday. And later I saw advertisement of their performance in *Irish Times*, as if one of our performances, no mention of Drama League.

DUBLIN. 18 APRIL. (GOOD FRIDAY). I came up yesterday about Robinson's engagement and to see last rehearsals of *Dragon.*[55] I had written to the Gresham for a room and they gave me one when I arrived. But the Hall Porter told me in an agitated whisper that there is a strike ordered for next day of hotel servants, and they may have to close. I asked the housemaid about it and she said it is about length of hours; that they are kept every fourth day from 6 a.m. till midnight, and other days till 10 o'clock.

This morning I found the Management putting up a notice saying all guests must vacate their rooms by 1 o'clock (the girl clerk consulted me about the wording of it and was delighted because what I approved was what she had wanted, and she had made a bet of 6d. that if I were arbitrator I would say so). So I went out lodging hunting, and was rejected at six houses, all full, but at last got (what looked better than any of the others) rooms at 71, Lower Leeson Street. With all this walking I was tired and glad to have a quiet afternoon.

And as I was coming by Merrion Square, Sir Robert Woods was just coming out of his house. I told him it was Providence, for I was just wondering if I might call so early or if I should send in a fee and consult him about an imaginary broken arm. He hadn't much to tell about the pictures. Carson seemed not to have gone into the case at all or to know anything of it except from my letters, and the others had asked if any of the spoil might find its way to Belfast! And he hadn't heard from them since. He and Sir M. Dockrell had for this purpose of the pictures joined the Irish Unionist Committee though they are really Independents; but whenever Ulster was talked about they were turned out!

I had found a note from Harris saying Robinson wants a two or three years contract. And in the afternoon Robinson called and I told him I didn't think he could have it, but we talked amicably of business. He had written me that if I came up on

Thursday, the rehearsals I would see would be on Saturday and Sunday, and now says they had one last night and were expecting me, but didn't even telephone to say it was on. He is vague as ever I am afraid.

I am reading Charlotte Brontë's *Life*.[56] Three sad deaths one after another, and caused most likely by living in a churchyard. And what splendid flowers of genius from these short lives.

20TH. Yesterday I first went to the Theatre and had another talk with Robinson about his contract, saying that even in marriage settlements each side had for practical purposes to consider the other a possible rogue, and that if he had to safeguard himself against capricious eviction (such as Miss Horniman's of N. Connell because Miss Allgood in her holidays had recited for a Woman's Suffrage Society), so had we in case he should take to drink or use the Theatre for the purpose Lord French is said to use the mansions he hires in London. So he gave in to a year.

Then Harris came in and he is down on Robinson because—an astounding thing—he had suggested the players putting on *The Liberator*, and as their own speculation, and they had so for three nights without any leave from us or arrangement with Harris who also thinks he should not be paid full salary when not working, and at first I said he should get it. But later in the day, when I reflected that there are now three blank months in which he would be doing nothing for us, it is hard that our low funds should give him £5 per week. And so when I arrived at evening rehearsal, finding him alone I "did the hardest thing first" and spoke to him, and he agreed to £2.10s., so now all that unpleasant business is off my mind and I can work with him.

19 APRIL. *Dragon* rehearsal went well on the whole, though words are rather shaky and the Queen bad, Mrs. MacS., being English, has no respect for words and hits with extraordinary perversity on the wrong one to accentuate in each sentence. Some of the others weak, but Miss Magee charming and the King splendid, makes up for all. And Seaghan has made a fine scene and Dragon, and there is so much good-will it reminded me of old times there. Back from dress rehearsal at 11, pretty tired.

I told Robinson in speaking of the Theatre that we must have two horizons, one, the far one, the laying of it "on the threshold of Eternity"; the nearer one the coming of Home Rule or whatever the new arrangement that must come may be when the Irish from America and elsewhere will come back to see their Country.

We must keep the theatre something we should be proud to show.

21ST. To Rehearsal, it went well.

Yeats came to tea and brought *Cutting of an Agate.* He is disappointed at the reviews of his poem and I had told him it . . .

BOOK FOUR

21ST APRIL 1919. [con'd] Yeats . . . would have made a better and richer book if he had kept it back till he could put in his rebellion poems—and he agreed—but does not know when that can be. He is still interested in his philosophy.

I went later to Marlborough Road and called on Jack Yeats and his wife.[1] He is in better spirits, is having a show here and one in London, and showed me a reproduction in "colour" of a donkey—has had several letters about it and is getting £50 for it. He told (we were speaking of the Lord Mayor's good qualities) how when the joint expedition to Maynooth at the conscription time was starting, he (the L.M.) was determined to make Dillon[2] and Healy[3] come together. They were standing apart from each other, Dillon glowering with his arms folded, and he said to Healy, "All the motors are now filled and I must ask you and Mr. Dillon to go in the only one left". Healy said, "I've sometimes had to eat crow in my lifetime and I haven't liked it,—but if I have to eat crow again I'll do it!" and so they went off together.

COOLE. 24 APRIL—EASTER MONDAY. After a quiet morning I went to the *Dragon* matinée. A very small audience (the weather lovely) but the play went well and smoothly, not many 'fluffs' for a first performance.

The evening was good, a £35 house, applauding pit. A little puzzlement as the play began, and the Queen was bad, still mouthing her words, but the King soon brought laughter and the Princess charm, and from that time all went well with increasing spirit and applause. Douglas Hyde[4] and Nuala and Stephens with his wife and two children (my little party) and Jack Yeats and his wife were all together, and I sat with them for the first act, but saw B. behind and grew nervous at having a critic near, and I moved to the back. The scene and dresses made a lovely effect, Seaghan's scene and my own choice of dresses. The King in the sleepy scene was a delight and I was glad we had not Donovan. At the end great applause and many calls for "Author"—and I made my bow more confidently than when I had last done so as Kathleen ni Houlihan. Douglas Hyde liked the play very much, but Stephens was enthusiastic and his children shouted with delight, that pleased me best of all, and I took my tram home with Craoibhin and Nuala contentedly.

Next morning I went out before breakfast to get the papers. *Irish Times* dull—*Independent* much better than usual, *Freeman* splendid; "Indeed", I said, "all the papers are so good they must be going to die!" It is long since I have had such ungrudging praise. I met Bodkin who said Stephens had been telling him the play was the loveliest thing he had ever seen.

Business meeting in the afternoon at the Abbey, report of year's finances not good owing to influenza chiefly. However, we are a little to the good but with the holidays before us we must be careful. Anyhow my play required nothing new but an india rubber ball and a cocoa nut.

I dined with Yeats at the Arts Club and he came to see *Dragon*. But he was listless and did not like the grey curtain or the Queen's acting, and spoke only of them and did not say one good word, yet I think he must have liked it. But I did not enjoy it so much as the night before.

WEDNESDAY 23RD. I went out in the rain for some shopping and to the Abbey to say goodbye to the Players, and then to Broadstone and a tiring journey to Galway, where the children were spending the day. They met me with news that "Quinn had been shot", Florimond Quinn fired at, but not killed or even very severely wounded—though many shots had lodged in back of neck and head. Diveney who was walking with him, just outside Raheen plantation was also wounded. It is said it is because he had taken the Galway Avenue grazing which Nolan had given up, but there had been no trouble. Nolan gave it up because of his brother's death, Florimond's was the only offer for it and he had not been threatened or warned. It was a cowardly attack and said to have been settled at a meeting held without leave inside our gates on Sunday. Margaret was of course very much upset. And Richard was disappointed that I had not brought him a fountain pen he had given me a commission for—I thought he had changed his mind and said he would get it in Dublin, and I was sorry. We motored here and got home at 8.20 and they told me all about the shooting, and it is a troublesome business and may bring more trouble. And nobody asked about my play, or had looked at any other paper than the *Irish Times*, so the Tuesday night seemed a long time away!

Today I am busy with house and garden and the children have gone to picnic at Garryland.

25 APRIL. All the men talking of Florimond Quinn's escape. "It was the branch of an ash tree saved him" "there's a bad clan

going about". Peter [Glynn] thinks English law very fair and wonders they "can't be content with Dominion Home Rule".

Richard's fountain pen has come.

1 MAY. Richard left yesterday, Margaret going with him.

6TH. I have been reading and just come to the end of Inge's *Plotinus*[5] a wonderful philosophy, really a new statement of Christianity—except that his idea was the ascent of the soul, its return to God. And the coming of Christ must have been the answer to this, the showing how the divine life might be lived on earth. Perhaps He had come to the Hebrews because of their more passionate cry, in psalms and through the prophets.

6 MAY, 1919. A lovely day, and Katty and Joey have come over from Roxborough[6] to tea with the children.

Before that I had a visit from Florimond Quinn. He is a good deal shaken by what he has gone through and seemed to have a difficulty in remembering names. He has many grains of shot in his head and neck and back, and showed me the holes made in coat and hat. He talked for a long time saying the country was in a worse state than he had ever known it and the Government are doing nothing to make it better. He says that last Friday at Killamoran, beyond Garryland, there was another attempt at murder. A man called ——— was fired at; he had been given a farm a long time ago by Wilson Lynch, long dead, but it is only lately he has been called on to resign it. He was fired at in his cart, the first shot struck him much as it did Quinn in back of head; he turned and seized a gun he had with him, and then another shot was fired which cut the jugular vein. The boy with him got him home and he is still alive. Florimond himself has had threatening letters since the attempt on him. He will not have regular police protection because the herds he has on another farm are strong Sinn Feiners, and though great friends of his would not serve him if he came there guarded by police. He asked what my opinion was. I said I could not give advice to a man either to put his life in danger or to give in to bullying. He did not say definitely he would give up the farm but asked if Mrs. Gregory would be satisfied if he did so. I said he could write and ask her. I told him I believed this business would pass over as it seems likely some form of self-government will be given to the country, and no Government could tolerate this sort of irregular intimidation and these attempts at murder; but he said that was all very well, but a man might be made an end of while waiting for that. While we were at tea there was a knock at the hall door and Catherine went to see who it was. She found two policemen and went on to the kitchen where she reported this, and said "they say they want to see the servants, and I don't know who the servants are". This pleased Marian. They wanted to know at what time Quinn had left, and by which avenue he had gone that they might see to his safety, but I did not know. I walked to the white gate and looked out at the Galway avenue, the park so fresh and beautiful.

7 MAY. I had a bad night waking and thinking of this business, but sunshine and the children healed me by degrees.

This evening John Diveney told me that this morning the priest—Father ——— came to their house and said that F. Quinn had called and asked him to come to a meeting between him and those who object to his keeping the farm—those in fact who planned or made the attempt to kill him and who now had asked him to meet them. Father ——— had assented and set out, but on his way had changed his mind, and sent by the Diveneys a message that he would not go. He would have had pleasure in helping to arrange matters, he said, had he been asked to do so at the beginning, but he would not go unasked except by Quinn.

It is not known yet what was done at the meeting but Q——— had his sheep taken to Cahirglissane today and evidently means to give in, and it is evident also that T. D——— has refused to herd for him except on the Gort Avenue. It is said that the conspirators mean to ask the Bank for an advance to stock the farm which they intend to take. They want to get a claim on it, J.D. says, and demand purchase later. They seem to think Margaret will let them have it but of course she will not, and I feel it would be a bad service to the new Ireland to reward and give in to these instigators of an attempted murder.

Two head of cattle have already been put in, and J.D. thinks we ought to get the police to take them to the pound and see who claims them, but I don't think we have the legal right, the land being still Quinn's.

8 MAY. J.D. told me this morning of the meeting with F. Quinn and I wrote to the District Inspector. A couple of hours after that three policemen came down with a note and asked me to send "The Steward" with them to warn off trespassers should there be any, and then they would act. Their orders are to protect our men and in case there should be a big crowd to send to the barracks for help. I said they probably knew more about the Steward than I did as I had not seen him for some time. "Health" . . . said the chief policeman, I said "We'll call it health", at which they smiled, but I promised to send for Mike John, and did so. Then two more, armed, arrived and said the D.I. said we ought to give up any firearms and ammunition we had in case of

a raid. So I am to send Guy's gun and Richard's rook rifle and the cartridges to the barracks tonight. The police said "these Sinn Feiners" but I said I did not recognise them as such. I didn't believe they would be approved at Head Quarters, I called them rather land-grabbers.

To District Inspector, Gort.

8 May 1919.

Dear Sir,

I am told that yesterday there was a meeting between Florimond Quinn (who was lately fired at on account of having taken a farm here) and three of the group who want to get it; that they refused to allow Quinn to hold any part of it, though allowing him to keep land he had taken in the previous year; that they have arranged to meet him on 10th May and refund him the half year's rent he had paid Mrs. Gregory; that they will then stock it themselves, and that they intend today to come in and begin fencing it. I cannot tell how much of this is accurate but I think it would be well to have the part they threaten to fence (Galway Avenue and Fourteen Acres) watched today, as it would be more satisfactory to keep them out than to let them make a beginning.

Of course Quinn has no legal right to let the land to them. They have not asked for it from me or Mrs. Gregory, and should they do so of course it would be refused to men by whom, or at whose instigation, that attempt was made to take Quinn's life.

I shall feel much obliged for any help you can give me in the matter.

Yours truly

A.G.

8 May, evening.

Dearest Margaret,

This afternoon I found a deputation at the door, three elderly men, Thomas Fahy, John Hanlon, and Patsy Regan! I was much taken aback, couldn't think what they were going to ask for. They explained that they had come as a deputation from "some of the tenants". I asked for names and they hesitated, said Hayes, Donohoe, and then said, hastily, they didn't remember the rest, there were about twenty. I asked what they had to say and Regan said:- "It is about that farm that Florimond Quinn has surrendered, they want to be given it".

I. "Who has he surrendered it to?"

Regan. "To these tenants."

I. "Who did he take it from?"

Regan. "From yourselves I suppose."

I. "And when you had Castletown farm from us would you have thought you had a right to surrender it to the men, say, of Crow Lane?"

He. "And was it not surrendered to yourself or Mrs. Gregory?"

I. "No, certainly not. So that's an end of that business. It would have been a great piece of impudence of Quinn to give it up to anyone else."

R. "He asked them to a meeting, and at the meeting he gave it up."

I. "Did Father Cawley attend the meeting? Did Father Fahy? Did any priest? You know they did not and would not."

I then went on to say that supposing it were given up to us, that I for one would never consent to let those who had made that attempt on Quinn's life profit by it. They declared that none of our people had done it, that it was an outsider, and tried to make out it was done from Caherglissane, where Quinn had had trouble long ago. I said it was this troop here who had the name of doing it, and that it was hard not to believe it now, for that the first question asked whenever murder was attempted was who would profit by it? And we know now who expected to do so. By this time they were very apologetic and I think ashamed of themselves, said they had only come because they didn't like to refuse, and that they thought the attempt the greatest disgrace that had ever come upon Kiltartan. I said that if these young men wished to show their innocence and right feeling they would guarantee to Quinn their protection, and would promise to protect his herd. We parted amicably, they saying I need not be afraid to walk outside the gate as not a hair of my head would be harmed, and I saying I never had been and never would be afraid to do so. I don't know what the next step will be. Florimond had apparently behaved very badly, but his nerves are shaken, and his wife and his sister—who is a nun in Kinvara—have been lamenting around him. Three policemen appeared in answer to my letter and asked that the Steward might go to Galway Avenue with them, to warn trespassers off and they would support him. I said they probably knew more about our steward than I did, that I had not seen him for some time. One of them murmured "Health", and I said "We'll call it health", at which they grinned. I hear he has been in Gort for several days and he must be bad not to come down, for he generally enjoys a crisis. I sent for Michael John who followed them, but no one was sighted. Then two more policemen came to say the D.I. wished me to send in our firearms, "a double-barrel gun and rook rifle", in case of a raid. I said I was afraid of their being sent to Dublin and our not getting them in time for the holidays, but they said they were sure they would be kept in Gort if I made a special request, so I have sent them with a note to the D.I. I feel better now there is a clear case of right and wrong, and no question of any compromises. And also, my pity for Florimond is evaporating and I am glad you have his half year's rent.

Daphne and Miss Arbuthnot have been here to tea, of course delighted with the gaiety of the chicks. Pip and Tonks have been gnawing portions of a dead donkey. I thought it was Sammy and felt upset, but John says Tommy was popped into the big hole at Raheen.

9 MAY. I have not told anyone but I put it on record here in case of necessity, that I asked F. Quinn if he knew who had fired at him. He said "When I saw him I was sure and certain it was but I am told now it was not."

I told the deputation yesterday that I believed they would see the day—though I might not live to see it—when murder would be looked on as a crime as disgraceful as sheep-stealing. That this would be under self-government, when informing against wicked crime would not be mixed up with the idea of supporting English government. Their answer was, "Oh, there is no man here would do such a thing as steal a sheep!" The police called early to know how we had got through the night.

Bagot came later, was much amused about the sheep stealing.

Coole, 11 May.

Dearest Margaret,

There wasn't much news from the fair. John said he saw 'the lads' gathering, and kept an eye on them, and that they did buy some stock. But he also saw Florimond who said there was no truth in the story that they were going to pay him his money. He also said it was by their invitation not his he had met them, and that he had not surrendered the farm to them, but said he could not do so without hearing from Mrs. Gregory. John reproached him for not holding out at least for the Fourteen Acres, but he said what could he do, they were all against him. He is weak and I'm afraid a little shifty. Bagot said he never gave a conviction when on the Bench. John heard from someone else that the lads mean, if you don't accept Florimond's resignation, to take it under him, let him be "their landlord." John says he walked home with Michael C——— who said that you had told him when he was paying his rent, of the attempt on Florimond, and had said that you were sorry those young fellows had not come to you, and you would have given them the land! I said that was impossible, but John says C——— certainly believes it, he must have got a wrong impression, and he thinks he probably told it and that this made the troop so certain of getting it. (He also said you had promised to look at the fence of his field; and this is the fence through which cattle are coming into Galway avenue.)

When the chicks were riding yesterday I called them to come to pond field, where the primroses are a wonderful sight and the fallen crab is covered with blossom, and they were very happy there. On my way back through the garden I met Lady Gough, evidently come to condole. She said "These things pass over". She asked us to lunch today and I said (for Anne's sake) we would go, but it is pouring now (10.30) and I don't think we can get to church. I hadn't told Anne, as I didn't want Cat to ask to come, so she won't be disappointed if we don't. Hugo is away for a few days, but Guy still there. No letter from you, but they are very slow coming. That one you posted on Friday wasn't here till Wednesday or later. John regrets the days of the Monsignor who on an occasion like this would "shake the chapel walls and make your body creep", but says Father Cawley spoke very good at Labane, and said the man that made that attempt on Quinn would have his arm stuck to his side before a twelvemonth.

Coole, 21 May.

Dearest Margaret,

Yesterday on the way back from Cregclare we met Florimond, who had called here and was on his way to Labane. He stopped to speak to me. John Diveney being present we had no confidential talk, but I don't think he had anything more to say. He asked "Will you be satisfied if I give up the land? They are going on at me, and now they want me to give up Cahirglissane as well". I said, as before, that you were the one to deal with, and asked if he had written to you. He said "no" but he would write today. I told him that the demand for Cahirglissane showed that they were encouraged by his weakness in telling them he would give up our land to them, and that if he continued to give in he would not be allowed to hold any land at all. He said "That would mean the workhouse". I said he must balance the two dangers, and suggested his having police protection. He said as before, his herds would not work for him then. I was rather stiff with him, because of his bad conduct in meeting the men who had threatened him, and promising them our land. I pity him of course for he says his wife is continually begging him to give it up, and no doubt his nerves were shaken by the shooting. If you write to him I think you might say much as I did, that those who are trying to drive him out are the last we would let profit by their threats and the attempt to kill him. I hear there are quarrels, that they are "in three splits", and it is just possible that if they were convinced they would not get the farm they might let him alone. And please let me have a copy of what you write as there are sure to be rumours about it. The Tillyra fight is still on, Regan's cattle have been driven and he himself has had a beating.

Coole, 26 May.

Dearest Margaret,

I have your letter enclosing one for Cahill. I am keeping it in case of need, but I think that at present it is better to let it lie, I suppose Florimond had not written when you wrote. The longer he delays the better, and I am inclined to think you had better write only to him, very stiff about not giving in to let the land to those who threaten or attempt murder and not offering to let him off his half year's pre-paid rent. I have consulted J. and he says it is getting so late now for the would-be tenants to purchase stock he thinks they may give Florimond leave to stay on for this year! Any delay is good, for there must soon be some change in the government of Ireland. If an Irish Parliament makes a law for the cutting up of demesne land, we must give in to it, and if not, we can carry on, without having the attempt to grab it mixed up with politics and nationalism as at present. J.D. was talking to one of the priests, he is very indignant that this attempt has been made without a priest having been consulted, and says, "If they are going ahead without being said and led by us, let them tear one another's throats out". He had brought down a bill last night with announcement of Kiltartan races for Thursday, "The celebrated Kiltartan Course" . . . but not mentioning where it was except "within two miles of Gort", so one must suspect it was Galway Avenue. Luckily Marian forgot to give it to me or

I should have had an extra bad night, and this morning we hear the race meeting has been proclaimed, so that is all right. There is also a split between Ballyanneen and Corker, and there was some fighting last night.

The horses were busy with tillage last week, and Tom O'Loughlin and James Diveney (it was a slip of the pen calling him Micky Fahey and an insult to M.F.) have been cleaning kitchen garden walks which were beyond my man, and weeding over the garden (if you like I will pay them as you had not been consulted). This week they will be at the Avenue, and we hope as J.D. says, "not to break into the horses by sending to Gort" so I'm afraid this letter can't be posted till tomorrow. Iseult came yesterday after Kiltartan mass, and in the afternoon we had picnic over the lake, the chicks delighted . . . luckily there were six wild swans! Nora had called on her and I am to pick her up to return the visit today when we go to Cregclare (with Cobji who is convalescent) for some plants. The chicks like Iseult, Catherine gave her a pressing invitation to "Come to our house for a night" and I think it would be a kindness to ask her for a week after she leaves Ballylee, but won't till I hear from you. I told Nora of her birth, as she met her here, and am glad she called after that.

28 MAY. The night before last old Pat Diveney of Ballinamantan was fired at in his house. "John, the brother, was sitting in a low little chair you might have for reading the paper in and the shot passed over his head but Pat was wounded in the face about the eye. The police think the gun must have been put resting on the ledge of the window and it made no report. It was about the old lawsuit and the quarrel and the ploughing up of the land. It is terrible the way they are now firing at one another, and the Almighty God must have a hand in it that there is no one shot dead".

29 MAY. ASCENSION THURSDAY. Marian back from Mass, says a priest who has been here for a long time gave "a terrible sermon" on *The Voice of thy brother's blood crieth to thee from the ground.* He told them they were bringing disgrace on the name of Kiltartan (didn't pretend to think it was done from another parish like Father Cassidy) and had "a face like death, setting before them the law of God".

It was with snipe shot Diveney was hit; and they think he will lose his eye. No one heard the shot, perhaps because the muzzle of the gun was within the house. "There was a great troop of police at Kiltartan Cross. One had the face of a devil and was holding the butt end of his gun". I say this shooting will not be put down till the people—the farmers—determine to do it themselves and they can't do this while they think it would be helping the police and soldiers and the English Government. But Marian says "in my opinion it is all because the most of the land is divided, and they are in a hurry to snap up what is left". When J—— went to his dinner today his mother said to him, "This is the place for company; there isn't a soldier in Ireland but is in it. There they were, soldiers and police at the Cross of Kiltartan—lorries of them coming from Oranmore and from Galway".

M.J. says "It is hard for the doctor to say did any shot go into P.D.'s face at all, when he doesn't shave but every seven days and is the same as a wild man or a bear".

Father Fahy from Kinvara had been to see T. Diveney and said he had been asked by the men at Kinvara to say that F.Q. must not keep on the land, but at the same time he did not wish to give any trouble to Lady Gregory, who is so simple and kind and saved the Union from being brought away to Loughrea.

9 JUNE. M. says Father Cawley yesterday gave a tremendous sermon on the state of the parish, threatened, and said he knew the gang, thirteen of them, and some married men among them. And if they were prosperous today they may not be so in another year.

M. today telling me of it, says that "he is well able to put a curse—he put a curse on Florimund Quinn at the time of the Amalgamation of the Unions, and if he wasn't a rich man he would break up entirely now with the losses he has had".

7. This delay is best over taking up the Gort Avenue (that is what I had already written to M.) and then F. may be allowed to stay on. They are afraid of Government buying the land, and soldiers being put in. And it is late to buy stock—and then Father Cawley's curse.

11 JUNE. J. says three new beasts have come on the Galway Avenue and he hears were driven in through the gate by P.H. I asked if he was one of the thirteen and he says "*One* of them! If there was but three in it he'd be one and a half". I said it was a comfort to think it is F's grass they are eating, but he says "Even if he was a man from the North I wouldn't wish to see him robbed!"

LANE PICTURES.

(*Independent* 2 June).

The report of the Director of the National Gallery London issued on Saturday, makes no difference whatever to the collection of pictures which Sir Hugh Lane, by his codicil left to Dublin, and which are in the custody of the Trafalgar Square Institution, although quite a lot of information is given regarding bequests and donations, and also loans of pictures to and from the gallery. What has happened to the request which the Irish Unionist Party made some months ago to the Chief Secretary that he should receive a deputation which would urge upon him Ireland's claim to these pictures? Has Mr. MacPherson given the Irish Unionist members the same curt refusal as he and Lord French gave to the request that they should receive a deputation from the General Council of Irish Co. Councils to discuss with those Ministers Irish Bills now before Parliament? If so, the Ulster Unionists are heaping coals of fire on the Chief Secretary by covering him so profusely with compliments.

39, Merrion Square, E.
Dublin.
3 June, 1919.

Dear Lady Gregory,

A deputation concerning the Lane pictures was arranged while the Chief Secretary was in London, but he was so pressed for time that he could not see them.

I am sure it would be more convenient for the Chief Secretary to receive the Deputation in Dublin, and if you agree I shall be very glad to attend, and if you like, introduce it.

Perhaps we had better arrange it through Mr. Atkinson.

Yours faithfully,
R. H. WOODS.

Coole, 5 June, 1919.

Dear Sir Robert,

Thank you very much for your letter. I am inclined to think that a deputation in London, with Sir E. Carson, or even his Ulstermen on it would make more impression on the N.G. Trustees than anything we can do over here. We have done what can be done over here in the Mansion House meeting and the Corporation resolution. And wherever the deputation is received I think it essential you should be on it, for besides the great weight of your name, you understand the whole case.

Would it be possible to arrange for the deputation to be received at whatever time you are next in London? I should think Mr. Samuels or Mr. Henry could arrange this privately with the C. Sec. I do think we ought to make full and prominent use of the Carson party, even at the risk of a little delay.

A.G.

39, Merrion Square,
Dublin.
6 June, 1919.

Dear Lady Gregory,
Many thanks for your letter. I shall try and arrange for the Deputation the next time I am over in London.

Yours faithfully,
R. H. WOODS.

8 June.

Dear Sir Robert,
Your note is a great ease to my mind—many thanks. I do feel it would be a pity to lose the chance of using Ulster as a battering ram.

Yours sincerely,
A. GREGORY.

39, Merrion Square, E.
Dublin.
21 June, 1919.

Dear Lady Gregory,
The Chief Secretary spends so much of his time here that it is not easy to catch him in London, but when I go over next week I shall try and see Captain Craig with a view to arranging for a Deputation if possible.

Yours faithfully,
R. H. WOODS.

14 JUNE J.D. hears "*they* are saying now that it is late in the year for buying stock—and that they intend to come and see Mrs. Gregory with an offer that they will allow Quinn to keep the farm till the end of his 11 months on condition that it is given to them afterwards".

I said that in that case the right thing for Mrs. Gregory to do would be to refuse to see them, as her words to Martin Cahill on the subject had been misunderstood and misrepresented, but to ask them to make any proposal they wish in writing and she will answer it in writing. There will then be no mistake as to those who wish to profit by the terrorising of Quinn and so no doubt planned it; and also no mistake as to our intention of refusing to let any of that group profit. As to myself, I said, I do not think we could do a greater dis-service to Ireland than by giving in to them.

19 JUNE. Yeats came yesterday, having arrived from London at Ballylee. I asked if there was any more news about the Lane pictures, and he says Ricketts said "Hold on to them and you'll get them, they are getting very tired of the whole matter". I have written this to Sir R. Woods.

SUNDAY, 22 JUNE. This was from Sir R. Woods today. I am writing to Poppy Gough to try and see Lady Carson about it.

27 JUNE. Yesterday morning Marian said she heard a shot fired about 10.30 the night before. She had lighted a match and looked at her watch, thinking it odd anyone should be shooting. Mike Fahey coming into the Park today says it was young Martin Nolan of Corker who was fired at and wounded. Glynn says Doctor Sandys took eighteen pellets out of him and that this shooting is a holy shame. But they all have a twinkle in the eye as they speak of it being Nolan! It is supposed to be on account of the Diveney feud. He had cut the hair of the mane and tail of Matty Noone's pony to disfigure it—the Noone's being proud of their turn out.

Margaret ill with influenza. I sent for Doctor Sandys at 9.20 last night she was so feverish, she is perhaps a little better today.

Typing and arranging diaries and Catherine's lessons and looking after M. and the children.

28 JUNE. Sir R. Woods writes:

"House of Commons
26 June, 1919.

"I saw Captain Craig today and reminded him about the interview with the Chief Sec. It is mainly owing to the fact that he spends most of his time in Ireland that it has not come off. I told Captain Craig that my presence was really unnecessary and that what we really want is that the Ulster men should speak. He has promised to look after the matter on the first opportunity, but it would be well to let him have a copy of the pamphlet so that he can refresh his mind on the matter."

Yours faithfully,
R. H. WOODS.

"The interview may take place next week."

I have sent pamphlets, typing the Corporation Resolution about building the Gallery as a P.S., and to Bodkin about having articles ready for the Irish papers.

Margaret better.

J.G. thinks it a pity young Nolan was let off so easily, "I'd be better pleased if his two legs were swept".

29 JUNE. Last evening we heard by the firing of guns at Gort Barracks that Peace (with Germany) had been signed.

30 JUNE. Tim says "Martin Nolan is sitting in a chair, there are shots in his arm and in his side that cannot be taken up till the swelling goes down. He has no great harm; and as to who shot him there is a mystery, but it is certain it was not a man from the North or from Kinvara or any far place".

1 JULY. Margaret better, and has gone with Olive, Guy and Hugo for the motor tour.

Sir H. Doran writes (after my long efforts) returning £4/10/- of Tim's £6/5/- for cutting turf, rather a triumph.

Poppy Gough writes she has seen Lady Carson who is to stir up Sir E. about the pictures—that is a help.

2 JULY. An amiable letter from Sir James Craig. I had only met him *once* that time when as recorded he was not so very amiable.

Anxiety about strawberries for jam for R's holidays and the other year [sic]—but Willie Trench thinks he can send some.

Catherine's reading lessons going well; at last she is getting a grip, and can spell out words she has not met before.

And I find her on the sofa with *Kit-Kat* in her hand instead of having to search her out and persuade her to come in.

And I have except for that lesson and a visit to the garden been writing letters chiefly over Theatre all the morning. The chicks made off to hayfield where we spent yesterday afternoon, by themselves.

39, Merrion Square, E.
Dublin.
1 July, 1919.

Dear Lady Gregory,

You sent the pamphlet to the wrong man. Sir James Craig is not the Secretary, and probably will take no notice of it. The Secretary of the Irish Unionist Party is Captain Craig.

Yours faithfully,

R. H. WOODS.

Ministry of Pensions,
London, S.W.1.

Westminster House,
Millbank, London, S.W.1.
30 June, 1919.

Dear Lady Gregory,

I am very much obliged by your kindness in forwarding

further particulars on the subject of Sir Hugh Lane's French pictures. As I have repeated on every occasion on which we have met, you and your colleagues may count upon my hearty support; it will be a pleasure to accompany any deputation to the Chief Secretary on the subject.

Yours sincerely,
JAMES CRAIG.

Lady Gregory,
Coole Park,
Gort, County Galway,
Ireland.

39, Merrion Square, E.
Dublin.
4 July, 1919.

Dear Lady Gregory,
I return you Captain Craig's letter. I think it very encouraging that he takes a favourable view of the matter.

Yours faithfully,
R. H. WOODS.

House of Commons.
7 July, 1919.

Dear Madam,
I am in receipt of yours of the 3rd inst., enclosing pamphlets setting forth the case of the Lane pictures. I hope for a Deputation to meet the Chief Secretary in a few days.

Yours very truly,
C. C. CRAIG.

To Lady Gregory.

House of Commons.
8. 7. 1919.

Dear Lady Gregory,
I took a deputation to see the Chief Secretary re the Lane pictures today. The Chief Secy. is very sympathetic and asked me to have a statement drawn up giving the salient points of the case to lay before the Cabinet. I have written to Sir R. Woods for this. The Chief Secy. will then urge the Cabinet to consent to the passage of a Bill legalizing the Codicil to Sir H. Lane's will which would effect the return of the pictures to Ireland.

Yours very truly,
C. C. CRAIG.

39, Merrion Square, E.
Dublin.
9 July, 1919.

Dear Lady Gregory,

I have received the enclosed from Captain Craig and shall be glad to do as he requests. I think however it would be better if you, who know everything so much better than I, would do this for me. It would probably gain a very great deal in its accuracy and force.

Yours faithfully,
R. H. WOODS.

Lane Pictures Committee,
Dublin.

Hon. Secretary,
George Atkinson, R.H.A.,
97, St. Stephen's Green,
Dublin.

Dear Lady Gregory,

I have received your card and your letter with enclosures addressed to the School of Art, and am giving the statement immediate attention. Something might be added to your draft as to the sympathy of prominent public men in the matter, and of the promises of support made to representative deputations by Mr. Duke and Mr. Shortt.

I hope to have the draft in Sir Robert Woods' hands tomorrow, and if it is agreed with him that any amendments or additions are of sufficient importance to submit to you, I shall send the revised draft to you at the earliest moment.

I think it is important to get this matter through, before the Party becomes involved in any fresh political development that may arise.

Yours sincerely,
GEORGE ATKINSON.

POST OFFICE TELEGRAMS

Lady Gregory, Coole Park, Gort, Galway.

Just received letters will prepare statement at once writing
BODKIN.

3, Wilton Terrace,
Dublin,
14 July, 1919.

Dear Lady Gregory,

I have been away from home for the last couple of days, so only received your letter this morning.

You and the deputation certainly seem to have done good work. I will prepare the statement you wish immediately, and send it in the course of the next few days for your approval or correction. I think I have all the necessary material.

Mrs. Gregory's point is, I think, one of the best we can make (among a great many good ones). I had not overlooked it. It is a lawyer's point.

With compliments and kind regards,

Yours very sincerely,

THOMAS BODKIN.

4 JULY. Would have been put out by Sir R. Woods' letter yesterday morning had not my mistake in writing to Sir James instead of Captain Craig brought me such a nice letter from him which I have sent to Sir R. to see.

It was a quiet day; writing letters, theatre and other business—and typing a bit of old diaries, and I took the chicks to Moran's field and left them there with the haymakers and they got another big bunch of bee orchids. Then when we had taken out tea to the little Hehirs who were weeding, they took a fancy to weed themselves and with real hard work cleared a long walk of groundsel. Anne said "If Richard were here he would help", and I said "I wonder" and Catherine said "No, for girls always do more than boys, because *they* mostly shoot!" Very true for a five year old.

Then J. and Tom Diveney came to say they believe F. Q. is to be allowed to keep the farm for the year, and that his cattle are to be put there to-morrow. He had been to Blake the lawyer who said he could go to the ringleaders for compensation and he could sue the three who came here—T. is taking credit for having told Hanlon this, and so magnified the amount of compensation to be claimed that "it would have left them bare on the road". He sent for the others, and anyhow, they are giving in. Margaret's reception of them and "stiff talk" is also supposed to have had a good effect. It is a mercy and puts off trouble at least for a year.

9 JULY. Strawberries from Clonodfoy for preserving yesterday—60 lbs., and then Mrs. Bagot brought 8 lbs.—and with our own 17 pots already made there will be plenty for the winter. The chicks much excited dancing around.

10 JULY. Captain Craig's letter saying the deputation had been "sympathetically received" and that the Chief Secretary wants a statement to lay before the Cabinet which he will urge to legalize the codicil. A great advance! I have looked up notes and

dates and sent them to Bodkin, hoping he and Atkinson will prepare the statement, and have written to Sir R. Woods.

15 JULY. There was no answer from Bodkin and I guessed he must be away, and on Sunday I (having a chill and sore throat that kept me from church) worked at one and finished it yesterday and sent it off to Atkinson, and then had a wire from Bodkin saying he has just got my letters and will prepare a statement. Just as well I sent mine, as anyhow it was very short and gave I think all the necessary points.

Packing for the chicks to go to Burren, Anne says, "Grandmama you must be out of breath with minding us so long". Catherine really has got on—she gets through a page of "Kit-Cat" every day though it is like teaching a squirrel. A day or two ago when I pointed to a wrong line she said, "Oh, Granma, I'm 'shamed of you!" and then stroked my face lest I should feel hurt. I shall be quite alone now, as in old times.

16. Bodkin and Atkinson both write they're working at a statement! So there will be three!

Carr, a farmer of fifty was struck on the head with a hurling stick last Sunday week after Mass at Tirnevan by a young man, Quinn, who came behind him and struck him before the congregation. He has since died. It was first a dispute about land, but "it was the women did it all", Peter Glynn says, "talking at one another—the whole world knows that".

I have finished typing my diaries and have begun looking through my letters to Yeats.

22 JULY. Have been to Galway for three days. Peace celebrations only marked as far as I could see by closing of the Bank and Post Office.

I have had a draft from Bodkin (of the statement), it was rather long and feeble I think. Today Sir R. Woods writes that he likes the one Atkinson has sent him (mine I suppose) so I am asking to see it again.

Yacht Wayfarer,
Kilgarvan,
Borris o Kane.
19 July, 1919.

Dear Lady Gregory,

I heard from Mr. Atkinson yesterday and returned his draft today. I made a small suggestion which he will probably carry out in a marginal reference to the subject of the paragraphs.

I think it is very good.

Yours faithfully,
R. H. WOODS.

Malchi Quinn came this morning in low spirits, says a grave has been dug before Martin Nolan's door, and it was decorated with flowers "'ere yesterday" (Sunday). Marian says there are no two farmers speaking to one another in Kiltartan, except the Noones and Quinns who had not spoken to each other for 20 years until now!

23 July. Yeats came yesterday and read his essay for the *Irish Statesman*,[7] he had written it instead of taking the Chair at the Plunkett debate at the Abbey—but thinks now that would have been less trouble.

Atkinson sent statement, mine, with marginal index by Sir R. Woods' suggestion—but writes, "a mistake in the date was inserted by him" which is important. I am glad he has sent it off, it is certainly better than Bodkin's. This may have been my last statement of the case after so many!

(Nov. 1, 1921—alas no!) (Feb. 1924—alas indeed)

Writing about it and plays (to Yeats and Robinson) and some other necessary letters till 2 a.m., and how my head aches!

BOOK FIVE

1 AUGUST, 1919. I took charge of the children at Burren for a week—Margaret going to London—and then I brought them back.

29 JULY, to meet Richard and he arrived next day, well and bright and happy. It is just as R. [Robert], used to come, he was taken up for the first day or two with thought of cricket and talk of school. But yesterday he took his gun to scare the crows that are attacking the potatoes, and cut branches to make pen holders and had a hunt after a trespassing rabbit in the garden. I read to him a cricket story after he was in bed last night. It was that day 18 months the news from Italy had come. It is a great happiness seeing that room occupied, the little dark head lying where the little fair head used to lie in holiday times long ago. Yesterday's *Irish Times* had a note saying the Irish Unionist Parliamentary Party has just found a statement of the case on which they base their request for legislation about the Lane pictures—and that MacPherson has promised to bring it before the Cabinet.

So my statement has gone a step further. I have looked through a good heavy packet of my letters to Yeats. And I have been putting together ideas for a play of change of character through playing of a magic fiddle.

18 AUGUST. I have been twice at Burren with the Darlings, while Margaret was here. Richard and Anne can swim now. Troubles at Tillyra. E. Martyn[1] submitted his case to a Sinn Fein Court in Gort and it was given in his favour. But when the grazing tenants who had been put out brought in their cattle again, it was driven off and the owners beaten "and those that bid for hay at the Tillyra auction without leave are in their beds since". Edward says Sinn Fein talks of calling out the Volunteers to put down the Cattle driving.

Today I have been as usual gathering fruit for the children and have arranged nets in the vinery for the ripening nectarines to fall into; and have covered plum jam, and written a scenario for my Aristotle play.[2]

No news of the pictures, and this evening reading Gilbert

Murray's "Appendix" on his Plays I find a verse:

"A crooked spirit, a churl's door hard set
"Against Love's knocking, nimble to forget
"What true men brood on: Hardly shalt thou find
"In man, though brothers of one kith and kind,
"One true friend to the dead. For coveting
"Is fierce, and duty but a gentle thing;
"And the old magic of the eyes hath sway
"No more, when the live man hath gone his way
"And the house is not."[3]

The session is ending, and I am anxious.

Alec Martin has written that Martin Wood's *Life* of Hugh is unsatisfactory, and wants me to see if I can do anything to it.

20 AUGUST. Rock was to have come and cut our oats with his machine. But he had been turned back by the police and military from Crusheen on his way to Ennis Market, which is closed, where he was going to sell his cabbage plants. So today he has taken them to Kinvara market, but has not much chance of selling them because of the drought. Though he could have sold them in the boggy Clare district.

30 AUGUST. Back from Dublin. I stayed at Sandycove in Harris's[4] cottage. A lovely sea on Sunday and a quiet day. I read through the MS. of Martin Wood's memories of Hugh—very painful to read, very unsatisfactory. Well, I have broadened my shoulders for another burden, and will write the *Life*.[5]

The Abbey very encouraging, most splendid House Show audiences for *Dragon* and Dunsany's *Night at an Inn*,[6] and especially for *John Bull's Other Island*,[7] such enthusiastic delight. And ours is the only theatre in Dublin where real Drama is being given, one has *The Maid of the Mountains* and the others variety shows. The sight of the Abbey audience makes one glad to have been born.

I must put by my "Bellows" comedy and do Hugh's *Life*.

On Wednesday I was sitting in the theatre watching the rehearsal of *The Saint*[8] and the author—Desmond Fitzgerald came in and sat near me and we had a talk. I asked if he had written much, and he said "only when I was in prison" (He is Sinn Fein member for the Pembroke division). He said he had been chained to de Valera as they were taken to the English gaol. I told him my sympathies were ever republican, but that such is the irony of Fate, I am praying for the health of Carson, because he is working for the return of the Lane pictures to Ireland. He said, "then we must all pray for Carson's health, for I remember when I was living in Paris the thing that seemed to interest the French in Ireland more than any other thing was the possession of those pictures. They used to say is it really true that Dublin has the Renoir and the Manet?"[9] I asked about Sinn Fein policy, if they would accept Colonial Home Rule. He said, "Would we get it?" I said I disliked politics and kept out of them, and he said de Valera hates them and longs to have done with politics and to begin the work of building. He had looked forward to being with his wife who he had seen but little of. And then he was taken to gaol and then when he escaped he was hoping for it again, and then he had to go to America. He spoke of him with enthusiasm, his sincerity and honesty. I told him of the shootings and outrages and he said, "It comes of there being 90,000 young men in the country with not enough occupation". Just what I say. We were much in agreement, or so it seemed. I told him it was our intention to give over some day the Abbey to a National Government.

Sir R. Woods was away, I have no news about the pictures, but see from Capt. Craig's letter that at least the matter isn't closed.

"29, Brompton Square, S.W.3. 23 August 1919.
Dear Lady Gregory, Excuse me for not acknowledging sooner the Statement composed by Mr. Bodkin re the Lane Pictures which you sent me on the 16th Inst.

I received the statement safely and it will no doubt be of considerable value. Yours very truly, C. C. CRAIG."

3 SEPTEMBER. Yesterday morning Professor Vendryès, an editor of the *Revue Celtique*, came for a night.[10] I have a bad cold, and was alone so asked Yeats and Mrs. Yeats to dinner, and wrote to Edward Martyn asking him if he could come and drive him to Kilmacdugh so he brought his motor and took him away for the afternoon, a relief as my voice was nearly gone. And E.M., came back with him and stayed to dinner and Yeats stayed the night to help me with Hugh's life, dictating to me some recollections this morning. Edward is very angry with the people, calls them Hottentots and says he will let his land lie idle rather than let them take it. He thinks we shall get the Pictures "because the English will never give Home Rule". I say, then we'll get them on the principle of the Beadle in Oliver Twist "when a pauper asks for money give him something else" and he won't ask again. Vendryès is much puzzled by the complexity of Irish politics—no wonder.

12 SEPTEMBER. After quiet days with the chicks at Burren reading *Life and Times of Cleopatra*[11] and helping Richard in

his play, I came back.

13TH. A tiring day. Fair of Gort—and W. Bagot came at 3 and asked for food—Mary having gone to confession in Gort! Then Mr. Vere O'Brien with Captain and Miss Ward and his son. Luckily Yeats came and entertained them. But after they left he argued for "a free hand" in settling for lectures, and in finance. I would not give—or take—that. All about an extra guinea Harris lays down as minimum for "lets" and Mrs. T. Smith refuses. I offered to contribute towards a fund for it but that was scorned.

Bagot very anxious we should apply for compensation for malicious injury for boards taken from Balinamantane—and succeeded in getting J. Diveney (rather excited after the fair) to swear on the Testament, and at the risk of £5 for broken oath, that he could testify in Court to having called the police and with them discovered the theft.

This while I was engaged with the O'Brien party. Bagot had made a great point of its being a *New* testament—thinking it may be that something in the old dispensation might nullify the oath—and Marion couldn't find one but brought the Bible "that has all the childrens' names in it" as an extra safeguard.

All very well, but next day he says "I wouldn't wish it known it was I went for the police. I might get a blow of a stone one night from behind a wall". Very true—and anyhow, it was not malicious, it was simple theft.

And while Mrs. O'Brien, upstairs, had been looking shocked at hearing we had engaged an actor who had refused to take the oath of allegience her chauffeur, having tea with Marion, was telling her it was by the soldiers the police were being shot and that the soldiers would have you robbed if you walked the streets of Ennis having two shillings in your pocket.

16TH. Margaret wrote putting off her coming till tomorrow—so it will be too late to start in the malicious injury claim, and so best.

39, Merrion Square
· Dublin
16 September, 1919

Dear Lady Gregory,

I saw the Chief Secretary a few days ago on another matter, and took the opportunity of speaking to him about the Lane pictures. He brought the matter before the Cabinet and they have written to the Trustees of the National Gallery on the principle of *audi alteram partem*. There the matter lies for the present.

I told the Chief Secretary that of course the National Gallery people would fight the matter, and that it would be a grave dereliction of duty on their part if they did not do so, so I am sure he will be prepared for their adopting a hostile attitude.

Yours faithfully

R. H. WOODS

17TH. On Saturday several of the Gort shops were searched. We were told how the police were gathered around Stephensons—and waiting for him to get up, which he did not until 11 o'clock.

Three police came here to know "if we knew anything more about the planks about B-mantane" I said we did not, but there was a rumour they had been taken and put down as a dancing floor for the Sunday dance in the tent at Kiltartan Cross. They asked if John Diveney would be willing to come there and identify the planks—I said I was certain he would not, as it would stir up the anger of every young man in the parish. They said they supposed it would. I took them to the garden for some apples and damsons—they liked them very much, and tried to get some into their pockets, but I said their costumes did not seem to have been made for such purposes, and I would send them in a basket which much pleased them. I told them the country would never be right till there is a National Government that honest people will support, for now no one will give up ill-doers to justice, lest they would be helping the police and the soldiers and the English—all felt to be in the same basket. They quite agreed and hoped a settlement would soon come.

Searching masses of old letters of Yeats' in search of scraps about Hugh—and finding one here and there.

24 SEPTEMBER. I left Coole with Richard on Saturday—a bad crossing and tiring journey.

On Sunday we went to Chelsea old Church and in the afternoon to the Zoo with the Pope Hennesseys[12] and had tea with them. Richard very happy, photographed the animals and had tea in the nursery. R.P.H., at intervals talked of the Dominion Home Rule League he is working on. He thinks it is making some way, tho' whenever Horace Plunkett[13] comes over he sets the Government against it by boring them to death talking in parentheses. R.P.H. had been given a command in Ireland but went to the W.O., to ask to be sent anywhere else, and found there an Ulster man who said "You are quite right, I wouldn't go there myself to shoot down my countrymen", and got him on to the

War Council.

On Monday I was with Richard all day, Maskelyn and Cook, and shopping. Tuesday, Madame Tussaud and saw him off at Waterloo. He seemed happy with the other boys and waved his little hand to me till out of sight—God bless him, my Darling child.

Alec Martin came in the evening. I had been shocked to get a letter from Martin Wood's sister, saying he had had a stroke, and can neither write nor speak. It was probably the disappointment of the 2 publishers refusing the book that brought it on, but Alec M. feels sad lest his letter may have helped it—But I think not, and I am glad I wrote him 2 such nice ones.[14]

Alec M. says Grant Richards wants to come. Witt had seen M.W's and thought it hopeless.

27 SEPTEMBER. Railway strike today, so bought some provisions. I walked to the Tate, a long walk, feeling a desire to see pictures. But it is now "Ministry of Pensions" and "no pictures 'anging there" the caretaker said.

I went to see Mrs. Childers, Erskine[15] is in Ireland, looking for a Dublin house where they will settle. She gave me an account of the gun-running (looking so delicate and fragile—she is kept in bed). It was Mary Spring Rice's[16] idea and they got a yacht and Darrell Figgis[17] went over and bought the guns in Liege, and they waited for them off Dover. "The British Navy was all about and I went downstairs with 2 sailors and we packed away the bunks and fittings to make room for the guns. . . . Then the tug came and they were transferred to us. When one bundle was being lowered to us the sailors who held it said: 'this is ammunition—it will explode if it touches anything'. We went on up the Welsh coast and lay outside Milford Haven, afraid of Custom House officers. Then for Holyhead and across to Ireland and sailed about the bay and outside Howth till the boat came when Erskine said 'I am going to do it.' It was just the hour when the tide was highest. We saw someone run up to a height and wave to us as a signal—it was a young officer whose name I cannot tell. . . . Then we saw the Volunteers coming down and when they saw us they broke into a run. The guns that had taken 6 hours to get on board were unloaded in a few minutes. As we left there were cheers for 'the lady at the helm'—it had been put into my hand.

"Some members of the Government thanked us when we came back to London, they said it was the best thing that could have been done, to show the South could take up arms as well as Ulster."

29 SEPTEMBER. I opened the *New Republic* of 10 September a few evenings ago, and saw there was an article on Renoir[18] and thought I would not read it so late, for it would touch on that harassing matter that so often disturbs my sleep. But yet I turned to it and my eye fell on the last sentences, telling how congratulations had been sent to him by Irish "artists and amateurs" when his "Parapluies" was hanging among the old Masters in Trafalgar Square. I have kept the number and will have it printed in the Dublin Catalogue should I be still living when the pictures are restored. But as I feared my night was troubled, by those "tiger thoughts"—dismal, rambling, horrible thoughts or dreams. The National Gallery I used to feel pride in and where pictures bequeathed by my husband still hang, seemed to have turned to be no better than a thieves' kitchen.

The Trustees should have belief in my word and my opinion, when the case of the Layard Pictures was going against them, they asked for my evidence, and I, having been much at Capello with my husband, as Trustee, and Sir Henry our host as trustee, and Sir Frederick Burton the Director—was able to write that, having heard much talk of Gallery matters in the presence of the very pictures in dispute, could say with absolute certainty that they were destined for it. And this statement was thought of some value, for when later I was in New York a copy was sent after me, and I was asked to swear to its truth. The best hours of a day were given up to this, for the British Consul to whom I was directed to go, had a Mitcham address not to be found in any telephone book, where all such information is looked for, and it was at last through letting questions loose in Nassau street that one hit the mark. That there was a telephone in the outer office I knew later for a clerk was discoursing through it of some dance or party of the night before, while I waited on a bench at the door like a suppliant. After the oath was taken the suppliance was on the other side, for I was asked to pay some fees through my taking it that had at that become due—I had in my pocket but enough to pay my fare home through the city, but poverty sharpened my wits and I remembered a word in the covering letter which lay on the table, and pointed out that he, the Consul, was better equipped to recover the money from the true debtor, the British Treasury, than I.

And as to the fate of the Layard pictures, it bears upon our case. The moral right was with the Trustees, there was no doubt in the mind of anyone who had known the Testator and spoke honestly as to his intention to the last that they should go to the Gallery which had been one of the chief interests of his later life.

But legally, though without doubt by the accidental omission of one word in the Will, the word 'family' before 'portraits' the Court inclined to think the case would be lost. It is in Hugh's case the converse; the legal right is with the National Gallery, the moral right, the intention of the Testator, on ours. To redeem the pictures for the Nation, the Treasury paid a sum of money to the covetous heir. It may perhaps in like manner bring back the Trustees to honesty in our cause.

The strike goes on,[19] but so far we have not suffered except by the shortness of milk. I do not walk so far that I cannot come back again on foot. I have my work to do on Hugh's book. Yesterday I went again to see Mrs. Childers, but by ill luck brought up the proposal of Dominion Home Rule as set out by G. L. Pope-Hennessy and others and which it seemed to me possible to be accepted "on account". But she fell on it and rent it, declared it made her ill and was putting Ireland into a worse captivity than before. And that torrent of words made me resolve to go back to my rule of never talking of politics with a woman—as indeed I have no desire to meddle with them at all, but to do such work for Ireland through the theatre and the gallery as I can.

30TH. Letter from Grant Richards, four days in coming from St Martin's Street and now I am trying if the telephone will be any more rapid.

12 OCTOBER. A week of the strike—and a week of a heavy cold have overthrown my hope of getting on quickly though I have done some work every day. I went to the City and hired a typewriter and I have at last got a typist for 2 hours every morning.

Una P.H. came, excited from her visit to Belfast—the bigotry of some, the Nationalism of others—an old colonel saying at the meeting "I don't care what you call them, Sinn Feiners, or Nationalists or Dominion Home Rulers they are all milk from the one cow, all traitors and scoundrels—" and she had brought a Liberal English M.P., to see Biggar[20] who had been talking so reasonably on the Nationalist side—but when the M.P. asked him what they would like to do he said, "to cut the wrists off you so you'd *have* to leave go!" This same M.P. had been in the same train as Carson when it came to a full stop because of the strike. He had taken a car and motored on and caught the boat—Carson had taken a car and sent a telegram to the meeting and turned back to London.

17 OCTOBER. I came yesterday to Newbuildings and found W.S.B. very much better than when I had been here before, he goes out in a pony chair, and has been shooting, he is soon

publishing his new volume of his *Diaries*—up to now the beginning of the War (some of his stories are illustrations of Bernard Shaw's *Heartbreak House*). There is a great deal of the recent history both of Egypt and Ireland, all George Wyndham's private conversations about the Land Bill. I don't think it will be so acceptable as the last it is a bit overweighted with politics, and to lighten it he has put in some personal sketches and scandals it would be as well without. He allowed me to read it on condition (1) that I should not tell anyone I had done so—they would be offended and (2) that I would not ask for any alterations as it is "too late". However I did ask to have Frederic Harrison's name taken out as to talk of scandalous rumours about Chatworth—this for F.H's sake—and he promised to do it. Also I objected to his description of Asquith at a luncheon in Downing Street "with cunning gooseberry eyes and flabby over moving under lip" for the sake of his own dignity—having been his guest, and this he promised to take out. But he was obstinate about John Dillon's story of Asquith being so ignorant of social usage as to give his arm to his own wife to hand in to dinner—He says "I must leave that to show he was bourgeois". There are inaccuracies in what he says of me and of Hugh and of Yeats, but I didn't venture to touch those. He had his lawyer there and Mr. Philip and is much worried at this lawsuit with, though less excited than in March and says now he doesn't mind if he loses; anything for an end of it. Newbuildings looked lovely in the Autumn colouring and I got rid of my cold.

24 OCTOBER. I returned on Monday afternoon, found a mass of letters and have been trying to answer some of them ever since. On Tuesday Mrs. Norman Grosvenor came to tea and told me a good deal about Hugh, more than anyone yet.

WEDNESDAY. I had an appointment with Lutyens, the secretary writing to me as "Angus Gregory Esq" and on paper 17, Queen Anne's Gate, making the appointment for 11—so I went there, too early and walked about looking at Queen Anne's statue and at my old habitation Q.A. Mansions and then on the stroke of 11 rang, and found only a charwoman who said "Oh, they've been doing it again, they're writing to people on this notepaper, but Sir Edwin[21] is at 7 Appleton Yard". So I had to walk across the park (no taxis available) to St. James's and then kept asking for Appleton Yard which was like a bee in a bottle, not to be got at—but not by 11! So I arrived fearing I had lost my appointment but he wasn't quite ready. He came in and said "I never thought it was you who were coming, somehow I thought it was your *son*". I could only say "Oh! He is gone—"

and he said how sorry he was. We talked of Hugh then. It is lucky I saw him at all for he sails for India on the 30th and is full of business. He showed me a tablet he has been commissioned to make in memory of Hugh by Miss Harrison.

I went to the Irish Dominion League by appointment with Una, met Sir Horace going out looking very pleased with himself, and says he has "a new plan" (Una says it is to have *another* conference and that he is a great stumbling block—none of the Cabinet will see him, he is so long-winded). I found them in sole possession and then ——— came in. They are hopeful of the Committee now sitting if Long and F. E. Smith can be got rid of and Sir Archibald Goddes be made Chairman, they are trying to work this through the American Press.

I went on to see Alec Martin at Christies. He has had no answer from Martin Wood's executor brother about going over the papers. I had lunch at a Lyons Restaurant (6½d like Hugh) and being out for the day went on to the Grosvenor Gallery to see if there was a tempting painting for Margaret—Didn't find one tempting for anybody. Jack Yeats, 2 little pictures of a carman and a dog—boy about to beat. I remembered that Francis Howard was Secretary and that he had been in Paris with Hugh, so asked for him and he took me into his office, couldn't remember much, but said if I would let him see some of what I had written he would probably do so, I am to go and see him again. Then suddenly he said "I am told Martin Wood's people intend to publish his book themselves".

I went back to Christies to tell A. Martin this. I suppose an injunction could be taken out to prevent it, but didn't know how to go about it—who to consult. Then suddenly I thought of Witt—one of the chief subscribers—a lawyer and a friend of Alec Martin, so I proposed his consulting him and he got him on the telephone, and Witt wanted to see letters that had passed, and I hurried home to get them together and sent them. I also sent a note of what Grant Richards had said "Alec Martin made a mistake in telling Wood he would not use certain parts of his MS. without his leave. That Manuscript was paid for, it belongs to the Subscribers, it belongs to Martin".

39, Merrion Square E,
Dublin
24 October 1919

Dear Lady Gregory,

I do not intend to go over to Parliament just yet, but I have not lost touch with the Government over the Lane Pictures. I got a message telling me that the Cabinet would consider the matter today, and I at once saw Mr. Atkinson and got him to send you the telegram you received yesterday.

As soon as I know what transpired at the meeting I shall let you know.

Yours faithfully
R. H. WOODS

TELEGRAM

22 October.

Gregory 13, Royal Hospital Road, LONDON. S.W.3.
The Cabinet considers question Lane Pictures on Friday it is essential that some authority on the matter should see Chief Secretary at Irish Office at 10.30 Friday morning can you attend.

ATKINSON.

Very tired that Wednesday evening, and at 9 o'clock a knock at the Hall door, and I opened it Kathleen being out, and got a telegram asking if I could attend at the Irish Office at 10.30, Friday morning, *re* Lane pictures—which the Cabinet is to consider on that day. An anxious night—and on Thursday morning I sent my answer that I would attend, . . . then I lost a little time in writing to M. Woods with (Mrs. Hicks) to get that off my mind, didn't send it as A.M. had written to executors. And then I set to work with cutting books etc. to make my case again about the pictures, and in doing so I saw that all the enemy's efforts to prove that Hugh makes the building of a gallery the test and touchstone are upset—or rather recoil—through his going to Mrs. Duncan on his last day in Dublin and urging her "to get the Corporation to give me assurance" to the effect that they would build *a* Gallery on any site.

I only went out to take A. Martin some letters he wanted, and he was not very violent—though he hadn't heard from Witt but only sent him the letters. He is quite anxious to go and face the executors himself and tell them what he thinks of them—and declares "we could take out an injunction in five minutes". So my mind is easier as to that. Anxious about the picture interview, but slept well. This morning (Friday 24th) I set out before 10, and got in good time to the Irish Office, Old Queen Street—had to look for it as I had never been there before. I was asked to wait a few minutes and then an Irish looking young man appeared, and not knowing the Chief Secretary's appearance and remembering how I had ignored the entrance of Lord Mayor Sherloch at our first meeting because he was so small. I smiled and shook hands with him; he, however took me through another room to a third where was Macpherson, dark, severe looking—dark hair brushed straight back. He seemed troubled, said "The Trustees are going to fight." He said "Here is their statement—they make a very strong case—I don't know how I'm going to meet it." He began reading about Hugh's treatment in Dublin etc., but seeing it was a long MS I suggested his beginning where Hugh made his Will as we don't dispute anything before that. So he skipped to it and we soon got on to the codicil, which they don't deny was written by him. I went on with the case. I was relieved to find there was nothing of the "New facts" they mentioned in their letter after the Mansion House Meeting. It was just "the old sea-serpent done up again". "He had expressed his interest in the making of a London Gallery with so many of his friends including Witt, Aitken and McColl". Then I interrupted and took out my paper of selections—pointed out that there was never any promise—they have no documents but the one in which he especially says he will make no promise. Also I showed him how McColl had juggled his dates, writing as if his 1914 conversation had been in 1915—and then giving my point that suppose he had made the final building of the Gallery a test, he had on his last day in Ireland charged Mrs. Duncan the Curator of the Gallery to urge the Corporation to do it. He was very much taken with this and indeed with all I pointed out—read the codicil again carefully and at the end said:

"I am myself absolutely convinced he intended this codicil to be carried out when he wrote it and to the end of his life." But he said "I have Curzon against me, and I don't know if I can succeed". Then he said if this fails a private member might perhaps introduce a Bill, "or I might ask for a sworn enquiry". I begged him to do this, to say that we on our side would welcome it, for I said neither Curzon nor any of the others would like to be put under cross examination by Sir Edward Carson, "and Carson would do it" he said, "he told me so" (it would be fine the trustees being examined as to why they didn't hang the Renoir and the Daumier). I told him also how the whole of Ireland was uniting on this question and what Desmond Fitzgerald said about them. He said, "It would be a scandal if it were set aside on a technical point." So I got up to go and asked when he would let me know the result, and he said not till tomorrow morning as he will be kept busy till 7 tonight—"For I have another task" he said, "sitting on this Irish Committee", I said, "I hope you will give a measure large enough to be accepted". He said, "I don't know what to do, I am a Home Ruler, I made stronger speeches for it than anyone in Scotland—I didn't ask for this appointment—I didn't know I had been made a Secretary till I saw it in the papers—I am doing my very best to find a good settlement, I assure you of that." I: "Where is the use of your saying that, when Lord French is calling out that no settlement will be offered until law and order are restored which he has so signally failed in doing?" (Here he shrugged his shoulders and made a face at an imaginery Lord French), encouraged by which I said, "Lock up your Viceroy", and he murmured "he is made so angry by all the murders".

I: "It is worse for us who live among them." Then I told him of Desmond Fitzgerald, when I asked if they would accept Dominion Home Rule, saying eagerly "Would we get it?" and about DeValera being so passionately desirous of a settlement under which they could begin the rebuilding of Ireland. He said, "I have said over and over I am doing my best, and I have never had one word either from newspaper or individual saying they would accept anything less than a Republic." I said, "That is a definite policy, it is so with all bargains, each and all demands the utmost—they ask for a republic and Lord French for Military rule." He seemed very depressed and said, "I don't know how I can bear it, it is weighing me down", I said, "You are not the only one—George Trevelyan's hair turned white in his Chief Secretaryship. The Nationalist papers had coloured cartoons then and he said to me it was extraordinary how they reproduced the shades of his hair making it greyer little by little—And yours has not yet begun to turn." And I said, "Give so large a measure of Dominion Home Rule as will touch their imagination—and then bribe Ulster." "You know Ulster is very bitter"—"Yes, they are bitter but they are business men and they have good heads. Put taxation on them, as part of England, that you remit on us in Connaught." *He*: "How can we give government into the hands of Murderers?" *I*: "The murderers are the extremists to be found in every party, they are not an essential part of Sinn Fein."

He: "Oh yes they are."

I: "I've seen the '48 in France. Do you remember how Lamartine turned the most violent of the revolutionists into a national guard and how well they kept order?" and so I left, thanking him for his patience. The Secretary smiled on me as he ushered me out and said, "Will you get your pictures?" and I said, "If we don't get it this way we'll turn on Sinn Fein."

A wet afternoon but I set out for tea with Ricketts and Shannon but my first experience of the crowded underground train, stood squeezed unable to move, but all were good humoured. R and S very sociable and kind in their beautiful rooms. We talked a little about Hugh and they were sympathetic about the life and the pictures, and I grew more buoyant.

25TH. But had a troubled wakeful night.

26TH. No news of the Trustees. I had a wakeful night and wasted thought that might be better used, in following their thought centre but last night some radiance came through sleep, one dream of a coming journey in dear company and in a beautiful country.

28TH. No news yet—I went to Mrs. Grenfell on Saturday, she said she had things to tell me about Hugh, but when I got there she was going for a doctor, her baby had been scalded by an upsetting saucepan. I went again next evening. She had very little to tell and was attending to the baby, who is going on well and I played charades with the children.

28TH. TUESDAY. I have letters from Alec Martin, enclosing one from the Wood trustee, seems amiable, and one from Witt saying he "knows what we can do", so I think that may be put from my mind.

Irish Office
Old Queen Street, S.W.
29 October, 1919

Dear Lady Gregory,

Mr. Macpherson is not yet in a position to tell you the decision on the Lane Pictures question as the matter is still under discussion. As soon as there is anything definite to communicate he will write to you.

Faithfully yours

Lady Gregory. S. WATT

8, King Street
St James's Square
London, S.W.1
29:10:1919

Dear Lady Gregory,

I have had a long chat with Wood tonight. His first point is that Grant Richards should not in any way tamper with his brother's MSS., secondly he feels that he ought to return the money, and thirdly he hinted that he might publish the book.

I gave him clearly to understand that Grant Richards would not even see the MSS again, that it was the wish, I felt sure, of my subscribers that the money should be retained and I gave him clearly to understand that his brother clearly understood that nothing was to be published without your authority, and that this must stand. I told him that I had heard rumours that it was their intention to publish the book but that if you objected I should take steps to prevent it.

His case is that he could publish his brother's own personal side. I told him that I did not think the book would exist at all if all the extracts from letters and diaries were deleted.

However, the next step is for you to meet him and this he says he will arrange to do and at once. I want you to be *very friendly* in your interview with him and see what impression he gives you.

I told him that you were being put to much inconvenience in not having the letters etc., and I asked him to let you have them as soon as possible.

I have to go to Grimsby tomorrow but shall be here on Friday I hope. At the moment I feel very depressed owing to the extra pressure of work and the very bad weather.

Yours very truly
ALEC MARTIN

In the afternoon to Lavery. He could tell but little. But he is still interested about the pictures, and Lord Ribblesdale is to dine with him and he will speak to him. And he is to paint Lord Curzon, and I said if he can't make him give in, he can put a pimple on his nose. He had been at Belfast opening an exhibition of pictures and says "My wife, who has more observation than I have, says everyone in Belfast is Sinn Fein". He agrees with me as to bribing Ulster.

Yeats came in the evening and read me the preface he has written to his essays, a letter to me. I like it, am pleased with his acknowledgment that I am doing the work of the theatre and with the ——— "you and I and Synge".[22]

His only Irish news was that G. had told him Sinn Fein thinks of shooting Cabinet Ministers now as well as or instead of policemen—Carson is on the list, and Curzon and Macpherson but Griffiths is holding them back. A terrible state of war.

31 OCTOBER. The next morning, Wednesday, I had a note from the Irish office from Mr. Macpherson's secretary, saying that the matter of the pictures is "still under discussion". So I sent Kathleen with a note to Sir John Lavery (and an annotated copy of the pamphlet) marked Urgent, and begging him to see and speak to Lord Curzon, that and prayer seemed all I could do. The afternoon was wet, but I made my way to see Ida Cunynghame, walking to Sloane Square, taking a 'bus to Victoria,

changing into one for Marble Arch, getting into a wrong one there and walking the rest of the way to Gloucester Terrace. I had a talk with her—not very rich, but getting a leaf or two for my garland. Then home by tube and underground, very tired and draggled.

ON THURSDAY 20. I worked at the book till 4 and was alone in the house, and just going out when there was a knock and I opened the door to a stranger—Mr. Wood—Martin's executor. Alec Martin had written me to be "very friendly" to him should we meet, and I was—but I never saw a stranger I liked less—a smiler—besides being a lawyer and publisher in one. Above his smile his eyes hardened, and for all my nice words about his brother he said he would publish the book if it had but five readers, and then he asked where he could get the manuscript. I said Mr. Martin was the person to go to, but I felt uneasy as it was on the corner table and had he seen it I felt he might have seized it and I have no right to give it. Again going out he asked when he would have it—tonight? I said Mr. Martin was away, he could have it Saturday. He asked "Who has it?" and I said, "Mr. Martin will send it" and he said, "He says you have it" rather threateningly—but I said "He will send it to you" and he left. I felt shaken but he was the very picture of a rage and I was glad to have him out of the house.

Then I set out to see Gerald Kelly[23] and had tea with him and Filson Young[24] and a Spaniard and some lady. After tea we went to the studio and Kelly showed me that portrait of Hugh more striking than before—because it looks as if he had been already then beyond the boundaries of the world. And Kelly talked of him and his kindness and his ways. I came back, tired but sat up to close on midnight going through M. Wood's MS., and making a catalogue of what should be taken out of each chapter, should he publish it. All that he had taken from material given by —— —— or other friends, who do not want it published in the common interest. I thought with that out he might if he liked publish the rest, its poverty would make it harmless. But today, 31st, having worked again typing this through the morning, I went to see A. Martin. He, after all his advice of being friendly, says the man is a rogue and he had turned him out of his room (that is why he came to me) and that he won't give him the MS. at all—or at least only in exchange for the papers he is keeping back. "But set your mind at rest" he says, "not one word of this statement shall be published." So I came back happier, bought a nice pair of gloves (much needed) at Ha———— in Sloane Street. Went in to see Mrs. ———— and when I was at tea their son came in and we had a long talk about Hugh.

2 NOVEMBER. Yesterday, Saturday, I worked and Clara Huth Jackson[25] came in to tea, I was glad to have someone to congratulate (on Honradin [?] marriage and her sons) after condoling with so many. Later I went to the Childers' for Erskine C. had a letter in *The Times* supporting Lord Southborough's[26] idea of a conference with Sinn Fein, and saying that Griffith[27] in a speech at Manchester in October had said he had no desire the quarrel with England would be continued for ever. I wanted to know what Griffith had said, had he really said this, and E.C. got out the newspaper report except that it went on—"Let England make us an offer of a *Free Republic* and all will be well." So that hope went out. But Mrs. Childers thinks his speaking in England at all is a great concession, as they have been refusing to convert England, have put their trust in America. A Major Malone M.P. was there, back from Russia and telling them that all we hear of Russia is lies.

3 NOVEMBER. Yeats came here last evening and I read him the bits of his letters I am putting in the memoir. And I read the little bits I had just written about my visit to Mrs. Grosvenor (I had lunched there) and he liked it very much—a pleasant talk. This morning I had a letter from Sir John Lavery telling that Lord D'Abernon[28] had been there "very strong for the retention of the pictures" but "the Dublin Gallery could have the pictures on loan whenever it liked and for as long of course that is the—[idea] an ungracious one—for we would never let them out of Ireland again." I answered without alluding to this proposal for they are sure to ask him how it was received, and our case is so strong I would much rather go ahead. But we shall have the pictures back certainly, thank God.

4TH. This morning Lavery encloses without comment Lord Curzon's letter—insincere—for what had that old connection to do with the codicil—and brutal as an answer to Lavery. I wrote to Captain Craig.

5, Cromwell Place
S.W.7
2 November, 1919

Dear Lady Gregory,

Since getting your letter with enclosed pamphlet, I have been confined to the house and have been unable to see Lord Curzon. I have, however, sent him the enclosed.

Lord d'Abernon came here today and was very strong for the retention of the pictures saying that he, with Witt and

MacColl, has sent in a very firm request to the Cabinet to refuse application for their return.

I could not move him from this, the most he would promise was that the Dublin gallery could have the pictures on loan whenever it liked and for as long.

If the present movement fails I think it would be wise to get the pictures to Dublin in the hope that time may bring about a change.

Yours sincerely
JOHN LAVERY

5, Cromwell Place
S.W.7
2 November, 1919

Dear Lord Curzon,

Lady Gregory, the Aunt of the late Sir Hugh Lane, has asked me if I would see you on the matter of the French pictures, now in London, which originally formed part of his collection for Dublin. As you are doubtless aware the Dublin Authorities of that day refused to build a suitable gallery for the pictures which so disappointed Lane that he changed and gave the pictures to London who in turn received them coldly or without, what seemed to him, proper respect and he returned in his last will to his original intention of leaving his entire collection to Dublin.

The feeling among artists in Ireland—where I have been recently—is very strong, because the pictures are much needed there for educational purposes, because they were collected for Dublin and because it was his last wish as expressed in the autograph Codicil to his Will.

I am writing in the hope that when the question comes before you, which I hear will shortly be the case—you will deal with it sympathetically.

Yours sincerely
JOHN LAVERY

The Rt. Honble.
The Earl Curzon of Kedleston, K.G.

1 Carlton House Terrace
S.W.1
3 November, 1919

Dear Sir John Lavery,

I know all about the Hugh Lane case having been the original intermediary between him—the Trustees of the National Gallery of whom I am one. Knowing as much of the case as I do I am afraid that my sympathies are not what you would desire!

Yours sincerely
CURZON

13, R. Hospital Road
3 November

Dear Sir John,

I am deeply grateful to you for your advocacy, it is a real help and support and must have its influence.

I saw the statement sent in by the Trustees, doubtless the one referred to by Lord d'Abernon. I went through it clause by clause with the Chief Secretary, comparing it with the sworn statements of our witnesses. He said at the end "I am absolutely convinced that he meant the codicil to be carried out at the time he wrote it and at the time of his death". So that is encouraging. Our case is in the hands of Sir Edward Carson and his party, who ask for the legalising Bill.

Whatever may happen please accept my very best thanks.

Ever yours sincerely
A. GREGORY

13, Royal Hospital Road
4 November, 1919

Dear Captain Craig,

About the Lane pictures, I hear from Sir John Lavery that Lord Curzon is as belligerent as ever. But he writes 2 November: "Lord d'Abernon has been here today, and was very strong for the retention of the pictures, says that he, with Witt and MacColl, has sent in a very firm request to the Cabinet to refuse application for their return. I could not move him from this, the most he would promise was that the Dublin Gallery could have the pictures on loan whenever it liked and for as long".

I imagine by this that they see their case is weak. If they formally propose this compromise, Sir E. Carson would be the best judge as to whether to accept as he would know what are the chances and difficulties of a bill. Of course if we got the pictures to Ireland we should never let them back again, they must know that.

It would be much more satisfactory to us in every way to have the codicil legalised, and I especially feel it due to Hugh Lane's memory. There is a practical reason also which I would suggest for consideration. The codicil was quite simple in its direction that if the Corporation had not provided a Gallery within five years the bequest would go to the Trustees of the National Gallery (Dublin). They will I believe extend the five years limit in consideration of the war, but they will doubtless fix a time limit. If "a loan" is granted, there will be no limit, no alternative destination. This might lead to confusion and endless delays.

Mr. Macpherson was very kind and understanding, and I feel very hopeful.

A.G.

7 NOVEMBER. Yesterday to Putnam to talk business with —————. He advised me to have nothing to do with Grant Richards. Mr. Stein very nice and kind but not able to put his poems into words except to Cottage pie.

Margaret writes of the group of men at ——— having seized the red flag Joey was carrying—and taken it and spat upon it. She says "No wonder every decent person is leaving the country". But when is the ——— going out.

BOOK SIX

9 NOVEMBER. Fog in London yesterday. I came to Ayot St. Laurence G.B.S., met me at the station and motored me home, the light flashing on the narrow lane and the hedges, still brown and yellow and bronze. The house full of comfort and fires. He had just been writing a review of Chesterton's book on Ireland,[1] read aloud a good deal of the book in the evening—the review will be better. Talking of the Dublin statues he says he had, when a child, a dream one night that he went out and went through the garden and at the end of it opened a gate and saw the sky all filled with wonderful light, and in the centre was God. And He was in the form of the statue of William III in College Green.

I have been consulting him about my book and Grant Richards trying to get it. He strongly advises Murray and tells me to go to Murray at once. It was he, he says, who helped Grant Richards, who had been secretary to Stewart, to start in business. At that time it was almost impossible to publish plays and then G.R. set up and came to ask him for something, he gave him his plays *Pleasant and Unpleasant*[2] and they were a great success. But then G.R. went bankrupt and he took a great deal of trouble trying to get this through, and says he would have got through but that the binders who had part of his stock and to whom he owed money, sold it off to pay themselves.

But Charlotte says "G.B.S. is like that, he never will speak ill of anyone. But Grant Richards treated him very badly, owed him hundreds which he couldn't pay and because he had spent the money on his wife's extravagances—paying thousands for a pearl necklace for her. And G.B.S. was poor then, and though I had money he wanted some of his own. Eusebia (or whatever her name was) left him afterwards and wouldn't come back—went off with someone else."

He is very indignant at the King's proclamation ("a lying proclamation too, because we are still at war") ordering all work to cease for 2 minutes on Armistice Day.[3] He asked what I thought and I said I thought it dreadful, I felt it an impertinence. We who love our dead will think of them—as ever—and those whose work is hindered and have none to care for will think impatiently. But I am sorry he sent his message to the *Daily News* calling it "tomfoolery", it will be misunderstood. He meant the "tomfoolery" of the King stopping factories and upsetting business by his royal word. He says he was in such a rage about it when the *Daily News* request came that he wrote it hastily.

I told him of the pictures and Lord D'Abernon's hint and he says it is just what he expected, for lately he has noticed a certain set are running them down, saying they are hardly worth keeping and that he encourages them in this; for which I'm not at all obliged to him.

I have been to church alone. He says he likes churches and often goes into one, but doesn't like the Liturgy—I say I like the Liturgy but not the sermon. We didn't have one today, a miracle.

10 NOVEMBER. Yesterday afternoon G.B.S. drove me to Cherry-Garrard's[4] in the afternoon and left me there for a while and came back for me.

After dinner I read some of the memoir—he thought it a very good opening "a very promising memoir", but that there ought to be more about Hugh's childhood. And he was struck with what Hugh had said to Duncan about "possessing" the pictures he gave to galleries, and his hatred of waste.

He talked afterwards of what Wilfrid Blunt had written of Morris and of his being without love for anyone (except the invalid daughter) and said it is often so with men immersed in their work, they have no room for another strong affection.[5] The first time he saw Mrs. Morris it was a shock. She was lying full length on a sofa, her long limbs covered, and looked death-like—like clay. He was trying the other day if he could remember anything she had ever said and could not, except that one day when he had taken a second help of some pudding, she said "You seem to like that pudding", and when he answered "Yes", she said "There is suet in it". That word aimed at his vegetarianism is all he can remember. One evening Morris came in to where he was—I forget the place—with an air of terrible depression and seemed under an intolerable trouble but said nothing. After a while G.B.S. said "I wonder why you don't at your Kelmscott Press, print the *Pilgrims Progress*", and as he hoped, Morris at once started up, threw off his depression, became excited about the idea saying how he would like to do it, how it could be carried out; his interest in his work had driven away whatever thought oppressed him.[6] He thinks Sigurd[7] a very fine poem indeed and spoke of his "beautiful prose"; but says people didn't think much of what he did because he did it too easily, just as they don't think as much of a singer whose lovely voice comes out easily as of someone who shouts till he bursts a blood vessel.

I told Cherry-Garrard that G.B.S. had been giving me such wise advice and he said "I always find out what she wants and then advise it—that's an easy way to get a reputation".

When he first came to London, the Trevelyans and Stanleys[8] made a sort of little circle of appreciation of him, Lady Stanley especially. C.G. was asking about Sir G. Trevelyan[9] and G.B.S. said "He is very old—I hear he cuts pictures out of Punch and sticks them a book"; and I said, "He told me he was collecting everything you had ever written and keeping them together, that must have been the origin of the story".

I asked about his learning to "Jazz", as the papers say he has been doing. He said it was when he went to the Fabian summer school last year, the pupils took up dancing and used to ask the Principal(?) to dance, but he said he couldn't, and to ask him, "as I was a sort of Head Patriarch there" and he couldn't. But he was afraid the social side of the life would dwindle so he learnt, and now he dances with whoever asks him.

He is very much interested in Dean Inge's *Outspoken Essays*[10]—he has written the review. I said Inge was making him a Christian, or he Inge a rationalist and he says some of the sentences in the essays are curiously like some of the preface to *Androcles*. I came back here this morning. A letter from Margaret enclosing me one from Mr. Johns saying there is a case of scarlet fever at Winton House, the boy had already been segregated for a cold when it developed. But it makes me anxious.

This evening a depressing letter from Captain Craig[11] in answer to mine—such a want of clear thinking and no allusion to Carson or the proposed compromise.

G.B.S. asked me this morning if I belonged to the Academic Committee. I said Yeats had written me some time ago that I and Drinkwater[12] had been put on it, but I had never received any intimation and had forgotten to ask him about it. He said he had proposed me after Mrs. Ritchie's[13] death and Gosse[14] had got up and said "I was under the impression Lady Gregory was already a member of this Committee—name Yeats." Binyon[15] had proposed Miss May Sinclair[16], but he had never heard of her or read one of her books, so he looked wise as if considering, and then noticed that Gosse had exactly the same expression. So he confessed this and Gosse said "I am exactly in the same position". However he had afterwards bought one of Miss Sinclair's books and found she was a woman of great ability.

11 NOVEMBER. Captain Craig asked me to come to the House of Commons at 4, so I did and found him and had a long talk. He seemed very ignorant of the picture matter, suggested a "Press campaign" but I gave him a list of all those who had written for us and the papers that had taken our part in 1916. Sir E. Carson is away, and anyhow he is unwilling to put the matter before him, "he is so busy". But I told him this was the crisis of the whole matter when the important proposal of compromise has come, and that in fact I want to know how much trouble he is inclined to take. Craig was vague as to what has been done, but says Macpherson is very much in earnest, but he is ill and away this day or two. He says it is quite likely the Cabinet, being busy, won't want to bring in a Bill and that if they refuse no private member could take it up, they would block it. We agreed that if Macpherson fails in getting the Cabinet to do it, we had better accept the loan, though I'm afraid if the Cabinet refuse, Curzon will stiffen and repudiate d'Abernon.

Craig talked very stoutly of how Ulster would never give in, and Sinn Fein won't get Dominion Home Rule, and if he had his way he would lock up the rest of Ireland for 5 years, and then when they had learned behaviour begin to treat with them. I said I had noticed the statue of Oliver Cromwell was very polished up outside.

I bought some Xmas toys and went to the Royal Hospital, found Lady L. and Hermione making toast for tea. Lady L. says she would take no notice of Ireland, but tell them when they had come to agree among themselves they might be spoken to. I said they might retaliate that the English Parliament is not in agreement, the majority approve of a measure or policy, just as they do with us out here they can pass it without the consent of the minority. That ended that subject and we talked of Hugh.

12TH. No appointment, so wrote letters and did some packing and bought a dressing jacket for Ala. for Betty's visits. Dined Orpens, Cecil Armstrong there. He told of Mahaffy's son who said "I don't know if I call Miss J. by her Christian name or not—I used to at Florence". Some one said "You should call her by her full name until she asks you to do otherwise"—"Yes" he said, "that is the rule I make with Dukes". He also said of London, "All my friends live in Park Lane". Armstrong said Mahaffy should never have been a clergyman, but became one to help his advancement, and it went against it, for at the time he might have been Provost there was an outcry against a cleric, and Traill was put in. Orpen[17] told anecdotes of Tyrrell, how when a waiter asked if he should bring a large or a small whiskey said, "I am very short sighted, I'm afraid I would hardly see a small one on the table."

Orpen looks ill and has been ill. He complains very much of the Hotel at Versailles where he is still painting the scene of the Peace Conference, it is long since a fire has been lighted there.

13TH. Today to Murray. He received me very amiably and likes the idea of the book. His son there looking all the better for his share in the war, a Major with a D.S.O., I claimed cousinship through Maude Brassey and his wife Lady Helen. I wanted a copy of *Saints and Wonders*[18] to give Mrs Chatteris, and asked for it downstairs, but after a long delay Murray himself came down to confess they hadn't one (it is being reprinted) but would let me look at the one in the file if I liked. To the Goupil to see Ezra Pound's portrait by [Wyndham Lewis][19], a sort of mixture of David and Goliath. Then to choose Xmas boxes for the chicks, and I sat for a little time with the Orpen children at their tea.

Ulster Club
Belfast
13 October, 1919

Dear Lady Gregory,

I fear nothing can be done by me in the matter of the Lane Pictures until the House of Commons meets.

In the meantime if you can bring any pressure to bear on anyone who can influence Lord Curzon in our favour it would be well.

I shall not be back in London until some days after Parliament re-opens.

Yours very truly

C. C. CRAIG

Margaret missed train.

Macpherson's letter and Craig's look as if I needn't stay.

Murray was at the other extreme to Grant Richards who wanted the "Balzac young man". He said, "There is nothing I admire so much as a young fellow who by his own industry and in an honest profession makes a large fortune." "Like those Smiles writes about" I said, "but Smiles' fortune makers I think spent their money on themselves, whereas Hugh gave all his to Dublin Galleries."

FRIDAY 14TH. I packed and then seeing in *The Times* that Birrell[20] had returned went to see him. He asked for an account of my "various enterprises" and this took so long that I stayed to lunch. As to the pictures, he speaks with comforting warmth of the trustees and calls Lord Curzon "a vulgar brute—but hardworking". He is rather afraid that D'Abernon's proposal not being in writing they may shuffle out of it. As to Ireland, he knows nothing now of politics but says there is no enthusiasm for Home Rule to be roused in England they only want to give it for their own convenience. I said the police murders were I believe not Sinn Fein policy but by an organised gang of extremists and he said "There is always a gang of that kind ready to take up extreme measures when hope of political help dies, and that hope has now died". He has finished his life of Locker and was interested in hearing of what I am doing and burst into indignation at the way Hugh had been treated about the Museum. I said T. W. Russell[21] had said it was Birrell himself "the Castle" that had approved Count Plunkett, but he said, No, it had been done without his knowledge or authority, and he and the Under Secretary, Dougherty had "raged" about it when they heard. He did not know much of Hugh "a figure that flitted across the memory", but knew what his work had been.

I left in the evening, very tired—but had an easy journey, 3rd class not crowded, reading *The Millionaire Mystery*,[22] and a calm crossing.

15TH. I arrived to find Westland Row in snow and with difficulty got a cab to the Gresham and had a couple of hours' sleep. Then Harris, and a theatre talk as to "Captain Alan Duncan"[23] not a success and decided to put Dossie Wright in his place.

The Matinée of *Androcles*[24] a pure joy. Horace Plunkett came and sat next me for a little—has nothing hopeful to say about politics, told of the threatening letters he had had since his speech—(I had seen a copy he sent to G.B.S.)[25].

Sir Philip Hanson there and I asked if we didn't deserve credit for keeping going so long; he knew what our finances were when he looked into them, and he said indeed he did. And Lady H. gave me a reminiscence of Hugh.

Then I went on to Sir R. Woods. He is going over to Parliament at the end of this week, for about a week, a great mercy as he can look after the picture matter. He would have been over sooner but couldn't get a room. He also had heard how the Cabinet had broken off the picture discussion and turned to other work in the middle of their meeting—probably on account of their defeat in the Commons on the yesterday afternoon.

Androcles again in the evening, and had tea with the Players, in the Green room—like old times seeing Power (as Ferrovius) Robinson walked home with me, says that the Government chose a time just after the two minute's silence on Armistice Day to make their descent on Dail Eireann, with soldiers and motors and to arrest its members.[26] Also that it had sent a "chit" to the papers forbidding them to publish any of the reports of Dail Eireann's activities in constructive policy and economics which they are working at, lest they should get credit for it in England.

Grant Richards Ltd. Publishers
8, St. Martin's Street
Leicester Square
LONDON W.C.2
4 November, 1919

Lady Gregory,

Dear Lady Gregory,

I can quite understand that the delay is extremely irritating but I confess that I do feel I ought to have the first chance of publishing your book if we can come to satisfactory terms. I say this not because of the fact that I have already been put to a good deal of trouble over the book, that my travellers have worked on it, and that it has appeared in my list of announcements for three years, but also on account of my friendship for Hugh and my intimate connection with his affairs.

Sincerely yours,
GRANT RICHARDS

13, Royal Hospital Road
14 November, 1919

Dear Mr. Grant Richards,

In accordance with Mr. Alec Martin's wish I tried to make up my mind to publish the Memoir with you. But it can't be. I am past the age for changing publishers—it is like changing ones dwelling house—the thought upset my work. I consulted and showed your letter to two friends, whose opinion you would respect, and in accordance with it, and as I am leaving for Ireland today, I yesterday offered the book to John Murray. I should have preferred waiting to do this (according to my custom) till it was all written—I can write better without any change or complications on the business side and I am sure you will feel as I do that to write it well will best serve Hugh's memory.

A.G.

We have had a letter of remonstrance about *Androcles*.

DROGHEDA AMALGAMATED SOCIETY OF TAILORS

Dear Sir,

At a special meeting held the Abbey plays was discussed about the part of the tailor.

The members think it is out of place and little making and if you could remove it from the play they would feel obliged. An early reply will much oblige. And pardon me if I am intruding.

I remain

Faithfully yours

P. SMITH, Secretary

The Manager
Abbey Theatre.

17TH. Yesterday I went to see the Gogartys[27] and had tea there. He told me of the boat coming direct from America with goods and Liverpool interfering and demanding its dues. He says the Government is deliberately trying to keep industries down in Ireland. Una [Pope-Hennessy] had told me the same, that the Furness Company intended to open a branch in Cork and was requested by Government not to do so—"they don't want the South to be too prosperous". Gogarty says Ulster is "their left arm" and they keep the income tax low there to keep it on their side. He thinks there will be no settlement offered that can be taken, and that disorder will increase, and *Englishmen* will be shot as well as the police. I asked if all, or at least 75%, in Ireland could not combine in resisting some law; they could not all be put in the gaols. But he thinks not, because some districts are so kept down by the military.

18 NOVEMBER. Harris and Robinson yesterday and arranged to get Dossie Wright back in place of "Captain Alan Duncan" who sits in the office biting a pen at £3/10/- a week, while Miss McGowen at 27/- does Robinson's correspondence.

Bodkin to lunch—*re* Hugh and then I went to Dundrum in rain and hurricane to see the Yeats.

18TH. Yesterday I went to theatre and rehearsed *Bogie Men*[28] and then to Harcourt Street Gallery. Had a nice talk with Starkey. D. O'Brien here when I came back. Evening, *Man who Missed the Tide*[29] rather crude, the old actors missed, but Shields very fine in last act.

19TH. To Coole. All well, only Anne and Catherine here.

25TH. Had the Shooters in to lunch. Mr. La Touche told me he had seen Lord French a few days ago. He had said he had not the least hope of the new Cabinet scheme of Home Rule being accepted in Ireland "but it *will show the goodwill* of the English people"! So it is to be a mockery.

26TH. A note from Sir R. Woods.

27TH. Today this note in *Independent* (see Newspaper cutting).

28TH. I have been given a note to one of our grazing tenants:

Kiltartan Sinn Fein Club
26 November, 1919

Sir,
At a duly constituted meeting of above Club the following resolution was adopted. We the members of the Kiltartan Sinn Fein Club call on all those who partake of the lands of Coole Demesne to surrender same when present tenancy term expires. You are, therefore, requested to comply with above and have your stock removed off said lands on or before 1 April 1920.

John Hayes, Martin Nolan, (Hon. Secs.)

I am not to tell to whom it was written as J.D. says all the grazing tenants have had the same but are not inclined to give in and Thomson says "the half of them might be dead before six months". Also, reassuringly, that "a man" was saying to him, "there isn't a young chap in the whole of Kiltartan has the courage to fire a shot". But he says "We have a rotten Government and as to the police in Gort you might as well put a dozen of schoolchildren in their place."

8 DECEMBER. Papers full of the attack on the MacNamara shooting party.[30,31] Marian back from Limerick says the police there are said to be "awful", very tyrannical there, but never going to any place where there is outrage or danger. When there was some street rioting the other day they went into the Reading Room where 2 men were reading—beat and dragged them out, and hacked a picture of the Siege of Limerick (Marian hears it cost a thousand pounds!) to bits.

9 DECEMBER. At church on Sunday the soldiers came with fixed bayonets, (there were two at the church) as if protecting us. It seemed unnecessary, as if we needed it; I didn't like it. Sir William Mahon[32] seemed to gloat over it as if it prevented rebellion.

Grant Richards writes again, sending copy to G.B.S.

8, St. Martin's St.
London W.C.
9 December, 1919

Dear Lady Gregory,
I must apologise for not having answered your letter of November 14th. Its arrival synchronised unfortunately with illness in my family which has made it very difficult for me to attend to things properly.
I will confine myself now to acknowledging the receipt of

your letter, telling you that its contents surprise me in view of the fact that I have announced the Memoir of Sir Hugh Lane over and over again in the last three years, and that I am consulting my Solicitors as to my position.

Sincerely yours
GRANT RICHARDS

15 DECEMBER. Yesterday, Sunday, made bitter and barren by these letters of Witt and A.M., and by having to answer them.

17TH. Sinclair writes to Robinson "The authorities wouldn't let me do *Rising of the Moon*[33] round Tipperary. They considered it seditious.

19TH. Wrote today to Macpherson.

21ST. Margaret and Richard came yesterday evening. He is so well and boyish and gay: my darling.

22ND. A terrible shock and shake.

16th December 1919

Dear Lady Gregory,

I greatly regret to have to write to you on a subject in which I feel no personal interest and in which I should very much prefer not to interfere—that is, the publication of Hugh's life, the writing of which I understand you have in hand.

I have never had anything to do with the matter, but I know it was arranged originally that Mr. Grant Richards' firm should publish the Memoirs. Various changes have taken place since then, and I understand you prefer that the work should be published by Mr. John Murray. Mr. Grant Richards informs me that he has announced the Memoirs over and over again for the past three years, and he now feels it a slight that the publication should not be done by his firm.

As I say, it is a matter in which I feel no personal interest, but in the circumstances I should be glad if you could see your way to let his Firm publish the work you are writing.

With kind regards

Believe me
Yours sincerely
J. J. MEAGHER

Lady Gregory
13, Royal Hospital Road
Chelsea

(Postcard)

10, Adelphi Terrace
W.C.2

11 December, 1919

I should leave Grant to get what comfort he can out of his Solicitor. There is much to be said for writing the book first and consulting the authorities afterwards. The book not only has a chance of being written, but of being a work of art instead of a collection of memoranda.

G. BERNARD SHAW

21 DECEMBER, 1919. Margaret and Richard came home yesterday.

Last night she told me that she thinks of selling Coole, because there is no society for the children here, and it is not fair to let them grow up without it. She would like a small house with a trout stream and with a good neighbourhood, people, and where a syndicate could give Richard shooting.

It was a shock to me. I said she might be able, as I was, to ask companions here in the holidays—and she is in any case keeping a house in London. We parted kindly.

This morning she spoke again, said she could not do it without telling me. I said I had thought it over in the night—which had indeed been a wakeful one—I said it is to Richard she is responsible that he will be of age in 10 years, and that he ought to have the opportunity of knowing what the sale meant before deciding on it, or he would not forgive her.

I had thought in the night that perhaps she only meant to sell the land, and would keep the house, even if closed for a while. But she says No, if she sells it will be "Coole" house and all, that selling the land only would be a money loss, and we should require to have caretakers. I asked if she would let me stay here as caretaker—I could nearly pay, could at least do so for house and garden, till Richard is of an age to decide. She said No, if she does not sell it she will have to live here "but I know I would not have courage to do what I think right, we can stay here—and the children will marry peasants".

Oh, what can I do?

Coole Park
Gort
Co. Galway
19 December, 1919

Dear Mr. Macpherson,

I am, as you will understand very anxious to know how the matter of the Lane pictures stands. It will be very kind if you will ask your Secretary to let me have a word that I may know if there is anything that can be done on this side.

I have only now been sent a letter to Mr. Yeats from the late Rt. Hon. W. F. Bailey, chief Land Commissioner for Ireland. He was very well known and his word would have some weight with anyone connected with the Irish Government, and I think with the Prime Minister. Mr. Yeats had mislaid the letter in changing houses, but here it is:

3, Earlsfort Terrace
Dublin
17 January, 1919

"My dear Yeats,

One day shortly before Hugh Lane started on his last voyage to America he came here to see me, bringing with him a pair of Chinese statuettes as a present. We talked about his French pictures, I remarked that it was a tragedy that such a proffered gift should not have been accepted by Dublin. He replied that this was largely due to misunderstandings—that there were mistakes and misapprehensions on both sides and that if the matter came up again he thought things would take a different turn. "Then" said I, "there is still a hope that we may get the pictures?" "Certainly" he replied with some fire, "give and take, give and take, an agreement will be come to on the question of a site for a gallery and Dublin will get the pictures". He added that too much had been made of this site question. I never saw him again but he left me strongly under the impression that he intended that the pictures should come back to Dublin.

Ever sincerely yours
W. F. BAILEY."

I myself am now writing a memoir of Hugh Lane and as I piece the story together everything confirms my conviction that his intention when he made the codicil and to the end was that the pictures should come to complete the collection in the Dublin Gallery, the making and perfecting of which was the purpose of his life, and that in justice to his memory that codicil should be made legal.

I know you are doing your best for us and for this I again thank you.

Sincerely yours
A. GREGORY

BOOK SEVEN

8 JANUARY, 1920. DUBLIN. Xmas and New Year and Richard being safely over I have come to see *Golden Apple.*[1] It went well last night though rather slowly. This morning I made some cuts and alterations.

9TH. I went to Plunkett house to see Miss Mitchell[2] (about Hugh) but found A.E. alone, and we had a talk. He gave me his poem "Michael"[3] which I had cut out of the *New Statesman* and liked so much. He says some lines of it came to him in a dream—and he was puzzled and then soon after (being in some country place) he saw it all and wrote it as it is.

He is trying to find time to write a book on the present impulses of the world connecting them with some invisible force in the universe—they are Anarchism, Socialism, Nationalism and Imperialism. He sees nothing practical to do just now except ones own work. He looks forward to the time when Brian, who is learning wireless, and Dermot, who is learning science, will support themselves and then he can paint enough pictures to support himself and be free to write or do as he likes. He believes the Government are trying to provoke a rising.

A while ago Col. Hutcheson[4] of the War Office who had been on the Staff(?) in Dublin, came over and telephoned him that he wished him to convey a warning of this to Sinn Fein, and told him Tanks and war materials of all sorts were being sent over with this in view. He, Col. H., had been to the Castle, where it was denied and he asked to see their orders, which they refused to show. He then got from the War office an order to see them, and they were as he had heard, orders to make the most of every disturbance, and then use the most violent means of suppression.

He took me to tea at the Irish Book Shop and Miss Mitchell came, and Stephens, who we met, went and brought his wife. Kerrigan just back from America says all countries are in the same state of violent unrest as Ireland, but they have only mercenary motives, while Ireland has the idealism of Nationality. A.E. says the same.

11TH. Such a splendid Matinée yesterday of *Golden Apple*, crowds of children. I was afraid they would find the play too long but they didn't seem to and laughed and applauded. My little party was Stephens and his wife and children, and Bobby Childers, and Craoibhin with his daughter and Mrs. Hyde. Between the acts I gave them tea, and the children lemonade and cakes. All went well except the change into a cat—clumsy—I think the little four legged beast would be better, as done at Miss Wilson's school. Ruth Badham and her child there, and Eily Shaw and Hugh Law and other friendly faces I hadn't seen for some time. I was dead tired (a very bad night) and could hardly have got to the performance but that I had invited Iseult Gonne,[5] and there was a fine audience of grown ups and some children, great applause—three curtains at the end. Iseult told me of her engagement to a boy—18½—poor girl—but it may be the beginning of a new life for her.

SUNDAY. She came to lunch and then I went to Miss Purser's[6] and was caught in a storm.

MONDAY. Home.

20, Birchin Lane
E.C.3
12 January, 1920

Dear Lady Gregory,

I am much obliged by your letter of the 8th instant; my original letter (of which I enclose a copy) was addressed to you at Chelsea.

I hope I made myself clear,—I shall of course be greatly interested in the Memoirs, the more so as I think, and thought all along, that you were the best person to write them. The question as to who published them would not have interested me but for the position Mr. Grant Richards feels himself to be in, and for which quite possibly he may have some ground if the publication goes elsewhere.

With kind regards,
I am,
Yours sincerely
J. J. MEAGHER.

Lady Gregory
Coole Park
Gort, Co. Galway

Coole Park
Gort, Co. Galway
13 January, 1920

Dear Mr. Meagher,

I am very sorry Mr. Grant Richards should consider it a

slight my continuing to work with my old publishers, and I am also very sorry poor Martin Wood should have suffered the slight of having his manuscript rejected after the long announcements of which Mr. Grant Richard's speaks.

I feel sure in rejecting it Mr. G. Richards felt he was doing what would best serve Hugh Lane's memory, just as I feel I am doing what is best for it in my turn.

I hope you understand that I came into the matter quite free, the M.S. having been also rejected by Chatto and Windus, and the subscribers' money having been paid to Mr. Wood.

I look forward to seeing you when again in London, there are some little matters connected especially with Hugh's last money troubles I want to ask your help in.

Sincerely yours
A. GREGORY

WEDNESDAY. Darling Richard left for school with Margaret. On Tuesday Margaret went to see Scott Kerr and arranged about sale of land—we are quite agreed about it and it is what Robert approved.

22 JANUARY. Have been alone with Anne and Cat, working very hard at Hugh's book.

Margaret writes today "Richard tells me he made up his mind definitely a few days ago to become an engineer! So I am entering him at Oundle no harm done by it—but he didn't much like the idea of not going to Harrow, but I told him it didn't mean that, only gave him his chance."

I am glad the darling child wishes to be a worker.

An exodus from the county, the Goughs leave this week and Lough Cutra is to be shut up till they see how things are, and Hugo is still in the Irish guards, Ld. Killanin has had trouble at Spiddal, and has dismissed all his men and gone to London. Edward Martyn is said to have sold Tullyra. The Lopdells (because of their motors having been searched or put out of action the night they were going to Roxboro' dance) are going to live in England. ——— empty and closed Amy has let Castle Taylor and lives in England. I will stay here I hope till my life's end, or rather I hope it will be kept open by Margaret for the children and I shall be content anywhere. John Diveney when I was going children and I shall be content anywhere. John Diveney when I was going to Dublin hoped I would come safe back. I said I hoped so, as I had come back so often and he said "Dublin was such an awful place." And the papers give such a list of crimes in London I am anxious about Margaret.

Coole
15 February

Dearest Margaret,

Not much news, Scott Kerr hasn't written, but I suppose he has to you. John has just the same story today, poor old Cahel standing for hours in the wet, while the youngsters were inside. He hears they are going to get a surveyor to look at the land, and to offer £8000—S.K., asked £12,500. However, though he talks of them as moneyless, he says it is now called "Regan's Committee", and that they Cooneys who are rich are in it, and Fahey who has money, so it may be as good to deal with as the other in the end. He asks for "two fields" for himself and Thomas. I said I had nothing to do with the sale and don't know much about it, that it was in Scott Kerr's hands. He spoke of writing to you. I think he ought to get something. He says this Regan Committee won't give him or Thomas anything, and they had declared they won't give Malachi Quinn anything. However, there are sure to be quarrels whatever happens.

I see the Land Commission has been settling soldiers on an estate, giving them ten acres each and a house. That would make the demesne rather too thickly populated to be pleasant.

The Archdeacon led me into the vestry after church to say the Monument (as I knew) had been vested in the church, and that they will insist on its being fenced round, that a little bit, a yard or two on each side belongs to them, as well as the little plantation at the back. He says it was Richard Gregory who made it, I thought it was Sir William's parents, and wished to be buried in it, but that the people would not allow that because it was not consecrated, and he was buried at Kiltartan and then the body was brought in during the night and buried in the monument. I am glad it does not belong to us, that we are not selling it, but it is rather troublesome about the fencing, I thought its own little wall was sufficient protection, but he says not. S. Kerr had written to Whitney and Moore about it, and they rang up the Church Body, and the A.D. went to see them about it.

Frank writes that his house was raided but he had heard they were coming and sent his gun to the barracks only keeping an old useless one to amuse them and they did no harm. I didn't see the Bagots after church as the A.D. kept me, but John says their hall door won't shut since the raid, and the Bagot's gun was in the house all the time but well hidden.

A. G.

Coole
5 February, 1920

Dear Mr. Macpherson,

Now that Parliament is about to begin again, I feel renewed hope and anxiety as to the fate of the Lane Pictures. My hope is in you, the first Chief Secretary who has taken a share of our burden, and I know you will do what you can.

Sincerely yours,
A. GREGORY

Irish Office
Old Queen Street
S.W.
10 February, 1920

Dear Lady Gregory,

I am sorry the consideration of the Lane Picture question has been so protracted. I am still fighting and am not without hope that we may yet be successful.

Yours sincerely
IAN MACPHERSON

Lady Gregory

15 FEBRUARY. The chicks gone to London. My Sunday is lonely. We had a quiet time, rain outside but they were cheery within. The day before Margaret left with Richard she put the sale of the demesne land into Scott Kerr's hands—rather sudden—but we are in accord about selling it, and Robert had intended to do so, rates and taxes getting higher and trouble about letting greater. I have written to Macpherson, the session beginning again. I am working hard at the Memoir—have just got through the hardest part and have a pretty clear narrative to work over. Scott Kerr made his first move yesterday, had written to "a few of the principal ex-tenants to meet him in Gort at 12." J. saw me going in at 1.30 and staying an hour or more reports that the "principal tenants" were standing out in the rain, while S.K. was shut into the office with Hayes and Donohoe and the other young disturbers. Regan the only man of substance with them—and their solicitor, Hogan. "All the schemers inside and all the decent men out on the Mall"—not a good beginning. John says today the well-to-do men are offended—£12,520, asked and the wall down avenue to be made—"but the wall upset them entirely".

19 FEBRUARY. Sir Thomas Esmonde[7] writing on another matter (about a play), says: "I wish you luck in your efforts to get back the Lane pictures. You will get them back all right if you

keep pegging away. It took me eight years to get back the Irish Gold, ornaments, but I got them back, and you will get those pictures back too."

Cromwell House
Dean Stanley Street
Millbank
London, S.W.1
13 February, 1920

Dear Madam,

Sir James Craig has asked me to acknowledge your communication of the 12th instant and to assure you that the matter shall receive his early attention.

Yours faithfully
C. H. BLACKMORE
Private Secretary

Lady Gregory
Coole Park
Gort
County Galway
Ireland.

5, Morpeth Mansions
Victoria Street
S.W.
20 February, 1920

Dear Lady Gregory,

You may rely on my doing what I can with regard to the Lane pictures, and I will write to Lord D'Abernon and perhaps Lord Curzon, whom I know best of the National Gallery trustees.

Yours sincerely
T. P. O'CONNOR.

House of Commons
14 February, 1920

Dear Lady Gregory,

Yours of the 12th inst. duly to hand. I have to see the Chief Secretary soon, and will bring the matter of the Lane Pictures before him again.

Yours truly,
C. C. CRAIG

1, Carlton House Terrace
S.W.1
20 February, 1920

My dear O'Connor,

I am sorry I cannot take your view of the Lane Pictures case. But having been in it from the start and having indeed conducted the original negotiations with him, I know too much to render this possible.

Yours ever.
CURZON

5, Morpeth Mansions
Victoria Street
S.W.
26 February, 1920

Dear Lady Gregory,

I have received the enclosed letter from Lord Curzon in reply to mine re the Lane pictures. But so far have not heard from Lord D'Abernon, who, I believe, is abroad at present.

Yours sincerely
T. P. O'CONNOR

Lady Gregory

21 FEBRUARY. A kind answer from T. P. O'Connor about the pictures, promising to write to d'Abernon and Curzon, I wrote to him in return. A letter from Margaret not so kind, saying she will never forgive herself for her weakness! that is in listening to me, and not selling this house. But it is of Richard she has to think—it is he who might not forgive the sale. A nice letter from Mr. Jayne. And the *Morning Post* begins an article with "Among the most perfect plays of the last twenty years are the one act plays of Lady Gregory and Miss G. E. Jennings."

Yesterday's post brought me fees for plays, nearly £5, will help my labour bills. But also a letter from Alec Martin. Executor Wood is now threatening law to get back that MSS, I wrote a placable letter.

1 MARCH, 1920. Regan's Committee having made a bad offer that could not be accepted for the land, the other tenants began to make themselves heard and Father Cassidy proposed trying to get all to unite. He applied to Scott Kerr who wrote a letter stating the terms. His meeting was held after Mass yesterday. He made an address telling the terms, and saying that there was arguing going on, but "if the lady that is selling the land sells it to the Government, you can't argue with it." Then Regan's Committee was asked to go into the childrens' catechizing room to decide if

they would let others join their committee, half and half. They kept the congregation waiting half an hour, and came out, Regan "like a lion raging, waving his arm and saying 'There will no man go on our committee only two, and they to be chosen by ourselves. It was we got the graziers out of the place!' Then there was arguing, just like you'd hear it at a fair. One half told the other half they were no Sinn Feiners. They said they were, and Hayes boasted 'We that got our sons to put their names to that notice'!

Cunningham tried to say something, but one of them shouted him down. "You that reared a son to go about the country shooting people". (A great shame to bring that up to him!) Shaughnessy the widow's son that had joined the army for a while tried to speak, but someone called out "Let you not say a word, you that wore the jacket!" And he said, "If I did, I threw it off as soon as I came back, and that's what you wouldn't do!" Regan, Cooney, Fahey, Hanlon, young Hayes, Donohoe are the one faction. "And most of the decent men on the other side, and Father Cassidy was seen walking down the road after with them, the Ballyaneen men."

Left Coole 3 March for London. Heard of F.S.T's murder at Athenry.[8] 4th to Dublin. Saw *Player Queen*.[9] 5th to London.

29, Brompton Square
S.W.3
2 March, 1920

Dear Lady Gregory,

I regret that I have no further news with regard to the Lane Pictures beyond that I had a conversation with Mr. Macpherson a day or two ago, and he informs me that the matter is still before the Cabinet. He did not seem to know what their decision would be.

Yours truly,
C. C. CRAIG

39, Merrion Square, E
Dublin
9 March, 1920

Dear Lady Gregory,

I am not at present in London but shall be going over at the end of next week. If I hear of anything I shall let you know.

Yours faithfully
R. H. WOODS.

5, Morpeth Mansions
Victoria Street
S.W.
11 March, 1920

Dear Lady Gregory,

Thanks for your note. I shall always be happy to see you if you will first of all ring me up some morning about 11.30.

Yours sincerely
T. P. O'CONNOR

Lady Gregory
13, Royal Hospital Road
Chelsea.

14 MARCH. Work done. Sent MS of Memoir to Birrell to look at, as I had arranged to see Witt and wanted to know how far it was towards being ready for publisher.

Took it to Murray and gave it to Lawrence to read before submitting it to Murray. Saw Witt, about letters in hands of M.W.'s executor. He will try to get them back—was amiable, we didn't speak of pictures. Saw Solomon to gather memories of Hugh, also Mrs. Reeves. Self and chicks to Balys. Neville Geary to tea, Kindness from Mrs. Chatteris; tried to get at T.P. O'Connor *re* pictures but he is away till Thursday. Very tired. On Friday lunched at 10 Adelphi Terrace. Mr. Colthurst there—"has sold every security he had and is putting all into developing his property at Lucan, making a market garden and is claiming the river for electricity". He has been seeing Sinn Feiners. Not only they, but various young Unionists are longing for a settlement that will leave them free to work at the reconstruction of the country. But he is afraid the Volunteer Army is thinking a fight inevitable; it was with difficulty they were persuaded to swear allegiance to Dail Eireann.

The talk turned on Darrell Figgis, whom Mrs. Shaw likes but he (G.B.S.) doesn't. He said "the worst of victims is they always let you down. There were some horrible tortures of political prisoners at one time in Portugal, and some of them escaped. We were getting up a meeting to get up sympathy for them, and before it I and W. were to meet them before Apsley House and bring them to it. When we came there we could not see them. There was rather a crowd laughing at something that had happened and we saw some very fat fair fresh looking men shouting and holding their sides with laughter and we said what a contrast they were to the thin and tortured victims we were looking for, but then one of them stepped forward and said "Are you Mr.

Shaw?" and we found they were the victims! Of course you couldn't get sympathy for them on the platform. And now it's just the same thing. I went to see films meant to help the starving European children. There was one showing the Children of Vienna in 1914, playing out in the Platz. Then the starved Vienna children of today, and they appeared just the same, looking quite happy and healthy, except that instead of playing in the city they were bringing bundles of sticks in over the snow and looking as if they enjoyed it as much as any other game. I told them, as I had told the organisers in the Portuguese time, if you want to get sympathy there is no earthly use in going to reality, you must get actors to dress up and play the parts". He said "Ireland would be let down as a Republic, with a shabby little embassy in London". I said, "No, she wouldn't, for you would be our Ambassador entertaining as you are now, with whipped cream!"

I went on to see Epstein's Christ[10]—the Christ who "his 70 disciples sent against religion and government"! and to John's pictures, and met Knewstub there and asked him to try and sell the John picture of Yeats.

Now the first day of a new week, I must try again to get some advice as to picture matter. I have written to ask Macpherson to see me.

16 MARCH. No answer from Macpherson. Una says he is to go out of office. T. P. O'Connor is away. I have written to Lord Killanin he might help in the House of Lords and to Mrs. Grosvenor—she might help with Trustees.

Yesterday, my birthday [15 March], the chicks brought me up little presents, a black china bear and a yellow bowl and Richard wrote wishing me happy returns. I took the chicks to Maskelyne and Cooks leaving them there with Ellen and Delia—all happy.

17TH. Alec Martin last night. Told me but little of Hugh, just his kindness in taking him motoring and other ways. He is very much pleased at having recognised a Carpacio in a picture in the Wentworth collection named as Dürer.

The owner was indignant at his changing it, "Where's my Dürer? I have always had it as Dürer", but was pleased when it brought in £30,000.

17TH. He had in his early days been sent to a Scotch laird's place to see his pictures. He said of one of them "that is a Hals", the owner said "No, it is not. The Director of the Scottish National Gallery has been staying here lately for a fortnight, and he valued my pictures and said that was a Van Dyck, and worth not more than £200." Alec M. said "2 or 3 thousand would be nearer it". But the Laird was very snubbing, took him into a hall, with sportsmen, and seemed to look on him as an errand boy and he was very glad to get away. The Laird then wrote to Christies reproving them for not having sent a proper expert. Alec felt this very deeply, for it was the first time he had been sent out. The pictures were sent to Christies and the picture was pronounced a Hals and sold for £5,000. He said to the Laird "I shall be much obliged if you will write to the firm withdrawing what you said about me as it is very injurious to me". He did write, but grudgingly and ungraciously.

Just before he came, I saw in the *Evening News* a paragraph on the Tate and the new gallery to be built and that "the wonderful Lane collection will hang there". It roused me to write to Carson today, not having heard from Macpherson.

13, Royal Hospital Road
Chelsea
17 March, [1920]

Dear Sir Edward Carson,

The enclosed cutting is a new evidence that the Nat. Gallery Trustees are trying to maintain their grip on the Lane pictures. I heard from Mr. Macpherson and Captain Craig a couple of weeks ago that the appeal for a Bill to legalise Hugh Lane's codicil is "still before the Cabinet". It has been for some months in that stage.

Last November Lord D'Abernon said to Sir John Lavery, who pressed for the return of the pictures to Dublin, "the most they (the Trustees) would consent to do would be to send them to Dublin on loan" a practically unlimited loan. I sent this informal proposal on to Capt. Craig, asking him to show it to you, and I sent it also to Mr. Macpherson. I thought that if the Cabinet means to reject our request for a Bill we had better accept the loan, and press for a Bill at some further and more favourable time—the offer may be withdrawn if the Cabinet refuses.

But I said the decision ought to rest with you, because you are the chief force on our side for his ———— is to you, on the Trustees side—and I believe he would give in if he realised you were personally taking up the matter.

I am here but for a short time, and hope I may have good news instead of further hope deferred to take back to Dublin. Please forgive me for troubling you.

Sincerely Yours
AUGUSTA GREGORY

EVENING. Mrs. Grosvenor has been here and I read her some of the story and she liked it. And she is sympathetic about the pictures, took pamphlets and will write to Lord Brownlow, Lord Plymouth, Heseltine, perhaps Lord Ribblesdale, such a help!

20 MARCH. An answer from Carson today saying he is laid up with a cold but when about again will talk over the matter with his colleagues—that is more hopeful.

5, Eaton Place
S.W.1
18 March, 1920

Dear Lady Gregory,

I have received your letter. I am at present laid up with a severe cold but when I am about again, I will talk to some of my colleagues on the subject of your letter.

Yours sincerely
EDWARD CARSON

Lady Gregory
13, Royal Hospital Road
Chelsea.

I went yesterday to the city to see Meagher. He didn't tell me much about Hugh. But he told me to remember he had written urging me to publish with Grant Richards. G.R. had told him "executors have power to keep back the papers of the deceased"—and he was afraid of what he calls "friction", that is the keeping back of the papers from me!! I told him he need not be anxious, the Wood executors having already done that! Meagher himself would, he says, give them all over to me if he had them in his hand and had always thought it was I who should write the book.

To Christies then to see A. Martin, who is sad because Witt won't hear of giving up the MS and is pushing on for law. But Witt told me that from what he heard of Wood he would never face a court.

50A. Albemarle Street
London W.
18 March, 1920.

Dear Lady Gregory,

This is a whisper; but I must write to say how very much I love your book. It is a beautiful piece of work, courageous, charming, witty and written with feeling and vision. You won't mind these adjectives from this neophyte in letters, will you?—but I feel very full of them just at present. I have written such a report as will I hope ensure its publication here, a very sincere report I need not say. I am little nervous about some of the references to current Irish politics and I think you might anyhow consider whether they are really worth while, for they date the book—which is a lasting piece of work—and as an Englishman whose heart is Irish I lament beyond words the disgraceful and humiliating condition of things now in Ireland and am sure it will soon be ended. The other part is—the father. It strikes me you are rather hard upon him. It may be you have good family reason for this feeling; but judging from the facts you give, to an outsider it does not look like fair play, and after all Hugh Lane would not have been himself without the paternal essence.

Your book has made me remember vividly the one visit I paid to Lindsey House, and causes me to regret that among the interesting people you have introduced me he was not one of them. You have championed a cause well and have portrayed a character—the wants and weaknesses, as well as the strength and the light—with brilliance. And that is all I need say—and must say—at this present. It will age my heart if A.St. does not publish this book.

Yours ever
C. E. LAWRENCE

20 MARCH. Home—and G.B.S., came a little after 4, hoarse from a cold and lecturing and going on to another lecture. I was sad at his having come but in a few minutes Birrell and Tony who I had expected later came in, and Birrell was delighted to see G.B.S., didn't often come across him, and he and Tony had been to *Pygmalion*[11] and talked of it and G.B.S., said how troublesome Mrs. Campbell had grown; he had three times at rehearsal had to send her out of the theatre and the other actors didn't like the way she treated them, telling one that no one with such a face as his had any business on the stage. He told us that he has been writing about Tree and that Lady Tree is delighted, thinking it alludes to a part he ought to have given her (which it didn't). The sale of pictures also he talked of and how the high prices for Old Masters are given by the same men who take boxes at the opera and send their wives there plastered with diamonds just to show their solvency. Nevill Geary came in and G.B.S. had stood with him for Marylebone Co Council and greeted him warmly—quite a pleasant little gathering; but then the chicks were rather wild, especially Cat, who made Tony her prey.

Guy had been to tea the evening before and we had acted charades. Lawrence's letter appreciating the Memoir a great cheer up. I have got the MS back to take out the "political allusions he thinks J.M. would object to."

21ST. Catherine went to Balys and I took Anne to Mudies. Sent maids out and stayed in afternoon. R. Pope Hennessey to tea, upset about Mayor of Cork's murder,[12] cannot think who it was done by, he is Sinn Fein. And he hears from Desmond Fitzgerald that Kelly's mind is affected (the Lord Mayor of Dublin) through his arrest and imprisonment. Murder of the mind of the one, of the other's body.

Letter from Lawrence telling me to hurry with my MS as "the iron is hot" so am alas! taking out some of my most personal bits about the rising and the treatment of T. Kelly and the like.

John Murray
50a, Albemarle Street
London W.1.
20 March, 1920

Dear Lady Gregory,

I am very sorry I missed you yesterday. I don't generally escape till 4.30; but I felt "done" at 4 and so fled into the Park to sit in the sun and bathe my nerves for half-an-hour.

I return the M.S. It would be well if you would revise it as you say. Thank you for the way in which you have taken my remarks. Send it back as soon as is well possible.

Ever yours
C. E. LAWRENCE.

20 March, 1920.

Dear Lady,

Send it back as soon as you conveniently can; but make those revisions first. The iron is hot.

Ever yours
C. E. LAWRENCE

23 MARCH. Letters from Mrs. Grosvenor—very cheering. Lord Plymouth writes: . . . "I do not think it fair to approach the National Gallery Trustees individually asking them to act upon their own personal opinions in a matter where their duty is to act as Trustees for the Nation. Their action as Trustees cannot be governed by sentiment but by motives of generosity or if you prefer the expression 'moral right'. Legal authorities having settled what the position of the Trustees is, it becomes the duty of the Government to carry the matter further if they think it desirable and fair, and by a deliberate Act of Parliament they should restore to Government that to which they think Dublin has a good moral claim. The responsibility for that decision should not be placed upon the National Gallery Trustees. . . . I hope I have

made my views clear. The Government must take full responsibility, and I should acquiesce at once in their decision."

Lord Brownlow writes: "The National Gallery have no power to relinquish property which is legally theirs, but of course *Parliament* can do so, and I can assure you that any Bill introduced for that purpose will not meet any opposition from me. As a personal matter I should be very glad to see them removed from the National Gallery, which is a collection of Old Masters and not modern pictures and to my mind an unsuitable place for Sir Hugh Lane's French pictures."

Mr. Heseltine says: "My own feeling in the matter is well expressed in the memorial by 150 Irish artists to the Prime Minister of 29 January, 1917. I am one of the Trustees who "view sympathetically the claims of the city of Dublin" but only the Treasury can authorise either the National Gallery or the Tate Gallery Trustees to carry out any terms not in accordance with their "primary capacity". I have never been able to understand the objections raised by the friends of Sir Hugh Lane to a *loan* to Dublin; it would not achieve the complete wishes of the testator, but Dublin would have the pictures, which is the chief thing."

24TH. Yesterday morning, being put in spirits by those letters I telephoned to Macpherson. He "couldn't be seen all day—at a Committee all the morning and House of Commons all the afternoon". I asked if I could not see him at House of Commons and the answer (evidently referred to him) was "yes" at 4.30. I went first to Putnams about *The Dragon*, which they are going to print in U.S.A. I wanted to add *The Jester*[13] to it but Grubb thought it would make difficulties with Talbot Press. Then to House of Commons. Had to wait a good time at the barrier and then appealed to one of the policemen who looked amiable, for leave to sit inside which he gave me. The other who looked a mass of fleshy insolence I wished in Dublin. Then I was taken through corridors and up staircases and found the Chief Secretary looking I thought more natural, less stiff and pompous. He said the question had been brought up 3 times in the Cabinet. It is divided, half and half, Balfour and Bonar Law being Scotch are for us, because the want of witnesses would not be illegal in Scotland. All the lawyers are against us, because "they can't stand any tampering with the law". He thinks it may be our best strategy to negotiate a loan, because Curzon is so violent on the matter that another argument may finally "put his back up".

I read him the 3 letters. He was impressed by them, thinks they strengthen our hands very much. I asked if he would like to keep them, and he said "yes, very much, they will be a great help". I asked if he would show them to Sir E. Carson and he said "certainly". I urged his trying to get the fear of Carson into Curzon, it would make him collapse. And I said if he cannot get a Bill we would accept a loan, as we would never give the pictures back and could bring in a Bill at a more favourable time. I think he has really worked for us. He said Craig "has been at him about it" so that either isn't lost.

Then to Regent's Park to Una's party for Wyndham and Lady Susan. I arrived late, but so much the better, sat and talked with Wyn and Tony, and made acquaintance with Lady Susan, very round and fat and pleasant. She said "ever since I have known Wyndham I have heard of nothing but Lady Gregory". Tony brought me home in a taxi. Una is excited and indignant as I was, at the military raid on that O'Grady house.

This morning more telephoning and it resulted in my going to see T. P. O'Connor at quarter past twelve. He also thought the letters important and was much wakened up by hearing of the state of our business in the Cabinet. He will see Shortt (who Macpherson had said was one of our enemies) this afternoon, and will also bring influence to bear on Lord Crawfurd.

He bemoaned the state of Ireland, "England has gone stark staring mad, and Ireland is nearly as mad". He asked for one of the pamphlets. I had sent him one so lately I had not brought it now.

I went on to Mrs. Grosvenor to tell her how helpful the letters had been and that Macpherson hoped she would write also to Lord Ribblesdale and Crawfurd, and this she will do. I found she had still one of the pamphlets I had given her, so I carried it off and went back to Victoria Street and to Morpeth Mansions and up in the lift and gave it in at T.P's door.

Home very tired, found the children finishing lunch and wrote letters from then till 5 when they came in for tea.

Then Una came in for a long chat, pleased about their hopes and prospects at Rostellan.

She says that when Sir Hubert Gough urged friendship with Russia to Lloyd George he said: "I wish you success in bringing it about, I would like to do it, but you don't know what I have to fight against."

27TH. On Thursday I packed and went to Bank, meeting Mr. Scovell in Piccadilly just as I had in Galway Square the day I was leaving. He is gloomy, says the railway (but it was I think the road) between Cranmore and Galway was blocked the day he left and that the Finevara sale has fallen through, the smaller tenants (who have no money to give) insisting on a share and breaking the agreement made with the larger ones.

I telephoned to ask if I would find Birrell at home and he asked me to come at once to lunch, so I did and told him of the Trustees' Letters and the interview with Macpherson and he thought all looked hopeful and agreed with me that there be no public discussion in the present state of feeling about Ireland. He spoke of Mrs. Humphrey Ward's[14] death, had admired her social work, but never could read her novels. He says her son is gambling away great sums of money—the money she has made.

Back to Royal Hospital Road, hoping to see Margaret but she only sent a wire saying she had found "charming smugglers cottage with cook" at Folkestone. To Newbuildings and having been misdirected as to trains didn't get there till 9.30, got a good welcome then and yesterday we walked, Dorothy and I with Wilfred's bath chair, all through woods bursting into leaf and bloom, and had lunch out also.

He is very much better than I had seen him for a long time, enjoying talk, the incubus of the lawsuit over, tho' there is still tiring business connected with it. He says it is all for the best the stud being taken from him, it costs £3000 a year and he is not able to look after it as he used. He would I think be quite happy if someone else would take the whole stud over from the official receiver but is afraid it may be dispersed and come to nothing. I said he had done a great work in having established it, and being able now to give it over in a flourishing condition, and he says it was never in so good a state. I wish some American would buy it. He has had no remonstrances about his *Diaries*, I told him Birrell had said he was in bad odour at repeating private conversations but had not heard of any of the victims themselves complaining. I asked if Mrs. Asquith had written, but he said she had only sent him a bundle of election posters from Paisley with "From loving Margot" on them and I said "she couldn't say more than that". We were talking of Mahaffy—I told about the "cocks and hens" story that he said had delighted the Kaiser, and he said Frank Lascelles had told him that his influence with the Kaiser has gained by telling him rather stupid and coarse anecdotes.

28TH. Yesterday began well with a letter from Murray "I have been reading your life of Hugh Lane, a most unusual biography of a most unusual personage, and am much attracted both by him and by the way his story is told. I have not yet finished it; as I grudge skipping and my leisure moments only occur at night, but I am satisfied that I should like to publish it . . ."

Such a relief! Now I can finish it with spirit and courage! I worked at it through the morning. W.S.B's criticism helpful, he is delighted with the three first chapters, but thought the fourth rather confused. I spent the day making a new beginning to it. I also read some of W.S.B's memoirs of his early life, quite delightful, and we talked with interest of how things might have turned out had he remained a Protestant, had he become a painter under Watts, or a monk as his mother wished, or an Indian Civil servant as his guardian suggested. Such a bore he would have been now as I told him! I was reading a bit of Doughty[15] and I said I wondered how he had built up his style and W.S.B. said "He was a scholar—he had never read anything but Elizabethan or pre-Elizabethan literature". Then he went to Arabia and having learned Arabic he wrote a sort of literal translation of it (like my Cuchulain) and with that and the Elizabethan influence his style grew, "you may have noticed (as I had) how much richer and simpler his style is in the 2nd Volume than in the first. But no one read the book, I was the first to read it and I thought and think it the finest piece of English prose of the century. I showed it to Morris, and he read it through and was delighted and gave it to Burne Jones and that set took it up and after ten years it became known. Then he wrote some poems and when they came out Garnett, who grieved at not having given the Travels a better welcome, received them with exaggerated enthusiasm. They were no good at all but Doughty became convinced his true gift was poetry and has written this new rubbish *Mansoul*".[16] He read at lunch out of doors the sonnet he had written for [the] Shakespeare Centenary at the request of Gollancz and which had (fortunately) not been printed with the rest. It ends with a voice from Stratford asking who are "these lewd boys who call me to join this mumming, I have left the stage."

He says he did not publish the *Diaries* without serious consideration. It was Lloyd George's call to "hang the Kaiser" that decided him. "No one would pay attention if I said I knew on good authority what had led to it. We must give all the story to have it credited."

W.S.B., looking in his Diary for the account of Lillah McCarthy's visit, read that I had been here (last March) and had read the *Jester* to him which he had liked and "I am more than ever struck with Lady Gregory's intellectual superiority to every woman I have ever known, it is not a man's intellect, it is a woman's but she has a power of continuous original work and dramatic construction. . . . etc." Oh! Dublin.

31 MARCH. The last evening at Newbuildings, I was reading

the *Memoir* of W.S.B's early life again—a brilliant entry into life. I gave him one of the Hugh Lane pamphlets to read at his reading hour (midnight), and when I saw him in the morning I found he had been interested and would speak to Lord Ribblesdale[17] when he comes; and will write to Lord O. Beauclerk[18] to speak to Lord Lansdowne[19], says he has become such an Irishman since he married he will probably be glad to help.

Back to London—went to see John Murray and settled about the Memoir for the Autumn and held out for more pictures till he, or his son, promised 12 pages instead of 8. He asked me what my politics were. I said I kept out of them on account of the Abbey Theatre. But Lawrence says he said to him when he had sent the M.S., "Lady Gregory is a great rebel" this after all my elisions! I saw Alec Martin, after my tea at the Nicholsons, he fears Witt is still threatening for a lawsuit with Wood. He had tried to restrain him but Witt said if he didn't like his advice he had better go to someone else.

Margaret came in next morning—she has a letter from Scott Kerr saying there is a bad prospect of sale. All the county in a wild state since F.S.T.'s murder. Lough Cutra has been demanded and Castle Taylor and they want only to take our grazing instead of purchase (just to get in as tenants) and he thinks if the Regan gang buy it they will be shot. She is going to Dublin to see Whitney and Moore but can't go to Coole till after the holidays; much better she should not.

I brought the chicks here (Sandgate) yesterday. Richard had arrived in the morning, is bright and well and with two prizes was so proud.

7, Audley Square
W.1
31 March, 1920

Dear Mrs. Grosvenor,

Many thanks for sending me the memorandum about the Lane Pictures. I am afraid that as at present advised, I do not feel in a position to support the transfer of this gallery to Ireland.

Yours truly
CRAWFORD BALCARRES

The Hon. Mrs. Grosvenor
30, Upper Grosvenor St.
W.1

30, Upper Grosvenor Street
W.
2 April, 1920

Dear Lady Gregory,

This is disappointing but I always felt him a very tiresome person.

I have not yet heard from Ld. Ribblesdale.

Yours very sincerely
CAROLINE GROSVENOR.

5 APRIL. Easter Monday. Yesterday was quiet. Cloudy. Richard still not well. I took the others to church and in the afternoon they walked to Folkestone. Mrs. K. the cook had seen a paper saying there was "terrible work in Dublin", and I was anxious—Margaret (perhaps) probably there—and the chicks and the ———— I couldn't get a paper even—Relieved to find this morning it was an attack on Income Tax offices and police barracks and apparently no lives lost. Macpherson ceasing to be Chief Secretary, a blow on the Gallery side, he seemed in earnest and now we must begin all over again.

6 APRIL. A letter from Margaret, saying the land is to be put up to auction in Dublin. She tells of French being fired at and Aggie having received a threatening letter, and Meldon having sold his land etc. She says "Of course one is endangering the children's lives probably and certainly ruining them financially and socially by keeping on Coole—but that is now entirely your responsibility".

8TH. A bad night and a weight on my heart. I cannot think it right to part with Richard's heritage and break up the children's home.

BOOK EIGHT

SANDGATE—8 APRIL 1920. Margaret coming today.

GRESHAM—DUBLIN. 13 APRIL. Margaret told me of negotiations about the sale—the only offer under £7,000—Scott Kerr unsatisfactory, says "the value of an estate in Galway is what you can get for it "and then *began* by asking our minimum price £12,600! He says he "has the tenants well in hand" and that they have now combined—but we know very little of what is happening—I said "Would it be of any use my going over to Coole?" and Margaret said "Yes"—so I decided to go at once.

We had a talk of plans. She has set her heart on buying Celbridge, and says if she could do so she would keep Coole as well and let Richard decide when he grows up which he will choose—I would be quite satisfied with this, I only want to keep his home a resting place in this stormy and uncertain and broken up world, and let him judge whether it is a burden or a boon. But it will be hard to keep up the house—I will do my best—I am happier for the talk.

I said goodbye to my darling Richard and the others, and got to London at 10—had a bad night and morning of headache—set out in the evening (Sunday) for Dublin—train rather crowded with troops—I sat up in the corner of my 3rd class carriage very tired—a rough passage. At Kingstown I bought the papers and the news of the hunger strike turned me sick.

To see Keller—a long talk with him. He thinks we should take £10,000—if we got it which is doubtful. But if much less is offered thinks we should not "throw away the place" though it would mean a fight. No account from Scott Kerr of his meeting with the tenants on Saturday offering 20 years purchase. In the evening a telegram saying they have taken till next Saturday to consider the matter and he has written. Meanwhile the general strike for next day on behalf of the prisoners ordered—so I shall be kept here—no trains—the Gresham staff are to leave at 10 a.m. and the hotel to be shut.[1] I bought a loaf of bread, a box of dates and 2 oranges and left them at the Abbey as I may have to take refuge there.

Went to Hibernian Academy and saw the "Homage to Hugh

Lane" rather blatant, and all turning their backs on him "amusing", Jack Yeats says "too amusing". A very fine picture by Jack himself there "The Market Day" I think the best he has done—marked £315; I wish someone would buy it for the gallery.

The Abbey quiet—Robinson hopes that his *Whiteheaded Boy*[2] is to be put on in London by Fagan. But he had met last week Iseult and the young man walking to the station—they had been married in the morning and were on the way to London. He sees nothing but disaster—the boy's father having died in a madhouse and he is but 18.

Harris came in. He advises us not to be in a hurry with the sale, to take £10,000 but not less—believes things will improve in the next year or so. He says Lord French was drunk when he gave that interview that has been published and that he is known to drink.

I went to Jack Yeats' exhibition—rather sketchy.

Evening to the Abbey to see Drama League give *The life of a Man*[3] Tchechov, very gloomy yet impressive. Edward Martyn there; he has not sold Tillyra as the Hemphills will not give his price and he believes there will be Government sale for estates—hears English profiteers want to come and settle over here.

Excitement in the street and everywhere—"Stop Press" editions giving news of the prisoners on hunger strike and the ordered strike outside.

This morning (13th) I expected to be turned out—but the housemaid says they are not ordered to leave yet. I say I think the one day strike may make the Government give in—but she is doubtful, says "the military are very cruel". I saw Dr. O'Dea, Bishop of Galway here and through the porter asked to see him, and have been having a talk. He is gloomy, hopes nothing from England, talks of last chances. Advises us not to fight at Coole—yet agrees we should not throw away the place.

Harris has been—says he and Keller talked over our affairs last night. I asked what they had said between themselves as to price. He had said we should not take less than £10,000. Keller had said that if £8000 is offered we should split and take £9000, but not a penny less than that.

14TH. I went to the Abbey found no one there—sat in the Greenroom and read Andreyev's *Maskers*[4] and *Sabine Women*[5] a gloomy diseased mind I think, though the *Life of Man* which I saw on Monday was impressive tho' gloomy.

I walked to Merrion Square hoping to see Sir Robert Woods. He was out but Lady Woods in and I had tea with her and her daughter: and stayed talking and they asked me to stay on to dinner. Sir Robert dining at Trinity, but I saw him for a moment and he said "We can't get the pictures—they won't look at the Bill in the Cabinet—Macpherson told me so". He applauded my success in getting at the trustees. Lady Woods was sympathetic about that, and about the hunger strike.

The streets crowded, all shops shut, people not dressed as for Sunday and not with any look of enjoyment. There was tension, a watching for papers, but these had no news save continuance of the strike. Lady Woods asked me to stay, but the Gresham will still keep me and I will dine with the Woods.

This morning the housemaid says "No deaths, but they are sinking". It is terrible. I had prayed so hard last night for them and awoke to find myself praying to *America*—I don't know if a cable there would be of any use.

Mr. Edmunds in the hotel and I got hold of him to consult about the sale. He says he must have more particulars, scoffs at M. saying Income tax would come to more than rates; will go and see Keller.

M. told Keller, Coole was a white elephant and that she wished to bring the children up "in a well kept house".

2ND. Have been at the Abbey listening to a run through the words of *Lost Leader*[6] a fine beginning—a poor end. Aeroplanes passed over with a loud rumbling constantly, taking Mountjoy in their sweep. They seemed like vultures hovering waiting for a death. I said it would make a fine end to *Lost Leader* if Parnell could say "I have learned that my generation has passed. I have no more to do I will leave it to the lads in Mountjoy" but we would all be sent there I suppose if that were done, and Robinson looked gloomy. Mrs. Martin[7] said her son (he had been a prisoner in Germany) had just been to the prison and thought there was a death near, "he saw the priest going in with religious pictures". Coming back, after a cup of tea Mrs. Martin made for me and a stale bun, I saw the posters "Prisoners dying". I thought to get Russell and H. Plunkett and cable to John Quinn[8] in New York, but Robinson says H.P. is lying up this week, and I couldn't walk so far as Russells.

3.30. Waiting at the Gresham; a constant quiet tramping of feet on the pavement, all going towards Mountjoy. No voices except the news boys now and again "Stop Press" and the buzz of the aeroplanes.

Stop Press says the Lord Mayor has been asked to go to the V.R. Lodge.

16 APRIL. Later the hotel manager, delighted, told me the prisoners had been released—such a mercy. I met Craoibhin and

his daughter, bicycling back from Mountjoy where they had been in the watching crowd and a man had called out to them in Irish that the Government had given in; then Miss Mitchell, radiant, we rejoiced together. It had been a terrible strain all day.

I walked to Kildare Street and Edmunds and Keller discussed our sale and made calculations. W.E. calculated that he if buying would give £9200 and there should be £1000 bonus. Then he said "why don't you go to the Board?" Keller said they are not buying, they have no money. He said "Oh, they can get it if they want to go to Doran, let Lady Gregory herself go to Doran", (he told Keller outside not to let Mrs. Gregory go to him). I felt more hopeful after the letter. Keller said it had been a great help, and the possibility of the Board, which I had always wanted, raised hope.

I went on to tea with the Hydes and Craoibhin walked with me to Merrion Square where I dined with the Woods.

Craoibhin says he thinks De Valera[9] would now be repudiated if he came over to Ireland, because of his offering guarantees the same as those of Cuba. Col. Moore[10] tells him that neither De Valera nor Griffith[11] nor McNeill[12] have power now it is all with the Volunteer army. I asked who were its leaders[13] and he tried to remember the name of one of them "a man with one Irish and one English name who was with me in the Gaelic League" (this must have been Cathal Brugha)[14] but couldn't. It, the army, believes there must be a fight, but seems to hope not for a battle but for guerrilla warfare, making the Government of the country impossible. The Republic has seized their minds. He had known nothing of this idea until in the Rising he saw the flag green, white and yellow, hoisted at the National University and heard "Up the Republic"! He said then "That cry and that flag have taken possession of the imagination and I don't think it will ever be got out of it".

The Hydes were to have had people to dinner but had put them off "How could we eat with the prisoners starving?"

Sir R. Woods and his wife and children entertained me—all kind and pleasant, tho' he is not hopeful about the pictures, the Cabinet rejecting or "not looking at" the bill; the Ulster party not caring about it. However I read him my Trustee letters and he promised to work again when he goes to House of Commons next week.

Next morning Thursday, the strike at an end! . . . I went to Keller[15]—he had a letter from Scott Kerr saying our offer of 20 years purchase is being considered but that there is not much chance of an offer anywhere near our figure. Keller thought I should go to Doran at once and rang him up to know if he could see me. He answered that he was very much occupied—had deputations and Irish business—but could see me for 10 minutes if I would come and stay in the waiting room. So, I took a cab and set off. As we passed Suffolk Street there was a great crowd and the car-driver said "There's another raid going on" and pointed out the Military and their armoured car. He didn't know whose house they were raiding, but I see in the paper it was an architect's and a solicitor's.

At the C.D.B. Office I had only a minute's wait when Sir Henry came down. There was only one chair and he sat on the table. He was, as he used not to be, hard in manner and absolutely refused to "touch the estate", they had no power—no money—never meddled in estates where negotiations were going on. I pleaded but he was firm and told me of places they had had trouble about. A long story of one in Mayo where they had sent a boat to help in developing fishing, and had just heard it had been burned. All this time I was praying—praying to the unseen to help us beyond the world and suddenly he said "Of course if the Land Purchase bill that has been promised comes in then we would buy it!" (thank God!) And he went up and wrote a letter that I might use.

As I went out I said "Mr. Edmunds tells me we were arrant and abject fools in refusing your offer of £652 for Lisheen Crannagh—but I had never heard of it. Would you renew it?" He said, No, he had offered too much and it had been rejected—but he said "Our first offer of £300 will stand". I asked if he could not make an advance on it and he said "No, but you may write to me—But not Mrs. Gregory—she is too smart for us to deal with". Poor Margaret!

And Keller when I brought back the letter thought I had done very well in both cases. Mackie had telegraphed about L. Crannagh that they only offer £150! and will hold on to their land. So the sale to the Board would be much better.

Then to the Abbey to arrange Abbey Programmes with Robinson, but luckily not much business so I got to the hotel and caught 1.30 train—getting half a cup of tea at the Broadstone. I telegraphed from Mullingar that I was arriving, but there was no one to meet me at Gort, and I learned at P. Office that the telegram had not come. The wires they thought had been cut or kept by the military who had taken possession of them during the strike. So I arrived home on foot and wet with a heavy storm.

J.D. thought there was going to be an even worse offer made, the "committee" wishing rather to go in as grazing tenants.

There is no reconciliation, just that clique still wanting to buy—"no more united than that stick in your hand".

Today, Scott Kerr came.

This morning, after a good night, I awoke or half awoke with the feeling of having taken my bundle of troubles to another place—a place where one learned in some higher air how to deal with them down here. As I awoke enough to define the sensation, to translate it into words, I thought with a feeling of turning it into comedy, that sometimes business debated in the Lords is brought down to be put into action in the Commons.

But then, drowsing again, those I thought of as helping me in that Upper House were those who had but lately gone from my company, Robert, and Hugh and John[16]. . . .

Perhaps it was this that made me, when Scott Kerr said the offer for the land was bad, and that he "relinquished the sale", feel that rebuff was less a defeat than a victory. For if we can sell it to the Board, it is the poorer man who will profit and as I think the most worthy, and so may be laid the foundation of a lasting peace.

Coole
Saturday, 17 April

Dearest Margaret,

Scott Kerr came here about 2.30. The offer had been raised to £7,500. He could not get them to raise this, though he thinks it possible they might give another £500. So he told them that closed the matter as far as he is concerned.

He had heard from Keller that I had seen Doran, so I showed him the letter. I think he was a little taken aback. He had been speaking of "waiting a couple of months to let things simmer". He had no idea that the C.D.B. would buy. He was rather annoying too about price, basing it upon "what Mrs. Gregory gets out of it is £500 a year". I said rents alone £626, but he said "rates have to come out of that", and waved it by. Of course I will say nothing of the C.D.B. until I hear from you. He advised saying nothing about it, but I incline to think it is as well to let it get about, for if any oppose the idea they will know the Board won't be friendly to them when it comes to dividing of land.

Then he proposed letting the grazing at once to the "Committee". I said the Board might object to having them landed in; that I thought we ought not to make any lets without consulting them, or at least Mr. Edmunds. He said delay would be loss of money, which of course I know. I asked if we would lose much if we let it all lie for a winterage, and he said he gets more at Castle Taylor for a winterage than for summer grazing, but that of course our land is not so good.

He says Ballinamantane was in the sale but that now it is over there is no reason it should not be separately disposed of. I asked about "Union" and he says Father Cassidy tried to get them all together at a meeting to unite, but they refused. He had proposed our stocking the land ourselves, but that was before he saw the letter. I think we are just as well out of him. He is muggy. He is very proud of his two sons, they are now coming to Ashfield.

He says there was trouble threatened at C. Taylor, small tenants demanded land, and threatened and I think began cattle drives. But the Sinn Fein Committee, which is very strong, intervened and said they would help them to get the land, but would have no cattle driving. I heard in Dublin Sinn Fein had declared against it.

I am writing this to post this evening. I daresay I may hear more tomorrow. He was astonished also to hear the Board would buy Lisheen Crannagh—I wish that were settled.

18TH SUNDAY. No news but that Thomas Diveney has had a threatening letter warning him against working for F. Quinn; and Rock and Cosgrave have had a permission to keep on Inchey sent them by young Hayes! At Church, the Bagots. No man allowed to work for them, except the gardener and he having been seen chopping sticks with Mr. B., has been warned not to do it again.

They drove themselves to church and Lally could not let them put up the pony in his yard and "would not answer for it", so it had to be stabled in the barracks. Mr. Bagot broke down in talking to me. They demand half his land. The police are anxious, but he refuses protection, but they have now got some flares to let up in case of need.

This morning at daybreak I awoke with such a clear conviction of what had crossed my mind now and again, but not for some time, that *Visions and Beliefs*[17] might at this time be a cause of offence and make our difficulties harder, that I came down and wrote Mr. Grubb asking him to cable to Putnam to keep it back for a while.

20 APRIL. Yesterday and today quiet though weather stormy. I wrote for plants and got gravel for the garden walks from the stone crusher. Margaret has wired assent to sell Lisheen

Crannagh to the Board.

Coole
21 April

Dearest Margaret,

I had your wire yesterday, but didn't do anything, expecting your letter which came this morning.

It is puzzling about the Crannagh wall, for Edmunds said the Board was to build it. I had asked Godmother to find out if he was in Galway and she writes that he was yesterday morning, but motored off somewhere, but Mrs. E. thought he would be back, so I am going in by 2 o'c train to try and find out something definite. I, like you, would rather the Board got it than the tenants, for I think it would have a better effect here.

As to Coole, Keller said he had consulted North, who thought a Dublin auction would be useless. I think that clique would be the only bidders as they seem to have intimidated the rest, and J.D. (who I am consulting confidentially) is of the same opinion. He says Malachi Quinn has suggested to him, that the three parish priests should be asked to negotiate. But this would be risky, as they might not accept our reserve. Or if nothing else turns up, I might perhaps see Father Cassidy and find out what he would hold out for.

I am going to post this letter somewhere else, so I can say that I think we are well out of Scott Kerr, for I asked him before he left what he thought we should accept, and he said "Schedule 8", basing this on the income he sticks to of "clause 5"! He had said when he came in that it was possible the bidders might go up to 8. So you see that if they should do so, he would recommend us to accept, and probably resign if we refused on the ground of our wanting too much. If I have not a high opinion of him (I don't mean to say he is bribed, but I think probably Hogan is too much for him) he has not a high opinion of us, for Keller says he wanted him to see you in Dublin and he refused saying "When I deal with ladies I like to have everything on paper"!!

All this made me think the Board our only hope, but if you won't deal with it I don't know what to do. The 1st May will be a troublesome day I think all over the country. I was hoping to have some settlement in hand before then.

I asked John this morning what Malachi Quinn had said about B-mantane, he says "Mrs Gregory asked him £1,700, and he couldn't think of that. He offered £1,200. Then she offered it for £1,500 in cash and he couldn't give that. If he was sure of being able to get a bit of the demesne land, in exchange for which he would give up his land in Kiltartan, I think he would rise a hundred". (That would be to £1,300, this a puzzle also, as you say you had not made the £1,500 offer. I had not said a word of it to anyone).

Keller and I put £750 as reserve on L. Crannagh, not with the least hope of getting it, but lest a further drop should encourage the Coole people to think we would make a similar drop in offer to them. I will try and settle something about Crannagh with Edmunds, as you think it best to get rid of it. I would go to Dublin if you think it any use trying to deal with the Board. I shall stay in Galway till Saturday so you could wire there.

I sent off the crates on Monday but saw them coming back on the cart—the Station Master said the English Railways won't take any goods for the next week or fortnight.

Mrs. Bagot was coming to tea but I am putting her off as I am going to Galway. She seemed very depressed on Sunday but writes that she has not "the heart of a lion"!

23RD FRIDAY. Sitting at the Gresham quite sick with anxiety and apprehension, waiting for an interview with Sir Henry Doran: on Thursday I had a letter from Margaret in answer to mine enclosing Sir Henry's offer of purchase. She says she distrusts the Board and goes back to the idea of a Dublin auction, which Keller had thought hopeless, as I think also and J.D. reports. I had written to Ala to find out if Mr. Edmunds was in Galway and she writes that he is, so I decided to go and consult him. In my hurry I took the 2.00 train and had to wait 3 hours at Athenry. However, the fresh cold air and enforced idleness sent away a horrible headache and I read *Arene Sanglantes*[18] feeling much like (as I do especially at this moment) Gallard, the torero, when getting ready for the bullfight.

Cromwell House
Millbank, S.W.1
22 April 1920

Private

Dear Lady Gregory,

Your expressions of regret on my departure from Ireland, even though that regret is to some extent actuated by the uncertainty still attending the fate of the Lane pictures, are very gratifying to me, and will certainly strengthen my desire to do all I can to assist you.

A deputation to my successor would not, in my opinion, be of service to you, but I will myself bring the matter to his notice, and that combined with your zeal and energy will, I feel sure, give you the best promise of success.

I am pleased to learn from your letter that there are still many people in Dublin who can appreciate the pictures at their true worth, even to the extent of giving them preference to the Home Rule Bill.

Yours sincerely,
IAN MACPHERSON

Lady Gregory
Coole Park
Gort
Co. Galway

I had tea with A. and then walked to Mr. Edmund'shouse and he overtook me just as I got there. He was tired I think and it was less easy to talk to him with Mrs. Edmunds listening—and he said we had better let in the Regan set to the grass lands and let the Board fight them later "we always have a fight" . . . But this would be the beginning of strife that I want to avoid. And if the Board's offer failed, we would be left face to face with the enemy. At last he said I had better get Sir H. Doran to buy the land at once, that the Board has money £450,000 but are keeping it back because they want to force the Government to bring in the new purchase Bill. So I came up yesterday afternoon to try if that can be done, but S.K. had said before it was impossible.

Mr. E. said about Lisheen Crannagh that he could build a wall for £100 and that we ought to take that £300—says he did not tell Margaret the wall would cost more than £300 but that it would be worth more to us. But Margaret's letter says Sir Henry definitely refused it, and the Crannagh people can't begin their tillage till this is settled.

I wrote to Sir Henry saying I was coming to see him and have just telephoned (10.30) to C.D.B., but he is not there yet and I am waiting. So much depends on this—peace or war—with perhaps disturbance that will strengthen Margaret's wish to get rid of Coole—Waiting on others is terribly trying.

I think of all the arguments—through so many storms, through a 150 years or more, Coole has been a place of peace. We came through the Land League days and through the sale of the outlying property without war, without police protection or any application to the country for Compensation—for there were no outrages. This was partly due to us and partly to our old tenants whose interest would be served by this purchase, division by the Board. Coole has been not only a place of peace during all that time, but a home of culture in more senses than one. Arthur Young[19] found Mr. Gregory making "a noble nursery, the plantations for which would change the face of the district" and those woods still remain: my husband added rare trees to them and I have added acres and acres of young wood. Richard Gregory collected that fine library: William's father died from famine fever brought on through his ministrations to the poor. He himself had a highly honoured name in Parliament and in Ceylon, loving Coole all the time, all through his lifetime. Robert loved it and showed its wild stern beauty in his paintings; left it through high mindedness and fought for France and Italy. I have lived there and loved it these forty years and through the guests who have stayed there it counts for much in the awakening of the spiritual and intellectual side of our country. If there is trouble now, and it is dismantled and left to ruin, that will be the whole country's loss. I pray, pray, pray.

GALWAY 25 APRIL. On that Thursday morning in Dublin I went out thinking to do a little shopping, but only got to the Theatre and sat watching the rehearsal of *The Good Natured Man*[20] and succeeded in getting the holes in stair carpet—or the holey bit of stair carpet cut out—to be replaced by a spare bit. Then very anxious and shaky to C.D.B. office—a little wait in the waiting room and then Sir Henry came and brought me to his room. I said, "This is an unequal interview, for I can't think of anything in the wide world I can do for you, and you can do so very much for me". We talked first of Lisheen Crannagh, he said he had not contested the case at first and had offered too much and then was vexed when Margaret asked more and had been "rather short", and apologised. He was still hazy about it—and I was anxious to hurry through it and get to the bigger matter of Coole and he agreed that he would give the wall and £300 and possibly more.

Then I told him of our trouble, the small group who wanted to buy the land and kept others out, and had offered a price impossible to accept, and that now they want to get hold of the grazing and would never go out again without a fight, which we are not able to take up. He said, just like Edmunds "Oh, you must let it to them—you must have proper agreement drawn up by a lawyer and make them sign" which, I told him, would be very unfair not only to us but to the respectable old tenants who had been shut out by Scott Kerr's bungling, if we gave in to them. He went on about "proper agents" . . . We were like Juan

Gallard and the bull—he pawing around and I trying to stick in a "baton" whenever I had a chance. Then he told me of the impossibility of buying just now; they are having a special meeting of the Board on Tuesday to assent this. They are inundated with landlords rushing up to beg them to buy, because their land is demanded by moneyless men who can never pay. But the Board will not go into their fight and so on, till at last I said in despair: "What you have to do for us is to buy our land before the first of May and let the grazing yourself." At last he said quite suddenly "I will do it if possible—I will put the case before the special meeting if you will write me a letter. It is a special case and I will do my best to get it through". And peace and joy and relief seemed to rush into me—over me—with that.

Coole Park
Gort
23 April 1920

Dear Sir Henry Doran,

Will you very kindly give us your help by putting this request before the Board. We sold, as you know, the out-lying land at Coole to you some time ago. We now wish to sell the grazing portion of the Demesne lands inside the gates, retaining the house, woods and sufficient land for our own use. This was decided on by my son, the late Major Gregory, on his last visit here in 1917. We had not had any trouble but he foresaw the breaking up of Estates, and also the necessity of tillage, and this land had for forty years or more been let for grazing. We had never found it ourselves.

Last January, Mrs. Gregory to whom it now belongs, decided to carry out his intention, and it was offered to our neighbours—our old tenants—for sale.

A small group of six or seven tenants thrust themselves forward and against our wish, and that of the Parish Priest, tried to get the purchase into their own hands, keeping out more desirable purchasers. The sum they offered was quite inadequate and we refused. The negotiations are now at an end.

This group now wish to be admitted as grass tenants. We believe this, if allowed, will cause friction and trouble and much ill feeling. You had held out hopes to us of buying the land in the future, but I now appeal to you to, if possible, take it at once for cash, as the grazing question will then become a part of your general arrangement and be out of our hands and there is likely to be no trouble as they will be unwilling to offend the Board. I shall personally be most grateful if you can do this.

May I draw your attention to the fact that through all the troublesome times of the last forty years we have never had to ask compensation from the County or for police protection. We have been, in comparison with many other Estates, the centre of peace and goodwill. This was in part owing to the liberal opinions and just dealing of my husband and of my son, and in part to the good behaviour of the majority of our late tenants—not I may say of the small group who are now trying to get hold of the land to the exclusion of the rest.

I make this proposal subject to the approval of Mrs. Gregory to whom I am writing.

Any particulars about the Estate are in the hands of our Solicitors, Messrs Whitney Moore and Keller.

Yours sincerely

Sir Henry Doran
Congested Districts Board
Rutland Square Dublin

Then back to the Gresham exhausted but triumphant to write my letter, which he wanted at once. Then to Keller, and had to wait for him—went for a cup of coffee and back again and at last he came. He was amazed at my success, he had had no hope of any solution though he had written a letter I had not received, proposing advertising the land for sale. I went through my letter with him and he had it typed—and I wrote to Margaret and to Lord Oranmore,[21] the only member of the Board I knew, asking his support. Sir Henry had said, "I will write to Mr. Edmunds to-night about it and Lisheen Crannagh"; so I thought I had better come back to Galway and see Mr. E., before he answered it. So I posted my letters and bought some little tomato plants I saw on the pavement, and had some tea—and caught the 7.30 train and got to Galway at midnight. I had written outside an envelope to Margaret "Offer being equal, would you prefer Lear's Daughter or La Planche?" and Ala handed me a wire from her saying she prefers La Planche if ready cash is given. So that is all right. Yesterday morning, very sleepy after my short night, I got up and after breakfast went to C.D.B. office and happily found Mr. Edmunds there. He clapped his hands and called out to me laughing and expressing joy at the surrender of Sir Henry—though he is not sure he can carry it against the Board. We talked over some details. He had not yet heard from Sir Henry.

I was quite ill all day and worn out, couldn't touch food. Sarah gave me beef tea and said "And the Missis thinks when you are coming that you will eat all Galway!" There was a quarter of lamb for lunch, and I had not let her know that I didn't touch it.

Slept well and better this morning, but will be anxious till Tuesday is over. Sir H. said he would wire.

TUESDAY 27TH. Sunday quiet—the new Bishop Ross, an Ulsterman looking like an Inquisitor read his sermon, an Easter essay. On Monday to C.D.B. office again but no letter from Doran.

I left for home—Miss Kincaid was at the station and I thought of asking her if she knew of a French governess—and she does know of a possible one—a girl staying at Lady Coghill's.

Margaret wired "entirely agree with everything" so that is a comfort.

Two of the Lisheen Crannagh men came to ask about tillage and I referred them to the Board and they were bewildered, could only propose "a few of us to go to Galway", but I typed a letter for them to send on.

Lisheen Crannagh
Gort
Co. Galway

Dear Sir,

We, tenants on the above lands are informed by Lady Gregory they are being purchased by the Congested District Board.

We are anxious to set to work at our tillage without delay, as we have lost a good deal of time, and if we cannot begin tillage this week there will not be much use in doing it at all.

We are advised by Lady Gregory to write to you on this matter as she cannot interfere with the Board. She believes that you might find it possible to send one of your representatives here to look at the land, and to say if there is any objection to our tilling the portions as have been used by us during these last years.

We are yours respectfully

Martin Burke has just been here now on the way to post the letter in Gort, and asks if I can say a word for him to get a little more land. He says 7 of them want land—and Mackie said he could cut it into 6 but not into 7. I said "He might not, but the Board that has half Ireland divided would cut it into 7 divisions or 17—as easy as you'd cut potatoes".

Anxious waiting for news from Rutland Square; have written

to Bodkin *re* pictures

Coole
Gort
27 April

Dear Mr. Bodkin,

I was not able to see you in a very hurried day in Dublin, but I much wanted to have a talk about our mutual pictures.

I was while in London rather encouraged by finding we have a good deal of support in the Cabinet against Lord Curzon, though it has not been enough so far to carry the Bill through. I also got (privately) letters from three of the Trustees promising not to oppose such a Bill, and I hope to have more, and so undermine Lord C. But then came Easter and Mr. Macpherson's departure, (which is a loss to us for I think he was sincerely helping us.) And then land business here forced me to come over at a day's notice, and I have been kept here and shall be for a while.

I wrote to Macpherson, asking whether he thought a deputation to the new Chief Secretary would be useful. He says in reply:- "A deputation to my successor would not in my opinion be of service to you, but I will myself bring the matter to his notice, and that combined with your zeal and energy will I feel sure give you the best promise of success".

I feel pretty sure, however, that we ought to make some demonstration in Dublin, and that this is a good time when we are being told we are to have liberal offers. These "liberal offers" are vague, and we might as well mention some definite thing we want.

I would like you to consult with Miss Purser about this, because you as N.G.Trustees and the alternative legatees, if the Corporation doesn't give the gallery within measurable time, are interested from both sides. What I thought of was, in the first place—but you and she are much better judges—a deputation from the "Learned and Educational Societies of Dublin". They would only have to repeat what they said in their petition (I enclose a copy) and to express regretful surprise that their request has met with so little consideration.

I feel certain that if we keep battering on we shall get the pictures though perhaps on "unlimited loan" (but this though I would accept I don't think we ought to mention, or they will water it down to a part of the collection which we ought on no account to accept). I don't think it at all a time for newspaper controversy (and Mr. Birrell was very emphatic about this) but I do think a new Chief Secretary, and a new Lord Lieutenant, should be confronted with the vitality of the matter.

We might have a deputation of artists to approach a new L.L. and then get another London deputation to the Leader of the House (Bonar Law I know privately is on our side.)

I should at any time come to Dublin if necessary, but I don't think there is anything special I could do just now. Please let me know what you and Miss Purser think of these suggestions.

A.G.

28TH. No telegram yesterday—no letter today—it makes me anxious.

The Independent says Frank[22] has been fired at—or rather "near" and his workmen forbidden to serve him. Tim says "some of the boys are asking when Mrs. Gregory is coming home, as they want to get the grazing". Marian, paying bills in Gort, comes back to say a man at Kinvara has been shot dead, in his house over a matter of dividing of land. On the other hand, Coen's walls that had been knocked down (as a shopkeeper holding land) in the fields close to us—have been built up again by 200 Sinn Feiners, his son being one.

Then Christy Griffin came, to measure childrens' bathroom for paper, and he gave me an account of the shooting of his pony. He had been sent a threatening letter desiring him to cease working for Mr. Bagot "this is final". He took it to the priest Father Fitzgerald, who pooh-poohed it. He and his brother and a man who helped them were driving to Ballyturin, had just passed the little bridge on the avenue, when "8 or 9 men, masked with all sorts of clothes, rushed out from the laurels, with a sort of a war-whoop, like ye'd hear of men in the war going over the trenches—and shouted to us to stop and to turn back and to put up our hands. I got down and went among them and I felt great courage, I told them we were working men and had nothing to do with land and that we had been at this job since January and they wouldn't ask us to lose our money. But all they would call out was "turn back" and they shoved the muzzle of their guns against us—here in my neck there was a black bruise. We turned back then and walked to the gate, but they were holding the pony. My brother felt weak and went into the gate house, and I and our man walked a bit of the road, and then I said I would go back to my brother, but he said he could not do that—he would go on down the road. When I got back to the gate we saw the pony rushing down with the trap, and giving a sort of a frightened scream—and just when he came to us he fell dead and we saw he was covered with blood. We had heard shots and they had fired shots after us when we were going away, but not till we were a good way off, and we had pellets put into us and we heard shots after that. But if I had known they were going to shoot the pony I would never have gone away, I was that fond of him and I would have sooner they had shot myself."

29 APRIL. No news from C.D.B., and I am anxious.

30TH. Last evening Mr. Edmunds came in, had walked from Gort and I gave him tea. He has heard nothing from Sir H.D., but seems sure it will be all right for us, that cheered me up. Girvan motored here from Galway for him, and had tea, and Mr. E. and I walked to middle avenue gate. T. Diveney says that Patsy Hayes, passing, "turned his neck till you'd think it would fall off" looking at us coming and will probably give out that we have sold to C.D.B.

No news this morning, but I am more serene. But I have just seen in *Connacht Tribune* that Frank Persse has been forced to leave his house—I suppose because of the proposed sale of Roxboro' lands to ex-soldiers—I am thankful he was not shot at.

2 MAY. A note from C.D.B., yesterday morning "owing to the state of the country the Board will not at present buy any lands." And so that immediate purchase is off—a sad blow and disappointment.

A letter from Keller slightly softened it. He had spoken with Sir Henry, who had done his best, and suggests letting to a couple of solvent men. I have hope that this may be managed quietly. After church today, Mr. Bagot said things are so bad with him that he is going to Galway tomorrow to put his case before the Sinn Fein Court. I said "excellent", I hope it may turn out well.

I planted lupins and hollyhocks on Friday and Tim and I watered them in the evening. But rain came in the night and there is a wet day—with hail stones.

22, Dominic Street
3 May 1920

My dear Augusta,

Forgot early post yesterday so was too late to write. A Hovis loaf by post to you, could not get one during war and did not know they were again to be had.

Mr. Barnett demanded 2/- for the hours after the first for which he gets 2/-. I refused said I could not afford it and that he was well paid every day 3/- which comes to £1.1.0 a week. I only get Mat (the 3/-) about once a fortnight and then! he made a face of disgust and about a minute after he bumped violently against a telegraph post. A lady in street came up "who are you?" I asked. "I'm Rose" you know we were raided the second time and have been for a week at Railway Hotel, but Frank paid his bill this morning and said we must look for lodgings Hotel is too dear. A party of men raided them broke pictures and did mischief gave them 3 days to clear out—said Frank was a Government spy—afterwards Sinn Feiners arrived and asked: "Did the men who raided you call themselves Sinn Feiners?" "Yes", "Well", said the S.F.'s "they are not they don't belong to us or any organised body". They could not get a car so Rose had to put on an old skirt, a shawl over her head and walk 14 miles into Galway. She then sent a motor and police for Frank—all their furniture in the house and her clothes she is afraid to go back for them. She was grandly dressed today must have got a new trousseau. She will come to tea tomorrow with little Geofrey and Kitty White who are with them.

Yours

A.W.

Roxborough
Loughrea
5 May

Dear A,

My house was attacked by an armed gang last Friday week who in the name of the Republic ordered me to quit as I was considered to be a Government spy. They fired thro' doors and windows and inside the house and terrified the children etc., I had no means of defence as my arms were in the barracks so thought it best to clear all my belongings out to avoid a repetition.

The only explanation I can imagine as to the origin of the affair is that, when the house was raided for arms last February, they came across some envelopes left by Dudley headed "On His Majesty's Service", and were handing these about and whispering to each other; having no land there is no other explanation.

The Sinn Feiners in Galway are very angry at the name of the Republic being used on the occasion and are ———— the better. We are in ———— with Roxboro' and Persse Park tenants here and had arranged everything with the latter when they repudiated the agreement, I suppose under some outside pressure so it is very hard to get anything through.

Your affecte. bro

FRANK PERSSE

WEDNESDAY, 5 MAY. No word from Margaret or about the grazing. It takes patience.

Mrs. Bagot came to tea. The man who milked their cows has now been ordered off so they must milk as well as chop wood. The demand is for all the land except 50 acres and a bit of bog, and would cut them off from the water. Bagot won't have police protection—But the "flying boys" from Oranmore circle over them and drop messages and have arranged a code and sometimes motor to tea and help them to chop wood.

7TH. Rain yesterday—planted onions. Putnam writes, rather cross at keeping back *Visions and Beliefs* so it is to appear. Nothing yet from Margaret or from the tenants. Working at Hugh's Memoir.

8TH. With second post came a letter from Margaret, telling me to do what I thought best about letting the land, so I feel free now to make some effort. Also there came a telegram from Edmunds saying, he was "attending Lisheen Crannagh at 4 o'c. to take up possession." He didn't say to which side he would come, so John rowed me across and we watched both sides—John went landwards, telling me to "keep an odd eye on the horse pump". After over an hour Edmunds appeared and I sent boat for him, and we walked over the farms—and each tenant gave me a piece of sod from his field, and I gave it to Edmunds so possession passed to the Board. It was a loss of late years it had fed stock for a while but though shooting the scrub had been a great amusement to Robert and all those holiday boys in the old days it was a romantic addition to Coole but times change and we must lighten the ship.

I consulted Edmunds about negotiations, letting of grass with Regan and his group and he entirely approved. He believes the Land Bill will be in before a year is over; so I have sent for Regan.

Coole,
10 May

Dearest Margaret,

First about Malachi Quinn. He came yesterday evening. He will not go a penny beyond £1,200 (cash). He wants to know at once because it ought to be ploughed if he takes it.

As things go I suppose you ought to accept. It will certainly be a relief to one's mind not having it.

He is very sad about the stolen mantel-pieces. He is not

taking on the callows till we know if any grazing agreement can be come to (none at present). He has stipulated for a reduction anyhow, because they have been and still are flooded, it has been such a wet year.

Please write to him direct about B-mantane, and let me know also.

I had sent word to Regan on Saturday that I would like to see him about the grazing. He is "spreading dung" and says he was only one of a committee, but would come on Sunday; he was seen later consulting Hogan his solicitor in Gort.

Yesterday afternoon a dozen or more of them arrived, the old friends, Hayes and Mulkere, and Regan's colleagues Hanlon and Fahey, and some young Nolans (including the Corker one!). I brought them into the breakfast room and said I had heard from Tim that some enquiries were being made about the grazing and when you were coming home, and that you had written that I might see to it. Regan immediately shouted "Why wouldn't she give us the grazing when we asked for it from Scott Kerr. She refused then and we won't take it now." I said that of course we would not give it during purchase negotiations, and he began shouting again, but I said it was no use going back to that, I wanted to tell them how things stood now. I then read them Doran's letter saying the Board would buy as soon as the promised Bill comes in; and also his message through Keller that we had better let the grazing for eleven months to one or two solvent men who could sublet to others. He was evidently much taken aback, but he was like a crocodile unable to turn and went on calling out, "Why didn't we get it when we asked it? Why was our purchase offer refused? We made a very fair offer, that should have been taken."

I said I would go away for a little and let them talk it over. When I came back they had come outside and Regan, still sole spokesman, repeated "We will not take the grazing. You had a right to take our offer for purchase, it was a very fair offer."

I said Mrs. Gregory had her son's interests and I my grandson's to consider; that he, Regan, would try to do the best for his children, and we must do the best for ours, and that not one of our advisers, lay or legal had advised us to accept that offer. At this he said nothing, and there was "slight applause" from some of the others—none of them had spoken at all, and they left.

I took the full responsibility of having gone to the Board so if there is any resentment against that it will fall on me. I was quite amiable and gracious all through, but I wish you could have looked in, for you would fly to the arms of Doran and the Board with joy rather than see Regan dividing it. I feel pretty sure that there will be a split, for confronted with the Board he is no better than the rest, and they will probably break free from him and make us a grazing offer. If not, we shall have to leave it for a winterage in the hope of improvement.

When I went out to leave them alone, I walked down by the barn and saw faces peeping out and then the door closed so I opened it, and there were three young men, young Regan, pleasant looking, and another I forget who, and a very handsome and attractive young fellow Patsy Hayes!! I had a talk with him about cattle driving and said Sinn Fein Headquarters was against it, and he said he believed so, but that without it they would not be getting the land (and that of course is true enough). I spoke to him about Ford, and said they had no excuse for driving his cattle. He said, Yes, he was the only one who hadn't obeyed the orders of the Committee to take their cattle off. I said, the land outside the white gates was never put up for purchase, and that we meant to keep it, probably not for letting (John says we must keep those fields for our own stock now Lisheen Crannagh is gone) so that no one would benefit by his being driven out. He said "He had to be punished". I said he had been punished enough by two drivings. He said "Well, I don't think so". However, I asked him to try and stop it, he made no promise, but was quite frank and civil. There was a rabble of youngsters and boys on bicycles at the corner of Shanwalla, and John tells me that they finished today and let off their high spirits by chasing off Florimond's filly, which had again found its way back from Duras!

I am going to Galway in the morning to see Anderson, for I can't afford time for toothache! and I want to be all right before the chicks come. Tell Anne to bring a proper muzzle for Pip, because with little chickens out he must have one until we can be sure of his good behaviour. He is said to have stopped killing them but they are better watched at Mike John's than here.

Malachi says that the military at Roxboro' have been sent away, that the people told Arthur he might send them, that they "didn't mean to use guns", and would give him a fair price for the land, and that he asked £36, has now lowered it to £20 and they have offered £15. Bagot's case is to come before the Sinn Fein Court in Galway tomorrow, but he can't be represented by a solicitor, as it is against their oath to plead before an illegal Court; this apparently is not in the oath of a Magistrate! Mrs. Bagot was much excited after church at hearing from the officer there that the 10th Hussars are going to Gort, this is the officer Edmunds was so taken with at Ennis. Molly had met Katey, Katty and Dudley at a dance given by the flying men in Galway. Dudley asked Molly to introduce him to some partners, and she introduced Miss Anderson who was sitting close by, and Katey said quite loud, "Take care who you introduce to Dudley, you mustn't introduce everyone!" Molly was furious! She said Katty was badly dressed and didn't look well, but Katy looked extremely well in a purple dress, a fur coat and gold crown.

10 May, 1920

Dear Sir John Lavery,

I have been watching eagerly for your return, I trust in very good health and strength. The African sunshine must have been a very pleasant change from London.

I must ask you to forgive me for so soon troubling your peace. You have been so good and helpful in the past it makes me presumptuous, indeed I am inclined to think that in this matter of the Lane pictures you have been more helpful than anyone.

You will remember that you wrote me last November of your having seen Lord D'Abernon and pleaded with him, and that "the most he would promise was that the Dublin Gallery could have the pictures on loan whenever it liked and for as long".

I, like you, felt that this was a proposal that should not be lightly set aside, I took it to the Irish Unionists in the House of Commons, who have the proposed Bill to legalise the codicil made by Hugh Lane in hand, for their consideration. I was called back to Ireland just then, and you had gone abroad, and the House of Commons party thought it advisable to go on with the Bill.

Mr. Macpherson, who was I think very sincere in working for it and believed in the justice of our case, told me in March, just before he went out of office, that it was still before the Cabinet, and had a good deal of support, Bonar Law and Balfour amongst others being for it.

But Lord Curzon is the stumbling block. And anyhow with the present pressure of business I am afraid it will be a long time before it could, even under more favourable circumstances, be got through.

Mrs. Norman Grosvenor kindly wrote to three of the Trustees, Mr. Heseltine, Lord Plymouth, and Lord Brownlow, asking them not to oppose the Bill, and each answered in a friendly way, saying in effect that although the responsibility lay with the Government they were inclined to meet our wishes. I think by this that those I may call our enemies Lord Curzon, Mr. Witt (Lord D'Abernon was one, but you seem to have brought him round to the loan) have not very secure support and might even welcome an agreement.

Meanwhile, we keep hammering on, Mr. Macpherson promises to coach the new Chief Secretary on the matter. Sir E. Carson makes promises. Dublin is already arranging a deputation to the Chief Secretary, and if a new Lord Lieutenant comes he will be greeted with one. We are keeping the Trustees aware that we are not allowing the case to flicker out. But I, as Hugh Lane's Trustee in the matter, feel that we ought to accept a loan such as Lord D'Abernon proposed. He was not in London when I was there in March, and threatened land trouble keeps me here just now. But in any case your mediation would be most acceptable and effective. We cannot formally approach the Trustees, we should have another formal refusal. But if you could complete your former kindness by seeing Lord D'Abernon again, and finding if the offer is one his friends would sanction, and is for *all* the pictures (there are rumours they will try to keep the Renoir and some others back, and to this we could not assent), I should at once advise my fellow-workers to close with the offer. You would be doing a great service to Ireland in doing this.

A.G.

12 MAY. My letter to Margaret tells of this. Working hard at the Memoir and it seems really near completion. I have put my pride in my pocket and written to G. Moore.

Coole Park,
Gort
Co. Galway
12 May, 1920

Dear Mr. Moore,

You wrote, as you know, some things that gave Hugh Lane annoyance I am sure you were sorry for this later. And I know from what he said and wrote to me that his anger had already died away.

I don't know if you would like to make amends for this by writing something in a more friendly manner now, for the Memoirs of him, the writing of which I have been obliged to take over. It would of course be of value to the book, but I did not think of asking it until lately [when] some of those who cared for him, Mr. John, Gerald Kelly spoke of his pleasure in your company when you came to Lindsey House. I thought then of asking you to come and see me, but I had to hurry back here to attend to our land business.

A.G.

17TH. To Dublin. Letter from Margaret. . . . "if there are no grazing rents there will be no money for rates or wages. . . ." I met Frank at the Broadstone and he came for a talk at the Gresham. He said he had written to Margaret that she should not sell Coole—partly on account of me and because Richard would resent it—"a father might do it but not a mother". A great relief to find he has my opinion. I had never spoken or written to him.

18TH. Rehearsing *Damer's Gold*[23] Kerrigan putting great life into it. I went to Sandycove and Harris going away, stayed the rest of the week there so quiet by the beautiful sea.

WEDNESDAY EVENING. *Hyacinth*,[24] *Shadow*,[25] *Minute's Wait*.[26] A good audience, and laughing as much at Hyacinth as if it was all new. Very cheering—but upset by another letter. Frank said "I must consider *you* (which of course is the *only* point there is for keeping it)". And she talks again of buying Celbridge. Lady Gough says it had in the Decies time such an atmosphere of culture!! Poor Richard, I seem to melt to nothing when I think of his birthright being sold in his infancy.

19TH. Rehearsal, and to National Gallery to see Stephens and to Director's room and to tea with Bodkin about deputation to Chief Secretary, and to Miss Purser about photograph for Hugh's book. Very tired.

20TH. My darling Robert's birthday and I wrote a nice letter to Margaret, and I pray constantly that she and I may both live "in the Light that consists in willing the same thing with God"! Five of us only—and we might make such a harmony.

SATURDAY 22ND. I went to the Castle, got in with difficulty through chained gates and police, and saw Mr. McMahon. He is against a deputation, but tells me to write him a letter he can show to Hamar Greenwood who is "by far the ablest Chief Secretary they ever had in Parliament—and also very vain and would like to be appealed to".

To Galway—arrived 6 o'c., and went round to theatres trying

for one for Race week, the players are so set on it, but they have been let for months and could only get Town Hall for the week before races. Very tired.

23RD SUNDAY. To church and walked a long way with A's chair and then took a car and drove home.

I didn't hear very much in Dublin. Stephens thinks Sinn Fein should certainly accept Dominion Home Rule. He says they are afraid to arrest Griffith as he says if anything happens to him there will be heavy killings. The police, he says, they shoot as spies. Erskine Childers says England is holding on for the 18 millions a year—they know they couldn't get it if they let Ireland go. He was laughing over the official list of outrages—unfair and malicious many of them. Kerrigan was there, had been at De Valera's great Madison Square[27] meeting to which he came with an escort of Staff officers of the American Army.

Poor Alderman Tom Kelly's mind is still affected—he has delusions, fancies there are people coming to take him, has to be kept in absolute quiet.

I went to see Sir H. Doran—he isn't sure the Land Bill will be put through "the Government may trick us again", but I met Edmunds in Galway yesterday and he had just heard from Wrench that it is being prepared, and thinks it will come through, even if the H.R.Bill is abandoned.

I have written to McMahon—And to Wilfrid Blunt to write to Lord Ribblesdale. Stephens' letter this morning about Lady Greenwood makes me hopeful, I am writing to her. Oh, when will the last letter on this matter be written!

Newbuildings Place
Southwater, Sussex
26 May, 1920

Dear Lady Gregory,

Here is the extract from the early unpublished Diaries which Mr. Blunt thinks is the one you refer to. He is expecting Lord Ribblesdale next week and will give him the pamphlet and your letter. He thinks it will be better than writing about it. We are thinking of you much in all this worry and he will write when he has seen Lord Ribblesdale.

Your affecte
DOROTHY CARLETON

Chief Secretary's Office
Dublin Castle
26 May, 1920

Dear Lady Gregory,

I am desired by Mr. McMahon to acknowledge the receipt of your letter of the 24th instant regarding Sir Hugh Lane's pictures. He hopes to write you further in the course of a day or so.

Faithfully yours
W. DOOLIN

Private 24 May, 1920.

Dear Mr. McMahon,

I do not like troubling you when you have so much important work to do—but this matter is also of importance in more ways than one.

I daresay you hear echoes now and then of the disappointment, discontent, and I may say bitterness felt at the continued witholding of Hugh Lane's pictures from Dublin by the Trustees of the London National Gallery. Appeals have been made to them by representatives of the Learned and Educational Societies of Dublin, including the Provost of Trinity, the President of the Hibernian Academy, the Chief Commissioner of National Education, The Principal of the Alexandra College, and the Chancellor of the National University of Ireland. Another appeal was signed by artists who are represented in the Municipal Gallery, including Sir William Orpen, Gerald Kelly, Max Beerbohm, Briton Riviere, W. Rothenstein, W. Nicholson, Wilson Steer, Mark Fisher, George Clauson and Augustus John. The Prime Minister was appealed to by Irish writers including Douglas Hyde, Katherine Tynan, Stephen Gwynn, T. P. O'Connor, Standish O'Grady, George Russell (AE), W. B. Yeats, James Stephens and Bernard Shaw. Sir John Lavery not only signed a petition but wrote to the papers supporting our case. Sinn Fein, though not as a body, making an appeal was very strongly represented at the great Mansion House meeting of 29 January 1918, presided over by Lord Mayor O'Neill, where a resolution calling upon the Government to "take steps to ensure the restoration to Dublin of these pictures which Sir Hugh Lane destined for the Dublin Municipal Gallery" was passed, having been spoken to by the Lord Mayor, Sir Robert Woods (M.P.) Canon Hannay and "On behalf of Sinn Fein" by Mr. Shawn T. O'Kelly.

Five years have now passed since the death of Hugh Lane, my nephew and whose trustee I am in this matter, and England still keeps the pictures. The Trustees keep to their argument (which we have never contested) that they have a legal claim. We have a moral claim—

I give details in the pamphlet I enclose. We ask Government for a Bill to legalise the codicil, which would be legal in Scotland even as it is, without witnesses to a signature that has never been disputed.

Mr. Duke when Chief Secretary received our deputation with sympathy and promised help; but it was War time and he was unable to do anything. Mr. Shortt also expressed sympathy. Mr. Macpherson has been our best helper so far, for after he had received a deputation from the Irish Unionist Party representing among others Sir Edward Carson and Sir Robert Woods, he drew up a Bill and laid it before the Cabinet. Having gone into our case and the comments on it of the National Gallery Trustees, who tried to weaken it, he said to me, "I believe in my heart and conscience that Sir Hugh Lane intended this codicil to be carried out at the time he wrote it and at the time of his death, and I think it would be a scandalous thing to lay it aside because of a legal technicality". I saw him just before he went out of Office, and he told me (privately) that the Bill has been three times before the Cabinet; that half the Cabinet including Mr. Balfour and Mr. Bonar Law are for us; but that each time it has been turned down by the violence of Lord Curzon.

Lord Curzon is one of the ten trustees of the National Gallery. Of the other nine, three have been written to by a personal friend; these three, Lord Brownlow, Lord Plymouth and Mr. Heseltine, have written (I gave their letters to Mr. Macpherson who still holds them) saying that while they have no legal right to give up the pictures they would not oppose the Bill. Of the others, Lord Crawford is against such a Bill, so is Mr. Witt; Lord Lansdowne and Lord Ribblesdale have not yet been personally approached, nor Mr. Benson. Lord D'Abernon, whilst against a Bill, has proposed to Sir John Lavery a compromise by which (though through a clumsy method leading to confusion) we should get the pictures to Dublin. Thus, Lord Curzon, while professing to represent the Trustees in the Cabinet, has by no means a unanimous body behind him.

I have never doubted our ultimate success because I have faith in "The Invisible Witnesses", also I believe that some day a measure will be offered large and liberal enough to make a friendly Ireland, and that if not already settled, this question would then be settled, for all the intellectuals, all the idealists and all who care for the dignity of Ireland lay stress on it. But as to when it will come—one thinks of the old Yankee Song when things are going badly and hope deferred made the heart sick—"*Abraham Lincoln give us a man.*" So when we heard of Sir Hamar Greenwood's appointment, ———— our hopes rose. We feel from all we have heard of his strong personality that he would be able to sweep away difficulties and that we may yet have his portrait in the Municipal Gallery as one of those who has helped Ireland. We believe that he could if he would carry through that delayed Bill. And I want you to advise us as to how best to approach him.

The Learned Societies are talking of a Deputation, so are the Writers and Artists . . . Please tell me what you think advisable? And please forgive me for so long a letter.

Yours sincerely
A. GREGORY

National Gallery of Ireland
Merrion Square
Dublin
22 May 1920

Dear Lady Gregory,

Lady Greenwood (the Chief Secretary's wife) has just been with me, and we were talking of the Lane pictures. She is very sympathetic in the matter. I mentioned that you were arranging a deputation to her husband. I think if you wrote to her you would find her most anxious to assist in obtaining the return of our pictures. She knew—and liked Hugh Lane. All good luck to you.

Yours very truly
JAMES STEPHENS

27TH. Margaret came on Tuesday and yesterday Horace Cole and wife came to lunch and stayed to tea and dinner.

She has gone—and was kind.

29TH. Today an ugly letter from George Moore—it is hard to understand so ungracious a mind.[28]

121, Ebury Street
London, S.W.1.
27 May 1920

Dear Lady Gregory,

In answer to your letter asking me to contribute to a Memoir which you are compiling of Sir Hugh Lane's transactions, I cannot think of anything that I could write about Sir Hugh Lane except what I have already written. I always looked upon Lane as an extraordinarily clever picture dealer, apt at buying, and equally apt at selling works of art; but when that is said, there is really nothing more to say, except perhaps, that if he had lived he would have died a millionaire. I put forward this view in one of the volumes of *Hail and Farewell* and Sir Hugh Lane took advantage of my absence in Palestine to frighten Heinemann with the threat of an injunction if he did not cancel some ten or a dozen lines describing one of Lane's very clever deals. If I had been in London I should certainly have refused to cancel the passage in question, and I think the restoration of this passage in a new edition of *Hail and Farewell* will meet the case as far as I am concerned. If you like to have the passage for your Memoir, you are quite welcome to it. I have not forgotten that you, too, wrote to Heinemann begging him to withdraw or to mutilate a passage in *Hail and Farewell*.

With many thanks for your proposal, which I regret that I cannot accept.

I am sincerely yours
GEORGE MOORE

W.S.B. sends me the bit about the influence of an early home that comforts me, also hopes of Lord Ribblesdale.

J. Diveney says Murty being offered his field would not accept accept it without consulting "those that won it for us, the boys that drove the cattle. Without them Farmer Quinn and Malachi Quinn would be in possession to our lives end". M. J. Laurence, J.D. and John Hehir came and paid them $\frac{1}{2}$ year. John said they had grumbled about our stock having had a month on the land—and that £2 each would satisfy them, so to have all easy, I myself gave them this.

SUNDAY, 30 MAY. John came in after breakfast when I was alone in the house, the maids having gone to Mass and says there has been an outrage—the old steward's house—old Richard Gregory's—burned down in the night. The Hehirs heard the noise and steps passing, but did not dare even to look if their calf that was in the shed was being burned—but it had been let out and was safe. The only object one can imagine was that it was to warn Hehir and M.J. and the others from tilling the land. Tom O'Loughlin had gone straight off when the offer to his father was made to consult Donohue, and he was seen very drunk last evening. I would rather think it was done through drunkenness than malice. Very sad and dread writing to Margaret.

Breakfast time had been cheerful, with letters from McMahon and enclosing one from Lady Greenwood about Hugh's pictures. To church. Afternoon the D.I. and Head Constable came to make enquiries about the burnt house. I said I had thought when I read of the terrible burning of Kilmallock barracks yesterday with 2 policemen in it that it might stir up other branches to do likewise and the D.I. said he believes the publication of outrages is an incentive to crime, just like the cinemas.

Margy Moran then, for linen for her little nephew who was scalded—I got him toys as well and sweets and jam.

Chief Secretary's Lodge
Dublin
28 May, 1920

Dear Lady Gregory,

Many thanks for your letter and the pamphlet. I badly wanted a copy of it in order to be sure of what had already been done in regard to Sir Hugh Lane's pictures. I have always been greatly interested, as he discussed the whole question when we were members of the same house party not so very long before his death.

Let me say at once that I would like to be able to do *something* towards getting the pictures back to Dublin where I have always thought they should be. Perhaps this is one reason why you would not have to convert my husband! Between us we will at any rate make an effort.

Oddly enough you do not have to make my acquaintance, for about fifteen years ago another old school friend and I were staying with Olive Persse and we all went over to Coole from ——— Chase and enjoyed lunch with you. Your son showed us pictures and Mr. W. B. Yeats was staying with you at the time. It was before I was married and so you would naturally not think of me as the same person even if you remembered the visit at all.

I hope next time you are in Dublin you will come here to lunch or tea and we can discuss a plan of further campaign.

Yours sincerely
MARGO GREENWOOD

P.S. Please excuse the results of bad blotting paper

Chief Secretary's Office
Dublin Castle
29 May, 1920

Private

Dear Lady Gregory,

Further to my letter of the 26th instant Mr. McMahon desires me to inform you that the Chief Secretary is going to interest himself in Sir Hugh Lane Pictures. Better still, Lady Greenwood has promised to take the matter up personally with the big London people on her next visit across the water.

This is of course for your own information only.

Faithfully yours
W. DOOLIN

Lady Gregory
Coole Park
Gort, Co. Galway

31ST. Mike John and J.D. say Gort is furious about the burning, that if it is found out who did it, they will get punishment and that Coen "turned black-blue" when he heard of it.

2 JUNE, WEDNESDAY. On Tuesday evening Martin Cahill came to canvass for District Council, supported by his friend Shaughnessy. They belong they say to Gort Sinn Fein, and condemn Kiltartan Sinn Fein for the burning of the house. I did not think I had a vote, but they declared I had, so yesterday thinking I ought to take my share of responsibility and Cahill having a good name, I walked to the Schoolhouse and voted for him, being kindly welcomed by an old Cahill and by Bartley Killean reminding me how I had succoured the mother of one and the father of the other in hospital and in times of trouble. And they said the burning of the house was a disgrace. Then I went in to the school house, there was young Hayes at the door, I said, "Oh, *you* here?" "I'm keeping order" he said, with rather an injured air. I said "I wish you always did that" and he grinned, looking away. Coming out I said, "Did you think it was *right*?" But then a woman came to vote and I came away. Hehir's wife near to death last night again—her temperature up to 102—the doctor lays it upon that midnight terror.

I heard of Mr. Jayne's death;[29] a warmth gone from the world.

3 JUNE. Tim says he had meant to vote for Martin Cahill "a respectable boy". But "when I went home my wife has more sense than what I have, and she said John came to her and that he said it was best for me vote for Cahill *and* for Donohue—it was as good to have one good and one bad." And he did so! And

both have got in. Marian says Father Considine at the end of the service laying down some maxims said "And the third thing I have to speak of is injustice—the burning at Coole" and banged his book and said no more.

Working at Hugh's life and have finished my *postscript*—that is finished practically the writing of the book. I am thankful! Now should I lose life or mind, it can go to the printers as it is, and I think good.

4 JUNE. Have written to Sir E. Carson and to T. P. O'Connor. No letters this morning. Mike Lally came to say the Mail car from Galway has been held up.

4 June, 1920

Dear Sir Edward Carson,

The New Chief Secretary has been approached on this side about the Lane pictures and is, I hear, sympathetic—But your help is much needed. Mr. Macpherson told me before he went out of office that the Bill for legalising the codicil was still before the Cabinet but whenever brought up was turned down by Lord Curzon. He speaks as representing the National Gallery Trustees but at least three of them, Lord Brownlow, Lord Plymouth and Mr. Heseltine have written letters (to Lady N. Grosvenor) I gave them to Mr. Macpherson, saying they are ready to accept the Government decision. I am not sure what line the others take, but Lord D'Abernon proposed a permanent loan some time ago (to Sir John Lavery). Lord Curzon has not, therefore, a unanimous body behind him. Is it not a moment while we are being offered things we don't want that this, which all parties want, should be given? Appeals to the Trustees or to the Prime Minister have been made by representatives of the Educational Establishments of Dublin, among them the present Provost of Trinity; Judge Madden; Doctor Coffey; Dr. Starkie; Louis Preser; Miss White; Mr. Lyster; Mr. R. C. Orpen, and by writers and artists including Sir W. F. Barrett; Mrs. Hinkson; George Morrow; Dermod O'Brien; Standish O'Grady; Sir William Orpen; George Russell; Bernard Shaw; W. B. Yeats; Rose Barton; Sir John Lavery, Augustus John.

You can do, if you will, what all these have failed in. Please do so for the sake of your old constituency and College, Trinity, and of your early connection with Galway.

Yours sincerely

A.G.

8 JUNE. I felt so free of the Memoir on Monday evening that I got out my old notes *Aristotle's Bellows*[30] and I found them fuller than I remembered, I think I may make a comedy. But today Sir John Lavery with D'Abernon's enclosure turn me back. I have written to them, and to Sir E. Carson, and I must now put something more into the memoirs of Hugh's intention at the last—his last directions to Mrs. Duncan.

Such lovely weather and the children so happy, playing with kittens and gathering and pressing wild flowers and plants, and sowing their little gardens. We have begun lessons but yesterday it was in the garden and the kittens were co-opted as pupils, and it turned to a picnic with lemonade and barmbrack and bananas. But today the lock of apple house (key lost by Tim) has been taken off and we can get at the apples.

9TH. Have written to Macpherson, endless these letters seem. Yesterday old Niland came and the children picked gooseberries for bottling earning 1/- each, 2d a bottle! I was stirred up by that wretched D'Abernon's bad note and worked over 3 chapters in the Memoir, leaving out (I think) "The Fight for the Pictures" and making simple statement of our case as strong as possible. Old Niland said about the burning of the house "it was done by blackguards that begrudged the 6 acres of land you were giving to the labourers". This covetousness will do more than anything to ruin Sinn Fein.

13 JUNE. SUNDAY. A quiet week, getting drawing and dining rooms into order again gives us a more settled look. The chicks good and happy, riding round the garden and finding the first strawberries.

Yesterday W. Blunt's letter rather cheered me—though it makes me realise the difficulties still before us. I have written to him—a letter I want him to send to Lord O.B.

I have still been working at the Memoirs trying to take resentment out of "The Fight for the Pictures"—I think I shall leave out that chapter keeping but a few sentences.

J.D. says 19 cattle in Nathy—may have been driven there or may have come through gaps in the wall. He wants Thomas to be made head and I have written to Margaret but no answer.

Old Niland says "All Gort is with ye—if it wasn't for you letting them have sticks from the woods a third part of Gort would be dead."

Newbuildings Place
Southwater,
Sussex
11 June, 1920

My dear Lady Gregory.

Lord Ribblesdale has just been here and I found him quite prepared to help when the time comes; He has already read the pamphlet and understands how much it is a matter of honour more than law—I think you may count on him to do what he can though he is not sure it is possible. Curzon is as you say very opposed and the legal people are of course all against you—

In haste

Yours affecte
W.S.B.

Coole Park
Gort
Co. Galway
12 June, 1920

My dear Mr. Blunt,

A great many thanks for having spoken to Lord Ribblesdale about the picture question. It has given me fresh courage hearing he is so sympathetic, and especially that as you say he understands "how much it is a matter of honour more than law". If all the trustees understood this is the real point I am confident they would urge the adoption of the legalising Bill now before the Cabinet, but I fancy the one solicitor among them, Mr. Witt, keeps their eyes on the legal claim (which we have never contested). You have done Ireland a service in thus helping us, for there is a very sore feeling of disappointment here at the little regard shown to the appeals of our "Intellectuals", from the Provost of Trinity and the Vice-Chancellor of the National University to Orpen and Lavery among artists, and among free lances, Douglas Hyde, Yeats, George Russell and Bernard Shaw.

I've written of this disappointment in Hugh's Memoir where I say of the Trustees "Yet they had been set a noble example by those in charge of the Dublin National Gallery, the residuary legatees of Hugh Lane's Will, for that promise of ten thousand pounds to the Red Cross Fund for a picture by Mr. Sargent might well have been contested in law and advice was not wanting that this should be done. But those legatees, knowing Hugh personally as they did, were certain that it was his wish his splendid promise should be fulfilled, and so carried out that wish to their own loss, except in honour."

We are at a moment when all help will tell, for the new Chief Secretary, Sir H. Greenwood, is now taking up the case. Mr. Macpherson had already brought it before the Cabinet and pressed it. He, a lawyer, having gone through our appeal and the statement or defence of the Trustees very carefully, said to me "I am absolutely convinced in my mind and conscience that Lane intended this codicil to be carried out at the time he wrote it and at the time of his death, and I think it would be a disgrace if it were upset and advantage taken of it on a mere technical point". Some at least of the Trustees are sympathetic. Lord Brownlow, writing to Mrs Norman Grosvenor says "The National Gallery has no power to relinquish property which is legally theirs, but of course *Parliament* can do so, and I can assure you that any Bill introduced for that purpose will not meet any opposition from me". Mr. Heseltine writes to me "I am one of the Trustees who view sympathetically the claims of the City of Dublin, but only the Treasury can authorise either the National Gallery or the Tate Gallery to carry out any terms not in accordance with their primary capacity". Lord Plymouth writes to her [Mrs. N. Grosvenor] "the Government must take full responsibility and I should acquiesce at once in that decision".

Yet each time the Bill is brought before the Cabinet I understand it is opposed even with violence by Lord Curzon as representing the Trustees. I doubt that he even represents a majority, for Lord D'Abernon had proposed a compromise, though an unacceptable one.

I wonder if you could stretch your goodwill so far as to ask Lord Osborne Beauclerc (I don't know him well enough) to put the matter before Lord Lansdowne? I don't know what his views are, but he is as it were the only representative of Ireland on the Board and I think would not refuse his aid in this case, so important to all of us over here.

BOOK NINE

Gort
21 June, 1920

Lady Gregory,
Madam,
I have pleasure in enclosing you the jottings you have asked for in young Cunningham's case.

Yours most respectfully
P. DUFFY

Cromwell House,
Millbank, S.W.1

Private 16 June, 1920

Dear Lady Gregory,
I duly received your letter of the 9th June about the Lane pictures. I have not forgotten the matter and am doing what I can to help. You will realise, however, that it not so easy now for me to interfere in a question of this sort.

Yours sincerely
IAN MACPHERSON

Lady Augusta Gregory
Coole Park
Gort
Co. Galway 17 June, 1920

Dear Mr. MacMahon,
I don't know if Sir H. Greenwood has yet been able to take up the matter of the Lane pictures. But I should like him to know that yet another of the National Gallery Trustees, Lord Ribblesdale, is (I quote from a letter from Mr. Wildrid Blunt whose guest he has been) "quite prepared to help when the time comes. He has already read the pamphlet, and understands how much it is a matter of honour more than law. I think you may count on him to do what he can."

Therefore, as I have already pointed out, Lord Curzon who blocks the Bill in the Cabinet and is looked on as representing the Trustees does not really do so.

A. GREGORY

Chief Secretary's Office
Dublin Castle
18 June, 1920

Dear Lady Gregory,

Mr. MacMahon desires me to acknowledge the receipt of your letter of the 17th inst., and to state that he notes that Lord Ribblesdale is quite prepared to help in the business of the Lane pictures.

You will be glad to know that Lady Greenwood is actively taking up the question and Mr. MacMahon would be very much obliged if you would kindly send her to the Chief Secretary's Lodge, Phoenix Park, half a dozen copies of the pamphlet which you already so kindly sent to him.

Yours very truly
W. DOOLIN

Lady Gregory,
Coole Park
Gort,
Co. Galway

15 JUNE 1920 Heavy showers today, good for the garden—Mr. Edmunds came and planned his wall for Lisheen Crannagh—I hope it can be built without mortar—it will look like a theatre scene at the Abbey. Four half windows have been stolen from Ballinamantan, I told John to speak to Coen, head of the Gort Sinn Fein Club, about these thefts and he did so and Coen said they would try to get at it at their next meeting—and that all the Gort people are indignant at anything done against us.

17 JUNE. Yesterday thunder and some rain. I heard from Yeats that he has gone to London, and wrote him a long letter about the pictures, telling how the matter stands in case he is asked—for he has lost touch with it. Now I have written to Mr. MacMahon. Rita Edmunds and the chicks very happy.

18 JUNE. A fine day and Rita helped with chicks' lessons—and except for a bit of temper from Marian no annoyance, and I begin to make out a scenario for *Aristotle's Bellows*, but not sure if I have enough plot, tried to invent a sort of Cinderella love interest but *couldn't*—But I doubt if the Dublin audience cares for one.

A Cunyngham girl came about chickens and I asked about her brother in gaol and promised to try to get him out for harvest. I had already consulted Mr. Edmunds and he thought I must wait for an amnesty, but I think (and the Head Constable thinks) that harvest might serve.

19TH. MacMahon's note more cheering than Macpherson's. Scott Kerr seemed quite impressed by the Sinn Fein Committee he is dealing with—very young men with very good heads.

22 JUNE. The chicks went to Galway today for a few days to see Godmother and dentist—I was busied with their departure and now have written about young Cunyngham, without much hope, yet one must try.

23RD. Lady Greenwood's letter pleasant, like the opening of a door.

Chief Secretary's Lodge
Dublin

Dear Lady Gregory, 22 June, 1920

Many thanks for the extra pamphlets. I wanted them in order that those people whose influence I am bringing to bear should be fully acquainted with the facts. When I was in London for a week, I went and had breakfast with my husband at No. 10. And I had a talk with the Prime Minister about the pictures. I am not dissatisfied with this preliminary.

If you are in Dublin later on perhaps we could talk more fully on the subject than is possible in a letter.

Yours sincerely
MARGO GREENWOOD

Tempers about downstairs, I asked Mary what she would do when she and Marion met in Heaven. The house very silent without the chicks.

25TH. Yesterday and today making scarecrows, putting down wire, fighting pigeons, squirrels, jackdaws, and M.J. says "the boldest of them all" the blackbirds—are attacking strawberries, gooseberries, currants.

2 spruce trees have been cut down near the natural bridge and carried off—by the usual group. Limerick trains stopped by the strike against carrying munitions. Working a little at *Aristotle's Bellows*, but before that had to make out Income Tax papers, depressing. Evening in garden making bird and squirrel scares.

27 JUNE. A peaceful Sunday—the post brought me Hugh's letters, obtained at last by Witt from Executor Wood. I have read them, and find very little to use—but a sentence about Lord Curzon asking for the pictures and Hugh refusing to give them, this I think will keep him from boasting of having had to do with the matter. Went to church and took strawberries and roses and passion flowers to little girl Johnson and a bottle of port A. had given to me to Peter Glynn, who has been ill.

Read *The Times* and *The Nation* and feel hopeful because *The Nation* thinks the proposal for Sinn Fein representatives to meet Lloyd George may come to something.

A knock at the hall door, and I found 2 little Killeen girls looking for Marian—but she was taking her Sunday siesta. It was raining and I brought them in to wait, and showed them the rooms which they were interested in—especially delighted with Anne's dolls that open and shut their eyes—and they had bread and jam and honey and milk in the breakfast room, and then went away, the rain clearing, one with a box of dates, an unknown luxury—and one with a box of sweets.

Later, after tea, Dr. O'Malley whom I had once met at the Workhouse was walking with a friend and stopped to ask the way to the Lake, and I asked them in and they also were pleasant, and intelligent about books. The friend (from Galway) had read some fairy stories of Yeats's and mine.

Then I picked strawberries and sent them to the chicks. Now I have been reading *Chez Swann*[1], it gives me an idea for the opening of *Aristotle's Bellows*, a family scene. Yesterday or the day before I read a report—a short paragraph in *The Times* of a lecture by Inge. He said we should not speak of "a future life" but of "Eternal life"—this is but a part of it. It has made these two days finer—links in so far-stretching a chain.

28 JUNE. Rain, and not so quiet a day for Swift came to say the new lock of the Kincora gate had been taken off—in preparation as it seems for more timber stealing. Mike John hears it was X. and Y. who took the spruce trees. I am sorry about X. yet it is better all these ill-doings should be but by a few and not several. We can but put barbed wire on the gate and give them trouble at least. No use asking the police to come, for the H.C. said to John "If we watch them, they watch us, coming and going."

I typed bits from Hugh's letters—not much to use, but telling more about his "neurasthenia" at the time of his Will—and about Lord Curzon's "pressing" him to give the pictures to London and his refusing.

No trains except an occasional goods' train—Limerick seems to be cut off and there are rumours of "killings" there—but we only got Saturday's papers today (Monday).

29 JUNE. A holy day (SS. Peter and Paul) showery and cold; I worked at Hugh's Memoir, putting in bits of the letters—and a little at the *Bellows* but I can't get on very far without getting tired and fits of yawning, I suspect I like the children's interuptions because they give me an excuse to break off. I scared birds

or meant to, but the strawberries were attacked for all that—and, I saw a squirrel coming down the roof of the vinery and Mrs. ——— came and stayed to tea. She had got yesterday's paper telling of the "arrest" and carrying off of General Lucas,[2] and the death of poor Lady Dudley.[3]

30 JUNE. Peter Glynn hears the constable at Ardrahan was shot coming from church yesterday (the Holy day!) (but not killed). Also that no police or military were at Peterswell races, but that perfect order was kept and there were a few arrests made by the Volunteers.

Peter Glynn thinks the kidnapping of General Lucas "the best thing ever I heard since I was born"! And it delights me also; but he says "shooting a policeman is a holy crime".

I have done a little more work on *Bellows*—written rough chart for three acts—

Squirrels attacking fruit and coming into both gardens.

House of Commons
30 June 1920

Dear Lady Gregory,

Your note received.

So far as the LANE pictures are concerned, we are in the unfortunate position of having to begin all over again with our new Chief Secretary, and as he has practically not set foot in the House of Commons since he assumed that Office we have had no opportunity whatever of making him acquainted with the position with regard to the Pictures.

The matter however has not been forgotten, and I still hope that either in the shape of a loan or in some other way the Pictures may yet be returned to Ireland.

Yours truly
C. C. CRAIG

2 JULY. Yesterday a little more scenario of *Bellows*, and afterwards going through old jam, have about 40 good pots and some doubtful. Today Mary is ill and I made 4 pots with Marian's help of strawberries I had picked.

3 JULY. Yesterday evening I read in *The Times* an account of Harrow speeches—it brought back those old days when I used to go with William, and look forward to going to see Robert, and once I did so very happily. And when he was in the War I thought he would be cheered when he came down the steps with his Legion of Honour—but now there is but his name in the "Golden Book".

This morning Huntington writes sending a press-cutting of

Visions in an English paper—headed "Superstition still lives". He says the book must have come from N. York and is anxious to publish here. I have given leave (as I have before) because once published in N.Y. it is sure to be sent over in single copies, but I am sorry it should come out just now as it may give a handle to those who attack Ireland—and it may offend Kiltartan—yet it gives dignity to "Superstition".

Diveney came to say the office had been broken into, the door broken down and a ledger taken out of it and this is so. But it may have been some little time ago perhaps when the old steward's house was burned—Mary still ill, and Mrs. Bagot brought strawberries for preserving and I had to do them myself, Marian not being skilful—a tiring hour skimming them but result good.

Then netting wall against squirrels—and Corly the piper came. Says at Ballaghadereen races there were no police—Sinn Fein took things in hand. The public houses were opened from 11 to 12 and closed for the rest of the day. "Only one poor publican allowed to sell porter on the course—no whiskey—and you might die for want of a drink in the evening." Also they have seized and broken up the stills in Mayo.

Tim is glad the Ardrahan policeman was only wounded. He has "ever and always heard that any man that does a murder—takes away a man's life—can never close his eyes again when he sleeps."

SUNDAY 4TH. Church, and a very quiet day. Looking through Plutarch in the afternoon for what I could not find—a story of one of the heroes taken to a cave and affable to his gaolers, but after his release had them put to death. Yet I liked stopping at sentences—old friends. "I myselfe that dwell in a poore little towne, and yet do remayne there willingly lest it should become lesse"—and that splendid passage in Solon about the neutral.

The basket maker my only visitor.

Last evening I looked again at *Visions and Beliefs* and was comforted. It seemed to lift and enable—perhaps through the beauty of the language—what has been ridiculed as superstition—and surely it was made with reverence; this will be felt by those who understand.

5 JULY. I wrote to Lady Arnott asking her to help about Hugh's pictures—and to Mrs. Chapman about a possible route for the French governess I have engaged via Athenry. And C.C. Lawrence wrote asking for photos of me and of Coole for an article he is writing, and I wasted time looking through old ones. And I paid bills and had but a brief hour for *Aristotle*. But I felt

suddenly certain I ought to make a child's play of it, and this gave me an extraordinary feel of freedom, no bounds need be kept. I at once introduced a Dwarf to bring the bellows and bethought me of the first blast turning a good meal to its opposite. This evening fine, and in garden and quite late I found slugs were eating the little chrysanthemums whose lives I had saved when Tim was throwing them out and I came in to Marian who scraped down some soot and I went out again in the rain and saved many lives of plants; and Mike John returning from Gort, says he was speaking to some of the real Sinn Feiners who don't acknowledge the R. group and that they intend trying both to get back the chimney pieces and other things stolen from B-Mantan and to arrange that the grazing should be let. I had been praying very hard for this last night—at least for peace and "the coming of Thy Kingdom—in Coole—in Kiltartan—in Ireland."

9 JULY. Wednesday evening the children came back from Galway, not arriving till half past eight—very well and gay—delighted with strawberries and cream I had ready—and then when Maggie was going, showering flowers on her and Flaherty the chaffeur, and then after 9—insisting on coming out "to see" and try the gooseberries. And at 10.30 when they were in bed another motor appeared with Mademoiselle Poidevin who had got to Limerick, and found there would be no train (strike) so took a motor—£5/10/- for me to pay! She seems pleasant and nice with the children and Anne has had a sewing lesson today besides little French sentences now and again.

I had headache already when she came, and that little fuss made it worse. A bad night and in the morning a letter from Margaret saying she cannot go on paying taxes and rates on Coole and "as you have chosen this course"—will I please tell her what to do! . . . Another bad night and headache.

Two Sinn Feiners of the Ardrahan Club called yesterday about the missing chimney pieces of Ballinamantan—they are trying to find the things—they were Murphy (son of the Mason) and Howley, good young fellows I believe. I asked them if I could make an arrangement through Sinn Fein to let the grazing, and they said I would have to go to an arbitration court. They think the case a good one but that it cannot be helped except through the Court. T. Diveney came to show me letters from the Transport Union to which he belongs. They have insisted that the Kiltartan Sinn Fein Club who prevented him taking Inchy should pay him £1 a week for loss of his employment. So they have given in and allow him to take Inchy,—but say he must put a notice in *The Galway Express* that it's by their permission. If they do, it may help us to get compensation for loss of our grazing.

To the Honble. Lady Gregory
Coole Park, Gort.

Honble. Lady,

Possibly you are acquainted with Professor John McNeill, if not, I expect you would be known to him by repute in the literary world. Please, for Justice sake, write to him immediately and explain all the horrible treatment Mrs. Gregory and you have been subjected to by local cowards, mention the burning, house breaking, thefts & c but no names, ask him to communicate with the Volunteers in Ennis, Athenry and Galway, the few in Gort could help to place the criminals, but are too weak to act. Those in the centres named would be ready to spring into action if they got word of such injustice. I expect you could give an interview to any of those who would investigate the case and you would be no further troubled. Had you taken this course earlier it would mean a difference of hundreds of pounds to Mrs. Gregory and you I am sure.

Do not delay—and mention all facts—how outside property was sold for benefit of local tenants &c.

I am, yours very faithfully

JUSTICE

8.7.20.

John and Hehir and Mike have also approached Sinn Fein—who have advised them to stock their fields and guaranteed that the cattle will not be driven, and that if driven they will be responsible for them. I think all this hopeful and would gladly go to their Court, which is following justice—if Margaret doesn't object.

Not doing much of *The Bellows* but just keeping it alive in my mind.

11TH. Trying to make out if I could arrange for Margaret to sell Coole to C.D.B., and I buy back house and garden and a few acres if they take the woods for foresting. But the woods must be saved or the place would not be itself. But my figures are not very encouraging—with my certain income not much over £500. But if I could save the place and house for Richard for 10 years. (21 APRIL 1928—Yes, I have done this, he has just been home for his first holiday and worked) J. hopeful about being able to stock his farm and is going to buy cattle at Tubber Fair tomorrow. Gort Sinn Fein tells him that there may be driving of his cattle, but if there is, they will be brought back again and he will be at no loss. It makes me hopeful for our grazing.

On the other hand a letter from Wilfred Blunt rather a blow. "Lord O. Beauclerk wrote to Lord Lansdowne about the Lane pictures and the answer is unfavourable—Lord L says 'I am afraid I cannot help in the matter—the whole question has been discussed again and again . . . we should not be particularly anxious to send pictures to Ireland in present circumstances'—In this last phrase you probably get his real chief reason."

Coole Park
Gort
Co. Galway
16 July 1920

Dear Mr. Coen,

I have been thinking of bring the matter of our grazing lands before your Committee. You probably know the facts. We offered a large portion of our grazing lands for sale last January. Negotiations with a small section of our late tenants were opened by Mr. Scott Kerr who acted as our agent in the matter, but the offer made was not one he could recommend us to accept, nor could our solicitors, and the negotiations were closed. We then offered the land to the C.D.B. who gave their promise to buy as soon as the new Land Bill now in preparation comes into operation.

I then offered the grazing for this year to those who had been in the negotiation, but they said they did not now wish for it having made other arrangements for their stock. It had been held by others last year, and I enclose one of the notices served on these last November (I have retained the registered envelope and the name of the receiver). This notice prevented those of last year from taking it again, and the land is lying idle. It hardly seems fair that those who do not themselves require the grass should keep others from taking it.

I should be very grateful for your opinion of this matter.

A.G.

Coole
13 July.

Dearest Margaret,

Chicks are well, eating quantities of fruit and no sign of pains—and getting on well with Mlle. She is only 17, very fat and cheerful, plays football and skipping with them, and yesterday when it was wet, hide and seek. She gives Anne a French lesson and a sewing lesson from 12 to lunch time and of course teaches them little words and asks riddles in French at other times. I like her very well, being so young; she is intelligent, and has energy or she would not have come so far to see other countries and learn English, for she doesn't speak as if they were poor, her father is in business and she is the only child. They still do their little English lessons with me, and Rita came back yesterday, and gives Catherine her sums and they are all very merry together. Mlle breakfasts with them, and in the evening has a little "collation" alone, but now with Rita.

I had a long talk with Mr. Edmunds yesterday, and told him our circumstances. I had written out a list of questions for him: "Is this possible? 1. C.D.B. to buy whole estate. 2. For them to reserve woods for forestry. 3. To sell house and gardens to me, with say 20 acres grass (back and front lawn etc.) and useless part (Shanwalla) between white gate and house. 4. At what possible price. 5. Failing my being able to buy could this be let to me from year to year with option of purchase, and at what rent. 6. What would rates probably come to on this."

He was very kind and talked it all over. He said the Board would buy the estate, but wouldn't much like having the house, as so many they have taken over had been white elephants on their hands. He was doubtful as to their reserving woods, but thought if I could do so they might be quite a good investment, with all that young timber coming up, and that enough timber could be sold each year to pay for their upkeep. He could not say what price would be, but says there is an easy way of paying "through stock". I can't say I understood very well and didn't take time to go into it. As to letting it to me, he thought I should do better by buying. He could not tell what rates would be except that the property would be so much smaller it would be rated much lower than at present.

He believes that if I could get hold of the Chief Secretary and the Under Secretary (MacMahon who I know) and Lady Greenwood (who attended an important Board meeting in her husband's train and clapped all he said and is supposed to have influence) and Lord Oranmore and made out the case, they might quite probably buy it at once, without waiting for Bill. They have plenty of money.

I had been trying to work out how far my income would go, and think I might just manage to run house and few fields and garden. If we left this I should want anyhow a roof of my own where I could have the chicks whenever they liked to visit me and of course I would rather spend everything here and avoid what I so much dread, the break up that I think would be a blow to the children, rather perhaps a shock and possibly a grief to Richard later. It would be for ten years at most till he's of age. I don't suppose I shall live for that time, but I don't think I could spend whatever sunset years are left to me in a better way. And this would leave you quite free to do what you think best in making another home for them. How much do we pay for insurance? I forget. I have the Yeats portrait to sell, and perhaps some other things. If I did fail to keep going, I should at all events have done my best, but I think I could manage. Do you think this is a possible way out of the difficulty? I hope so. There would be no gossip about it, just a family arrangement. Edmunds says there have been several similar cases—one member of a family selling a place and another buying back in part.

I am afraid prospects of letting the grazing not good—John says one of those who wanted it think rent too high as it is late in the season. Much love and I do hope we may do what is best.

18 JULY. Rather a troubled week—Margaret writing about Ford, whose fields she had given to J.D., and she can't get Celbridge and talks of "making a home in London for the children."

I have begun a sort of preliminary negotiations with Sinn Fein. Lennox Robinson was here. We drove to Tillyra. Edward (Martyn) told how having driven from Dublin in his motor, with a good many rugs and parcels inside, Tillyra was raided by military who made a search in the belief General Lucas had been hidden under them! Also his Dublin house had been raided, because Paul Farrell having borrowed his upper room for a rehearsal of *The Enemy of the People*,[4] and the windows being open, the shouts and strong language in the scene of the meeting had reached the windows of Kildare Street Club and the authorities were informed he was holding a Sinn Fein meeting! He says de Valera and Griffith[5] have but little power, that Michael Collins[6] of the Volunteer army, and of whom he knows little or nothing, is the man. He thinks however, Griffith a great statesman. He had known and liked de Valera when he was teacher at the little Tawin school. Here next day, he talked of John McCormack (the singer) who had been one of his choir boys at the Pro-Cathedral. He was rather insubordinate and was put out; and he was not popular, because he used to play ball with the police!

Have done a little—perhaps not more than 10 or 5 minutes to half an hour at *Aristotle*—each day some one.

19TH Wrote again to Lady Arnott about pictures, yesterday tranquil and a rest.

20TH. Yesterday wet and heavy—yet rather good. Chicks played hide and seek through the rooms with Mlle and Rita—Catherine did a little French lesson, her first with Mlle, and helped me to cover jam. I wrote to Murray about getting papers from Will and read a long play, *Crossed Souls*,[7] I think good. All seemed to get on better. Today also good, we picked black currants for preserving, and the chicks rode and Kathleen Bagot came to tea and Mlle taught them many games. "Planting *les choux*" among them.

An encounter in the morning between Mary and Marian *re* the turning off of some hot water, I feel like Mr. Pickwick between the two armies in the sham fight. But all cooled down later.

21 JULY. I wondered the last day or two why I felt so peaceful—as if all would go well—and this morning brought a nice letter from Margaret saying it would not be a bad idea to sell to me—but that she will keep what she can of Coole—so I hope now all will go well and that we are both "willing the same thing with God." Letter writing and returning 2 plays I had read—possible ones—and chicks lessons. And at lunch time Mr. W. Fogarty a Land Commissioner came to see Lisheen Cranagh and came in to lunch and back to tea and was pleasant, and the chicks and Rita and Mlle. were very merry riding Pud and Tommy and the cob. Poor *Bellows* only had a few minutes though.

25 JULY. A wet Sunday—most of the days have been wet but the chicks keep up their spirits and with Rita and Mlle keep the house alive.

Mr. Fogarty told me he had slept at the Ennis Hotel the night before and at 10.30 the Volunteers had come in and cleared the bar. All went out quietly. They asked if he was staying at the hotel, and did not interfere with him.

Today some of the chief Sinn Feiners of the neighbourhood have been to see me—Stanford, Coen, Shaughnessy, P. Cahel—this in consequence of my letter to Coen. They asked me to state the case which I did; they advised the Arbitration Court and I talked it over, and said I would put it before Mrs. Gregory when she came. They are very civil and sympathetic. Margaret had written, I had the letter this morning, saying she would not go to an Arbitration Court, but she may change. However, I told them that I would prefer selling to the Board, though I'm afraid they can't take up the grazing question unless we bring in the matter of the sale.

I told them what I had written Una, that I would prefer a Republic; but that were I a politician and with influence in Sinn Fein I would say, accept Dominion Home Rule. One of them said, "When all the people of the country ask for freedom we must have it." I went on "I wrote also that I would do this because some day the Dominions will become Republics and then Ireland would automatically become one." They were amused at this idea. They are pleased at the success of their Courts, and not afraid that they can be put down. I liked the young men, and thought well of them.

27 JULY. The morning has begun rather gloomily—My appeal for Cunyngham's release refused and J. Diveney's cattle have been driven. Swift (ex-policeman) coming to report breaking open of Kincorda Gate to drive out J.D.'s cattle says: "Ireland is worse than ever it was in living memory. In the Land League time they only shot landlords, but now they are attacking the forces of the Crown!"

29TH. Richard and Margaret arrived, the darling! Anne and Catherine and Rita very proud of mounting their "horses", Charlie, Puddah, Black pony, and trotting and cantering about. I am proud of having them so well and happy.

30TH. I had a talk with Margaret about sale; we are agreed as to selling as much as makes it possible to keep the rest, house and perhaps woods.

In the evening a better talk—she told me of buying Rivercourt at Hammersmith, "so much better for the children than the present house and the year would be well balanced for them, school and companions there—home and country here."

Alec Martin writes saying the Wood executor is getting chancery to order the return of the manuscripts. A troublesome business. I have written Murray etc., I may have to finish off with a rush. Poor *Bellows*!

4 AUGUST. Yesterday morning J.D. came to say the rooms over harness room have been broken open—their locks broken—and 23 fleeces stolen, also the carriage rugs. A very painful and disagreeable occurence, besides the money loss. I think it must have been done by outsiders, don't think the Republican Group did it—for Hogan their solicitor wrote that very day asking us to submit the purchase question to an Arbitration Court.

This we are not inclined to do—but I thought we ought at once to try and hurry on the C.D.B. to take the land.

And Edmunds came late and stayed to dinner, and he was so very certain this should be done—and so kind offering to come himself to Dublin with us—it was comforting, and we settled to go next week.

I had showed Margaret the evening before my picture scenario of the *Bellows* for I had been reading Gay's *Beggar's Opera* she had brought over, and it gave me new energy for my intention of putting in a song or songs somewhere—and I am already making them—to the tunes of "Bells of Shandon" and "Shule Aroon".[8]

20 AUGUST. Alas! I went to Dublin and to C.D.B. and had to write to Margaret "Failure"! Micks said it was impossible to purchase, that they would lose 50% on it; if they gave £10,000 in cash they would be paid back in stock. . . . Lord Oranmore, at the Board meeting then sitting, sent out a letter to the same effect. I was up against a stone wall, no pleading or argument could help . . . Two days ago Margaret talked it over, for I had another letter from Hogan summoning us to an Arbitration Court to give reason why we preferred selling to the Board than to his clients. Such irony when the Board won't buy.

And yesterday, when Margaret had settled to go away and when Micks had wired "impossible" as an answer to her letter offering to sell for stock, I had to say she could not go till she had come to a decision whether to go to the Court, or what to do.

At last she decided to motor to Tuam and see Concannon and to ask Frank to come and spend a night, and I came here to Burren leaving her at Coole. It is a troublesome business and I feel for her, and for us all.

The fleeces stolen have been recovered and returned to us by the Volunteers—they have told us who were the thieves.

In Dublin I stayed at Sandycove writing almost all the day at Hugh's Memoir and on Saturday before I left I posted it to London—tired but so glad it is off my hands and complete.

At the theatre splendid audiences—a joy.

11 SEPTEMBER. A long time without writing. I had 10 days at Burren with the chicks—lovely weather—a pleasant change. I worked very hard there and here on *Aristotle's Bellows* and have really finished a rough draft, in dialogue.

Also the proofs of Hugh's Memoir are arriving, and I have been correcting them so I feel, for once, that should I die there is no work on hand that it would grieve me to leave. And the same day—4th—that I got Hugh's 1st proofs I had also the book of *Visions and Beliefs* published at last. And that day also I began writing dialogue for the 3rd Act of *Aristotle*. Rather tired since then. And Terence McSwiney's long dying makes me suffer.[9] I read the service for "a sick person", though there seems but little chance of his recovery, night and morning, and have ordered the Abbey to be closed should he die, but that is little to do.

25 SEPTEMBER. Burren. Not much change. Land purchase still unsettled. Galway "in a bad state". Lee tells me there is firing over their head at night. Margaret was told by Mrs. C. the D.I.'s wife that there is to be no enquiry into the police reprisals.[10] Burren peaceful so far. A policeman said to have been shot at Ennistymon yesterday, and Ballyvaughan barracks burned.[11] I am still using the prayer "for a sick person when there appeareth small hope of his recovery" for Terence McSwiney and the Cork prisoners—all still living and suffering. Richard very well in this wonderful air.

27 SEPTEMBER. Going home today (I still call Coole home!) better for having been here, have slept better and lost headache.

But proofs are more troublesome to correct.

Stories of shootings and burnings by the Military always. Today Mrs. Scovell coming in says houses were burned in and near Kinvara last night. Arabella wrote from Galway 21st "At 11 o'c. last night the maids heard shots at a distance. They say it was the police attacking Lee's pub over the way, which is decorated with a line of Sinn Fein colours and that they knocked at the door (besides firing at windows) and Miss Lee who was alone in the house, her brother sleeping elsewhere (to hide possibly) had to come down in her nightdress to let them in; then they helped themselves to drink. I hear the bullet marks are there but have not heard the other side yet. Probably they got some provocation, in any case it was a savage act". She writes 23rd: "Glad Richard was away last night for at 11 o'clock firing, at 11.15 a great crash, probably a lot of shots but it sounded like a wall falling. The postman said a house nearly opposite Deasy's fish shop has been fired into. It is next door to Walsh's pub that had been attacked the night before and belonged to a man who left Brennan's Drapery and set up a drapery of his own and had "Outfitter to the Republicans" over his door. A raid at Post office (in this street) today. 2 armed men with rifles, soldiers, were standing at the door. Don't know if they found anything, probably not, as Brown (Postmistress's husband) has gone out of the country and probably took his papers. He is a Judge of the Republican Court".

25 SEPTEMBER. And again: "Last night J. Lee's Pub nearly opposite here was raided. The house was empty as the old sister and little niece who were there when it was attacked before, now sleep elsewhere. Lee has not slept there for some time. The lower

windows were well fastened so a ladder was brought and they got in through upper windows, broke up things, set taps of bar and spirits running and stole chairs which they threw out of top windows. We hear the *Galway Express* office has again been entered and everything broken up. They were a whole day at Queen's College, but it was a legal military entrance. What kept them so long was that Doctor Walsh refused to open the safe, and they gave him till 5 o'clock. I did not hear if there was anything found there. Doctor Walsh was arrested but let go again as they had no evidence."

In Margot's *Autobiography* she says General Booth wrote in her book "What is life for but to walk in harmony with God. . . . and to spend and be spent for the temporal and eternal weal of this suffering world".

28 SEPTEMBER. Yesterday evening I came home. I had been told that Feeney's house in Kinvara had been burned in the night—the Sunday night—and we passed by the ruined walls in the town. A little farther, at the cross roads, there was another ruin, McMerney's the smith. His house had also been burned down in the night by soldiers and police. He and his family had found shelter in the cart shed. It seemed so silent, we had always heard the hammer in the smithy and seen the glow of the fire. And he was such a good smith—I remember how Robert used to send his hunters to him. "One of his sons was said to be secretary to a Sinn Fein Committee". Today Malachi Quinn came to ask for sand for the building up of Burke's house at Ballymacwiff—burnt also by military and police. They had gone to look for one of the sons and he was not there. Then they told Burke to take whatever money he had out of the house, and then set fire to it. First I said I must ask Margaret's leave for the sand and wrote to her. Then I tore up the letter and gave leave. There were children in the house, Malachi has taken two of them to his. They say Gort would have been burnt on Saturday by drunken soldiers arriving from Ennistymon, but three of the old police restrained them.

30 SEPTEMBER. I was quite ill, could not sleep or eat after the homecoming—the desolation of that burnt forge, and all one hears. Edward Martyn's beautiful little village hall burnt down. C. Griffin says on Monday night two lorries of military came into Gort "firing and shouting—and the people brought out their furniture from their houses expecting the burnings to begin." "Black and Tans and police and military" burned Burke's house, "an officer with them. But are there any *gentlemen* among them?" Griffin takes their part, says it brought tears

to his eyes when five bodies of policemen were carried through Gort, one only 25. Terrible on both sides, but it was in Clare they had been shot. Police they say were fired at near Ardrahan, but not wounded or killed—that was the excuse for the Sunday burnings.

1 OCTOBER. No post today.

Peter Glynn told me today "There did two car loads of the Black and Tans come into Gort late yesterday evening—they were a holy fright shouting and firing. They broke into houses and searched them, and they searched the people in the street, women and girls too that were coming out from the chapel, that they came running down the street in dread of their life. Then they went into Spelman's to drink and got drunk there. It is terrible to let them do that. Look at McMerney's they burned all the bedding in the house and every bit of money he had. And at Burke's the same way, burnt all in the house, and nine acres of oats. They would have burned the hay but didn't see it. Mr. Martyn's beautiful hall they didn't leave a stone of, and at Ardrahan the same way as at Burke's they kept the boys running up and down the road for near an hour and a half and they all but naked while they were chasing them up and down, and girls the same way. It is a holy crime—it is worse than Belgium. What call have they coming to Gort that is such a quiet little town? Jack Hehir that went into Gort in the evening with a message from his wife that is sick was stopped near the town and made put his hands up and was searched".

Marian has just brought me back a book "Chez Swan" that I had sent to go back to Mudies.

There was a "regiment of soldiers with their bayonets standing at the Post office door and no one could go in—and the shutters up as on Sundays. They were said to be searching the letters inside" Tim is trembling "There is no one is safe".

2 OCTOBER. No letters yet, J., says the military opened all the letters that came in yesterday, that time they were in the Post Office. The Black and Tans left last night. "They searched a good many houses and found nothing, but any pictures they saw that had anything to do with Sinn Fein they tore and broke them. Young Hayes was trying to slip away from them but they fired and hit him in the thigh. They went singing about the streets 'Irishmen come into the Parlour' and 'Who fears to speak of Easter Week'. There were not three people in Gort went to bed last night, but sitting up through the night-time keeping the lights quenched. Carr X. that is a policeman's son was the Captain over the Black and Tans, a tall young fellow. He was wearing a white

cloth over his face and holes cut in it for the eyes. Prospect was searched twice. But Stephens says it would have been worse but for Carr X. being in it, he has friends he would not wish to face in the town."

"The reason for Burke's house being burned was that he had driven cattle in Druimhasna, and the police say they felt (heard) shots there one night. There are others living near say there were no shots fired. It was 7 o'clock in the night time they burned the house, and the wheat and the oats. A slated house and as well furnished as any house you could see. The boy they were looking for was in it, and they covered him with their revolvers, eight of them, holding them to his head and his body, but the Captain said 'We can do enough harm without killing him' and they began the burning".

Mike says the military had stopped the mail car yesterday and opened most of the letters; mine opened was one from Galway telling "At 12.30 last night the Post Office, which is a nest of Sinn Feiners, was riddled with bullets, also my grocer's shop (2nd attack on him) Heaney our bacon merchant and others".

M.J. says the Black and Tans fired 12 shots at Hayes but only one hit, in the shoulder, and that they broke all the pictures and furniture at F's.

Glynn says "they stole a piece of tweed from B's shop, and a gold necklace and a watch from a house in Church Street. Carr, their officer, made them put back the tweed, and the watch and the necklace they brought away. They drank in every bar and went about drunk in the evening shouting and singing. Savages they were. And after they had left the town police got drunk and went drunk about the town with their revolvers—a holy terror."

3 OCTOBER. As I passed Merney's yesterday, driving to Burren, there were men building at his house (I am sending him £5).

Margaret had a letter from Concannon saying the Regan set will only give £8000 at most, without building wall, and including timber. Concannon had been confident of £10,000, so it is a blow. Margaret is so anxious to sell at once—and yet this is too low to accept. I had heard that Shaughnessy and some of the volunteers had purposed coming down today to talk about the grazing, and I asked Margaret to come and see them as it might lead to a sale, but she would not but said I might do so and try what I could do. So without unpacking my things I had them put on the car again and went back from Burren getting home at 9. I pray for a settlement and peace. "Thy Kingdom come, Thy Will be done—here in Coole—in Kiltartan—in Ireland."

I had a letter from A. opened and apparently censored with blue pencil it says "heard Military had taken up Post Office no letters of any sort."

R. writes (Wednesday 6th) "I didn't get your letter of the 30th till last night, though I got the letter you wrote on Saturday on Sunday—your 30th letter was opened by the military (as were all our letters yesterday) and perhaps as it was full of the account of burnings etc., they held it over."

But she writes in it Doreen (her nurse) has seen the soldiers and is much disgusted at their being "little boys, not even Scotch!"

4 OCTOBER. Shaughnessy and Cahel of the Volunteers here about land, but only wanted to know details, acreage etc. . . . I asked about the Black and Tans, if it was true they drank, they said yes; "they arrived drunk and drank in most of the bars while they were there. They stole in Gort many things—a bicycle and such like and would have done more but we have a good D.I., who kept them back."

5 OCTOBER. John took my letter to McMerney's. They told him the attacking party had come about midnight and had begun by firing into the kitchen through the windows but that they thanked God there was no one there. Then they broke in and dragged the boys out, ordered them all out, and poured oil about, and set fire to the house. One of the soldiers had told the wife to go back and save her money and clothes and she was going in, but a policeman dragged her back. They had saved nothing at all.

9 OCTOBER. The Land sale has been arranged by Frank. He met Regan and his committee here last Wednesday—and again today at Gort and carried it through. £9000 including the timber. They will not build the wall Margaret wanted, or promise any certain acreage to the workmen but "will give them fair play, and Frank says if we are not satisfied they do this we will bring them before the Arbitration Court.

I wish it could have been to the C.D.B., that the poorer and better old tenants might have a chance, but as it abandoned us there was nothing else to do.

Richard has gone back to school, much the better for the long holiday, full of life and vigour. The house very lonely without the darling. We all went to Galway with him and Margaret to see them off.

Yesterday afternoon Anne had a fall from Black Pony, who shied at the sight of Catherine picking berries in the bushes. Poor little Annekin her elbow looked bad and I sent for Foley, the doctor. He came and said it was dislocated. He had brought, as I had asked him, chloroform and gave her some sniffs and she did not feel the setting, and is better today—but we have put off going back to Burren, and she needs much care. He was at Athenry when our messenger got to his house and didn't get here till 9.30. He said he had been held up at Clarenbridge while a party of Black and Tans went through the village, firing indiscriminately into houses. In one house they fired up through the ceiling. They ended by going into a public house, drinking 11 glasses of whiskey and throwing down a shilling as payment. He spoke of the "reprisals" when Burke's and McMerney's and other houses were burnt down—"There was no ambush of policemen, there was not a shot fired at one. One of the police who went to Drumhasna that night told me that when they got there they saw three men walking in the fields. They followed them, trying to come up with them. On the way they found in a quarry 2 revolvers, that might have been left there by anyone, for there are many hiding their weapons now. Then they fired at the three men, there were no shots fired back, that was all the firing. There was no ambush. That was all the excuse they had for the burnings."

He has just been again, this evening to see Anne. Her arm is going on well, but will need massaging for a long time. I said he must have been tired when he got home last night and he said "I was hardly in the house at all, there was some bad work last night." I could not have him tell it before the children but when he came down he said, "Those Black and Tans that were in Clarenbridge went on to Maree that is a couple of miles farther. They dragged three men out of their houses there and shot them—Keene and two others. They are not dead, they were wounded, I was sent for to attend them, then they set fire to some of the houses and burned them down". I asked if anything had happened there, if these were "reprisals" and he said "nothing, except that a good while ago, last year, a policeman was disarmed there but not hurt". He said "I used not to believe the stories of English savagery whether written or told, I thought they were made up by factions but now I see that they are true"—he said also "they are savages, they are out for loot. In Galway they went into Whelan's Medical Hall and took a fancy to a Kodak, but it was £5 and they said that was too dear. In the night they came back, broke the window and took it. And the next night they brought it back broken and took another. I told Whelan he ought to make a public complaint, but he said 'they would break in every night of the week if I did that'."

Gort is quieter. Peter Glynn says "It is the police are the worst for they are always drunk now they have nothing to do".

Very much worried about illustrations to Hugh's *Life*. Murray and Emery Walker between them seem to have decided against the French pictures—and I must have two of these.[12] And Walker has told Murray I will myself bear the cost—this without any authority from me! Letter-writing on this took me a long time. I don't want to offend Murray and think by his letter he is offended.

Then Frank came, and says sale is through, the money to be lodged in a fortnight. I am glad it has not lingered on, but it is rather a shock feeling I cannot cut a tree for firing or bring in a cart of maiden earth for the garden outside the white gates!

MONDAY, 11 OCTOBER. I had to tell J.D. yesterday, for it would have been cowardice not to, that there was no land reserved for him or other labourers in the sale only "fair treatment". He was very much upset.

Coming from Church the exits of the town were barricaded—carts drawn across, and soldiers in a group—they let us pass without question. I hear they took all the men coming out from Mass into a house, and searched them. There were two officers in church, heavy faces—We had "God Save The King"—it has been sung ever since the military were sent to Gort—one lesson and all but one psalm cut off "because the soldiers must be back for their dinner" but it remains. The drivers outside. I wonder if they recognised it. I thought of the Afghan in "Mr. Dooley's" *Journals of the Olympic Games*[13] saying as he hears it. "I don't know the name of that chune but it's mighty like the one they were playing the time they chased my grandfather through the streets of Cabul"!

A. writes "Barnett saw a soldier (not sober) beating his horse because it had trodden on his toe, and every time he gave it a blow he said 'Now will you tread on my toe again'"? (reprisals!)

12 OCTOBER. Robinson, telegram last evening saying Dollard could let us have one of the photographs I want for Hugh's *Life* eases I hope the Murray situation, such a blessing.

Out gardening, transplanting peonies while the chicks planted wallflowers in their little gardens. The doctor came and says Anne must keep her arm quiet for some time to come.

I asked the doctor how his Maree patients are. He thinks they will recover though one was very badly wounded. Another dragged out was better. The looting goes on in Galway, the jewellery shop robbed. He thinks Government intends to get rid of the Black and Tans, because two very bad characters he knows, one Moycullen who had been in gaol for killing his mother (O! *Playboy!*) have just been added to them, and he thinks they will get such a bad name at this rate that it will be impossible for the force to be kept up. It seems a long way round.

The Hanlon girl from Kiltartan comes asking for a bit of land—as if I could give it! She says Hanlon, one of Regan's men, was taken from his bed on Wednesday night (the night of the meeting here) beaten and ducked in the river by disguised members of the other faction, they said there were 4 more to be served the same way. I am very sorry land violence should begin again.

BURREN, MONDAY 18 OCTOBER. We came here last Thursday Anne and Catherine and I—the sea breeze good for Annekin after her accident. All quiet here, the police being moved away to Lisdoonvarna where they and others from outlying stations are to live in the Atlantic hotel. There were shots on Friday. I asked a man who looked like an ordinary policeman what they were. He said "the Black and Tans are come, they are firing. If they get drunk they'll burn the whole place tonight." However, all stayed quiet. My chief trouble as to my last proofs, Murray's printers by a mistake printing the whole catalogue of Hugh's bequest (I had sent for names of painters only) with Langton Douglas's preface and the Will in full.[14] The list of pictures troublesome too.

20TH. Yesterday rather good, for Margaret wrote "Poor little Anne . . . she will find you a most comforting nurse. I don't know anyone so perfect in a sick room"; and "Sir Horace Plunkett said with great energy 'What wonderful work Lady Gregory has done for Ireland'—so I said with equal enthusiasm 'Wonderful work she has done for us all—a wonderful woman in every way'!" and C.E. Lawrence writes "You need be in no qualms about the book. It has yourself in it, and where yourself is, it marches to the music of Kiltartan". Three compliments on a day!

All quiet here and the police gone. Reading Miss Edgeworth's *Waste not want not* and *Lazy Laurence* to the chicks, they were delighted, it makes up for *Mrs. Wiggs of the Cabbage Patch*[15] which they lamented the end of. My "Week's Diary" is in the *Nation*[16] that came yesterday.

At the Post Office Gaynor showed me the order that no parcels for Ireland will be accepted in English Post offices from today.

21ST. The Police barrack was burned down in the night, the walls stand and are smoking, the roof has fallen in. A mercy it was empty save for one man who was not injured. A. writes from Galway "They say Walsh the publican was shot last night and his body thrown into the docks. I don't know if it's true. . . . I hear police think Joyce has been murdered or he would have returned home."

Murray; rather down, but Murray says he is getting photographs from Dollard of the French pictures—so I hope that is all right.

And Miss White writes asking leave for *The Dragon* at the Alexandra—her girls having set their hearts on it—so that is rather comforting; I want to have plays ready for the young generation.

22ND. Mrs. Duncan sends complete list of pictures "given and bequeathed" a help though rather late.

EVENING. The Black and Tans have come, they have been at the barrack and at the quay "sixteen of them"—the children hope there won't be any more burnings and echo what they hear "it can't be until night". Their lorries have been racing about—but all is quiet now (9.30). I think they have gone.

24TH. A rather trying day at Coole, to meet Frank, and try to insist on good terms for the workmen, as the Committee have written to them to "bring £200" to Gort (which they are not inclined to do until they know what is to be had for it). F., grew grumpy after lunch attacked me for having spent money (my own, earned!) on planting instead of "keeping it for Richard to spend". But Richard may love trees too—and they can't be grown in a minute. Then M.Q. came and was quite abusive at "the old tenants" not getting the land which they had refused to offer for! Rain came on and a long drive back here. Poor Grandmama! . . . but the chicks delighted because I brought apples.

We were at church, Mrs. Scovell and Stanley, the two children and I, a congregation of five. A strange Litany astonished me, then Mrs. S. sent a copy across. I tried to join and indeed might have, but that it was so manifest that the crime of murder and superstition and other sins prayed against were set down as those of Ireland, that it seemed almost an exoneration of "those appointed for the Government of this land."

I am reading Garibaldi's *Defence of the Roman Rèpublic*[17] very comforting, because so many a praise of Italy's fighters and martyrs taken from its contents could stand as justly for ours. "Men who would have been called to make her laws and lead her armies and write her songs and history when their day came, but that they judged it becoming to die there in order that her day should come." I go on saying daily the prayers for the Lord Mayor to Him "with whom do live the spirits of just men made perfect, after they are delivered from their earthly prisons."

26TH. The day began well, a letter from Frank, saying our workmen are to have fair treatment in the land division, a great relief.

My 2nd "Weeks Diary" was in the *Nation* and I think helpful. After the chicks' lessons I worked a bit at the *Bellows*.

AFTERNOON. Mrs. S. called, stayed some time talking of "country newses" from the English point of view—then incidentally said, "The Lord Mayor is dead—there has been a wire"—I said "He was a brave man". She gave a superior smile and said: "I believe his sisters are rather . . ." "Rather what?" "Rather rowdy"—I got up and opened the window and spoke of Catherine's copybook and didn't sit down again and she left, and I looked up at the hills for a while, towards the west. "It is not a little thing a man to die, and he protecting his neighbour".[18]

27TH. Very quiet; no newspapers at all have come to Burren. Harris in a letter from Dublin "does not know what the effect of the Lord Mayor's death will be, but the military all seem fully prepared". Old Tierney, having talked of the attack on my father's yacht—about 80 years ago—says the funeral is today in Cork; but I hardly think they will allow the body to be brought to Ireland. I go on reading *Garibaldi and the Thousand*[19] this not so near to our case as the Roman Republic.

30TH. Quiet days—the chicks picking blackberries and harnessing the go-cart to Tommy and digging shell fish out of the sand.

I have sent off *Aristotle's Bellows* to be typed, probably the last play I shall write. I am face to face with my memories, or whatever I have gathered from my life.

Yesterday "Punch" had a caricature of "The Irish Volunteer army" that degraded type that helped the bitterness in the land war and before. I felt the Lord Mayor had not given his life in vain if even to contradict that, for his portrait must be also in those Dublin papers; it is, they say in all the American ones. Reading Garibaldi still, with envy.

31 OCTOBER. J.D., from Coole—The Black and Tans have been several times at Gort, shooting and destroying. Three policemen have been shot or shot at near Castle Daly. Then Doctor Foley came. He was very excited, and said houses at Ardrahan had been burnt down last night and that the Black and Tans are spreading terror and ruin. He could not speak explicitly before the children . . . but I saw him for a few minutes alone and he said that at Clarenbridge they had got drunk and had assaulted a widow. And a man there,—Casey—had come to him yesterday saying "Don't let your Misses walk on the road, they

are out for drink and women," and said he and his son had been dragged from their houses, put against the wall and while held there his two daughters were assaulted. Foley thinks the attempt succeeded to violate them. I begged him to get the facts and write them down, that I may send them to Massingham. He says even Unionists are shocked at Greenwood's falsehoods in the House of Commons. A bad night.

Today I wrote to G.B.S., begging him to come over to Coole and examine into these Black and Tan horrors.

I wrote to Margaret saying the workmen ought to be given their houses and an acre or two,—and that if she did not feel the same way I would use the Crannagh £300.

The chicks so good at lessons, spurred by fear of the Italian governess, Catherine reading her page off, hardly needing a prompt.

5 NOVEMBER. A. writes "The milk girl says a young woman was shot yesterday at Kiltartan by a lorry of passing military—it seems dreadful—they are very careless with guns."

Then Ellen told me it was Malachi Quinn's young wife who had been shot dead with her child in her arms.

Ellen says her mother's house near Athenry was broken into by military the other night, she was made get out of bed, but she was not assaulted. Poor Malachi Quinn; he had trouble enough to bear, and was sad last week when he came to see me . . .

Foley said it is dangerous now to be on the road, and it was dangerous to stay in the house at night.

When I pray "God save Ireland" the words come thrusting through "Gott strafe England" in spite of my desire not to give in to hatred.

5 NOVEMBER. We came back from Burren, late, for rain had kept us back. J. had been the two nights at Malachi's house—says the little children said "Mamma's asleep". Malachi was in Gort when it happened, they sent for him. Marian had been there also, says "you could take up the three little children in your arms together" and there was another coming. There were 89 cars at the funeral. "Burning would be too good for the Black and Tans" J. says. Tim says they have been firing continually as they pass, his sick daughter cannot sleep, "the day they killed Mrs. Quinn they had fired at Donoghue's house as they passed and killed some fowl"—"It is to show their authority" Tim says. They say now that it was not done by them, but the dying woman herself was the witness, told her mother and the priest that she had been shot by the Black and Tans. "They fired at Callinans house as they passed on, and broke the windows. The old police

in Gort are ashamed of them. They stopped a man the other day turning up the road and robbed him of £50, he had just sold calves and was bringing it home."

"Malachi cannot stand alone—he has to be led 'linked'— They were so happy, they had just got in the harvest, just dug the potatoes and threshed the corn and were ready for the winter."

6 NOVEMBER. A letter from poor Malachi in answer to mine "My God it is too cruel"!

J. says Father Considine had never preached a better sermon since before the War than he did on Sunday, praising the young men of the parish for not having joined in any of the attacks on police, and begging them to keep patient; The police came down the road after and thanked him.

The next day a Holy day (All Saints) and pig [fair?] "There were a great many people in Gort and on the road. The Black and Tans came dashing out and began to fire shots from Lally's down so that the houses shook. Swift, that was bringing up water from the river in a tin can, said he could hear the bullets singing over his head as they passed. An ambush! in a big open country like that!"

8 NOVEMBER. I asked the Archdeacon after church about the Black and Tans. He began by saying there was a hill or at least a slight incline near Malachi's house which might have helped an ambush, and that there was no robbery or drinking while they were in Gort, and praised the Auxiliaries who have been there and he had chatted with through the evening says also that if Gort doesn't kill it makes bullets, and that men from Lough Cutra and Gort were at the Castledaly police ambush. Then I told him I had heard of things stolen; "O, yes, when they raided a house they often carried things off, they looked on it as loot". "And if they found drink, they thought they were serving their cause by taking it—drinking". Mr. Johnson put in "there are bad lads among the Black and Tans" and The Archdeacon said "The police are drinking too"; just as I had heard.

"They were Black and Tans in the lorries on Monday. They had come out from Galway for the day and when they were leaving Gort they began firing in the street."

As we set out for church I asked J.D. how long he had Ford's field for. He said till April. I said Ford had asked for it again and I had promised to write to Mrs. Gregory. He burst out:- "Isn't my money as good as another's" excitedly, and I said nothing till we were at the White gate coming back, and then asked him if Mrs. Gregory had not told him how angry she was at his having deceived her in saying Ford didn't want to keep it on—as he did.

He blustered, but confessed she had. I said I did not know if it would be let again, that I thought we might want it for ourselves. He said "If you want it for yourselves I'll say nothing—but if anyone else gets it—I'll. . . ." I said, "What will you do?" He said, "I'll fight my battle", I said, "then it is a threat"—That was all. I am very sorry—an ugly revelation of character and just when I was doing my best to help him. No letter from Margaret. Poor John.

9 NOVEMBER. L.R. writes about a possible Fund to help the homeless we may play for "though probably by that time we will be among those asking for charity. All the theatres are hard hit but we are especially so, and I think it's because the military now often go to a concert and hold up the whole audience to search them, and our audience is more Sinn Fein than most audiences so it naturally doesn't want that."

A. writes "After the wedding (a Black and Tan officer to a widow) the Black and Tans formed an arch of revolvers for the Bride and Groom to walk under and then fired (blank) cartridges. Being Saturday all the Market was filled and the old women stampeded in terror. Later the wedding motor ran into a lorry and the bride fainted."

Malachi Quinn came to see me looking dreadfully worn and changed and his nerves broken, he could hardly speak when he came in. There had been aeroplanes flying very low over the place all day and as he came from Raheen one had swooped and fired 3 shots over him. He believes they shot her on purpose—they came so close. He was so fond of his wife "she could play every musical instrument". It is true the messenger sent for a Doctor was shot from another lorry, wounded in the leg.

R.D. came to tea—she says the Black and Tans are a bad lot but thinks them justified in flogging (the Archdeacon said "scourging") because they say they had found a paper with sixteen names signing it, on the guard of a train, saying a convoy of soldiers was going to Galway and that the boys there would know how to be ready for them.

I am troubled by another talk with J.D. who still keeps to his threat of not allowing Ford back into the field he got from him by his misstatements, "It is not ye I threaten, it is Ford". I have not told Margaret.

12 NOVEMBER. Mrs. Randolph Warren has been here for a night, finds it hard to believe about the burnings etc. A pleasant day's talk about her travels and U.S.A.

A. writes "Shops all closed by order of the Black and Tans 'in honour of the brave lads who gave their lives for England and the police who were murdered by their fellow-countrymen. If this order is not obeyed not a house will be left standing,' or words to that effect—I did not see the posters".

A few days ago the cutting about Hugh's pictures stirred me up to write again to Lady Greenwood.

SUNDAY. 14 NOVEMBER. Too wet for church.

Reading Miss Edgworth's *Rosamund*[20] to the children and they are looking at the big Bible prints.

Yesterday morning I awoke with the words in my ears: "And the Leaves of the Tree are for the Healing of the Nations", ah, if we could but find that Tree!

BOOK TEN

15 NOVEMBER 1920. Una [Pope-Hennessy*] writes about Terence McSwiney: "You could not see the face of that man in his coffin, looking like the face of a starved child of 10, without feeling the most awful moral wrong had been done—It overwhelmed you."

18 NOVEMBER. A. writes from Galway that there had been a raid in the University, and some students who had not saluted the flag there were made to do so. The paper says "forced to uncover while the National Anthem was sung."

The children were in the wood cutting sticks and heard a great many shots—4—close together. Swift told them it was the Black and Tans.

I was so angry at the official report of Eileen Quinn's shooting—beginning "the enquiry was open to all but few chose to attend it". I had heard none but the family and the witnesses were allowed to it and I asked the Archdeacon after church if he had heard it and he said "No, no one was allowed in but the witnesses. I sat outside with—" I forget whom.

Reading H. James's letters[1]—very charming reading—yet, near the end of the second volume I begin to wonder what was wrong with them, there is an unsatisfied undercurrent either in my mind or his in spite of his pleasant surroundings and the work he liked and his many friends. I think it is that he being severed from his country was as it were sterilised—not "in the pedigree" of his nation, as was his brother,[2] and Howells and Chiltern and the rest. And he might have found more sap and substance among his own people a new people whose soul has been but imperfectly revealed. He has found such wonderful subtlety of expression and wastes it, I think, on what often seems at the best a fly sucked dry—it is the web that interests one.

Aristotle's Bellows[3] came back typed yesterday and I am rather hurriedly sending it to Robinson today, Mike Lally saying there will be no trains tomorrow.[4]

A proof came of the Max Beerbohm caricature of Hugh displaying pictures to the people of Dublin. I had asked for it, and the rejection by Bond Street dealers one, to put in the same page. Then, having left that out, Grey suddenly sends this, filling one page. I assented, writing a card, but thought in the night that what was now wrong (and I felt there was something wrong) is that the two together appeared as caricatures of Hugh, but this one alone is a caricature of the Dublin people and I myself being sore about that "Volunteer Army" libel of Punch, I would avoid hurting others in the same way. The anguish of this possibility had gripped me in the night and today I sent a telegram—braving Murray's wrath, which need not be excessive as the money loss falls on me—to cancel it.

That, and having given Mike John £40 towards his purchase of land, makes me feel more serene.

20TH. Dr. Foley here yesterday. He says the family of the girls violated by the Black and Tans wish it hushed up. There has been another case of the same sort in Clare—but there also it is to be kept quiet. Peterswell has been undergoing its reprisals. A man Foley had long known—an old Land Leaguer—had come to the dispensary to have his back treated— "I think there was hardly a worse scourging given to our Lord—the whole back black and blue with bruises and the Blood drawn in some places."

Other men there were beaten "one thrown on a dung heap—a Black and Tan put one foot on his face to press it into the dung, and another on his stomach. And then he and others treated the same way were thrown into the village well to wash themselves."

"There is an old man of 70 living at the side of the mountain. He had come down to the village and went into Hayes' public house. He had 18/6 in his pocket—a Black and Tan came in and called "Hands up". He put up his hands and the Black and Tan took the 18/6 out of his pocket and walked out with it".

I am told "no one but witnesses were allowed into the Quinn enquiry. The President of the Court looked like a gentleman and was well mannered but after the first he had nothing to say, an officer with a dark countenance and a Scotch accent took it all into his hands and the other seemed afraid of him. The Archdeacon sat outside on a bench, with Father Considine. The Head Constable was in the house while Mrs. Quinn was still alive, but asked for no statement from her. It is their custom to ask that even when told a patient wasn't fit for it."

I was just sitting down to write this when "Mr. Nevinson" was announced and came in, with a Doctor Watson. He is writing for the *Daily Herald*. They had just come from Scariff where those four young men were shot in trying to escape the day before yesterday. He is certain they were not trying to escape—the shooting was on a bridge, where they would certainly not have been—he is sure they were shot in cold blood. They stayed the night—pleasant visitors as we talked of many other things—and it is a great relief to my mind that these horrors are being made known by so competent a writer. He said, "Those 'Nation' articles of yours have been of the greatest use." I said, "They are not known to be mine" and he said, "Oh, no, but *I* know". Foley told me some of what he had said to me had been recognised by a friend of his. He said I was welcome to tell all he told me, that it ought to be made known. But he thinks if the Black and Tans hear I am doing this, revenge and loot may bring them here.

22 NOVEMBER. Reading of Henry James's life, last night, his spacious Canne (although these midnight letters must have been a never lightened weight)—I put my own life beside his—and wondered, for a writer, putting capacity aside, is ease worse or better for one's trade? It was Sunday, when in the morning I usually write to my friends—apart from business—but I had seen the night before reading *The Times* that a play "The Dragon" was to be put on at once at the Aldegate—and the saving of the title of my poor Dragon, worked so on my mind I had, to have it free for the Church service, to compose and type a letter and a telegram to Murray.

Then with the chicks to the garden and to church with Anne. When they were out after lunch, I began to compose a letter about getting compensation (!) for poor Malachi Quinn. He had been on Saturday evening to ask me to help towards this. I had consulted the Archdeacon after church, and he did not think it possible because it was not "malicious injury" and said "the bullet if fired in the air might have come perpendicularly down and struck her" (I said it was odd if the fowl at Mrs. Donohues next door had also been perpendicularly struck). After I had written a draft of this I went out, going at 4 o'clock into the nut wood. Presently I saw 5 or 6 dogs of sorts running through the bushes, then lads 6 or 8, big and small one carrying a great bunch of rabbits strung on a stick over his shoulder. I called to them and they stopped a moment, did not answer, and went on. I turned back to meet them at the gate, but they turned up another path though still keeping in sight, and standing, and then moving as I came near. I called to them to come back, that it was cowardly to run away—that if they were doing no harm they must not be afraid. However, I had to give up the chase. Then I met the children, coming from Shanwalla wood, where they had seen boys catching rabbits—the same I think, for they had yellow terriers and one black and white. I felt terribly upset—it seemed like what we had heard of the French Revolution as it began, and lately in Russia, the peasants making themselves free of the woods. I felt so helpless; the police are out of the running, and the Volunteers are being chased by the Black and Tans. It seemed as if I must give in and consent to give up Coole.

I grew more tranquil reading to the children, and looking at their treasures, dogwood and furze, and knowing that having found they can be happy and occupied in woods and fields, they will never fall into the separation from the earth that makes the country an intolerable prison to the town bred.

Mike came in later, I saw him. He said there had been parties of boys all through the woods and fields—he had sent some away. He thinks they imagine that all land and woods have fallen to the purchasers—and these having had leave to clear their fields from rabbits, then came in to us. He recognised a few, and I have written today to Jordan, their father—explaining to him that the woods are still ours, and asking his son to acquaint his companions with this fact. I also wrote to Regan, asking him to tell those he admits, to respect our boundaries—and telling him also that I have now no feeling but good will to those who have bought our land.

I have also now re-written my letter to MacMahon. All this has led me a long way from Henry James, and his subtle analysis of "the Anglo-Saxon and its American enthusiasms." No wonder it is Kiltartan I must take as the dye into which to plunge my hands. M.C. coming to lunch, says she was at a dance in Galway on Saturday. One or two of her military partners came in later, and said they had been to the railway station to ask to be taken with some of their men in the train—and that, being refused, guard and firemen must be dismissed. One said "It would have been a great sell if they had taken us! we wouldn't have known what to do! We didn't want to go anywhere."

23RD. E. says the Black and Tans have been very busy round Athenry—many young men—3 friends of hers amongst them, were dragged out and whipped with a thong. Her sister's house was raided one night, in search of two young men—but they weren't there. They have told the mother of one of them that if her son is not given up her house will be burned.

She reports no trains running at Athenry—and rumours of "great killings" in Dublin. Today we have no post save one card from Galway—no paper. "There was great firing on the road last night"—the maids frightened—"30 shots a minute," M.J. said.

24TH. That news of the murder of officers[5] in Dublin is terrible and of the firing on the crowd. We seem to have grown used to the taking from their homes and shooting the young men of the countryside by "uniformed men"—for these killings in Dublin seemed more terrible for a moment, yet they are in the same list, on the same basis.

Marian went to pay the bills in Gort yesterday. They told her the Highlanders had come there and had "done bad work the evening before" beating men, driving them before them, following them even into the Chapel, "until the Clerk locked the door.—All the shops had to be shut—no one was allowed to go into a house after it had been shut unless he had a key—man or woman."

P. today says to me they are a "bad crowd"—they beat women and children as well as men, with the butts of their rifles—Belgium, where are you? This is worse than Belgium ever was. The postman told Marian this morning that the officers of the Highlanders told the people last night it would be on their own heads if anything happened, as the men "are let go free to do what they like for their last evening in the town". So everyone left the street, and shops and houses were all locked.

25TH. Mr. Edmunds motored from Galway yesterday, brought a sack of flour I had ordered in case of a strike. He began with "what do you say to the murder of Dublin officers? when I read of it I saw red—I wished to go out and kill someone" and so on.

I said it had made me feel sick with its horror, and that it was perhaps from its being never one's own class, and perhaps to me the Gresham surroundings, where I sometimes stay—that made it into a vivid horror and shock—And after a while as we talked I said perhaps those whose own sons or friends or kindred had been seized at night and dragged out and shot, would feel their tragedy more terrible—though in substance it is the same. And I quoted my King Brian; "Death answering to Death like the clerks answering one another at the Mass". And to myself I wondered why the English should claim the monopoly of the scarlet vision. I told him also of that old man scourged at Peterswell. He said he thought the floggings worse than the murders.—I said they were worse for the characters of those who inflicted them, a shot might be fired in the heat of passion, but it is always a question if even schoolmasters, even parents, can be trusted where beating is concerned. And now the weapon in the hands of the stranger, and those coarse men let loose to flog who they would, strangers to them, and often innocent of a crime, must be brutalized by such actions. He agreed or seemed to, and spoke fairly enough against reprisals and in favour of a settlement.

Today we hear Father Considine has had a typed threatening letter, (although the Chief Secretary had spoken with approval in Parliament of his sermon against crime,) his protest against Mrs. Quinn's death and his evidence, have given offence.

26TH. I went to Gort to have my signature (*re* Lisheen Crannagh sale) witnessed by the Commissioner of Oaths. He said Father Considine's letter ordered him to leave the town within 24 hours. I asked about the Highlanders. He said that on Monday night some of them who had been drinking had gone through the streets beating those they met with their rifles. Hogan the Solicitor has been arrested in Loughrea.

Today the telegraph boy tells me young Coen (who helped to get our wool back) and young B. and another have been arrested. The children came to Gort and bought Christmas presents!

Then M.J. came back from Gort, says others have been taken, Gibbs—and young Mahon—they are looking for others who are not to be found. The police say to their fathers "its better for them not to run, they'll be maybe only seven days in our hands if they stop and let us take them."

He passed a lorry with "4 boys from Gort in it—military with them, and a lorry of police behind, and flags flying." P. says that the Scotch are still in the town, they "wouldn't be as bad as they are but their officers are bad—letting them get drunk and beating all they meet. To be beaten on the back, and the neck, and to have a prod of a rifle in the head, a man might as well be dead. There could no worse happen out in Turkey. I don't know in the world what to say to the world—it's a holy fright."

Tim says his little girl met a lorry yesterday, having a yellow flag—that is Orange. They say 200 Orangemen are to be sent for, from the North to go through Ireland."

28TH. MacMahon writes advising me to write to Lady Greenwood about Malachi Quinn.

Yesterday was wet, and very peaceful. The children with me all day almost. I cut out the counties of a railway map of Ireland and they painted them and began putting them together, and Anne said her "William First as the Conquerer known" almost through and earned her 5/-. Then Catherine had to get a shilling for good reading, and promise of another when she has finished the book. They played "I spy" through the house. I went through letters of Sir A. Lyall's and begin to see him in my "Memories".

Today letters late—and ups and downs. Society of Authors have written Jeffrey asking him to change the name of his play "The Dragon" but says if [he] holds to it I have no means of redress. Yeats writes enclosing lines he has written and has, without telling me, sent to *The Times*,[6] I dislike them—I cannot bear the dragging of R., from his grave to make what I think a not very sincere poem—for Yeats only knows by hearsay while our troubles go on—and he quoted words G.B.S., told him and did not mean him to repeat—and which will give pain—I hardly know why it gives me extraordinary pain and it seems too late to stop it . . . and I fear the night. After church the Archdeacon advised me to write, as MacMahon advised, to Lady Greenwood—on the ground of the Chief Secretary having spoken with some sympathy of that death. Another reason against the poem.

Our Bank Manager has been here, I asked him about the Highlanders and he says "just a few of them got drunk and beat people in the streets". He spoke again of that robbing of £60 and says a poor man from Peterswell whose house and possessions were burnt down has been to see him—a pitiable case—and that he was absolutely innocent of any crime or approval of one. He says that at the Fair the other day his clerk was kept busy signing deposit receipts, I think 128—they had never had any such number in one day—"but all were afraid to walk the road with money on them because of the Black and Tans."

Lennox R., writes "I read 'Aristotle's Bellows' two nights ago and—as the Americans say—I take off my hat to you. I read it to a young man who was staying with me and he said 'one of Lady Gregory's best'—I agree with him, though *The Image* still, I think, remains my favourite. I think it should go very well on the stage. What a pity we haven't Kerrigan. Celia is beautiful—as your young girls always are—there's the little Princess in *The Dragon* and the girl in '*Golden Apple*'—But your philosophy is very good. I have thought of the play constantly ever since I read it." This is a relief and a pleasure—finding I'm not "quenched" yet! He has read sadness into the philosophy which isn't there, it is the sudden mechanical violent change—(as say in Russia) that makes the mischief. It is better to do it, make changes, little by little "the same as you'd put clothes upon a growing child" (but I think that is a line I left out) "and leave it to the Man who is over us all".

30 NOVEMBER. Yesterday fine and peaceful. I wrote out extracts from my Diary for "*The Nation*"—for we still need an enquiry. Today tells of the fires at Liverpool—Consequent I should think on Griffith's arrest. Well, we were brought up to revere Moses and the Ten Plagues of Egypt. Worked through Sir A. Lyall's letters. Today I am typing the H. James fragment to send to J. Quinn.

Giving out fruit for Christmas plum puddings though so doubtful that there will be anyone here.

1 DECEMBER. An officer quartered at Cork wrote yesterday asking if he can get a mirror such as those at the Abbey . . . "May I add what a joy the Abbey is to a tired person in these troublous times. I have seen nothing like it since I was at the Art Theatre in Moscow 1913."

It was a peaceful day—no letters or papers. Chicks still delighted with Swiss Family Robinson. I said to Nevinson that I thought the description of food and meals in a children's book is always popular—answers to the bedroom scene in the modern comedy.

2ND. Worried still about Yeats' poem—and as it hasn't yet appeared I have wired and written begging him to suppress it—saying I dislike it personally, but would not think it right to keep it back because of that, but those Sunday killings, made it a bad moment to appeal to *emotion* in England—and no wonder. Yet we were brought up to revere Moses, flinging his Plagues, his only weapons against the armies of Egypt.

3RD. Whispers on the countryside tell of anxiety, Marian tells me, about the two Shanaglish boys who were taken away and have not been heard of. And the men who took them—military or Black and Tans—came back with them to Coen's in Gort, and bought a rope.

Writing "Memories and Meditations" for I feel as H. James did as the War went on—page 402 Vol II of his letters. And I also am "in time of War"; and see on page 418:— "If you have got something to do stick to it tight and do it with faith and force; some things will, no doubt eventually be redeemed".

4 DECEMBER. J. says it is feared there was "bad work", that the two Loughnane boys from Shanaglish were done away with. "A man MacGill, took notice where a lorry had turned on the road, where it was narrow—and had knocked down a part of the wall, and he wondered to see it broken, and looked behind it, and there were two boys lying, their heads near one another, and dark clothes on them. He went home and it was three days before he could rise from the bed. He told others and when some went to look there after, the bodies were gone and no word of them."

5 DECEMBER. In Henry James's appeal for Belgian refugees "Times Supplement June 23" he writes

> ". . . people surprised by sudden ruffians, murderers or thieves in the dead of night, and marched out terrified and half clad, snatching at the few scant household goods nearest at hand,

into a darkness mitigated but by the flaring incendiary torches—this has been the experience stamped on our scores and scores of thousands whose testimony to utter dismay and despoilment, silence alone, the silence of vain uncontrollable wonderment, has for the most part been able to express."

Is not this just what I have been hearing of from the cross-roads, from Maree, Peterwell?

The mason R. here, says the Black and Tans came back to Shanaglish after two days, looking for the Loughnanes, "said they had escaped, and every one believes they were done away with." It is drink that urges them. He saw the lorries leaving Gort the day Mrs. Quinn was shot; the T.'s in their car firing, and two of them were lying back "lifeless as if drunk".

6 DECEMBER. J., says "there was news brought to him last night that the bodies of those two Loughnane boys were found, near Murty Sheehan's cross roads, in a pond that is back from it towards Ballindoreen. It is said they had no clothes on them, and had the appearance of being choked. It looks very bad, but those Black and Tans can do what they like, and no check on them. Look how the Head Constable was afraid to take a deposition from Mrs. Quinn before she died, and he in the house."

The Connacht Tribune has an advertisement of "German toys in great variety at lower prices"—to be had from—Belfast. Going to the woods with J., he says "At my dinner hour I met two boys from Shanaglish. It is true about the Loughnanes. Friends had gone to the place they were found, and saw the bodies and they knew them, although they could not be sure what way they met their death. The flesh was as if torn off the bones. God help the poor mother! There is one sister but no boy left in the house."

The Abbey has lost £500 in the last quarter—chiefly in the last month, since Curfew came in, and the raids became incessant. We must close till Christmas, and after it, until better times come.

Alec Martin writes saying he and Witt think my "Postscript"[7] injudicious, would like it altered or left out—just two months after I had sent it for their opinion and it comes too late—though I will write to C.E.L.

7 DECEMBER. Marian hears the two Loughnane boys could not be recognised—that "the bodies looked as if they had been dragged after the lorries. When the men in the lorry came to Coen's shop for the rope they took a bottle of whiskey too, and when he asked for payment all they did was to point a revolver at him. The bodies were brought home last night. When they

passed through Gort at 6 o'c., the dead bells were ringing. God help the poor mother, that is a widow!"

"Father C. has sent a notice that any sick calls in the night time are to be sent to the other priest, for he himself will be fired at if he goes out. He knows why they are threatening him, and will tell it bye and bye."

A letter from Lady Greenwood, very kind has

> "gone fully into the Quinn case with my husband, who did, as you say, most sincerely deplore it, and is as anxious as I am that the application for a grant will be sympathetically received. I do not think I am raising false hopes if I say that I expect to be able to write again shortly to tell you that the grant is to be made to the bereaved husband."

7 DECEMBER. J. says "the two funerals passed last night going to Shanaglish. I don't know was the mother there, but the sister went to see the bodies after they were found. She could not recognise one of them, but when she saw the other she called out that it was her youngest brother. It is not known for certain how they came by their death. There are some say they were burned. For Murphy went out into the pond after they were found to bring them in, and when he took a hold of the hand of one of them it came off in his hand. They are giving out that they had to do with the Castle Daly murder, but it's strange that if they knew it was boys scared off, they burned the houses that were near." M. says "It is said when they were taken they gave impudence to the Black and Tans.

It will never be known what way they died. There is no one dare ask a question. But the work they are doing will never be forgotten in Ireland."

8 DECEMBER. M., having been at Mass, says lorries packed with military are passing. "Those boys were winnowing at their mother's house when they were taken, they had been looked for before but had been away, but came back. It is said that the mother came to Gort barracks and asked where they were, and was told they were safe in prison. Another whisper is that the police or soldiers came back a day or two after they had taken them and said they had escaped, asked if they had come home." S. doesn't know how they met with their death but says those "Black and Tans are a terrible class—one of the old police in Gort said to me the other day, as I went to draw my pension, pointing at one of them 'That is what we have to put up with now!' The standard reduced, little chaps of 5 ft. 6—and with no character. There are two in Gort that were

sent up from Kilcolgan where they were suspected of having stolen £120. Filling their pockets from the people in the name of Law and Order".

M.J., says "that Plumber that comes here told me he heard one of them say he was put in Gaol for 7 years for killing his wife, but had only served two of them."

9 DECEMBER. Malachi Quinn here, I read him Lady Greenwood's letter and he was grateful. He says Burke's house that had been burned down and been rebuilt by the neighbours has been raided again in the night by the Black and Tans. He hears they threatened to burn it again, but that the Ardrahan old police have said that if that is done by the "Castle Police" they will all in a body resign.

He knew the Loughnane boys—"One of them may have been a bit in it, but the other was as innocent as myself. It is said they were hanged, and that Gill saw them hanging when he went in over the stile, but that he went back on it and was afraid to say it."

Tim and G. working in the garden tell of it. Tim says "it would break your heart to see that funeral, the two hearses and the poor mother between them. She came from her house but she could not recognise her sons. She had come to the barracks before that looking for tidings of them, and some say she got none, and some say she was told they were at Renmore barracks; and the next day she got tidings they were found. Some say that one of them was bayonetted through the heart. Such a thing could hardly happen in savage lands out in Turkey." J. says "There was an enquiry at the barracks yesterday, and we heard nothing since. It is hard to know what happened. There is no one dare trace or tell".

The "*Independent*" gives Mr. Henry's "printed reply" in Parliament, that "he was informed they escaped from custody and had not since been heard of".

J. says "They say they dragged the eldest boy out and beat him—and the other took his part and they beat him too and the mother looking on."

10 DECEMBER. Today's "*Independent*" reports "The sister gave evidence of making enquiries at Leneboy barrack, where she said she was told by the Commanding Officer that her brothers had escaped".

The Commissioner of Oaths witnessing my signature, said "the soldiers had sent to Mrs. Loughlane's house a couple of days after they had taken the boys, to say they had escaped, and asked if they had gone home—just a bluff".

Gort Hall (S. Colman's) raided last night, and one prisoner taken—he had a letter in Irish in his pocket.

M. says "the B & Ts went into Frenchs' house and took a pair of brown boots and some books. Then they went into C. who is employed by the Post Office and were taking his bicycle, but he said 'I will lay my complaint at the barracks if you take Government property,' and when they saw it was a red bicycle they left it. He and French complained about it and they were sent for to the barracks, and the officer brought out Black and Tans and said 'Tell me if you recognise them' but though they knew them well they would not say it, knowing if they did their house would be burned in the night."

12 DECEMBER. The C. Taylor's chauffeur coming here with O. told "the police in Ardrahan say they found a head and a hand in the same place as the Loughlans were found, but they did not belong to their bodies. It is from the police that comes." As to the proclaiming of counties she says "not to harbour a rebel! and who would give up any one they were sheltering in the house?!" I think of Brownings "Italian in England":

the State
Will give you gold—oh, gold so much!
If you betray me to their clutch,
And be your death, for aught I know,
If once they find you saved their foe.

And it was in England that rebel found sympathy.

13 DECEMBER. Mrs. Pickersgill said yesterday the B & Ts are shooting both Castle Taylor and Crowdane woods without leave, and carrying off the game. J., says "They were in Gort again last night stopping and searching people that had been at the Rosary and were coming away—making them open their jackets and searching them, boys and girls alike."

The basket maker says "Yes, and children too they searched, and a few nights ago they looted Crowdane lane, going in and bringing away even clothing. They are a terrible class, we are haunted by them killing and burning and looting, whipping you off in the dead of night. Look at what they did to those Loughnane boys—and one of them come but lately from school—tying them with a rope to the lorry and burning them. And they burned Kilkelly's barn after, because it is there they were waked, burned it to the ground. And on the Holy day they were looking for the other Loughnane, the comrade boy, that dreamed where they were to be found; and they said if they got him he would never be at the inquest to give evidence. Worse work they are doing than ever was done by Cromwell. (For I was told it was a cousin of these boys who dreamed their bodies were in that pond. And when one of the searchers put down his hand in the water he clasped a dead hand).

"It is the district Councillors they are looking for now—at Ballyann—and up on the road they went to Donohre, but he was not there, and they said they would call again."

J. said "Whenever the Black and Tans come to the town, 8 men of the old police go to keep guard over Father Considine's house. What now will happen if they go in and shoot him? Will the police shoot them again?" M. says, "all the Drumhasna workmen who had returned to work for Ashtown have been forced to do so—the Black and Tans going to their houses and threatening to burn them down if they wouldn't."

I had not heard of their meddling in land disputes before, and this whole reprisal business there seems to have come from no greater crime than cattle-driving.

15 DECEMBER. News today of the burning of Cork.[8]

Cunningham, coming with a goose, says his mother "is not fretting now about the boy in prison—he is safer there than he would be at home. Look what a terrible death they gave the two Loughnane boys—my sister Delia knew them—there was one of them very delicate. And the Black and Tans are passing the road every day. They would not be so bad but they have drink taken".

16TH. I asked J., if it was true about the Ashtown tenants being forced to work, and he said "Yes, there were notices put up saying if they did not their houses would be burned down. Co. coming later to see me about the rates, says the same thing. J., said "Is Lord A., in the army? He must have the great influence to make them do that for him." C. says, "What are they at at all, taking away and murdering the two sons of a widow? There are some of them leaving Drumhasna now and coming to Ballylee. There have provisions been sent there today. It is likely it is to bring prisoners to him; they will find more facilities there, to bring them over the bridge and drown them in the river. For Drumhasna is as Cromwell said, without a tree for hanging or water for drowning. A bad class—for it is not drink that urges them it is cruelty." Mr. Edmunds motoring us to Galway says with pride that 15 officers of the Guards have volunteered to come as privates among them. I say if they come to stay it would be an improvement to have at least gentlemen.

In Galway A., tells me her nurse is engaged to a Black and Tan but he says "I am not like the others—I am a University man and it was a great shock to me to find what sort of men they are. I am not like them, I don't like killing people." He was at tea in the kitchen but took only half a cup of tea and was so excited by it "you would think he had taken something stronger" Maggie says. He had had shell shock.

I see in *The Times* of 14th the Martial Law order—Gen. Macreedy's "Great Britain has no quarrel with Irishmen . . . her sole enemies are those who have countenanced, inspired or participated in rebellion, murder and outrage"! General Tudor in the same paper, calling for recruits "draws attention to the magnificent service which is being rendered to the Empire by the Auxiliary Division of the R.I.C., their influence has been of the greatest value. With their comrades in the R.I.C., proper they are lifting the terror of the pistol from the people of Ireland." This after Croke Park, Cork, the Loughnane brothers. A., says Doreen's fiancé had suggested that Mrs. W. should get a permit from the Black and Tans—"What for?" "Oh, to keep them from raiding the house."

19TH. Gort yesterday to receive Margaret and Richard, the latter so well and is so bright and cheery.

20TH. T. Diveney here, wanting a letter from me to the Transport Union. He has been writing there. The car man told me yesterday to "take care what would you write, for three times in the last week or so the Black and Tans stopped the car and took the letters and went through them, and if you were saying anything about them your life wouldn't be safe."

"They put up a notice in Ardrahan that if Lord Ashtown's workmen did not go back to work by the 1st December their houses would be burned. It was about land the dispute was, and they would not work for him."

21ST. Captain Turner called yesterday, told Margaret two men had been found examining the barracks and had run away when found—and they had fired after them but missed; and that "no one has any idea what a bad state Gort is in"!

Old Niland says he has "a grand pair of boots" given him by one of the old police—"they haven't much use for them, they're getting the time idle enough."

24TH. News of the invasion of Aran,[9] and three men shot. In Synge's *Playboy* Peegeen Mike says: "If I'd that lad in the house I wouldn't be fearing the loosed kharki cut-throats, or the walking dead." And the Lord Chamberlain's censor had ordered this passage to be cut out "together with any others that may seem derogatory to His Majesty's Forces". It is likely those forces are being spoken of this Christmas Eve in Aran in yet more loaded words than even Synge's fancy could create.

26 DECEMBER. Mr. Johnson says they are overpowered with work at the Bank—all the people are bringing in their money to put in deposit, to save it from the Black and Tans, since the robbing in Kinvara of £200 from Flattery about a week ago."

J. says, "The poorest creature has some fireside to come in to. But God help the boys on the run."

Father Considine preached yesterday advising the people to keep no money in their houses "and don't be telling me you must keep enough to run the house. If it's taken you'll get no satisfaction." The Wren-boys have been here—4 sets of them—not very well up in their lines about the Wren but all singing "The Soldier's Song".[10]

Margaret back from church says Miss Daly told Captain Turner what I had said about leaving out "God Save the King", on the ground that it turns our mind to politics when it should be turned to religion. And he said "If you do that is very simple. I would order it on again!"

A., writes that Dillon said in joke to a countryman coming to his shop "Have you brought me a turkey?" and he said, "If you want turkeys it's to Leneboy barrack you must go—it's there they'll have the queer Christmas dinner"! M. says "Why wouldn't they, going into houses and taking sucking pigs and whiskey and everything they take a fancy to, and walking off with it."

29 DECEMBER. The chicks have been very happy through Christmas. Their railway out of fashion and billiards in. The Christmas Tree party quite pleasant and easy.

Last night I asked Margaret what she was going to do about A., and C., for the Spring—she said "Nothing, unless I get River Court—there is no room for them in the present house." Poor Chicks—I must do my best for them. Harris has twice written that I should go up to Dublin about the Theatre—"it is very slack"—but as we must shut till Curfew is done with (having lost £500 through it) that can wait.

Mike to say two larch trees have been cut in the nut wood, and dragged, with a horse, to the lake, and put into it to float away to Cranagh, but the wind came the other way and they are at our side, and we are getting them up. They saw 2 men one of them young Glynn, going away from them. It is rather heartbreaking—this treatment from our neighbours.

31ST. Mr. J. came to tea—he says £200 was taken from Lydon at Duras, and the rush to lodge money at the Bank goes on—£2,000 having been brought "from the mountains" by one man, but probably others had joined with him to get the higher interest—5%. Yeats writes in consternation at the idea of B & Ts going to Ballylee and wants "the name of the Commanding officer in Gort for George's solicitor to write to"!

1 JANUARY, 1921. A clouded night; but today I am more tranquil. I have had a talk with Margaret—she says that Coole takes £800 a year to keep up and brings in nothing so that we cannot keep it and her London home and she and the children could not stay here all the year round. So after discussions I agreed to her plan of trying to let it for 7 (9) years, to Richard coming of age and he can decide then about keeping it. Burren will be kept for the summer and River Court be the home for the rest of the year, there is a good day school for A., and C. I shall be glad if this can be carried out. It is quite different from an irrevocable selling of the place. And I am thankful that even Catherine is now 7 years old and they all know the happiness of the country life and could return to it, as I have done with content. So I think this may bring a better understanding. For myself I may buy a little home—Beach House at Burren—that is to be with the children for the summer holidays. M. talks again of giving up Coole . . . But for my sunset it doesn't much matter—I shall just work anywhere while mind and energy last—and after that—what does the last phase matter, except to be in no one's way.

S. here. He says the Black and Tans are simply robbers "not looking for prisoners or revolvers, but out for loot. Men who joined the army for plunder and have taken this job of a year for plunder" an English friend of his in the R.D.S. in charge at Lisdoonvara says "none of them should be let out without a keeper". Aran had been so peaceful that the police had been removed to other places, it did not need police. Then these B & Ts visited it, shot and killed one man or more, but chiefly plundered, taking even the womens' wedding rings. This they have heard from a man in Aran connected with their business—and their Aran maid has had the same account from some friends. (I see in the paper that after a while on the Island they got drunk—) Sir Alfred Lyall wrote me in Nov., 1900:

> "So far as I can see we may now be in for another Century's estrangement between Irish and English . . . Nor do I see what remedies we have to try, since Home Rule has less chance than ever in the present temper of the English who are becoming accustomed to the use of force, and their determination to be dominant wherever they dwell. This Boer War must now, having fallen into fierce methods, leave traces that will last

long, and we seem likely to be driven to Cromwellian expedients for quieting an obstinate resistance. The close reality of these things puts me out of humour with my literary dissertations upon the heroic poetry of ancient days, where distance lends enchantment to the stories of slaughtered men and burning towns."

When S. spoke of the B & Ts method, X. said: "There is one good deed they did, burning Burke's house. He was intimidating Lord Ashtown's labourers and they forced them to come back to work and saved 14 acres of oats for him". The Labour Party should be interested in this strike breaking experiment. They had destroyed all Burke's harvest save one rick of barley that was out of sight.

X.'s police friend tells him that the next two months will be the worst yet—the rounding up of men and what it leads to.

J., says "Some that passed me yesterday through Gort were wearing ladies' furs around their necks that they had robbed from some house".

3 JANUARY. Yesterday M. had an argument with the new D.I., Captain Blake about the B & Ts—she objecting to "licensed murder" though opposing Sinn Fein. About Mrs. Quinn's death he said it was not done by a B & T, but by one of his own police; they know who it was.

5 JANUARY. To Galway yesterday— Margaret saw Mrs. M., an officers wife, yesterday who told her the stealing by the B & Ts (and Auxiliarys) is disgraceful. Her husband knows as a certainty that one officer at Renmore barracks has made £1000 by looting. Her husband means to use strong measures and dismiss those who rob in future. She said Arthur Persse had been to look for police protection as he expects trouble about his land—but it was refused because he had gone to the S.F., Arbitration Court.

F. says this is not true—what he went to Galway for was to ask for Hogan's release from the internment camp—as his land question can't be settled while he is kept there.

M. Quinn here today, it is true Burke's house has been raided again, but they couldn't find the eldest boy, and only dragged the other out and thrashed him.

The piper here—had been ill in the workhouse at Portumna, but was well treated except in tea— "Did you hear talk ever of the fair-haired tea?"—but he had complained to the doctor, and he had ordered the nurses to "put a colour on it" next day.

"The Black and Tans are queer hawks, you wouldn't like to be under them any hours at all. The less of them is the best. But I was in a herd's house—a well-off house near dad Ffrench's and they came in and searched the house and brought the man away. In the night time we heard a great beating and hammering at the door and I knew what they were by the nature of their talk. I lay shivering, stretched in my little bed, but they heard me moving and did no harm. They asked me who was I and I said a poor dark man and they asked did I carry a gun and I said I did not. They had brought a great many bottles of whiskey from some house in Ahascragh and they put them on the table and were drinking them, and they asked me did I like whiskey and I said I did not, but I'd take a little, for I was shaking with fear of them. And they filled out the full of a tea cup and put it on the dresser and told me not to let the cat get at it, and they went away.

"Up in Roscommon where there was a land dispute they shot the cattle that were put upon the land. And they put something in whatever they shot them with that left them no use for eating but they had to be burned . . . In two or three places in Roscommon they did that" Frank says D. goes out shooting under police protection lest the B & Ts could see him when he is near the road and fire. F. advises him to carry a Union Jack as they could not fire on that.

8TH. Ed. writes that his —————— to the Archdeacon.

10 JANUARY. Chicks with colds, but gay—Richard painting and this morning looking at the pastels and paintings upstairs, and also asking if AE and Jack Yeats ever come now.

14 JANUARY, 1921. On Monday I had a long talk with Margaret. By her showing we cannot keep the woods—she thought not the house—that all must go ———— land and rates so high. We went through and through. I asked how much she thought she ought to give to keep the house going. She said, nothing, that it would be only for the Christmas holidays. I awoke in the night and thought it over and over—taking it to the "Higher Court". I could not and cannot see it right to abandon it, if it be possible to keep it—a place of rest and security for the children in the midst of a changing world. I thought and thought and decided that if I could sell some things I might keep it; Yeats portrait by A. John—and my writing table, and the books given me by authors. I talked again to her next day and we walked out to see how much we could cut off and what we could keep. We planned out keeping Nut Wood, Pond field, Shanwalla, to Lake farm gate—tillage fields and the strip of trees beyond them and plantations. This would make a little demesne about 350 acres, wooded and romantic and beautiful, tho' any who know the old woods would miss the extent. This she thinks—even this—

would come to £300 a year in rates and taxes. Then what makes it the more desirable I thought that perhaps the 300 acres woodland we sell might be taken for forestry and so be kept as woods—a great advantage instead of selling them to farmers or timber merchants who would cut them down and turn in cattle. I should be quite satisfied could this be done and would try hard to attain the £300 a year by selling things and try to do the rest out of my income—under £500 a year outside my uncertain earnings!* I would be sorry not to keep the place so many have loved, I told M. that Anne would be the one to miss it most and to this she agreed.

If this plan is impossible—then House,.Gardens—back lawn, field, Shanwalla she thought £150 rates and taxes.

She is against my selling the writing table—but doesn't grudge the books. I feel more peaceful having a clear understanding. I have written to Robinson to try and find out about Forestry purchase probabilities.

We, Anne, Cat and I motored with the ——— to Galway and spent the day with Godmother.

* 22 APRIL, 1928. This idea was only carried out six months ago, though I have been paying all expenses in these last years, and without having to sell anything my plays & books have carried me through.

BOOK ELEVEN

JANUARY, 1921. Mr. Reginald Geary The Black and Tan (engaged to A.'s nurse) is very indignant because during a few days when he was away ill his fellow B & Ts had stolen his blankets!

16TH. Yesterday, in the woods with the children, looking for primroses we heard a dog hunting and the children said that down by the lake the day before they had seen men with dogs, and rabbits they had caught. I have told Mike, and he says young ash have been cut in the more distant plantations. There have been no petty sessions for a long time and the Volunteers have been taken away or are on the run—so there is no law at present. It reconciles me to losing the woods, if we cannot mind them.

19TH. M.J., says Gort is quieter "not so many Black and Tans kicking about as there used to be."

The police came this morning, a troop of them on the lawn, two at the door to ask for the permit for shooting to be given back. I didn't think we had one, for all the guns were given up to the barracks long ago, but searching the silver box found one, a permit for Richard to use his single barrelled gun (also in the barracks) and this I surrendered. The police acknowledged that the neighbourhood is better, and hoped it would not be necessary "to take more lively measures". While they were here an aeroplane was circling overhead.

Mike has found some youngsters with terriers about the woods, but warned them off. All we can do is to claim our right to the woods, until some law is established in the country.

Reading *Robinson Crusoe* to the children. Writing about Sir A. Lyall. A cheque for £43 from French U.S.A. for plays (£15 for *Dragon* at Cambridge) fills me with hope of being able to keep Coole.

I had rather a miserable night, bread bill being so high I thought I must surrender!

I had written vehemently to Yeats, seeing he was going to a meeting at Drury Lane of Theatre Managers, to promise performances for "ex-warriors"—and we must keep the Abbey free from Black and Tan sympathies—so was relieved by his answer.

20 JANUARY. Tired from a bad night, but a quiet day, the

usual round, looked at the papers, ordered dinners and gave out stores—taught the chicks for an hour by the hour glass. Anne read part of a chapter of the Gospel, Catherine reads her lesson and writes a copy; geography for both and a little French. Today they worked at their samplers. I wrote letters for post, and worked a little at the chapter on Sir A. Lyall[1]—the children drove Puddah to post the letters. Lunch, out to see Connelly mending vinery door, etc.—then an hour or two at Lyall article, beginning to type it. Made list of apples for garden for Dicksons. To the woods; tea; *Robinson Crusoe* to read to chicks while they roasted chestnuts, and again after they went to bed. Reading Lyall's book on Tennyson.

22ND. Mike found three of the Gort women who are allowed to take away fallen branches, cutting young ash with saws, which he took from them, also Mrs. Cooney's son and another youngster with dogs in the woods, trying to get rabbits out of a wall.

Received from Murray a first copy of *Hugh Lane*. It looks well, light in the hand and well printed; a mistake or two at first glance, one mine, one the printers, but a relief it is ready, so small and tidy when I think of the immense litter that went on growing for a year. Raftery here to mend a crack over window. He told me of the reprisals at Sixmilebridge, I said we are pretty free now of the Black and Tans but he said "We are not free of them yet. There were some of them in the town yesterday, four of them were going about the streets very drunk. I was flagging a side walk before Fahey's shop, and one of them stopped and looked at the walk and asked me what was I doing, so I told him. Then he said 'What do you call that?' and I said it was a shovel, and with that he kicked it into the street. Then he began kicking the rest of the things about, a bucket he near kicked in through the shop window. He came back again with the others, and they kicked everything about and the language they used was not fit to be listening to. It is terrible to put arms into the hands of those men. The soldiers of the military are not like that, but if they saw you in a hole would give you a hand out."

He seemed as if shaken with shame as well as anger when telling this, and I thought of the old verse:

"To deal with such men is but pain
For either must you fight or flee,
Or else no answer make again
But play the beast and let them be."

J.D., from the market says cattle are gone down because of the order against exporting, on account of the Foot and Mouth disease in Wicklow, "and everyone is uneasy, for one time before when it broke out there were cattle ordered to be killed that were never near the place where it was, and cows in calf that were never near it; but there were many prayed at the time that the English might never die till they would be in want of a bit of butter or a sup of milk."

Yeats wrote a bad opinion on *Aristotle's Bellows*.

25TH. Yesterday with the children to Roxborough, a very pleasant glimpse of the old home, though a little sad to look from the garden at the mountain side, now sold. Arthur says there are poachers and timber cutters coming in, but that there is nothing to do, no law to appeal to, he agrees that the Sinn Fein Courts were wonderful in keeping order. We passed the blackened walls of the Howley's house. The woman—J., does not know where, the two boys on the run. Today Mr. McNicols, the Horticultural instructor, came to give advice about pruning and said how much improved the garden was since his last visit. He is trying to get the farmers to plant more fruit trees, but they are not inclined to in this time of unrest. He himself was anxious to be back in good time lest he might meet a lorry. He is told of a day on the Headford road when a lorry stopped whenever it met a young man on a bicycle, and each time pulled the cyclist off, strapped and beat him, then put the bicycle under the wheels of the lorry and went on. He spoke in horror of the Loughnane case; thinks it the worst and most brutal of all.

Mr. Johnson later, delighted with Kinglake's first volume and took two more.[2]

29 JANUARY. Basket maker here—says the B & Ts have left Drumhasna "a bad class, they haunted by night and by day with the wind of the word they would have set fire to many a house in Gort, but the D.I. kept them from it, and they had to content themselves with taking what they could, and destroying any picture of Pearse, or any ballad." "It's time for me to go on with my ballad collection". "It is not", he says, "to find one on you they might whip you away". "We can't say nothing", says J.D., talking of Tom O.L. "The two Hayes have almost killed Peter Glynn, on a quarrel about right of way."

31 JANUARY. Peter says "they are gone out of it now and time for them. Killings and burnings, homes destroyed and families scattered."

3 FEBRUARY. The children have been laid up with colds and now I have one, not good for much but didn't like to stay in my room.

Looking over *Aristotle* a little—have put the cats' speeches in rhyme.

4 FEBRUARY. Yesterday, coming down with a bad cold, Patrick Murphy the mason asked to see me. Captain Blake, the R.U.'s car had run into his cart and the mudguard was broken, and he has been asked to pay £12.5.6 for the mending. He had pulled his cart to the side of the road when he heard the motor, but it dashed on in the middle, as is the R.I.C., habit. I gave him a letter testifying to his good character and industry, for with 4 acres (until Lisheen Crannagh was sold, when he bought a few more) he brought up his family on what he earned as a mason. He says the Black and Tans came one night and carried off a new bicycle of his son's from an outhouse. It had cost £16. He put in a complaint to the Head Constable but got nothing.

Poor little Catherine had earache last night and cried pitifully, but warm oil in the ear, and a flannel bag I made, with hot salt in it got her off to sleep. But I have such a bad cold! and it is raining.

5TH. Down, stupid with cold, but had felt when I awoke that Lord Northcliffe must be written to about supporting the picture claim so wrote a draft and then made blunders in the copying, but got it off—A. wrote also to a forester.

Dear Lord Northcliffe,

You were good enough to give me a sympathetic hearing some time ago when I asked your help in getting Hugh Lane's French pictures back to Ireland, and you gave immediate help by putting a statement of mine in *The Times*.

The pictures have not yet been restored. This is how the matter now stands. The National Gallery Trustees say they have no power to give up property legally bequeathed to them. Several of the Trustees however, Lord Brownlow, Lord Plymouth, Lord Ribblesdale, Mr. Heseltine have expressed their willingness to accept a Government Bill enabling them (by legalising Hugh Lane's unwitnessed codicil) to give them up. Lord D'Abernon, has proposed a compromise, but not one we could accept. Mr. Macpherson, when Chief Secretary, went into the matter, examining my statement and one drawn up on behalf of the Trustees by Mr. R. C. Witt and Mr. MacColl. His conclusion was that he was "convinced that Sir Hugh Lane intended the codicil to be carried out at the time he wrote it and at the time of his death". Mr. Macpherson then prepared a Bill and brought it more than once before the Cabinet. It was I understand still before it at the time he left office. He told me privately that the Cabinet was equally divided—the lawyers against any tampering with legality—the Scotch, including Mr. Balfour and Mr. Bonar Law for it, because the unwitnessed codicil would have been valid in Scotland. He told me also that the real obstacle was Lord Curzon's violence whenever the subject was mentioned. (He had asked Hugh Lane for the pictures and had been refused and is bent on getting them now). Sir Hamar Greenwood on succeeding Mr. Macpherson promised his help. I have not made any new appeal of late, because I was waiting for the publication of this book, which I venture to offer you, as it gives the facts more fully than has yet been done. But now it is likely that interest in the question will revive. You were good enough to offer the help of *The Times*, of course the most valuable we could possibly have; a few words in it now might turn the scale.

Mr. Macpherson might probably give more exact information as to the prospects of his Bill. I gave him the letters written by friendly Trustees. You have been doing so much for Ireland in these unhappy times that I feel the more confidence in making my request.

A.G.

SUMMARY of the CASE. Hugh Lane being angry at some ungracious treatment in Dublin connected with the Gallery he had founded there, made a Will in which he bequeathed to the London National Gallery Trustees a group of foreign pictures he had intended for the Dublin Gallery. Later, being reconciled to Dublin, and but a few months before his death, he revoked in a codicil this bequest, leaving the pictures according to his original intention to Dublin. This codicil is in his own handwriting, is signed and initialled by him; he put it in a sealed envelope addressed to his sister who had charge of his Will. Many of his friends have given evidence, some in sworn statements, that this codicil was according to his intention. But the signature was unwitnessed, and a Bill legalising it is necessary before the London Trustees can abandon their claim.

6 FEBRUARY. Deaf and dull with this cold, but read to the children about Moses' troubles in freeing his people—and then looked for this scrap I had written last year and copied it.

6 JULY, 1919. For myself I have tried to do my work apart from politics, my formula has long been "not working for Home Rule but preparing for it"; and whatever may be done or left un-

done by Government I hope to go on with the endeavour to do for Hugh Lane's pictures from those who are holding them from us (as I believe against his intention and desire).

As to the form of Government I would prefer to see come into being I have but little right to speak, for there remain at most but a few years in which I may enjoy or endure it. Yet it is my persuasion, my confession to myself—though not as yet to others—that among us "the essential forms of temperance, courage, liberality, magnificence and their kindred" would best thrive and grow under a Commonwealth. That word, as its kindred one "Republic", has a high and noble tradition that stirs the imagination, as "Dominion"—"a territory, region, district, considered as a subject" could never do. For if, as may be in the British Dominions, imagination is prone to turn towards Westminster or Windsor, it is in part because of the constant inflowing of men and women born and bred in the Kingdom of England. But those of our kindred who come to us over the sea are not from a Kingdom, but from the great Republic that has been their refuge and has become their home. Mr. Roosevelt once talking to me of Ireland's difficulties said:- "We are too far off or she might be taken as a State'. We can do those things." But though that may not be, I am certain America would give the little Republic that delighted ungrudging welcome, that having no savour of patronage can give help that has none of bitterness.

I know that some who now, as they would not a while ago, countenance the word "Dominion", and yet tell those who have "Republic" on their lips that such a cry is but a waste of breath, a thing out of measure. Yet, over here are some who prophesy that what is impossible today may be possible tomorrow; and I remember a poet saying to me a long time ago "A prophet is an unreasonable person sent by Providence when it is going to do an unreasonable thing".

A.G. 7 JULY, 1919.

6 FEBRUARY, 1921. And yet one day last summer as I was talking with some young Sinn Fein Volunteers who were bravely doing their best through their Courts to restore law and order, I said, "if I were a politician, which I am not, and if I had authority, which I have not, I would say, Accept Dominion Home Rule. For in the course of years all the Dominions will become Republics, and then Ireland, their fellow will be one among them."

A. GREGORY

13TH. Ups and downs, still ill with cold. About sale of Coole Margaret writes 8th that "Nicholas says a let is impossible and 'it is sheer insanity to keep it' which I told him I was perfectly aware of, and said if sentiment prevented one from doing what was the only reasonable and obvious thing to do, that we should keep house and garden only—just your suggestion in fact. . . . If I ever had any lingering doubts about Coole they have now gone for ever, but I am prepared to do whatever you want with the house and a minimum of land so long as it does not permanently injure the children's future". Not very encouraging, but I had written to try to get acreage and rating of woods. Then, two days ago, Mr. Edmunds and Mr. Johnson called, and I consulted them, and both said the Valuation office is the place to get this information from, and Mr. E. promised to get it for me. He is vague as to woods being bought, but I had found through Robinson that Mr. Ponsonby is head of Forestry department and told Margaret and she wrote she was to meet him at dinner—and yesterday second post her letter about meeting him came, and filled me with hope and joy!

This rather dashed later by Frank coming and telling me she is taking Celbridge[3], but that I am not to be told at present.

Mr. Johnson said the Black and Tans are back at Gort, "on a visit". And today, going to church, John tells me they burned several houses near Kinvara for no known reason. Mr. Edmunds said he had dined with the officers at Ennis and they had abused the Government for not giving them their way, "that is, letting them shoot 50 S.F., men for every one shot by S.F." He tried rather feebly to take their part; but Mr. Johnson said "There are very bad lads among the Black and Tans."

Trying, through my dullness and cold, to write of Sir F. Burton.

14TH. Mrs. Watts, 13 Birch Lane, Longsight, Manchester, called, she is on a mission to find out what is going on. We had a talk and she stayed to lunch, and then I sent her to see Father Considine, as I would like her to see the mother of the Loughnane boys, and he might manage it.

Tim says: (and J.D., the same) "The B & Ts arrived on Friday at Burke's, Ballyvohane, near Kinvara. Three or four boys were playing cards there, they took them out and beat them cruelly, knocking down a wall on one of them, and breaking his arm." It is not certain if they burned the house, he believes they did. J.D. says Mrs. Quinn's house near the same place was burned the same day with all its furniture, and that £80 hidden in the pillow of her bed was found and taken away by the invaders. No reason was given for the attack.

Mrs. Watts says she has been looking for a Unionist to put the other side of the case but hasn't been able to find one!

J.D. says "you'd be sorry for the boys on the run. There is young Staunton, some one that saw him was telling me he is nothing but skin and bone. There isn't a house but would be open to them but what can you do? There are a great many spies about."

19 FEBRUARY. Mr. Edmunds here last night and says there has been a great scare, a bomb thrown into Eglinton Barrack yard, the explosion caused a panic. But it was thrown by a Black and Tan who came back drunk, and was indignant at finding the gate closed. There is a bad feeling now between them and the military. They burned a house down because the two boys are said to be out and out Sinn Feiners. But the old man and their father had not been mixed with it, and the military are angry because he used to supply the mess with chickens.

DUBLIN 25 FEBRUARY. In Galway I settled for the chicks to go for morning school to Miss Anderson; and gave them spades to dig by the sea afterwards and so left them to come to Dublin. I had a chat with Robinson who met me and came to tea, and we went to see Drama League in *The Witch*[4] at the Abbey. John Dillon there. I said we had not yet got the Lane pictures, and he said rather gloomily "you will be a very remarkable person if you do get them". Harris came yesterday morning, is to get account ready to see how long we can go on at the Abbey.

In the afternoon I went to see A.E., and we had a long talk, interrupted once by the telephone, on which he was told of the destruction of another creamery at Inver, Donegal. He is not very hopeful, thinks Sinn Feiners so embittered now by all that has happened that they will not accept any connection with England. The most hopeful feature, he thinks, is the coming over of Unionists, as Mr. Herbert (?Vincent W.B.Y.) of Muckross and many others. Some visitor asked him the other day to introduce him to Unionists and he couldn't think of one. As to his interview with the Prime Minister, he thinks he is a pleasant openminded man, ignorant, reading nothing, learning everything by conversation, but of no use because he is not Prime Minister in his own Cabinet. This he judges of by his own experience as a negotiator. He had he thinks convinced him that the withdrawal of 18 millions a year would prevent any proper economic development, and Lloyd George had been very much interested in his argument and said, "No one ever told me that before" and that he would be prepared to deal liberally on that scale. But when he met his Cabinet all went to dust. General ? had told A E that there is a letter in existence which would ruin L.G. (Not one? no more than this) and the few who hold it have all been given big offices.

He had just been reading Hugh's *Life*, which is but just out, and likes it, likes the "crowd of miscellaneous bits and opinions, which gives so clear an impression of him." Mrs. Duncan (at the Abbey) delighted with it, thinks it gives a very clear impression, at least to those who knew him. Sara Purser also pleased with what she has read, and Harris "wonders how I have been able to do it". Such a relief it is out! and I am trying to get the pictures demanded back in the reviews. *The Revolutionist* at the Abbey with a large audience all much interested in the play . . .[5]

Mrs. MacSwiney was there, I went to meet her in the Green Room, such a charming face and manner—"a sweet girl" she would have been called a while ago. I told her with what pride we gave this play for the first time, that we felt we were laying a wreath upon the grave.

SUNDAY 27TH. Splendid audiences. Yesterday's matinée the stalls were not full, but so many people were standing in the Pit that I sent for Robinson, and we brought all we could find places for to the front. Last night all places full, many turned away at the door. We had already decided to play it again next week, and R. announced this from the stage. I feel so happy that we have been able to keep the Abbey going if only for this one week, the production of a national play of fine quality by one who has literally given his life to save the lives of others. For by his death and endurance he has made it unnecessary for any other prisoners to protest through hunger strike; he has done it once for all. It is strange to see the change in political thought now; the audience (in spite of Robinson's request in the programmes for no applause during acts) cheering the revolutionist who stands up against the priest's denunciation, denounces his meddling in return. They applauded also fine sentences "Life is a divine adventure; he will go farthest who has most faith".

We had a reading of *Aristotle's Bellows* the company delighted in it. W. Shields is going to "have a week's sickness" to work at it, the highest compliment he can pay.

Harris has gone through accounts and says we can play on for the present without borrowing, though we have dropped about £150 a quarter. But last week's £170 on Lord Mayor's play should help to reduce this. Nice letter from Birrell and from Ricketts about Hugh's *Life*. The Duncans like it—and I have been to see them to ask their help about reviews here—that is, to get the papers to demand the return of the pictures.

I have a note from Lord Northcliffe's secretary—I had written to him and sent the book.

Yesterday I went to see Jack Yeats's pictures.[6] He is increasing I think in beauty of colour and in richness. "The Tinker's Fire" a lovely thing, he says he has to put high prices on now, because painting a big picture takes so much more out of him. Then to Mrs. Childers—she has "gleams of hope" chiefly because some people are coming over to Ireland to see for themselves what is being done.

2 MARCH. COOLE. Came home yesterday *via* Galway. I went to tea with Sarah Purser on Sunday, she is much pleased because I had written of her good work in getting up the Hone-Yeats exhibition which had been Hugh's first acquaintance with their work. And this I had done without any hint from her or others, but just from finding from the old catalogues what she had done. She told me of a French newspaper paragraph telling of a bequest to the Louvre, carried out by the executors, though not in legal form. She, anxious as we must be about the country, hears that the extreme Sinn Feiners now declare they will fight it out this time, even if the rest of Dublin is burnt down.

Monday morning at the Abbey they were rehearsing *Aristotle*; very cheerily.

In Galway I found the chicks well and merry, and liking school, so will leave them on. [I went to see Mr. Cruise about Malachi Quinn's compensation—so very small—but he says there is no use in trying to get it increased.] I said the interest on £300 would not even pay a servant to take the wife's place in housework, but he said the father of a boy shot by mistake had only been given £150.

I said the policemens' families were given much larger compensation which seemed hardly fair, but he gave the, I think inadequate reason, that the County Court Judges fixed these. He asked what policy I would propose? I said I was no politician, I have no taste for politics, and besides this I had to keep out of them, because I could do my work better about Hugh's pictures, and especially in the Abbey which I think so important. He said, "yes, that is of great importance". Then presently he said, "I once sent a play there and it was refused!" He told me the plot, a dispute about a right of way, but I didn't remember it. We did talk politics a little, or rather a possible settlement. He says the Government cannot give in because Egypt and India would then think they had but to murder policemen to get their self-government. I said the present troubles were doing as much to injure the Government in India and Egypt as anything else could do, and he assented. I told him that I had said to the Volunteers that I would prefer a republic, but were I in authority would accept Dominion Home Rule because the Dominions will one day be republics. He blames S.F., for rejecting the present Home Rule Bill,[7] says if they would accept it the Government would give them almost anything they want; and blamed people for objecting to it who had not read it. I said I had not read it, but that it was so strongly objected to by the three provinces that I did not see how De Valera could, if he would, accept it and keep self respect. I told him what A.E. said, that the Prime Minister is not master in the Cabinet. Then he asked if De Valera would be master enough to carry a settlement against Michael Collins. (Of course one feels that he may have to shed Collins and Lloyd George Bonar Law, before any settlement can come). We parted in the room cordially enough, but on the steps he renewed an offer to send me back to Coole in his own car. I had refused, making excuses, but when he pressed it I said "the real truth is I would lose my character if I went home in a police car". He seemed hurt, but I explained I had all through kept free from official surroundings, I was working with Nationalists, and they have so often been deserted or betrayed. I told him of G. Wyndham's offer of £5, and how Lady Aberdeen had asked me to dine at the V.L., offering not to have my name put in the papers ("people often dine with us whose names are not sent to the papers") but I had refused on this ground. He defended his B. & Ts—yet read me a letter from the Schoolmaster at Kilchriest begging for protection, as he was threatened night and day, and ordered to leave within a week. I was surprised and said, "Is he a Unionist?" But he said "No, the threats are from the Forces of the Crown". (I heard afterwards he had spoken at a farmer's meeting in favour of the division of ranches).

All quiet here, but J.D., says "a lady has been staying at Lally's Hotel who went about, to Shanaglish, and to M. Quinn's and other places—and the police arrested her a couple of days ago and took her away." He thought it might have been Mrs. Watts; but she had left the day after she was here.

I asked again about Mrs. Quinn's house at Caheraboneen. He says the young men were stripped naked, thrown down, a heavy stone put on their backs to keep them from moving, and then flogged, "They will never be the better of it. And there is no one knows what it was for". They had taken her money before burning the house.

Captain Blake the R.M., "has a bad name. He will let poor Patrick Murphy off nothing. He came in his motor a few days ago and followed him to Lisheen Crannagh and asked did he pay the £12 and when Murphy said he was a poor man he said 'You'll be a damned deal poorer before I've done with you—for I'll make you pay every penny of it.'"

A pleasant letter from Yeats about the Hugh Lane book met me, and cheered me very much. He thinks "it will be a most powerful influence" and thinks too "it may bring the pictures back to us". "It gives me a great impression of intellectual energy and not only in the writer" . . . And he says "the poem given on page 138 'To a Friend',[8] it was meant for you, not for Lane" so I feel the richer for that!

Also Northcliffe's secretary sent me copy of a letter in last Monday's *Times* by "A Friend of Lane's", and giving my own summary of the case as I wrote it to Lord Northcliffe. This puts *The Times* on our side, yet agitates me lest a controversy should begin. I wired and wrote to Miss Purser to get (as I had already suggested) S. Gwynn to write about pictures in *The Observer*, and quote her French paper paragraph, and I wrote asking Yeats to watch for any chance of helping. Sent off crocuses from the chicks' garden to them. The place very still without them—not a sound.

Coole
Wednesday, 2 March

Darling Anne and Cat,

These crocuses are all from your own little gardens, I know you will like to give them to Godmother yourselves. The little bunch tied up are Cat's; the two daffodils, the only ones out, are from your little garden path by the swing, I never thought they would bloom so soon after transplanting.

Delia met me at Athenry, and the carriage met us at Gort, luckily, for there was a heavy shower going on. John had got the car ready, and when the rain came he had only just time to change. Pip was at the door, but received me very quietly, I think he was disappointed that you had not come. Mary says he missed you dreadfully and cried for several days. He goes out a good deal with Mike John, and hasn't hunted the chickens, and looks well fed. Mary gave me some delicious raw rabbit livers for the kittens, and I had a warm welcome from them, I don't think they had been given anything except their milk and Tim's bread. They jumped for joy when they saw my parcel. I put it on the vinery floor and they began to tear it, each seizing a piece. They look very well, Tiger quite a giant, and like most giants rather a goose, for when I went across to the other vinery to speak to Tim, he left the meat and followed me, thinking I had something more, and when I took him back there was only one little bit left, hidden under the paper, but I gave him that. This morning they walked round me while I gathered the flowers.

It seems so strange and lonely not having my chicks, but I am glad you are having the school and sea air, and indeed everything you can wish for! Richard's letter was in the carriage to meet me, please send it back, for my collection. There are twelve lambs, I haven't seen them yet; and we have planted six more little apple trees, the Mr. Gladstones among them. Tell Godmother I won't write to her as I am writing to you.

Goodbye, my chicks, much, much love from.

GRANDMAMA

3 MARCH. Seeing in the paper last evening that this was Jupiter's month I wondered if that would have any effect on me, for March has brought good and bad; my birth, my marriage, my mother's death, my husband's death. I had looked through *The Times* and seen nothing about the pictures, but late in the evening I saw a paragraph, written I should guess by Witt, Curzon and D'Abernon, saying the Trustees intend to keep them, and this agitated me, as such things do when one is alone. But later yet I thought it is best they have said this, we know where we stand. Today I have written to MacPherson asking about his Bill, and to Birrell asking if he would write a review in *The Daily News* with a word to help the case. This morning a letter from Margaret saying there is no chance of the Forestry Department buying the woods; and that she has no money to pay labour or coal.

Then a letter from Stephens, stirred up by Langton Douglas[9] and very angry at what I said about the irksomeness of the Gallery and "it is with pleasure I relinquish your acquaintance!" I am sorry.

A.E. sends a nice letter and a nice notice he has written for *The Homestead*,[10] and with a delightful comparison of the Trustees to the Black and Tans. What else will the day bring?

4 MARCH. (my wedding day, 41 years ago!) It brought nothing more, being a pouring wet day, but troublesome letter

writing, to poor Stephens, and to Langton Douglas (asking him to say anything harsh to me he might think I deserved, but to comfort Stephens). And I wrote also to Birrell asking if he could manage a review with call for pictures in *Daily News*—and to A.E., and to Mr. Edmunds about the land; and to Ian MacPherson[11] asking about the picture Bill. Very tired in the end, and troubled still about Stephens, though this morning I take a more ironical view—for after all, if he said "No one ever showed me a picture" and now says, "L. Douglas showed me hundreds"—which does he expect to be judged by?

Today's *Times* has in the Index "The Hugh Lane Pictures" and an illustration of one of them, so they are moving. I have sent the memoir (returned by Stephens!) to Lady Leslie "Winston's Aunt, Shane's Mother" asking her to stir up Winston to help us, and get the Bill through the Cabinet with a rush. Ah! if we get them what do little worries matter! And with a great effort I got to work again on Sir Frederic Burton.

46, Gt. Cumberland Place
W.

My dear Lady Gregory,

Thank you *so* much for sending me dear Hugh Lane's Memoir. It does "grip one". *Of course* I will do all I can about the pictures. I am sure they will eventually reach Dublin—but one must just go on hammering away. Winston is in the East—but I expect will be back in time to help. There are others one tries to influence—and I promise you I will let no opportunity slip by.

There is a foolish argument made, that in any case the pictures are safer here than they would be in Dublin—but any excuse will do!

Yrs. Affec
LEONIE LESLIE

5 MARCH. Mr. Johnson came to tea yesterday, says the purchasers of our land have sold all the timber to Martin McDonagh for £230. I would rather he had it, for he will most likely cut it all at once and the Park will become tillage fields, better than leaving it nibbled at for years. But I wish they would spare the trees by the river.

A "Trustee letter"—Witt probably—in *The Times*, and one on our side from Mrs. Grosvenor. I have written to Sir E. Carson, and to Poppy to see Lady Carson, and to Lady Leslie again. Curfew in Dublin now to begin at 9 o'clock, this will I think mean closing The Abbey. Mr. Johnson said the Black and Tans had been back in Gort, making arrests. I asked D., today and he says they took away Donohue and Hanlon and the two Hayes and others, and searched many houses, L. Dooley's among them, asking "if any of the wild class had been given harbour in this house." While three officers and a sergeant were talking politely to Katy and Laurence in the front room, two Black and Tans coming in by the back door had ransacked the bedrooms and thrown all the clothes out of a chest, and overhauled even the child's cot.

March 5, 1921

Dear Sir Edward Carson,

I am afraid this is not a very good moment for a renewal of the Lane picture demand, Ireland being out of fashion, but the appearance of the Memoir (please accept the copy I send with this) has brought the matter up. "A Friend of Lane"—I don't know who this was—wrote the letter I enclose in last Monday's *Times*, and the statement by the Secretary of the Nat. Gallery appeared next day. It was a mistake saying a majority of the Trustees are for returning the pictures; Lord Ribblesdale I believe is, and I gave Mr. Macpherson letters from Mr. Heseltine, Lord Brownlow and Lord Plymouth (to Mrs. Grosvenor) saying they would not oppose a Government Bill legalising Hugh Lane's codicil. There are, therefore, these four at least against Lord Curzon who, both on their Board and in the Cabinet, is our violent opponent. You, as I have always believed, are the only one who can overcome him.

Mr. Macpherson's Bill legalising the codicil was before the Cabinet when he went out of office, and I have heard nothing of it since, though Sir H. Greenwood promised to take up the matter. Sir James Craig when I last saw him promised to do his best, his last words to me were, "We won't give you Home Rule but we'll get you the pictures"—but now he is gone.

I have given the case in pages 218–237 of my book, and in the appendix.

It would surely help towards the unity you and I myself and many others long for—if you who have done so much for the North will by getting the matter through earn the gratitude of

Dublin, and of Galway, which had a share both in you and in Hugh Lane.

J., back from Gort says, "all the men carried off by the Black and Tans, the full of a small field, were brought up to Peterswell and a sergeant who had been wounded in the Castle Daly ambush was brought around to look at every one of them, but he could not identify anyone and so they were let go free. The Black and Tans were in Gort till evening, a very bad looking troop, with little ribbons hanging from their caps and faces that were not shaved since Christmas, and nothing could be more drunk than what they were, staggering about the street and letting their rifles drop out of their hands. If those had brought away any prisoners with them they never would have reached Galway alive."

7 MARCH. Tom Lee had asked for onions and cabbages to plant at Mount Vernon if there was a cart going there, but that this was doubtful "as Clare is going on very bad and the roads are being ripped up." However, there was one in Gort today and we sent them. A card from Miss Purser saying she had done my errand to S. Gwynn, so I hope he has something in *The Observer*.

I wrote yesterday a letter for Robinson to show Healy of *The Irish Times* and ask him to write an article about the pictures. Today I ordered a copy of the *Life* to be sent to Macpherson to whom I had already written. A quiet day, working at Sir Frederic, and in the garden.

10 MARCH. Two quiet days, working at Sir F., but rather tired. Today Sir E. Carson's letter cheers me, he has committed himself more than before—and Macpherson's also, showing the Bill is not dead.

5, Eaton Place,
S.W.1
9 March 1921

Dear Lady Gregory,

Thank you very much for sending me a copy of your work on Hugh Lane. I fear the present moment is very inopportune to re-open the matter of the pictures held by the National Gallery. I will, however try and get some opportunity of discussing the matter with the Chief Secretary. I quite agree that it would be a useful achievement to secure the pictures for

Ireland and I have very often expressed my views to the authorities in that direction.

Yours sincerely
EDWARD CARSON

Lady Gregory
Coole Park
Gort
Co. Galway

Private

Ministry of Pensions
Cromwell House
Millbank, S.W.1
8 March 1921

Dear Lady Gregory,

I received your letter about the Lane pictures on my return to Town from the North. So far as I can ascertain, however, I am afraid there is no prospect of the Government taking up the Bill during the present session, and in the circumstances it is difficult for me to give you any helpful advice.

I shall, of course, continue to do what I can to help.

Yours sincerely
IAN MACPHERSON

Lady Gregory
Coole Park
Gort
Co. Galway

Tim lamenting the state of the country says, "And the King could stop it with a word, but maybe, poor man, he is afraid of his ministers."

11 MARCH. Review in Literary Supplement[12] calling on National Gallery Trustees for their defence. I am rather sorry. I have written to T. P. O'Connor and Sir R. Woods. A wire saying *Aristotle* is to be played on Patrick's Day so I will go up. A. writes "Miss C. told the children police and Black and Tans are having a dance in the Parochial Hall tonight, where prisoners are; the prisoners are to be locked up in a back room."

Coole Park
Gort
Co. Galway
11 March

Dear Sir Robert,

This is just to tell you how things stand in the picture matter. *The Times*—meaning friendliness put in a letter from an over-zealous "Friend of Lane"—I don't know who—asking for their return, and saying "a majority" of the Trustees were for this. That is incorrect, only 4 of them are, so far as I know, and a statement from the National Gallery says they mean to hold on to the pictures. Today I see in the Literary Supplement a review of my book (friendly) and calling for an answer to our claim—so controversy may arise, which I am rather sorry for just now.

I wrote to Mr. Macpherson asking what had happened to his Bill. He answers "I am afraid there is no prospect of the Government taking up the Bill during the present session. . . . I shall of course do what I can to help". (So the Bill is not dead anyhow).

I also wrote to Sir E. Carson and he replies: "I fear the moment is very inopportune to re-open the matter—I will however try and get some opportunity of discussing the matter with the Chief Secretary. I quite agree that it would be a useful achievement to secure the pictures for Ireland and I have very often expressed my views to the authorities in that direction."

I am not altogether dissatisfied with this—as Sir H. Greenwood is pledged to help us.

Yours sincerely
A. GREGORY

House of Commons
16 March, 1921

Dear Lady Gregory,

Thank you for letting me know the position concerning the pictures. I was not unprepared for it.

I am afraid there is little prospect of getting anything real done for our unfortunate country at present. The general attitude is that we ought to be looking after our own affairs. I have no doubt we shall get them sooner or later if only for shame's sake.

Yours faithfully
R. H. WOODS

15 MARCH. Galway. Came in here and gave the chicks my birthday party yesterday, very successful, with games and balloons, and my matches blazing stuck in a pineapple defied counting my years (69) so that leaves them guessing for another year.

Irish Times had L.R's excellent little article, very cheering. I sent the maps and rates to Mr. Edmunds—rather cast down, rates alone on Coole coming to over £200 a year.

17 MARCH. Came up on Tuesday and Robinson met me and came to tea. He had been to Limerick lately and one of the Carnegie librarians told him she had been in Courthouse where Sinn Fein prisoners were shut up. She heard suddenly a noise that alarmed her from the prisoners' room and called the assistant (?) who went in and found Black and Tans had broken in, one was holding a lighted match, by the light of which he and others were kicking the prisoners. No one seems to have hope of the Government making efforts for peace, the hanging of the six last Monday is a bad beginning of the week.[13] Harris says ——————[14] was as innocent as he is.

Yesterday to a short rehearsal of *Aristotle*, Will Shields only able to come for a short time, and to the dress rehearsal in the evening—it went very well—the players love their parts. Seaghan has made splendid cats' heads out of old felt hats, only the pigeon is more black than white (!) and has to be painted.

News of Margaret having taken Celbridge . . .

18 MARCH. Yesterday passed pleasantly. I took Hugh's *Life* to Starkey at the Municipal Gallery, and he was much pleased. I read him what I had given of his memories and he was pleased with that also. The Gallery looked lonely without the French pictures, how I see them again in my mind's eye. Then matinée of *Aristotle* went well though a small audience. It was beautifully acted, not like a first performance, all working together, and Miss Delany very fine when she bursts into "Oft in the Stilly Night". Fanny Trench was there and I was glad one of the family should see it and my call at the end!

Then Robinson's tea in the Green Room (with my barmbrack) very pleasant. Jack Yeats very appreciative, that pleased me best. And a young man who praised both it and the *Life* said that "Dermod O'Brien[15] says it shows *two* charming personalities, Hugh Lane's' and Lady Gregory's own". Evening performance also pleasant though poor audience—but they liked it. And *Bedmates*[16] that follows is delightful; it would have a great success in India where the "Pax Britannica" has been worked so long. Hindus and Mussulmans being assured that each would murder the other were it removed.

20 MARCH. Friday was quiet. I went to look for apples for the chicks and for Easter Eggs. Evening performance nice but small audience. But in the evening I saw Literary Supplement,[17] audacious untruth signed "X" (Witt I should think) that Hugh at the

time he left for United States was "bound by promise to Aitkin and McColl to give the pictures to London if a Foreign Gallery was built there". "Bound by promise" is new, and the condition they used to claim was "in whichever city most appreciation was shown, the test to be the foundation of a Gallery". It made me feel sick and shaken. And at first I wished myself at home where I have the cuttings of the old controversy. Then I wrote to Mrs. Duncan asking if she had them; took the note to the theatre and Alan Duncan was there, and took it to his mother, and later I had a telephone message asking me to come to the Gallery at 11 next day. A dreadful night! First I saw no one to write but myself, and that seemed horrible—drawing a new controversy on me; and if I quoted anything from the book I would be supposed to be advertising it. Then I thought Yeats might write—but he is so far away—so I began making notes for a letter to send him. Then in bed, I thought A.E. might be better; I got up and made notes for him. Then later, or earlier, for it must have been the morrow morning, I thought we must have two letters—one quoting from the old letters of Aitkin and McColl from Yeats, and a fiery one of moral indignation from A.E. I got up and made more notes. In the morning to Gallery—and there were the cuttings I wanted! And Mrs. Duncan typed from my dictation, slowly, but so much better than my own tired hand. Then to A.E., rather bewildered at the sudden call. And H. Plunkett came in, rather cross at finding him talking with me—and in a distressed manner fell back on Miss Mitchell (he had co-operative business on his mind). But A.E. will do it, and have it for me to see on Monday morning before I go.[18] Then to Abbey, and good Robinson had been to National Library and copied bits of McColl's article in *XIXth Century*[19] giving their case away, so I sent this also to Yeats.

Today writing to Northcliffe's Secretary. A meeting with Robinson and Harris in the office and we decided we must close. Even at 9 o'c. Curfew we can't carry on but at a big loss, and now from today it is to be at 8.[20] Robinson will try to get the Players into a tour with *Whiteheaded Boy*. Failing that I don't know what we can do for them. It will be very sad. *Aristotle* still liked.

Extract from letter 26 March, 1921.
Mrs Lingard came up greatly excited saying the Sinn Fein Hall (the house I began to buy before I took this on lease) was burned. Anne rushed up begging to go and see it, so we went. Only the walls and roof left, windows and floors gone and we could see flames creeping up back wall, a disgraceful thing and there was no one to check the fire and wind was high. A mob of

boys were tearing stones out of a wall and throwing them into house and doing as much damage as they could. There was only the caretaker in when fire started and she got away. A little girl of 10 or 12 told me it was done by 13 Black and Tans.

AT MORNING MASS
(Ireland—1921.).

For them that die today,
  Lord Christ, I pray!
Enemy and friend—
  Lord, give them a good end!

Thy Body broken was
  On the hard, high Cross:
The Blood of Thy dear Heart
  Flowed on the blind man's dart!

Lord, be not wroth in mind
  With them that slay, being blind!
To the just men, slain,
  Make good the death of pain!

In the White Christ, lifted up—
In the Sacrificial Cup—
In breaking of the Bread—
  Three-fold, my prayer is made.

Lord, unto all give peace,
  Succour, and soul's release!
For enemy and friend—
  This, my prayer to the end!

ALICE FURLONG

BOOK TWELVE

20 MARCH, 1921. (continued) I wrote to Mr. Price, Lord Northcliffe's Secretary about the pictures, asking if an article would be possible to close the controversy, as there are no new facts to bring out on either side.

Then to lunch at the Hydes, very pleasant, though he is not hopeful. I asked what Sinn Fein would accept. He thinks if Dominion Home Rule, with no tax to England, but even without army or navy, were offered, that Dail Eireann could not refuse to put it to a plebiscite, and that it would be accepted. But he fears England will not offer this, and thinks they will accept nothing else. The young men are determined not to let the matter go on to another generation but to fight it out now. They are not afraid to die—"See how those six died on Monday! They were sustained by faith, by patriotism, by religion. As Sir Robert Woods[1] says in a speech reported today, 'They don't look on killing as murder—in this cause and that, is a thing that cannot be too often said'." He says many more of the Crown forces are being killed than are made known. And Sir Horace Plunkett said yesterday that many more Sinn Feiners are killed than are known; they don't report their losses. He (Craoibhin) is only afraid of all the young men being killed. He is sad, no wonder, and much of his fire is gone.

Then to Harcourt Street Gallery to get a pamphlet from Mrs Duncan to send to Price, and with Fanny French for the rest of the day. It had been announced in the morning papers that Curfew is to be at 8 o'clock, and I was looking at my watch now and then that I might leave in time. But suddenly Fanny exclaimed that it was just on 8, and I found my watch had stopped! A moment's consternation, but then we looked at the paper and found the new hour doesn't begin till tomorrow.

Craoibhin says Dublin is full of Government spies, two or three well-dressed women at the Shelbourne, others on trams; it is not safe to speak a word anywhere.

TUESDAY, 22 MARCH. Yesterday morning I went to A.E. He had been worried by constant business but had written me a letter, the beginning splendid, for as I had never before known, he himself had asked Hugh in those last Dublin days if he would bring the pictures back to Dublin, and had an assurance that he would. But after that, A.E. had gone into mild argument, not very good. He knew it was weak, and asked me to write a draft for him, and I sat down and did so. But perhaps it may be too strong in its moral indignation—or too frivolous with its poultry yards quotation!

Then I asked him what Sinn Fein would accept. He said he was trying to negotiate and didn't wish his plan mentioned, but thought what Hyde had said was correct. I asked for something I might use, and he wrote down a few lines and gave them to me. Then I wired to Yeats to quote McColl and Aitken (for I thought he had better nail the lie to the counter in that way). Then Theatre. The players know we have to stop playing. This 8 o'clock Curfew settles that. It is very sad for them and us. And there was a letter for me from G.B.S. refusing a lecture for our Theatre fund. He says he is overworked and I'm afraid it is true, but I wish some of his work could be given to Ireland. Then I marked Gallery pamphlet and sent it with my letter to Price at *The Times* office. Then I dictated a letter to *The Times*, just giving what Hyde and A.E. had said, for with many plans proposed no one seems to get at what Sinn Fein would take. Then to say farewell to players, but there is some hope they may be taken into a tour of *Whiteheaded Boy*. I thanked them for their work in *Aristotle*, and they were very nice.

Then to Galway, found the chicks well.

COOLE All well here.

Old Niland today says "Bartley Hynes that was living up the road from Kinvara to Galway had his house burned, and the furniture and the hay and corn, by the Black and Tans. And there is a woman, an O'Donnell, over in Peterswell, and she having but the one son, and they pulled him out of the bed and brought him abroad in the street and shot him, and they brought her out that she'd seen him shot. And she took the son in her arms and he died in her arms. About twelve days ago that happened. They didn't give no reason at all for what they done.

"At Stanton's house, up from Kinvara, they took £20 worth of a pig and threw it into the lorry and brought it away; and fowl they took and they burned the house, a fortnight before Patrick's day. It's for robbery they are out and for killing. They were firing in Gort four nights ago, about forty shots around the street, and a bullet went by Pat Lally's ear as he came out of his own gate where he was watching ewes. They are like wild animals that came from some place, or savages out from some island.

"Look at the way the rates are gone up, that the less man that will have land will be the best man in the end. What way can they pay them? It was in the prophecy of Columcille that a man would pay twice but he wouldn't pay the third time; and that he'd shoot his cow in the door before he'd give it up to them.

"In Cromwell's time there wasn't half as much done because they hadn't the way of doing it. What was Cromwell's army only walking Ireland? But now with their lorries there's not one of them has to walk half a mile.

"And what can the Sinn Feiners do? It's as good to be standing on the ground firing stones at the moon as to be trying to knock rights out of the Government, unless that America might come at them. And if America would stir and go out against them, sure the Japanese are watching themselves".

Mona Gough writes in answer to my letter that Lady Carson "has promised she will speak to Sir Edward herself about the matter of the pictures, and told me to send a message to you that she would do what she could. The Baby is a most delightful child, *very* like Sir Edward!"

24 MARCH. Rather a blow, the Literary Supplement this morning without Yeats' and A.E.'s letters; and a letter from the Private Secretary saying he can't do any more at present. Probably the enemy have used their influence. However, trying to "turn a defeat to a victory" I reflected that it might after all be better to send the letters privately to one or two of the friendly Trustees, to help that split in the Board; so I wrote to A.E. to ask for a copy of his, and I have the rough copy of Yeats', the one I sent him, which he says he had typed and sent on, but doesn't want to be asked to do any more controversy.

Yeats writes March 22, 1921. 4, Broad St, Oxford.

My dear Lady Gregory,

I had what you sent me re-typed and signed it and sent it off in good time. It was an excellent letter, much better than anything I could have written. I have not been through the material since 1917 and have not that material now (even if I wished to revive it in my memory) so when X replies, if he does reply, please answer him yourself. I must keep out of it. When I go to London at the end of April I want to give my whole mind to work for the Theatre. That I may do so I must finish other work between this and then. I am writing verse, and turning aside to write even that little note for Miss Allgood, which anybody else could have done, was a great loss of nervous strength. If I carried on a dispute now with McColl I would not write at all because it would fill my mind. I do not even open my letters till the day's work is finished. I leave them on George's mantelpiece so that I may not be tempted. By good luck yesterday was an exception for I had brought on a bad headache through eyestrain and could not work. When I am writing verse I must not break the momentum, for if I do I lose the poem. I came here to live because I knew that if I did not get out of every kind of public life I would lose my poetical power. Years ago I had so much passion it did not matter what I did, but now emotion has to be brooded over in solitude to get it to the intensity for verse. I am trying to write, in the next month or so, enough verse to make the book published by my sisters large enough for publication by Macmillan.

I send you a letter of Maud Gonne's about your play which came today. The first paragraph about Desmond Fitzgerald refers to some relief from great discomfort I was able to secure for him through Lord Henry Cavendish. Lolly writes also great praise of your play, indeed I have heard nothing but praise. Lolly says her little girls who went into town on Saturday (to the Abbey I think she means) came in for three "ambushes" and had to lie flat on the tram. She adds "the military and B and Ts are always shooting up there (on the north side) and saying they were shot at. We had first hand evidence that in three cases they threw a bomb first themselves to start the fight. (Rubbish)

Yrs ever
W. B. YEATS

My letter on "The Irish Situation" is in *The Times*[2] and the *Independent* has it today, headed "Dail Eireann and Peace—What Lady Gregory heard"—but it is for England I thought it might be useful. But *The Times* is very down on Sinn Fein today, and the boycott of English goods. Very wet. Dressed dolls for Workhouse children, and wrote another appeal to G.B.S.

24TH. Yeats' note such a relief! (from Editor of Lit. Supp. saying it will be published next week)[3]. For after all yesterday was a heavy day, and I had disturbed dreams last night—one that I had lost my sapphire ring, but after a long time I saw it shining through the darkness. So may it be with the pictures!

A letter for Margaret from Elvery's shop, and one for Anne from Guy have arrived marked "Censored", but not mine.

Power says "The name of the Black and Tans will go from generations down the same as Cromwell. Out in Shanaglish they burned a picture of the Redeemer—'Is this another Sinn Feiner'? says one of them and he pulled it down and threw it into the fire".

Peter says "The town is filled up with police and Black and Tans these last days. In dread they are something might happen at Easter, and they have a notice put up that if anything is done the town of Gort will blaze.

"But there might come some change, for in England gentle and simple would seem to be wishing for peace.

"There was a schoolmaster in Kilchriest brought out from his house and beaten because he was teaching Irish to the children".

28 MARCH. Yesterday, Easter Sunday, I went to church and then to the workhouse with toys and sweets and Easter eggs for the children (delighted) and tobacco for the old men.

Seeing that Sir Philip Sassoon was made a Trustee of the National Gallery I began composing a letter to him, and have been writing and typing it, and now it is too wet to send to post.

A writes re burning Sinn Fein Hall, and rising. It was burned by B. & T. "Contained the offices of the Transport Workers Union, and some of the oldest carved and cut granite in the town."

30 MARCH. Anne and Catherine came yesterday. Well and bright and pleased with everything, Pup, the kittens, the garden, then to pick primroses and cut sticks in the wood. But a wire tells that Richard won't be home till next week.

This morning A.E's letter tells me his picture one will be in *The Times* but unluckily in the part he wrote himself he has got a couple of mistakes; he thinks that his talk with Hugh was "within a few days of his writing the codicil" and also that he told his relations his intention. I have always said he never told me. But A.E.'s name will carry weight, and he won't be accused of telling fibs.

1 APRIL. Peter said yesterday that young Hargrove and Fitzgerald who drives the motor had been taken away by Black and Tans, and they were looking for young Cooney but couldn't find him—"All the youth of the country are being brought away".

M., telling me of the state of Limerick (she has just come back after some weeks in the county) says there is no doubt at all that Lord Mayor Clancy (as well as O'Callaghan) was murdered by the Crown forces.[4] Everyone loved him, she says. "He taught Irish to the children in the school and if he met a child on the road would get off his bicycle and speak to it. The young men are put against walls and struck on the head, and often go with bleeding wounds to be attended to in the hospital." She was pointed out one who had never belonged to any organisation and had been treated like the rest, his head cut open. "That dance at the Guillamor's house was for a fund for the boys on the run. They had a password coming in, and a spy came in, one of the Auxiliaries, and when he did not give the password at the door, a shot was fired, and then the destruction began." She was told of one young man of whose body "like the Loughnanes" very little had been left. He had been run down by bloodhounds sent after him.

Malachi Quinn was here this morning, very dissatisfied with the £300 compensation for his wife's death, and is going on with his claim for malicious injury.

He says his yard was fired into by Black and Tans again on the 19th February; and that another day they shouted as their lorry passed the house. He had been in Galway the other day when a policeman's funeral was going through, and as it passed the people walking in the streets were "welted with ashplants, and the old people knocked over like rabbits"

Regan said "They talk of a gang of murderers, but the whole youth of the country is in it".

Yeats's and A.E.'s letter in the Literary Supplement[5], and look well—and I *pray* they may bring conviction to the Trustees.

Afternoon post brought circulars from Robinson I have made spills of them; quite useless and untrue about the foundation of the Theatre. Miss Horniman made the *building*, not the Theatre, and we bought it from her when she stopped her help. The Theatre—the Irish National Theatre—was in existence before her—we did not "take it over" from her. An afternoon working in the garden, and at "Sir Henry Layard," calmed me down.

5 APRIL. Robinson wrote yesterday wanting me to lecture for the Abbey 12th or 19th. So I wired 12th, though not knowing if I can get away in the end.

Today we expected Richard but he didn't come. Then Regan came, in a state of fury. M.Q. had refused to give up possession of Ballinamantane (says he has it until 29th). Last night his cattle were driven to his yard and his windows broken. Then he called in the police, and they have arrested a young Donohoe (innocent, Regan says) and are looking for others. It seems the beginning of bad work—they will retaliate—After all my prayers for "Thy Kingdom come—In Coole, in Kiltartan, in Ireland".

7 APRIL. Robinson's wire about the matinee is cheering. I've written to Sara Allgood.

Yesterday Regan, Hanlon, Donohoe, down again, abusing Malachi Quinn—wanting I know not what. Regan I think afraid of his sons being arrested.

But Tim says Malachi was "beaten with a hurl" and that his door was broken down as well as his windows, and that he knows who the doers were. I preach to both sides the wickedness and folly of this private quarrel over a month's grazing, when the great battle is going on in the country.

13 APRIL. Reading Strachey's *Life of Queen Victoria*[6]. Poor Prince Consort—I remember in my childhood the riddle "Why is he the tallest man living"? "Because he reached all the way from Dover"—And the other "Why is he like the letter P?" And our English Governess Miss Chaplin, saying he spent his time "pottering about the Palace looking for candle ends", and my father saying that driving in London in a hansome cab he had taken his hat off, the roof being low, and was bending forwards, and the Prince passing by thought it was a salute to him, and delighted, took off his hat with a bow.

Working through the Layard letters. I must try and get on with my work now, it will help towards keeping the home.

17 APRIL. The quarrel between M.Q. and his neighbours settled, such a mercy! He wouldn't take his cattle off Ballinamantane, and they drove them and broke his windows, and he called in the Black and Tans, and they searched Kiltartan houses for the boys "on the run", and I feared reprisals on him. But in Court yesterday a settlement was made, he getting the best of it; £20 and twenty acres inside the demesne and "no whistling or shouting at his servants or workmen". In consideration, he withdrew his summons.

21 APRIL. Frank here today. He says there was an agitation begun to have the Castleboy land sold, and the Kilchriest schoolmaster made a speech, for which the Black and Tans gave him a great beating (the beating I had heard of) "and he deserved it, it was no business of his", "But what business was it of the Black and Tans?" "Oh I suppose to please Arthur". He rather approves of my keeping Coole, thinks I should be able to manage (but doesn't know how small my income is!) and doesn't think M. will be able to run Celbridge, and may be glad to come back.

The chicks very happy, going up on the roof with J. Diveney to get jackdaws' eggs from the nests in the chimneys, and playing with the goats tethered to eat the grass on the tennis ground. Richard has done wonderful patterns with his meccano, and has begun learning shorthand!

24 APRIL. Mr. Edmunds here yesterday, from Kilkee. All the passengers had been searched in the train in which he was for a part of the way, he himself searched and had to hold up his

hands, but they didn't find his revolver, which was in his bag with papers. But they took and carried off a priest, Father M. and said they were searching for him and another man. Edmunds hears (as A.E. had hinted) that there are negotiations going on between North and South. The Northerns find it will be a very expensive business running an independent Parliament, would like to share it. And they feel the boycott of their goods by the South, having just bought a large stock after the war.

BOOK THIRTEEN

24 APRIL, 1921. I tried to bring T. to reason about accepting the twelve acres of land the Committee offer him, and at one moment he said he would, and then that they must come in person and offer it, and blustered and threatened that he would "allow no man ever to put a head of cattle on the land." I could but propose arbitration, and he half assented.

25 APRIL. The children drove to Gort and brought back news that a Burren girl there said the road had been broken up between Burren and Curranroe. She had to take her bicycle into a field and so get round the obstruction.

29 APRIL. Margaret doing up tennis court and rather inclined if Celbridge fails to keep this on, when I would take a house in Dublin where the children could come for classes.

7 MAY. We left on Monday. Richard and I came through a tiring journey safely here (64 Rutland Gate) and he went on to school in the afternoon. Darling child, they (the Huth Jacksons)[1] liked his "friendly pleasant simple little ways". We lunched with Mrs. Gough and I made acquaintance with Rotter. 64 Rutland Gate.

8 MAY. A wonderful week of kindness, luxury, courtesy.

Among events, Yeats' lecture on the Theatre, lunch before that at the Queen's Restaurant with the Fagans, when Horace Plunkett gave £100 to the Abbey fund. And I had just been a little cross with him because he would talk incessantly through lunch about his "plan" for a constituent assembly to ask for Dominion Home Rule. A good one enough I think, but it bored our hosts. And I could not sign it, as he asked, had an excuse of not meddling with politics but thought in my heart the matter should be settled by the man in prison.

Yeats' lecture not very good. He didn't get fire. However the audience liked it and an American lady said "I had never any idea that Mr. Yeats could be amusing"! He was probably less amusing when, he having asked for questions, I suggested his saying something about the fight with the Castle over *Blanco Posnet*, and on hearing my voice he exclaimed "I had been for a long time wondering where some bright beams of intelligence were coming from among the audience, and now I see it was from Lady Gregory"!! (No applause!)

He brought some new poems here and read them to me, "On the present state of the world".[2]

Fritz Huth Jackson says an American said to him "We have luxury without comfort, and we have courtesy without manners".

C. says when Eton was challenged to play Downside at Cricket and wrote back asking "What is Downside"? the answer sent was "It is what Eton once was, a school for the sons of Catholic gentlemen".

Claude Phillips[3] here this afternoon, friendly, and I was glad he spoke nicely of Hugh, saying he would have done work even so much greater had he lived till now, for I want to be at peace with all the world. But he has not recanted about the Rembrandt, but hasn't seen it since its cleaning in Berlin, and was very much struck with it in the reproduction in Hugh's *Life*. Sir F. Burton had, after long asking, come to see a picture of his which might have done for the National Gallery, but came when he was out and refused to give his name to the maid, and so to his great indignation, was denied admittance. Browning used often to come to his house to hear Tosti[4]. He was the only poet who understood music and he was pleased one day when Tosti kissed his hand. George Moore used to call often at one time, and would dally in the hall, chatting with the maid on his way, and asking for coffee when he had come to tea. Phillips made him very cross one afternoon when this was going on and said to the maid before people "You ought to be pleased at Mr. Moore talking to you so much, he would not do that to everyone", and she tossed her head indignantly and said "Yes 'ee would to any 'orrid dirty creature 'ee met". And after that George's visits ceased.

Dr. Munro[5] wants to free Scotland, spoke with bitterness of the eviction of the small holders for deer forests, and of the vulgar people who came to take them. I said "And Balmoral"? and he said "Yes that was a terrible cloud". Claude Phillips, after Dr. Munro had told some strange ghost stories, told that he had once stayed in a house taken by Mrs. Adair; the house was filled with a large noisy fashionable party and he was put in a small room off the hall. In the night he felt a chill of horror and saw a long procession of white-robed figures, like nuns, pass by. He, terrified, rushed down to the butler's room. He never spoke of this, fearing ridicule, to any of the party, until twelve years later meeting one of them he told it and the other said "Of course you know it was an old convent, and that hall was the refectory". But he had never known that.

14 MAY. That Sunday, 10th, I dined with the Studds. Mary asked me if I thought the worse of her for having become a Catholic. I said no, she was bound to kick, to make some new departure when her children were off her hands. She had never expressed herself fully in life (I didn't say through two common-minded husbands). But I said, I, knowing what the bondage of the mind imposed by the R.C. Church is especially in Ireland, I should have blamed her had she, who was free born, put the children into that bondage. She said that is what Herbert had said (and it made me think better of him than before). When she had first spoken of changing he had said "Don't do it till the children are grown up", and she put it off until then. Her daughter Mary has changed her Church, but not Dorothy or Jim—or Horace!

11 MAY. With Yeats to lunch with Una [Pope Hennessy] and on to his Reading at Mrs. Herbert Jackson's house—Very smart, and brought in £39 for the Abbey.

12 MAY. My lecture, after the long misery of thinking of it—And to think, and go over it without interruption, I had in those last days to wake myself up at 7 o'c and work at it before breakfast—perhaps too much, for my nervousness grew and when I got to the platform I was actually trembling so that I had to lay my hand on Robinson's chair to steady it. I began in this nervousness, terrified of losing the sequence, of using wrong words (as I sometimes do in talking) terrified of forgetting altogether what I had to say. And thinking I might have to use my notes all the time I was afraid to put my glasses on—I can read better without them, and so I could not see the faces of the audience and I felt that my voice was dead and flat. When at last I ventured to look I saw that they were interested and pleased, and I saw Birrell's kind face beaming, and then I took courage to speak out, and got through well I think. Yeats wasn't very comforting, said he was disappointed in my voice at the beginning, but that it improved later, and he thought the matter very good, but that I should have begun with amusing anecdotes (and I had hated his doing this—and keeping to this—in his lecture). Many people said "beautiful"—that meant nothing. Birrell said, and it sounded sincere "it was *very good*", and that he was going home to write a play if he could but think of an emotion to drive it! Una was best she said "You really need not have given us so much—it was packed with matter" (and it was under an hour). And there had been real laughter and applause nearly all through, and as Molly and Sally gave a beautiful performance of *Gaol Gate*, I

think the audience had no reason to complain. But I couldn't sleep and am only just getting sure the ordeal is over.

We have made: Lectures, £175.4.8, (but expenses of lectures, about £30, will come out of this). Matinée, £84.11.7. W.B.Y. reading, £39; Donations, £172.13.4. In all £471.9.7. But I think anyhow we shall be able to pay our £500 debt to the Bank.

Fritz Huth Jackson[6] told me (as we spoke of a tax on pictures sold, for the benefit of the artist) that Huth, his uncle, had seen at Agnew's a picture he liked very much and had given £700 for it. Afterwards he had the artist (Fritz forgets or didn't hear his name) to dinner, and asked what he had been paid. He said Agnew had only given him £40 for it. Huth went back in anger and told Agnew he must either give the artist a part of the profit or take back the picture. He said all right, he would take it back, so Huth got back his £700 and sent a receipt. Some time later he learned that an American had seen the picture and asked its price, was told £760. He said that seemed high, but Agnew said "I am only getting £60 profit, I gave £700 for it, I can show you the receipt" and showed it! Ruffian!

Yesterday, Friday, 18th, I came to Ayot St. Lawrence. Charlotte Shaw had advised my coming by 4.15 train, but being Whitsuntide, Tiny persuaded me to go by an earlier one to avoid the crush, so I waited at Hatfield for a couple of hours, and the time passed pleasantly enough as I went into an antiquarian's shop, bought a brown stoneware flask in the likeness of Lord John Russell, with "The Spirit of Freedom" on it. Then the owner, Mr. Speight showed me his wares, and gave me tea in a charming summer parlour. He had begun dealing simply because he owned a house opposite to the one he lived in, and thought he might as well utilise it. G.B.S. and Charlotte came to meet me, he back from his Scotch lecturing, had immense audiences. I asked what his moral purpose was in speaking to the Scotch—what he was doing for them. He said he wasn't doing them any good, that was the worst of it. He had gone to lecture for the Fabian Society of Edinburgh, and when in Scotland some time ago he had an audience of working men and tried to help them; now he had a paying audience of many of the well-to-do; but he must have set up that Fabian Society for ever and ever.

He is pleased that *Heartbreak House*[7] has had a good run to a steady house in America. After it had been accepted, the producer, a man with a German name, wrote to him, many compliments, but saying he found it necessary to make several cuts. G.B.S. sent a cable saying he was returning the £500 he had been given in advance, as he would not allow this. The answer was "Producer sacked. Play proceeding", and no cuts were made. He says you must either have a light play to go a couple of hours or one that will take at least three hours and that the audience will remember through their lifetime. *Methuselah*[8] is to be played in three nights and a matinée, and no one may take a ticket for one performance only. Yesterday he had a cheque from Spain to his astonishment, the first money he had ever had from there, it was for "the inevitable *Pygmalion*". A collected edition of his works[9] is coming out at £1.1. a volume, and he is writing prefaces, giving his autobiography in that way, all that need ever be told of him. Now that his mother and sister are dead there is no one to be annoyed and he can tell the tale of his father's drunkenness. I say it was his father's dreams when he had been drinking which, speech failing at the same time would not let him tell out, that are now being expressed by him!

We have been for a motor drive. I asked if he was ever nervous lecturing. He said not now but at the beginning his hands used to tremble so much he could hardly hold the notes (just like me on Thursday!). He used the same lecture all through Scotland, quotes some preacher—Whitfield—"No sermon is any good till you have preached it forty times". At Newcastle having an hour to spare before the train left he had remembered that Bewick had left his collection there,[10] and rushed to the Museum and found the beautiful plates of birds and made some notes. Some names he had not known as "Night swift" for the jay (?). He says little owls that have been introduced to this neighbourhood have driven away or killed the nightingales. These owls fly both by day and night, and at night hearing only the nightingales' song, they make for them.

In the evening I read *Aristotle's Bellows* to them. Both liked it. He said it was "a wonderful thing", "homogenous like a poem", and the language richer even than before—that if it is published with *Dragon* and *Jester* (which he remembers from my reading it two years ago) it will make a wonderful book.

5 MAY. This morning he said he had sent for an old novel, his first, that has never been published, that is wanted for his collected edition. He was not able to get his first novels published for a long time. *Love among the Artists*[11] (I think) was at last published in a Socialist Review (*Today*?) merely to fill up space. All the novels were refused both in England and America. He thinks it was because he came at an unlucky moment. Stevenson had just published *Treasure Island*. The Education Act passed in 1870 (?) had taught people to read, and publishers who had been putting their capital into George Eliot &c found to their surprise

that a story "that in my boyhood would have been published in the *Boys Penny Magazine* was what the public really liked. Macmillan and Chatto and Windus (?) read my novels and said they would like to hear from me when I had a new one, but didn't think these good enough. *Cashel Byron* was founded on a friend, Beatty, who used to take me to boxing matches. My ideas of property were very vague. I think I gave my heroine a fortune of £40,000 a year from about sixteen acres. I offered *Man and Superman* to Murray, but he wrote back, refusing it, saying that while recognising the talent of the work, he found it subversive of all the principles he upheld" (very right of Murray!)

Lunch with Mrs. Phillimore,[12] at Kendals. Lady Connell had said at a lunch her husband was at in Dublin "one must approach George Moore with *circumcision*". She had seen Ellen Terry at Stratford, who said, speaking of her husband "I used to pay for myself. Now I am a kept woman"!

6 MAY. I read the Preface to *Methuselah* this morning—the "nine months of gestation" in ? pages, and he read the last act to-night, a history of the race—a philosophy of its life—terrible in parts but leading to the freedom and life of the spirit at the last. He had tried to humanise his people, wrote a sort of domestic drama as a continuation of Eden, but Granville Barker said it was wrong, and he saw then that he must keep to this subject of the continuance of life.

At dinner he had spoken of Henry James, said they had given some of his plays at the Stage Society, some beautiful dialogue in them, but something that failed—a pessimistic philosophy, somewhat akin to that of George Eliot. He had written this to H.J. when a play about a young man followed by a ghost that gets him at last was sent in, and told him he should make his young man stand up against the ghost and get free of it. But H.J. was not very well pleased, seemed to think he was but making excuses for not putting it on at the Stage Society. He had been at the tragic performance of *Guy Domville* at the Theatre. "It began well, with very good dialogue, but it was a Catholic play, and the second act was very bad, a drunkard behaving in a stupid way, pouring glasses of wine into flowerpots, treated more as a novel. And just at that time audiences were in a booing habit. But the tragedy was that H.J. only came to the Theatre at the end to ask how the performance had gone, and someone said the audience was calling for the author and dragged him on to the stage, and he found the booing going on, though I and others clapped as loud as we could, for it was disgraceful behaviour, and not more than half joined in the booing. Next day I wrote for the

Saturday Review[13] a violent attack on this, and praised the play up to the skies, and so did Scott in the ——— He was a Catholic. Alexander came on the stage but did not act as he should—was almost apologetic, he ought to have told them they didn't deserve a decent play and he would never give them one again. The first night of my *Widowers' Houses* I came in to see half the House applauding, half booing, but I didn't mind. And I have never felt nervous at the performance of my own plays. The only times in my life I felt really nervous was at the Opera in Dublin when my mother sang—though she always did well, yet I used to suffer from anxiety.[14]

"I wrote *Arms and the Man*, or rather finished it quickly for Florence Emery. She wanted something to save her from the failure of that play of Todhunter's, and asked for leave to do *Widowers' Houses*, which she had already played for Grein at the Independent Theatre, and I said this would suit her better."

The MSS of Inno . . .? his first novel, never published, arrived today, all written in the most beautiful clear handwriting. He wrote five novels in all, without enthusiasm or much hope of their being taken. "I bought sixpence worth of paper at a time, and wrote five pages a day, just to form a habit, but I was thought to be indolent, but I was sometimes so tired of it that when I came to the end of my five pages I would stop even in the middle of a line".

17 MAY. This morning when I went down I said to G.B.S. "I am happy to find that in spite of having travelled through the ages in your play I was still able to say my prayers". He said "There is bad news in the papers—but Margaret is not hurt", and told me of the shooting of Captain Blake and his wife and the two officers,[15] and then I saw a telegram from Margaret for me "Sole survivor of five murdered in ambushed motor". It was a bad shock—the thought of the possibilities . . . And then, though she is safe thank God, it is impossible to know how it will affect her outlook and the life of the children, and through them mine. I was quite broken up—went into the air for a while, and then when I came back, kind G.B.S. made coffee for me and spoke comfortably and wanted me to stay, but I thought I might be wanted at Coole and must get to London. Then he offered to motor me up, but I wouldn't let him waste his morning, but accepted the motor, and on my way sent a telegram asking Margaret if I should return. But in the afternoon an answer came "No need, many thanks". I thought she might want to leave Coole at once. There were two letters from her here (at Rutland Gate), about land worries, and I'm afraid

the Thomasin difficulty that I think could have been settled with a money gift, and told her so. And now Black and Tans have been brought in to drive his cow off the fields, and the purchasers were afraid to take up the land, and he put the cow back again.

Lady Gough came to see me this evening, and while she was here Fritz H.J. came in. He said he had been told at lunch at the Bank of England by some man who knew Captain Blake that he was "a terror"—a very harsh and violent man, who had gone over "to make it hot" and was bound to find trouble. He had boasted he would take the blood of Michael Collins. Poor Murphy can corroborate this. (He had dashed into his cart on the roadside, broken it up—and then demanded money from him "robbery with violence".)

18 MAY. Fritz H.J. at dinner talked of the Blumenthals and what a remarkable thing it was that a little Jew music-master and an uneducated Australian should have been able to keep the most exclusive salon in London. He knew that Duchesses had tried to get there in vain. (I was pleased as I had been one of those admitted)! Talking of Lady Lyall he said someone had told her that the influenza was spreading rapidly and her reply was "How can you wonder when so many people will eat Canterbury lamb!"

I went to see Alec Martin today. He is pleased with the *Life* and thinks the dedication is the greatest compliment he has ever been paid. He told me that Freeman Smith, the Head of Lenygans, came to see him and said he could give evidence as to Hugh's intentions about the pictures; so I went to look for him, but in vain. Then to see Murray and Lawrence. There were Pall Mall placards with "Lady's Story of Galway Horror", and I bought one . . . Dreadful to read and think of. But no word from M. yet.

Milner, dining here about the time of his resignation, had said that Lloyd George had become quite impossible since the peace—gives no attention to anything, forgets everything, promises everybody. He put up with him as long as he could and then sent in his resignation.

22 MAY. Newbuildings, Sunday. Not much progress. I had on Friday a letter from A., who had seen Margaret and gave more details about the killings—terrible! And on Friday a letter from Margaret herself. . . . All seems crumbling, yet I will not leave Ireland and will try to hold Coole for a while at least that the darlings may still think of it as home.

W.S.B. has not been well; has suffered pain and is easily

tired—yet we have been out all the morning in the woods, he in his pony chair; and had lunch under the trees, a peacock coming to be fed, and a blackspotted lamb to look on, and Dot, the favourite spaniel, setting up a loud cry for his food.

He is pleased that there is to be an American edition of the *Diaries*.[16] The publisher wants prefaces, and he shrinks from writing these, thinks the exertion too great, says his mind grows confused when he takes the pencil in his hand. I suggest his giving some extracts from his diary since the *Diaries* were not yet published, bits of letters about them, rather than make the effort of a formal introduction; and he asked me to make some notes, and I have done so, one being that the diaries would never have been written at all but for his habit of early rising.

He has not had pain since I came, but is weaker than last year, sleeps more, dropping off in the middle of conversation. He says he will not live through, or to, another winter, and wished he could drop off like his little dog did, in sleep, without any pain. He says he has lived his life to the full, good and bad, and is content to go. Neville Lytton[17] is coming on Tuesday for the night, and he is to see Anthony, now quartered in Dublin (and kept shut up in barracks!). And I think he is much more at peace since the lawsuit is over, and the Arabs, all but six, gone.

He read an account from his Diary of May 1918 of a talk with Winston Churchill not yet to be published, very interesting, showing how much fear there was then of not winning the war; and yet more because he definitely tells that before the war the Germans had asked the Cabinet more formally if England would keep out, if in case of war with France they respected the frontiers and only took some African colonies. He, Asquith and Grey, these three, had refused to do this, and decided to go in and make Belgium the excuse. So we seem to have gone to war to save France from losing a Colony! He is sympathetic about Coole, thinks I ought to keep it on.

On Tuesday, after Ervine's lecture, Robinson and I went to see *Major Barbara* at Hampstead and met the Shaws, and they came and sat with us. A full and very fine play and the Salvation girl's appeal to the ruffian so moving that I asked G.B.S. what he would do if any of the audience called out they were being saved!

F. was furious at Ervine's lecture, so bad, but thought mine "better than Yeats" (L.R. says) and "the revelation of a beautiful mind", so I have that to live up to!

It is peaceful here today after the shock last week, and I have more time to think, and feel I ought to go home lest the children should be brought away from my keeping.

Col. Fisher has told at the War Office how well M. had given her evidence, and of her "wonderful dark eyes".

On Friday I found Mr. Freeman Smith at Lenygans. He knew Hugh well, spoke of him with great affection and says that on the day before he left London to sail for America, he came there, had tea with him, and talked of the pictures and said he was "giving them back to Dublin in a codicil. No—I don't think he used the word codicil, I think he said he had altered his will that they might go back to Ireland". Very good testimony. I asked him to write it to me, in a letter.

WEDNESDAY. 25 MAY. I came back from Newbuildings on Monday. I had a little talk with W.S.B. before I left. He spoke of Egypt and Nationalism and said "The British and Americans, the English speaking races, may be the best in the world, but it is not right that one race should try to take hold of it all, that would not be for the world's good, it is much better that there should be the feeling of race. In the forests of South America you may see twenty different varieties of tree all growing up together, struggling against each other for room, but no one sort dominates the other—and that is all for beauty". He says he is willing, even ready, to die, has lived his life fully, and has no belief at all in a future state (yet some slight belief in the transmigration of souls, believing the little dog, Dot, to have the soul of one he lost forty years ago). I said "Well I believe we shall meet again, and I will say 'I told you so'; but if we don't you will have the worst of it, for you can't say anything to me!" I found here a nice letter from Margaret, asking me to forgive the first, a great comfort to me. Ruth is going over to her till I come.

I dined at the Huntingtons, meeting old Putnam and Lady Bonham Carter and Shane Leslie and Lord Grey. I told Lord Grey of having written to Roosevelt long ago what he had said about him and that the answer had come from Roosevelt, in hospital after he had been shot at in the election, and that he had been pleased.

Lady Bonham Carter said she had had a letter a while ago from that lady who had been arrested at Gort, because the police searching her trunk had found a private letter to the Bishop of Manchester telling of the state of the country and had lodged her in Galway Gaol. She had said in her letter that Captain Blake had been very rough.

On Tuesday I lunched with the Murrays, Lady Helen doing the honours, old John very deaf, young John pleasant, Lady Brassey and I doing the talking.

A French friend or agent to F.H.J. at dinner. He said to Fritz that France was determined to "crush" Germany.

Dr. Hector Monro came on Monday to talk to a few women and two men on "Auto-suggestion" and afterwards when he asked for questions some lady asked if rheumatism could be cured thereby, and he said that had been done. Then I showed him my wrist and said "I used to have beautiful hands, and today when I went to buy a pair of gloves I asked for 'the largest' and when they offered 7½ I said 'that will do'." He said "They can be cured" touching the wrist. Then after they had gone he said "you have done so much for me (I don't know how except that he is reading *Visions and Beliefs*) that I would like to try to do something for you", and so these three evenings he has given me "treatment". He tells me to sit or lie in an easy position and lay down the hands and relax the muscles. Then to make a picture in the mind of myself quite well and free from pain or swellings, and try so to drop off to sleep. His idea is that as the child is formed in the womb or its features determined by some idea building it up, so if we fix our minds on the ailing body as a body in perfect health, it will change by degrees to that ("as ye believe so will it be unto you"). He tells me of cures he has seen, and believes this mode will make a revolution in medicine in the next twenty years. But my poor wrist has been enlarged so long (one sees the beginning even in Kelly's portrait) that I have to try. I found it very hard to "get a picture" at first. Then, half-asleep I saw myself beside a river, standing on rocks and someone that I thought was an angel came and said "We must not let these hands go as they are across the river", and touched them, and I saw more life coming into my body and energy. I can recall this image now when I am quiet and close my eyes. (And now in 1928, reading this, I see that hands and wrists are almost as slender as ever!) April 1928.

(I did not go on long with that effort; yet however it may be, I have been wonderfully free from rheumatism for a good while back. I am not sure it may not be from not having had much time to think about it, but however it may be I have been taking a cold morning bath, which I had given up years ago because it gave me stiffness and pain. And even my hands are better, I can put on my sapphire ring, though afraid to keep it on just yet. But I have not been thinking about the poor body at all, but rather, since my Passion play, about the possibility of living in Heaven while yet upon earth, and I would say with some success and an increase of charity and serenity—but that it is not a fair trial when the children are my only companions and so good and gracious as they are. November 26, 1923.)

27 MAY. G.B.S. yesterday gave his lecture for the Abbey and read two acts of his new play *Back to Methuselah,* and some of the audience were pleased, others would have liked a continuation of his lecture better, Lady Gough fell asleep. The play read well, the bit about the feeding on the heavenly manna very fine, Dr. Monro's idea is in the phrase "imagine to create". Today I have been to Lady Orpen to ask if Orpen would do a poster for the matinée.

The Fagans to lunch and Charlotte Shaw, but G.B.S. came late, but we fed him when he came, in the garden. Clara told us of Sir A. Mond after the war had begun, becoming very British and saying at a meeting "I was born in England and I am an Englishman." When questions were asked after the meeting an old coster said "I have a cat: Now if it kittens in a banana box, will its young be bananas or kittens?"

She had been talking of a very enthusiastic review G.B.S. had written of a book of Vernon Lee's *Satan.*[18] He said "The reason I wrote it was that when I was a young man and very poor she wanted to help me. I would not accept her help, but when this book appeared I saw my chance of repaying her. It is interesting, but her ideas are those of George Eliot."

He liked the house, took real enjoyment in the beauty of the prayer carpets and the Japanese screens, and other lacquer.

28 MAY. I went to dine with Nevill Geary and to *A Bill of Divorcement.*[19]

This morning I awoke free from pain, my wrist and hand quite easy. I am so glad, for Dr. Monro's sake more than my own. Even though it should get bad again, his treatment will have had some effect and please him.

And then I had a letter from Margaret, gentle, and she has not decided on anything yet except against Galway, but I think accepts my staying at Coole. Lady Courtney to lunch, Lady Prothero to tea.

29 MAY. F.H.J. said last night (although his father owns coal mines and he is the Director) that the coalowners are now behaving very badly, have no largeness of mind or insight at all, and he is delighted if there is legislation coming to force them to terms. He spoke of the popularity of Karl Marx, he is almost always quoted at Labour meetings, and his conclusions would be right if the big capitalists owned the big businesses. But since limited liability, they are owned by many shareholders. Sir Hugh Bell for instance said he did not own more than two thousand of the shares.

30 MAY. Sir C. Ilbert, talking of indiscreet diaries, and too

discreet ones, says he once found Birrell looking at a new volume of Grant Duff's[20] and said "There must be something about you in it—look at the index". And he did, and found his name and looked at the passage and it was "Dined at The Club. Sat next Birrell. Sir Alfred Lyall was opposite but unluckily I couldn't hear a word he said." Poor Birrell!

A New York Millionairess came in, sat on the sofa behind Tiny and laid down the law with an expressionless face. Then she turned to me and asked if I knew the Lady Gregory who writes Irish plays. I said I was that person, and Tiny corroborating this she turned to me and said "I saw some of them in New York. But there is no humour in them". "No humour!" "No, they are not humourous!!" (She may have mixed them up with other plays—but even so!)

I dined alone with Fritz H.J. He being a Governor of Harrow, has written to Dr. Ford to ask what is the best house, and if Richard can get into it.

He was himself brilliant at Harrow. Yates Thompson had been here in the afternoon, and F.H.J. had said later "How I used to hate that man's name! I ran up the school very quickly and whenever I got a remove or took a prize the Headmaster used to say 'No one has ever done that before except Yates Thompson'." He said "There was a dinner at the Head Master's, (Butler) I was asked to, and I sat next a little old gentleman, and I didn't know who he was, and talked to him a good deal, trying to put him at his ease. He asked what college I was going to at Oxford. I said Brazenose. 'Why Brazenose and not Balliol'? 'Oh I don't know, my grandfather was there, and there seems no reason why I should not go'. (my father was given his choice of three years there or a three year's trip round the world and he chose the trip). 'Well, tell your Headmaster tomorrow that I have advised you to go to Balliol'. So I told the Headmaster next day that this advice had been given me by the little old man I had met at dinner. 'What'! he said and jumped up 'Do you know who he is?' 'No sir'. 'This is most important. He is the Master of Balliol, Jowett. If you like I will write to your father and tell him of this and recommend him to send you there. It is an extraordinary chance for you'. 'No thank you, sir, I won't trouble you, I can write to him myself'. I couldn't understand all this excitement. However I wrote to my father and he put my name down for Balliol. But in my last year at Harrow I got brain fever—had worked too hard—and the doctors said I must give up work and make a voyage round the world, and so I did. When I came home I had been a year and a half without opening a book, and I went up to Oxford and told Jowett this, and that I didn't know if I could pass in. He said 'In certain cases we can dispense with an entrance examination and I will dispense with it in your case. But' he said 'I must just give you an examination in Scripture history. Who was Jacob?' I told him what I knew of Jacob and he said 'That is quite enough. You may consider you have passed'. He was very kind to me though not to everyone. I was with him one day when an undergraduate came in who he had sent for to reprove for some fault. He didn't like him, and he was very unjust to him and harsh. He said to me 'You are interested in political economy and so am I. Come and breakfast with me every Wednesday and we'll discuss it together'. So we did, but he didn't get very far, he only got as far as Riccardi(?)". I said "Like the Labour Leaders and Marx". He said "Yes just like that". "I read other books but he always went back to Riccardi. It was he and I together who founded the Balliol Sunday evening concerts, a great success. Joachim and all the chief men came and played for us, they had nothing to do on Sunday, and got their fare and were put up and took no pay. Jowell liked the concerts because he used to entertain weekend parties, and when he was tired of them on the Sunday evening he could walk them all into the concert." (The only time I met Jowett was at one of these concerts, I was staying with Madeleine Shaw Lefevre at Sommerville and she introduced me to him).

He told me that at the beginning of the war he and Tiny were abroad and when he read *The Times* the Monday before the August Bank holiday he said things looked bad, and hurried back.

He went at once to Lloyd George and told him there would be danger of a great financial crisis, and that would be a bad thing for England to begin the war with, and recommended a moratorium. Lloyd George took up the idea, but was absolutely ignorant of the subject and asked him to take the matter in hand. He asked Cunliffe to dine with him, and Sir R. Holden, and another Smith? and his lawyer, Herbert Smith, had already proposed dining. Then another financier arrived as they were sitting down to dinner (which he had ordered originally for two) and the cook said there would not be enough, but as they began four more appeared asking for food. He said they must go and dine out and come back afterwards, and so they did and stayed till 2 o'c and prepared a scheme to which they all put their names. Next morning Cunliffe telephoned wanting to withdraw, but he had signed the documents and duplicates and they wouldn't let him off. F.H.J. took the scheme to Lloyd George who was much interested, made him explain it all and especially wanted to know what a Bill of Exchange was, and when he got an explanation sent for typists to take it down, four typists one after another taking it down in shorthand, then going off to type it. Lloyd George said "I will take this to the House of Commons to explain, but you must come there yourself in case I want to consult you". So he got hold of a couple of Bills and brought them but they were not needed, Lloyd George found his statement was accepted all right.

I asked if he thought the war could possibly have been averted, and he said no, he thought not then, when Belgium had been attacked. But he does blame Lloyd George for not having made peace at the beginning of 1917 when the terms offered were quite good. They would have accepted but for America coming in, they thought the victory would be quick, never contemplated the long delay. Had the Germans won, one of the conditions would have been the taking over of the whole railway system of England [and?] manning it with Germans [until?] [an?] indemnity was paid.

BOOK FOURTEEN

1 JUNE. Yesterday evening people to dinner, Gerald Goal? and his wife, and Ramsay MacDonald. After they had gone Fritz said MacDonald had given them a very interesting account of the days before the war. Lloyd George had had all information that came to him sent in duplicate to R.MacD. and had kept him up one night till 2 o'c trying to persuade him to join the Cabinet. Fritz spoke of his fine speech against war, and he said he was hampered by knowing too much, information that he could not disclose.

He (R.MacD.) talked to me of Winston Churchill, thinks he has no good qualities at all. Someone had gone to see him on a birthday and he was sitting before a bust of Napoleon and put his hand on it and said "when he was my age he had won the battle of—" (I forget which). He told us what he himself had done about the insurance of merchant ships. He had gone to Lloyd George at the start of the war and told him it should be done. L. G. asked him to attend a Cabinet meeting and tell his plan. He went down to Possingworth and wrote it out himself, his Secretary, Maurice Hankey, having got out of doing it. He took this and read it to the Cabinet; Kitchener was present and said he was against it. F. asked why. "I don't understand why we should insure ships that don't carry munitions or food". F. said "if a ship takes even a cargo of things quite useless for war, say ladies' blouses, from New York to Rio, we should subsidise it, because we want ships to bring provisions to a central port. That ship can't go back empty, it will bring foodstuffs to New York, where we can get them". But still Kitchener would not consent. (I quoted Dr. Johnson "I have furnished you with an argument, am I bound to furnish you with an understanding also?"[1] Then Winston Churchill said "I am for the scheme", but he noticed a sort of shrinking, a hardening against Churchill. However it was accepted and carried out. And now a German book has been published in which it is said that one thing that shows England had intended to go to war is, that this scheme for the insurance of merchant ships was all ready on the breaking out of war. "But I never got credit for it".

"Nor for the moratorium" said Tiny.

He had written to Dr. Ford asking what would be the best house for Richard to go to, and if there is still time to put down his name for a good one. And yesterday at a meeting about a new tea room for Harrow he met Ford, who said he had had his letter, and they talked and seem to have both been of opinion that Vassall's house is certainly the best, if not filled up; and he asked Vassall if he could take Richard, and he said he didn't know if it was possible but would look through his list. (And Richard did go there in the end). F. says "Harrow is now so strong on the scientific and engineering side that Armstrong and Vickers when they know a candidate for their works is a Harrow man, let him in without any examination. And Eton says 'We would be as good at science if we had Vassall'. The examiners' confidential report speaks of the great keenness of late in all the work. But the classical side is sacrificed to the modern; only about a hundred classical scholars now in the four hundred."

This morning I heard from Coole, and have decided to go home at once. Freeman Smith's fine letter about Hugh came yesterday!

COOLE. 4 JUNE. On Wednesday morning I had decided to come home, and it was a busy day. I went to look for something for the chicks and bought a croquet set, which has proved a success, the tennis ground luckily ready for it, and they have exciting games. Anne and her Mama against Ruth and Catherine.

I lunched at the 30 Club by special invitation, having given up my membership when the war began. It has grown fashionable, and I liked looking at the array of beautiful dresses, V-necked, short-sleeved, pearls, smart large hats. Julia Maguire was next me, pleasant and vivacious. She said Winston Churchill, when a friend of hers asked him how they could have appointed Hamar Greenwood to Ireland said "No decent man would take the job". Lady Clifford, back from Nigeria, looked ill but is going back there and says the work is interesting. Tiny and I went to see Max's cartoons, and I had a nice little talk later with C. E. Lawrence at Murrays. He wishes he was Irish and could come over here. Rather comforting. Dined at Lady Courtney's, sat next Lord Parmoor and a Miss Ellis, both pro-Irish, but not inspiriting, and after dinner a Mr. Basil Williams came in, and Lady C. put him into an arm chair next me and we talked—he is on the Peace with Ireland Committee. He abused *Whiteheaded Boy* which he had seen at Oxford "vulgar and vulgarly acted—a new type of Irish," a man with him had said "if these are the Irish I would rather keep away from them". I talked conscientiously but without joy, and then the Parmoors got up to go, and offered to take me in their motor. And on the way home Lady P. said Massingham was (or was not) looking well. "Massingham! Was he there?" "Yes, at the other end of the table, between me and Lady Courtney". And I had not known! I nearly cried, especially as Lady Courtney had made me tell at dinner what Tiny had told her about the American Millionairess saying my plays had no humour, and it sounded egotistical. Poor Grandmama!

At 64 Rutland Gate I had seen several men leaving Tiny's boudoir, and Dr. Monro brought a tall wild looking Highlander to introduce, who said he was proud to shake hands with me, and that they were going to help Ireland!

I left sadly enough the house where I had met with—been encompassed by—so much kindness, and had grown so much better in body, and had also begun to recover self-respect!

A tiring journey. But Mr. Johnson chanced to be at the Broadstone in the morning, and got me tea, and he scouts the idea of danger for Margaret and says they were "Clare boys" that were in the ambush.

Coming back from Galway and near Athenry, the train was stopped—"A military search". Soldiers who had got in at Galway, I thought as passengers, produced rifles and ordered everyone out, and all luggage out, and with some demur people scrambled down the six or seven feet drop on to the line. I looked and saw I could not attempt it, or if I did get down with help, could never get up again, so I sat down and stayed there, the only one who did. Soldiers passed and repassed and pulled out suitcases and parcels and threw them out for search, but they passed as if I and my little fish bags (fresh mackerel for the workmen) were invisible. I looked from the window and could see the luggage opened and the men searched, pockets and inside coats and waistcoat "hands up"! Once they took out a pocket book and read its contents hopefully. But they found nothing. "They never do" said one of the young men. The passengers scrambled back and we went on, and I got home, and found the children well and happy at the sheep shearing, and M. looking sometimes as if the terror was with her, but tranquil and told me all the story of the ambush.

She had had that morning a letter signed "I.R.A.", apparently a threat, wanting her to give money to T. Diveney. She very properly sent it to Nolan in Gort. He answers that it has nothing to do with the I.R.A. but is probably written by a young chap at Coole who is giving trouble and they will investigate the matter. T. Diveney has settled with the Constable, that is a mercy.

J.D. says Captain Blake was "very stiff" and that Mrs. Blake "made him stiffer again". M. says both he and Mrs. Blake had attacked Father Considine and had a scene with him, in his house.

6 JUNE. P. says "There was shouting and firing all the night in Gort. Black and Tans and Highlanders about the streets, but not one of us but must shut his door at seven, and lock it and not open it again". J. says "Whatever they are after there was twenty three lorries full of them counted passing the road last night".

M. and Ruth, coming from Archdeacon Daly's say 200 military or police are encamped at Ballyturin. There were rooms commandeered in Gort last night, two at Mrs. Lahiff's, for officers. Nothing is known yet of the Blake's people, no relatives have come forward to claim their effects. The Basket maker came begging. I gave him £1 to buy rods.

7 JUNE. P. hears the Black and Tans have gone up to Chevy to make their camp there and that "they went around the country between Gort and Peterswell, and took the men out and beat them".

Tim says "The lorries passing are terrible. And there was a dog in one of them—a big black dog".

J. went to Gort for the post—rode—at 5 o'c and isn't back yet. 8.30. Marian hears our woods are to be searched for "boys on the run."

9.30. Marian hears from Johnny Hehir that all who were met on the road were taken away to fill trenches.

8 JUNE. J.D. returned, says he had just been to the post office and had the letters in his pocket when the barrack gates opened and a great troop of them came out, military and Black and Tans. It seems as if the police are out of it now, and it is the military who are in command. "They said I was to come with them to do some work, and I said I had all Lady Gregory's letters in my pocket, but that didn't save me. They took every one they met, about forty in all, bringing them out of the shops or from the street. There was one little man of a chemist, a delicate little handful of a man, and they brought him out, but it would have killed him to come along with them and when we were brought to the barrack those that were behind managed to shove him out at the back and he was the only one that escaped.

"They put us in the lorries and brought us past Lough Cutra, and there were two sheep killed on the road, the lorries running over them.

"We came to where there were three or four big trees cut and thrown across the road and trenches dug in it, and we weren't long moving the trees but the trenches were very long and we had to go into the bog filling them up. But they didn't mind if it was a stone of no size you would bring back with you, they were good humoured enough. They kept us at it till dark, and we got nothing to eat".

W.S.B. writes asking me to write a preface for the *Diaries*.

10 JUNE. Lady Ardilaun's letter promising £500 to help the Abbey a pleasant surprise, I had written from time to time telling her what our finances were.

Lord FitzAlan's speech at Belfast reported in *The Times*[2] of 8th. He confesses that "Crimes, horrible crimes, have been committed by members of this force" (the Black and Tans) and says in excuse that "this force was hastily enlisted and hurriedly set to work without proper discipline". The first time an Official has confessed to this.

An aeroplane today passed low, firing shots. J. says "We didn't know what the military were until Sunday week, when the roads shook with all the lorries going up and down. And there's more of them today bringing up the mountains quarters of beef and quart bottles of whisky and barrels of porter. No market allowed. There was a man yesterday brought in a few potatoes to sell, and they were being weighed, and the military came and stopped it, and said there was to be no weighing, and locked up the weighing house. The streets of Gort are full of them, some good and some bad, and half the small shops ruined with the people not being allowed to come into the town."

Talking with M. yesterday she proposed letting or giving the place rent free to the Pickersgills. Today I have asked if I may not try and keep it for a year. She may get tired of Celbridge even if she gets it, and the children be without a home.

11 JUNE. Robinson writes "Matinée cleared £140," so that was worth doing.

Lord Monteagle writes to ask if I can see him in Dublin on Monday. I can't, but it looks as if there might be some "peace with Ireland" move on.

M. hears "the murderers have been taken in a trench on the mountain with rifles and ammunition"; says it must have been from an aeroplane the trench was seen, they can see any shadow from above. I am in terror lest she should be called as a witness. She says there is no likelihood, and the only one she could identify is the one who led her away.

12 JUNE. Sunday evening. I have finished writing the preface for W.S.B. but don't know if it is any good.

The maids yesterday met a great troop of Lancers as they

came from Mass. Ellen says they were squeezed against the wall, and then a lorry came, and the horses went wild. Today eight lorries passed them as they came back from Mass, the occupants laughing and firing shots over their heads. Marian says there were 140 men taken and examined, but only seven sent to gaol. Feakle men, and some were flogged.

Yesterday by second post a letter from Lady Ardilaun with her cheque for £500! So the Abbey is safe for a long time, I hope for ever! Such a joy. Lecture misery and matinée fuss wasn't thrown away—we shouldn't have had this without it:

13 JUNE. I sent off the preface to W.S.B. and began looking through his letters, Catherine had pain in her face and I spent the afternoon with her, but she is better.

Hanlon and Coppinger were here, asking my help about a pension for Mrs. Coppinger. Hanlon said they had settled with T.D., "he had bad advisers"—I suppose the Transport Union.

14 JUNE. Jordan (the butcher) hears the burnings are over "and that's a good thing, it was terrible to be burning houses over the mothers of little children, and they as innocent as the leaf on that tree".

15 JUNE. A very hot day. Writing letters of thanks to A. John for his pastel and to Fagan; and to Yeats and teaching and reading to the children, and housekeeping. All my party went to Lough Cutra to lunch. Looking back on the day, my mind dwells with happiness on a few friendly words with Hanlon and Coppinger who I met by the lake; grateful to me for my advice about old Mrs. C.'s pension. It is to these people I am drawn, it startled me to find how much. G. and O. and even R. seem shadowy beside them. I would, as in early days, wish to serve them, wish to have them for my friends.

17 JUNE. Yesterday quiet and hot, I went through a box of W.S.B.'s letters. This morning no post, and Mr. Anderson coming later says the mail car was held up between Oranmore and Clarenbridge by I.R.A. and he was three times held up by "the other side" on his road, and was late. I said "What the locust hath spared the cankerworm hath eaten".

18 JUNE. A telegram came last evening, "Manuscript received. A thousand thanks. Wilfrid Blunt", so he must like preface, a great relief. Mr. Edmunds turned up just at dinner time, from Co. Clare, where there are many barricades, of stone near the sea, of trees to the east of the county, and he was delayed, but the people turned out and helped him over.

Working through W. Blunt's letters, the political part, so absorbing then, seem so external now.

19 JUNE. Mrs. B. to tea. The telegraph wires cut, both sides of Gort. G. tells me that "the English object to De Valera because he got up the Easter Rising", and that "whatever the English are, they have enough fine feeling to resent a stab in the back"; and secondly because he is not Irish but Italian! They would prefer to negotiate with some other leader and he agrees in both of these opinions.

I've written to Sir John Lavery with Freeman Smith's letter about the pictures. By what road am I making the return journey to our heavenly home. That is from Plotinus.

20 JUNE. Old cracked Mary in her rags says "They are terrible in Gort and out beyond, and firing down the second next boreen near Kelly's, and out in the borders of the town, and if they got any person lonesome down the road what would they care about them?

"I was out gathering a faggot for the fire and two of them came up to me, soldiers, having black gaiters and guns at their shoulders. 'Have you any money' they said. 'I have not' I said 'I haven't one penny if you gave me Ireland'. 'I wonder you wouldn't have some ha-pence to give us' they said. But when they saw I had nothing they went away".

Young H. and F. hunting through the fields, yesterday and knocking down walls. No law to appeal to. "The men who could have been called to make her laws and lead her armies in prison or dead" as in Italy, in Trevelyan's *Defence of Roman Republic.*

22 JUNE. M. came back from her two days in Dublin, went to Galway on the way, as she came back there were military at Galway station on the platform examining passengers' luggage and asking their name. When she gave hers to a young officer he said "It may be rather unpleasant, but we want to know if you can identify photographs of the men taken at Feakle, and tell if they were among those in the Ballyturin ambush". When she got to Gort she went into the Post Office, and another young officer Mr. Plowden who was there said "Oh, there is some business you can help us with. I think I have it here in my pocket", fumbled, then said he had it at the Barracks and asked her to go and wait for him there. She waited for some time at the Barracks in the Victoria, and John said "It must be to identify any of the prisoners you are brought here". Mr. Plowden then appeared and brought her in; showed her five or six photographs and asked if one of them was the boy she had seen, and who had led her away. She did not know any of them and said "These look such ruffians and he didn't". There was one of a young man, not the boy she had seen, and she said "He is more the type

as he isn't such a ruffian", and Mr. Plowden said "Then you think that may be him". She said "No certainly, I don't recognise it, I am sure it was not". He said "I am showing you these as it is easier for you than to go to Galway Gaol and look at the prisoners through a slit in the door". She told me this when she came back, and I was very much upset, thinking it might endanger her life having been taken to the Barracks, and the object guessed; they might think she had recognised or given evidence, but not being alone with her I said nothing. Afterwards she came to the garden with me and said she is very anxious and very indignant, and wishes a complaint made at Headquarters, as they had promised at the Enquiry she should not be asked to identify anyone. And in any case this was a very unsatisfactory way of having an inquiry, no witnesses present, no words taken down that she could see and correct, leaving her just at the mercy of this young man's intelligence and memory. She thought of writing to Colonel Fisher in Galway to make a complaint, but is afraid the letter might be opened and the military indignant, and can't go in, as she might be suspected of going to give information. I offered to take a letter but then she said it might be better not to write, and I offered to go in and see Colonel Fisher and tell him how unfair it is to her to put her at the mercy of a boy like Plowden, who had even twisted her words, though probably without bad intention, while she was there, and she begged me to do so.

SATURDAY 25 JUNE. So next day Thursday, I set out by the 2 o'c train rather sorry for myself, having sore throat still and slight headache, and my eyes very painful. There was a three hours wait at Athenry, but I was glad of that, went to the Hotel and lay flat on a sofa till 4.30 and then had some tea and felt more rested. In Galway I took a car and left my things at A's and went straight to the Police Barracks asked to see Mr. Cruise (Chief of Police). "Away on leave". "Colonel Fisher?" "He's gone away". "Who is in command"? "General Chaplin". So I asked the Head Constable to ring him up. But the answer was that he had gone out fishing after tea, and they didn't know when he would be back. "Who is in command of the Police"? "Mr. Sidley". They didn't know where he was but said he would be at the office in twenty minutes. I waited an hour, then left a note for him (I had known him when he was at Gort). I went back to A.'s. At 9.30 he appeared, but I had forgotten he was one of the feeble folk, rather slovenly, no definite statements or opinions, except that the matter was now in the hands of the military and the police. I said I thought it shameful that Mrs. Gregory should be put in danger as she had been, but he said "Oh of course they want to get all the information they can". I went to bed very downhearted, and prayed more than I slept I think.

At 10.30 on Friday morning I went to the Police Office again and telephoned to know if General Chaplin could see me, and when I was told "Yes" I took a car and drove to Renmore Barracks, where I had never been before. In spite of my telephone appointment I was received with great suspicion, was taken into an office to write my name, business, &c &c. Then after a while handed to one after another and taken through passages and around buildings. On the door of one there were printed notices put up. "We were lonely without you yesterday but this is our busy day so please be brief". Then a sort of Holy of Holies to which after renewed inspection I was admitted, a very tiny room, and a very fat man, the General, looking severely at me. I told him of the danger M. had been put in by being taken to the Barracks, even our driver knowing what it was for. I told him also that she had been just recovering from the shock, and that this had thrown her back into all its horrors. Also that she did not believe she could identify the only one of the men she had seen, saying, as she did to me, that she does not easily recognise a country face, and even finds it difficult with our own people; she had seen this was a pleasant faced youth, "a sweet boy" she had said over and over to herself as he was leading her away, and that if he were among a dozen or a half dozen others of the same type she could not, as she believes, pick him out or be certain enough to swear information against him. And I asked whether on the remote chance of her being able to do this he would think it right to endanger her life or cause the house to be burned, as might well happen if she was to be dragged in to see prisoners whenever they are taken. He said "But the officer (Mr. Plowden) has given us to understand that she did recognise one of the photographs". I was furious at this and said "Then Mrs. Gregory was quite right in saying that in such an interview, without witnesses or lawyer or shorthand writer, her statements were to be at the mercy of this young man's memory". Then he said he would go for Captain Harrison who is over the Intelligence Department. However after a while he came back alone and said "We have decided, after what you have said, not to bother Mrs. Gregory any more". I said "You make that promise, that she will not be asked to make any identifications"? He said "Yes, I promise that". I said "I have not said it is *impossible* she should identify, but that it is very unlikely." He said "It is all right, we will not ask her". He said also "The method was very wrong, the officer should have taken some less public way". (I was thankful P. had put himself in the wrong, and that finishes the matter.) He smiled upon me then, and offered to accompany me to my car, and we went through the approaches, meeting with salutes this time. I said "I suppose you are not able to enjoy the amenities of Galway."

He said No, he had always wished to be sent to Ireland and now wished to get away again. I said "A case of 'There's neither friend nor foe of mine but wishes me away'". He said "I am very fond of sport but never have had one moment for it". (I said nothing about his last evening's fishing!) I went back very light-hearted, and bought three dozen mackerel in the town to take home for the workmen's Friday supper.

The arrival at home not so fortunate, M. vexed because I had seen Mr. Sidley, and because "they would think she was afraid". So she was and so was I, and we'd have been superhuman if we had not been. But I feel, thank God, that her life is safe now; I believe it was in danger before.

(It was not till later I was told that the day after the ambush she had been sent a message from "them" that she was in no danger, that there never would be trouble here "As long as there is a Gregory in Coole" because of what I had done for the country—I believe my *Nation* articles though I did not think they were known of. December 1923).

Two pleasant things. Fritz Huth Jackson writes that Vassall will take Richard into his House. And G.B.S. sends me the just published *Back to Methuselah*. But I was so worn out last night, headache and eyes and fatigue, I had some bread and milk and went to bed at 8 o'c.

SUNDAY. 26 JUNE. Ill last night and today. But afternoon post brought news of Lloyd George's letter offering to meet De Valera, so hope brings me back to life.

30 JUNE. Yesterday to Ardfry, with the children; a lovely peninsula, remote and still. The children bathed and found bee orchids. The peace news is still good. Though when I read out to M. that De Valera had asked Craig and Sir R. Woods and others to meet and discuss the matter, she said "He represents nobody" and Ruth echoes this.

7 JULY. Watching for news from the peace meeting. Nothing bad so far.

11 JULY. Foxrock. I had set out yesterday to go to Dublin, to the Gresham, for the Carnegie committee meeting, and in passing through Gort the boy ran out from Post Office and gave me two telegrams, one with an invitation from Horace Plunkett,

asking me to stay here; the other from Sally Allgood from Brighton, "What glorious news of peace!" I got the papers at Athenry saying Friday's conference had lasted till 4 o'c, a long adjournment in the midst, probably waiting for an answer from London, and that De Valera has accepted Lloyd George's invitation, and there is to be a truce.[3] Robinson was at the Broadstone with the evening papers, giving details of the truce—please God a lasting one! But I am still anxious—as I have been—I who was so hopeful all through the dark days! On Friday I could do nothing through these Conference hours, but as I told M. "say my prayers and write to John Quinn". I am in such terror of this breaking down just at the last! I had wired acceptance to Sir H. "though without toilettes" as I hadn't brought an evening dress for the Gresham. Robinson brought me here in a taxi and I found as fellow guest, Lady Fingall and the three Scotchmen, Sir John Ross (over 80, humpbacked and infirm but with a sympathetic mind and "would like to live longer, things are so interesting") Sir William Robertson who I haven't talked to, but Sir H. says is an entirely ignorant and uncultured man; and Colonel Mitchell, a rather pedantic man, had been in the war for three years. These are the three Dunfermline men into whose hands Carnegie confided his millions for the good (according to their lights) of the United Kingdom. X. says the Committee that works with them is yet more ignorant and is especially prejudiced against Ireland, and he has instructed me this morning before breakfast, that we are not to oppose them but to try and get what money we can, and have the spending of it left to our own judgment, libraries of course, but he talks of other uses as well. I try to cling to a library for Galway, in connection with the University, and with branches through the county. However at breakfast I happened to tell of the good work done by the Sinn Fein Volunteers and Land Courts before the military dispersed them, and they seemed interested and Sir Horace said afterwards "That was a good beginning". His own hope is in letting Sir W.R. beat him at golf, to get him into good humour, but he is afraid he will play so badly that it will be impossible. But in the afternoon Sir W.R. said to me "I have been given a hint that Sir Horace is a bad loser, is greatly put out if he is beaten, so I'll take care to let him win some of the games"!

Sir Horace is a little sad at not having been invited to the Conference, but I told him truly enough that he has done very much to make it possible, by holding on to the Dominion Home Rule idea which no one would hear of at first, and keeping his little office open in London.

I had been cheered as to work by a letter from John Quinn who likes very much my little H. James essay, which he had not acknowledged and I thought he despised. And W.S.B. sent me a note from Knopf[4], saying my preface would be a "material help to the book . . . it is first rate." So I shall go on writing with more courage.

Margaret went to inspect Burren. Not much wrong with the roads but water very scarce.

Lady Fingall[5] tells me of the illtreatment of young men by the military in Mayo, told her by Sister Bernard of the Foxford Industries. They were stripped naked on a bridge, beaten with rifles, indecently treated and then thrown over the bridge into the river. They escaped alive but with what memories! She went to Lord FitzAlan and an enquiry was insisted on. General Macready[6] was present and the facts were proved. He said at the end to the officer who had been in command while this was done "You were wrong and in any future case of the kind you will be dealt with severely". Then to the others "If any use is made of this for propaganda I will myself frame the answer to be given in Parliament".

During the Conference the crowds in the Dublin streets outside the Mansion House were saying the Rosary, praying for peace.

BOOK FIFTEEN

COOLE TUESDAY, 13 JULY. Sunday passed pleasantly enough, Dermod O'Brien[1] to lunch, and we talked of Hugh and of the pictures. I went to see Robinson's Lodge and found Dolan there, and Will Shields, and Gorman[2] came afterwards, and we talked Abbey, and of our re-opening now there is peace. Robinson proposed *Playboy* for the opening week, but I wouldn't have any contentious play at this moment of goodwill. For the same reason I said we would put off *Revolutionist* (Terence MacSwiney's play) for a few weeks. Dolan says: "The boys in Ballykinlar nearly went mad with desire to get out and see it" when we put it on before.

I talked a little with Sir H.'s Secretary Mr. Heard, a thoughtful gentle man (Lady Fingall calls him Martha) and looking always as if he was being led to execution. At dinner Sir H. asked who I would like next me, and having I thought, done my duty by the delegates I chose Smith Gordon of whom I knew nothing except that he is a Sinn Feiner. But in talking of tree planting I found he is head of the Sinn Fein Land Bank, and he says Barton is over the Forestry Department of Dail Eireann, and that they will look into the matter of our woods if I send them the facts when they get to work. He had been for a while teaching ancient history at the University of Toronto, and we talked of the choice of books for the Libraries. He agrees about Trevelyan's Garibaldi books, and would like "if they could be put into any intelligible language" to give Meredith's *Vittoria* and *Sandra Belloni*.[3] And this led us to style, and others listening, I told Sir John Ross that it would be a fine thing to reprint North's *Plutarch*, which one can only get or not get in the expensive Tudor edition (I paid £8 for the one I gave Robert) and which is a so much finer translation than any other. He was interested but Robertson of course, and perhaps wisely, is inclined to oppose all he doesn't understand, and that is a great deal. Lady F. thought he hadn't been paid enough attention (I think because I hadn't chosen him next me) and walked up and down with him while he told his stories and laughed at their point, he emphasising these by poking her arm (this he did to me the next evening when I was the sacrifice!)

On Monday morning we motored to the Plunkett House[4] first to see the Co-Operative Library. The Librarian, Miss Marks (who spoke excellently on the matter), looked familiar to me, and I found it was she who had played Sibby so well in *The Dragon*. Then the Meeting. I was placed next Lyster[5] who at once began a resumé of Irish history, and was telling me that most of our woes derive from the abominable character of George the Third, when I had to turn my back on him, proceedings having begun. I was the only woman; Hugh Law, Father Finlay; A. E., David Barbour, D. O'Brien (who was drawing a sketch of me) and a nervous little man next me I discovered towards the end was the Librarian of the burned Cork Library, begging for £100 to make a temporary shelter for the books until a new building can be provided. A reasonable request, but Sir W.R. refused, was very bullying and domineering and sneered at his want of a definite plan and would only consent to the request being referred to the London Committee next Friday. I found the poor man, Mr. Wilkinson, after the meeting, actually trembling with rage and disappointment. He said he had found it hard to keep his temper (so had I, and I think others) and he told me in confidence that it was difficult for him to explain the want of a definite plan, but that wooden military huts had been offered, but could not be accepted from the military, but that now with the peace, it is possible they may be accepted, which would help things on. Later I spoke to Colonel Mitchell and he at first thought the grant impossible; then came back to say I might write a personal letter to Sir John Ross. I did this in the evening, and talked to him, and he promised to help. But in saying good bye to Sir W.R. I mentioned it, and he flew out at once "I can't do it. I never heard a worse case—no definite plan". I was sorry I had spoken, but in the morning thought (as usual) it had been for the best, and asked L.R. to see that in drawing up the report they put in some such sentence as that our Committee would agree to the grant being conditional on a definite plan, and time limit, and that should satisfy them.

As to other matters at the Conference, I only spoke (except about Cork Library) to say that Connacht has no library at all, and that I suggested Galway University being its centre for the county, there being already a (poor) library there. Father Finlay, later, said Moycullen would be the best centre! And a letter was received from the Archbishop of Tuain, hoping the books chosen would be such as would satisfy the priests and heads of families, and that the Jesuits should have a hand in the choosing A. E. said nothing at all; said he knew nothing about the matter. I asked him what he thought of peace prospects. He is anxious, but says they (Sinn Fein) adopted some suggestion of his, to acceptance of the National Debt Loan, which they had intended to repudiate. Sir H. was gloomy and tired in the evening; took me up to see his revolving roof bedroom, and then sat down and lamented, said the Delegates had not been worth their bed and bite! I told him of the visit long ago Gertrude had paid at Sir George Jenkinson's, when Sir Michael Hicks Beach had come there for a meeting, and had voted against Sir George, who in revenge had told his butler before dinner "No champagne for Sir Michael Beach", so he sat dry until Lady Jenkinson offered him timidly a little beer; and he had his revenge at breakfast, finding a pin in his hot roll, which he stuck in the lapel of his coat and showed to everyone who came in.

Sir Horace, more courteous, gave champagne, and played golf again. I asked Sir W.R. how it had gone, and he said "Oh, I let Sir Horace win a game, he is like a child, so pleased when he wins it's a pity to disappoint him!" My own unfortunate good manners led me to sit on a verandah with Sir W., who told me stories of himself and Carnegie, and was just beginning "Mr. Carnegie on one occasion at Skibo introduced his housemaid to the King". "Oh!" I cried "Mr Carnegie himself, on our first meeting, told me that"! "Oh, did he. It was the first time I suppose a housemaid had ever been introduced to a King. Mary". Mr. Carnegie said . . ." However I turned it off and learned with more satisfaction that Carnegie had not left him anything (nor to Sir John who I wouldn't grudge it to) and that what rankles is that he left money to John Morley.

Bonfires lighted on the hills for the peace were a help to detachment and these were still blazing in the early morning.

Sir Horace motored me in with Heard and L.R. and I left my things at Plunkett House and did a little shopping. Mr. Heard, meeting me in Grafton Street relieved me of my parcels, including a new door handle for Ruth's room, Sunday picture books for the children, and two cucumbers. But he met me again at the doorway of Plunkett House coming in equally laden, fruit and cakes for them. And after all I didn't find the children at Coole! They had gone to Burren the day before; but I'm glad they are at the sea.

I have been losing my taste for novels, but going up to Dublin I had read a part of *Diana Tempest*,[6] having begun it on my last journey to Galway. And I thought to finish it coming down in the heated train, having the long journey in a crowded carriage where I must sit straight up. But taking it, as I thought from my bag, I found Emerson's essays, also paper covered, in my hand instead. But an old idea came to mind, of a poem about the Risings from century to century, and an old woman lighting a candle for the hero of each; and so I made a beginning, scribbling on the margin of the New Republic (a dull number) and then on on a half sheet that was marking the Emerson. I don't know if it will come to anything (A pennorth of clips, a little present to myself, such a comfort)!

Today letters, and this. And Mary the Dance came this morning and improvised upon the peace sitting outside the hall door and I must type out what she said. (I think it was in allusion to rumours of General Smuts lending a hand). "The man in the skies is settling down things; he is coming from very far out; from South Africa or maybe from India; there is gold buckles all over his clothes; there is gold rings in his ears.

"He'll settle down everything, and he'll begin work, and all drink will be stopped.

"Ah let me alone! He is going through the world, through the skies above, and there is no one will see him till the day he'll land in Ireland!"

Tim says two boys, H. and N. "came to the house and asked money of us for the men that are gone to fight for Ireland in London. We gave them two shillings. I suppose they spent it in drink, but if we didn't give it the house might be burned over us".

15 JULY. Rain last night, all rejoicing. Peter heard it in the night "a golden shower for the world". And the truce has been kept; and *The Times* has a picture of De Valera's arrival at Euston, and he has been with Lloyd George for three hours, and they were to meet again today. "God is in Heaven,—All's right with the world".

Sending fruit and provisions to Burren. And working over *The Image* for Putnam. I had not looked at it for years, and it pleases me, it has harmony.

20 JULY. These last days were filled with hard work, getting those plays reading [ready] for volumes, revising them, getting my mind back to the time of writing them, that I might make notes. *The Image, Shanwalla, Hanrahan's Oath,*[7] I am fairly well pleased with them all. Of the *Three Wonder Plays*[8] I like my little *Jester* best, perhaps because it hasn't been acted yet, the bubble hasn't touched a curtain, I cast out the *Wrens*, I hadn't read it since its performance and it seemed mechanical, and that more knowledge of the history of the Union voting than is general would be needed in an audience. Perhaps one day if plays of

history are acted in or for schools as they ought to be, it would have its chance. I wonder if a little company acting only historical plays might go round the provinces of Ireland? All seems possible with our new hopes. [Sir R. Woods' letter confirms these. He writes thanking me for copy of Freeman Smith's letter "I agree as to the very important possibility of introducing a clause legalising the Hugh Lane codicil. It has been present in my mind, and I hope when the time comes I may be able to do it. The outlook in Ireland is brighter than it has been for a long time past".]

Molly Childers writes "Erskine returns tonight. I am like Leonora 'wischen Tod und Leben.'[9] I have not yet begun to hope. But it may be even now, out of this apparent impasse, that we may bring hope. One can judge nothing. I feel that there are powerful forces for good at work in England and helping us. But whether they are powerful enough we cannot yet know. Please write and write and write, now more than ever".

Burren. I came here yesterday to be with the children while M. is in London. I am rather—very—sleepy and idle today—those last days were too tightly packed, and on Sunday afternoon that I had counted on, parties of children came asking for fruit. I had only currants to give them, but had to sit in the garden while they picked. The boys thought the green apples "not sour", so these helped to fill their pockets.

Mineog has just been talking to me at the window, wants to sell me a load of seaweed or mangold leaves for the cow (when she comes). As to the hope of peace he is grumpy and says "we got the land cheap, and we have got good reductions. We don't want to be ruled now by bank clerks and shopboys".

S. talked of the insufficiency and jobbery of the Boards, the C.D.B. especially, boats built and rotting, ice kept till it melted, an official being paid to market it; little work and big salaries "and I'm afraid in the future big pensions."

22 JULY. Thursday passed, and no post has come to give news of that talk in Downing St. There is a mist, turning to rain. I have been reading *Lives of the Fur Folk*[10] to the children, and reading Santayana's rather depressing *Little Essays*,[11] and Turgenieff's *On the Eve* and *Virgin Soil*[12] (because I hear that at the Minster Libraries they like his books) and trying to write that wretched *Memoir*, that refuses to take shape. It is a sleepy place but peaceful.

23 JULY. The papers came last night, but disappointing. "No basis for a Conference".[13]

25 JULY. Monday. It is rather like being on board ship, so little communication with the outer world. There was a post

today, the first since I came a week ago; but only a Gort one, and a cheque from the Abbey to be signed, as I haven't told anyone to write here. But a Saturday's paper was brought yesterday by Geoghagan, motoring from Gort with his "Missus" and I laughed in S.'s presence and he couldn't or wouldn't see the joke—to read that De Valera and his friends had travelled to Holyhead in a "semi-royal carriage" given them by the L.G.W.R.[14] and that their luggage had been exempt "though that of all the other passengers was searched"! These passengers must have felt as indignant as those war-loving travellers to France when they were left huddled in the waiting room at Boulogne, and saw G.B.S. brought through in ease and state!

I am reading Santyana's *Little Essays,* a curious mixture of indignation that anyone should think ideals come from beyond the World, and belief in what one may call the unpunctual power of these. I am trying (being in a way in gaol, where I often think I should be free of distractions) to get on with, or rather get on to, my memoirs, trying to approach them from one or another side, not very satisfactorily. Today I have been doing a new scenario. And my time is not quite free. I hear the children read, and read to them for an hour or so in the morning and again after lunch, and I try to get through arrears of letters, writing them on chance of a post, and I seem easily tired. But by working on I may some day find myself on the right road.

26 JULY. Mr. S. by some miracle got yesterday's *Independent* and sent it in. It seems hopeful though no statement has been made yet. Mme Markievicz has been released.[15] They talk of the New Year for the settlement, but it seems long to wait.[16] This is not like other revolutions a breaking down, it is a building up.

29 JULY. Yesterday such a storm, and I spent most of the day with the children, and towards evening supplies came from Coole, and a horn of plenty from "Godmother" for them. And there is no bad news in the papers. I am reading Turgenieff still, last night *Fathers and Children,*[17] and with all that talk of destruction as it is, makes me feel that for such a long long time this matter of a separate nationality has possessed us that there has not been yet time to turn to other matters, religion, education, economics and that there may be a new revolution when the mind turns to these.

30 JULY. Richard came back yesterday, looking so well and bright. And the papers say things are going well and that a "basis for a conference" is agreed on.

1 AUGUST. M. has been here, says Celbridge is now for sale

and she has written to ask price. As her heart is set on it this may be for good, she will put her energy into making the best of it. As to myself my first feeling was of relief, that if this is to be purchased, as was not before possible, it may become a home, and I need not keep Coole after all, with its anxieties and loneliness, with the burden of keeping it in order and paying its taxes and rates and labour, more than my income will cover, and that I must sell treasures for or earn. I shrink from having my last years cumbered with thoughts of management and money. But this passed quickly and it seems more in harmony with my life than taking ease to take this increased responsibility, for Richard's sake especially, that he may if he will, and chooses to work for it, inherit and keep the place, even though diminished, his father and those before him loved, and that once gone, sold, dismantled, could never be regained. The little ones love it too, and it would be a shock to them to know it gone. And Coole with its associations has been of some importance to the country through a century and a half, old Robert Gregory's planting so as to "change the character of the county" as Arthur Young[18] says; his son Richard planting also and gathering that noble library; his other son William gaining respect for his large share in governing Ireland; William's Robert dying through his endeavours to help his famine stricken people, taking their fever as he fed and tended them; my husband's honoured representation of the county in Parliament; my son making visible through his art the beauty of what had been looked upon but as barrenness; dying and leaving a gallant record because he would not let others fight for the country's safety while he stayed at home. His little Richard inherits a fine tradition. And who can say how much of it is bound up with the woods and solitudes that have been loved by all of these? For Ireland's sake also I keep it, I think the country would be poorer without Coole. And I read the other day, but I forget where, "to care truly for a bit of land anywhere the world over is a liberal education".

3 AUGUST. Miss Q. said yesterday they had been afraid even to look at a Black and Tan when they were in Gort, "They were often half drunk, they didn't mind what they did, they took what they liked from houses and shops, there wasn't one of them that didn't steal. At Dairebrian they put a man down in a hole and hammered him down into it, beating him on the head and shoulders with a rifle. At Peterswell they took a man—a man there was nothing against, and threw him on his face and put a man sitting on his heels and forced him to crawl along the ground".

Leech brought yesterday's paper, but no news of a decision. It makes one anxious.

Santayana says "A native country is a sort of second body, another enveloping organism to give the will definition. A specific inheritance strengthens the soul . . . But happiness and utility are possible nowhere to a man who represents nothing and who looks out on the world without a plot of his own to stand on, either on earth or in heaven. A man's feet must be planted in his country, but his eyes should survey the world".

If the just settlement should come and the lasting peace we pray for, the long awaited dawn, it will find some part of the dream, some chords of the harmony, even now in being. Hugh's Gallery, wanting yet its building, its body, and the return of the treasures kept from it; the Abbey "shabby" perhaps as the Leader used to call it, in spite of the new curtain and rosy walls, but alive and vigorous; the new University with De Valera as its Principal; the Gaelic League more powerful in its politics, more successful Craoibhin thinks with the language, though the romantic and imaginative side has been rather pushed aside. The Feis Ceoil also, doing homage to the ear. All these are things Parnell's nation had not got, and all must help to our enrichment. The country parts, the provinces, need more. There is increase of wealth but not I think of intellectual strength.

I gave one dreamer's dream twenty six years ago in *Kincora*: "Ireland, Ireland, I see you free and high and wealthy, wheat in every tilled field, beautiful vessels in the houses of Kings; beautiful children, well nourished in every house". Is there much change in the vision since then? For the beautiful vessels were but a symbol of all beautiful art.

6 AUGUST COOLE. Home on Thursday, and tired yesterday, getting papers and housekeeping into order. M. coming from Galway races, says the young men there are drilling at night.

Alone but finding it hard to get to writing. One's thoughts take the excuse of a change to get away from the work in hand.

11 AUGUST. Two days ago I had a letter from Margaret sending the cheque for workmen and saying "I suppose you will be paying altogether after the holidays? Whether one goes to Celbridge or to River Court is immaterial, so far as *my* keeping on Coole is concerned. It is both useless and impossible financially, but if you care to keep it on, the gain of having you there and the breathing space it gives is far greater than the loss of added income by the sale of the land, and the temporary doing without family things that will in the course of things be part of the children's life wherever they are". So that new beginning is coming near; for I do not admit that Coole is "useless".

I am anxious about money to carry on Coole and I am beginning to work hard at my memoirs. I have gone back to calling it "My Education", it groups better so. And I am troubled about what workmen to dismiss.

Mr. Johnson came to tea yesterday, says there is drilling going on at Kilbecanty and Peterswell (and no doubt in all British Barracks!). But after a terribly anxious day McKeon has been released and peace seems nearer. Last night I felt so extraordinarily happy it seemed there must be some reason!

There had been some pleasant things, news that Richard is coming tomorrow for a couple of days. And Robinson writes that the Theatre must have cleared £150 last week and he says "I took W. Rothenstein to the Abbey tonight, and I wish you could have heard his praise of *Aristotle*. He was charmed with it. Will Shields was wonderfully good, the others not quite so good as the first time, a little nervous".

And M. wrote (about my keeping up Coole) "Thank you so much for charming letter. I feel if we are *each* doing what we believe right about the children's future such a happy time ought to be still there for both of us".

16 AUGUST. M., Richard, Guy, have been here, Friday to Monday, all went well. Richard very contented, trying a mechanical boat Guy had brought on the lake, and mending his musical box and rummaging among his treasures. He and I were alone for Sunday afternoon and went out in the boat with Mike John, just as I used to do on Robert's Sundays thirty years ago! Yesterday just before they left the post came and news that De Valera has refused Lloyd George's terms.[19] A great blow though one still must hope.

Marian had told me yesterday there has been drilling at Lydican. And J. tells me today that he and his brothers were called there on Sunday night and kept and kept till 10 o'c, drilling part of the time, but a part was taken up with electing a Captain. There were two men from Cork and they "gave a great dressing to them, and said Kiltartan ought to be ashamed they were all fighting over an acre or a half acre of land, and doing nothing for the country, that might want them more than ever it did before. The two names put up were N. that stole our stones, and Paddy Cahel that befriended us about our wool, and there was great voting, Regan and his party for Nolan, and Ballyanneen and Castletown and Gort for Paddy Cahel. So in the end the two were made Lieutenants one for Corker side and the other for his own side and Castletown".

M. terrified, the 100 or under men had grown by report to

3000, and J.D. and Johnny Hehir to "all our workmen"; and they did not go in a military spirit but "to oblige Paddy Cahel with their votes", an urgent whip having been sent to Johnny per two bicycles. He has been walking on air ever since. "The Cork man was very much put out at the arguing, and declared if they would not be said or led by him there might come someone they would be said or led by". When he had gone they told M.N. he had no right to be in it at all, being under the Crown. "Had he been in the army?" Oh, not at all, but in the Courthouse and put under bail and is under it still for breaking M.Q.'s windows. "It is Paddy had a right to say that while the Cork man was there; but that's what's wrong with him, he's too bashful". "R. was in it, and he an old man, sixty eight, to support his crowd, and he was put drilling, and you could drive a wheelbarrow between his two bow legs".

Mike Lally this morning (I heard him coming and brought him out apples), asked what I thought of yesterday's paper. I said I thought it was not good, but there are some good men in charge who have brought it as far as this, and I hoped would bring it to a good end. He said he hoped they would, but he had seen three lorries of soldiers coming up the road this morning.

J. tells me of B.'s garden being robbed "and the young trees broke and flung over the wall; that is a robbery of revenge for the entertaining of the military".

I am glad to be alone while this anxiety is so sharp. Knopff sends proofs of the Blunt papers preface for correction.

17 AUGUST. Yesterday afternoon I had hoped to get to *The Wrens* revision again. (Putnam wants it in the book). But after lunch I went to the garden to bring in some apples for Burren, and then sat down to correct proofs of W.S.B's preface, and found he—or Dorothy—had put in so much that was written in a different style to mine that I could not leave it so, yet feared he would be hurt if I changed it too much. But I worked at it till my eyes and hand were tired, from 2.30 to 7.30, and am not yet satisfied. The simple and personal effect was spoiled and it is hard to get it back without throwing all the new lines overboard. However I have put the greater part into inverted commas. And it was as well to have something to absorb me on a wet afternoon, with no good news yet from Dublin.

18 AUGUST. I worked again at the preface, and finished it, and gathered fruit and wrote some letters and set to work on revising *The Wrens*. Anxious still and no news, and M. writes indignantly having "heard our workmen are drilling" and talking of sending the children to Galway, "as a ship may be sent there to

take away Loyalists". A nice review of *Hugh Lane* in the *New Republic*, and of *Visions and Beliefs* in the *Tablet*. P. says the soldiers in Gort are again carrying arms, and that if no settlement is made there will be killings and burnings through the whole country, as seems likely enough. Last night I kept thinking of Finn's best music—"the thing that happens". And last winter's sufferings have helped to get this offer. But going through it all again would be a vain and terrible sacrifice.

20 AUGUST. Yesterday rather gloomy no news of possible peace. In the apple garden I found the little tree that had been loaded with apples, that I was fighting the wasps over, had been all but stripped, as well as an espalier quarender near it. A thief (*the* thief) had been over the wall and carried them off. We could but build up the weak places in the wall, and put broken bottles, but he is too good a climber to mind that. In the evening I was more peaceful, had been copying bits from old letters to W.S.B., and they give glimpses of the old life here, that will be just what I want if I go on with the "Education". But at half past nine Mike John came to report that the other garden had been invaded by boys who had taken the screws out of the new lock in nutwood gate. He had found them among the apple trees, a young B.F. who he captured, while an older B. ran away. He had known someone was inside by their dogs scratching at the gate, so a little rabbit hunting had gone on as well. This made me more heavy hearted. I, alone, can only go on living here if I have the goodwill of the people, and indeed I have done nothing to lose or lessen it.

The day has ended more cheerfully; for this evening Paddy C. came with a young M., I having asked their help about our trespassers. I told them that ever since the sale of land boys with dogs had been hunting through our woods and fields, so that on Sundays I could not let the children out alone; that I had hoped the Sinn Fein Courts when set up again would remedy this, and that I understood they were opening again now. That these boys who took the lock off the garden gate had dogs with them, and as we now know who they are I can ask what is to be done. They said yes, but advised me to see N., Lieutenant of Volunteers, as the culprits parents are "in his crowd". Then they said it would be better still to write to Pat McInerney who is Commandant, and he would either take the matter up or see that Nolan did. They are hopeful of a settlement. C. showed me the new orders they have received for keeping the truce, giving a quotation from a French paper giving them praise for having kept it so well up to this. I was walking back with C. and he said "Headquarters say they will never forget to your ladyship what you did for us". I asked what they knew I had done and he said he didn't know, "but that is what is said at Headquarters". I suppose they have found out the authorship of the *Nation* articles; and though I had not spoken of them or claimed any credit I was pleased.

24 AUGUST. On Monday to Burren for Catherine's birthday, I stopped at McInerney's smithy and saw him read letter, and he promised to see to it, asked if I wanted "anything done to them". I said No, only to prevent them from running through the woods in future.

The birthday very cheerful, Catherine delighted with her writing desk and her cake with my cat on it and all her presents, and the others with their water pistols and books &c. Guy came back with me for the night; is afraid there will be war "doesn't see how De Valera can eat his words" and is afraid of trouble here. But I had been brought a message after the ambush saying "as long as there was a Gregory in Coole they need fear nothing". McI. here, I was grateful for what I had thought fit to do for him at the time the house was burned, and besides that "it was from Dublin they had got word of my help". (suppose the Nation articles).

I was tired yesterday and came down early to write to A. an account of the birthday for Guy to take to post, and I didn't do much all day, typed a few letters and all the afternoon, 4 to 7.30 was taken up entertaining the Archdeacon's daughter and grandchildren.

Anxious this morning. Robinson wrote that he heard "Childers was despairing on Friday". But today's paper is more hopeful.

Typing letters, paying house books, seeing walks cleared in woods, and nets put up to catch the falling nectarines.

27 AUGUST. Quiet days. Yesterday picking and packing fruit for Burren and typing my letters to W.S.B. Rain today, and the paper gives De Valeras rejections and Lloyd George's indignation thereat.[20] Yet both must wish for peace and L.G. is evidently in a hurry for it. I had told J. there would be pressure put on De Valera by the 30 interned prisoners and their people, and he says Mrs. Fitzgerald told him yesterday that her son had sent to ask for his clothes and other things, as they are not to be released, and she is indignant. And others say that if their sons "are going out to do that work again they will put them out the door". I hear that T.L. has been warned to "let Coole alone"; so I hope the apples will be safe. I am reading a nice, neglected, letter from Great Falls Montana, from Mrs. Mitchell.

1 SEPTEMBER, (1921) After a good many days of rather irksome typing and arranging of Wilfrid Blunt's letters and my own (I have stuck the passages I have chosen into the Carnegie Report books in sequence) I have this morning waked up and written a little preface to the letters which rather pleases me; and then began the quite delightful task of writing a heading to each letter. I don't remember having seen this done before. I will have it in italics and it will prevent me from putting in passages that don't contain matter for a heading. Also I have spent two or three evenings and a part of Sunday in making up verses for the blowing out of the seven candles, lives lost in each of the seven centuries' rebellions against England, only doggerel I'm afraid, and the last two verses which I composed first of all in the train as I came from Dublin after I had seen the bonfires for the truce, don't quite fit in with the rest; but we'll see. (Note. This poem has been published as "The Old Woman Remembers".)[21] Small thefts have troubled me (out of the Volunteers jurisdiction) strangers over the walls who took the most unripe of all the apples, those that don't come in till Easter and mysterious vanishing of plums and pears. (December 1923, I now find the last robbers were the squirrels). Poor M. when she writes harps on the sins of Ireland "like the dropping of water in a very rainy day". And I am anxious, as the time draws near for me to take over the place. My Yeats portrait still unsold and I have not enough money to begin with confidence, and sad because the Abbey isn't playing, through Robinson taking his holiday at the wrong time, and I can't leave the place just now to start the plays, and with Dail Eireann sitting we should be making well and doing a service.

4 SEPTEMBER. To Burren yesterday, the children bright and well. Coming back late we saw drilling going on in a field near Kinvara, all dark coated, marching, preparing. I stopped to give McInerney some apples, the house is still unroofed. They had begun to rebuild but the Black and Tans had come in a lorry and said that if the roof was put on they would burn it down again.

Today I have finished my verses, the Old Woman Remembers.

About the apples. John says that at the drilling McInerney walked up and said to the leader "What about the raid on Lady Gregory's garden"? "I heard nothing about it". "Well I heard about it, and it's you have to deal with it". And since then X. and Y. and Z. have not been out drilling.

6 SEPTEMBER. They had very hard drill on Sunday, 1 o'c to 8, very hungry before it ended, looking for a bit to eat at Swift's gate lodge.

Today's paper and yesterday's keep one anxious, the Cabinet council at Inverness tomorrow, the English Press cross at De Valera's vague answer—Yet L. writes "I was at the last public meeting of the Dail—one's heart had to go out to De Valera, he spoke finely with tremendous sincerity". But the Kinvara oyster woman, speaking of last winter, and hoping such a one will not come again says "Wasn't it a woeful time"!

Getting my papers into order for Miss Cuffey, (who is coming to type them) and have more material than I remembered; the war folk lore as well as the Rising.

8 SEPTEMBER. A Mulloo child coming into the garden for apples brings her little terrier. "What is his name?" "Rebel!" This evening at dusk four young men on bicycles came looking for apples. I took them to the garden to fill their pockets; they said they came from Ballygar to Gort. "Are you drilling?" "Well, a little of that".

9 SEPTEMBER. X. says "There is a party for a settlement and a party that would like to go on. There is plenty of money, and some of those boys that were on the run are for going on again. And there are some others that say "Why wouldn't we have a chance to die for Ireland". And some of the Volunteers are now wearing uniform, X. and Y. and Z. I asked how he would like to be called out to fight. He said "I wouldn't like it. I would sooner be killed at home".

16 SEPTEMBER, 1921. Sandycove. Last Tuesday Anne's birthday at Burren, my Kites the chief success. The darlings very gay and well.

On Wednesday I came to Dublin. Before I left home J. showed me a typed paper from Volunteers asking for money, in the first place to buy arms, and then for reparation of burned house &c. Daly at Athenry says "Are not they good men, De Valera and the rest at a bargain? I never thought they would hold out so well".

To the Abbey. I saw Dolan and tried to hurry up plays, but can't get one on till 4 October, *The Lord Mayor*. A heartbreak that all these good weeks have been missed and the theatre let to outsiders who have profited. I went in to see Dolan's class, it was rehearsing *Spreading the News* with great spirit.

Yesterday early to the Abbey and talked over casts and business with Dolan. We are to put on *Revolutionist* the succeeding week, and Dolan is to give over some of his stage management to a helper to have more time for learning his part. I made a vain effort to get Yeats on the telephone. Went to see Molly Childers, and sat with her and the boys at their lunch. She said she was "more than ever hopeful" yet I thought her, and young Erskine, rather in a low key of hope. She praises De Valera's absolute unselfishness and honesty, says Michael Collins is a fine man with a good head, and magnetism. Yet she is uneasy lest they should ask too much of Lloyd George and bring about a break. She says what the leaders fear is that if the English forces (and these will especially for aerodromes be very large) are kept in Ireland there will later be another outbreak, and they want a lasting peace. They are full of plans, are for prison reform, so many of them have suffered in prison they know the bad results of the present system. Robert Barton[22] had been put in a punishment cell and for a month on punishment diet, bread and water, and every third day porridge which was "rotten" and he could not eat, so that meant a day's starvation. He had led a strike "down tools" because the Irish alone among prisoners were not allowed to speak either to others or each other, although this was allowed to the lowest criminals.

Then at rehearsal of *Lord Mayor*, quite promising except that the girl "Maire O'Brien" who has three proposals in the course of the play, is hideous. I told Dolan as he himself, in his part, will have to make love to her he had better choose someone more personable.

Then Yeats, and we went for tea to the Hibernian. He is much pleased at having a son.[23] He is still working at his Memoirs.

I read him my verses "The Old Woman Remembers". He said at once the verse about Sean Connolly must go out, it breaks it (This is what I felt myself but had not courage to do). He thought also "What did we ever win with tears" confused. I don't think so, but will put "by" for "with". He said "You have not the momentum you would have if you had given your life to writing poetry, but it has some charm", and he was still reading it over when George came in. So I am relieved, for I was afraid he might scorn it altogether.

A beautiful moonlit night here by the sea.

This morning it is a shock to see the Conference at Inverness is cancelled, De Valera claiming to represent "a Sovereign State".[24]

COOLE. 18 SEPTEMBER. After I had written that on Friday, Yeats came in, very gloomy about the breaking off of the Conference and says "Now I understand why Maud Gonne has just gone to Germany. I knew it must be a political errand, and of course it is to make a German alliance". I said Germany could do nothing to help us and could but turn France against us by showing sympathy. Then he thought she might be trying Russia; but there also there would be no help to be got.

He took me to lunch at the Bonne Bouche, but we both felt downhearted, and sat in the Hibernian for a while. I told him of my trying to keep Coole, paying all myself, and he thinks I am right, "there is no country house in Ireland with so fine a record", but is afraid the want of enough money will be a burden on my mind.

Frank had come in the morning, I wanted to consult him about practical things, what bits of my little demesne I should let; and whether the proposal I had made to M. was a fair one. He says yes, but he thinks it will be impossible to carry on if I keep even the workmen I propose, and then urged me to shut it up, dismiss all workmen, put a caretaker in the house and only open in holiday time, and take a flat for myself in Dublin "where you will be happy and have no weight on your mind". But abandoning Coole is no part of happiness to me. I told him my object is to keep it for the children whenever they want to come home, and to give Richard the chance of keeping it on if he wishes to when he grows up. He refused to look after it, but will come and see about letting land. This also had been rather depressing, and I proposed to Yeats that we should go and see A.E. and we found him at Plunkett House and he was more cheerful. He says De Valera's claim to "a sovereign country" means the repeal of the Union. Ireland had been made by the act of 1785 "a sovereign country" independent of Westminster. I begged him to get the *Bulletin* or some other Sinn Fein voice to say this, for the English would be less alarmed at "pre-Union status" than "A Sovereign State". He thought this possible and said he would speak to some of them he was to see in the afternoon. He believes should the settlement come, there will be for five years at least a wonderful Government of integrity, and thinks very highly of the leaders. Michael Collins had been to see him, to talk of Economics, and he thought him very straight, a powerful mind "a tall handsome fellow with a sense of humour, a very good head and memory. He keeps no notes, but if he has promised to be at a meeting two months off, there he is at the appointed moment. He is writing, or has written, an article for the *Manchester Guardian*, putting the whole matter on a higher plane. And as to Madame Goone's mission to Germany, he says she and her whole family went a fortnight ago; they wanted to hear music at Beyreuth, and found it would be very cheap because of the depreciation of the mark.

He doesn't think negotiations will be broken off, and left us with better courage. Yeats came to the Gresham and we had tea.

He is taken up with his *Memoirs*, and behind them, his philosophy, a philosophy of the history of the soul and the race. He had made, and wrote down for me on a telegraph form, a little poem in the train the other day, because leaving for a journey always depresses him, and he turned that to use, and made the verse "Through the winter time we call our Spring" . . .

Then Harris our Financial Adviser came to see me, and when I asked what he thought of the breaking off of the negotiations he said he hadn't given it a thought, it didn't mean anything, he had made a bet that morning that all would come right. And when I asked Seaghan later on at the Theatre what he thought he said it would be all right, and seemed to think it a very good sign that Lloyd George had gone to bed!

I saw rehearsals at the Abbey again, trying to find a girl for *Revolutionist* and some others, and will come up again to see last rehearsals of *Lord Mayor*.

Yeats came again and gave me dinner at the Gresham, and we sat late talking pleasantly enough, it seemed like old times. But he has been very much cut off from Ireland, and if he "can't stand England" talks of South Italy.

SATURDAY 17 SEPTEMBER. I got up at 6 a.m. and left by early train for home. The papers more cheering, De V. having sent a rather cloudy "surprised" telegram to L.G., who will probably find another cloud in which to meet him. I had only just come back when P.C., now Commandant of Volunteers came to ask for a subscription "to buy arms". I said I had seen in the appeal they sent round that it was wanted also for reparations, and that I didn't think they would need arms, there would be peace. He said he thought so too "but if we do want them". I asked if money could be applied to restoration at the giver's wish, and he said certainly, and I gave £1 to show my goodwill, but said I could not approve of killings on one side or the other, or indeed of capital punishment at all, remembering Shelley . . . "Whether death is good or evil, a punishment or a reward, or whether it be wholly indifferent, no man can take upon himself to assert; and so it seems to me that while we live in that unfathomed ignorance it is too terrible a responsibility for any man to take on himself, the sending of another out of the life we know, unless it may be in the certainty of thus saving other lives." Yet this "unless" leads one very far, and I am not certain that I was quite honest, for I do think if war can ever be justified these surprises and ambushes called murder were justified to break the government by England that has been destroying both body and soul, and my heart goes out to those who have taken that responsibility and have risked their own lives—or lost them, while I have been but "the hurler sitting on the wall".

The children with M. and Ruth and Patrick all home, the little voices sounding again through the house!

19 SEPTEMBER. Yesterday, Sunday, we, Richard, Anne and Miss C., went in the boat in the afternoon. She wanted to photograph "the wild swans", and did just get a snapshot of two, one on the water, the other flying, startled by the boat. A heron looked at us from a rock, and then, also uneasy, flew across to the island; there was flight after flight of wild duck, I had never seen so many, the long absence of guns has made them brave. The lake was very silvery and beautiful, I was glad Richard was there.

Today the news a little disturbing, De Valera more conciliatory, Ll. George keeping hard. Mme Markievicz saying in a speech "we are going to have a Republic". E. Martyn came over in the afternoon, never very hopeful. But home affairs are better, for I have had a long talk with Margaret about her own plans, perhaps a country house instead of River Court and then about our arrangement. She is to let Coole to me from year to year at a nominal rent, as we agreed. And though I must pay all expenses in and outdoor, taxes and rates, she will let me have the stock now on the land (as I had let the estate have it when W. left it to me) and will pay a year's wages for one man, Mike John, as he must watch the woods while they are unsold. And we are in agreement and I feel more peaceful than for a long time past.

21 SEPTEMBER. They have gone, darling Richard so well and radiant. I said to Ellen I never remembered seeing him in a bad humour, and she said she never had. Anne and Catherine and I alone to keep house.

22 SEPTEMBER. Girvan going to Galway called; a rush for grapes and flowers &c for "Godmother". Then J.G. with Coen's bill for M. . . .

25 SEPTEMBER SUNDAY. A rather good day. Mrs. Watts wrote a very nice letter about Hugh's *Life*, and offers to give Watts' original sketch for a portrait of himself instead of the copy of the sketch bought by Hugh for the Gallery. *Revue Universelle* with a nice notice of *Visions and Beliefs*. And McNicols, the Horticultural Inspector came unexpectedly and gave a great deal of advice about the apple trees, and thought the garden very much improved all round, and was astonished to find three trees of Cox's Orange Pippin laden, and a very healthy tree bearing Ribstone pippins, and so many of those immense baking apples, and said we should gather and store all apples now, which I had wanted to do, and Tim had held out for October. So next day, yesterday, the chicks and I and John and Glynn spent

the morning [Sept. 26] picking apples, A. and C. up the trees, and getting hampers full. And in the afternoon we drove to Tillyra, and Edward sent them to the Castle with Owen, and let them play the organ in the hall and gave us tea and was very pleasant, thought Catherine very like Velasquez Prince on horseback;" approves of my keeping on Coole but thinks I have great courage. He is not very hopeful of a settlement, but he never is hopeful, but he praises the leaders, De V. and McNeill and Barton especially. And indeed one feels more pride in being represented by them in England than by the British Cabinet in Europe! He says George Moore is really angry about Miss Mitchell's life of him,[25] and told him 'Boyd is to do the official life'; but Edward says "that will make no difference, Miss Mitchell's will always be the real one accepted, she took the only possible way of dealing with you, treating you as "Mon ami Moore". Edward is sorry he didn't build a Theatre twenty years ago, and "put the key in his pocket". Countess Plunkett took the room she had lent him away, ostensibly because he had put on *Bricriu's Feast*,[26] she said it was meant to ridicule her son's poetry! (The *Independent* has just in reviewing this poetry, placed it above Yeats)[27] He is anxious about money, has fears of his investment in the English railways, and is very crippled with rheumatism.

28 SEPTEMBER. Sunday was peaceful. There were sports at Kilbecanty where "the Volunteers kept great order". And on Monday and Tuesday we again picked and stored apples, Anne and C. up in the trees, the storing a problem, for the Volunteers' rule is not yet established enough to keep us from pilferers. Anxious days, no answer yet from L. George to De Valera, and Mme Markievicz still makes speeches promising Republic. I wish the irresponsible speechmakers could be put under Hanrahan's Oath. (of silence.)[28]

30 SEPTEMBER. Yesterday because of the strike I had to take a motor to bring me and the children to Galway "all the trains going random".

All sorry I think to leave the Indian summer at Coole. Mr. Nicholas wrote to ask for some of our apples for exhibition at Ballinasloe show. The drive to Galway very pleasant, A. and C. in high spirits. The journey to Dublin tedious in a crowded carriage; arrived 6.30. First to the Abbey and saw rehearsal of first and second acts of *The Revolutionist*, the actors promising. The papers give Ll. George's answer, inviting a Conference on 11 October, not asking De V. to withdraw anything, but reiterating that there must be no Republic considered. Very anxious we must be.

1 OCTOBER. Yesterday to the Abbey, did business and read plays. Then to see the Crimmins at the Shelbourne, and waited for tea, and met Lady Chance (Murphy's daughter!) but we didn't talk Gallery. Then to Mrs. Gogarty—she said Griffith had been there the evening before, "he doesn't tell us anything, but he was in very good spirits"—hopeful! Then to Mrs. Duncan with Mrs. Watts' letter. They are going to London—"you must get someone else for the Gallery"—but I couldn't say much of regret, for there is a dreadful picture by a Mr. Leech, flowers or flames given "in memory of Hugh Lane" and hung on the line; and I hope there will be a curator with strength of mind to resist such things. Then to a very satisfactory rehearsal of *Lord Mayor* and *A Serious Thing*.[29] I think we shall have a very good new company. And as I came out Ella Young told me De Valera has accepted the Conference invitation.[30] And this morning's paper says the Railway strike is settled,—by Dail Eireann.[31], through R. Barton, but a number in Portland Goal! and the Conference is accepted.

Yesterday was chiefly given up to kind Mrs. Crimmins, so little, after all she had done for me at Boston—taking her to the National Gallery and to a Matinée at the Abbey. Then I went to see Mrs. Childers, a good many people there. One young American lady said "Oh! I heard you speak at Vassar" and another "Oh I heard you at Brynmor", and they were so nice and said they wanted me to come again. Father Hackett there also, and is coming to *Lord Mayor* rehearsal. I was alone with Molly Childers for a little time and read her "The Old Woman Remembers" which she seemed to like. And she thinks I ought to write a letter to De Valera, or the Dail Cabinet, about the pictures. So I have been copying that this wet Sunday morning.

Harris thinks the new Government when it comes in will have great trouble with the Labour question, that Larkin will come back, they will have influence in America to get him out of Sing-Sing.[33] He says "I saw him being brought to trial. He was wearing a slouch hat and long sort of frock coat and was smoking a cigar. And all the way from the Custom House to the Court House there were people eight or nine deep along the streets pressing to take a look at him. They thought of him as a god". He talks of the amount of whiskey drunk by the priests at some house he goes to, and of the bad manners of a priest even at Lady Granards, and I told him of Nevill Geary saying of George Moore, when his mother wondered Mrs. Martyn could have him at Tillyra "he is quite a useful friend for Martyn, he cured Father Considine of spitting on the floor"!

4 OCTOBER, 1921. TUESDAY. Sunday was a wet day so I stayed in the house glad of the rest, and Keller came to talk about the Coole avenues. The agreement only gives us a right of way by Gort avenue, not reserving it for sole use, and we have no power to stop blocking of middle avenue. The agreement must have been very carelessly drawn. It is a pity.

Keller is disturbed at the prospect of a new Government, thinks land business will be no more, and "doesn't know what line to take". He had lunched at the Wicklow Hotel the other day, and seen a young man at one of the tables, on whose words all the others were hanging, and who when going and presented with the bill took out a handful of notes and threw one to the waiter with a great air. He asked who it was; "Michael Collins". I said to Dolan he seemed to be Dublin's "fancy man", and he said "That is the way with the hunted men". I had asked if our new actors were Sinn Fein and he said "Is not everyone Sinn Fein now"?

Yesterday, Monday, I tried to see the Lord Mayor about the statement re Hugh's pictures but he was presiding at a Corporation meeting and made an appointment for today. I came back to the Abbey and read plays, none good. And at dress rehearsal of *Lord Mayor* we had five priests in, not allowed to see real performances, and I brought them to the Green room where the players were having tea and the barmbrack I had brought from home. They were delighted with *Lord Mayor*, not so enthusiastic about *A serious Thing*.

This Tuesday morning, I got to the Mansion House at 11 o'c, and saw the Lord Mayor and read him my statement. He suggested my sending it to Lloyd George myself, but I told him I had been working almost single handed all this time, and it was time for others to take the matter up; that the pictures should be of more importance to him, as they are the property of the Municipality (or should be) than to me. And he said he would consult the Dail Eireann Cabinet and let me know on Thursday.

Then I said I had very much on my mind those unfortunate interned prisoners kept shut up untried, winter coming on, and that they must feel it all the more at this time of excitement. He said at once "That is just what I have had in my mind for some days". I said I saw in the papers that the leaders will not *ask* for their release as an act of grace, and I thought perhaps some outsiders might be of use in doing so. He thought this possible. I asked if representative names, perhaps of Bishops, on a petition or letter to the papers would be of use. He said "No, not Bishops". I said "I meant Protestant ones". "No", he said "We have done very well without the Church all this time and we don't want to bring them in now". I asked if Horace Plunkett's people could be of any use as he is a little sore at being left out. And he has secretaries and organization. And I said that when Conscription was threatened I had myself got a few writers to sign a letter against it for the English papers. He said "I would do it straight off, but that now the Cabinet is sitting I would do nothing without consulting them". I said that was just my own feeling, we must do nothing without their authority. This also he will let me know on Thursday.

Keller said he had asked Hogan, just out from a meeting of the Dail, what he thought would be the future of the country. He said he believed that within three or four years of independence "there would not be a ballad heard, all thoughts would be turned to economics". He thought also there would be less individual liberty than in England, that Ireland would be more on the American model.

WEDNESDAY. 5 OCTOBER. That Galway disorder and the accidental shooting of an officer will go against the release of prisoners.[33] I think of the old story of the man digging to release his wife from the Sidhe in the hill of Knockmaa, and just as he came near to her his pickaxe striking her on the head.

Great excitement at the Abbey because Michael Collins has taken eight seats for tonight, is bringing on a party from a wedding. I went to Miss Byrne with the Diary copybook to type; and saw Jack Yeats back from Kerry.

A splendid opening night at the Abbey, a full house (but a good deal of Press &c) £40 in all; great enthusiasm for *Lord Mayor. A Serious Thing* I think fell a little flat, except in such passages as "its a curious thing that every country we occupy seems to be exclusively inhabited by rebels" (great applause). But it did my heart good to see all going so well, a real National Theatre. Martin Killanin was there, loudly denouncing the state of Ireland, only goes to Spiddal for a day now and then—no use going there unless he can have friends with him; looks on me as the last limpet clinging to the rock, would barely believe I am staying on at Coole; comes over to the meetings of the Education Board "but that will be swept away". Young Grattan Esmond also there, had been "turned back from three countries", including the Fiji islands, on his tour. Robinson came in the middle, back from Spain, a great triumph having the successful performance to greet him!

6 OCTOBER. Yesterday, Theatre. Tea at Gogarty's. Sir W. Wilkinson says there was a house and garden adjoining the

National Gallery sold during the war. No one thought of bidding for it for the N.G. and it would have given space for a new Modern Gallery. It might possibly be had yet, but most likely at a high price. It is a pity. He has also a scheme for moving the Pavilion at Clontarf (now beginning to rot because the lead on its roof has been removed) to Merrion Square to make a Print Room. There is not one, although most of the great mezzotint engravers were Irish. He had tried to persuade Lord Iveagh to do this, but "he is old" and it failed. Such a comfort to find anyone talking of building!

And Tom Kelly, who had Castletown long ago, and came to my theatre party in pre-Abbey days, has come back and wants to buy a house in the West. I hinted at Lough Cutra but couldn't be sure it was for sale. Then to Mrs. Duncan about Mrs. Watts' offer of Watts' sketch of himself. Tired to Theatre; a big audience, though Michael Collins who had ordered eight seats didn't come. Plays went well, or rather *Lord Mayor* did, and all seemed pleased except Holloway[34] who attacked Perrin in the hall, said the audience were being defrauded, and that he had sent me a list of good players! Perrin lost his temper and told him he mustn't come in again without paying. And today, the first I heard of it, I am told that I ordered this!

Today Thursday, I went to Mansion House at 11 o'c, and the Lord Mayor brought in Alderman Cosgrave, Minister of Home Affairs, who said my letter about the pictures had been considered by the Cabinet; that they think it better not to take up the matter until the Peace Treaty is being made in detail, and have sent it to the Minister of Fine Arts to keep till then. He asked if I thought this satisfactory, and I said Yes, if it is remembered at the proper time, and that I advised their pressing for the Government Bill (Macpherson's) to be got through, as, simply legalising the Codicil. It will avoid future legal difficulties.

Then the Lord Mayor said we were to do nothing yet about Prisoners' release; he will let me know when the time comes. I suppose they have some reason for this. I told him I had thought of either a meeting at the Abbey to pass a resolution, or a letter signed by all our playwrights, Yeats, G.B.S., Robinson &c. But he said "Wait" so I shall get home.

I said as I was going that I had never seen De Valera and would much like to see him, even from the window, when he comes as expected at 3 o'c. The Lord Mayor said "God help you!" I asked "why?" and he said "I oughtn't to have said that," and mumured something about idols. I said I didn't make an idol of him, but I had been fighting his battles, and he said "Oh, I know that". But then he called out "Here he is coming in!" and hurried me to the doorway he would pass through to the Cabinet meeting, and said as he came, "Lady Gregory—President De Valera". I said I was just going to his old constituency, west Clare, and he said he had never had time to go there since just after his first election, and I said there were many very proud of having had him as a representative. The Lord Mayor said "Lady Gregory was just wishing to see you", and I said "You have been so often in my prayers I wanted to see what you looked like". And indeed I liked his face, good, honest, with something in it of Lincoln.

In the street I met Lord Westmeath. He had just had a letter from Lady Gough saying they are going to auction the furniture at Lough Cutra and that "perhaps as nuns had it before they will buy it again". So I told him of Tom Kelly, and he thought sale to him would be a great help. So I went to the Shelbourne, but Mr. Kelly was out, and then to Mrs. Gogarty, to ask if they would all come for a night on their motor trip to see Lough Cutra.

Then to Theatre. I wrote to ask Yeats to let us do *King's Threshold.* A letter there asking if we could lend the Theatre on Monday evening, or rather let our players give a performance there for the Republican prisoners' dependents. We must have the stage for rehearsal on Monday, but I wrote offering it for the next Sunday, very glad to be able to help at all.

Then in the afternoon I went to see Edward Martyn, he is rather more hopeful than before, praising De Valera very much. He was excited at hearing of Kelly; wants to sell Tillyra.

He says "It was Casement who sent De Valera to Tawin and paid for the Irish school there, and I was supposed to look after it. Casement often came in to see me. And Mrs. De Valera used to act in my theatre."

Our players say De Valera once acted on our stage, though not for us, for some Company that had hired it.

8 OCTOBER. The Thursday evening very good, within a few shillings I think of £50. I said "What a pity we are not up to £50" but Robinson said "No, we should have to pay the dramatists a higher percentage then"! Audience enthusiastic. Someone in the green room laughed at their cheering the bombastic "sunburst" speech as read by Gaffney (in *Lord Mayor*) but to me it seemed touching that there were some who would not let the last words "God save Ireland", in even so farcical or sarcastic a context, pass without applause.

Home safely. The children, arrived before me, ran out to meet me, waving the American flag.

Alas. This morning when I went to the garden—was told there had been a robbery again, the apple house broken open. There were but few apples but they carried off a quantity of pears just put in. J.D. and Mike John heard them and waited at the gate and tried to stop them, but they knocked both men down and made off, breaking through the gate. New robbers I think; they went back towards Cranagh, carrying off the apples but leaving a knife. (Dec. '23. I am told now they had nothing to do with Cranagh).

8 OCTOBER. (EVENING) Just now, 8.30 I was alone in the drawingroom, and Ellen came up and said there were some young fellows at the door to see me. I went down and found P.C. (Commandant of Volunteers) and five others, asking for the loan of some beds and bedding for Raheen, which has been made Headquarters. It was a bad moment to come, for Marian and Mary and Delia had gone to the Mission in Gort, there was only Ellen in the house, and only Marian knows where there are portable beds, (I'm sorry I didn't show them Margaret's four-poster, and the immense bed in my old room!) but I said they could have them tomorrow and they seemed content and will come for them. They are wanted "for about three weeks"—but how can they tell, poor boys! I gave them apples, bringing up with Ellen two baskets of the best from my apple room—"My God"! they said when they saw their size. My heart goes out to them and I pray they may never have to go into danger for they are all known now, their drilling has been open.

I asked Ellen then about the Galway trouble. She says they heard from Father O'Kelly's sister who had been at the dance, that it began with Auxiliaries trying to force their way in without payment, and this to "bring on trouble".

9 OCTOBER. At church today poor Lady Gough and Hugh, both looking sad, and they were disappointed I think that I had no buyer ready for Lough Cutra, Lord Westmeath having written them that I had, and then Gogarty had written me that Tom Kelly "Won't make his mind up for a year or two". I told them that if they had my faith they would keep the furniture in the house for these next months, for if the settlement comes there will be Americans with Irish blood coming back.

The Volunteers had been here while I was at church, only wanted one bed, and were pleased with an iron one and its bedding Marian had ready for them. She offered them a larger one from gunroom, but they said it would do very well, it was a small man who was to sleep in it. Marian was afraid it was too narrow, but J. says "Some of these that were on the run are drawn up as thin as a rod". Anne and Catherine happy skipping in the afternoon, and picking up apples and washing them in the tank, and indoors we read Pilgrim's Progress and stories from *Sunday* and looked at the Bible pictures in the big book.

The priest advised the people last week to get rid of any Ulster notes in their possession. J. says this evening the people are getting very anxious lest the settlement should break down, and their boys suffer as they did last winter—"and De Valera maybe off to France".

12 OCTOBER. A nice letter from Kerrigan[35] from U.S.A., saying he would like to come back and do work in and for Ireland; and that he has been reading *The Dragon*, "it is wonderful, it is the greatest folk play I have read. There is a wonderful quality in it" and so on. And he has been reading also the *Kiltartan History Book* "it has filled me with a kind of sweet sadness and longing for white roads and little houses". It will be a great help if he comes back.

Also a letter pleased me from someone in Dublin. "Kevin Barry's own Company will hold a concert in aid of war-stricken Volunteers in the Queen's Theatre on October 23rd" and asking "permission to produce your beautiful little drama, *The Rising of the Moon*". I am so glad to give it.

And the "Prisoners' Dependents Fund" secretary has written "We are very grateful to you and gladly accept your kind offer" of the Abbey performance of *Revolutionist* for them. I forget if I wrote that a priest asked leave, writing from the Friary at Glasgow to give *Workhouse Ward* "at one of our Confraternity meetings"; and that also it is a pleasure to give.

The Conference has met, but no news except of its formal meeting.

A letter from Margaret saying the houses in Kent were too small, and that Kent is "almost as depopulated as Galway", so it is River Court, and I am glad as the children can get better teaching there. They are very good at lessons now.

16 OCTOBER. Burren. Yesterday was lovely and we came here, but rain today. We had gathered in the orchard apples, the children asked for a tree for themselves, and I gave them a well laden one, small bright coloured sort of croftons, and they were delighted picking them and storing them in the little cupboard in their dining room wall. They had been happy these last days also with a little frog they found in one of the garden water barrels; made a floating garden for it, of large leaves and pink lilies, and then gave it a mousetrap for a sort of Noah's Ark, and finally a board supporting grass in which were slugs, and they say it has

eaten all but two of these! I suggested letting it out, but Catherine is reading for her lesson, the "Look about you Country Book" and it says frogs like a quiet pond and she says "the barrel is a quiet pond".

18 OCTOBER. Weather broken, but the children seem happy, and it is rather a rest to me from small distractions. I am going through my old diaries, and now think it may be best to run them on, or the parts worth using, and not group as I had intended doing. I asked Mr. Scovell if he would give the children some arithmetic lessons. I am too weak in it to teach with confidence, and he readily assented, and they have been with him these two days. The first day they had felt the hour long, and I had asked that it might be cut down to half an hour, but today they enjoyed it. And Mrs. Scovell has offered to teach them a perhaps even more useful accomplishment—bread making.

Mr. S. now speaks of the Sinn Fein Government as if certain, and without animosity, just as all must be, a little anxious. Pride must have a fall and I had been rather proud of having had my help to the Volunteers recognised, and of having lent the theatre and Players for a Sunday performance for Republican Prisoners' dependents, and rather expected a word of acknowledgement. But the *Independent* gives the speech of General Mulcahy,[36] Chief of Staff, I.R.A. at the performance, with his words in large type "It seems to me that we have been deserted at the present time and all through the fight put up in the country by our poets and by out literary people". I wonder if he has seen Yeats' poem,[37] and A.E.'s on Brixton Prison, and his pamphlets (my *Nation* articles, not being signed, don't count).[38]

I heard Lloyd George had said "Talking with De Valera is like talking with Oliver Cromwell". So last night, reading Lord Rosebery's speech on Cromwell I looked for the affinities. Perhaps they are in these passages: "A man who combines inspiration apparently derived from close communion with the supernatural and the celestial, a man who has that inspiration and adds to it the energy of a mighty man of action, such a man as that lives in communion on a Sinai of his own, and when he pleases to come down to the world below seems armed with no less than the terrors and decrees of the Almighty himself" . . . Or this "On the field of battle he is a great captain, ready, resourceful, and overwhelming". (De. V. had put a barricade to hold but held it to the very end); off the field he seems to be a creature of invisible influences, a strange mixture of a strong practical nature with a sort of unearthly fatalism, with a sort of spiritual mission.

S. Gwynn writes attacking De V. for asking for "a total surrender of judgment" on the issue. But I think the appeal was perhaps but the steamship one "Do not speak to the man at the wheel".

19 OCTOBER. G.B.S. wrote to the children, in return for the scarlet Croftons they sent him, some lines, and on such charming postcards, Reynolds' Angels, and Age of Innocence, Stein's Grace before meat, a girl's head by Grense, De Hoogh's Dutch courtyard, with a child. They are delighted.

Perrin writes the Sunday *Revolutionist* went off well, and made £84. 16.

This is G.B.S.'s poem:

Two ladies of Galway named Catherine and Anna
Whom some called acushla and some called alanna,
On finding the gate of the fruit garden undone
Stole Grandmama's apples and sent them to London.
And Grandmama said that the poor village schoolchildren
Were better behaved than the well brought up Coole children
And threatened them with the most merciless whippings
If ever again they laid hands on her pippins.

In vain they explained that the man who was battening
On Grandmama's apples would die without fattening,
She seized the piano, and threw it at Anna,
And shrieking at Catherine "Just let me catch you"!
She walloped her head with the drawingroom statue.

"God save us, Herself is gone crazy" said Marian,
"Is this how a lady of title should carry on?"
"If you dare to address me like that" shouted Granny
"Good-bye to your wages you shan't have a penny!
"Go back to your pots and your pans and your canisters"!
With that she threw Marian over the bannisters.

"And now", declared Granny "I feel so much better
That I'll write Mr. Shaw a most beautiful letter
And tell him how happy our lives are at Coole
Under Grandmama's darlings' beneficent rule"!

Working through the old Diaries. Some scraps of conversation interesting, but some must be left out for kindness sake. I had forgotten I had done so much for Southwark and great Ormond Street; great blocks filled with the record through the years 1887–91. The foreign travel dull; guide books; I wrote names of pictures that I might remember them to please W. more than for my own pleasure. And the Coole part, "the trivial round, the common task" as even then I called it and the helping of the poor would be of no interest to others, though this last is of great interest to me for I see how the cards have been shuffled. In my later life it is I who have been the gainer, it is my work that owes so much to the people.

Reading *The Young Exiles*[39] to the children this evening. There was wonderful harvest moon over the sea.

A wet afternoon and worrying over accounts, don't know if I'll be able to carry on, but having about £500 in Bank I can manage for a year anyhow.

And I had to write a long letter to Mr. X. of the Galway County Council, having with extraordinary folly consented to look at his poem "Fingal"—Ossian put into verse—Macpherson's *Ossian*—the children calling me out now and again to their game. I have finished reading old diaries.

22 OCTOBER. Murray's accounts received. Nothing coming to me (for the first time) "corrections" in Hugh's life, and £6 for the two extra plates, leaves me owing him £29.4.11. Not encouraging towards paying my way at Coole. *Cuchulain* and *Gods and Fighting Men* and *Saints* having been reprinted bring in nothing this time. However last night I thought over the diaries, and made some notes and begin to see a shape for the memoirs.

23 OCTOBER. I sat with old Tierney for a little time yesterday afternoon. He is anxious, longs for peace and a settlement, hopes there will be no more Black and Tans, "the worst class that ever came into the country, the English will be ashamed of them when they come to know their pedigree". I felt a little dwindling of confidence because of De Valera's telegram to the Pope,[40], [41] seeming to reject any less offer than a Republic. And today J. coming from Coole tells me "things look bad" and yesterday's paper (which he hadn't brought me) says De Valera is being given till 11 o'c tomorrow to withdraw it. John says "no offer for rabbits, no price for them and no one buying anything. Keane hasn't a bit of bacon in his shop, afraid to bring out money, no one knows what will happen". A rough cold day. I read to the children and we went to church, and had the Scovells to tea. There is a good sentence in a speech of Wickham Steed's in *The Times* of last Tuesday "Ideals are points of concentration for the magnetic forces of the mind, and it is magnetism that drives the world".

28 OCTOBER. The days go by, all beautiful without, sky and sea; but great anxiety about the Conference—Heaven or Hell! Though even this delay shows there will not be absolute agreement should a peace come, the ideals are too high, too clear cut,

to be carried out without opposition when the opposing force that holds all Ireland together is removed. I give the children their lessons, and write letters, endless letters, today about a possible exhibition of Vienna children's work in Dublin, and judgement on a play, and home affairs and Dublin business. In the afternoon I work at the Diaries, cutting and pinning into copybooks, and sometimes getting a vision of the whole but often discouraged. I want it to be a book that can at least be put on the same shelf with *Poets and Dreamers* and *Cuchulain*, and the material seems a long way from that.

A. writes "I read a story the other day that reminded me of you. A little girl was ill, very dull and lonely as she could not get about, and her sister was at school but used to write every day to the invalid whose cheerless days were much brightened by the letters. Afterwards she went to school herself and then for the first time realised how good it was of her sister to have written regularly when there was so little spare time at school. It's wonderful how *you* can find time to write, and such interesting letters". Poor A. I don't think I have missed half a dozen days in these years in writing to her. She is very patient in her invalide's life.

Mrs. Watts' offer of her husband's sketch of himself has been gratefully accepted by the Municipal Gallery, and *Hyacinth Halvey* has been acted with success at the Birmingham Church Congress before eight Bishops, and the lesser clergy in their ranks. Sara Allgood is coming back to the Abbey. This is all pleasant to think of.

30 OCTOBER. Sunday. Mr. S. is anxious, says the Volunteers have sent round to all houses a day or two ago to take a list of all tools, saws and the like, and that it is said the truce will soon be at an end. J. coming from Coole does not seem to have heard this, but says there have been lorries of Black and Tans on the roads these last days, but that some of the boys who were on the run, and their leader, say there will be no fighting, that an agreement will be come to.

2 NOVEMBER. A merry teaparty for the children's Holly Eve. Not much in Lloyd George's speech; anxious still. This morning brought Yeats' *Four Plays for Dancers*[42] from him, and a letter, and the proof of his "Thoughts for the Present State of the World".[43] And a letter from Mrs. Duncan saying Atkinson of the Art School will arrange for the Vienna Children's Exhibition I had written to her about. And R. sent a play *Insurance Money*[44] which he thinks would offend Ulster, but I think a very fine comedy and that as to offending Ulster it would take a good deal

to make up for the Ulstermen wrecking the last Convention.

3 NOVEMBER. The Scovells hear trenches are being dug.

5 NOVEMBER. Yesterday morning M. letter going back on the agreement she had written was a shock at first. But perhaps it will be better in the end. The sole charge of Coole would be a heavy responsibility. And I hope still to save a part, though perhaps a smaller part for the children. I wrote draft of a letter today over and over but didn't send it till today, and hope it may be for the peace and harmony I desire. But I remember a sentence I wrote long ago "Every new rejection is a new lease of liberty".

I read, and wrote a long note on, an interesting play *The Crimson in the Tri-Colour*, the antagonism sure to break out between Labour and Sinn Fein, and sent it to Robinson. (April 1928. This was the first play I had seen by Sean O'Casey[45])

I had tried in vain to begin writing, that is, to write the beginning of my memoirs. I have now chosen the title, *Seventy Years*, and thought that will give me a sort of plan, but in vain, till two nights ago opening Plutarch at the life of Marcus Crassus[45a], with its simple statement, it gave me an impulse and I began to write a paragraph "At the midnight hour between the fourteenth and the Ides of March (date) a girl child was born . . ." I don't know if it will stand, but last night I wrote a new paragraph, on the cover of the New Republic "the reason of this little girl's story being written". I don't know if it will help.

10 NOVEMBER. Gresham (Dublin). I left Burren at 9 o'c yesterday morning, a storm blowing, the sheep huddling for shelter against the walls, then rain for the rest of the way. Home, and ran to the garden to see what the men had done, digging brambles out of the top border and now clearing grass from around the apple trees. Then on to Dublin. Rain had stopped on this side of Mullingar, and Robinson met me at the station. He had seen Smith Gordon, who had been over for the week end with the delegates as financial adviser (and who had brought Michael Collins to the Abbey on Saturday evening for *Devil's Disciple*, but R. to his grief had not been there!) S.G. said he hoped there would be peace by Easter, seemed cheerful on the whole, but said they are "having trouble with the Church".

The Abbey then *Courting of Mary Doyle*[46] amusing and well acted, though rather poor dialogue in patches. *Yellow Bittern*[47] also, not very good, the voice off being at least to me inaudible as to words, and the audience seemed cold.

EVENING. The Carnegie Committee rather dull, the Provost in the Chair, but I had a little talk with A.E. afterwards. He says the Sinn Fein leaders are straight men; that they ask when a post is to be given who they can find that is efficient (and L.R. said the same speaking of S. Gordon's appointment). He said also that the Belfast *business* men are for an agreement on economic grounds, even Barbour who was the chief opponent at the Convention has been corresponding with him on economic matters and seemed quite reasonable, but unluckily got ill and couldn't go to the (new?) Conference. A.E. has been trying to write a book for over a year, on the taking of the "Over Soul" as one's adviser rather than the people around, but has been too much interrupted by these economic enquiries to go on. "I am not known as a poet or artist but as an economist".

He and I had both spoken at our Committee for having a say, or at least giving advice in the choice of books to be bought with the grant given. The Provost had called out against a grant to Kilkenny because when he was Bishop there the people, in spite of there being a library, read nothing but newspapers. I said there was a new intelligence in the country now, and that if books bearing on the subject of the rebuilding of a nation, and the work before them, were given they could certainly read them. I said I would choose Plato's *Republic*, and More's *Utopia*, and Trevelyan's *History of the American Revolution*, and the *Life of Alexander Hamilton* and the story of Napoleon's creation of the Code and of a new government for France, and A.E. warmly agreed. I was afraid to mention Trevelyan's Garibaldi books as Father Finlay was there, but A.E. afterwards told me he had found a farmer in the South reading one of these with great enthusiasm and saying "This is Ireland over again".

A very nice letter from Kerrigan about *Aristotle*, and cutting from Indianapolis saying how well the *Dragon* had gone there.

Talking to Atkinson about the exhibition of Vienna Children's paintings this he is as anxious for as I am. He says the Dail, reorganising the teaching system, is going to strike out drawing, thinking it sterile, and this he says it is as at present taught. But this exhibition may show them how children can learn to express themselves through it, and he agrees with me that they may take a national pride in trying to emulate Austria. He, also, touched with and struck by the national stir of the mind. And later, at the Abbey, I sat and talked with Larchet while I had some tea and biscuits, (having forgotten to get it at the hotel) he said he had been working very hard of late, the Dail employing him to draw up a method he believes will teach music to children in the easiest and most natural way. Then Casey, the author of *The Crimson in the Tri-colour* came in, and I had a talk with him about his play, and when I said we could not in any case put it on now, as it might weaken the Sinn Fein position to show that Labour is ready to attack it, he said "If that is so I would be the last to wish to put it on". And he is a strong Labour man, and is collecting names to sign a message to Larkin in Sing-Sing.

Such a fine audience at the Abbey! *The Courting of Mary Doyle* extremely amusing and quite excellently acted; so I left Dublin this morning in very good spirits, and (although the papers say Ulster is obstinate and may wreck the settlement) I think it will be hard to kill the spirit that has awaked. It is a different Dublin to that we found in 1899 when we began the Theatre and later when Hugh talked of his Gallery, and I used to say the Dubliners were like water lilies in a pond and amazed when a new idea came splashing to disturb their complacency—or serenity.

I came by the early train to Coole and drove on here (Burren). J. says an arbitration Court has had a sitting to decide claims of purchasers of our land, but it had been adjourned. And that the Lough Cutra workmen who were to cease work last Friday, came in on Saturday morning and said they would not give up their employment, said they had no other way of living, though they had been allowed to buy what land they can but it can bring in no money for some time. They refused to leave and the steward (who told him this) had sent to Gort for Ruane and Shaughnessy "and they came and told them to leave the yard and go home and we know what the police are, and I never saw police or any others deal with a body of men and get obeyed like those two did, and they were very brave lads to come and face them as they did". A tyranny perhaps beginning, but still one must remember that "to a nation at war the order must be 'march' and not 'develop'". That will come with the peace.

The chicks had driven Puddah a long way on the road to meet me, very bright and well.

BOOK SIXTEEN

14 NOVEMBER, 1921. A letter gave me a troubled day. I am trying to do what is best for the children by keeping their home while I can, but this gets me into more tangles than I expected.

19 NOVEMBER. Leaving Burren today, and a nice letter today "you stay at Coole for your lifetime if you can afford to keep it. If not, I will sell everything you can't afford to keep".

21 NOVEMBER. COOLE. The Scovells and Keller came on Saturday for the Lough Cutra auction. Yesterday I motored to Roxborough with Keller. Arthur is rather gloomy about the prospects of the country, and when I said the leaders were doing so well and are honourable men, he said "Yes, but will they last? That is what I am afraid of, that they will have their throats cut. Both farmers and labour will be up against them". Such a change in a year or two, his hope being in the Dail Eireann Cabinet. And he is very much down on the C.D. Board and says all the Boards ought to be cleared away.

24 NOVEMBER. Guy is staying here, says the Volunteers are looking after Lough Cutra, keeping people out from the auction who have no business there, keeping excellent order. And they have just reported that the boat stolen some time ago has been discovered, sunk in the lake, from whence it can be recovered. I asked what they would expect in return for these services. He said "I suppose they do it for an advertisement", but that Hugo had gone to them for help, and he may be expected to give something in return. And, like Arthur, he says "But will they last? That is the danger that they may not always keep order".

Anne and Catherine went to the auction yesterday to see Guy's horse and puppies, and had tea with him "in a private room", very much pleased.

26 NOVEMBER. The auction well over. Bennett says King's County is "cleared out", he has sold the contents of 400 houses there. I have bought three chairs from Lough Cutra for the children, brought from the Dresden house.

27 NOVEMBER. The week passed pleasantly, the Scovells pleased and pleasant, a holiday for her after her nursing of the Mineog child. All were nice to me, and the children were gay as

possible, finding the house filled exclusively with their admirers.

The Gort avenue fields are being laid out for a coursing match, a cruel sport I think, but old "Mary the Dance", coming from Gort, says that is not so, for that "God Almighty likes to see the hounds following the hares and routing the fox out of his burrows because that is according to their nature". Father C. is spending his time overseeing it, said "it is very hard to make them get up any sort of amusement". He says he has hounds of his own and goes to all the coursing meetings in Clare. The "coursing Committee" keep sending down for poles and for laurel branches, and I am glad to give them, and go out to show where they may be cut without injury, even with good result. Yesterday they sent me two hares, I sent one of these to Jack Yeats and in thanking me he says "I wouldn't care for the coursing, I agree all hunting and coursing is horrible, though what old Mary from Gort says is half true. But there was a time when nature did not require the aperitif of cruelty. You may have heard how in India in a long drought when the beasts were tamed by the agony of thirst, a young subaltern was sitting by his tent door, having a cup with a little water in it hanging in his hand, and a hare came out of the edge of the jungle, staggered to him, buried its little boney face in the cup and drank. There is not a living man who could look on such a sight without some wrinkling of the emotions, because of some throwback to the great days. Sport itself comes from the same thing. Beauty brings emotion, emotion is uncomfortable, therefore bring down beauty as it runs".

Not much time for writing, but I have copied out and altered what I had written for my first pages, and I think they will stand, and that perhaps at last I have got my "point of view".

Marian says there are Volunteers from a distance being quartered in many of the houses around not drilling but teaching signalling and such like.

29 NOVEMBER. Robinson has written gloomily of the reports from London and that Smith Gordon[1] is back in Dublin and doesn't expect to have to go over again. And this is the day of the Ulster meeting of Parliament—God and America help us! Robinson wrote that their players have filled the Gaiety in Dublin, even lessening our audience, and he asked them to tea to meet our players and for all their good reception, or because of it, they said that if we came to play in Belfast we would not escape with our lives!

I am a little comforted by an article in *The Times* on "the Church in Australia"[2]; it is separating or wishes to separate from the Church of England. "Its case for 'Freedom' is based, to an important extent, upon the desire to meet the needs of the native-born Australian in a land whose growing national sentiment cannot be ignored by the thinkers of the Church". They may give up the oath of allegiance next, and so save Ireland.

Marian was in Gort to pay house bills and says a young man came into Coen's to order a hundred Volunteer caps, and so many were not in stock but were telegraphed for, to be ready for an inspection by De Valera next Sunday.[3]

SUNDAY, 4 DECEMBER. It is not known yet if De Valera will be at the meeting or what is the prospect of peace. "There were a great many lorries yesterday, with soldiers, going the road to Galway". And today after Mass "the Volunteers, the strange ones, that are at the camp, thirty of them, marched together from Mass, but didn't speak to any of us". I put up a basket of my best apples to be placed in De Valera's motor had he come, but it is uncertain.

5 DECEMBER. Monday. The children came in from a walk with Delia yesterday afternoon said they had looked over a gap in the wall and seen the meeting, a great many Volunteers being drilled and some girls drilled too, and a great crowd. And a very tall man was standing in a motor and made a speech, "he had a lovely voice but we couldn't understand what he was saying, and Delia said it was Irish". Later Mary came in and said there had been some trouble, that police had "put a hand on De Valera's motor and the Volunteers had seized them and carried them off to the schoolhouse". This morning Mike Lally says it was military who turned round in front of De Valera's car and the Volunteers were vexed that he did not get a free passage and carried off two policemen to the schoolhouse"; and that De V. had gone there afterwards to have them released.

X. says of the meeting "We waited a long time for De Valera, not knowing would he come or not, and such a gathering of Volunteers was never seen, men and officers. The officers are mostly strangers from Clare or from Cork, you would know them by the accent. He came at last, and was well guarded with seven cars of Volunteers. He didn't speak more than about fifteen minutes, first in Irish and then in English. No word about peace, but that war was being forced upon us, and what we all had to do was to stick together and to obey our officers, for they were all men he knew and had tried. His voice was good, but he looked very pale and wasted with the ways he had gone. As to the disturbance, there came two lorries from Gort with military, and they stopped at the gate of the field where he was to go in, and the boys didn't like that, for when De Valera's motor came there was no room for him to get in, and they went and told the military to go back, and they turned away then. It was after he had spoken that an officer came and said to our officer, Reynolds, "I don't like what those four men up there are doing. Go up and take some others with you and send them away; and be sure you search them first". He spoke sharper than we do, and we knew he was a Clare man. Reynolds went up then, and some others with him, he had his revolver and a short gun as well, and we could see them go up to two military officers, and they told them to come along with them, and searched them, and brought them away, eight of them taking charge of the two. They went quiet at first, but one of them got very headstrong and didn't want to go on.

After that we were let move about and I went next the mall. Then the two officers were brought up and put into one of the lorries and they brought them to Kiltartan, but one of them stooped and whispered to two soldiers that were standing abroad in the Mall, as if to send a message to the barracks. And when those two soldiers had gone as far as Mullo's house, our man went after them and brought them back, but then let them go. The two that were brought to Kiltartan were put in the strange woman's house, and they asked the Volunteers what right they had to bring them there, and they said they didn't know, they were but obeying orders. Then the one that had been headstrong said so was he obeying orders, he was a detective and had been ordered to keep a watch on De Valera and follow him wherever he went. After that there was a noise heard of lorries, and we all knew well that noise on the Kiltartan road, and when it was heard, their captain did what he ought not to have done. He ran out and down by the chapel and over the wall where there is a big drop, and going over it he broke his leg. It is long he had been on the run before. But the two privates stopped there with the prisoners, and the Black and Tans and police got out of the lorries and took the prisoners away and went to look for the captain, and searched Mrs. Hanlon's house, but they could not find him.

Then a great troop of lorries, military and Black and Tans drove into Gort, and at the turn of Crow Lane they let off shots that would knock the heart out of the people".

I said I hoped there would be no outbreak here or there that might set the war going again, and he says "The Volunteers are going to keep all quiet until the 1st of March".

6 DECEMBER. The day began sadly, news of Fritz Huth Jackson's [4] death in *The Times*. I had not known of his illness, and it was a sudden grief, for he had become a real friend and

was so kind last May. I wrote a telegram of sympathy to Tiny, but could not send it, or letters, cob laid up and black pony busy, and heavy rain through the day. A telegram came from Robinson late in the afternoon "Agreement reached London", and I thought it must refer to some agreement with Sally Allgood or another, and that he had written about it and the letter had not yet reached me. But at tea time it flashed across my mind "it means peace". I looked again at the telegram and what I thought was a smudge was "in" London. Peace at last![5] Catherine went down to tell the maids, and they cheered and clapped.

9 DECEMBER. "The load is gone off many a mother's heart" J. said yesterday. I sent to ask Cunningham at what date I had first tried to get Bernard out of gaol, that I might look up the correspondence, make another effort, and write to the Castle again. And today I found it, and set to work to type copies for use, and was cheerily half way through when the paper came with news that De Valera is advising the Dail to reject the Peace Treaty![6] I had already posted a letter to Alderman Cosgrave about the Lane pictures, saying he had assured me that should a peace settlement be arranged, this matter should not be forgotten, and that now "that happy moment has come". I was thinking of writing to Lady Greenwood as well but this startling fact made my courage begin to ebb, and efforts seemed useless. However later J. told me the stationmaster had talked of it to him "and thinks De Valera only said that the way he wouldn't be showing too much joy at the Treaty. And others said the same thing; and with what they are saying in Gort we needn't be afraid. And there are boys on the road saying they didn't think a great deal of De Valera's speech on Sunday". So I came back and finished my copying. He said also a Black and Tan had come into Stephenson's on Wednesday and asked the girl there if she believed the news of the peace, and if she was glad of it, and she said she was and he said "Well I'm not, and my mother won't have as fat a Christmas as she had last year, when I sent her two turkeys and a goose and a ham". "And did they cost you anything?" "Not a penny"!

Mr. Edmunds here yesterday, much discomposed by the Treaty, supposes he will have to leave "and my life's work will be lost"; but hopes for foreign employment. I said it would be some time before the work of the C.D.B. could be closed, but still he was sad.

Writing letters, and reading Robinson's play[7], and with the children, and haven't written one word of my own work these two days, and very little on the days before. But they are very happy, sending for Christmas presents and "earning" money to pay for them.

10 DECEMBER. Writing about young Cunningham, and other things. P. says the Black and Tans were "thieves and a bad class, but the natives (the police) were worse again, setting a bad pattern, leading them to houses and pointing them out, and they of our own country". No one seems much troubled over De Valera's objection to the Treaty. G. says "Ah he said that on account of the American money—Republican bonds that 'ill be worth nothing".

Connacht Tribune reports a case tried in Dublin where the accused could only speak Irish. He was accused of murder and said he did kill the man with a stone. The Judge said he had better plead not guilty that the facts of the case might be stated, but the interpreter having spoken to him said "He tells me he would not like to say he did not kill the man when he did kill him"; and then he had said he "did not mean to do any harm to McDonough more than he would to the Mother of God". That is akin to the literal truthfulness of De Valera.

11 DECEMBER. At church today, and said the General Thanksgiving with a full heart. The Archdeacon stopped me to ask if it was true De Valera had come to lunch with me last Sunday, and when I said No, he said he would have no objection to meet him himself, and thinks he must have seen him at Blackrock school in his boyhood, and supposes he will resign and be made Premier instead of President. Quite a change from his old "Rebellion is as the sin of witchcraft" days.

J. says the prisoners back from internment are against the continuance of war, especially those from Derrybrian, who "got fierce treatment, were often dragged from their beds and flogged by the Black and Tans, because it was thought they gave shelter to the Clare boys. And so they might give them bed and a bit of breakfast, and they'd make off for the day then".

We had arrived early at church and while waiting I read as is my habit the Tate and Brady psalms; my favourite

"The trees of God without the care
Or art of man with sap are fed;
The mountain cedar looks as fair
As those in royal gardens bred".

But going farther where in the plagues of Egypt:

"From fields to villages and towns
"Commissioned vengeance flew[8]"

my mind went back to last winter and the reprisals.

Meanwhile Father C. at Kiltartan had said very little about the peace, just that he thought it likely it would be all right. But had in his sermon given "a terrible dressing" to four of the young men of the parish who, though he had been given the use of the fields by the coursing committee for the coursing match he has been getting up, was sent in by these a bill for £35. The four denounced being unpopular, the congregation enjoyed the sermon. Marian is astonished to hear that Insurance with other departments of Government will be in Irish hands, says "Isn't that a good thing?" I say "Yes, very good, and they are good men who are making plans for all, though I don't suppose they will please everybody"; and she says "How can they? There was a little boy asked by the Bishop at the Catechising 'Can God do everything?' and he said 'No', and the Bishop said 'What is it he cannot do?' and the little chap said 'He can't please the farmers'".

I wrote to R. J. Kelly about Bernard Cunningham.

13 DECEMBER. J. says "there are a great many Black and Tans about Ardrahan and they say they are going about like mad the last week with anger, and if the Government don't interfere or take away their rifles they'll have some of the people shot".

15 DECEMBER. A bad beginning to the day. First MacMahon's letter saying there is no chance of getting Bernard Cunningham out of gaol. And then a telegram from Robinson "No decision yet". I had hoped and believed the Treaty would have been accepted yesterday.[9] Marian says "If it is not, as sure as you live De Valera will be shot".

18 DECEMBER. Richard and Margaret came yesterday; the three darlings safely together for Christmas. That is something gained.

No news from Dublin yet. J. says "That Irish Parliament is very slow, a great deal of talk; caged in and no reporters at it". Old Niland came for his Christmas box and said "It is all on the turn of a halfpenny".

Sara Allgood can't come to the Abbey, has engaged herself to the Everyman.[10] Says it is because of the long delay in signing her contract, she could not wait. But she might have written to me. It is a blow.

19 DECEMBER. This the day of the debate; no news yet. P. hears in Gort that De Valera was bribed not to let it pass—"there must be bribery somewhere. But if it doesn't pass there will be holy murder".

Tim laments any change at all, Mrs. Gregory having told him Lord Ashtown is going to leave and that "there is not a grand person left in Dublin".

I have been sent an invitation to the World Congress of the Irish race in Paris, "the first assembly of this nature to take place in the past seven hundred years".

22 DECEMBER. Waiting, waiting, while the Dail talks. A letter from Yeats about giving over the Abbey or rather putting it under the new Government, but I don't agree with him that they would leave it in any way under our control, or subsidise it unless it was entirely in theirs, and I am for giving it up altogether if they will have it. But they may prefer a larger one.

26 DECEMBER. The adjournment of the Dail gives one breathing time and hope![11] and Christmas has passed peacefully. I miss the workhouse children now it is closed, after so many years. Robert used to come with me to give them toys and the old men their tobacco, and last year I had Richard and Anne with me. Our Christmas tree here, Guy and Olive staying in the house, Bagots, officers, M.F.H., etc. Today the wrenboys came, knowing but few lines about the wren. Some sang the Soldiers Song, and two of the groups gave a song about Kevin Barry being hanged in Mountjoy gaol "for Irelands' sake."

4 JANUARY, 1922. On St. Stephen's day G. walking in the woods saw two young men with guns, who seeing him "ran like hares"; and these had also been seen by Mike and by S., a Quarter master in I.R.A. and they had followed them in vain. There have been many boys and young men coming in with dogs, killing rabbits or taking timber, and I felt as if the woods were slipping away from our hands. But yesterday evening the children Richard and Anne, were out at dusk in the nutwood with their bows and arrows and say they met a man who told them they need not be afraid of him (as indeed they were not) as he was one of the I.R.A. "one of its police" and was taking care of the woods "for her ladyship". And I find that there are four of them told off to do this, C., S., M. and another but not wishing their names to be given. This brings fresh courage to me and gives me hope.

Margaret ill still with what we thought diptheria, but it is only septic sore throat, but the children must not go near her.

7 JANUARY. Richard's birthday yesterday. I did not think to live to see it, and I am happy in seeing him and the others so happy together, so simple and strong.

The Dail—J. says "Ah, bad cess to them, shewing one another up the way they are"! And there is grumbling at De Valera, as Peter said "All the fighting to begin again, and he maybe out in France".

SUNDAY. 8 JANUARY. I was getting ready for church when

Anne came up to say the telegraph boy was coming and was calling out that the Treaty is ratified.[12] I ran down and got L.R.'s telegram. Such a relief! The little boy had fallen off his bicycle with excitement on the avenue and had shouted the news to the maids coming from Mass and they had cheered. He said "This is the first time I ever was sent with a message, and I brought the best message that ever was brought"! and I gave him a shilling in addition to his apples. Mine had been the only message to Gort, and had been given out, everyone delighted except the poor Bagots who foresee the vanishing of officers. We met a motor lorry leaving Gort in charge of one soldier and I said to Guy "There is the army in retreat!". And we went to the Barracks after church (where I had said the General Thanksgiving with a full heart) and got Richard's gun and cartridges back again.

BOOK SEVENTEEN

11 JANUARY. 1922 Dublin. I came up yesterday in time for first performance of Murray's *Aftermath*.[1] L.R. met me at the Broadstone and came to tea. He had lunched with Desmond Fitzgerald and had spoken about turning over the Abbey to a National Government, said we had thought of doing so in Redmond's time, and had heard they were now going to establish one. Fitzgerald said there was no idea of taking the Gaiety or doing anything on a large scale, that he hadn't heard of any definite plan and that of course the Abbey is the National Theatre of Ireland. So we need not be in a hurry but just go on with our work. He had told Robinson that De Valera has been so upset and worried these last two months that he is hardly himself, and is seized on by the extremists, Mme. Markievicz and Childers, and made their mouth-piece. The evening papers had the news of Griffith's[2] election as Prime Minister.

As to the election of Reynolds[3] to the Municipal Gallery it is said to have been because his brother was killed in the Rising and he has six children. . . .

(APRIL 1928. He had proved himself quite a good Curator, very attentive to his business and energetic about the fight for the pictures).

I went to Plunkett House and had tea with A.E. and Miss Mitchell. He had been at the last big debate at the Dail, thought Griffith's speech extraordinarily fine, did not think he could have spoken with such fire and on such a high level.[4] De Valera he thinks "has a simple nature and mind and is not well able to assimilate the tangles and arguments with which he is loaded by his following". Mme. Markievicz delightful in private life, has always high spirits ("hoyden" puts in Miss Mitchell) but loses her qualities on the platform. He had a very interesting talk with Frank Gallagher who is against the Treaty and wants to keep republicanism alive because he thinks there is danger of the young men losing their idealism, their soul, if this idea of freedom, of a free nation, the most spiritual they had ever attained to, is lost in mere industrial and material undertakings. He, Gallagher,[5] said so pure and spiritual a force had never been attained to in this country. A.E. says that it is as science can set free the energy contained in the atom, that this spiritual force can be liberated by the breaking of material interests. I told him of John Shawe Taylor's fear long ago that where land purchase was obtained idealism might be quenched— "I thought it today"—he had said once when he had ridden over to Coole "when I saw the houses look so comfortable, the haggards so well filled. Will they be able to keep any enthusiasm for anything beyond that?"

A.E. had been to Belfast lately, says the new Parliament is a nest of jobbery and extravagance. Barbour[6] who had been an enemy at the Congress has now come round and is quietly working at a scheme for unity. Some man he knows who went back to the North when it set up for itself now writes begging that he may be given work anywhere in the South.

He says there is great confidence in Michael Collins; that Mr. Douglas of the White Cross says he has "more intellect and more humanity" than anyone he knows. And of Smith Gordon "a cold mind, absorbed in economics", says he at first disliked him, thought him rough and overbearing, but now says "he always turned out to be right", and thinks him "one of the biggest men in Europe". And Mrs. Duncan says Lavery told her (when speaking of the Gallery) that he is the one to get things from the Government, they have such an immense opinion of him. A.E. read me some humbugging verses he himself had written to Stephens, one on his "Take me" poem to De Valera, and one by which he cured Stephens of his constant irreverent and patronizing allusions to God, one ending by telling God he might come and sit on his knee "and call me James". He has never mentioned the Divinity in his poems since then.[7]

At the Abbey performance a lady with a party in the second row of stalls smiled and nodded to me. I couldn't think who she was, but after the second Act I went round, she was Mrs. Alfred Lyttelton. She introduced me to a tall lady with many diamonds looking like Queen Elizabeth—sitting next her "Her Excellency"—and she—Lady Fitz Alan[8] stood up and said how much she had heard of me and how glad she was to meet me and asked many questions about the Theatre, and was much interested to hear that Murray, whose play was on, was a National schoolmaster, had been one in a Cork village when his first plays were written. Mr. MacMahon, the Under Secretary, was next her, and said something about my letters to him. I said "You were not able to release my prisoner. Shall I go to the Sinn Fein Government about him now?" "Oh, we can release him" he said. I said "Can you really do that?" "Yes, we'll get the boy back". "Is that a promise?" "Yes it is". "Then give me your hand on it" and he did. "Now", I said "her Excellency is witness"! So it seems I shall have good news to bring back to poor Mrs. Cunningham.

Margaret's letter this morning says Guy is laid up at Coole with rheumatic fever.

Carnegie meeting was easy this time, and short, chiefly the Provost doing sums and asking Robinson questions about them. He asked me to sit next him, and when A.E. suggested that a list of books should be made out that bear on the present situation of the country and sent as a suggestion to local committees, he said "Lady Gregory made that suggestion last meeting", and approved. Sir H. Poë came, his first meeting; and hadn't a chance of saying anything. Mr. Wilkinson was happy at getting £1000 to keep Cork library going—so was I. A.E. walked as far as St. Vincent's Hospital with me, happy about Brian in India and his wife's improved health, and quoted Epictetus "No married man can be a stoic".

I went to see Nurse K. about Katie T. and she gave me names of other suitable hospitals, as their own Matron "is high and mighty and scorned poor Katie because, as a candidate for nursing, to give you an example, she called the Porter 'Sir!'"

But Miss Kelly thinks she is just the sort of country girl who turns out well. Then to Smith Gordon at his Land Bank, and he promised that if I send him a letter about the Lane pictures he will put it into Michael Collins' hands, for as Lavery thinks the Cabinet won't refuse him anything, he may as well ask for the pictures. But about our sale of woods to the Dail he is not hopeful, says nothing at all can be done while the Provisional Government is in office, and till after the election. And he is doubtful about the election, thinks if the British soldiers are removed some of the warlike Volunteers may insist upon a Republic.

13 JANUARY. I went to see Molly Childers in the afternoon. She looked troubled but, with someone there, didn't talk politics, but asked if there was any play coming on at the Abbey that would interest or amuse Erskine. When her visitor had gone she spoke with some bitterness, not of the insults to Erskine but of the Treaty "it is the first time in the history of the world that a sovereign nation (Ireland) has given up its sovereignty, except the Boers, and that was only when all of their people who were left were in concentration camps". De Valera had been to see her, and she spoke of his great nobility and honesty. She said also that no one is bound (in this she meant the people of Ireland) by a treaty imposed by force as this was. I said as I was going that we must always be grateful for what she and Erskine had done in

helping Ireland, and that I was very sorry for the discourtesy shown him. She said there had been verses against him in the *Freeman* that morning; But Bobby said "We don't mind those things, we like them", very stoutly. I am sending him places at the Abbey for next week, *Lord Mayor* would interest both him and his father.

During the second Act of *Aftermath* I sat in the hall and talked with Larchet.[9] He says his work for the Dail is completed; that in future singing at sight is to be compulsory in the schools. He had been at one of the Dail debates, found it so exciting that the hours passed unnoticed. He had not been greatly impressed by any speaker, but thought Griffith spoke extremely well; Miss McSwiney[10] with great clarity and manages her voice well. De Valera looked worn out, sat with his greatcoat buttoned up to his ears though the room was stifling. All the Pressmen and a great many of the Deputies were smoking. He, like others, thinks De Valera is stuffed with arguments by the extremists, and finds a difficulty in assimilating or expressing them. He was walking home with Professor ———— and had asked what he was carrying so carefully in his bag and he said "What I would like to give a dose of to De Valera—sleeping sickness. He has not slept for a fortnight and is worn out".

L., when I asked how it was Michael Collins had not been recognised or taken during all that bad time, said "He was quite well known to the police. But when the Dublin Municipal Police were first armed, three or four of the worst of them were shot, and then the others made an agreement with Sinn Fein that they would not carry arms (unless compelled) and would not give any of them up or point them out, though when taken about in lorries with the military they would have to point to the number of a house containing wanted men. It is a certainty that five times Collins was sent a warning when the house he was in at the time was about to be raided, and all those five times the warning came from the Castle. He was often here at the Abbey Theatre during that time, generally on a Thursday evening, in the pit, I knew him, and a few, perhaps three or four did. But he had always a strong bodyguard around him. I don't believe he killed anyone with his own hand but he planned the ambushes. Those officers killed in Dublin were all spies. Those at the boarding houses went there to try and make acquaintances and get invitations to ceilide and such things. I hope there may be an arrangement now, but we would be better if all those women were out of it. It is to a county Galway girl Michael Collins is engaged, and a commandant of the I.R.A. is engaged to her sister."

Robinson, walking back, says Smith Gordon is very low and gloomy.

14 JANUARY. Telegrams yesterday from home asking if I could take Richard over to London as the threatened railway strike would prevent his return to school next week; so I will meet him at Broadstone tonight and take him on. Poor darling, he misses a couple of days at home with the others and will have to wait five days in London.

I dined with L.R. at United Arts Club, Smith Gordon and his wife there, and we talked of books, S.G. loving Meredith and L.R. Henry James. I don't feel an enduring love for any novelist but would like more volumes of Trollope. S.G. told us of the raiding of his Sinn Fein Land Bank by the "Auxiliaries". They took away over £2000 and he is trying now to recover it. It was taken from Michael Collins' account and anothers, I forgot who. They seized the books and found under what names these were kept and took the money. S.G. asked why they did not take it straight off without these formalities. They said that would be stealing. He said he didn't see the difference, but one of them said "you will find that under head. No 0 (some letter and number) of the Regulations as to the Peace of the Realm." "and that floored me". When he found they intended to stay in possession for nine hours he proposed to his assistants to play Bridge, and so they sat down and played, the police coming in and looking on and giving them advice. L.R. had seen them raiding a public house opposite his rooms one night. They broke down the door and carried off among other things £40 from the till. I hoped they would be held upside down and their pockets shaken out before they left. On the way to the Abbey, just over the Bridge, there was a great crowd, I asked what was going on and a young man said "It's the Tans", and some motors passed containing them—on their departure!

There was no booing or applause, just a sort of delighted murmur, a triumphant purr.

I had been to see Edward Martyn in the afternoon in his warm little flat; very crippled, but more cheerful than I had seen him for a long time at the exit of the "Tans". He is all for the Treaty and blames De Valera's doings here as much as he had admired them in America. He will listen to no excuse, says "he is jealous of Griffith" "I met him in Gort at the time of his Clare election. I was doing my marketing and he and another" (I forget who) "had come to hold a meeting there, and I talked to them in their motor and I said 'You will get on all right as long as you hold to Griffith and keep with him' and I saw a shadow pass across their faces".

I spoke of De Valera's honesty and his belief that he is doing the best thing for Ireland, but he wound up as he began "It's all jealousy of Griffith".

He says M. Collins made an inspection of the Volunteers all through Ireland before he went on the London mission, and came to the conclusion that we were not in a position to fight. When they brought the signed Treaty back (and this I had heard from others) no one in the Cabinet made an objection. But suddenly some days later De V. sent his protest to the Press. He says of course the police knew Collins by sight, but what could they do? He would walk down Grafton Street but he had always an escort at hand, and if there was an alarm and he blew his whistle a hundred men would appear, and while a scrimmage was going on he would be far away "and what could an army do against a man like that?" He had begun as a Gaelic League organizer in Kerry. And now he is being followed by detectives.

I wrote my letter to Collins about the pictures, and left it with Smith Gordon.

15 JANUARY. 13, Grosvenor Place. I did some hurried shopping for the journey and packed and looked in at the Abbey matinée and coming back to the Gresham saw a long line of lads, some quite young boys, lined up against the wall in the hall. I asked a waiter who they were and he said "Prisoners after being released". I spoke to one of them, asked what he had been put in for. He said "Murder —suspected". He had never been tried, had been all the time in Belfast Gaol, said it is "fine" to be out again. I bought a box of cigarettes for him and saw him dividing them with the others. I see in papers that "men" suspected of having been in "the Cavan ambush" have been released in Belfast, the authorities there refusing to "release" them, but handing them over to the Imperial authorities.[11]

A long wait at the Broadstone for Richard (there was cheering on the other platform for prisoners going home) and then he arrived safe and cheerful. But there was "no train going on to Kingstown", and we had a rush to get a cab and drive to Westland Row, and caught the train from there, and arrived this morning. And now I see the strike has been put off for a month!

19 JANUARY. This evening at 5 o'c my little Richard went off from Waterloo, very cheery with the other boys in a Winton House compartment. I think he liked his days here, the servants kind, and "Captain Gough had said he was to have everything he wanted", and the car such a blessing! We went to "Shoulder

Arms" the Charlie Chaplin film, and Babes in the Wood pantomine and Mme. Tussauds, as he said he hadn't seen the Chamber of Horrors—harmless looking poisoners not seeming to know what to do with their hands, standing about like actors at rehearsal, but something in the air made me feel upset. I was better pleased upstairs where G.B.S. is sitting in the harmless company of Charles Dickens.

And at Bank of England they showed Richard the calculating machine, and today when he had failed to get engineering books at Harrods we went to Hatchards where he got two he liked; and Mr. Humphreys greeted us and there was a friendly feeling there.

Except Baly I've done nothing of my own, and except Una for a few minutes, I've seen nobody.

20 JANUARY. I lunched at 10 Adelphi Terrace, so very pleasant. G.B.S and Charlotte and Massingham, who I hadn't seen since that dreadful evening at Lady Courtney's when I didn't recognise him. He asked about Ireland, and my little bits of Dublin-gathered news fitting in, he said, with what he had already heard.

G.B.S. full of the Molière lunch and meeting at which he had spoken.[12] The lunch was given by "The Government"—the Commissioner of Public Works, "I suppose because Molière wrote 'works' they thought he came into his Department." There was a difficulty in getting anyone who could talk French to sit next the guest of the evening, so he was put there. Then at the speeches Professor W. P. Ker stood up to speak "giving one word of French and running through the whole French Dictionary in his mind before he ventured on another". He himself had made the witty speech about the four great men, Dante, Shakespeare, Goethe, Molière I had seen already reported. It was Paul Bourget who had said to him that these great men reflected the qualities of their nations, but he could only say that he had travelled in Italy and never met a Dante, and if there were Goethes in Germany they must have had influenza when he was there; and as to Shakespeare, look at our leading men and see which of them is like him. If they had worked at the Versailles treaty Dante would have approached it from his attitude of law giver; Shakespeare as an Englishman was a born anarchist; Molière alone would have given expression to the mind of the people. When he had hoped, as he was sometimes called the English Molière, that he was not a twentieth century but a sixteenth century Molière, he had mentioned how he had once teased and perhaps offended his distinguished friend Hugh Lane asking if his great Titian was a twentieth century one, and who had painted it.

He has been writing a long preface on prisons; says (and Massingham confirms it) that the criminals are made in prison, put in for some small fault like selling newspapers in a railway station and destroyed there.[13]

"All the inhabitants of all European countries were proved in the war to belong to the criminal classes. Queen Victoria belonged to those classes, that is proved by the account in Strachey's book[14] of the first request she made when assured she was really queen; to have some hours quite to herself and her bed taken out of her mother's room; and then she bundled her mother out. Like the criminal she saw no medium between complete freedom from authority and absolute despotism".

E.S. had sent him "a dreadful play" to criticise, and he had written her his opinion of it; that she ought to have given up that old opinion of the Irish upper classes that the peasant was ridiculous, that there was something ridiculous in poverty, in dishonesty, in dirt. I said it was the Gaelic League that had changed that, changed the table of values, made it ridiculous not to speak bad English but bad Irish, though they refrained from ridiculing the speaker; and they agreed. "She had made Flurry Knox marry the niece, the young lady, and I wrote to her that he was nothing but a stableboy, and that if Molière made Scapin no better, anyhow he didn't marry him to Hyacinth".

I asked when he would come back to Ireland but he said "No, I'll not go. I would be treated as the common enemy". I said De Valera had promised to join the others against a common enemy, so he might come to unite the two parties. He said "I am growing fonder of England now, as Napoleon grew fonder of France than of Corsica because he had conquered it. One always loves the country one has conquered best, and I have conquered England; they hang on every word from my lips. There must be few English gentlemen left for this country, and they will have to come from Ireland, they have none of the old graces here".

They talked of Dean Inge. Shaw had gone to lecture on Ruskin (as the chief and original anarchist) soon after he had written a review of Inge's *Outspoken Essays*[15] and was amazed to hear that the Dean of St. Paul's had insisted on coming to propose the vote of thanks. He did it badly, stumbled and said a few words of deep depression and melancholy. But he wrote a nice letter afterwards and said that his shyness had been so great he had not been able to say what he thought, "but like all animals in captivity I appreciate kindness".

Massingham (delighted at this) had heard Inge preach in St.

Paul's; he read his sermon, but he could not but listen to every word. He said in it that perhaps St. Paul had never seen Jesus and also that he could believe in the Resurrection, but that the Ascension was impossible, because one knew that Heaven is not in the air, but as the disciples believed it was, he had made it appear to them he was going upwards. I told of Rassam and Sir H. Layard. When the beautiful Prince Donka in gauzy raiment was drawn up to the flies—Rassam had turned, awed, to Sir Henry and said "Is that the Holy Ghost?".

After lunch Massingham spoke of India; has heard the Prince's visit was a complete failure, that his very handshaking qualities had been fatal there and shocked the people meant to impress.[16] G.B.S agreed and said different countries should be differently treated, and in some it might be necessary to make an impression by cutting off the heads of a hundred men. I told of the Dublin attorney long ago "I don't think much of Spencer[17] with all his bows and politeness. Give me Abercorn[18] scowling at you over his beard as if you were dirt".

Massingham thought they ought, if they wish to keep India subject, to have executed Ghandi. I said another leader would arise and he said "No, you can't so easily replace a saint" (W.S.B. when I told him this said "Yes, he is a saint".) G.B.S. said they ought to have built a sort of Eiffel Tower and put him in the top where he could not be expected to address the people. I said he would have been as dangerous there, as dangerous as the Mahdi was in his grave that he was dragged out of.[19] Massingham hears from his authorities that India has no more use for England, has learned all it has to teach; wants to be left alone. He and G.B.S. agree that it will go, and the Empire is breaking up, and that Ireland has taught her methods invented by her so successfully to the other countries in revolt.

G.B.S. talked [Mark date*] after he had gone of his own poverty. Says they are living much beyond their income. He is now publishing his own books and his last two years' profits come to £29! And half the small theatres don't pay, and from the large ones he had to accept bills instead of ready money. I said the Abbey might lift up its head, and he said "Yes," and that some provincial ones pay—not the Everyman. But *Methuselah* is selling very well indeed especially in America, and I told him he must go to lecture there.

22 JANUARY. I lunched with Birrell, he was glad to hear Irish news. He had been very much against a "Governor" in Ireland, knowing, as I do, how vulgarity would crowd around; and was relieved when I told him Massingham said the Governor was to

be O'Connor (but that was only humour—it was Tim Healy in the end). "An appointment of my own, I made him judge, but if he is to live at the Viceregal Lodge vulgarity will go on as before". He says Winston Churchill can say nothing too good of Michael Collins "but then I suppose they are birds of the same feather".

I came in the evening to Newbuildings, found W.S.B. looking fairly well and we had a nice talk, he so interested in hearing about Ireland. He had sent a telegram of congratulation to the Lord Mayor. We had another talk after dinner, he was interested about Dizzy's *Life* that I had been reading and said he would send for the last two volumes to begin with as I have been doing. Then he dozed off, and after a while (I had kept quite still) he awoke calling out for help and I ran to look for someone, found a nurse at the end of the passage who went to him. He often gets these attacks of pain—it is cruel. He said "I have always felt that you have done more for Ireland than anyone else. You showed its poetry and beauty, you destroyed that association of vulgarity and ridicule with its people". But I told him, as I had told Shaw and Massingham yesterday, it is to the Gaelic League that praise belongs.

He is afraid Egypt will be internationalised "and that will be worse for it than anything", and he had been already certain the Prince would do harm in India, having begun his democratic habits in the Colonies. "There ought to be one prince for them and others told off for the subject peoples". I said I felt for the poor Prince he is like the cat in Alice in Wonderland, one day there will be "nothing left of him but the smile".

The house here looks so fine, the old oak doors and woodwork, the blazing oak log fires, the bunches of everlastings, the sun today shining in. But the owner is again in pain.

24 JANUARY. Gresham, Dublin. W.S.B. said goodbye to me "we shall never meet again", and again thanked me for the preface. He said my visit had done him good, and he was not in pain when I left.

A tiring evening journey to London. No porters or cabs at Victoria "because of the fog"; but at last a taxi driver consented to take me, finding I only wanted to get to Grosvenor Place. Guy and Margaret, and Sara Allgood to dinner. I took S.A. to Guy's sitting room afterwards and read her the "Old Woman Remembers" and she cried and kissed my hand kneeling, and begged to be the first to be allowed to use it.

Yesterday (the sad 23rd) I went to see Lawrence at Albemarle St. and Huntington at Bedford St., and talked of the new volume of plays, and bought some "delicatessen" for the children at Fortnums, and packed, and came over last night, not sleeping at all until I got into the boat at 3.30, and then so soundly that I didn't know if it was rough, as I believe it was. Papers cheerful about the Collins-Craig agreement.[20] M. had crossed in the same boat as Collins, says he looked "shifty" and she had been told never looked anyone straight in the face—the first word I have heard against [him] since the peace.

26 JANUARY. COOLE. I arrived in Dublin, on Tuesday (The day before yesterday). Found the Theatre in a ferment, the London correspondent of the *Independent* having reported Miss Allgood told him "it was not quite correct to say that she was immediately taking over the Abbey Theatre, but she added that it was her intention to do so. Count Plunkett while Minister of Fine Arts approached her on the matter, and on Sunday night she discussed the question with Lady Gregory, who is anxious to hand over the Theatre to the Irish Nation to be run as a real National Theatre". Fitzmaurice who had been about to sign a contract had told Perrin he was not going to sign one for Miss Allgood; and some friend of Harris' had gone to his office to express indignation, and said she would never go to the Abbey again; and Robinson would have been bewildered had I not been happily there to explain. I had asked Sally about the rumours of a National Theatre and she had said "I was with Mrs. Childers, and she said what a splendid thing a National Theatre would be, and she rang up and sent me to see Count Plunkett, and he said it was a very interesting idea, and if anything should turn up about it he would let me know". I had said I didn't know what could be more national than the Abbey, and that we hoped some day in the future to give it over to the State. And that was all.

So L.R. and I were interviewed by the *Irish Times*, and I wrote an interview for the *Independent*, and it was all for the best, giving us a chance of telling how we stand, without the risk of being snubbed.[21]

Tired with this I opened a letter that had been laid on the desk for me, and nothing could have better pleased and cheered me. For it was from Michael Collins, an answer to the one I had written him as I was leaving Dublin ten days ago. And he says "I would like you to know that I raised the question in London yesterday. Some of the advisers of the British Government seem to think that legislation would be necessary before these pictures can be removed, but the opinion was divided. I found however that the attitude towards the return was not unsympathetic, and I am raising the matter again after further enquiries have been made. I most sincerely hope that we shall be successful in securing their return".

Such joy to think that at last and after nearly seven years of fighting for these, and for how many of these years alone, a strong hand is lifting the burden!

McMahon's letter (saying he could not yet write definitely about Cunningham's release) was a disappointment, but not a hopeless one.

A small audience at the Abbey, *Dragon* and *Gaol Gate*, and performers rather nervous on a first night, but Barry Fitzgerald magnificent.

L.R. said "They say the real Michael Collins was murdered, that this is someone personating him!"

Yesterday morning as I arrived at the theatre boys were running and a band was just ceasing to play, and we saw a long line of military leaving, marching by the river.

Robinson says H. has been over and said he had heard a conversation during the negotiations between Lloyd George and Winston Churchill as to the preparations to be made for war in Ireland should they break down, which disquieted him so much that he had gone to Scott of the *Manchester Guardian*, and he, a great friend of L.G. had in consequence come to London and stayed there till the Treaty had been signed, using his influence for making it pass.

Coole. A good welcome from Anne and Catherine, a real homecoming.

It is said the military sold guns in Gort before they left, a very fine one among them, and I am writing about ours.

There has been no trespassing or shooting in our woods, but a good deal at Lough Cutra. Guy told me a party from Clare had come with guns and shot all through, and knocked down the steward who tried to stop them, And Mike hears a party from Gort went and shot there last Sunday.

SUNDAY, 29 JANUARY. Church today very empty but for a new group of police come from some distant part. Bagot at the door said Black and Tans were expected today, but their motor had been stolen at Kilchriest. He also heard Mr. Cruise had been fired at near Galway (I think not true).

The first Sunday for years there was no "God save the King". We had the Royal Family prayers, but these I used sincerely, putting in place of Royalties the new Government of Ireland.

31 JANUARY. Anne has just come in waving a rabbit she has shot, having been out with Mike John.

A. writes The I.R.A. are giving a dance at Lenaboy and have

asked several loyalists including the Bakers of the hotel. Miss B. was the girl whose hair was the first to be cut off on account of the military and Crown Forces being customers of the Hotel, and they have not asked several of their own faction. Maggie thinks perhaps they are only going to pay off the loyalists by leaving them sitting all the evening—wallflowers. I said perhaps it was a new gunpowder plot to blow up the loyalists. I am having the stone seats made for front of house, and getting to work a little in the evenings at "Seventy Years".

8 FEBRUARY. M.B. heard a priest in the train say "Nearly all the Protestants are gone, and the rest are trembling".

Mr. Edmunds says an old fisherman at ——— said to him "the sun never sets on England—because God wouldn't trust her in the dark".

A. writes "Maureen heard an old man say as he pointed to the Sinn Fein flag floating over Lenaboy 'look at that now! Wouldn't you think it was an angel from Heaven' "!

13 FEBRUARY. A. writes "the Connaught Rangers went off waving a Sinn Fein flag and singing rebel songs. The Black and Tans sang God save the King and waved a Union Jack—both in the same train".

14 FEBRUARY. Frank here today, thinks well of the new Government but is uneasy about the elections, he said "farmers will vote for it but what use will that be if a farmer's three sons vote against it"; and that the young men believe a republic will free them from taxation for war debt and pensions. He had asked Miss G. if she was a republican and she said No because she hates De Valera, "Why?" "I was taught by him at school and all of us who were taught by him hated him". And Peter says "I always knew De Valera was a *lad*. Look at the way he got out of gaol and got away for America, and never told how he did it. It was the Government helped him".

The men say there is bad weather coming, they see wild geese flying overhead.

20 FEBRUARY. Snow since then, and hailstones today, so their warning was justified.

I see in a letter (I had written about lecturing in America) "As to Ireland, I had a week or two of extraordinary happiness thinking all was well with the country, and the rebuilding about to begin. Then came the unhappy split, and there may yet be chaos. It is hard to say how the elections may go. But you will know that from the papers, and I don't lose faith and hope".

Thomas D. who was in the garden today says the Sinn Fein delegates from here are to vote for a Republic: They expect De

Valera to win at tomorrow's meeting "and the young chaps that didn't fight yet say they are ready to die for Ireland and they should get their chance". John H., and M. the Gort draper, M. the carpenter's son are delegates from here.

Mrs. Yeats says their Irish maids are always uneasy after dark in Oxford, because of reading in the papers of all the (English) murders, and if there is a knock at the door go together to open it, and ask who it is with great caution.

3 MARCH. Mc. Nicolas the Horticultural expert was here a day or two ago, a Mayo man and Irish speaker, and says he has been going about the country constantly and hasn't heard six people say a word against the Treaty.

And today D. says "there is no man or woman with a house over them that would stir a step for De Valera. He got a very poor welcome in Ennis all the applause he got was like the clapping of little children. There was a band sent from Crusheen to play at the meeting, but they met outside the town some one that heard Dr. Fogarty's sermon and told them about it, and but three of them went on to the meeting, they said they would not help the man that was trying to upset Ireland. But all of us that were called for the drill at Lydican in the summer were made take a big oath. I forget what way it went, it was swearing to the republic, It was one Reynolds from Cork that gave it to us, a big man with a voice you would hear beyond at the limekiln".

6 MARCH 1922. My husband died on this day, 30 years ago. Thank God this is still a house for his child's children.

But it is true that in our twelve years that we were together, as well in Robert's life, there was never, as it seems, such an opportunity as now for putting our hand to the rebuilding of Ireland. In the Land League days as I look back on them, and as I read old letters, his and mine, I wondered first at our anger, our want of faith and hope and charity. But then thinking calmly as I do of those past days I do not see that he or I could for any motive save a hope of present ease have joined with Parnell and his men, or consented to give up to grasping hands the lands that had been bought and cultivated and wooded by his great grandfather.

In 1866 he had joined with Sir C. O'Loughlin[22] in drawing up a Bill to give increased stability of tenure to Irish tenants. "We sent copies to the tenants' associations and from all of them I believe we received assurances of their complete satisfaction with it. It proposed to discourage annual lettings and led(?) to the granting of loans. Where there was no written contract a lease of twenty one years was presumed. Compensation in case of ejectment of a young tenant was enacted (except in case of non payment of rent).

These were the main provisions which would have resulted in the final granting of loans, and we would have had peace in the land for twenty-one years".

11 MARCH. We heard bombing all one day, but the bombs were being thrown into the river by the departing police.

There have been attacks on police in Galway. A. writes that she hears the Clare National police were sent to Galway, and say the Galway men are too slow, and they will show them what to do. But K.D. says "I hear by talk that it is the police that were spies and led the Black and Tans to houses that are shot, and that it would not be safe for them to stop in the county". He says "there is a bad name coming on De Valera." And I suppose it is on account of the two armies in Limerick that the station master refused to take M.'s carpet yesterday, says only food stuffs are taken "because of talk of strikes".

19 MARCH. The week brought my birthday, my three score and ten achieved. Thank God I have been able to give the children a happy and peaceful home until now.

But it is an anxious time. De Valera is "getting a bad name" but none the less there is uneasiness "no one can say what will happen or what way will things turn out". And the night before last J.M.'s house was burned down in the night without warning (some quarrel about land), wife and children and all in bed. All escaped and saved most of the furniture, thought they heard the noise of a motor and saw the light of a motor, and then found it was the light and roaring of the house itself burning. "The Black and Tans were better than that; they'd drag you out of the bed and give you a kick out of the door".

Trying again to get Bernard Cunningham out of gaol. The children good and happy, Anne shooting, Catherine playing with the kitten and riding Tommy and feeding the sheep with ivy and watching the lambs and a pigeon's nest that is half made.

22 MARCH. Power says "I seen De Valera when he was in Gort. He has the cut of the Spanish, long and lank. British troops in the North now, they'll be down upon us in the South."

26 MARCH. An anxious week. Belfast and its Specials, a part of the I.R.A. in mutiny; Ballydugan burned down (land dispute), all anxious; the convention of the mutinous part of the I.R.A., being held today. A. has written of shops being entered, provisions commandeered by I.R.A. and the fishwoman says one of them asked her for a fish and when she refused said "I'm hungry" and she gave it. But this is hardly true for I see in today's *Tribune* the barracks business arrangement about contracts.

It is the children's last week here. They have found a thrush's nest with eggs.

28 MARCH. Yeats came yesterday, rather a cheerful report, that De Valera is "beaten" and that there may be union; the Constitution framed is so democratic that it must be accepted.

J. from Burren says the people at that side are "leaning very heavy" on De V. but only afraid that if he is beaten he will bring on war.

Yeats says he was asked what he thought of the Irish Race Congress in Paris as he went out for the debate there at which all sorts of schemes were proposed, and he said "I'm afraid the Provisional Government will find it rather an expensive wife, all whim and no responsibility".

1 APRIL. He says "Oxford being the home of lost causes is now violently democratic".

An attempt theft last night, harness room broken open. J.D. and J. Hehir saw lights and very bravely went in and found M.R. and M.D., who made off leaving a bag filled with what they could collect. Poor M.J., his son seems to have treated him most cruelly, as does his wife.

I wrote to "The Officer in Command, Gort", and two officers came out, one from Galway one from Attymon, and took notes of the case. I spoke of the Galway barracks having been taken over by Republicans but they seem to think it doesn't matter, that all will come together again. I feel more satisfied now I have actually met our new upholders of law and order. (It was not till later I discovered that these were themselves Republican officers, to whom by mistake or purpose my letter had been given. They were in the Barracks, the Regulars in the Workhouse turned into a Barrack).

BOOK EIGHTEEN

4 APRIL. The children have gone, and the house is very silent, and my heart is heavy.

As to the breaking into harness room, J.D. said yesterday Paddy Cahel had come down and said R. and D. are intending to get witnesses to swear their sons were not the miscreants.

He seemed anxious the case should be withdrawn, said "No one knows where we are or what sort of a court we'll have or where we could send them if they were convicted", and that is true enough. J. proposed their fathers, Rock and M. should come to me and undertake to keep them out of mischief for the future, and I should have been glad if this could have been done. But this morning J. was sent a message to come to the Barracks and when he left me with the children at the station he went there, and was asked by another officer to give his evidence, and did so, and they said they would arrest them. But M.J. on Saturday when I told him I would not send the report of the robbery to the Barracks by him had said "I'll be glad to bring it. They deserve it. I went to bed early last night and I heard M. and the mother talking downstairs and then he went out, and he wasn't back till late. He was in it". And then he told me how badly his sons had been behaving to him, and that a little time ago he had for a fortnight never been let into the house, but had bought bread and tea and eaten in the yard. Today he says he knows nothing about it, or whether M. went out or not. But I would not in any case ask him to bear witness against his son.

Yeats is very angry at the *Freeman* office not having been guarded directly after they had published the report of the Army mutineers convention.[1] He had said at the time "The *Freeman* Office will be wrecked" and says the Provisional Government ought to have known that and guarded against it.[2]

I asked J. just now how the case would go against our robbers (the lads who had broken into the harness room) and he says "let the best horse lep the ditch, and let us see now what way will they govern Ireland. And all the neighbours are saying it was the Great God made the cow calve just then, the way we would catch them at their work".

5 APRIL. R. the father, came yesterday morning in great grief, crying and begging me to forgive and help his son who was with M.D. arrested last night. I asked if he would sign an undertaking to keep the boy (aged 23) from such misdeeds in future, and he said he would indeed. And then M. and J. came and both signed it. I wrote then to the officer in command telling this, and begging, as a personal favour, that they might be released. But this could not be done, although the I.R.A. officers decided to let them out, on bail with a small fine, and one agreed, but the other refused, insisted he had not been there "didn't care if they put him in gaol for ten years". His father says he has been wild, and others say crazed, since he was on the run from the Black and Tans. It is sad.

Father Cawley came to tea. He is for the Free State but cautious, and says De Valera has a great name still among the people. He spoke of the Black and Tans, and a young man they suspected of having been in the Headford ambush. They found him by opening a letter in the post, and took him to Oranmore, shot him, but not dead, tied him to a lorry by the feet and drove off. His mother went to ask for his body at the barracks and they showed her the feet but there was no head.

It was only by his boots, he says, that one of the Loughnane boys was identified by his sister, "it is not known if they were burned when they were dead or living". Joyce the schoolmaster at Barna was suspected and they wanted to get something in his handwriting. A deaf dummy called at his house, wrote a note asking for a drink of water; then some question that Joyce wrote an answer to and this the "dummy" carried off to the barracks.

Yeats has been writing a little new song for *Pot of Broth*. It was a pleasant ten days visit from him. I read him *Consuelo*[3] in the evenings.

The house is silent without the darling children.

Yeats says of Moore "he discovers nothing, as Joyce does. He only lays tremendous emphasis on two or three already discovered facts."

10 APRIL. I have been alone and working hard at my "Seventy Years". I have taken up all the MSS to the large playroom table; and I have typed the whole *Pot of Broth* for Yeats, he had no copy of it. And I have arranged my Dun Emer sets; and had many letters to write. I don't know how it is they never cease; again today from breakfast to 1 o'c with only fifteen minutes in the garden away.

Yesterday after church our carriages hadn't come, and I walked to meet them with the B.s and when we came to the turn to the Barracks I said "How things are changed, I am going to the Barracks and you turning away." I went to ask about some prisoners.

I had not been at the Barracks for years. The reception room looked very smart, done up perhaps by its last inhabitants, the 17th Lancers. Lieutenant L. who had called here was there, and a Captain Burke, very good looking, very smart in his new uniform, and I think country bred. Both very kind. Yeats walked over in the afternoon, hadn't seen the papers for four days, and we had a long talk, and I read him some chapters of *Consuelo*. It seems as if the army is going with De Valera. Twelve Republicans took Renmore Barracks from ten Free Staters (said to have been unarmed) and of these some stayed with their supplanters.

11 APRIL. A nice little letter from Catherine yesterday. Old Niland here today, says there was an attempt to rob the Post Office yesterday. The I.R.A. were called, the thief made off, climbed a wall, swam the river; they fired but didn't hit him. They are searching for him still.

Q. here last evening, wants land from M. and threatens to stock it "though I don't want to use violence" and to insist that the price should be left to his valuer. I referred him to Frank, and showed how easy it would be to shoot me through the unshuttered window if he wanted to use violence. He is down on De Valera and declared there is nobody with him.

I went to the Garden, J. says "we have the frost banished, the rain has it bet", and a few drops turned to a shower. And then I spoke of old Niland's story of the theft in Gort, and he says that wasn't the way it happened. "It was the two officers from Gort that went to Ardrahan ere yesterday and took the money for dog licences from the Post Office, about £30. And yesterday three motors came from Galway with Army men or whatever they were, to get it from them again". "But what about the man that climbed the wall and swam across the river and was fired at"? "That was Captain Lennard, that put you into the carriage on Sunday"! It's very hard to know what is going on. P. as usual down on De Valera and says "it is his men are doing all the robberies, where he has no money to pay them".

I have worked on at the memoirs, have got to the end of the "Sheltered Years". There is not much shelter now!

12 APRIL. A. writes from Galway: "Maggie heard seven shots last night at 2 a.m. Notices were put up last night to support the Republic and not to enlist in Free State army or Civic Guards".

13 APRIL. Gresham. To Dublin with Yeats for Abbey and Carnegie meetings. Yeats went to see the Gonnes and says Mme. G. is hopeless about the country and deplores the military spirit and domination that she used to applaud in her early days. At breakfast the papers are filled with De Valera's denunciations of Griffith and Collins, and his assertions that only those support the Treaty who are in dread of the "immediate and terrible war" threatened by England.[4] This will not help his cause in the country. Yeats thinks Gandi the only great saint and leader of the present time. He spoke of Lenin's belief that the destruction of all may lead to the forming of a new and better life. He says "the mystic sees the goal plainly but not always the steps to it". I say Gandhi must already be living in part beyond the world, and quote "She's an old dweller in high countries, but not from me; here, she's here", which he didn't know and was pleased with. He says Gandhi has pure moral force; is not concerned with external things, can fast when there are outrages, is not dragged into a political party as he would be here.

He finds some intelligence in Iseult's husband and says he wrote to the *Times Supplement* pointing out an error in Keats which had never been noticed, but which S. Colvin[5] at once accepted. He can't remember the verse but "the word that should be lore has always been printed as love, and it just shows that poets are supposed to be unintelligible." And I quote the old German preacher at Therapia "that is poetry, it hath no meaning". Y. asked who it was that had no peace because he slew his master, and I told him Zimri,[6] and that I used to apply it to John Dillon after the split with Parnell and he says that is what he is going to do.

The Carnegie meeting rather dull. After all my fighting for the £1000 for a temporary house for the burnt out Cork library, they now say they don't want it and won't take it, and Wilkinson thinks they may never rebuild the Library, all is chaos. Horace Plunkett says the English and Scotch Trustees scoff at anything being spent on libraries or books in Ireland now in this disturbed time, say it is thrown away, and he wants the Committee to support him, and I suggested his telling them that Vassar College, the first women's college in America was founded during the civil war. And there are good reports from Donegal; the libraries a great success because of a good librarian, a self taught man.

The Abbey meeting fairly cheerful. We have only lost £400 on the year, to end of February, and that includes part of the Black and Tan time when "rebels" avoided us, thinking as I used to say, our pit would be looked on as a fishpond.

People are cheerful over the Conference tonight; Yeats saw A.E. and he is hopeful that all will come right. I went to the Hibernian Academy, such a fine portrait of De Valera by Lavery, enough to help the breaking of the Treaty; and "transit troubles" had kept Griffith's and Collins' portraits from arriving, whether for good or bad. For Griffith's at least would make but a poor show against this. I met Atkinson who says the Vienna children's Exhibition was a very great success, was crowded; crowds of schoolchildren came, and there is already the practical result that a very bad scheme of teaching drawing that had just been adopted for the National schools has been given up. Also there is about £200 profit to send to Vienna. And the same pictures at Belfast only brought a profit of £30.

Read two plays *Kathleen's Seamless Coat*; and *the Drapier Letters*,[7] an imaginative piece, I think powerful.

14 APRIL. Yeats didn't hear anything of the Peace Conference but heard a rumour that Griffith had been fired at. He heard a good deal of firing as he passed through Stephen's Green, coming home late, but no one seemed concerned. Mme. Gonne told him a great many of the boy soldiers are brought to hospital wounded by accidents, and that one sees them walking about with guns used as walking sticks, their hand over the barrel, and several have had hands blown off, poor lads.

At his club he had heard two conversations. One was between the Public Prosecutor and a Resident Magistrate who said to the P.P., bemoaning their prospects, "And what do you think of it?" and he said "Oh I think of Coué, I keep saying 'I'll be better, I'll be better'". He, the P.P. had some wit Yeats says, for he spoke of the English "with their tongue in their cheek and their heart in their sleeve". Then another tête à tête near him. One told of an old lady a friend or relative of his who had left some pictures to the National Gallery, and it has refused them as not good enough. "And I am employing an expert to look at them and see that the National Gallery did not change the pictures in the frames"! (This I say is reductio ad absurdam of De Valera's suspicions of England). Robinson came in later, hears O'Hegarty of the Post Office under the new Government says all is going well in the Conference,[8] that all will be settled and that Collins is in high spirits. Then I get the evening paper (there was none published this morning) and it says that in the early hours of the morning four hundred armed men seized the Four Courts[9] and hold it. Then Sir Horace's car came to take me out to Kilteragh. He says the Conference has been put off for a week because so many of the members are to speak in the country on Sunday, and that orders have been sent out to the army to allow free speech. But whether this will be obeyed is doubtful. Sir Horace is very depressed, the I.A.O.S.[10] badly hit, first by the Black and Tans destroying the best creameries, then by the fall in agricultural prices, and finally by the state of unrest.

Such a dreadful portrait of Edward Martyn in the I.R.A. but Yeats says "it represents Edward's own view of literature—the lines are there—what does grace or comeliness matter"?

15 APRIL. Kilteragh. So comfortable here, luxury, and the quiet after the Gresham, and the view of mountain and sea. Sir Horace looking ill, and living on Benger and at his typewriter didn't come down to dinner. We had two men from the North, David Barbour and Mr. Adams, fairminded and workers in or helpers of the I.A.O.S. H.P. telephoned after dinner to *The Irish Times* Office for news, nothing further, but uneasiness about Sunday and the seizing of the Four Courts. And the Conference has come to no decision; only "hopes there will be no interference with meetings".

This morning H.P. has been talking about his I.A.O.S. and gave me the pamphlet about it to read, and liked my comment that the creameries might claim help as they had been lightning conductors to carry off some of the animosity of the Black and Tans. He is afraid it will die out unless the farmers support it better, for the English Government grant has now come to an end, and it isn't known yet if the new Government can or will renew it. But Hogan is very much in favour of it. I said that what would bring the farmers to feel the direct benefit of the society would be to make a new call and effort not so much to keep it going as to extend it to develop the Co-operative store idea, crushed almost altogether by the traders up to this. The farmers would feel the advantage of co-operation every Saturday, every day of the week, with this, instead of having to wait till the end of seasons or years. And my mind clearing as the idea grew, I think that there is encouragement in the decline of the priests' influence which was used on the side of the shopkeepers. Monsignor Fahey would have killed the effort near us. And the Parliamentary party that was against it is also maimed now. I took our sale of land as an example. The people are complaining, suffering, because of the high prices in the Gort shops, yet they dare not raise a finger because many of them to buy the land have borrowed money from those very shopkeepers who make their large profits out of them. I thought one town might be taken to begin with, the people released by the Organisation or a Land Bank taking over the debt. It is on good security all of it or the traders would not have lent, and at the same time opening co-operative stores, bringing an immediate fall in the cost of living, and giving new confidence and support to the I.A.O.S. It may be but a dream. He asked if I knew of any young man who would help the work "Any Shawe-Taylors"! But I had only known of one possible helper "and he has formed an attachment that is keeping him from work".

Sir H. is troubled also because he can't get rid of Z. who has taken to drink "and alcohol while it stimulates the imagination impairs the judgement".

Sir H. at his typewriter all the afternoon working, writing, catching at every straw, Yeats, the O'Brien boys, who may help to breathe life into the Society. I told him if it must die it would be a good moment when the new Government begins; he can lay it at their feet and show what he had done and that if its continuance is worth while it is for them to take up his work. And he seemed to agree in this. Yet (just as I have done these seven years about the Lane pictures), he writes and writes, because one letter out of all those may be the winning one.

16 APRIL. EASTER SUNDAY. H. Plunkett said he had been to the American Consul's office on some business on Thursday and had found the anteroom full, (the office also full and door closed) of people wanting their passports for U.S.A. visa-ed, many young men from the country. L.R. said yesterday that Desmond Fitzgerald[11] had been telling him of the odd way the delegates had been dealt with in London; allowed the day free, nothing to do, and then called up perhaps at 3 o'c in the morning for a visit to Chequers or a Government meeting. At Chequers all their tastes and habits had been carefully enquired into before they came.

This is an anxious day, no news yet. Last night near midnight H.P. was in bed when a message came up that men in uniform had come to ask for the loan of his motor for some members of the I.R.A. who were ordered to Bray. He lent it, (thought to himself they would carry it off if he didn't) on condition his chauffeur should drive it. He did so and brought the car back about 2 a.m. They had been to several other places besides Bray "under orders".

Just now the butler came to say there are no papers this morning, hears they were brought to Harcourt Street station, but burned there.

Mr. Hearne says the I.A.O.S. *must* go; is heavily in debt, and the guarantors will have to pay up, including farmers. Sir H. builds on Hogan[12] being interested, and has supplied him with literature "that will keep him reading till he goes", but Smith Gordon told him yesterday that Hogan has no power; that Collins is indifferent to agriculture, and Griffith and O'Higgins[13] actually against it, and they are the only three that matter, though they occasionally consult Cosgrave.

Easter Sunday. Conservative Evening. John Dillon and Professor Henry[14] came to lunch. Dillon looks impressive in his old age; an El Greco type, and talked all the time, stayed till 4.30, very interesting all he said. No news from Dublin but he had been awaked in the night by a burst of firing that lasted some time, but has not heard what it was. And as he left Dublin the streets were lined with Republicans, awaiting the funeral procession of one who was shot accidentally[15]—or while trying to escape—by Free Staters.

He takes a gloomy view, hates Griffith—"a liar", thinks better of Collins "because he knows nothing about him"; had seen a good deal of De Valera after the Mansion House Conference; doesn't think him honest (the first I have heard say this) but not so dishonest as Griffith. De V. had asked him to join them when he proclaimed his Republic and set up Dail Eireann "but I said, you cannot fight in open war, you must end by organised murder and I will never countenance that". As to the state of the country "the curates are all gone mad and the Bishops have lost authority, no one cares for them. I cannot foresee the future of the Church. There must be bloodshed before this trouble is settled, that accursed English Government knows that and will not interfere, wants to see us disgraced in the eyes of the world. They will most likely put Sir Henry Wilson[16] in authority in the North with 20,000 English troops, and 50,000 Orangemen. Then when there is an excuse they will come over the border; the I.R.A. will not be able to stand against a regular army. Whenever the trouble in Belfast slackens Sinn Fein sends men to stir it up again to keep it going. The Belfast Catholics would be ready to go into the Northern Parliament but the priests won't allow it. Devlin[17] would have gone in, but the priests would have prevented his election. Craig told me he wished to come in with the South, but he couldn't get support at present.

"It was the executions after the Rising that led to it all. If the leaders had been kept in prison until after the war a settlement could have been made and accepted. I was shut up in Gt. George's Street for three days by the Sinn Feiners, and the first day I got out————told me there were going to be executions, and we went together to the Viceregal Lodge and found Wimborne[18] there, and Lady Wimborne, holding a rifle and ready to leave. He promised to do his best and said 'I have been disgracefully treated, I was told nothing, I have no power'. Then we went to General Maxwell,[19] and I protested against the executions and he said 'Mr. Dillon, these men have shot English soldiers, and I have come to Dublin first to put down the Rebellion and then to punish the offenders'. 'But the Rebellion is over now'. 'Yes and I am going to punish the offenders, four of them are to be shot tomorrow morning. I am going to ensure that there will be no treason whispered, even whispered in Ireland for a hundred years'. 'You have been trying to do that for years'. 'Well, I am going to do it now. There will not be a whisper'.

"I went back to Wimborne and he promised to do his best. Next day I heard the four men had been shot in the morning and I went to him. He was very angry said 'I dined with General Maxwell last night and he promised that only two should be killed'. Then I went over to Westminster and when I saw Asquith he said 'I am going over to Ireland'. 'What on earth are you going for?' He said the wires had been cut and he was going to see what was going on. It is well he did go, for the military were having their way, they had made a list of fifty for execution. Then it was cut down to 35, but Asquith stopped them. It was to please the military leave had been given for these. I saw Lloyd George about it too, and I said 'Maxwell is a brute'. 'No', he said 'he is not that, he is an ass'.

"Redmond's speech was the great misfortune, promising the help of Ireland for the Empire. That is a word that is hated in Ireland. It has always been so; there has been actual joy at any defeat of it."

I told of my old nurse and the cheering she remembered hearing for the landing of the French in '98, and he said "There was an uncle of mine who laid down his head and cried when he heard of the victory at Waterloo. There was nothing to be done after that speech but to go with Redmond to see Kitchener and put Redmond's ideas before him—a separate regiment, Commissions sent to Gaelic Society, other societies, permission to recruit themselves, and have their own officers. Kitchener listened for a few minutes and refused to do so. Then Redmond said 'Then what will you do?' He said 'If you send me 5000 men I will say thank you. If you send me 12,000 I will say I am much obliged. If those five thousand are killed I will ask you to send another five thousand'. He fixed his blue eyes on me as he said this, and I said 'Then there is nothing to be done, we will not come again', and we went out. Then when Conscription was threatened I went to Lloyd George and he said he had to do it, because men were refusing to enlist in England unless the Irish were forced.

"Parnell would have got all we wanted but for the woman. Have you read the life? It is a wonderful love story. It would have been all right if it had not been made public. No man is allowed to stay in public life when that is so". (I said "Kings are an exception I suppose, for George IV reigned to the end of his life").

"Lord Melbourne was all but driven out by such a scandal. Dilke was driven out, Bishop ———— tried to arrange with Parnell, he might have given her up for a while. But Chamberlain wanted to destroy Parnell. O'Shea had been his agent for a while and he bribed him. O'Shea refused to give up the action. When he told Parnell that it is likely he had Chamberlain's bribe in his pocket. I always refused to attack him on moral grounds, but only because he had unfitted himself to be leader of the party. If he had lived a little longer he would have had no follower left. It is a curious thing, the people thought it was a made up story until he married her, and then they were shocked. And so little did he know this, that he proposed to Bishop ———— to bring Mrs. Parnell to the Longford meeting.

"No doubt Carson has a hold over Lloyd George, but he has lost his power since he took the judgeship. Devlin met him the other day in the lobby, and Carson held out his hand and said 'Will you shake hands with your old enemy?'. And as he did so Devlin said 'And what about your new enemy?'. 'Ah', he said 'I asked my dear Smith how he could say such things in direct contradiction to what he had said before and he said, "My dear Edward, haven't you known me long enough to know I have never said anything I could not throw over within a week?"'

"My staff at Ballahadereen have all been drilled since the Treaty. I asked one of them the other day, a lad, if there was much support for the Treaty and he said 'I believe the Civil population are supporting it', with the air of a Field Marshal."

I went to tea with L.R. at the Lodge, Will Shields and Dolan there. They say yes, De Valera, or Republic, has more of the army than the Free State has. One of them was told this by a Free State Captain.

17 APRIL. No news of any importance. Sir Horace went in and out of Dublin, had a talk with A.E. and I asked what he said about the present troubles, but he says "I don't know. I was so much taken up with the matter of the I.A.O.S. I never asked him" and he sat down again to type letters about it.

(I think of a play that might be written on one who believes all is good, finds all—all that is good.

"To live this day as 'twere my last". No, I would live this day "as 'twere" my first—in Eden.)

Just now to turn his mind from it a little I asked if he ever thought of writing his memoirs, and he said two publishers wanted him to do so, but he didn't feel that he could "I know nothing of literature or music I am interested in nothing but my work". I said people wouldn't want to hear details of his work in a biography, they know roughly what he has done, and anything necessary could be put in an appendix. I said "They will already, when they buy the book, know that; they will want to know what sort of man you are and how you came to do it". "Oh but I am only interested in the work". Then I asked how it did come to him and he said: "I left the University having managed to take a second in History. Then I became agent to my father for a while. Then a doctor said that both my lungs and my elder brother's were affected, and that our only chance was to go for a while either to South Africa or Colorado. He chose S.Africa, and he died on the way home after a painful illness—the consumption had attacked the knee. I went to Colorado, I bought a waggon and a pair of mules in Denver, and went on to a ranch. When my health was quite recovered I came home. My father had died and left me independent. I had always wanted to do something for Ireland, and having leisure I looked for what I could best do. I saw that farming was the chief industry, but that all the energy of the people had gone into tenure, into getting the land, and not to making the best use of it. I found that in other countries, abroad, the best methods had been brought into use and that they ought to be introduced in Ireland and I tried to work for this. Then Dillon and the Parliamentary Party were down on me". I said "Because they thought that would distract the thoughts of the people from the political side". "Yes, that was just it. I could not have done it had I not been a wealthy man. I had Anderson as Secretary for many years. I spent eight dreadful years in Parliament. They were necessary but I did not like the work there. And the hardest work was taking those long Drives" (I had reminded him of these) "to hold a meeting; and then no one turning up for an hour, and perhaps very few then. After a while the Development Committee, with Sydney Webb and others, helped and gave me a grant. That Society is all I care for. And now today I get a letter from Anderson, objecting to the economy scheme we had drawn up reducing the expenditure to £10,000 a year. He says we must spend £15,000. And someone else writes saying we must not spend more than £8000. No, I am not selfsacrificing, it has been my great interest, all I care for. You are right in saying that if it must end this would be a good moment for it to make its bow, for the curtain. But there are many in Ireland whose hearts are bound up with it who would suffer very much in seeing it fail".

(And G. Heard had told me it is hopelessly in debt and *must* come to an end.)

Later, in conversation with Heard he said "They think we want to give up self help. It is quite the contrary. We want the new Government to give a grant to the Society on condition the farmers themselves subscribe".

I told him this was the clearest summary I had heard, telling the gist of his efforts. But he said he had already said it in other words—and read me several pages. . . .

Last night talking of Dunsany he said someone had said to him in America "I told your nephew I knew his uncle, Horace Plunkett, and he said 'Yes, we are not much alike. I often wonder how the eagle came to be born on the Plunkett stock'"!!!

18 APRIL. Abbey last night. *Lord Mayor* spoiled by Nolan being put in Dolan's part and paid extra while Dolan idled about.

Larchet thinks things will come right. Fahy T.D. told him or "let out to him" that De V.'s army is ninety per cent the young men lately enlisted. And he thinks the Four Courts will soon be abandoned, because a good many of its garrison are workmen taking a holiday and that can't afford to stay without pay. They have levied contributions on the shops so far and that will not get them friends. Cathal Brugha[20] had been to the Abbey on Saturday week, "a small insignificant man, but determined looking." He thinks it is the loss of Griffith that leaves De Valera so vague.

Sir H. has shown me a letter from his nephew Mr. Ponsonby, from Thurles saying he had better not come there as he had intended, as his house has been raided three times; the first for motors, which he could not defend. The raiders have not entered the house, as it was barricaded. He says he is on the border between the Free Staters and Republicans, and while they are engaged with each other, thieves are having their opportunity. The third raid was interrupted by I.R.A. forces who drove the raiders away. He thinks they have chosen him for attack because he has more to be taken than in other houses. Sir H. is very indignant with any "peace prophets" (I'm afraid I've been one). But I hope if all these raids have been made by thieves, I think both armies will combine against them.

Sir Horace motored me to the Gresham and Harris came in. He had spent Easter in Wexford, says the "independent army" has come there, has commandeered provisions from the shops, a shopkeeper he knows told him he had already given £20 worth, and didn't know how long his stock would last. Also, but I don't know if this was done by men in or out of uniform, every window in a house belonging to a Protestant has been broken—"reprisals for Belfast", and it was the Protestant shopkeepers who were the first to have provisions taken.

At the Broadstone Frank met me, to talk of Malachi Quinn's letter (he has written saying he wants the land). He says Roxborough has been raided, the guns taken away, but a promise that they will be returned when done with. Arthur wrote him a bare statement of this. He heard from someone else they had got to the cellar and had drunk too much. He said "You will be safe because you are popular, we are fair game but you are known to be always on the side of the people". But it is not I.R.A. I am anxious about, but miscellaneous thieves.

At Athenry there was a boy stretched on a bench—to be moved into train. I asked Daly if it had been an accident; "It was a bomb—in Castle gar" was all he knew.

All peaceful and quiet here, at Coole. Free State Army is in the Workhouse. Independent in Barracks.

21 APRIL. COOLE. All peaceful. I drove to Ballylee yesterday; moved plants in Garden today. Peter says De Valera is coming to speak in Gort tomorrow and "if he gets his way there will be open war in Ireland" and that the Republican army haven't a penny, and that a good many boys last week have joined the Free State.

Working at the *70 Years* very hard yesterday, but have got into the second part, the lonely life, and having done that will get on better.

22 APRIL. Mike John back from Gort yesterday just missed hearing De Valera speak. Mr. Harry Boland[21] was speaking, saying "the Republic would give them everything and the Free State gave them nothing, and that we have the English beat and well beat". "There was a crowd of women around them, De Valera was sitting in his motor and Stevenson along with him; very few men, the men were passing by doing their own business it being market day". "There's not a father or a mother or a married woman or man but is against him".

23 APRIL. After church I went to see Mitchell's widow—he died two days ago. Miss Quinn told me about the "robbery" of Post Office. Captain Burke and Lennard had come and asked for the dog tax money, £25, said they were "under orders" to get it.

She and Mrs. Mitchell speak well of them both and like them, and Miss Quinn herself made up the money to £25 as it was not so much. Both these Republicans at the Barracks and the Free State soldiers at the Workhouse are very quiet and well behaved. She also said De Valera had a poor meeting and no cheering. J. says there was a band from Crusheen but no one to meet them at the Station. De V. said in his speech that he would never give up fighting for the Republic. "Up the Republic" was whitewashed on one of the walls. (And has been renewed from time to time. February 1924).

The Bagots said Lady Clonbrock was sitting in her motor outside the door at Mount Talbot when the raiders came there. She refused to get out when they demanded the car so they lifted her out, and she had to go home in a carriage drawn by a workhorse. Katy had written that the raiders at Roxborough "behaved well—for them; did not come into my room or disturb the children, not as they behaved at Mount Talbot", and Bagots say they were very rough there, dragged Mr. Talbot across the hall though he was ill, and that he is now in a Dublin nursing home and his wife has died from the shock. Mrs. Mitchell heard Roxborough had been raided again, and a motor carried off. I asked the Archdeacon if we ought not to protest against the Belfast killing of Catholics,[22] but he had already done so in the name of the parish, adding it to some resolution.

24 APRIL. Strike today, labour protesting against the quarrel and army rule.

Mr. Johnson here, says Hayes has had to sell all the land he bought, after all the disturbance they made to make us sell. He gives a good character to Lennard and Burke, but says the official I.R.A. are very well paid, but the Irregulars haven't a penny, and they took I think twenty boxes of biscuits that were going to Limerick, from the station. He spoke of the robbery of the people by the shop prices, and says Lipton, intending to open a branch in Gort could not get a house, the shopkeepers uniting to keep him out, and he will have to build one if he wants to come.

Malachi Quinn here this evening just as I was coming from the garden. He gave me Frank's letter to read and said "That doesn't suit me. I see ye have stock on the land". I said "Yes, our own stock". "Then I will drive it off". I said "I don't think you can do that, there is still law and order enough in the country to prevent it". "I tell you I will clear it off". I said "You should make your threat to a man, not to a woman" and walked away. A troublesome business, I think he is half crazed, and no wonder.

Mr. Johnson said there had been a good deal of cattle driving in Co. Clare, and Lord Ashtown's had been driven at Druimhasna, and the windows broken.

A. writes from Galway "De Valera passed this house about 11 on Saturday night. A boy went round ordering people to put candles in their windows; 'Support the Republic', 'Uphold the Republic' is painted on walls and the town decorated with Sinn Fein flags. The meeting went off quietly, De V. advocated 'Force'. Two of his admirers went to Tuam to hear him, but came back very down on their luck there was such a poor meeting there. He lunched last time he was in Galway with the Bishop but this time with some firebrands of curates in the house that Father Griffin lived in. Even the little shops that do not close on Sundays were shut yesterday".

26 APRIL. Yesterday morning J.D. told me the cattle had strayed again and the stones seemed to have been moved, so Malachi must have driven them. I wrote to Frank asking him to try and arrange a sale with Margaret. That, and cold and cough, and the papers—M. Collins' Meeting obstructed and De V. breathing war, made me sad. I worked at Memoir, got "Letter Box" chapter through. And letters from the three chicks cheered me up.

28 APRIL. John this morning to report cattle have again been driven and that Malachi came to his house last night threatening that if he and Thomas put them back he would shoot them—very violent. Johnny Hehir says he came on to their house and told him that if he put the cattle back "I'll give you more than the stick this time". I said I would not have the stock put back just now, as there may be some settlement by next week, and I see the I.R.A. in Clare have denounced cattle driving, and probably Gort may do the same, but we don't know yet which army is in power there.

Then Peter tells me "De Valera is banished from Gort, only six men left in the Barracks, some are gone home and some joined the Free State army in the Workhouse", so that is hopeful. He says they had no money and "went borrowing bread from the shops" but the Free State men get twenty five shillings a week.

F. writes "A wild crowd came to interview Arthur at Roxborough and force him to sell. One of his grounds of refusal then was that his family had been in possession for three hundred years, whereupon a voice shouted 'You had it long enough'! You might say the same to Malachi if he urges his claim on this ground."

A. writes "The Masonic Hall has been seized by Republican

troops and their documents carried off".

The plumber, just now, says there are sixteen men in the Barracks, the others went and joined the Free Staters at the Workhouse, and that a great many through the country are joining the Free State.

30 APRIL. Yesterday one of the young bullocks, frisking with the others leaped twice into the air and fell down dead (they think blackwater). It is most fortunate Mike happened to be there, near the lake. Had it happened in the field Malachi drove them from we might have suspected him. And a lamb died last week. I was too dull with cold and headache to work at Memoir so tried to make up my accounts for the half year from 1 November. Heavy enough, I can't go on unless I earn more, or sell, or both. But I'll get on to November anyhow.

A nice letter from Catherine by afternoon post, but the papers give news of more killings of Protestants in Cork[23]—reprisals again. "Death answering to death like the clerks answering one another at the Mass".

I awoke early and thought how sad it is with all this violence that we cannot have peace even within the demesne, and I have been writing a letter to Malachi.

8 o'c. But John says he put his cattle on the land last night and they strayed through a gap and he has been collecting them to put on again. However I sent the letter, a last effort towards peace.

And I did not know whether witnesses should or should not be sent to the Court yesterday (the harness room case) and the witnesses were not eager to go, and I had intended going to Gort to find out which army was to conduct the prosecution, but couldn't with this cold. And now I hear they were vexed and that it is adjourned for a fortnight. Lennard and the Workhouse army that chased him through the river great friends, the "coolness" only lasted about three hours!

Yeats was here, sad about the state of parties and the quarrels; he said "this is the country you and I have spent twenty years working for".

I read him what Robinson says in his letter "A.E. is very disheartened, wants someone to write a play about how the generations for 700 years fought for the liberation of beautiful Cathleen ni Houlihan, and when they set her free she walked out, a fierce vituperative old hag. I feel almost inclined to write the play and leave Ireland for ever the day before it is played, but I really feel more optimistic than A.E." Yeats is afraid the reaction against Nationalism that must come will do great injury to India and other countries, the cry for "liberty" must die away, may have been already dying, and this scene of confusion and discord will hasten it, this quarrelling over things that mean nothing. We agreed in the comfort of being out of England where we should have to hang our heads whatever causes may have contributed. I read him Una's letter saying how contemptuous the Germans are of us and "what we want to know is, what do you think of Ireland?" When there is lunacy in a family, I said, one doesn't write to ask members of it what they think of its state.

Brennan had talked to G.Y. of Cunningham's imprisonment and said "It may be that my own boy had as much to do with shooting Baldwin, or it may be the gun went off of itself. The Judge said at the trial he didn't know why one was brought up if the other wasn't brought up. But my boy would have been gaoled along with Cunningham only that I had sold twelve pigs for £84, and I paid the whole of that to a lawyer I employed".

I sent my letter to Malachi but without much hope.

1 MAY, 1922. A. writes "Last night the maids saw Crossley tenders with Republican soldiers in uniform armed with rifles sitting back to back as the English soldiers did. They don't know where they went to; it does not look as if the Labour strike had alarmed them. We hear the Custom House was raided and Mullins Stores in Nune Island was seized. I met Soman coming from there, his office and papers left and he has got the key of it. A lot of whisky there in store but he says 'Bond is not paid on it so they won't touch it as they would be destroying their own revenue. Did you ever hear anything so absurd?'"

2 MAY. In the afternoon Malachi sent a copy of his answer to F. and a bill (not for me) no other acknowledgement of my letter. Donohoe and his "crowd" have twice sent an offer to drive off his cattle, which they would do with glee, but I don't want to begin that battledore work, and will leave it to law and F. and M.

This morning Mike comes to report that Malachi has now stocked one of the callows (not in the sale) with sheep.

Mike, back from Gort, says the National Bank is now guarded by regular troops, and there is a machine gun on the roof of the other Bank. No wonder, as the papers tell of Bank robberies everywhere, and of railways up in Tipperary, and De V. calling out the election must not be for six months; but a proposal by troops not Rory's but five Gort irregulars with Mulcahy and Collins that they should unite and have a free election.

3 MAY. F. writes (enclosing a letter from M.Q.) "Roxborough was commandeered yesterday, both house and lands, including live stock; the I.R.A. are to pay the workmen, servants

&c. I suppose by selling the stock. Arthur and family came up yesterday and are crossing to England".

It is a shock. Roxborough seemed so safe and permanent; and now they may never come back. The papers say they, the I.R.A., are irregulars and that they demanded it for refugees from Belfast.[24] M. Quinn's defiant letter a trouble too, though F. says "the matter will not be difficult to arrange if M. wishes."

Molly Bagot came to lunch very low, had been to Clare to say goodbye to the Studderts who are leaving, taking their furniture. The Macnamans had auctioned some and intended to auction the rest but I.R.A. came and ordered them not to. She told me also of Mr. Bradshaw the Kilchriest clergy man's house being entered and robbed.[25] On the other hand A. writes "They say the Republicans in Dominick Street have been given to 9.30 to clear out but they are still holding the fort with guns in their hands at the windows. The Free Staters got back the Custom House and Millers Stores, under McKeown, a blacksmith, who lived a couple of miles from Medellis in Longford.

A nice little letter from Richard is a comfort, though he draws a little picture in it of "A Misty Day"!

4 MAY. Nothing today. I am thinking of my three little ones at River Court, and Richard leaving tomorrow.

5 MAY. Postman says "the Truce is signed" but no details. A. writes "The buildings have not all been retaken, only Custom House and Bond Stores (Millers) but the Free Staters have ordered the others not to stir out, so they are in a sort of way interned. It is said Free Staters have retaken Roxborough from Republicans".

6 MAY. But the Truce is only signed for four days.[26] No news of Roxboro' but *Connacht Tribune* says Arthur was handed a paper saying the place was taken because he is "A Freemason and Unionist" (he isn't a Freemason) and that Woodlawn house and estate have been taken on the same grounds. But it is empty of furniture, and Ashtown is away.

A. writes "Madell looked in at window of Masonic Hall and saw the Irregulars at dinner with knives and forks, but only potatoes in a heap on the table. They are interned by Free State". Mike brings a rumour that Houston, Lough Cutra gamekeeper, and Sullivan, Garryland caretaker have had notice to leave (both Protestants). But it was personal, someone wanting their house or land.

7 MAY. Sunday. To church and Guy was there from Lough Cutra and came back to lunch. He says neither Houston nor Sullivan have had any notice to quit, it is an invention.

He had arrived in Dublin on Tuesday, drove to Kildare St. Club but found it occupied, though a young man on the steps with a rifle told him there was a room he could use if he was a member, but luckily he didn't, as all members were excluded later in the day. He went then to the Shelbourne, found Arthur and Kathie there, they told him Katy and the two children had left for England two hours before the raiders came. They were prepared, as after Mr. Bradshaw had been raided they thought their turn would come next, and had been packing and hiding away valuables and whiskey. When they came they were quite civil, but handed Arthur a paper saying his house as that of "A Freemason and Protestant" must be given up to shelter Belfast refugees (but no refugees seem to have arrived there). He asked them not to occupy the drawingroom and they agreed. They were allowed to take their personal luggage, but Kathie was carrying a Waterford glass jug she valued away from the drawingroom and one of them met her on the stairs and said "Oh no young lady, that won't do", and made her put it back. Arthur went to Whitney and Moore, and they, or Frank, got in touch with Hogan, and he sent orders to the regular I.R.A. on Loughrea not to allow any cattle from Roxborough to be sold. (Mr. D. Browne, also at the Shelbourne had been evicted in like manner, in Mayo, and his cattle have been driven away to be sold). And Arthur had just received a letter from the intruders asking him for a cheque to pay his workmen!

Bank robberies go on, and my name for R.O'C. is Rory of the Tills.

8 MAY. I read in Montaigne last evening that Epaminondas refused some means of gaining wealth, preferring to "fence with poverty". I have had that thought, that the muscles of the mind may be strengthened by the battle. Yet I would take any means in harmony with my instinct and judgment to save the home for the children. And my half year's accounts show that my certain income would not pay more than rates taxes, labour and repairs. All the rest I must earn if I can, or sell what they will not really miss or regret.

X. writes "The Labour exchange near this was raided in broad daylight yesterday and £50 unemployment money taken. The night before a great attack on G. Post Office, but they did not get in.

Yeats came over and we sat in the garden, in the sun. Later I was reading *Consuelo* to him in the library when a motor came to take him back to Ballylee for some visitors. The people say the fine weather is come because of the truce.

Richard's cricket bat and racket sent back from the Post Office with Customs declaration forms (in French!) for me to sign and fill. I had forgotten England is a foreign country now.

I walked in the wood, the bluebells out.

9 MAY. X. writes "Canon Berry says H. Anderson the dentist went as usual to Gort, was held up and asked if he had been a special constable. He said yes, for a few days in 1916. They said "Don't show your face here again, we don't want you"; and took his motor, a hired one.

11 MAY. That is true. McNicholas who was here yesterday teaching me to graft apple trees, had met Anderson and his wife on their way to Galway on a farmer's car after the motor had been taken at Druimhasna. But he says being a special constable had nothing to do with it, there was a feeling against him because he had gone about a great deal with Sidley, R.J.C. last winter.

J.D. said Thomas had come from Mulloo's house and said Mulloo had heard that Shaughnessy at the railway station said a message had come that De Valera will go out of politics for five years. And this morning Mike has heard that he will "Lay down his arms for five years".

A.E. sent me his lecture "Past and Future" yesterday;[27] comforting because he believes in the future as I do, and is anxious about the present. I had said to Yeats the other day that is my feeling, just the converse of one's usual uneasiness about the future but confidence in getting through each day.

Evening. Alas, no settlement.

Yeats says McNeill thought there would not be one yet, though all sides, both army and civilians want it, except the few officers. These he thinks are the danger, they will fight and may have to be executed; and that it is a small physical force party that is keeping down the country.

13 MAY. Yesterday a nice motor drive with Guy to Ballylee and to Burren, sea and mountains beautiful. I went to bed tired, and at 11 o'c Mike knocked at the door "There's men downstairs knocking at the hall door. I think they are raiders". I told him I would follow him down, put on dressing gown and veil over my hair. He said they had called out to him to open the door. He said he hadn't the key. "Where is it?" "Upstairs in Lady Gregory's room" (it being in the door all the time). When I came to the door they were knocking again. I went to it and said "Who is there?" "Open or it will be the worse for you"—a young unpleasant bullying voice. I knew one would not gain anything by speaking to such men, so stood at the foot of the stairs. They kicked the door then and I expected every moment they would

break in the unshuttered window and come in. I prayed for help though without much hope, and stood still. After a while the knocking ceased, I thought they had gone to look for another door and whispered to Mike to come up to the playroom by the back stairs as we could see from there. But the door on back stairs was locked, and the moonlight was now so bright on front staircase I didn't like to show myself on it. We could see nothing or hear nothing. Once I saw a red light and thought they were coming back with helpers. But no one came, and I could see no one from any window, and at 1 o'c went back to bed and Mike to his. It did shake the nerves. Yet at the worst moment I felt it was right somehow I should know what others had suffered in like cases, and that I might be glad later to have known it. (February 1924. Yes it has given me more sympathy and understanding, for now that I am alone again in the house, so long after, I constantly feel a slight nervousness when I have gone to bed, a feeling that there may again come a knock at the door. And this although of those two men one is in gaol (for a more serious crime) and the other in the Civic Guards—something like Pharaoh's butler and baker!)

15 MAY. It is suggested that the raiders were the two under bail who were found robbing the harness room, and while thinking this possible I did not think it likely. But on Saturday their trial was again put off, Lennard being away in Galway, and Mike having come back said to me "I hope that case will be settled. If it is not I don't know what will happen, there will be bad work". I said "What will happen?" He said "Oh nothing to your ladyship—but terrible things will happen". Some one came up then and I did not see him again, but this seems a threat he had been sent with, or had given as a warning. So it is possible the two culprits had already tried to alarm me that night. I was troubled last night, lay awake wondering what I ought to do, wishing for peace, but doubtful if it would be right to show any weakness. And opening the prayerbook to read a Collect, the one I opened at was for St. John Baptist's Day . . . asking that we may "after his example constantly speak the truth, boldly rebuke vice, and patiently suffer for the truth's sake".[28] And knowing what the truth is, I suppose I must go on. On Friday night the Collect I had read was for the Ascension "that we may in heart and mind thither ascend and with Him continually dwell".[29] And I tried to fix my mind on that high country while I stood expecting the raiders to break in.

Yeats came yesterday for his sitting to Spicer Simson[30] who has come to do a medal of him, and I have put up here. He read me what he has written in his Memoir about his first coming here and about my work, and I am pleased especially that he puts *Cuchulain* and *Gods and Fighting Men* to the front, as I am doing in my own memoir.

Evening. Yeats came back from Ballylee with Mr. Simson and offered to come and sleep here for a bit when he is gone, and I am glad to accept.

Simson began doing a medallion of me "for himself".

Jordan ("Mr. Quirke") came asking for a little help; says he had his stall in the Square at De Valera's meeting and was skinning a couple of kids at the time, and the meeting was no great success "the people not paying much attention to it, and he said there would be civil war all over Ireland, and that every man should carry a gun". He thinks the Gort thieves who robbed the Station are to be arrested "Everyone down on the Free State army for not doing it before; sure they had them chased into the churchyard and it's well known who they were. Father Considine gave a great sermon and he asked where was the use of an army in the town if it wouldn't do that much. But they are well to do lads, if it was a poor man going to bed fasting they'd arrest him quick enough". But he says "There are a good many with De Valera in Gort".

16 MAY. Yeats came to lunch, and Simson finished his medallion and mine. Y. likes mine very much and has ordered one.

I asked M.J. what he meant by "terrible things", and he said he thinks it was "these lads" (the two M.s) that came the other night to frighten us on account of the case.

18 MAY. Yesterday morning I heard Bernard Cunningham is out of gaol and at home. Such a mercy at last.

Then Yeats. He had been to the Workhouse Barracks, and appointed to meet Free State officers here. Two came, Harrington, rough, but seems to have a good head; Fahy who didn't say much. I told them of the night alarm and asked for either a patrol or a couple of men to sleep in the house, and they promised these, thought it would be best. But at night having made a room ready with two beds, they didn't come. I stayed up till after 11, Yeats till after 12. J.D. till after 1 o'c. But this morning cigarette ends were found in laundry yard, as if they had been there. And J. going to Gort found they had come, but seeing no light in front of house had gone away after a while, but they are to come tonight. The Bagot girls also here yesterday to meet Mrs. Yeats. They looked pale and said in the morning a party of Irregulars had come and given Bagot a paper saying he was to give up his land and stock to them. He might keep a hundred acres, and the tenants on the rest should pay the rest to *them*. He might keep the house and personal property. There is a rumour later that they went back and apologised. (Yes that is true.)

Yeats had said to Fisher (English Minister of Education) who was boasting of the culture he had bestowed "You have made vocal the mouths that were closed by the Deity".

Mr. Johnson here, says they are not absolutely sure who the Gort thieves are, that is why they have not been arrested.

I read the beginning of my Memoirs to Yeats. He thought first chapter (3rd Person) should be condensed in places, but seems to like it; so far a relief.

19 MAY. Two young Free State soldiers came at 10 o'c last night, nice looking lads and strong, Mahony and Flanagan, one from Craughwell, he had been on the run last year, the other from Clarenbridge. They went to bed directly, 10.15 and this morning when I came down to breakfast at 9, I knocked at gunroom door, no answer, peeped in and saw them fast asleep their heads on the same pillow. As we finished breakfast they appeared and they said they had been up the last two nights and were tired. I felt more tranquil having them in the house.

Guy writes from Lough Cutra: "Captain Lennard paid us a visit in the morning and took forty acres of land away, land inside the demesne. He informed us that they had been very lenient with Lough Cutra. Whilst I was out in the afternoon he returned and said that the orders were cancelled and returned us Hugo's land".

21 MAY. Brady, Gort schoolmaster yesterday evening to ask about loan of Carnegie books, and I brought him to the library to talk with Yeats as to the sort of books Gort would read, and am glad to think of being able to help there. The paper was depressing—talk—talk—in the Dail. But after church today we heard there had been a telegram saying "the two parties had joined and made peace".[31] Typing for Yeats as of old, his "Memories" for book form.

Evening. The schoolmaster again, but with a wife—excited—Yeats says mad—about spiritualism. She talked incessantly and the Carnegie books were in the background, except that I gathered she is giving up her drapery shop and wants to try bookselling, and thinks they might help her. Brady confirms the news of agreement, has seen the telegram, that it is to be a coalition Government. When they had gone my head ached and I went to my room and read *Leaves of Grass*[32] and thought of De Valera as I read "Must I indeed learn to chant the cold dirges of the baffled, and the sullen hymns of defeat".

22 MAY. I said at breakfast that in looking through Whitman's poems of the Civil War it seemed to me that no one thinks the worse of America for that War; and why should we be looked upon as such reprobates for being on the edge of one? And it is much on the same subject, for the same cause. They fought as we are possibly going to do to avoid separation, and if they had the slave question as an excuse so have we the Catholics in Ulster. Yeats said he had always thought the American war a mistake, the South had a fine civilisation and tradition that had been broken by it; and America in humour, in religion even, had become standardised and so impoverished. And as to Ulster, he said, "I have always been of opinion that if such disagreeable neighbours shut the door, it is better to turn the key in it before they change their mind".

News of agreement between leaders in the Dail, but of burnings in Ulster.[33] Yeats read me his memoirs through the day, a fine book, rich in memories and in philosophy.

BOOK NINETEEN

23 MAY, 1922. J.D. was at Lough Cutra yesterday and says that some days ago the F.S. troops drove off cattle that had been put on the land by grabbers. They had done so before, and the cattle had been put on again. One of the grabbers, said to the Officer when they warned him that they would come back if the stock was put on again "It will take more than you and your handful of men. It will be the worse for you if you come". So yesterday they brought three lorries of troops and put off the stock again, and told B. that next time he would have them driven to the pound and not released till £1 per head had been paid. And A. writes from Galway "a Protestant farmer a few miles from this had land, stock and house seized. The Free Staters sent and had them restored, said 'We are going to deal with the land ourselves and don't alow others to interfere'." So that looks like the return of law and order. And I told Mike that with this in mind I would drop the case against those two young thieves.

26 MAY. Yeats says of some young poet "he is rather a dissolvent in conversation—earnest and looking for truth".

Yeats proposes my continuing his anthology of Irish verse, says he can't do it himself, he would give pain to people he must leave out. But I would not.

I have read "Sir Frederic Burton"[1] to Yeats and he likes it. G[eorge] Y[eats] writes "Lt. Byrne said there were men patrolling every night round Coole though he expected Lady Gregory didn't know they were there; and that 'Lady Gregory is the first person in the county that would get protection'".

28 MAY. Simson said of Epstein (he had looked at my bust)[2] "His tendency is to exaggerate the physical rather than the psychological characteristics".

A. wrote yesterday "While Nurse was putting me to bed we heard cheering and a band in the street. Nurse and Sarah rushed to the hall door and saw a large mob headed by a man dragging with ropes the statue of Lord Dunkellin from Eyre Square, some sitting on the statue as if on a sledge. The cook from the Rectory passed and told the maids she had been in the Square, a great crowd there, 'A Councillor' (this was young Larkin) 'made a speech after which they dragged down the statue. They went towards Grattan Road, probably to throw Lord D. into the sea'."

I asked Lennard about this. He said "It was madness. It was done by the Labour Party." I said they could have sold the statue (Foley's) probably to Lord Lascelles for a large sum. And I told him I had read so many of Lord Dunkellin's letters to my husband,[3] they were colleagues in representing the county, and the letters were full of interest in Galway, anxiety to have the Packet Station there, and to help constituents. He said again "It was madness". He says the robberies now are by ordinary thieves and that they are getting them in hand.

I had read my Layard[4] chapter to Yeats. He thinks it very good.

But now, 4 o'c, I have read my Lyall,[5] and he will have none of it, scoffs at his poetry, turns down his letters. And I remember that once I asked them to meet one another at dinner and Yeats would only pour out conversation on Irish things to Stephen Gwynn, their only fellow guest—ran wild, though he said afterwards in half apology "I know I ought to have talked about Indian idols". And Sir Alfred, though he wrote saying he would try to help the young poet to "come out of that Celtic Twilight" in which he fancied him obscured, said on a later day of some other Irish acquaintance "like our young friend the other night he talks too much". But now Yeats has his revenge, and alas the flatness of Sir A.'s letters and even of some of his poems show how great was the personal magnetism that made writers and statesmen and many brilliant and beautiful women proud to be known as his friends.

Coole Park Gort
Co. Galway
28 May, 1922

(Letter to my sister).

I had a visit last evening, about 10 o'c from Captain Lennard of the Irregular Force, about the case against young D. who was found burgling the harness room. I asked for news of Roxborough, and he said it was he who had taken it over. He said Major Persse was a fine man, and had taken it very quietly, and Miss Persse was a splendid girl, it must have been a shock to her to leave her home so suddenly, but he was acting under orders. I asked why Major Persse, such a fair man and large employer of labour had been molested, and he said "He was unlucky. The names were put in a bag, and his came out twice. Besides he is a Freemason and high in the Order. It is such men as he who can influence Craig and the English Government to stop the Belfast disorder. There are no Belfast refugees in the house, but it will be kept until Belfast is quiet. There are four men in it, they keep to the back rooms, I locked up all valuables in the drawing-room, I put padlocks on the door. The raids before that were not by us but by thieves. We have got back the arms that were taken then and the motor. We are using it, but will keep it safe and give it back. The stock is all right. The place was being eaten up by rabbits, there were three trappers being paid 20/- a week, I increased their pay to 26/- thinking to make them more efficient but they only kill 18/- worth rabbits in the week, they may be stealing some, I thought of getting over two or three trappers from England who would do the work better." I asked if they were selling old or young rabbits, as this is out of the season. He said "Both, they get 1/6 a brace for them. The tillage goes on and the steward pays the men out of rent that was owing on grass farms."

THURSDAY, 1 JUNE. Galway, I came on Tuesday, had a letter as I passed though Gort from M. an unpleasant one, so I am going back tomorrow. (18 February 1924. L. Cutra was no example to follow. They had endless trouble there, and were blamed by the F.S. soldiers as well as the community for taking up so much of their time and energy in this constant driving off of cattle &c. And in the last week's *Tribune*[6] I see some man fined for killing rabbits there says "it is a commonage, everyone is killing rabbits over it". And the treecutting also has been going on as well as shooting through the demesne. We have been better off all through, though we have not their retinue).

2 JUNE. GALWAY. Yesterday I walked to the end of the Claddagh pier to look for traces of the Dunkellin statue in the sea. Some boys and young men were sitting there and told me there was nothing left "all broken up or swept away". I was told also some of the broken pieces had been sold for a few pence by boys who had fished them out.

I came home today to carry out M.'s desire about driving off M. Quinn's cattle. I wrote yesterday to C.O. at Gort, asking him to come and see me. As I came home from Galway there was on the platform at Galway a troop of young soldiers who marched to the train with their rifles and got in. There was cheering, and a song (I could not catch the air) and cheers to the very end of the platform. I asked one who was looking out of the carriage where they were going. "To the frontier". "What frontier?" "Belfast"! At Athenry there were more uniforms and cheering. I said to Daly the porter as I changed for Gort that these young fellows were pleasanter to look at than the Black and Tans and that I hoped there would be no fighting where they were going. He said "There must be fighting if Belfast goes on the same way, it is terrible what is done there."[7] And he said a special train had come from Limerick filled with troops, who had joined the others and for the same destination.

All here so radiant, so decorated, the great white horsechestnuts in bloom, the smaller red ones, the crimson and the white hawthorn, lilac and laburnum, the leaves so fresh, the paths carpeted with the brown blossoms of the beech. It would have been a pity to forsake this home and leave it to desolation.

3 JUNE. I have been rewriting some bits of my Layard and Lyall chapters, with my new and delightful idea of using Yeats' criticisms as a sort of Chorus and so making crutches of the rod.

I have been out till after 9 o'c. Everything is beautiful, one must stand to look at blossoming tree after tree; the thorns in the Park that W. used to come over from London to see at this time of year best of all. I feel certain I am doing the best thing in giving Richard the chance of keeping this place, and in keeping it as a home for the others' childhood at least.

5 JUNE. Yesterday, Sunday, I thought and worked for a bit on a possible Passion play. I think of one that could be put into Irish and played in St. Theresa's Hall. Then church. Coming home I was told Lough Cutra has been in a worse state than before, cattle put on the land again, turf cut, a bog burned, (now it is said a wood burned as well), and that fifty of the Free State army are in the yard to protect the castle. This accounts for their not coming here.

The Cranagh men came to complain of our horses and cattle trespassing; this owing to Edmunds and the C.D. Board not having carried out their promise and contract of building the wall, it was left unfinished last year. But we must remove our cattle from the lake, though so short of grass.

I found Yeats here and read him my "Conversation" chapter. He liked it and was amused at my use of his criticisms.

Today he and George have been here, to consult about the Belfast degree being conferred upon him.[8] Mr. J[ohnson] came to tea, thinks Free State are not strong enough to take another case on, having their hands full at Lough Cutra. He hears mountain men are dividing up land at Roxborough, ploughing and sowing. The C.D.B. official, who went to see them said "You are sowing but you will not reap it".

8 JUNE. Yesterday I drove to Tillyra, Edward Martyn had left Dublin when Kildare St. Club was taken possession of[9], he thought there would be a battle and he would be in the line of fire. But he is pleased at having found no trouble down here. Then to Ballylee for tea. This morning I awoke very down-hearted about my Memoir, and thinking of it almost—indeed for a while wished—it might be destroyed; and I had been so uneasy lest it should be in case of a raid. However I worked at Roosevelt later, and felt more hopeful.

And then Yeats came, to stay a week, and I told him of my discontent.

Mrs. B. came yesterday to look for Margaret's passport, who wants to go and look at French seaside places, in case they cannot come back here. Guy has given her a bad account of the country.

11 JUNE. Lough Cutra bad still, they say, the cattle driven on the land at night though they have been put off it by day; the bogs being cut by all the country round, the Free State men taking their names, threatening punishment when the Courts are set up, not able to keep order now.

SUNDAY, 18 JUNE. Yeats left on Friday. We had a quiet ten days and he was encouraging on the whole about the Memoir, as he begins to see it as a whole; liked best of all what I had last read him—all I have arranged so far; my letters to Wilfrid Blunt and his to me. So now I can go to work with better courage.

The country has seemed quieter; and I look on it as a sign of peace and sanity Roxborough having been given back. Though now, having come from church Mr. B. told me there of Ballydugan house having been burned down. There are over 100 Free State troops at Lough Cutra, and they now mean to enforce the "pounding" of trespassing cattle. But M. of Lisheen whose bog the Irregulars had seized and from which they had been put out by troops, has now had 11 head of cattle driven off, and he himself has spent £10 on motors looking for them, and both armies have gone searching and they are not to be found "but as if the earth ate them".

19 JUNE. A.S.T. here. I looked at the papers to see result of elections and cried out "Oh, they have killed five Protestants!" and she said "I'm glad they have killed Protestants, it will show it is not only Catholics that are being killed"!!

The Officer (I think Republican) who came to ask her about the raid at Castle Taylor said he expected the next few months will be troublesome "If the Treaty is broken we'll have to fight the English, and if it passes we will have to put down disorder with the bullet, there will be opposition". He said "If any raiders come at night or disguised don't let them in. If we come it is openly in the daytime, and under orders".

20 JUNE. Girvin came about Cranagh wall, with news of Mme. Markievicz' defeat, and Mellows.[10] J.H. says "some wish Clare had been fought against De Valera, and some say he gave £100 to the Labour man against him to withdraw".

I have been reading Act III of *Brand.*[11] It has much of Ireland's contest of wills today.

21 JUNE. The longest day, and dark and cold as winter. I drove to Ballylee, brought news of the Treaty candidates' victories, Yeats is going on with the poem he began here "The rich man's house stands in its flowery lawns" . . .[12]

22 JUNE. More Treaty victories, but De Valera's protest sounds like another permit of quarrel. And the army is not at one. I said to Mr. Johnson that I did not suppose the Irregulars can go on very long without money, but he says "that £58,000 they stole from the Bank of Ireland will last a good while".[13] I worked at "Folklore of the War", and the Rising, and Conscription, dreading the end of the chapter . . . the Padua grave.

27 JUNE. F. writes "I got away all of the good furniture (4 vans) safely from Roxborough to Dublin last week since when there have been two more raids on the house and a lot of silver-plated things and china were taken together with blankets &c I have applied to the Republican army for Patrols as I was told the house would be burned if we got Free Staters to mind it".

27 JUNE. F.'s letter about Roxborough makes one feel disorder is still far from being put down. But on Sunday the Lough Cutra steward told me the F.S. troops had at last driven *all* the cattle put on the L.C. land into Gort pound, and that after a threat of sending them to be sold in Dublin the owners had paid 10/- a head to get them back.

Yeats came on Sunday, I read him my Folklore of the War, and the Rising and he liked it very much, a relief.

Yesterday I worked at that sad chapter, reading all the letters and notices. And that I have to go on with today.

28 JUNE. Girvin was here yesterday. He has news of his car which had been raided; hears it is somewhere near Tuam. He wrote to O'Connor, Solicitor to C.D. Board about it, who answered that he would probably get it back "as my brother" (Rory!) "is anxious all stolen property should be returned".

I finished my heavy task.

Mrs. Scovell's letter this morning is sad "27 June.

Dear Lady Gregory,

"Today my husband has had notice by post to quit the country in a fortnight or else take the consequences, as Ireland is wanted for the Irish. My husband asks what you think he should do in the matter? Of course I know we could not stay here to be subjected to this sort of thing.

"Personally I have great suspicion that one we were speaking of when you were here may be behind the scenes."

I wrote, typed, a letter telling of the raid on them and begging for protection at once for them and sent it to Yeats to take to the C.O. at Gort Workhouse. He did so and came on here afterwards. The C.O. had promised to do his best but was not sure if protection should be sent from Gort or other Headquarters. When Yeats arrived here a Health Assurance envoy was examining workmen's cards which had been neglected, but luckily I had just bought stamps for them. He said later editions of the papers than ours told of fighting in Dublin at the Four Courts.[14]

I read Yeats the last chapter I had written. He only suggested most of the Padre's letter being taken out, and was right in this.

29 JUNE. No English or Dublin post this morning.

I sent John to the Barracks with a note asking if protection had been given to the S.'s. He came back to say the Officer would call upon me at 3 o'c. He heard there was fighting in Dublin, but brought no *Independent*, taking *The Times* of yesterday for it! (Leah in place of Rachel!).

A smart looking young man came at 3 o'c, Captain Hession, said he was an ex-Service man. I said "How did they come to take you into the forces here?" "They couldn't do without us" he said; and that he belonged to a farmer's family on the Clancarty estate. He had sent my letter on to Ennis, which is H.Q. for Burren, last night. When I said Mr. Yeats had gone to Dublin he said "Dublin! He won't get there. There was a bridge destroyed near Mullingar". "Why?" "To prevent Dail forces passing". Then he said the Dail troops had come with artillery to the Four Courts and given the troops there an hour to surrender. They did not surrender, and the building has been "pounded" and fourteen killed, many wounded, but it is not taken yet. A terrible story!

He says of course the English will come back, and that there is fighting in Limerick also, "600 of our men gone on there from Ennis".

30 JUNE. No post but from Galway. Raftery's man, come to put up stonework for the flower boxes says the Irregular troops,

under Captain Lennard are sandbagging the Barrack, preparing to defend it. Some of the regulars told J. yesterday they can do nothing against them without orders. And Captain Hession did not think there would be trouble, the Irregulars are so few. 3 o'c. Mike, back from Gort, reports no post by midday train. "Great barricades put up at the Barracks, they are making preparations to fight".

Yeats and G. came in before tea. They had not left for Dublin having heard trains were off. They had come by Gort and brought a *Freeman* with news of the fighting at the Four Courts. Mrs. Mitchell told them it was completely taken, but that was not in the papers. She told them also that Gort Barracks will be attacked tonight. I hope it is not so. It is all terribly sad. Last night, being so troubled, I turned to "Prayers to be used at sea"—"that the inhabitants of our Island may in peace and gladness serve thee our God".

Just now I found Marian and Mary looking out. Marian said they had seen the horses gallop across the lawn and stand near the stables, quite still, "shaking their tails", and after a while gallop back violently, and that Mary had said "That means they hear firing".

I have been these last days looking through Yeats' letters and typing a bit here and there to use, and I read these to him. I had told him they were not very good letters, for we had both so much to say about the business of the Theatre, or of publishers or whatever work we were at, that they are taken up with that for the most part, both his and mine. He did not write to me in the leisurely way I see him sit down and write to others, taking up the sheet perhaps through three or four days to add a phrase.

But he and I are sad, thinking this unhappy contest will not be forgotten, will leave bitter memories. He thinks there will be a Republican rising again after some years. I still think that it will be made unnecessary by the Dominions becoming virtual Republics, probably throwing off the veto and the oath and the Governorship, even if they keep a link necessary for protection in case of attack in war, and give similar help in return; and I shall be content if the building of the country is allowed to go on. I think again of that argument between Brand and the Baillie—two rights—and the ideal one, the "kingdom not of this world" must always attract the imagination.

The people are already a little uncertain as to whether the Government ought to have attacked the Four Courts'' "if we don't mind them being stolen, why would they mind it?"

1 JULY. Peter says the Gort Barracks were not attacked last

night, because Captain Hession had to take troops to Limerick,[16] there is fighting going on there, and many lorries passed the road last evening taking troops there; that is what the horses were listening to. Half the men have been brought back from Lough Cutra, no papers or letters except from Galway, but rumours that the Four Courts have been taken "and Rory O'Connor the leader, taken and lodged in Gaol".

Mrs. S. writes gratefully and says they are taking my advice. I go on copying Yeats' letters, recalling many a little turmoil, that about Miss Stokes' lecture in 1903 just now, when he pulled up the red carpet to prevent the Viceregal visit "that would have split up the National Literary Society"—very faint beside the tragedies of today!

J. back from Gort without post says all there is quiet, though there are strangers, some of them Republicans, walking about, "tall men in uniform and every one with his revolver stuck at his side". No news from Dublin no telegram, "plenty of talk, but I couldn't tell you the half of it because the whole of it is lies".

2 JULY. Sunday. Marian says she heard firing in the night. She thinks bombing.

Yeats came yesterday to stay the night. He had heard that Rory O'Connor's constant question was "What would Trotsky do?" G. came laden with papers telling of the taking of the Four Courts and De Valera's seizure of the Gresham Hotel.[17]

8 o'c. Going to church I saw a cloud of smoke over the town from what was left of the Barracks that could burn, the walls only standing. The Archdeacon spoke of "this destruction going on" in his sermon in a very broken voice. And outside the door said the Irregulars had been given 48 hours to clear out. They removed what they owned, or what they could, and then set fire to the Barracks; a bomb burst at 1 o'c. H. very much upset, said they had then gone on to Lough Cutra, throwing down the wall along a part of the road that they might not be followed, had gone to the Castle where the Free State troops are, had fired about thirty shots at the windows and shattered them "a sort of sham fight", then gone on, it is said to the mountains. John had gone to look into the Barrack yard, said there were heaps of petrol tins lying about, and that all the people are very angry, "they are done for now". And he was told they had burned the Barracks at Ardrahan, Kilcolgan, Oranmore, and in Galway the Renmore and Eglinton Barracks.[18] The Gort people are so angry "because if the wind had been in a bad quarter, if it had blown from Loughrea, the whole town would have been burned". But he hears a number of the Irregulars at Loughrea

laid down their rifles and said they would never fight against their own countrymen. The Gort men are said to have gone to the mountains, to Chevy Chase, and that they will "make ambushes". I am so thankful there seems to have been no bloodshed or loss of life.

The maids rather late from Mass because there had been "a collection for the Pope".

Yeats went on re-making the poem about Ballylee he had begun to make here. In the stanza with the waterhens, he has made them "stilted" and some other changes. It will be a fine poem.[19] I told him he would be employed by the landowners who are moving from large estates to small to write poems showing they did it from virtue and not from necessity.

He says what he has always tried for is to satisfy the ear, not to sacrifice the meaning to the stanza—that is done rather for the eye. I read almost the last chapter of *Consuelo* to him, it keeps its interest wonderfully. And I saw John Gormally about his father's pension.

3 JULY. No post this morning. P. says the roads are all blocked, to Loughrea and to Galway and Eserkelly as well as to Ennis, but the Free State troops are bringing out men to clear them. He says the Irregulars "slipped away" having set fire to the Barracks, and when the Free Staters came there it was too late to put the fire out, all soaked with petrol and everything destroyed "oil paintings and carpets, the doctor's room a holy fright". And then some of the townspeople began carrying off doors and a bath and other things, but these will be taken back—"I ever and always said that De Valera would bring the country to ruin"!

6 o'c. I sent to Gort in the afternoon to try for a paper, but a message came back that nothing had come in, the bridge at Athlone has been broken. A priest had set out from Gort but was turned back. J. hears that "400 men have gathered into the big house at Chevy Chase", Republicans.

"One party in Gort are angry at the burning and another party are proud of it. You wouldn't know what to say". Mrs. L. says that "some of them that come to the counter and that wouldn't be given charge of a cat, talk as if they would take over the whole country".

TUESDAY, 4 JULY. No post. Tim has just come in tears to say two big trees have been sawed through, and have fallen across the road, outside our gates.

3 o'c. A McCallum boy who has just been in Gort hears that the Treaty and the Truce are broken, that Collins has resigned

"and everything left to De Valera".

7 o'c. Mike comes in saying "two travellers that came to Lally's, said there are Black and Tans watching to come into Dublin, and the half of Dublin is burned down". Stephen, later from Gort, for Yeats, says there are 15,000 English troops landed, (not true). Yeats spent the afternoon, I read him bits of his letters that I had typed, and we picked strawberries for his tea, and for G. and I read to the end of *Consuelo*.

Captain Lennard and other Irregulars are walking about Gort, as well as the Free State troops! "Some say it is a plan between the two parties to burn the barracks and keep the English out".

5 JULY. Tim hears the railway between Ennis and Crusheen is torn up. No trains passing. No post.

4 o'c. Mike back from Gort says the Republicans are walking about, and preventing the people buying bags of flour and that a man from Dublin says there are any amount of English troops in Dublin Bay, and that the Free Staters are beaten to their knees. K.B. has been here, bringing strawberries for preserving. She heard the Free Staters had left Lough Cutra and the Republicans have taken possession of the Castle, and Mike heard this also.

She says the railway bridge near Crusheen was blown up. And she heard a man in the signal box near Athenry had been shot and that Republicans had been in a train going to Galway, and Free Staters had stopped it and turned them out and got in, and went away in the Dublin direction.

But she heard a train had come through to Athenry from Dublin. The telephone wires have been cut. The Irregulars had gone up to some place on the mountain, but she doesn't know if they stopped there. J. who has spent the day cutting bracken has heard that "ere yesterday the whole of O'Connell street was blown up; and it is said there is a truce made between Connaught and Munster that none of its men will attack each other, and that it was like a little market around Coen's shop, the people buying what they could, but the Republicans had brought away a great deal of flour and other things to Lough Cutra" and that "the barrack in Dominick Street, Galway, was burned." That makes me anxious about A. (not true).

He says also that everything, the things put back, at Druimhasna has been stolen again.

6 JULY. Rumours of "a truce of a month in Dublin". The Free Staters have taken away the tree from Kiltartan road, not the other. Some of the forces are drifting home, M. from the Free

Staters and some from the Irregulars. A good time for John Quinn to have sent me Santayana *Soliloquies*.[20] I read them after breakfast instead of *The Times*; the *Lion and Unicorn* very amusing.

9 o'c. About 12 o'c a Mr. Charles O'Malley with two sons and a friend "from *Boston Post*" called. They had landed at Queenstown on Sunday, had got on to Limerick, fighting going on there, pretty quiet in the daytime, violent firing at night, but he thinks in the air, no one hurt. They had got on to Ennis by train but then had to take three outside cars to bring them on to Gort, many obstructions on the road; they had to get off and roll stones off; in one place a ditch had been dug. However they got to Gort, and don't know how to get on, no train and so many roads blocked. They heard that O'Connell Street had been burned down, the Gresham among other buildings. That the Free State captured some of the Republicans and the rest made off to the mountains; that a truce has been called to give the leaders time to make some agreement. Yeats, coming later, had met Captain L. who, while not confessing any defeat, said there had been a truce called. The O'Malley party of nine came to tea, happily Yeats and G. came, and little Anne Y. came with them, and was very gay. Then the Bank Manager appeared! We made islands in the dining room, an extra table for guests and the little one for Miss Anne, and all went well. There was no news of De Valera, but it was said all the leaders were captured. The Republicans seemed by rumour to be holding their own at Limerick. Captain Hession had called up Mr. J. at the Bank this morning for money, he was to take two hundred men there, and McKeown is said to be in command of two thousand. The Americans all pleasant, and it seemed quite a rush of life after our isolated week. Mr. O'Malley called out against the number of public houses in Ireland and the drinking. His wife told us of a beggar at Queenstown who importuned them, and when they had passed called out "A drunken sailor would be better than the whole of ye"!

7 JULY. Yesterday's news had seemed more hopeful of peace, but Christy coming this morning to do some painting says the signal box at Gort station was destroyed in the night and that all the railway porters have been given notice, and the road to Ennis has been blocked. He says there was a telephone message that Mme. Markievicz had been shot.[21] I said "Oh, I hope not"! but he said "she was out for it".

Tim says another large tree has been cut down and thrown across the road to replace the one the Free Staters cleared away. "A soldier" last evening had asked for a drink of water, and then asked which was the road to Galway, he was walking there. Later another came and asked the same question and was glad to hear he need not pass through Athenry "I don't want to go through Athenry". They say a good many are deserting. All bicycles are being commandeered in Gort, and F.S. men go on them towards Limerick. Christie is going home "by the back way" with his. Yeats came and I read him what I had since copied of his letters and we began to read the *Countess of Rudolstat.*[22] He spoke of our consciousness in sleep actually going away and receiving or giving advice; our waking life being perhaps the dream.

C's boy, whose family are Republican says his brother has been in Loughrea and heard the Republicans have been beaten and "all the leaders wounded". M. returns from Gort very excited about the looting of the Barracks by among others the shopkeepers of Gort. We got a little brown flour, 2 stone, but there is no white flour left, and no sugar, the Lallys just keeping a little bit for themselves. Our American friends, she hears left today for Kinvara to try for a boat to Galway, and if they can't get one will return to Lally's "where we have no food to give them". I had a letter from A. written 1 July. The mail car had come, had been two days on the road. And one from Frank dated 28 June "You might contradict the report that Arthur is a Freemason as he has no connection with the order. Also you might ask Commandant L. to return my evening shoes (a new pair I had never worn) which he was seen parading about in at Roxborough. I am sure also it was he who finished my evening clothes as he was the only one they would nearly fit". It is now said in Gort, M. says, that L. had been a Black and Tan. Lally said the townspeople of Limerick had held a meeting and ordered both Free State and Irregular troops out of the city. But I don't know if it was obeyed.

8 JULY. The first really hot day for a long time; heavy rain. Christie came to paint, says all quiet in Gort, and a man who saw a paper last Wednesday says things are not so bad in Dublin as we thought. "What things? Is it not burned"? "Well, he says the Republicans are put down".

6 o'c. Rain all day. J. back from Gort says there weren't twelve people there, but that flour is holding out, only sugar very scarce. It is said there is a truce "for two days". The roads are still blocked; the mail car driver talked of going back to Galway as he could; putting up at farmers' houses and going through byeways. The Irregulars had been for three nights at Lough Cutra. H. and his wife had to feed them. Now all have left—both sides. And the

cattle driven off had been put back again!

SUNDAY, 9 JULY. J. driving me to church said "Father Considine preached a great sermon at Kiltartan that made us late. He called on both sides to lay down their rifles. And he said he had seen a paper of yesterday that said Dublin was quiet, and Cathal Brugha had died in the Mater Hospital,[23] and the Republicans were gathered now in the Wicklow mountains". But Marian says he said there was fighting in Dublin and it is going on today but that Limerick is quiet. He (Father C.) said also that it was said two men had been shot in Galway, and anyway there was a dead man brought past Kiltartan this morning. Yeats had heard a Free State soldier had been killed in an ambush near Ennis. A Kiltartan girl to whom I gave a lift to Gort said some more trees had been cut down, blocking the road.

I read more of the letters I had typed to Yeats, and a chapter of *Countess de Rudolstadt.*

At church I was given Mrs. S.'s letter telling of new threats, and this troubles me very much. I wrote a letter to the O.C. at Gort, and Yeats will take it there tomorrow. The Free State officer had told them his men would not be safe at Burren, that it is a Republican district, though both he and the Republicans sympathize with the Scovells. It is dreadful.

"Burren. Friday 7 July

Just to tell you that we have received another letter today. I enclose you copies of both. Protection seems impossible to get and the worst part is that all are unarmed here. Locally it is loudly condemned and feeling ran so high that before it was known that the notice was not official a protest was being drawn up by the people, signed by old and young to be taken to headquarters protesting against it. All suspicion stronger than ever, always the same person . . . Only if there is any possible way that you may command of having us protected there is nothing more to say . . . I feel collapsing."

Enclosure, copy of 1st letter. Dear Sir, Take notice you are requested to leave the locality within a fortnight as you know we want Ireland for the Irish and if you do not comply with this warning you must bear the consequences".

Copy 2nd letter. Sir, I hear by authorised [sic] you got a warning to leave that locality a short time ago, but all your stratagems nor all the influence at your command would not do this time, if you are so fond of Ireland you may go down to the north east and we will convey you there.

P.S. Remember it is not child's play we will have this time so this is the final warning.

MONDAY, 10 JULY. I kept thinking last night of Mrs. S., and drove to Gort after breakfast to ask Miss Quinn who had brought the letter from Burren for more particulars. She rather reassured me, saying the Finevara people had offered to come and sleep in the bungalow within call of the Scovells, as protectors. I went on to the Workhouse but "none of the Captains are in". A hundred Irregulars have gone into Lough Cutra. Two men are said to have been shot, Free Staters, in an ambush at Castle Daly by Irregulars. Miss Q. sent for the copy of Saturday's paper that had been going round Gort, and it said the night before (Friday) had been the quietest yet in Dublin; told of Cathal Brugha's death, said the Irregulars were being driven out of their strongholds all through the country.

There was also an interview with the City Architect about the rebuilding of O'Connell Street in a new plan. Even a talk of rebuilding is new and cheering.

8TH. Yeats and G. came to tea. He had taken my letter about the Scovells to Captain H. who had sent him to the Republican officer "but don't tell him I sent you" to ask if he would take up the matter, as Burren is a republican district; and between them, they, or one of them promise protection. (D. had been told the officers and men are drinking together and going about together, Free State and Republicans). Captain H. had sent a motor to Loughrea for yeast. The first messenger he sent had been shot but this time the yeast had been brought back and distributed in the town (there was no bread to be had at Gillane's when I was in Gort). He brought also today's paper, and Yeats saw it. Not much fresh news but Irregulars being swept away or vanishing" and people writing to the paper about such things as irregularities of the post, very comforting.

I am still going through Yeats letters and he is making a poem about the bees, calling to them to make their honey at Ballylee.[24]

11 JULY. P. says a boat has come to Kinvara with flour, and the flour is being brought to Gort and there will be plenty now.

There is a pleasure as it were losing count of time, after my punctual life. No post coming; none going; the hour for sending to Gort thus fluctuating. And though breakfast at 9 and lunch at 1.30 are the same, the evening meal now I am quite alone is so simple that I can take it when I will—strawberries and cream last night, and a bit of brown bread.

Padraig Niland says "De Valera—it is he put Ireland to and fro". "They are not hungry now in Gort, but they haven't an inch, only what they'll want. Such tearing and such tattering there never was as when the Barrack was burned and the slates falling down".

Then R.D. She has heard from two places that Roxborough has been burned.

Old Niland had seen a Kinvara woman yesterday who had brought 100 eggs to Gort turned back with them unsold. One of the shopkeepers told him he had 1000 eggs rotting in his shop.

The one newspaper that came on Monday had been read by everybody. Even old Padraig had heard from it that "thirty Republicans had been taken prisoners in a field of wheat."

12 JULY. "The Orangemen might break out from the North on the twelfth" has been said. But Yeats says last Saturday's paper told that the Belfast authorities were prolonging the truce during which murder by those in their employ is to be stopped.

"Flour is come to Gort" P. says. And Yeats came, and had heard that a settlement has been made, and still more had not only heard but seen a train—an engine—with only one waggon—and only going as far as Tubber, but we greet it as the swallow that announces summer. And he says the burning of Roxborough is not true. I am so thankful!

FRIDAY, 14 JULY. I have seen a *Galway Tribune* of 8 July. Galway seems cut off as much as we are, but they have flour mills.

Dominick Street Barracks are not burned "because it might destroy the whole side of the street, and almost certainly the sweet and tobacco shop next door". A fortnight since any English or Dublin papers or letters have come.

Yeats came, depressed because his little Anne wants treatment and it may be difficult to get to Dublin. The basket maker came, says the Millmount bridge near Kilchriest is broken by the Republicans. Mr. J. told me they had been driven out of Loughrea and had gone to Kilchriest, and that Captain L. had been heard trying to get a farmer who has land from Arthur to pay the half year's rent to him—"under orders". "Whose orders"? "The Commander at Ennis, so and so." "Oh I know him well, I'll write to him about it", and the rent was not given over.

15 JULY. This morning as I came down Marian said "I think there will be letters, Mike saw the mail car coming, with Free Staters in lorries protecting it". And in half an hour Mike Lally appeared with a great bag of newspapers and of letters, and a whole salmon from A. from Galway. The first English letters or papers for over a fortnight; and the *Independent* of 12th with some earlier ones. Not many real letters, one from the darling children of the 5th, one from Wilfrid Blunt, one from Clara Jackson at Aix; but a quantity of circulars and advertisements,

seeming so futile, so superfluous just now. Mike coming from Gort in the afternoon said today's paper had arrived there, a few copies, sold at sixpence each, but he was not quick enough to get one. (J. tells me Mike said it was in a motor the papers were brought, and he seeing the people crowding round it, and having a gloomy mind, fancied it was a funeral, and that there was "a dead man in the car" and kept on the other side of the street; and when he found out his mistake all the papers had been sold).

Papers we have looked at and rumours seem to tell the same, that Dublin is in the hands of the Government, and all the most important places, but the Republicans, driven to smaller places, can do mischief and are doing it, to roads and railways. The breaking of the Kilchriest bridge breaks the road to Ballinasloe. Yeats and G. came to lunch, they had had the same papers. My children's letter so cheerful, they are at last going to school (no, to a governess) and it is "great fun". But I am afraid they will not get back for the holidays as things are now. I read a good deal of *Countess of Rudolstadt* to Yeats, and typed some bits from my own letters I have found a big envelope of, that he had given me; some about the Rising in 1916 and the shutting out of communication with the outer world—less complete then than it has been now.

SUNDAY, 16 JULY. Going to church I was told Edward Martyn had lent his motor to take a man who had gone out of his mind to Ballinasloe Asylum, and that at Ballinasloe the motor was taken, and Owen the chauffeur left to come back on foot. I heard also that the Free Staters had cleared Kiltartan road, but there has been an attempt to cut another large tree to fall across it "But it was the same cross-saw they had used at the Natural Bridge when they tried to cut a tree to keep the sheepwashing to themselves and it stuck in the tree in the same way. It is well known who they are that did it". J. heard but doesn't know if it is true that the windows have been broken at Roxborough.

At the church door Bagot said he had heard there had been a fight. He gave me an *Irish Times* of yesterday. And J. had borrowed an *Independent* for me to glance at in the carriage and return. Fighting still going on in Limerick, though Dublin quiet, and Republicans being driven out from towns, but are still strong from Limerick southwards. Later I was told there had been "bad work in Gort last night. Some boys that were going home from the Town hall where there was cardplaying had noticed three men hiding behind trees near the railway bridge, but went on home. A little later shots were heard, and then volleys, then there came knocking at Lally's door, and they were in dread to open it, but Mrs. Lally put her head out of the window and asked what was wanted and men there shouted 'the doctor, send out the doctor'. And then they said Republicans had fired on Free State men that were passing by the railway bridge and two were wounded and one was shot dead—a boy from Connemara".

This is terrible! I found Yeats here, and he said he had expected it; that Childers had said the other day "The ambushes have only begun", and that he has foreseen this settled policy of making government impossible so that the English will have to be called in, and then all Ireland will unite against them. K. said about twenty Republicans had joined the twenty or thirty in Lough Cutra yesterday. And Mike says that "ere last night he met a young fellow in uniform on the Lake farm, that asked him the way to Lough Cutra and if he could get there without going through Gort, and he told him the way. He might have been bringing messages or orders". I knew some might be killed in fighting, but I did not think one would kill another in that way in cold blood.

And in Gort last evening young G. was arrested and taken to Galway gaol. He had gone to Crusheen about a motor that his sister had travelled in and that had been seized. A rather confused story says he told the Co. Clare man he supposed to have taken it he was his prisoner, and some Republicans coming to rescue this man, he drew his revolver and shot one of them dead. M. reports the Kinvara road blocked with trees and a notice put up that whoever removes them may expect death.

17 JULY. P. says there was bad work again last night in Gort, firing but he does not know what happened. It is said the shooting on Saturday night was by Republicans in revenge for the one of their number that was shot by young G., and that they had meant to wreck his house, but it was watched by Free State men, and he himself taken to Galway gaol and his father has gone away. The poor Connemara boy who was shot was only 22. The Republicans who killed him "were well protected behind the railway bridge and some say one of them was killed, and that his comrades were seen going to the coffin maker. But it's hard to know, and nearly the whole of what you hear is lies. These Republicans are a terror, tumbling houses and knocking bridges. There were fifteen of them at first Mass yesterday. Why didn't the Free State men bring them away to gaol?".

J. says the funeral of that Connemara boy passed the road this morning, three motors, "Father Considine went with it. And the mother was there, a woman with a good grey shawl; and a grey-haired man that should be the father".

18 JULY. J. says the firing on Sunday night was only to send in children and idlers from the street; and that young B., a shopkeeper's son in the Republican army has been arrested as one of those who killed the Connemara boy. I had told him to ask about posts to Galway, if it is possible to send a parcel there. But Miss Quinn said the mail car that had been sent off in such a hurry on Sunday morning for the three hour's drive was seen on Sunday evening still at Clarenbridge "and not making a stir".

Then I am told by X. terrible news, if it is true. The Connemara boy had been "carried to the end of Crow Lane and put in the motor, and the flag wrapped around him and they gave him the last salute." When X. was in Gort he heard nothing of it and the motors had not come back. But later he was in Mulloo's house, and a little girl came in from the town for a drop of milk, and she said only Father Considine and Dan Burke had come back from the funeral, and had brought news that they went by Craughwell and whatever road they could till they came to Clarenbridge. And there was bad work there and fighting, and Captain H. that had gone with the body was killed. (Not true).

After breakfast I was reading Santayana, and it happened I had come to a chapter on war and peace: "Homer who was a poet said war did not disguise its horrors nor its havoc, but he knew it was the shield of such happiness as is possible on earth". And "peace itself means discipline at home . . . so vigorous an internal regimen that every germ of dissolution or infection shall be repelled before it reaches the public soul" . . . But it is terrible if it must be through war with one another we have to attain to this.

4 o'c. P. says "there is a flying column coming to put out those Republican lads. The Courthouse has been taken from them".

19 JULY. Mr Johnson came to borrow another Garibaldi volume, and Mrs. Bagot and Kathleen came to borrow novels and all stayed for tea. And their story is that the motors taking the body for burial had to go so far round as Moorpark beyond Athenry. And when they came near there were stones across the road, and Captain Hession and the others got out and removed them. Then a very little way farther on there were more stones, and as they began to remove them they were fired on, two men wounded and one killed, and Captain H. made prisoner.[25] The motor drivers tried to turn and the car containing the body got wedged against a bank, and as the fight went on the coffin was hit by bullets, and when the attacking party went off with their prisoner the dead soldier and the wounded one were put in the car with the coffin, and it is not known what happened after

that. Father Considine and Dan Burke came back and told their story. Someone said the Connemara boy's young brother had been eager to join the Free State army, but was so young his father and mother would not allow him, but as he pressed it they said the elder one who was willing to stay at home might go in his place. And when the news of his death came the mother cried out to the young brother "If it wasn't for you he wouldn't have gone"! And the boy said "If that is so it is best for me go drown myself", and he went out, and the mother was distracted, not knowing if she would find him alive when she got home.

(FEBRUARY 1924. Poor woman, I was told a little later that she but went home to her bed, and died before the week was out.)

It is said Sean McKeown's flying column has been at Athlone and other places and is coming to Gort to drive away the Republicans, and that some of these have gone off to the mountains. Mr. Johnson had seen a man who had been in Limerick on Sunday, who said the fighting is going on, and that the city will be destroyed. And J. going later to Gort was able to get hold of a paper, at sixpence, brought by motor, and it gives the same bad account of Limerick, though other parts of the country seem better, Mr. J.'s man said the Limerick Republicans have been strengthened by a body driven out from Cork, who have come to fight there. He (Mr. J.) says De Valera would be shot in the street if he came to Gort.

Yeats today here, had heard the windows at Lough Cutra are sandbagged. M. from Gort says a number of Free Staters have come to the Court House that there was a bomb exploded last night, and that "you might hunt the town for a pound of sugar." Yeats has written another stanza to his Ballylee poem.[26] I finished typing bits from my own letters to him, rather sad work bringing back so many memories, especially of holidays here.

20 JULY. Mrs. Keane got to Galway and back by motor, took my parcel to A., says a train was to run from Galway last night to try and reach Dublin. The road to Galway was clear, but roundabout. J. reports the Court House in Gort sandbagged. Free Staters arrived there last night. Reports from Limerick say seventy were killed there yesterday, but that is rumour. A Lough Cutra boy told him that "there are strange cattle grazing up to the hall-door." Old Niland has come again, has had no old age pension this last week, I gave him another five shillings.

J. says a motor of Free Staters on the road between Creg Clare and Castle Taylor dashed into a tree felled across the road, and one was killed others wounded.

21 JULY. A large post this morning, a heap of papers piled

up, several letters, one from Anne and from Catherine. I hurried to write letters for G. Yeats to take to post in Dublin. Yeats came in the afternoon; he less disturbed than I at the number of counties still under the Irregulars according to the Government announcement. But I feel that my darling children will not come back this summer.

I read on in *Countess of Rudolstadt*. At dinner I asked Yeats if he cared for Turgenieff, and he said "No, I never liked him, always detested his books, or at least disliked very much something in them, it is insincerity. I remember Henley[27] saying Tolstoy is like Homer immense, Turgenieff is a mass of insincerity."

A. writes 19th. "D. Wade here telling me about the raid at Fairfield. Eight men in a motor arrived 9 o'c at night, demanded food and beds, followed by others, forty in all; said they must have every bed in the house. They ate till 1 o'c. They went on next day to Raford where they spent two nights. When Ballydugan was set on fire they burned a box E. had packed and locked her and two maids in a meat house. The roof being wood caught fire from the burning house and E. called out asking if they were going to burn the two young girls (the maids) and then they were let out. She sent a message to Miss Graham in Loughrea to borrow clothes and was found sitting in her dressing gown". (This burning was on account of a land dispute.) C. Seymour, Engineer of the line told D. he is busy repairing and hopes a train will reach Athenry shortly; he is also repairing bridges at Oughterard".

A letter from F. from Dublin dated 6 July says "have no news from Roxborough since the fighting began as posts and telegraphs seem to have stopped. We are quiet here now except an odd sniper. We had a good view of the fight at the Four Courts and its destruction as we can see down on it from here. The war would have been over in three days if the Free State had not put gloves on which was a mistake as it allowed time for the buildings now burned to be occupied."

22 JULY. Another post this morning, no letters, but yesterday's *Independent* and the day before yesterday's *Times*. And J. tells me the old age pensions were paid yesterday "all the old people very proud". I should think especially old Padraig, who had just got his second five shillings out of me "on the head" of the stoppage.

The boy bringing luggage from Ballylee said there had been seventy Republicans at the foot of the hill yesterday, ready for an ambush, but no Free Staters passed by. But Yeats, arriving with Michael, says he heard they were gathered there but doesn't believe for an intended ambush. He also had a couple of papers today, and reading them is more confident, says the Government is working on a definite military plan and all is going well, a safe zone between North (which has been brought to quietness) and South where they are now beginning in earnest, as with Limerick and Waterford.

An old man had said to Edward Martyn that there is an old saying "A Spaniard will betray Ireland when the summer is winter but for the leaves on the trees"; and this June and July have been cold enough for that.

24 JULY. Yesterday, Sunday, peaceful. After church I was given a paper to look at for a minute or two as I drove through Gort. It told of Irregulars being driven out of Limerick, Waterford, and Castlerea.[28] And I think without much bloodshed.

But the railway bridge at Ballyglunin is said to have been blown up. There are very few Irregulars left at Lough Cutra "and they have killed but four sheep". Yeats' eyes bad, and I read a good deal of *C. of Rudolstadt* in the evening.

This morning is fine after yesterday's rain so we hope to get on with the hay, and there is a peaceful feeling.

I heard yesterday that "a few young fellows had been arrested by Free Staters, young Hayes and Coen and another; it was said letters had been found showing they were in correspondence with the Irregulars." Then that they had been let go. Then today no, that they are still under arrest, and that "these new Free State men come to the Courthouse are very firm." Yeats has just come in to say (7 o'c) the shot we had heard this afternoon as we were sitting outside the house was by its sound a bomb. And that from a quarter past four for an hour they had heard shots from beyond Ballylee, not an ambush but regular firing. There are bodies of Irregulars now going about, disbanded and some one had said "Take care are they hiding in the Coole woods". Yeats came to tell me I must have my mind prepared what to do should they come in here at night, but I had already decided to give them food if they wanted it, and hoped nothing more would be asked for. I have plenty of cold meat and I have been down to get out some wine.

25 JULY. A post this morning, but before I could look at my letters Marian told me there had been a fight last night where the firing had been heard. Some lorries were taking prisoners to Galway and when they came to the foot of the hill at Lissatunna a body of Irregulars were seen. I don't know which side fired first, but they were pursued through the fields and thirty prisoners taken. Then G. tells me of it, and that later again "at

10 o'c new time we heard a great rattling on the road, like the Black and Tans back again, and twelve lorries passed by our house bringing the prisoners to Galway. We couldn't know who they were, only John Hayes, the light shone on his face as they passed. And on Saturday night Fahy and Stanton were near Castle Daly on bicycles and they saw a lorry coming and went into a field, and they were called on to halt but they would not, and Fahy was wounded but Stanton got away. Three hundred of them came down from the mountain and broke into a house that is between us and Tillyra and made the people give them food and beds. Captain Burke that was here with Lennard that day and made prisoners, and young Coen from Gort that was just come from College. But J. H. Glynn's son is taken into the Free State army and was bringing the prisoners to gaol."

Mr. J. coming later says the new Free State men from Athlone are likely to keep order. Trained men could not be spared while there was so much fighting going on, and those in Gort were but boys—"whistled airs while they were guarding the Bank."

27 JULY. Some newspapers this morning up to Saturday 22nd were brought by a railway wagon coming from Athenry to see if the line is clear. The postman brought news that Lough Cutra is clear of Irregulars—the Castle—though there may be some about the place; other newscarriers say a machine gun was brought against them but no shots fired they were only a few and surrendered and Captain L. is a prisoner, I say "poor L." and Marian says "Oh, don't say poor—everyone hates him". I say that is just why I feel for him.

J. tells me later that he has heard a report that Mr. Edmunds ran his motor into an ambush and was shot; but this I trust is not true.[29] Yet I don't feel the accounts good enough to write and say it is quite safe for the children to come. It is the road danger that makes me hesitate.

28 JULY. This morning a letter from M. saying she has taken a house at St. Ives to take the children to for the summer. I did not know I should feel it so much. I had been hoping against hope they could come. My strength gave way, I had to lie down for a while, trying to realise it and not to break down. Then I wrote to M. making the best of it and saying that though I believed they would be safe here, there would be the danger of news of things happening that one would rather keep them from the knowledge of. Then I went out, heavy hearted enough, all had been prepared and ready, the tennis ground rolled and mown, the gooseberries wired in to keep for them, . . . And then John told me it is true about Mr. Edmunds, he has been shot, he and his chauffeur,

and not they say through accident but because of some division of land. A terrible thing, indeed it is better the children should be away.

29 JULY. No, the papers have come with the account. He ran into an ambush intended for Free State troops. He called out when they fired "It's all right, it's all right" (meaning that he was a civilian) and would not turn back. He had often boasted that he had never been stopped or attacked, but a bullet brought him instant death. It was a sad day. And Yeats who drove over to Ballylee said when he came back "There is fighting still, for a motor passed with a dead man in it".

I read all through to him a dull three act play that won't do for the Abbey. And in the evening finished reading the *Countess of Rudolstadt*. He has left today. I am putting together those of A.E.'s [George Russell] letters I have typed, and writing in between.

30 JULY. Sunday. No bad news even after church, but I must be a little downhearted, the gathering of my darlings for the holidays so far away. I sent for the Hehir children to take some of the gooseberries I had netted, and was glad to give that pleasure, though tears very nearly came when I saw some of the little red and yellow pears Anne and Catherine liked fallen in a heap. I could but gather them up for little Anne Yeats.

It has helped me to read in Santayana: "The art of life is to keep step with the celestial orchestra that beats the measure of our career and gives the cue for our exits and our entrances".

1 AUGUST. Cold and showery. Yesterday Yeats and G. came to lunch and for the afternoon. She had just come back from Dublin. She had met at Gogartys several members of the Dail. Michael Collins himself had come in near midnight in his uniform of Commander in Chief, with shining buttons—had walked there alone though his life is threatened. All seemed in good spirits and very confident that within two months the country will be quiet. They are a little anxious about Cork, there are good fighters in it, Kerry men, and it is feared they will not fight there but will get out and go through the country.[29] Yeats thought all the news good. I think two months a long time and think this new outburst of burning country houses a bad sign. On the way to Ballinasloe with Dr. Walsh (the priest who had been at Tillyra) they had to pull down walls sometimes and take the motor through the fields. They said there was a train running to Gort today.

This morning I was told that Kiltartan bridge was blown up the night before last by three bombs and is "the greatest shipwreck ever was seen". The train that was coming was signalled to go back, and we are more than ever cut away. And X. says he believes the Irregulars are hiding in our woods. Ten of them came through the place on Sunday night, before the blowing up of the bridge and were joined by others, not all from a distance, on the road. A girl of the Donoghues showed John her milk pans, quite black from the dust shaken down from the roof by the explosion.

2 AUGUST. A post this afternoon. The Dalys and Mr. Johnson here for tea say Captain H. is back in Gort, he was found marooned on an island and rescued. The troops in Gort are not allowed into public houses now. They are very well behaved and vigilant, examine strangers. And the little children in Crow Lane play "Put up your hands! You have to be identified"! Lough Cutra is none the worse for its two sets of occupants, the Free Staters were very careful, their officers locked most of the rooms lest they should use them. Captain Lennard when there used to say 'I like living in a lordly hall, but I'd like to see a lordly table'"! However they killed five sheep and commandeered milk and butter, and from the garden cucumbers and tomatoes.

Now Z. tells me there is serious danger of the Ballylee bridge being blown up. I said I would go over and tell Yeats; then remembered Mrs. B. is coming to tea so I have written a note to the C.O. in Gort and will ask her to leave it at the Barracks, I must not send one of the men. One is told over and over "The Government is confident" but we seem far from peace here.

6 AUGUST. This has been a better day. I picked fruit for little Joseph at the gate, and meditated that we are at the seamy side of the carpet, these burnings and breaking of bridges; and perhaps the pattern on the other side is growing to a harmony. And then, somehow I thought of those climbers of Mount Everest going through so much hardship and peril for the sake as it were of difficulties and dangers, and that we without any effort of our own are confronted with—surrounded by—both, and my courage rose.[31] So hearing hints that D. "a contrary sort of a fellow" would give trouble about my putting a new gate and removing his bar on the avenue, I stopped at his house coming from church and asked to see him, and he was quite civil, even pleased.

I found Yeats here, and told him of the rumoured danger to the bridge and he was disturbed, but decided to go and see the C.O. at Gort when he left this.

BOOK TWENTY

7 AUGUST, 1922. This has been a quiet day. A motor going to Galway for Mr. Johnson called motoring to Galway, and I sent a sack of peas and cauliflowers and some fowl and eggs and butter etc to A. Delighted to have the chance. We heard the train running "and whistling" said Marian. And J, going to Gort for oats for the fowl brought back a post, the first for several days, and with no bad news in papers or letters. M. writes an indictment of the country and says "I envy you your blind optimism", but encloses a nice little letter from Catherine, so well written—though my pupil! Then having worked very hard this last fortnight at my Memoir I found I had really got all the material roughly into shape and form. I thought to continue—for it really ends in 1918—with my diary kept since I took up the fight for Hugh's pictures. But reading it I find it is too near, there would be too many personal bits, talks with friends and the like, to cut out, and I think it must be left for a later volume, it is likely after my death. If this is so, I can begin rewriting each chapter at once and that brings me within sight of the end. Anyhow I think I am clear of confusion and can go straight on.

8 AUGUST. Yes, after a little re-arranging I took my first chapter "The First Decades" and spent a good part of the day at it. No post or papers to interrupt. And I thought it good—much better for a little cutting and re-arranging suggested by Yeats. About 7 o'c Raftery came about building my wall, and Danny Shaughnessy brought me some trout; and I took them to the garden for the last—all but the last—of the gooseberries.

9 AUGUST. Another peaceful day, and post came. T.S. told me he had been present at the "Republican argument" at Ballinamantane and that my "name came up"—someone wondered raiders had spared this house, but it was said "They won't touch her; she has too good a name at headquarters". I had the little Johnsons to pick gooseberries, and for tea. C.E. Lawrence sent me his new book *Mr. Ambrose.*[1]

10 AUGUST. In the hayfield we heard shots, rifle shots, from Kiltartan side. Then one or two from Cranagh, but Mike thought these were fired from some old gun "where the potatoes

are being destroyed with crows". The night before last he had met "a young fellow looking for his comrades that had gone astray on him". J. said lorries had been going up and down the road since yesterday. P. says "last night about 1 o'c I felt footsteps outside the house and I got up and looked out the window and I saw fifteen soldiers marching in step, and their rifles strapped to their shoulders. A while after that I saw ten more, and after that again four officers together. It will be a great blessing when peace comes to the country for the way they are now is a holy sin".

L. R. writes "I met a Republican this morning in a position to know and he seemed very hopeless, said 'the people did not seem to be ready for freedom', and that they had been betrayed by the priests and the shopkeepers". The papers tell of troops landing near Cork.[2]

11 AUGUST. The men say Ardrahan Barracks were fired into last night and that there have been a great many lorries on the road. There had been arrests in Kinvara and an officer told Yeats on Sunday that the Ballylee bridge was in no present danger, the Irregulars being a long way off. But they must have come back to Ardrahan.

12 AUGUST. A wet night; not getting on with the hay. News of the capture of Cork from the Irregulars.

15 AUGUST. On Sunday there was a rumour of Arthur Griffith's death. Yeats here. Yesterday's papers tell it is true.[3] I am sorry, I should have liked to make friends with him. He showed unworthy enmity towards both Hugh and Synge, but one must weigh against that his tenacity in keeping to the Sinn Fein idea, and his wisdom and moderation of late.

No word of what De Valera is intending now he is driven out of Cork; but Mrs. Mitchell wrote yesterday that the through posts are coming in although the telegraph wires are cut every night; and I am told this morning that the railway bridge near Craughwell has been blown up. Then the maids coming from Mass (Holy Day) say Kiltartan railway bridge has been blown up. And later John coming from Gort says Ballymacquiff bridge also has been destroyed, and it is said the bridge at Castle Taylor. So no train has come in, there is no paper.

16 AUGUST. Rain on the hay. Yeats came over; still making his poem on Ballylee, he likes connecting it with the Rising,[4] says "Lyric poetry is such a fragile thing it ought to have its roots in history, or some personal thing." He says he told Masefield long ago "You'll be a popular poet—you'll be riding in your carriage and pass me in the gutter". He had been looking

through M's poetry lately and thought of this, not liking it except a few of the gay early ballads. He says the Banshee was heard around Ballylee on Friday night—perhaps for Griffith's death.

20 AUGUST. Little Anne Yeats with her parents here on Thursday, and yesterday the Archdeacon's daughters and grandchildren and Mrs. Y.—very tired last night! I have been working very hard, especially over the Lyall chapter, and have wakened it up by an argument with Yeats, in the course of which Mr. Johnson arrived and had to be segregated. General news in papers good, Dundalk retaken[5] and progress everywhere. But continuance of ambushes, destruction, and what one must call murders everywhere.

Robinson writes from the Abbey—Wednesday night—"We are about £52 behind Horse Show last year which perhaps is not too bad considering how difficult it is to get to Dublin from the South—and indeed from the North since the line was cut at Dundalk—and then Griffith's funeral today.[6] The stalls are very empty and one misses the usual evening-dressed English visitors whom I was always snobbish enough to enjoy seeing. I remember last year we walked up and down Marlborough Street together because we couldn't find a seat; alas, we could find many a seat tonight. However we shan't lose money on the week I hope and there's no use in being despondent. Griffith's funeral was very wonderful today. I wrote for a ticket for the Requiem Mass but didn't get one so I gave up the idea of going as I had a lot of rehearsing to do, but about 12.30 I had a break in rehearsal and went out with Dolan and Miss Crowe on the chance of seeing something. We found it just beginning to pass Beresford Place and stood there and saw everything. It was splendidly done, so dignified and impressive, the coffin very simple, covered by the tricolour. The procession took nearly an hour and a half to pass and the crowd of spectators was immense. It seemed a wonderful ending after all those years spent in the office of an obscure journal in a back street in Dublin. Collins marched boldly at the head of some troops with Dick Mulcahy beside him. Michael looked very well and very much the soldier".

20 AUGUST. EVENING. Before church I was told there had been trees cut again, blocking the road to Ennis. And at the gate Mr. B. told me he had just heard the bridge at Ballylee had been blown up last night, so I was in anxiety all through the service. After it John said Yeats had gone to Coole, and had left a message that though the bridge was destroyed they were all safe.

Mr. B. said that last Sunday as they went home from church

they had without knowing it driven over a mine near Kilbecanty. They are told there were Irregulars behind the wall and in a shed with a machine gun and holding the wire, ready to explode the mine when the Free State troops were on it on their way to Mass; this is their revenge because of some having been arrested as they came out of chapel. However the F.S. men didn't go to Kilbecanty that day.

I found Yeats here. He said all were safe, and not a pane of glass broken. He said "Last night about 12 o'c there was a knock at the door, I went down. There was a man, not in uniform. He said 'What room do you sleep in?' I pointed up to it and he said 'That's all right, you will be safe there. Stay in the house'. I said 'Are you going to blow up the bridge?' 'Yes'. 'I suppose you will give me time to bring the children up into our room?' 'Yes, there will be plenty of time, the explosion won't be for an hour and a half. There will be three explosions, I'll warn you when they are coming'. We got the children and maids upstairs, opened the windows that the glass might not be broken, and waited, put cotton wool in our ears and the children's. Then we saw men running away and one came to the door again and called out it was coming, and went away saying 'Good night; thanks'. The explosions were not very loud, I had expected much worse remembering the air raids. Anne said 'Glynn (the carpenter) is making a great noise up in the workshop' and Mary said 'yes, he makes a great noise when he lets his hammer fall'". The miller had come to look at the bridge in the morning and said "It's a pity, it's a pity, it took a long time to make all that worked stone. They won't find many to help them in their work".

Yeats very indignant at his old poem written for Parnell's death and he hoped forgotten, being reprinted in the *Independent* as if for Griffith. I asked if he could see any trace of merit in it. He said "None". So I said he must remember that in judging young writers. It is just in the fashion of that patriotic day:

"Mourn ye on grass-green plains of Eri fated,
For closed in darkness now
Is he who laboured on, derided, hated,
And made the Tyrant bow".[7]

21 AUGUST. S. told Marian he had been to see his uncle at Kinvara and that "the houses on the road are full of them" (Republicans).

22 AUGUST. Pouring rain all day. Rumours of firing beyond Gort. Cheered by M.'s letter to Marian saying they will come back at Christmas.

23 AUGUST. They say there was fighting at Gortnacorna, and the Chevy woods were searched, and Irregulars driven towards Peterswell, and eleven taken there; one or two wounded and brought to Gort Workhouse-Barrack. "and two of your own tenants among them".

John brings back from the Post Office news of Michael Collins' death, shot at Bandon—"You have bad news to bring to Coole, her ladyship will be in a great way"—And indeed it was a great blow—my hopes had been so much in him and he had been so good about Hugh's pictures. I was stunned, I could not stay in the house but went and sat in the garden for a long time—found at last a little comfort in Mulcahy's fine call to the army:

> Stand calmly by your posts. Then bravely and undaunted do your work.
>
> Let no cruel act of reprisal blemish your bright honour.
>
> Every dark hour that Michael Collins met since 1916 seemed but to steel that bright strength of his and temper his gay bravery.
>
> You are left each inheritors of that strength and of that bravery.
>
> To each of you falls his unfinished work.[8]

But one wishes so much to have some direct work to do towards peace. (Just as I still feel today, 25 February, 1924, while typing this) (But now, corrections received at 25 April, 1928, I feel we are as peaceful as most countries, now Fianna Fail are in the Dail). Then I received a letter from Robinson written on Monday night (this is Wednesday) "Collins is safe, absit omen—and dined at Kilteragh on Saturday, he came in Lady Lavery's train, or rather she in his for she is his abject admirer. The Shaws were there too, G.B.S. was in great form on Sunday afternoon".

The basket maker says "They have De Valera's money in America blocked" (Supreme Court's decision to keep it from him).

I keep thinking "And the best labourer gone
"And all the sheaves to win"!

There is an interview (before the death) with G.B.S. in *The Irish Times*.

He says that from the moment the elections went against De Valera and Childers they had either to set to work to convert the Irish people to their views or to choose between the two other courses open to them "One was to subdue the country by armed force British fashion and coerce it to become an independent little republic whether it liked it or not. The other was to take to the mountains and live more or less merrily by brigandage in the manner of Robin Hood. . . . they have attempted the first alternative but having no war chest, they have been forced to tell their troops on pay day that they must live on the country, which means in practice that the leaders are to be Republicans contending for a principle and their troops are to be brigands . . . I have a friendly personal regard for Mr. Erskine Childers. Like all genuine Englishmen he is a born anarchist and will smash heaven and earth to have his own way unless there is a policeman standing over him".[9]

25 AUGUST. Yeats came over. A boy had said when he heard of the death "The Free Staters will all have to go home now". But the boy's father had said later it was "bad work and no one could think well of it."

I am told the sawmill at Lough Cutra has been broken into, a great deal of mischief done and bands cut and any removable pieces of machinery, crosscut saws, hatchets, taken away "it's likely to sell in Limerick".

Mr. B. says H.'s house at Lough Cutra has been raided. They took him out, blindfolded and threatened to shoot him, asked for his gun, and took away coats, a mackintosh and two others, and anything they could lay hands on. H. says "We don't hear half the things are happening, the people don't tell of it for they say 'Who is there to tell'?" and he said H. had "gone to the Free Staters and lodged his complaint. Two bicycles were taken from him among other things, and the Free Staters arrested two young fellows at Gortnaclocan. But now H. is said to be sorry he made any complaint".

28 AUGUST. The morning of Michael Collins' funeral. I have been reading over Housman's poem:

> They carry back bright to the coiner the mintage of man—
> The lads that will die in their glory and never be old". (A long list now!)

Then I hear "The Republicans are glad. K. was glad telling of it, and T.S. said 'isn't this a great victory'! But four of the Free State men and their Captain that were in the house were in a great way and they said 'The next time we go out we'll shoot to kill'! And one F. a great republican said 'I'd sooner have the British back again'. The Republicans think that if they got their Republic they would have no more rent, rates or taxes to pay. They are sure of that. Miskell's farm has been taken from him, or the most of it, two hundred acres, walled around, and he forbidden to put any more stock on it. He complained about his turf being cut, and they drove away fifty of his cattle then. Some say it is because one day the Republicans went into his house and asked breakfast, and the wife gave the worst breakfast they ever got in any place, and they said it would be a dear breakfast to them. Skim milk they got".

And A. writes that in Galway on the very evening of Collins' death (but they may not have known of it) there were sarcastic notices put up in Galway calling for recruits and signed "Michael Collins. God Save the King". "And when those boys were taken near this one of them called out 'Up De Valera', and one of the Free Staters said to another 'Will I shoot him?' And after that there was quiet".

30 AUGUST. The hay saved, all but a very little, so we need not watch the clouds with so much anxiety.

Two or three days ago Peter said "They say De Valera shot himself" and this morning Marian said "Everyone says he is dead". And G. Yeats coming to lunch today had been told in Gort that a man who had come from Dublin said he had been prayed for, "To recover or have a happy death". But the papers say nothing of this; all sadly filled with the Collins funeral.

31 AUGUST. The garden door broken open in the night by some drunken man they think. He walked along the wall and took some plums—might as well have them as the wasps. A little F. boy, said to be one of the apple robbers of last year, came and asked for some apples yesterday, said they were making hay. I told him it was better to ask for them than take them without leave, and gave him a basketful.

"I live in a poor little town" Plutarch says of his birthplace, "remaining there willingly lest it should become less".

L. said three lorries had gone up the road this morning and I told him Irregulars had been seen in the wood at Castle Taylor. He says "the Republicans are watching now for spies. I know two boys that have got very bad letters with threats, one in the country and one in Gort".

Mr. J. said the people say it was Childers that held De Valera back from going to Michael Collins' funeral. "They hate Childers."

H. says one of the Free State young soldiers who had slept here was at Kiltartan Mass on Sunday and she heard B. say "He ought to be kicked out of the church".

1 SEPTEMBER. They say in Gort that Griffith was made away with by a doctor and his nurses—"didn't he eat a good breakfast? What would make him die? They think De Valera is

maybe in a churchyard. There were said to be eleven put in Kiltartan churchyard the other day, not buried openly".

Yeats came for the afternoon, says "it is a pity when a country has only courage and self sacrifice and not intellect". I say "Rather sanity".

He had not heard, and liked very much, Pearse's little poem that I had translated and that is much in my mind of late:

> I am Ireland,
> Older than the Hag of Beara.
> Great my pride;
> I gave birth to brave Cuchulain.
> Great my shame;
> My own children killed their mother.
> I am Ireland
> Lonelier than the Hag of Beara.[10]

Speaking of that generation of the nineties (WBY)[10a] he said "They were succeeded by an inferior generation such as Belloc—Shaw of course above these, but I said to him once 'you are like Joseph, you have led your brethren to wealth. But it is at the expense of literature'. He said 'Well I have improved the newspapers'."

2 SEPTEMBER. I worked hard at "New Threads in the Pattern" trying to get all ready for typing in Dublin. It is said in Gort "there were three arrests for the doing away of Griffith"!

3 SEPTEMBER. To church, and heard "Miskell is in a bad way. For the Free State troops, on his complaint, drove the cattle put on his land to the Gort pound. And now the owners refuse to take them out and have told Miskell he must himself bring them back or it will be worse for him".

John G. was here about his father's pension. M. says that whenever he had a quarrel with his father he used to threaten to go to S. Africa "like the hens; when you hear them singing at night it's said they are saying they'll go back to Denmark. But they have forgotten it when morning comes."

5 SEPTEMBER. Packing and sending plate to the Bank. Mr. J. advises it. I think it right but I am a little sad, having kept it through these troubled years, liking to act according to my faith.

Yeats here this afternoon. He is anxious lest there should be weakness in the Dail.

He quotes the saying "See Jehovah and die" in the sense that an abstract idea held to will always bring destruction, as indeed it seems to be doing now.

6 SEPTEMBER. A tiring day, getting plums picked to save from wasps and sending nectarines to the children; and Mrs. B. brought two friends. Mr. J. says fifteen sheep have been taken from Donohue nurseryman.

7 SEPTEMBER. The piper here, has been in Connemara, says there was great suffering there for a while for want of food, railway lines pulled up and "the bottoms knocked out of the boats that were coming. They have one another nearly ruined. The devil a one robbed me but the De Valeras—took my little Christmas money on the road, putting a revolver into my mouth. They have finished us in our old days. I was never worse or less thought about, I wish they would let us die easy". But Lord Dudley had helped him, had come over to Connemara and had good fishing "No one with him in the world but himself. The divil the likes of Lord Dudley ever came to Ireland".

The papers say there is a report that De Valera and Childers have been taken. I went to Ballylee and Yeats says Miss Daly was told on the way to Dublin that he was to be one of the bodyguard when Griffith's body is exhumed. But it still seems incredible such a story as that of his poisoning could be true. The plumber was here, at the roof, and says he heard De Valera is dying of cancer "and looked very like it the time I saw him".

8 SEPTEMBER. Packing Anne's birthday cake and their books. Then the paper came and says the Government deny the "absurd rumours" as to Griffith's death. (Folk-lore)! Yeats came and stayed the night.

9 SEPTEMBER. Yeats reading Morley's *Rousseau*,[11] likes it better than any of his he has read, disliked the style and literary metaphors of some of the others. But he thinks Morley hasn't seen the real significance of Rousseau's character, that there is a division in ourselves between abstract ideas and images, and Rousseau was all images.

Yeats asks me if I like the brilliant red of the window frames in the old castle of Ballylee. I say I don't much like them but think they will be better when they fade. He is troubled and gives me all the reasons why they are the only colour that is right with the old stones and I agree politely but not convincingly and at last I say "When one's friends marry one should make up one's mind to have done with telling the truth", and he laughs and says "Quite right", but that the bright red was his idea, G. wanted bright blue.

10 SEPTEMBER. After church I heard that young F., a Republican, had been shot—wounded—last night by the F.S. soldiers. It was midnight and they called to him to halt and he did

not; then they fired a shot and he ran away, and they fired three more, and he was hit, badly wounded, has been taken to Galway. I asked Mrs. M. (the postmistress) with her children and sister to spend the afternoon here, such a lovely day, and they came and sat in the garden. They say most of Gort is Republican, and all Burren. They think a certain number being allowed to join the Government would be accepted as a compromise and bring peace, but if no settlement is made they believe the fighting will go on all through the winter. She said "You are in no danger, the people look on you as one of themselves". I said "But they can't now they are 'in splits'." "Oh, yes", she said "Both sides speak well of you".

12 SEPTEMBER. The postal strike has begun.[12] We got an *Independent* from Gort and it tells of the death of Wilfrid Blunt.[13] An added sadness and loneliness after a forty years' friendship. Yet he was suffering so much when I last saw him I felt he could not bear it long.

Yeats here yesterday, but we were both a little downhearted, no sign of peace, though he longs for some more evidence of strength. It is hard on the new Government having this postal strike with all its other difficulties. Meanwhile Miskell's little son came into Gort on Sunday to say his father had been kidnapped, carried off after Mass.

I have this evening finished—somehow—getting all my MSS straight and tidy enough for typing. But now no use taking it to Dublin with no posts to return it, I must try and bring a typist back.

KILTERAGH, 15 AUGUST [sic]. I came to Dublin on Wednesday. I was pointed out Miskell at the station, apparently released and being looked after by a couple of Free Staters. Trains slow, journey took 12.30 to 7.30 including two hours wait at Athenry. My letter ordering a room hadn't arrived, but R. met me at the Broadstone with a message from H. Plunkett asking me here, and I came on after the Abbey, a very charming performance of *Damer's Gold*[14]—Will Shields gave it a poetic quality, and all were good. Audience rather small but appreciative. Yesterday Carnegie meeting and business, and not here till near midnight. The Dail is sitting and people seem pleased with Cosgrave's[15] opening speech, and Mulcahy's,[16] and the firmness shown. The postal strike is hard on a new Government. Sir Horace is sad, dreads going to U.S.A. this winter—what can he say? "Can I say the country is gone into a lower stage of civilisation than ever before? Or is it just lust of blood that leads to this sniping?" A bomb had been thrown at Free State troops passing close to the

Abbey the afternoon I arrived. A.E. is more cheerful, gave me his last article to read, thinks a better time must come and that we should be ready to take up our work; thinks there may be a great intellectual awakening. Harris is gloomy, the big business houses hard hit by the strike. Lord Lascelles has given up the idea of coming to Portumma, and Lord Kenmare may be driven to leave "though it will break his heart to leave Killarney". Furniture vans engaged for nine months ahead are taking goods from the country to England. De Valera is said to be "Out" now as a leader; and a Republican told Harris "Childers is the man that understands war". Marquis MacSwiney has written to Father Murphy from Rome that "there is absolute evidence that Childers has been for some time in Bolshevist employ, and getting large sums from Russia, of course to carry on the war here." Then Dolan, coming with me to the station after the evening performance says a friend of his who is in touch with the Republicans says they will accept Mulcahy's terms offered in the Dail, and that there will be peace within three weeks. But I bought a little typed paper in the street *Freedom*[17] denouncing the "pretended Government" and accusing them of murder, torturing of prisoners and the like, signed Eamon O'Maille "Ct. N and E Command".

Evening. The walls have sentences painted in black on white bands "Fight clean, Mulcahy, call in your murderous troop". "Brugha refused to come under the Empire". "Ballina and Kenmare taken from the Imperialists" and the like. I bought a paper. There had been much firing in the night, an attack on the troops in the Four Courts Hotel, but no lives known to be lost. I had to stand for some time while a procession of Post Office strikers marched past. Not much interest shown in them, yet Labour may join them. Sir Horace says it is altogether a political move.

16 SEPTEMBER. In Dublin today some of the writings on the wall had been in part rubbed out but there were new ones "We will not come into the Empire"; "Men are dying on your prison ships in Dublin Bay Dick Mulcahy." Harris's typist looked tired, had been kept from sleep all night by the noise of firing. At the Abbey Miss Bushell told me the two Childers boys had come to ask for tickets for the matineé "as Lady Gregory always said they might", and she had given them, but Dolan hadn't been sure if she was right. I said, "Yes, she was right"; but was less well pleased when she told me they had said to her "What are you here? Why don't you put on a Republican play and you would have a full house. Why don't they (the F.S. Government) make peace? They began the war, they should begin the peace. They

said they would have beaten us by the 29th and that is near and we are stronger than ever. Do you remember when Father came to *Blanco Posnet* how tired he looked and pale? Well he is quite different now, quite strong, and when we last saw him as brown as a berry".

They saw me when I came into the Auditorium and I spoke to them, and later in the interval, gave them tea in the hall. Bobby kept asking if our part was quiet? If we had any rows? But I turned off to their work, his engineering and Erskine's science, and when Erskine showed me marks on his hand and face of the explosion of an experiment, I didn't even ask if it was a destructive machine. Poor children, I don't suppose they realise what this killing and maiming and destruction mean.

17 SEPTEMBER. A very stormy night, and I thought of the prison ships and all the sadness.[18]

People in the afternoon. A.E. came to call me from my room and we had a talk. He believes the trouble will go on for a long time, years perhaps, and will be even worse than now; thinks the whole world is in a restless state, and that the industrial system must break up. Yet he is ready with plans for the future, on the lines of Denmark. He says eight lines of his poem "Michael"[19] came to him in a dream, and the last line, and he could not think what he was meant to write in between, and then it came quite quickly.

Dr. Moorhead also came. I had not met him before. I sat between him and Mr. Fletcher, head of technical education, at tea. As we talked Mr. Fletcher said "The English don't look down on the Irish, it has been a mistake to think we do". I said "It is no mistake, look at the Punch caricatures, though just now for the first time improving". Dr. Moorhead flushed red and said "Yes, it is no mistake. I didn't know you were an Englishman". I told this today to Yeats and he said, John O'Leary said "The English despise us but they like us. The English don't despise the Scotch but they thoroughly dislike them".

19 SEPTEMBER. COOLE. I came home today. Yesterday on the way, the train was shunted and stopped outside the station at Athlone. A woman looking out of the window said there were coffins. I looked out then and saw them, three I think. Men were lifting them on their shoulders.

I slept in Galway. The nurse says a great many are joining the Republicans. Waiting at Athenry two women, children with them, were talking—I heard the words "The head and shoulders of one of them were sent over five fields". They must have been talking of the Cork ambush reported yesterday.[20] A very wet day. I saw Harris before I left Dublin but he says no typist will come down to Galway, they are afraid.

20 SEPTEMBER. The Yeats children came here yesterday to spend a week while the Dublin house is made ready. Yeats came with them, says they are flooded out, the heavy rain caused the water to rise so they had to wade about the lower floor for packing, and put their boxes on tables. While he was here Mrs. Y. sent his night things with a message he must stay here the night, she was sending the servants home. He has left today, rather sad, between the flood at Ballylee and the firing in Dublin. And I had no very good news to give him from there.

21 SEPTEMBER. A letter from Galway, posted 9th came yesterday, but they say the harness of the Mail car was stolen in the night, and it is not likely to go again.

Patrick says Miskell when he was kidnapped was tied with ropes to a rafter and "put sitting in some cold place till his hands gave way". He offered to give up all but a hundred acres of land but they want all. Some of the butcher's sheep and of another man have been stolen also. "There's a class of boys that are the scurf of the world that stop at nothing and are a holy terror. They'd stop you and rob you if you had a one pound in your pocket, the same as the Black and Tans. It was from them they learned those ways. A great shame it was, the English sending them here, but what did they care"?

22 SEPTEMBER. No paper today, the midday train did not arrive; the line they say had been broken somewhere, and waggons of pigs being sent from a fair upset. Mike met Houston at the station, he said there is a great deal of timber being cut at Lough Cutra and he cannot prevent it. He tried to, and they blindfolded him the other day.

I am typing some of J.B. Yeats letters. Reading Belloc's *French Revolution*.[21] The first French forces seem to have been rather like our Republicans "a somewhat lax and turbulent democracy". A shortage of officers too because so many of "the classes" had emigrated. (But it is the German war more than emigration that has left us without men in our houses who might now lead the Free State army). Robespierre and De Valera seem to be akin "sincerely convinced of the purest democratic theory, a man who cared for nothing else but the realisation of that theory . . . a politician and incorruptible".

23 SEPTEMBER. K. hears there were shots in Gort last night about 1 o'c. Doesn't know why, but "what do young boys want going out through the town at that time? But they say the Free Staters are only Connemara boys and don't mind them". Some

of these Connemara boys Mrs. Mitchell told me, have been learning since they came, to speak English.

They say that at Tubber fair some stolen cattle that were being sold were recognised by the owner, and the Free State men arrested two men who were with them. (26 September. B. says the house of the man whose cattle were stolen and who gave information and had them arrested has been bombed and burned down).

24 SEPTEMBER. The L.C. steward told K. that a fortnight ago he was beaten and two of his ribs were broken. He was standing in the yard chatting with the gardener and turned to go to his house, and when he had gone a few steps three men came up, gave him a sudden blow on the mouth that knocked him down. Then the others "strangers, low sized men, beat him with the butt of their rifles breaking his ribs". It is said he was supposed to have given information that led to some arrests two months ago. He does not know what to do, to go or stay. It is very hard for them to hold on there. A great deal of timber is being cut and taken. B. hearing this story said "You must have some sort of charm at Coole that keeps trouble away". I, hearing this, said I hoped it might last. When I got home Marian came out much excited to say some "Volunteers, Hall and another had come and taken a car and harness", said they were sorry but were "under orders, for a secret purpose, and would bring it back at 6 o'c." They were taking the best car, but she told them "it had been Mr. Robert's, and her ladyship would not like it taken", so then they took the old one. They said something about "a review" and that they would not object to the oath to this king in the Constitution, but would not take it to his successors, or so she understood. But K. says those he heard talking last night said the Ministers' salaries were too high, and that if the Republicans can beat them there will be no more rates to pay.

25 SEPTEMBER. At 9 o'c last night rat-tat-tat at the door. M. asked if she should open it and I said yes, and went down. There was a man I didn't know. He said he had brought back the car and was sorry to have troubled us, but they were "under orders for a review". I said I hoped it was not for an ambush and he said "Oh, no" and I said then it was all right as they had asked and not taken it without leave. But I now hear they went to Peterswell races and that it was probably only for their own amusement. And that a shop at Peterswell had been raided and everything in it carried off to the racecourse.

26 SEPTEMBER. The Yeats children left. Finished typing J. B. Yeats' letters. Reading Morley's *Rousseau*, and the Granville-

Bessborough letters.[22]

27 SEPTEMBER. Mrs. Johnson brought her children to get damsons and to tea, and said there had been firing in the night at Gort and some windows broken. The basketmaker coming later said there had been an attack by Irregulars who came they think from this direction, into the town and fired volleys. There was no return fire and they withdrew. One Free State soldier was wounded. There are Irregulars again in Druimhasna, they fired on a lorry of National soldiers passing. Three or four Gort men were arrested today on suspicion as they were leaving by train. A post this afternoon, two letters from Dorothy Carleton telling me of the last days of W.S.B. He had an Irish nurse, and near the end had given her his *Land War* book and said "Tell the people of Ireland I am sorry not to be able to do anything for them".

28 SEPTEMBER. Last night as I went to bed about 11 o'c I heard a bang, and after a little another, and one of the horses whimpering. I was a little uneasy but read for a while and lay awake till about 1 o'c. This morning I am told two bombs were thrown in Gort, but there is no news as to whether anyone was hurt. And as I was in the garden two rifle shots sounded. And as I came back to the house there were three or four shots louder "with cartridges". "But with people looking you between the two eyes and staring it's best not to talk of anything at all". Four of them were very near by. Soldiers out last night by the old road.

Then I hear that there were three arrests yesterday in Gort. And that the National troops were "very wise in not going out to return the fire on Tuesday night, for there were only a few men there in the lane, but it is known now there was a large party waiting near the Workhouse Barracks thinking it would be left undefended".

I took apples to Kiltartan school, open again, but only about thirty children there, it being a fine day several had been kept for the harvesting. I saw the broken bridge for the first time, and four of the five elms that were felled to block the road. It was fine enough to pull the baking apples for storing.

One of *The Times* I have opened has an article on "A Mystic".[23] "The mystic is like those stars whose motions are affected by some other star too far away to be seen with any glass, yet the desire which moves him is so strong, and to him so much a matter of course that it must, we feel, be for something real, as hunger presumes the existence of something to eat . . . perhaps the greatest gift such men give to the world is the conviction they communicate to those who meet them that their life is not an illusion . . . but prophetic of what man will be in a higher state of spiritual development. There is a convincing beauty about them like that of great works of art, and seeing them is believing what they believe".

29 SEPTEMBER. Some apples stolen in the night, and garden door broken open. Nothing of much value and it is lucky we had given the schoolchildren theirs. But a peaceful day gathering the remaining cooking apples, and working through some of the typed diaries (Black and Tan time). And the papers brought news that the Postal strike is over.[24] And in the Dail there was a discussion on peace which may possibly lead to it.[25]

3 o'c. Expecting letters today, but disappointed, none. The mail car had been robbed at Kiltartan.

1 OCTOBER. The summer over and the children have not seen the flowers or gathered the fruit. An anxious month, it may bring peace, or failing that a more bitter war. I think if the idealists among the Republicans could realise that against the high light of the desire for freedom are to be measured these dark shadows of covetousness and crime, they would themselves call for peace.

Reading Morley's *Rousseau* because of its bearing on revolution, but other things come in "he cherished that conception of the true unity of man's life which places it in a closely linked chain of active memories, and which most of us lose in wasteful dispersion of sentiment and poor fragmentariness of days".

This has been a good Sunday, the sun came out after church, the people looked in good humour, I felt so much at peace that it seems as if peace must be in the air! Two Killeen children came for apples, I gave them damsons as well. And a rather deaf young H., son of the harness maker in Gort passed, having been in the woods picking nuts, and I took him to the garden for apples, and I liked his brightening and excitement when I said he might have damsons—his sister is an invalid "and will be so glad of them".

It is said that stolen property from Dunsandle has been searched for in Loughrea and some silver has been found "in respectable houses". It is a good way of beginning to restore order, getting at the looters who are already held in contempt.

2 OCTOBER. The Postman's voice this morning sounded pleasant. He brought newspapers but few letters; said he got no pay during the strike "No funds" and grumbles at the cut, but has still £3.4.0 a week "for a couple of rounds on a bicycle" says M.

At Gort fair we sold lambs well, but cattle were down. More shots last night fired at Court House Barrack, where the Free State soldiers now are.

Glad of a letter from Reynolds saying he had "made a detailed report of your recommendations given me in our interview of the 14th" re the Lane pictures, "this report came before the Libraries Committee at their last meeting, and it was decided that the Town Clerk (its Official Secretary) be requested to formally apply to President Cosgrave to act in the matter".

3 OCTOBER. Many letters, one from the darlings. I was writing answers all the morning, and then drove Tommy through the woods to mark trees for firing and was cheered by the young plantations looking so well, and no signs of trespass.

There were some stolen sheep at Gort fair yesterday. They were detected and three or four men arrested by the F.S. troops. The thief had cut off the brand with shears and put on his own. Yeats writes from Dublin "People seem cheerful and I imagine the Government is greatly tightening its grip on the country . . . I have got Spicer-Simson's bronze of you, not very like but very vigorous and simple. It is perhaps only a little unlike to my eye because one never really knows any vigorous person's profile, one thinks only of their front face, talking or listening".

4 OCTOBER. Patrick says some more stolen sheep have been discovered in a barn belonging to Lee's brother-in-law, Hearn. They had been taken from a poor man, Donohoe of the neighbourhood. The Free Staters went and searched and found them and have taken L and Hearn "in two lorries" to Galway. "A good thing too, for it was no republicans but schemers of the sort that were robbing the country, and if they were let go on, there is no man at all would be left with nothing. I knew Lee's grandfather well that was one Crowe, and he got five years in gaol for stealing cattle, and went to America after. See now how it broke out in Lee".

6 OCTOBER. Yesterday too damp for outdoor work. I worked at MSS scraps, putting together some Roman notes, perhaps for future use, and some about R's childhood. The Amnesty offered to all Republicans giving up arms and looted property before 15 October may bring peace, or a last outburst of fighting.[26]

Looking through scraps I find this written before I began my book: "What is good in us is ever ascending, will at the loosening of the spirit be freed in its full volume; what is heavier than befits the spiritual life will fall into its place among material things.

"And so I question myself how far have I translated my dream into reality? Can I relate everything to the eternal purpose and harmony".

I shall be able to judge better when I read the clean MSS through. But not even then till the Diaries are read with them, they are not all yet typed. I find another note "We want the history of the pilgrim soul, telling to which of the eternal purposes it has been able to put the body".

McNicholas, Horticultural Inspector, came before lunch and gave me useful advice in the garden. Later I was superintending apple picking, and heard Mike had come to say he had come on Hearn cutting young trees in the quarry plantation. Hearn had fled on seeing him, and J. sent a cart to bring in the trees that had been cut. Just then four boys with sacks came to the gate to ask for apples, little Fahy and Killeen and two sons of Hearn. I let them all fill their sacks with apples and their caps with damsons and then I went to the yard and met the cart, seven young ash cut, and three sycamore. Just then we heard a motor and I was startled by seeing a man in uniform holding a rifle come into the yard, three more in the motor. He was Lt. Lynn of National Forces, a Clare man now at Gort, and had come to ask for "about half or a quarter of a stone of apples to make cakes". Such a mild request from such a warlike apparition! I brought them all into the garden and they filled their pockets satisfactorily. I showed Lt. L. the young trees just cut that he might be a witness. Mr. J. came later and I consulted him about prosecuting Hearn, as the Lieutenant had been vague about Courts, and he said there will be no Courts we can go to until January, but that I should get a solicitor to write to Hearn that the case will be taken up then. Quite an exciting afternoon, so many visitors.

A review in the *Athenaeum* of a book by Dr. Ritchie on Faunal Evolution[27] says: "Nature exterminates an animal: long she seems to ponder over the process, slowly the conditions creep in which render existence more difficult, time gives many opportunities for changing a habit, even for modifying a structure, so that new adaptation may turn aside the threat of extinction, only to incompetence of adjustment does nature mete out its reward". (And this applies to us landlords.)

7 OCTOBER. After a night's reflection I wrote to Hearn.

8 OCTOBER. Thieves were in both gardens, took all apples from apple house, a good many, but not good ones, windfalls, we had stored the rest. They broke a pane of glass and strained lock in vinery, but didn't care for the grapes, not yet ripe. I don't mind as the children are not at home to know of it.

I was sitting alone outside at the steps, when a big violent looking man appeared, Hearn. I hadn't seen him before. He produced my letter "Dear Sir, I am sorry you did not act as those nice little sons of yours did yesterday, when wishing for some apples they asked me for them, while you, wishing for some of my young trees cut them without asking. I did not tell the little fellows of this, although I was aware of it at the time, as I would not have them know their father had set them a bad example. I should be glad if you would come and see me on this matter. I have always wished to live in peace and friendship with my neighbours, but at the same time must protect the property in my charge."

He said or shouted "In general when I get a letter from a lady I wish to treat it as a letter from a lady but I'm afraid I can't do that this time. It wants an explanation. What does it mean?" I said "Just what it says. Some trees were cut and I am told you cut them". "Who told you that? It is either a concoction or a misunderstanding". I said "My keeper, whose business it is to look after the woods told me". "Did he see me cutting the trees?" "Either that or going away from them, getting over the wall where they were freshly cut". "I was never near the place. I haven't a sheepcock or anything that would require timber. It is a concoction". I said "It is possible it was a mistake. M.D. could not have invented it, he is a quite honest man". "I know he is that—and his son too" (!!!) Then I told him of my hearing blows of a hatchet one day and finding it was old Padraig Niland who had brought cart and hatchet, and when even he did so it showed how closely I must look after the woods I have in charge for my grandchildren. We parted amicably; rather a verdict of "Not guilty, but don't do it again". And now I am told that young C. had seen Hearn going into the plantation with a hatchet, and he had come later and asked him, C., for the loan of his jennet to carry away what he had cut! I think of Lord Morris's definition of Prima Facie evidence "If I saw a man coming out of a public house, wiping his mouth, I would say that was prima facie evidence he had been having a drink".

Three nice young fellows, Corly, Gillane and Stephen Fahy, came for apples later and I took them to the garden, plenty remaining luckily for gifts.

9 OCTOBER. I sent Mike for a walk round and he found hidden by a wall some young trees cut from Raheen plantation. John sent a cart for them and they have come, six young oaks, two quite substantial oak cut in lengths and a sycamore. But I mustn't grumble as we have had so little trouble so far. A rather idle day, but a bundle of typed MS came by afternoon post, 73,000 words Harris says. Very glad to have it safely back.

11 OCTOBER. Yesterday a drive up the mountain, a lovely afternoon and Lough Cutra looked beautiful and tranquil; though I am told Miskell's oats are rotting in the field; he has never come back since he was kidnapped and tied up, "and there

is no one dare put a hand to them".

Yeats writes about the pictures being housed in Dublin Castle. But I don't want to meddle with the question of housing them, only to get them back. I have just corrected the "First Decades", the typed copy, and think it good; a little anxious about the rest.

13 OCTOBER. No paper or post yesterday, the bridge at Ballinasloe having been broken. But today's post has come.

I am asked "What is De Valera doing and where is he at all, or is he out in foreign? Bad luck to him".

14 OCTOBER. J. and Patrick last evening met coming in at the white gate "a young fellow with a dark cap" a stranger. They said some greeting "and he answered in a very high up sort of a voice. It must be he was going to the woods, the river is too high to cross, bringing dispatches it's likely. How can you know where any party of them might be hiding?"

15 OCTOBER. After church B. told me Cloon bridge had again been blown up last night. The people had just begun to repair it and there had been a little footpath left after the last explosion, but now they say all has gone—Gort cut off from Peterswell and Loughrea.

I had heard unusual sounds last night, like two bangs, but had made up my mind to put down all strange noises to the horses, and having fed Sarsfield with apples thought he might have come looking for more, tried to think so. But it was just at that time Marian had heard it, and the Hehirs say their house shook. No good sign of the amnesty being accepted, it lapses today. And this evening in the garden I heard for a long time the rattling of lorries.

I wrote a little account of Hugh as a Nation-builder, having been asked to write something on building the nation for a forthcoming book (to be published in America). But breaking is not done with yet.

16 OCTOBER. Corrected typing Sir A.L. and H.J. and wrote and cabled to Pond, giving up the idea of lecturing in U.S.A., too much anxiety here. Then a letter from Reynolds of the Municipal Gallery asking advice about a statement he is to draw up for Cosgrave about the Lane pictures. I wrote to him, and for him, and for Yeats to see him. Then I sat by the lake at sunset and watched the wild ducks pass northward against the sunset sky, sixty-four in all. Then the first star came out and I heard the Angelus bell.

17 OCTOBER. Guy and George Gough this morning, with miniatures of the chicks and letters from them, and saying they are looking forward to coming back for Christmas.

The Cloon road said to be blocked with trees so that the people can't bring their turf to market.

Then R.D., a Republican had said to her "We will *never* give in to be ruled by those Free State lads". I sent off my letters to Reynolds and Yeats.

20 OCTOBER. Two hard days, L.R. having written to ask my approval of a statement asking the new Government to subsidise the Abbey; and also for a statement for the Government, about Hugh's pictures.

The Theatre paper was too much a S.O.S. and did not give an idea of the value of the property we propose to present to the Nation. And the figures were nearly all wrong, and though I didn't mind Yeats being given credit for "Collecting money in 1916 that helped to keep the Theatre going" (the £200 through his lectures) I thought the sum, over £2000, I had raised in 1911 to enable us to buy and continue the Theatre should be mentioned also. The corrections took some time and I wrote to R. but sent the statement to Harris to correct the figures. Then as to a statement about the pictures (again!) I clambered up on a chair to reach top shelf of MS compartment of press, and took down masses of papers, and others fell down (I had put all these away as done with after Michael Collins' letter). And I went through those about Hugh's codicil, and chose two full statements, one I had made at Sir R. Woods' request for Macpherson, the other giving the Trustees' refusal and Curzon's letters. Then I tore some pages out of my diaries, my interview with Macpherson, and letters, and sent these off. (Is this the last time?) (29 February, 1924. No, I wrote and sent statement etc to the Governor-General yesterday, asking him to get McNeill, Free State Agent in London to press the matter on Thomas of the Colonial Office). (April, 1928. And am still writing—working on!)—And 1 January 1930 I reported at President Cosgrave's meeting my effort for a favourable answer to Hannon's question.

I was so tired and my head ached, I made a "Sunday" of the afternoon, arranging my writing table, and read some of Horace Walpole's letters, and gathered apples for a present to Danny Shaughnessy. And my parcel for the children having come back (Guy had left too early) I repacked the chickens and plum cake and sent them off.

Today (20th) has been easier, and I got all through "Education on Politics" corrections. I don't know if it will be cared for, neither ancient history, nor new. And I got Peter to pot some marguerites for the winter, and John to take down the winter pears. But letter writing had kept me till lunch time. The papers tell that Lloyd George is out.[28] I am sorry. The Die-hards may give trouble over the treaty. On the other hand Bonar Law, as a Scotchman, had been for giving back the pictures, because the unwitnessed codicil would have been valid in Scotland. Letters from Anne and C. and their lesson marks.

Yeats wrote "I may not see Fitzgerald (about the Abbey) as the Ministers sleep in their Offices and seem practically prisoners there, only moving with a guard".

21 OCTOBER. A quiet day; worked through typed "Politics: Egypt" yesterday and "Folklore in Politics" today.

22 OCTOBER S.C. The B.'s in church, they had to drive through the fields the road being blocked. Marian says the Bishop's letter was read after Mass, "and all sat quiet though Mrs. Finn whose son is in Gaol turned and said to me 'Let them mind their own business'". And she doesn't think Father C. will read it at Shanaglish or Father O'K. at Kilbecanty.

Gillane; also Killeen and Hearn asking for a subscription for races, and their children for apples; and Raftery and little Tom came as I was tying coloured tape to the dahlias, to remember their colours when they die down.

26 OCTOBER. Galway. I came here on Monday to have my typewriter mended; two and a half hours wait at Athenry. I took typewriter to Flanagan who returned it next day, having screwed down the loose screws and cleaned it and charged £1.

On Tuesday evening I was startled by John Diveney coming in. I knew he couldn't have news from London, but thought perhaps Coole had been burned down. He was a long time getting to the point of his story, making the most of it for conversational purposes, but at last I found he had come in with Raftery, who had been shot in the shoulder by Michael Dooley who had with young C. cut four trees in the field just sold to Raftery, but that they thought was still ours. Raftery got word of this, met them taking the trees away in two carts, knocked them both down and they fled. As he led the carts, intending to take them to the Barracks, M. and C. came back with a gun, came within a few feet of him and M. fired at him. He caught hold of the barrel as it was fired, thereby his hand got some of the pellets but the main charge went into his shoulder. He turned to try and get away towards Gort but C. cried "Load the gun again"! and one or both said "If you go that way we'll kill you". He dragged himself to Coole, losing much blood. John heard him calling and saw him lying covered with blood, called the men, who carried him into the breakfast room, and the maids attended to him and gave him wine and sent for Father Considine and Dr. Sandys. The doctor bound him up and sent him to Galway to the County Hospital. His poor wife came with him. I went to the Hospital and got the house surgeon (a nice young woman) to look to him and sat a while and brought his wife back to have tea here, for she had the long drive before her, not being able to leave her children for the night. Yesterday, Wednesday, I saw him again, for I put off my return home until today. Some of the Free State soldiers had come from Gort to ask particulars.

27 OCTOBER. B. to lunch. He says a commercial traveller from Cork told him 150 Free State soldiers with their arms have gone over to the Irregulars. The papers say these have proclaimed De Valera "President of the Republic" again, and called a Dail of their own. Rather good I think as there will be some clear issue to vote on at the elections, a definite and not a shadowy Republic.

I lay awake thinking of Jacob Boehme's saying that we may live in Heaven even while in this world—; and in the thinking it seemed possible.

29 OCTOBER. Sunday. Yesterday Mrs. Raftery came to see me, says he is going on well. M. and C. were brought to him by Free Staters and questioned. They admit cutting the trees but say they or Micho—fired "in self defence"! I worked over "Among the Poor" and had the geraniums and chrysanthemums brought into the vinery; and read Horace Walpole's letters. Church today, and worked a bit at my account of Hugh as a Nation-builder. We passed on the road two of the Civic police, the first I have seen here.

30 OCTOBER. "The Civic Guards have seized all the treacle in Kinvara, where poteen was being made that poisoned the people".

2 NOVEMBER. Yesterday the Holy day, very peaceful (St. Colman's?) I worked at W.S.B.'s letters, and gave out apples. Today Mike reports having found G., M.Q.'s brother-in-law cutting a tree (ash) in the field M.Q. has seized. Says M. gave him leave.

4 NOVEMBER. Yesterday I was cheered by an excellent statement drawn up by Reynolds about the Lane pictures for Cosgrave to take to London. R., on the other hand writes that after all my trouble in sending documents for a statement D. Fitzgerald had asked for, it isn't wanted, they didn't know of Reynolds. But my hopes are again high.

Last night, looking over odd letters, I found that W. writing from Ceylon, agreed with his mother that "there is no getting over November, it is odious" and encourages her to leave home.

But this morning the garden is more lovely than in summer time, such an Italian sun and sky, and the silver stain of the copper beech shining through its gold.

6 NOVEMBER. Yesterday, Sunday, I "holystoned the deck" finishing and typing my article about Hugh's work in the building of Ireland (just as it is breaking around us!) At church the B.'s had driven through the field that is getting very much cut up, the road still blocked. Today, writing about the pictures to Lord Carson and Sir John Lavery. I worked on at typing of "The Changing Ireland" but found it more cheerful than the last chapters, the rather scattered interests in London; worked till close on 8 o'c.

KILTERAGH. 10 NOVEMBER. FRIDAY. I came up on Wednesday, not knowing where I should go, but when I arrived at the Broadstone, tired after the long journey, the two hours' wait at Athenry, the crowded train, L.R. was waiting with a note from G. Heard saying my room was ready here. So I was glad not to have to look for a hotel and went straight to the Theatre and had some tea, and then saw the first acts of *The Round Table*,[29] very amusing and well acted. And then Yeats who had come there to meet me took me to Harcourt St. Station, and G. Heard met me at Foxrock; every one very kind, and the rooms so comfortable, and the morning sunshine was on the mountains when I awoke.

As we had come down O'Connell St. from the station we had seen a small crowd, Mrs. McBride speaking on the treatment of the prisoners.[30] And at Athlone I had got the evening paper with account of the Dublin battle, an attack on Wellington Barracks.[31] Yeats said the Government are satisfied with the military situation but not with their own army, the discipline is bad. He heard Mulcahy is resigning and putting Dalton in his place, as an ex-service man and a better disciplinarian (but this he says today is not true). Today he hears or heard last night that they have shot twelve of their own officers for want of discipline. And that three soldiers have been flogged in the Barrack square. They were afraid the rest of the army would mutiny against them if they did not. The Irregulars are making a great fight now to prevent the Treaty being ratified. But the Government say they will have all leaders in gaol within a week, and the whole country quiet in a couple of months. He hears endless rumours. Miss Mitchell was told yesterday that there were 8000 men marching on Dublin. Yet things go on much as usual, though the Abbey audiences are very small.

This afternoon at 4 o'c I went into Brown and Nolan's to buy some carbon paper. One young man behind the counter called to another "Is it true about Childers"? The other said "Yes, it is official". I asked what it was and they said "Erskine Childers has been taken".[32] Half an hour later there were a great many little boys running about with the evening papers but not calling out anything, not even "Evening Papers" as usual, though I fancied they ran with some excitement. I went into Gogarty's for tea, to ask if he could help to get Katie T. hospital training, and he was nice about it and promised to do so. I told him what I had heard about Childers and he said it wasn't likely, and he felt sure Childers would never be taken alive, he had done such terrible destruction. I said it could hardly be true as the newsboys had not called it out "but perhaps they were afraid to", and he said "That may be". At Harcourt St. Station I bought a paper, and it was true enough, in a large headline. It gave me a strange feeling, almost of dream, that silence and swiftness of the boys, whether it was through fear or their own sympathy with the Republicans.

The Carnegie meeting had been interesting, Maguire the Donegal librarian giving his report. And Robinson has been asked by Sir Horace to go with him to Gibraltar, and I promised to look after the Abbey as much as possible while he is away. And I saw Reynolds about the Lane statement and A.E. to know if I might publish his letters; I had brought them for him to read, but he thinks them poor stuff and is against it but will think over them. I lunched and dined with Yeats in their fine house, they seem very well content. I am very tired.

12 NOVEMBER. SUNDAY. Yesterday I left Kilteragh. I went again to A.E. without any great hope of the letters. But he was very good, had pencilled out some passages, not many, and gave me leave to use the rest. And he was just writing me a note which he has given me leave to use also, saying as he had said to me, that he can only write what is worth preserving when moved to the very depth of his being, and the rest is trivial, worth nothing.

But he doesn't forbid it "if it is not ascribed to A.E., but to George Russell". Then I went in to see Yeats, he had written a good bit of his article on the Abbey for the American book and read it to me, and then read me his just finished poem, a wild and visionary one upon the sight of the moon.[33] It is drawn he says from his philosophy, and so from vision. It is beautiful in its wildness and in sound. I couldn't wait for lunch but went to the Abbey to settle programmes with Dolan for the weeks Robinson will be away. I think the plays have been rather too gloomy for these troubled times. I suggested *Dempsey*; Dolan said people were tired of it, though it hadn't been played for nearly a year. But I found that N. had been playing *Dempsey* which was enough to kill it, and with some pressure insisted on the part being given to W. Shields. Then I want *John Bull*, and the difficulty about that is there is no visible Broadbent. I wrote to Sir Simon Maddock who, as Mr. Maddock, had once played it well. But he is said to be "high in himself" since his title. Thinking over it in the night I thought Will Shields could do it if we could get Sir Philip Hanson to read the part to him; he is a natural Broadbent.

I went to see Harris. He had in his office a young man from Killarney who gave a sad account of things there, coal £7 a ton and food almost impossible to be had. Lord Lascelles wants to "clear out" and sell his land (just as well I think), and Lord Kenmare who spends £200 a week on labour, is losing patience, and his son and Lord Revelstoke pressing him to leave against his desire. On the other hand Harris having bought the house in which is his office, was afraid he would have difficulty in letting the ground floor, but has let it to a very good English company who are doing it up, spending a good deal, must have some confidence in the country.

G. Heard, told me but has not yet told Sir Horace for fear of troubling him, that one night about 9.30 the maid answered the door bell and without asking who was there (as he had told her always to do) opened the door, and ten men, Irregulars, came in. She called him down. They asked or demanded lodging for the night, were rather rough at first but he spoke gently and they became more mannerly. He gave them lodging, though not beds and in the morning gave them some food and they went away. He was rather expecting other parties to arrive, the Irregulars are said to be concentrating on Dublin, and the plantations round Kilteragh would make it easy for them to escape in case of surprise. So he told me not to be alarmed at any strange noise. However nothing happened, and I had a most peaceful and pleasant time there, though working hard in Dublin I was very tired at the end.

I had F. to meet me at the Abbey with Ordnance maps, to see what area of woodland we have to sell, for peace sake, and economy. He had not much new to tell about Roxborough; first the occupation by Irregulars, then their departure; then general looting, then the burning. But a great deal of furniture and all the family pictures had been saved, sent away. A great deal of the land has been sold, and there is more to go. Arthur has made no plans yet. Dudley will be of age next month and they can decide then. The steward has been left in charge and wrote a little time ago that he wanted a man to help him. They sent down Captain

White. After a few weeks and various threats a party of men came, put him on his knees, put a revolver to his head, asked if he had not been in the police (he had been a D.I.) said they would have no police there and gave him eleven hours to clear out. F. thinks the steward is "In with the neighbours", but he suits Arthur well enough as they only want someone to look after the tillage. Only the chimneys left standing at Roxborough.

In the train yesterday a young man told me he is Baptist Minister at Athlone, has been there for two years; when the English troops were there he was Minister to four denominations, Church of England, Wesleyans, Presbyterians, I forget the fourth. He gave a sad account of the drinking among these young Free State soldiers, says among the Tommies there were individual cases but it is more general among these boys. He thinks it is partly because there are no recreation grounds or reading rooms as there were for the others, they have no evening resource but the public house; says he saw two priests the worse for drink the other day saying good bye at the station to men (civilians I think) in the same state, and "going into the canteen for more drink when the train had left". I wish there was anything one could do to help.

SUNDAY EVENING, GALWAY, 12 NOVEMBER. At church there were but two or three faces I knew, where there used to be so many, kinsfolk and acquaintances; one Wade girl and Mr. Eraut of the Grammar school and Girvin of the C.D.B. Mr. Berry in his sermon appealed for more money from those who are left, to make up for the donations of those who are gone. There was one soldier there, in Free State uniform.

I went to see Raftery at the Hospital, looking well but impatient, he whispered to me that if he is not given proper care he would be ready to go to Dublin. I didn't understand this until I spoke to J.D. (who had come in with Raftery's man and two of his children). He said "one of the Coons was saying they made a mistake when he was in the hospital and treated him for the wrong thing". And "they are putting iodine on Raftery's arm; but aren't we rubbing iodine on horses all our life and what good is it but to take down swelling, and why don't they take out the pellets?" But the House Surgeon, Miss Faller, told me that when they X-rayed the shoulder they found the bone was shattered, and they are hoping the splinters will join, or if not a plate may be put in by an operation. But she thinks the arm will always be stiff and doubts his being able to do heavy masonry work. That would be a terrible blow. The House Surgeon spoke of "these dreadful agrarian crimes" and I said all the shootings and killings were very bad, but the Government believed there would soon be peace. She got red and said "I am a Republican" and that her brother is in Athlone gaol. I asked if we might not all work together for the saving of Ireland from its sad state, but she said "How can we work with these people". She thinks Collins and Griffith could have got more out of England if they had tried and held out, I said they had been able to judge better than we who were not there at the signing of the Treaty. But she went back to "the 3rd Dail was to have met on the Saturday, and on the Tuesday the Four Courts were fired on", and I was out of my depth, but could only think we might all work together, like body and soul (for she claimed the idealism for the Republicans) to make our country a part of the Kingdom of Heaven. And we parted kindly.

TUESDAY, 14 NOVEMBER, COOLE. Yesterday I went again to the Hospital and saw Dr. O'Malley. He said the bone was broken—"a fracture"; they found this under the X-rays. It is joining well he says; wouldn't give any date for Raftery's release, but when I said "I suppose we shan't see him till the New Year" said "Oh, he'll be out before that". So I comforted Raftery with this and told him that as he is a master-mason, O'Malley is a master-surgeon, and the ignorant are ready to criticize both. He said he would like some books, so today I've sent him some magazines and a Guide Book to the West with many pictures of buildings, and some little Irish patriotic poetry books and *Freckles*[34] and my own *Hugh Lane*. When I came home to Coole, I found a letter from M. saying the children all want to come back for Christmas, and she wants "an exact statement of the situation"—which is such a moving bog! But I am very happy that the darlings want to come. I found also a nice review of *The Image* volume in *Times Literary Supplement* beginning "There are four plays in this small volume and every page of every one of them is a delight".[35] That outweighs the *Morning Post* that used to be so kind to my plays, heading its review "Too much Ireland" and saying "we are heartily tired of her Ladyship"—written it may be by a Diehard.

Today much letter writing, and Madden and his man were here to prune the fruit trees, and I drove to the head of the boreen and went to see Mrs. Raftery and tell her of her husband. And the Piper here this evening, had slept last night at Gurteenbuie beyond Kilbecanty and was nearly lost, with his bad sight, in the field that has been a thoroughfare since the road was blocked; and didn't much like his hosts last night "a queer race, they are never going to pay rates any more, so I tied up my garters as the song says, in the morning and left them there". Carson seems by his letter to have "tied up his garters" as far as the pictures are concerned. He writes, 11 November 1922. "Thank you for your letter. I imagine it will be very difficult to do anything until the Government has become more settled in the South of Ireland. Perhaps then after all this long wait your efforts will be rewarded with success".

15 NOVEMBER. Writing letters, and a little bit to add to the A.E. letters; and out in the garden with N. He complains of Free State men coming and helping themselves in his garden and "giving impudence" when he complained, even in their Officer's presence. They accused him as an excuse of having hidden Republicans in his greenhouses they would otherwise have taken. I hope they are not going to turn into Free*booters*.

18 NOVEMBER. Micho and young C. have been let out from gaol, we suppose on bail, and came back last evening from Galway with members of their families and "shouting as if they had gained a victory over the English".

Such a nice letter from poor Raftery in Hospital about Hugh's *Life*.

19 NOVEMBER, SUNDAY. On Friday the B.'s said the road had been cleared by Free Staters. But today he said it had been blocked again, worse than before, and that it would take them an hour to get back from church. The news in yesterday's paper "Four men executed" because of possession of revolvers seems too sudden violence, too extreme a penalty, unless there is more explanation than has been given.[36]

Yesterday a telegram saying Mr. Harris, our Abbey Auditor, had died after a short illness. I grieve for him, so kind. And I can't think how the money business of the Theatre can be carried on without him.

Reynolds sent a cutting giving Sir H. Duke's ruling in some will case making pencilled alterations written by the testator and signed, but without witness, legal. Yet he did nothing when Chief Secretary to help us, in spite of promises.

Cosgrave having said in the Dail he will take the matter of the pictures up with the Government I have written yesterday to T. P. O'Connor and Lord Peel, today to Ramsay MacDonald and Asquith sending testimony up to date, and M. Collins' letter, and asking their help.

Reading this morning of the speeches on the Speaker's election (Whitman) brings to mind a visit to Sandy long ago when there was a discussion as to who would be the next Speaker, and W, pointing to Arthur Peel said "That is the man". And next day going back to London Knowles who was with us said he had been very much struck with the idea, he had not thought of Peel before; and W. said he had not said it lightly, he had always thought he would best fill the place. And so it happened not long after.

Stephenson came at my asking from Gort yesterday and we settled the old newspaper debt I could never get from him. We agreed on four years and he made it up to £9.17.1. and I paid it from his debt to me for fruit, a great relief. I had often asked for it, and he said he hadn't made up the account, and I think from what he said yesterday that he had been unwilling to do so through gratitude because of my having gone to the Provost-Marshal to get him out of gaol after the Rising, on the ground of ill health and general good character.

DUBLIN, MONDAY, 27 NOVEMBER. The Bagots say their road is blocked worse than before. I am told S. and Fahy have been taken in a field at Beagh. The F.S. men went without motors, surrounded the field and took them. F. had a revolver but S. none.

Because of the death of Mr. Harris and the Theatre wanting me I came to Dublin on Saturday. At Gort station I opened the paper and saw that Erskine Childers had been executed.[37] A shock, for I had but seen him in his home life, with Molly and the boys. I sent her a telegram of love and sympathy from Athenry.

I found all well at the Abbey, it had been a good week until the heavy firing on the Quays on Thursday night had frightened the audience, so that many would not leave the Theatre until towards midnight when a F.S. soldier came in and told them all was safe. So on Friday there had been a very poor audience, and on the Saturday no stalls practically, but a good and enthusiastic pit, for Shields was splendid in *Dempsey*. I had had a telegram from Dolan saying they couldn't get a Broadbent for *John Bull* and asking if they might put on *Arms and the Man*, and I wired to G.B.S. asking for leave.

Yesterday I went to church at St. Anne's; a large congregation, good music, twenty-two choir boys. The sermon on Esther—was she right in telling of the conspiracy; there was a correspondence lately in *The Times* headed "Should a doctor tell"?. "In the last twelve months a great Church in this country had kept silence when it ought to have denounced crime. Our own Church was not quite without blame, but not in the same degree". Then an appreciation of the Divinity: "His resources are infinite; his adaptability is marvellous . . . He is as well adapted to the twentieth century as to the first.!!".

I went to Kilteragh for the rest of the day, lunched with G. Heard. A nice afternoon, looking out dates and facts in the library (for the Memoir) the National Library being closed because of the state of the city. McGreevy came to tea and Mr. N. to dinner. We talked much of poor Erskine Childers. I had thought of asking the boys to Coole for the Christmas weeks. But N. said they had last week in some house spoken of their father's execution as certain "but it doesn't matter—the Republic has won it will be given in to at once" so they have "put away childish things". Poor boys. Norman is afraid their mother will bring them up in hatred. He had been working to save Childers and Molly had sent him a message that they did not wish for anything to be done by friends, they would not accept it. A.E. had done what he could, writing to Cosgrave and others, N. had known him very well. G.H. asked when he had last seen him, and he said about three weeks ago, had not indeed seen him but had recognised his voice calling out his name from a dark corner of the street. G.H. said he was just a mathematical proposition, plus bravery. They think he wanted to be taken, felt there was no more to be done. N. hears he came out on the landing when the F.S. men were coming up the stairs and lifted his revolver to fire at them, but a servant in the house flung herself across him and he could not fire nor could the others. He thinks the execution was illegal and unwise. Yet when they discussed what could have been done they said the prisons are so full and so often broken from they must have seen the difficulty of keeping him there; and there is no law that can enforce banishment. N. is afraid hatred will grow, sees no hope. Heard says A.E. believes we grow like what we hate. Yet they say the Government are themselves threatened men, under sentence, have their food brought to them in their offices. N. says De Valera has shown he has no statesmanship at all. He fears a small secret society will now take rule. Someone has heard that it was the army that insisted on the execution, Childers being the brain of the Republican army. One hears that Mulcahy, Fitzgerald, and another were against the execution, Duggan and two others for it. N. says De Valera is in Dublin, was all but taken at Harrington Road and also at the Suffolk Street Office the other day when he hadn't time to put on his coat, left it behind him, and hears he would not now avoid arrest, has been seen walking about. N. said Childers had seen A.E. three weeks ago, had denied having destroyed the viaduct, but said he had consented to the cable being cut "to test feeling in America". They are also afraid there will be trouble over the boundaries question, Bonar Law being pledged to Ulster and that may lead to a break with England after all.

I looked through Repington's first volume of Memoirs[38] in the afternoon very like its own parodies. And I noted there in 1916 at one of his fashionable gatherings "Lord D'Abernon said that a new collection of Foreign art was about to be started to complete the Tate collection. We all agreed upon the desirability of cheering up and lighting up London, having restaurant cars on trains and emulating the French". Our poor pictures!

Today business; to Keller about poor Harris's death, and to the Abbey where D. didn't arrive till 12 o'c—with so little time to get up *Arms and the Man*! And to Miss Renwick who will keep on our business for the present, and then back to Theatre to meet Millington . . . He is fairly cheerful so many printing orders are coming to the Brunswick Press.

TUESDAY, 28th [NOVEMBER]. Last night I felt that I must make some attempt for the release of M. McSwiney, said to be dying in her hunger strike.[39] I thought it possible that if I and other women who have been supporting the Treaty and the Government went on a deputation begging for the saving of her life and her sister's it might help the Government to do what they must themselves wish for, and release them. I got up with this determination this morning, but feeling it a heavy effort to make, yet thought out a plan. Then coming down I got *The Irish Times* and saw she had already been released, and she and her sister are in the care of friends and hospital—thank God!

Yesterday I looked in at Jack Yeats—but had no real talk with him. George Y. came in the evening. All I speak to blame the Government for the execution of the four young men, and the carelessness of the manner of announcement to their friends. She says Childers' last letter to his wife was censored before it was given to her. It is Z. she says who is the bitter one; Cosgrave and Mulcahy are more generous.

COOLE, 2 DECEMBER. Saturday. Home again yesterday. On Tuesday I saw Reynolds at the Gallery. He asked me to find out what President Cosgrave is going to do about the Lane pictures. I went to the Government Offices in Merrion Street and was shown into a small room where people on business were waiting. There were slips of paper on which we write our name, nature of business, who you want to see, and a note giving particulars of what you want to say. I filled one and sent it up, and in a few minutes a messenger brought me upstairs to Mr. Baker, Cosgrave's secretary. I said I had been writing to various people of influence asking for their help in the matter, Asquith etc; and that I wanted particulars as to when it was likely to come up in the Cabinet or in the House of Commons. He said he had taken my memo to the President who was at a Conference in another room, and who told him to assure me he had not forgotten the matter, had kept it in mind and that there would be no difficulty about getting the pictures back, the only difficulty was where to put them. I said I was afraid he underrated the difficulties, and that this would be a good moment to press the claim, Lord Curzon our chief opponent being away at Lausanne. I told him something of the violence of the opposition, and he took notes to show Cosgrave. I went away feeling something must be done at this side to show we are in earnest. And so in the evening I went to *The Irish Times* Office to ask what time Healy would be there, as I thought to come over from the Theatre. They said he was now in the Office but engaged and would not be free for some time. However I sent up my name and he saw me at once. He was doubtful, said he hadn't much space. I had asked him for a leading article. Then he said if I would write points for it and send them on to him he would manage to say something before the end of the week, as I pressed its urgency. Then on to the Theatre to see *Paul Twyning* very amusing and splendidly acted, but a very small audience, very appreciative.[40]

BOOK TWENTY-ONE

2 DECEMBER, 1922. (*continued*) Strange to see a long queue, more than could get in—waiting close by the Corinthian to see a Charlie Chaplin film, and they could not laugh more delightedly there than our audience did at Barry Fitzgerald.

I telephoned to Stephen Gwynn asking if I could see him next day, hoping he might put something about the pictures in his Sunday letter to *The Observer*.

Next morning, Wednesday I began writing my "points" for Healy. But then I thought of writing a letter as well to the *Irish Times*, for him to print and found his article on. So I wrote it and went to the Abbey to look if we could find costumes for *Arms and the Man*[1] to save the expense of hiring, but none were to be found.

I had asked Reynolds to come and see me, and gave him my letter to be typed at the City Hall, as it is Corporation business. I did a little Christmas shopping for the children and the house, and then went to the hotel to meet Stephen Gwynn at 6.30. He was rather depressing, said this was a bad time to raise the matter, that Ireland is in disgrace, all the Die Hards would oppose our getting the pictures, and agreed with Cosgrave that we have nowhere to put them. I said we had the National Gallery to house them if necessary for a while. Gwynn said anyhow he couldn't put more than a few words in his article. Then I gave him the cutting with Sir Henry Duke's ruling the other day, allowing an alteration pencilled in the margin and signed without a witness to stand, because it was evidently the intention of the testator. This interested him very much and he took the cutting. Then, to explain something I was saying, I gave him my letter to the *Irish Times* to read, and he became quite keen, said "it is very good copy, Healy will certainly print it. That letter of Freeman Smith's never published before makes it very important. I will write about it. Tell Healy that if he doesn't print it till Saturday I would like to see on Friday what he is going to say that I may quote it". So I wrote this to Healy, and left my packet very cheerfully at the office. And next morning, Thursday, my letter was in the paper and a splendid leading article; so I left

Dublin feeling something had been done. And wondering, as usual, if this has been the last letter I shall have had to write!

(April 25, 1928. And this I still wonder now and again for that letter writing never comes to an end!)

Dublin looked cheerful, many people shopping, and, the first time these two years, I did not see a single lorry or car with soldiers dashing about, very few soldiers at all, although on Sunday evening at Harcourt station as we arrived there from Kilteragh passengers were searched, or rather their pockets felt, McGreevy's among them though Norman who was carrying a brown paper parcel that might have held bombs was let pass.

G. Yeats had heard at Gogarty's the Government could no longer refuse to release Miss McSwiney when a resolution asking for it was sent from Cork by Michael Collins' sisters and Mrs. Mulcahy. And that a big offensive is threatened for the 6th December (ratifying of the Treaty). Also that they will not state the crimes of the four men executed, because then revolvers would be carried as before by those who have no criminal charge against them. Two of those executed were criminal looters, one had been a spy in the Government Offices and had betrayed the planned journey, the road to be taken by Michael Collins; the fourth was the man who had shot (when robbing a public house) Cosgrave's uncle dead. She hears also that St. Helena has actually been borrowed for the prisoners. Little Anne Yeats welcomed me. She had shouted the other day "Sacred Heart! The cat's eating the canary!" and the maids rushed in just in time to save it from the cat's mouth. But Anne is especially indignant because she says the cat had already had its tea.

They say Tim Healy has been invited to be Governor General,[2] and that it is no great compliment because "the first Governor General is sure to be shot"!

A night in Galway. It is quiet and Raftery going on well, the doctor says he will be working by the new year. Michael R. was at the station, is staying in Galway to be qualified for the Civic Guard! Now that M. is in trouble "he has his companion lost", and Gort is dull.

Raftery asked me to take him to a lawyer's office yesterday and we went to see young Kelly. And he asked me to write a letter about his purchase of the field.

3 DECEMBER. SUNDAY. Such a good night's sleep, and I awoke with the thought "whatever the Church's faults, there is no such manifestation of the Divine as Christ—so intimate in his companionship with those around him that we can understand his life, his teaching, can try to live by it; so perfect an example

yet so easy to understand."

I had read last night that sentence in Jacob Boehme "seeing that human life is an outflowing of the Divine Power, Understanding and Skill, the same ought to continue in it's Original, or else it loseth the Divine Knowledge, Power and Skill,"[3] and this stayed with me, so that in Church when the organ was played I thought that music is a shadow of the Divine harmony, and some who hear it may understand or be moved by it but a very little, and others better endued by nature or effort may absorb its entire beauty and force, and so it may be with us, born with or catching but a morsel of that "Power, Understanding and Skill" that is about us.

Last Sunday when I was away young H. and another lad had come to the door and knocked and Marian had come down. H. told her they were taking the car to Shanaglish for a gathering in memory of the Loughnane boys, killed by the Black and Tans. She remonstrated, but H. said I would have no objection. And when John told me of it as we came from the station I had said I did not mind as it was to honour the memory of those poor lads. I had given flowers to girls who wanted to make a wreath for them last year, and I daresay this was known.

In Erskine Childers' "statement" written in prison and now published he says . . . "we hold that a nation has no right to surrender its established independence, and that even a minority has a right to resist that surrender in arms".[4] I am glad to know definitely how he justified his work, yet I think his reasoning breaks down with the word "established". Even America was never persuaded by De Valera to recognise that, and the claim seems as unreal as to push on the hands to 12 o'c and call out that now the midday sun is shining.

Raftery *walked* here this evening from his house. He had got leave to come back with his wife for Sunday, but has to go back tomorrow. He was afraid his youngest child would have forgotten him, but she held out her hands to him when he went in at the door and he is very happy.

Among my letters here is one from Dorothy Carleton saying "Wilfrid's Prison Bible has been left especially to you".

Also one from Ramsay MacDonald saying he will help about the Lane pictures when he can.

6 DECEMBER. This afternoon's post brought the paper with heading "Birth of the Free State"—a birth so welcome after all the "Deaths" in headlines. And after some anxiety about Richard's entrance exam to Harrow Margaret writes that he passed fifth out of thirty-three, and will go into the Shell. Such a

relief that is over—the darling child! A good post.

L. Robinson writes "Sir Horace has taken the Childers business very much to heart; he got him out of the Navy to join the Secretariat of the Convention and they were great friends till Childers got extreme".

7 DECEMBER. Names of members of the Senate appointed by Government appointed, Yeats among them. Very glad.

These two days there are rumours of a fight at Clifden, very little about it in the papers, but Mrs. Mitchell hears eight Free Staters have been brought in dead, and Dr. O'Malley's brother wounded.

9 DECEMBER. Yesterday, a Holy Day, the Immaculate Conception, and I had more time for work at my MSS and so today I have finished the correction of the typed copies, two of them—a copy still in Harris's office for safe keeping. A good deal still to do, little bits to put in and some of the letters in Paul's bundle to type. Yet I feel that the hardest of the work has been done. 262,000 words according to typist's bill, written, typed by myself, and the new typing corrected; all easy for the executors should I die today!

EVENING. Mike told me he had found Tom O'Loughlin setting rabbit traps on the land Malachi Quinn has seized. He said Malachi had "told him to do so."

The papers bring news of Rory O'Connor and Mellows' execution "as reprisals".[5] That seems the worst step yet, the deliberate approval of reprisal. And a train set on fire near the Broadstone, passengers in it. I hardly think the children can come home.

11 DECEMBER. This morning I was told that trees had been cut and thrown across the road to block it between L. Dooley's and J. Diveney's gates. This had been done at 9 o'c last night. I wondered the Free Staters had not come. "Who would tell them? Whoever would tell them would be shot". So, there being a market at Ardrahan, carts and cars have been coming round by our avenues. Someone in a motor, coming to the house to ask which turn to take, gave me the *Independent* with account of Deputies' houses in Dublin being burned; children rescued from two, but one in hospital with burns.[6] It makes one sick at heart.

John has come from looking at horses. I want one before the children's return! At Ardrahan, with a mare that was given "a very good pedigree," "reared up beside the train and would live in a motor, would put her nose in it; and wouldn't have any plunder, any dash or any kick". Of others one he was offered was fidgety, too low, swinging the head up and down, and besides a

Rahasane man, her owner, "had too much praises for her, saying there was nothing was the equal of his breed. And I wouldn't like a huckster's horse, I like a farmer that has bred his own".

14 DECEMBER. Yesterday a letter from Putnams, saying *Three Wonder Plays* American edition out, and they are sending six copies. Also one from T. P. O'Connor about the pictures "I will do everything I possibly can in the matter". And a box from J.Q. New York with 23 fine apples for the children, a miraculous delivery as one side of the box was out! Quite a good post.

Today John renews his praises of "Fanny" as her owner who called yesterday had named her—"for honesty and quietness and keeping the middle of the road, and not shying or wanting winkers in the stable".

"But as to Hynes the huckster he was leading his horse beside his bicycle and it shied and made a lep and had him dragged off the bicycle into the road. He had too much to say about her, and would not let the reins of her into any man's hand." Mr. B. guessed the price of the mare at £22 though when he saw her at the station he said "Is there any go at all in her?"

16 DECEMBER. Yesterday with Madden at the Vine border for the morning. Then the B.s, and worked very hard, until 7.30 at "London Folk Lore". Too tired and didn't get much sleep.

J. thinks the Cooneys and Dooleys have quarrelled as after the Court in Galway, where they each had a solicitor, "each party went out by a different mall". Raftery here today, his arm stiff still but declares he feels well.

19 DECEMBER. Mr. B. showed me some letters about the trees felled and thrown across the road beyond Kilbecanty. He and others having had to drive round them through a field for some time it was becoming a bog, and they ventured to remove some of them. He had a letter with address stamped in black I.R.A. &c name signed, saying he had no right to have meddled. "We have the whole Island to think of and you only of your miserable trees" or some such words, and that if such things were done they would be obliged to "use Dick Mulcahy's methods" against whoever had interfered. He wrote back that he understood from his man C. that one of their number had assented to the removal. The answer was that they would take C.'s word for it and take no further steps. But the remaining trees have not been taken away.

I have paid £20 for Fanny. Dr. Foley writes "some animals were brought in since Monday. But none like the mare you got. One after leaving here ran away with her owner a 'nice honest person' I know for some time, and contradicted his testimonial".

"The schemer! I wouldn't begrudge it to him" says John.

I have been working very hard to get through MS corrections expecting the darlings tomorrow or next day; and this morning at 11.30 a telegram came that they had left London last night! There was just time to send for them—but they weren't there. But I hope to see them tonight.

A nice letter from A.E. "I have just received the *Wonder Plays*[7] and I promise myself delight in reading them . . . It was kind of you to suggest your imagination owes anything to mine" (in notes to *The Jester*)[8]. "But nobody would ever think you hadn't enough imagination to supply not only your own needs as a dramatist but a whole school. I remember what Goethe said in the conversations with Eckerman about ideas. They belong to those who use them and make them their own. I think I have strict ideas about honesty in money matters and have fairly honourable ideas about meum and teum but when it comes to the realm of ideas I am a convinced communist and deny rights of private property. We all exist in a mind which is the common mind of humanity and the power of using an idea is the right to it. Whether ideas well up within or I get them from without I know in the first case as surely as in the last they are communal world property I use. Still it is pleasant and flatters the outside man to be told that his ideas have had some influence though he is not entitled strictly to flatter himself about anything. Willie I think likes the Senate and finds good and reasonable people there. I refused nomination because I have very little spare time and it was a choice for me between literature and politics and I decided I could do better work with my pen than on Senate Committees. If I was more independent financially I would consider it a duty to go on and it would be a relief from writing as it is with Willie. But I would lose my soul if I went on writing about politics and economics in the paper I edit and then considered the same things as a Senator. I had a letter from dear old Standish O'Grady this morning. He is well but frail and old, living near his son Carew in Worthing, Sussex. He I think had finer and loftier things in his nature than any of us but he could never get them out rightly and he exists in splendid passages, an inspiration for a few when he should have been read by everybody. I have hopes next year will be more peaceful than this which is ending. James Douglas[9] is trying to bring about a settlement. If anybody could do this he could. He has the quickest mind I know in Irish politics, is most candid, kindly, unselfish and fearless and his election as Senator and as Vice Chairman I take as a good sign. It was Douglas was largely responsible for the drafting of the Constitution. The method of choosing the Senate was his idea, also the peculiar constitution of the minority. I am trying to write a romance of an original kind about the future in Ireland and the appearance of avatars, and what they did to bring the country into harmony with the god world.[10] I wrote the first page yesterday I wonder will I be able to carry out my ideas".

St. Stephen's Day, Tuesday. The darling children arrived this evening last week, well and bright, happy and simple as ever. M. came on Saturday, all very happy days, and yesterday we were all at Church, and had the Christmas tree very pleasantly though with only the Johnson children and their parents, and Rita and Georgie Daly, and all has gone well.

The only annoyance was yesterday afternoon, just as I was getting things ready for the tree, a deputation called; H., N., and a newcomer N. lately come to Burke's old cottage. They, or rather H., the only speaker, asked if they might give a dance in our barn (I had had a hint of this request coming). I said I was very sorry they had not asked for something I could give; that this was impossible as our hay is in the barn. H. said that didn't matter "We took a look at it as we came and there is plenty of room for us"! I said there was the danger of burning and I could not give leave. He said they would guarantee it to be kept safe, and went on to say they wanted to give the dance towards paying a Gaelic teacher they have had, so that it is for the Gaelic League. I said I had brought the first Gaelic teachers here long ago and was in sympathy with the League, and that though giving the barn was impossible, if they could get another place for the dance I would give £2 towards the fund. They said they had no other place, that they were getting Kiltartan school for one dance, but Father Cassidy would not give it a second time. That they were so sure I would not refuse that they had put it on the posters that it would be here. I said it was impossible, that even if I had no other reason I had not power. He said they would ask "the young lady". I said No, I would not have the unpleasantness of a refusal put on her; that she could but say as I did that it was impossible. He went on for a long time, saying his committee would "think bad" of my having refused. I asked who the committee were. He would give no names, said they were "young lads". I repeated my offer of £2, said that was all that could be done, and they went away, he muttering a sort of threat that another deputation would come. I was much worried, consulted Mr. J. He says H. and N. are both "bad lads" and at no good wanting to come here; that I had made a very fair, indeed a liberal offer, and that H. has no following and is not likely to come back. Yet I am sorry they came.

Finnegan here today says he heard three weeks ago and believes that De Valera was taken, in a priest's clothes, and is in the hands of the Government. I think they are more likely to let him stay out, and I have never lost hope he may come to a better mind—believing that like Cromwell he "was once in a state of Grace".

30 DECEMBER. Yesterday's paper had such a fine and beautiful letter from A.E. to the Republicans.[11] It gives me hope. There must be some who will listen or he would not have been able to write it.

And I was pleased because L.R. had written "A.E. is delighted with your new volume of plays,[12] especially the one with the little Princes" (*the Dragon*)—my own favourite at present, perhaps because it hasn't yet been acted.[13] The chicks were out "building a house in the wood" and I went out and met them there, very merry, driving Tommy.

In the evening as I was reading to them after tea we were all in the breakfast room. There was a sudden loud knock at the door and it startled us. Then Marian came to say she had asked who was there and the answer was, the same members of the Committee who had come on Christmas Day.

I went out, rather shaking, fearing a fresh effort to get the barn or perhaps a seizure of it. H. began "We are come again. We know that if you had power to do it would have granted our request". I interrupted "No, you must not think that. It is a mistake. I ought to have said it before. It is that I am a woman who has lost her husband and her son. It is not fitting there should be merriment and dancing going on here, it would not be respect to their memory. I could not have it". H. said at once "Why didn't you say that before—we would never have troubled you at all or said another word. We thought it was a made up thing, we didn't understand. We won't trouble you any more". Then I asked what I could do for them, and they said "just what you offered, to write to Father Cassidy for leave to use the schoolhouse and to give us what you said". I promised to do so. Then they said "the Committee thought" the young lady ought to give something, but I said I didn't know about that, but if she didn't I would give something on her behalf. So they said Goodbye, promising they would do anything they ever can for me. I have sent £3 today, and the letter to Father Cassidy, and hope all may go well.

John Quinn's apples for the children, 191 have arrived today.[14] Margaret and the children looking in old letter boxes for stamps, are finding treasures. When I got a permit for Richard to carry a gun the other day it was given without delay by "Adjutant H. (our late sub-agent)". And when John asked for an ammunition permit as well he said it wasn't needed "who is there to meddle with ye only ourselves"?

1 JANUARY, 1923. It was a pleasant ending to the old year, the children happy and merry. Mrs. Scovell came up (as she had done the night before to see them dancing in their dressing gowns) to hear the hymns on the gramaphone, and among them the Chimes for "the coming year". And Anne had learned a new hymn from the little poetry book I had given her (compiled by Roger Ingham) Bunyan's "Pilgrim"; and M. to whom she had repeated it before said "We call that Grandmama because it is so like her" . . .

"Whoso beset him round
With dismal stories
Do but themselves confound
His strength the more is.
No lion can him fright
He'll with a giant fight
But he will have a right
To be a Pilgrim" . . .[15]

This morning I wrote to A.E. I feel the New Year has begun well. My letter had the suggestion or hope of a new bond or motto for Republicans "Gan molais" "without malice" as in the old poems.

4 JANUARY. "The country's easing off" says Coen the rate collector. Yet peace, an agreed peace, seems far away.

Catherine in a letter to her aunt Ruth says "I am going to tell you a poem. It is called The Clouds.

The Clouds do sail on high
They fly at such a rait
Across the blue sky
And how the stars do twinkle
And how the sun dust shine
But the clouds run along.

Catherine Gregory, I made up this poem by myself.

7 JANUARY. Yesterday Richard's 14th birthday, the third seven years to begin with his entrance at Harrow. A big step from the private school—darling child. He is so merry and childlike and gentle still. Only the Daly's at his birthday party, but I think the children were quite happy. A letter from A.E. He likes the *Wonder Plays* better than anything except *the Image*.

I went to Ballylee, hearing from R.D. that she had been there and found a window open and a strong smell of tobacco from inside, so that she thought there was someone in it. The house has been entered, drawers and cupboards opened and the bed slept in, but I could not see that anything is missing. It may be used by a Republican on the run, and I wrote Yeats this, but did not advise any action that would be looked on as an "unfriendly act", as the burning of Senators' houses has been threatened.

EVENING. This afternoon "H. a younger H., and N. and M. want to see you". I went down. "We want to ask the loan of the boat to go over and hunt rabbits on the island." "Our island?" "Well, doesn't it belong to the Committee that bought the land?" "No, we didn't sell it as far as I know nor Inchy". "Well, we only want a day's sport, we brought the dogs, we'd do no harm." "I don't mind lending you the boat, but that is not admitting any claim to the island." "Oh no, all we want is the day's sport." "I hope all your sports will be as harmless as this, I'm afraid they are not." "Ah, you heard something." "Well I think with all the trouble in Ireland we ought all to do our best to keep good conduct. I pray every day 'Thy will be done, in Coole, in Kiltartan, in Ireland'". So they went to get the boat. But rain came on and I have just been to the barn to look, and it has not been moved, was probably too heavy, or the rain put them off.

8 JANUARY. This afternoon towards 5 o'c I went down to the lake, and saw the boat drawn up, the island party having landed, two of them were there G. and N. They had got about 70 rabbits on the island, half starved, a mercy to kill them; and a badger. I was sorry it had been killed. They thanked me very much for their day's sport, a lovely day, and they had, some of them, never been in a boat. I told them we had a difficulty about cartridges for Richard and they eagerly offered me some but had no 20s. I asked if they could give powder, and they said yes "but it mightn't suit; we make it ourselves". I said "You ought not to tell me that. I may give information of an ammunition dump," but they laughed and said "Oh, we know you of old." When I came back after a while they had gone, had left me a brace of rabbits, and John says are very grateful. They asked me to let them have the boat again tomorrow morning "for a couple of hours" and I gave leave.

13 JANUARY. SATURDAY. The week has passed well I think. The boat was put back after a second day's use, the group calling one evening while we were at dinner and leaving me some gunpowder for Richard. And today I have a letter from P.H. thanking me for my subscription to the Gaelic League in the name of

Kiltartan branch who "wish you happiness Prosperity and moreover a Peaceable New Year". Richard has been happy and has shot a pheasant as well as pigeons, the three chicks very gay all together. A nice talk with Margaret last night.

I had written to Yeats to try and see Tim Healy about the pictures and ask him to take the matter up, and if we could do anything to strengthen his hand. And yesterday Yeats wrote that he had seen him, and he will do it, and while Yeats was there dictated a letter to Lord Beaverbrook to use his influence with Bonar Law and Curzon "who look to him for financial support"; and the Dail and Senate will pass resolutions, and Lord Glenavy talks of an agreed Bill and wants to know if the Trustees would oppose it. And by the same post I had a letter from Lord Peel, willing to help. So today I have written to him, asking him to influence the Trustees privately, and to Yeats with list of Trustees for and against and lukewarm, and to T. P. O'Connor asking him to stir up the Press. (Are these the last letters I shall have to write?) (18 January, 1930. I have been writing to Carson today with his woodcocks—saying our own Government—Cosgrave—is taking the matter up.)

M. has been reading my Memoirs and makes I think a good suggestion of putting the chapters on Athenaeum friends at the end instead of the beginning of the "Twelve Years", and perhaps putting the letters at the end also.

15 JANUARY. A good deal of rabbit hunting in the woods, M. and the children heard it and told Mike and he talked of "a dog caught in a trap" and on further evidence walked the other way, so it is probably M. junior.

The paper tells of Gogarty being kidnapped,[16] and Cosgrave's house burned.[17] And rails were pulled up near Tubber on Saturday night, and there is a rumour of a broken bridge.

16 JANUARY. This morning, awaking, I thought there should be but one battle going on all through the world, that is ourselves, between the good and evil that is in us. I grew drowsy again in thinking of the badge those of us who take up the fight should wear—something common, out of the reach of none; Parnell has the ivy leaf.[18] Perhaps a blade of grass.

Richard and Anne have each shot and brought in a rabbit. Mike says the hunting in the woods yesterday was by boys who heard of a fox in a trap, dragged from some farmer's field being there and wanted it for a man in Gort who had a desire for a fox to stuff.

17 JANUARY. P.H. writes of a demand made by T.D. for money to do up his house, though I who got no penny from the

sale had given his brother £25 then and lately £10.

I asked E. how things are at her home. She says "Bad and it's said they will be worse, and that people will be lucky if there is any train at all left in a little while." I said I supposed they were all Republicans there but she said "a good many are leaving them". They had been told to do such dreadful things that they went to the Archbishop of Tuam.

I read in my passages from Plato: "He (the wise man) will look at the city which is within him . . . in Heaven I replied, there is laid up a pattern of it, methinks, which he who desires may behold, and beholding may take up his abode there. But whether such a one exists, or ever will exist in fact, is no matter; for he will live after the manner of that city having nothing to do with any other". And for the children's reading this morning I chose a part of the first Epistle of St. John.

EVENING. Dr. F. has been here, "beset us round, With dismal stories" has found the lamp from Lady Wallscourt's sitting room and much other loot in the houses of patients around Ardfry. The stones of the house are being carted away, "But nothing has been done to a house as bad as to Roxborough and Castle Hacket." And R. talks of the timber being cut at Lough Cutra, sees a cartload from it every day.

The children went across the lake in the boat. Richard shot a rabbit and they saw hundreds of wild duck.

Foley said an old man at Annie Redington's funeral said he remembered her father; Sir Thomas Redington's funeral, and that there had been 126 carriages; at hers there was only one, Edward Martyn's, and he was not well enough to come himself.

18 JANUARY. Post this morning, as it didn't come yesterday. Nothing very bad in the papers, only some railway breakages. And Lord Peel writes "I now find that the question of the Lane pictures will be coming up shortly for consideration by the Government. I will look out for this and will bear in mind what you say". And I am sent a cutting from the *Homestead*[19], a nice notice of the *Three Wonder Plays* by A.E. especially of the *Jester*. "A wise and delightful book". . . . M. says when she was speaking of the stoppage of trains through rails having been pulled up near Mullingar Anne who was somewhere in the room murmured "I wish all the rails were pulled up and we wouldn't have to go away from Coole".

But a bad evening—and night.

SUNDAY. 21 JANUARY. All well at the end.

We went by motor to Galway yesterday and saw darling Richard off. They had loved their holiday all together. Anne and

Catherine and I came home. Today we hear Gort Bank was raided yesterday. I asked the Archdeacon about it after church. He says it was about midday six armed men walked into the Bank; it was crowded as always on Saturdays with people doing their business. They made Mr. Johnson hold up his hands and took all the money they could find, amount uncertain, ranging from £130 to £900. (When the claim for compensation was made it was for £1400. May 1924). One Free State soldier was on guard. John hears another had just cashed a big cheque and put the money in his pocket. They made him hold up his hands but didn't search him.

I am quite alone in the house, maids and children out. Just now I saw four young men coming towards the door so I opened it. A Cahel, brother of Paddy their spokesman; they want to ferret out rabbits for a coursing match, and I gave leave; was glad it was something I could allow, and we are so overrun with rabbits it will get rid of a few, by a less cruel means probably than trapping.

I have wondered during this last week whether while we cry to God, to the Divinity, to help us, He the Divine, may not be crying to us that it is for us to help his work, and for that our faculties have been given to us. Yet I can see no other way in which I myself can help in the present troubles than by showing good will and the will for peace.

Yeats writes from London that he has gone there about the return of the pictures. The battle may really be won.

EVENING. Marian says there were four arrests last night, Q. of S—, Head, Regan and P.H. I had wondered he was not here today to ask for the boat. A wild bird to be caged, poor boy.

22 JANUARY. Yes, those three have been taken to prison, it is said for the robberies that have been taking place, the £6 from a farmer on the road, at Raheen gate; and robbery from Bourke's house at Cranagh and at Tim's and others, T.H. and a son of R. and of N. were given "a beating for these same robberies." I felt horror at the beatings, feeling there ought to be some trial or evidence, but X. says "There's not one of those that got it this time but deserved it, they had all a hand in the bad work".

But this method also was brought in by the Black and Tans.

Catherine called to me to know when they might begin learning Irish, and we had a first lesson. We had talked of it coming from Galway and they said they would love to learn it.

A telegram from Richard saying they had got safe to London. Madden came to tie up the vines, and I sent Guy's gun by him to Scott Kerr to take to London. Anne shot a rabbit with it before it was sent. We had got on all right through the holidays with this gun, the Free State permit and the extra ammunition from the Irregulars.

23 JANUARY. My thoughts with Richard today the day of his entry into Harrow. And at Padua—five years today since that grave was made.[20]

I took the children to the Convent to learn stepdancing. Sister Enda and Sister Columba teach it—"they didn't learn it here, but before they came to us" the Reverend Mother said. All the infant school learn only in Irish, speak Irish; the elder ones all learn it. Such a difference from that old day when the Reverend Mother wrote to thank the Turkish Ambassador for a donation she thought came from the Sultan because the letter was written in such a strange looking language she thought it must be Turkish (as they always remember the Sultan's charity in the 1847 Famine time). But he denied it, she took the letter to Monsignor Fahey and he burst out laughing and said that strange language was Irish! One of the older nuns there today said "It was you, Lady Gregory, were the first to bring Irish to this neighbourhood" and spoke of Miss Borthwick who had given classes at our gate lodge.

These floggings on my mind, I wrote to Yeats in protest. The young men taken away were flogged as well as those left "with a thonged whip". I was not surprised to hear H.'s house at Kilreecle has been destroyed. Hatred must grow—"death answering to death through the generations like clerks answering one another at the Mass".

The reason given to the H.'s father was the robbery from Tim's house, from the farmer at Raheen gate and from Burke of Crannagh, T.H. was very angry because his father told this to neighbours. He wished it to be given out that the Bank robbery was the crime they were suspected of—no crime in Republican eyes.

EVENING, 24 JANUARY. A quiet day working at corrections of the letters to W.S.B. I have been typing. This evening letters from Yeats, and I have been answering them, about the Lane pictures. Yeats wrote "I only learned an hour or two ago from Eddy Marsh that he and Lionel Curtis have been asked by the Cabinet to draw up a report on them. The report is to be sent to the Duke of Devonshire". The other letter (written before this) says "I have not yet found out if an agreed Bill is possible, but I have learned that our opponents rely now 'upon the sentiment of lawyers against Acts of Parliament changing the law in some special case'".

27 JANUARY. And today he writes from Dublin that he was "advised in London to let the matter drop until the Irish war is over". Rather a heartbreak . . . and "if we drop it now we must drop it for some months".

About my protest against the floggings here he says "I laid the facts before the highest authority and notes were taken, but these words were used 'There are men on both sides who are mad. War is terrible. Sometimes indefensible acts have yet the effect intended'". A troublesome letter from L.R. also about Abbey business, I spent some time writing to him and to Yeats. A tiring day, though the children are bright and happy—learned Irish words from Mike and rode and went out in the boat where they saw many wild duck. We read about "Sir Gibbie" in the flood. I began putting bits of letters to W.S.B. into the Egyptian chapter.

Inge says "Souls are members of a choir which sing in time and tune so long as they look at their conductor, but go wrong when their attention is directed to other things". And "Love is an activity of the soul desiring the good".

29 JANUARY. Yesterday a coursing match going off peaceably, no drink, and F.S. soldiers and civilians looking on—"Father C. a Judge, holding a red flag"—showed a more peaceful spirit. And Brady and another came to the church door to ask me to get some "properties" from the Abbey for a performance of the *Eloquent Dempsey* they are getting up. I wrote my letter to Yeats about the pictures, urging no delay and the resolutions for their return in Senate and Dail. I feel we can't go backward. I had worked so hard to get the effort made now, in the first months of the comparative independence of Ireland. I wrote again today and telegraphed—perhaps too much worried about it and my head aches. But my first Harrow letter from Richard came, a cheery one.

Marian says the account she has heard of the floggings—no doubt it has grown—is that they were lashed with "the cat"—a whip made of steel as used to be used. And that their shrieks could be heard in Gort. Quinn of Shragh has been released.

31 JANUARY. The month ends gloomily, for today's paper tells of the burning of Palmerstown[21] and the blowing up of Kilteragh,[22] where I had enjoyed such pleasant days; and the kidnapping of Mr. Bagwell[23] and what I think very bad, the Government proclamation that if he is not released in forty eight hours they will execute several of the prisoners in their hands. And it seems likely that if they do this Bagwell will himself be put to death.

Peaceful here, for Madden came to plant young apple and

plum trees and the children have just been giving a performance of their reel, and do it splendidly and joyously with the new record (Miss McCleod's reel). I began rewriting the first chapter of the Memoir, more simply, as for them.

A letter from Yeats too—more delays about the pictures . . . "Must I indeed learn to chant the cold dirges of the baffled and sullen hymns of defeat"?

2 FEBRUARY. I read *The Passing of the Third Floor Back* to try and get rid of vexation. And yesterday brought a rather better letter from Yeats, though he still holds back from a Senate resolution. But I have written him that I think it more needed than ever, if the Cabinet are going to appoint a Commission and take evidence, for I don't believe the Trustees, Curzon especially would like being examined, and they could withdraw their opposition with grace from a demand of the Irish Parliament. I have written to Reynolds also, suggesting that the Corporation whose property the pictures will be, should make application for this to the Dail and Senate.

Free State soldiers yesterday made a great clearance of cattle—seven goats—put on M.'s land and other land about Gort "that the owners hadn't been able to put a beast of their own on these two years". A beginning of law and order.

3 FEBRUARY. The children, out in the wood, near the apple garden, saw M.D. and a friend hunting with dogs. His trial long delayed, and suspicions arising "because why was Q. let out of gaol while H. and H. were kept in? Isn't his mother a cousin of one of the officers in Gort?" Mr. Bagwell's release or escape such a relief.

5 FEBRUARY. Yesterday, Sunday, I heard that M.D. and C. had been arrested and taken to Galway on Saturday, not long after they had been seen rabbit hunting in the wood. It isn't known if their trial is coming on, or their time up. Raftery came to see me, his arm much better. He had met M. and C. in Moran's field "on Friday with a bagful of rabbits and a spade." The children picked a bunch of primroses in the wood.

The meeting of the old I.R.A. men in Dublin today to try and arrange a peace kept me praying all day![24]

Today troublesome theatre letters, L.R. wanting to give contracts to more actors while we are losing money. Then worked at Memoirs and planted some silvers in Shanwalla. M. writes to Anne a pleasant account of Richard, quite happy at Harrow. Such a comfort!

7 FEBRUARY. R.D. here, says the anger against the Government is very strong about the executions and will probably turn

the elections against them. The whips used in the floggings here were not steel but whalebone taken from the Kennels, what are used on hounds. She thinks they were used with authority and that there is much feeling against it. (Margaret read in the English papers that the whips were made of steel.)

F. writes from Dublin: "the seizures at Gort have had a good effect, and the trespassers have taken off their cattle &c. We nearly every night have apparently a pitched battle near us here but nobody seems to be hurt and nobody knows what they are firing at". And L.R. writes from Kilteragh "I am all alone at the Lodge, it is rather dreary with the shadow of the ruin over it. Just as I wrote this came an explosion and a great outburst of rifle fire, God forgive us all." But I won't lose heart. And yesterday was rather good, for the papers (and rumour before them) gave signs of peace,[25] the 600 prisoners in Limerick gaol wanting to send an embassy to arrange it,[26] and Liam Deasy[27] calling for it, though only after sentence of death. Also the *Manchester Guardian* writes asking me for an article and offering £20; and C. E. Lawrence writes thinking he may put me in the way of selling books, and this would help me on. And I went to the Convent to see the children's last dancing lesson, very satisfactory; they do the reel perfectly and the nine steps of the jig and will carry that accomplishment at least back to England. We had tea with the Reverend Mother, all so friendly and kind.

14 FEBRUARY. All well to the last, Just going to Galway to-morrow to see the chicks off from Kingstown. A little anxious about railways, Liam Lynch[28] having called for a continuance of violence.

BOOK TWENTY-TWO

17 FEBRUARY, 1923. DUBLIN. A tiring journey yesterday, through tickets not being given—refused through—"You can't know what might happen before the end of a journey". So I had to take them at intervals, Galway to Broadstone, then to Westland Row, then to Kingstown Pier, then for Chicks and Ellen to Euston. The darlings very good and cheerful all through, and in the hour's wait at Broadstone I read them *Limberlost*[1] and they danced their jig on the oilcloth of the waitingroom. I got to the Hotel (Russell) at 10 o'c, after a walk from Kingstown Pier to the station, a walk from Westland Row to Dawson St., a long wait for a tram; very tired today.

L.R. came in with no sort of good news about peace or settlement. And Yeats is still in London "dining out" R. says and "sending for more dress shirts". But we had a satisfactory talk about the Abbey, I said that although I had agreed to his and Yeats' proposal of asking for a grant from Government for the theatre because they were two against me, I do not think it worth losing our independence for £1,300 a year (we who used to turn over £7000 or £8000!). That I very much prefer my old idea and intention of giving the whole theatre over as a gift to the Nation whenever we had a Home Rule Government. That we want a new impulse in it, new energy; and that now Harris is gone who used to keep me up in finance knowledge, I don't feel that any one of us is capable of dealing with that side.

He said he had been talking to Johnson,[2] the Labour Member, about the grant and had found him very sympathetic and encouraging. I said that encouraged me. That we must if we went on have a business man or men among the directors and that it would be much better to give it over altogether and if Johnson will make a people's theatre of it, that is what I always wanted and would be glad to see done. To my surprise Robinson quite agreed with me, and will ask Johnson to see me.

18 FEBRUARY. Yesterday morning I met Johnson in the Abbey Office. We had a long talk, Robinson there also. I liked Johnson, quiet and without affectations and with luminous grey eyes. He is very sympathetic to the Abbey. I asked for criticisms

or suggestions he may have heard, and he said there is a feeling there is too much repetition of old work. Also he said (this I think of himself) that more translations of foreign work would be good. He was interested when I told him of our wish and old promise to hand over the Abbey as a gift to the nation. However he doesn't think the Government could take it just now, perhaps after the elections. I told him we must put a business man in as Director at once, and he said it would be a good thing to have him chosen by the Government, and I said I would see McNeill about it. He believes there will be an enormous Free State majority at the elections. I said I was not sure of it at all, because though the farmers, heads of houses, all will vote for it, there is a likelihood of the farmer's half dozen sons, and especially his daughters, voting for the republic. However he seems confident. He is not for a republic himself, because he thinks the North less likely to come into one than into the present State, yet agreed with me that all the Colonies are so rapidly becoming republics that the road will be easier. I said Tim Healy's appointment as Governor-General makes it likely that native statesmen rather than imported peers will be called for in the future, and he said that is certain.

At 5 o'c I went by appointment to the Government Buildings to see the Minister of Education, Eoin McNeill.[3] I had to wait some time, there was a Cabinet meeting going on. And then he came for me himself and took me by stairs and a long passage to his office. I reminded him of his old kindness to me in giving me bits of the *Duanaire Finn*[4] for my *Gods and Fighting Men*, and he laments that the second part of it, even finer than the first, is still untranslated. He himself is hard at work, out of office hours, at a compilation and translation of the old Irish laws. (I was told he had said he is sure to be shot, and that is the best work he can leave done.)

As to the Abbey he is anxious we should have the subsidy, it is to come on in the next Budget debate. He is asking for it as an aid to an educational work, our teaching of acting and dramatic writing. He is by no means sure we shall get it, but thinks even a discussion on the Abbey will do it good, get more interest aroused in it. I told him of our desire to give it over. He was rather startled, said he didn't want to manage a theatre and was sure the Government didn't, anyhow for some time to come. I told him of the necessity of a business Director, and he thought it wise it should be someone acceptable to the Government, but not appointed by them. He suggested a solicitor called M'Cracken, Lady Arnott's solicitor. Then before leaving I said I thought Dail and Senate ought to pass a resolution asking for the return of the Lane pictures. I had spoken to Johnson about this, and he had agreed and said it should be in the form of a resolution urging our Government to press it in England. MacNeill said "We wished for such a resolution and had prepared it, but Mr. Yeats wrote to ask us not to go on with it". (And Yeats won't be here till Wednesday to ask about this.) So I said good bye. MacNeill is hopeful, says the present violence is "a sickness, a disease, it will wear itself out". And he is full of a plan of district schools on the plan of St. Enda, where boys could be educated without taking them away from their own home and countryside.

Robinson told me Yeats' "plan" about the Lane pictures was to get the *Dail* to pronounce the codicil legal. Glenavy was quite interested, thought it "a new point". But Cosgrave turned it down, said if one began that sort of thing it might lead to difficulties. I said it might be effective if the pictures were here in Ireland, but I don't suppose the Free State's writ runs in London. I think it would have about as much effect as The Pope's Bull against a comet—(or was it earthquakes?).

I went to see Tim Gormally in the Hospital, there had just been an operation on his other eye. He was glad of home news. So wet I didn't go to the Abbey in the evening. To bed very tired, a very bad night, worried chiefly about the pictures. And the mail train from Dublin to Galway had been wrecked in the morning.[5] Such a mercy the children are through their journey. Wreckage of the Government Stationery Office was the cause of the Friday night explosion, and there is a good deal of night firing. I met Craoibhin (Douglas Hyde) very glad he wasn't made a Senator. It had never struck me he could have been left out, but he says he had written to Cosgrave begging for a reprieve for Erskine Childers, and that Cosgrave, he thinks, having made up his mind resented it.

MONDAY, 19 FEBRUARY. Yesterday I went to see G. Yeats just come from London. She had been round to see Mrs. Gogarty with some message and had found her crying, having just seen in the papers that Renvyle[6] had been burned down. They had met Gogarty at a party at Lavery's a few evenings ago. A servant coming in had let a glass fall with a crash and every Irish person of the party had jumped, so said Lavery. Yeats is to be back tomorrow. While I was there, about 5 o'c, the armed guard arrived to stay the night. I went on to tea with the Hydes. He is depressed, sees no light, criticizes the Government but when I would not join, saying they are certainly doing their best, he agreed and says Cosgrave keeps them together by a sort of bonhommie. And that things are hard for them, they ought to have shot the officers at Sligo who looked on while the station was burned, but they can't trust the army.[7] In Mayo battles the firing is into the air, neither side wishes to hit anyone on the other. They want to keep both armies going, one side gets pay, the other loots. But in Kerry they want to kill. Hyde hears the Government now want (we agree foolishly) to arrest De Valera. They could easily have done so a fortnight ago, but were waiting to get Stack with him, and now Stack has gone. I reminded him of his telling me that when he first saw the flag of the Republic, green, white and yellow, put up he had said "That will run through the country it will swallow up all other movements". He said "Yes", and that he said at the same time "It will be hard to whistle the dogs off the trail".

Joseph O'Neill[8] who I met in the evening lamented that Craoibhin had come to the University. He has no influence there, there is no enthusiasm and he was so splendid in the country with the people, and would be splendid if he could be given charge of one of the new schools Eoin MacNeill spoke of. I went in the evening with Robinson to A.E.'s, several young men there, among them young Reddin[9] one of the new Justices. I remembered him as a little boy often coming to the Abbey. His house, or his father's for his sake, had been burned down the other day. He had lost among other things the MS of a boy's book about fairyland he had just typed, and also half the MS of a novel. A.E. said the loss of MS was more unforgivable than any other. When the Black and Tans raided Plunkett House they had taken one of the chapters of *The Interpreters*[10]. But I said he ought not to grudge that as it may have done them good, and he said Yes, that thought had comforted him. He has always held that you become like what you hate, and that is what has happened now, it is from hatred of the Black and Tans the Republicans have grown into their methods. "When there is all this hatred flying about I feel it coming at me as I walk alone. I say to myself 'I hate' and try to drive it out". I said "I feel the same, a sort of influence in the air. It is Broadcasting, I am a receiver"; and he agreed. Someone said "You wouldn't like to live in the Republic that would be set up" and he said "I feel like Goethe when he was asked if he would like to go to Heaven and said 'Well if all the people who don't believe in it are to go there I wouldn't mind'." Someone came in then and said there had been an explosion at 7.30 (see in today's papers it was the blowing up of a T.D.'s house, MacCabe's)[11] the children and their grandmother turned out at a moment's notice, the baby taken from its cradle and laid on the pavement close by. Some saw no hope. Reddin thinks things are mending, and I thought the signs are those of the iceberg in warm seas the resistance—or terror—may suddenly topple or fall. A.E. gave plots for plays, one that would suit G.B.S. The Englishman Chavasse coming from Oxford, abandoning his own language for Irish, wearing a kilt (which the Galway people point at as "a sort of English dress") meeting Miss Fox, who had also come from England adopted the Irish language and a fancy Irish costume; and then when they met, each had found the real ideal Gael at last, and they married! He also proposes a play to show the dullness of country life, to begin with fifteen minutes of husband and wife, each trying to say how dull it is, and each speech broken by a yawn. But I say if he put that on and was then called for as author he would confront an audience that had caught the infection.

A nice evening.

I proposed my plan of a republican party "Gan molais", as that could take in all but all sides into itself, a badge, white yellow and green with a little dark spot in the corner to remain there until in the natural course of events, and with peaceful pressure a republic is in being. Russell thought it a good idea, and so did most of the party, but there was no one to start it, A.E. saying he is an anarchist, and K. Reddin who much approved being an official, and J. O'Neill the same. Yet I think the idea better than this deadlock.

20 FEBRUARY. Doran's *Julius Caesar*[12] last night very fine, he as Brutus, all finely spoken. Tragic too the rejoicing over the dead Caesar. One could not but think of Michael Collins.

This morning Frank here. The timber cutting at Roxborough has been stopped by the Civic Guards, and he is hoping to get rents due for over a year.

Yeats back, and a long talk with him. He agrees to having resolutions in Dail and Senate re pictures, and agrees to my ideas about the Abbey; has a plan for peace but not to be spoken of. G.B.S. had said the other day this is what always happens in a great Empire, it is so powerful the nations it encloses lose power, become passive, atrophied. Then when it breaks up they cannot help themselves. Now in Ireland we are not allowed arms, whereas it ought to be held a crime for any man not to carry a revolver. The English in general are very down on Ireland, but the Government people much impressed by our Government, which as Yeats told them, is fighting their battles and doing with 30,000 men what they had believed would have taken 250,000 to do.

Miss O'Farrelly had heard there are to be sixty executions next week, I trust not.

To *Othello* with Yeats. I asked him about Goethe. He says his great quality, that struck Europe, was that he was the first modern with the idea of perfect culture, the perfecting of the individual. That in William Meister one can see that those with but one aim come to grief; it is only the man who aims at one end, a harmony of the being, that should succeed. (And this is what the Roman later letters show, he trained his mind as an athlete his body). But I don't yet get at what Matthew Arnold meant by his "suffering human race" lines.[13]

Today, February 1, [21] I took some books for A.E. to sign. He thinks three months will bring peace. Miss Mitchell says, and he assents, that it is the young women now who keep up the war, firing their revolvers from a pocket. A.E. thinks me right to stay quietly at home.

I asked Yeats last night about the executions. He didn't know anything but said "the Government are in a very stern mood". Today I ran in to say good-bye. Douglas had just been with him and is not without hope. The question is whether to deal with the war party behind De Valera's back or to arrest him and his followers first. They are impossible to deal with by reason. I said I hoped De V. would not be arrested, he is not in favour in the country but if executed (and there is a probability of that) he would take his place at once in the army of Martyrs. Yeats said the Government are afraid the stopping of executions and any overtures would be looked on as weakness; but I said any treaty that is made or essayed may have that accusation brought against it, and he agrees. He thinks if executions go on Senators will have to live in the Government buildings (or the Savile Club!). He will try to get the Dail resolution he stopped brought on, but McNeill is away until next week. At the Gallery Reynolds told me the Government are moving the pictures from the Mansion House to the Museum—more prisoners! A.E. said it is strange how almost all the violent insurgents are half foreign—"halfers" he calls them, Childers, De Valera, Cathal Brugha and so on.

Perrin came in here, says a rifle bullet came through the café window at the Abbey yesterday afternoon, troops pursuing a man who had thrown a bomb in O'Connell Street.

As I drove to the station there was some commotion where Suffolk St. joins Grafton St., a restive horse was being held by two or three men and men were running. My cab horse was restive also and the cabman lashed him on. There were still men running, and crowds about Dame St. "That was rough work" the cabman said when we came to Broadstone, "soldiers were firing". I told the bookstall keeper of it after a little, I had seen him talking to soldiers, and he said there had been an attempt to rob the National Bank in Dame Street. But today's paper says it was an attack on the Revenue offices in Dame St.,[14] a battle, Irregulars shooting from the roofs at the Guard while they were attacked by others in a lorry, and by some who had gone in disguised as business men.

A quiet journey, a carriage to myself all the way, but at Galway nothing to meet me (Flaherty's fault) and I took a car, and broke my umbrella and there was terrific rain.

This evening I am back at Coole. The house looks lonely without the darlings.

At Galway station there were troops going away and some seeing them off, nice looking lads, but some more flushed than by nature, and that is the real pity, the sin, the public houses are open to them.

At Athenry I waited for the Gort train for an hour. A woman from Craughwell lamented the disturbed times but said Craughwell is quiet "though it used to be talked about, the name was worse than anything that happened; they darkened the cloud over it for a time". Irish is not spoken there much now she says, though the two sons of Callinan the poet, old men, are living yet.

Rock and two other men got into my carriage, and Daly coming to the door told them some of the prisoners from the fight near Castle Hacket had been brought through by Athenry and had gone on by train, but about thirty of the seventy had gone by road. A public house had been burned, they said because a bomb had been thrown from it. Rock said "It is stronger they are getting" but another said "The Free State will sweep through the country". The third then said "There is to be an execution tomorrow" and one said "If that is so there will be more killings". Rock said to me he longed for a settlement "whichever side would win".

While I waited I had written some notes for my *Manchester Guardian* article "War in folklore"[15] as I now think of it. In Gort I stopped to ask for Peter Glynn's wife and he said she is "very slack" and takes nothing but arrowroot and a little milk but has taken most of the wine I sent. I asked what else she would like, he said when a little stronger he would like a chicken for broth. He was grateful for the firewood I had sent.

I went on to tell Mrs. Gormally about Tim's eyes. All well here and peaceful I am thankful to say.

Some Boy Scouts, asking for "a thought" for one day in the year, I wrote "Let our life be ruled by law and love. Law the serenity of order, love the joy of self-sacrifice".

24 FEBRUARY. Yesterday I had a nice afternoon, thinning the plantation in Park-na-Laoi. Today I have begun writing "War in Folk Lore" for the *M.G.* There were shots in Gort last night, no one knows why. And a rumour this morning that De Valera and Stack had been taken, but nothing of it in the papers. Bessborough[16] has been burned down. I am sorry as Enid Layard was connected with it, and there were fine things, and I am sure some of her embroideries there.

28 FEBRUARY. Rather bad rheumatism, a good deal of pain, but worked at my Folk Lore article and work outside. Amy arrived this evening, she is going to auction the furniture at Castle Taylor.

Mrs. M.J. came this morning wanting me to "get M. off"! Poor woman I was sorry for her, but she made no apology for him but abused the O'L.s and R. "a strange man that swam across the sea after ten acres of rotten land, and got on, making knick-knacks for the gentry, to cheek *my* son!"

2 MARCH. Amy Shawe Taylor has been here for a couple of days arranging for the auction, meaning to empty the house. We went there yesterday, it is sad to see the broken windows shuttered up, the garden wild. She sorted things to keep and was to finally settle with Joyce today, as to date of auction. But when I saw her this morning she said "I've been thinking, finding this place so comfortable and peaceful that we might keep Castle Taylor open after all, so I'll tell Joyce not to fix a date and I'll bring Michael over at Easter to look about him and see what he thinks". I am glad of this.

I asked about the Black and Tans having shot Castle Taylor woods when they were at large and she says "Yes, and gave a shooting party in May, when the pheasants were hatching!"

BOOK TWENTY-THREE

12 MARCH, 1923. This last week or so has passed quietly, no history. Some hope of peace moves coming to success. I have been a good deal in the woods freeing the little trees in Parc-na-tarav, and find my love for the wood work has come back as strong as ever, I so hope to save all the woods for the children. I have sold the Cuala sets for £135, that will help pay rates and taxes. I have been working very hard at the Memoir, spent all last week on "The Changing Ireland", getting it into better shape, and have begun on "New Threads" which wants enriching. Tedious work; and rheumatic pains especially in right wrist make me awkward and have given me some bad nights. Nice letters from the darlings.

15 MARCH. My birthday. The little ones not here to try and count my seventy-one matches so no cake or celebration. But in the afternoon parcels for a feast from Arabella and a cheque. No English or Dublin post. I had letters to write till lunch time and worked at "The Boer War and the Theatre" till after 4 o'c, and then went to the nutwood and worked with Mike, clearing young trees and cutting ivy. Came in after six, and a telegram came from Hammersmith "Many and happier returns of the day to a much loved and much needed Grandmama". The darlings! That has cheered me up.

18 MARCH. The day before yesterday when I was with Mike in the nutwood clearing rubbish from silver and larch I saw some young men, four or five, getting over the wall. I called Mike, he muttered there were "all sorts going about" and seemed unwilling to speak to them, so I went on and asked what we could do for them, and then Mike ran before me and asked if they had come from the fair and if they wanted to find their way. They said yes, to Kinvara, and he told them the way, though I was puzzled at their coming such a round instead of going by the road. Today John told me that on Friday his brother had called him from the garden and said there were some strange looking men going through the place and he and J.H. had gone after them and caught sight of them, saw they were strangers and is sure they were on the run. Mike must of course have known this.

There has been an election of Clerk to the Rural Council in Gort. J. Gormally was a candidate but only got one vote. A Fahy, P. Fahy, was appointed. "General Commandant Stanford" had recommended a candidate, but his name had been withdrawn, and I wondered at the Council showing themselves anti-republican. But I am told Fahy was also a republican "no one would have any chance to get in only one of that crowd".

23 MARCH. Mr. Johnson says the Fahy who got in was the better of the two, a quite good man "but he would not have been elected if they had not kidnapped a supporter of the other who was coming from near Kinvara, and locked him in a house till the election was over".

I don't know how it was in the night that peace seemed so easy, so simple, all as I said in my *M.G.* article "having their faces turned towards the realisation of Plato's dream". If the F.S. Ministers would but admit that—and they could not dare doing it even if they would—in so far as all wish for independence of England, where would be the quarrel? The Colonies are moving in that direction every day, Canada having signed her own treaty with Washington is an evidence. Are we not all republicans and could we not all agree to remain so "gan molais". And someone writing to the *Times* of 21st says (with intent to put the blame on England) that the most of the South was against the Treaty and those who signed it said they did so under compulsion; that the Free State was England's invention and an unwelcome one.

25 MARCH. SUNDAY. It has been a peaceful week, hard work indoors on the Memoir, splendid work out of doors with Mike and Melliney and Corly in the woods.

A couple of days ago I had a letter from L.R. He enclosed a typed order from the "Government of the Republic of Ireland" signed by Padraig O'Ruitleis, "Minister for Home Affairs", saying that because of the acceptance of the Free State, and the executions, and imprisonments "It is hereby decreed that the present be observed as a time of National mourning, that all sports and amusements be suspended, that all Theatres, &c be closed. . ."

Robinson[1] wrote that he had not taken it very seriously and heard later that there was a meeting of Theatrical Managers at 1 o'c . . . and at quarter to seven "rang up Mr. Armstrong of the Empire Theatre and found to my astonishment they were closing and that all the Theatres and picture houses were doing the same thing. So then I got in touch with Yeats and Government and went over to Merrion Square. The Government were debating their action and promised to let me know what they wanted done. I waited on and on, 'phoning Perrin not to open till I heard, till finally at 8.15 not having heard from Government I 'phoned the Abbey again and found that the army had arrived and made us open. . . . It was a good performance and a fair audience, well guarded by military at all entrances to the Theatre. During the show we took the portraits in the vestibule out of their frames and they are in safe keeping. After the performance the military left and the C.I.D. came but didn't stay all night. This morning I spent in Desmond Fitzgerald's office, all the other managers waited on O'Higgins who gave them great abuse I believe, and an order was issued to us all commanding us to open tonight. Fitzgerald has arranged that we are to be specially well guarded as we opened last night, and W.B. being a Senator makes us a good target, we'll have a guard all tomorrow. It seems queer that my stormiest moments in the Theatre have always been over the question. "To open or not to open". It must be written in the stars somewhere. The Government knew nothing of the matter till my 'phone to them last night. The Company have been splendid."

29 MARCH. Richard's first Harrow report very good—"He has more brains than most boys in the form". No Greek but "science good, very promising". Mathematics "Quite satisfactory, Good work".

5 APRIL. Rather a worried week, L.R. having given me a wrong date for Carnegie meeting, and a wrong address to send *Mirandolina* to (for Fagan) after my hard work on it and my only copy! And a good many tangles thereby. Read a little bit of Plato "A man . . . if in this life . . . having adorned his soul not with any foreign ornament but with her own proper jewels, Temperance, Justice, Courage, Nobility, and Truth, he awaits thus prepared his journey to Hades".

5 APRIL. I worked very hard at my M.S., over hard, it began to oppress me, and some days my head ached. But today I have I think done with really hard work; having absorbed some of the letters into other chapters, I have made one good little chapter I think of what remains, with some of Yeats' best. So I may have but some typing and patching to do now. At work still in the woods, pleasant work, generally not in for tea till 7 o'c or after.

A letter from the Dean of the Medical College at Pekin today, remembering "a delightful hour" of my visit to Smith College "which a group of us spent in Miss Jordan's room". She says the Chinese students "wishing to cultivate their command of spoken English through dramatics "have given my play *Spreading the News* and are going to present *Aristotle's Bellows!* so Kiltartan will flavour the English of the medical profession out there.

About Mr. Scovell's business Yeats wrote, April 3: "I have seen O'Hegarty, Sec to Post Office. He says "Gaynor will not be appointed. He is not the kind of man we want. I have his record here up to March 26. He and the priest have been to see the Postmaster General since that date they have made no impression on him. If he had they would have informed me'. You can tell this to Mr. Scovell, and he can get that man he thought a good man to send up his name". A great relief to the Scovells and Burren! (May 1924) But he was reappointed after all, O'Mally using influence with the P.G.

12 APRIL. I came up yesterday for Carnegie meeting. Liam Lynch's death in the papers, killed in the fight.[2] Six executions at Headfort, wrong I think—of men arrested in February.[3] Yeats thinks peace is near. He still has a guard in his house, a larger one than before.

15 APRIL. I dined with the Yeats' on Thursday. The door was cautiously opened on the chain and a voice asked "Who is there", I laughed and said "A friend", and a Guard in uniform let me in. I had a little talk with him on my usual line—where is the quarrel? and he agreed. Yeats had been threatened, owing to a conversation with Mrs. McBride, when he had refused to interfere for Miss MacSwiney, and has told her he will have no more political conversations with her. But now both she and Iseult have been arrested and lodged in Kilmainham.[4]

At Mullingar on the way up, I went to the waiting room and found it guarded and a soldier evidently wounded lying on a bench. But Dublin is quieter though there is some firing most nights, and there is real hope of peace. Yeats says that the five names in favour of peace in the captured document were of the military, and the six against it politicians.

At the Abbey I found an armed guard; there has been one ever since the theatres were threatened if they kept open. And in the green room I found one of them giving finishing touches to the costume of Tony Quinn, who is a Black and Tan in the play, and showing him how to hold his revolver. *The Shadow of a Gunman*[5] was an immense success, beautifully acted, all the political points taken up with delight by a big audience. Sean O'Casey the author only saw it from the side wings the first night but had to appear to make his bow. I brought him into the stalls the other two nights and have had some talk with him. Last night there was an immense audience the largest I think since the first night of *Blanco Posnet*. Many, to my grief, had to be turned away from the door. Two seats had been kept for Yeats and me, but I put Casey in one of them and sat in the orchestra for the first act, and put Yeats in the orchestra for the second. I had brought Casey round to the door before the play to share my joy in seeing the crowd surging in (Dermod O'Brien caught in the queue) and he introduced me to two officers, one a Colonel. (Yeats has wanted me to go with them to a *ball* given by the army, "good names being wanted"!)

Casey told me he is a labourer, and as we talked of masons said he had "carried the hod". He said "I was among books as a child, but I was sixteen before I learned to read or write. My father loved books, he had a big library, I remember the look of the books high up on shelves". I asked why his father had not taught him and he said "He died when I was three years old, through those same books. There was a little ladder in the room to get to the shelves, and one day when he was standing on it, it broke and he fell and was killed". I said "I often go up the ladder in our library at home" and he begged me to be careful. He is learning what he can about Art, has bought books on Whistler and Raphael, and takes *The Studio*. All this was as we watched the crowd. I forget how I came to mention the Bible, and he asked "Do you like it"? I said "Yes, I read it constantly, even for the beauty of the language". He said he admires that beauty, he was brought up as a Protestant but has lost belief in religious forms. Then, in talking of our war here, we came to Plato's *Republic*, his dream-city, whether on earth or in heaven not far away from the city of God. And then we went in to the play. He says he sent us a play four years ago *Frost and Flowers* and it was returned, but marked "Not far from being a good play". He has sent others, and says how grateful he was to me because when we had to refuse the Labour one "The Crimson in the Tri-Colour" I had said "I believe there is something in you" and "your strong point is characterisation". And I had wanted to pull that play together and put it on to give him experience, but Yeats was down on it. Perrin says he has offered him a pass sometimes when he happened to come in, but he refused and said "No one ought to come into the Abbey Theatre without paying for it". He said "All the thought in Ireland for years past has come through the Abbey. You have no idea what an education it has been to the country". That, and the fine audience on this our last week, put me in great spirits.

So yesterday that helped me when I went with Yeats to the Government Offices to see MacNeill. He thinks the Government will refuse to take the Theatre over. But they must give us a subsidy for now Harris is gone and I have been so much away we have overdrawn so heavily at the Bank that it will cash no more cheques. I had to speak plainly to Yeats and said I would not go on unless there is a business man put in to watch and control the expenditure.

And MacNeill promised to help towards having the resolution about the Lane pictures brought on, that has been so long delayed. MacNeill as kind as always, though very much taken up with the Brehon laws, which he is translating and editing. Yeats says the laws made by the Volunteers, the Republicans before the split, are wonderfully good. There is a whole book of carefully considered recommendations as to the Irish Fisheries. Lysaght told him all this work had been done by men on the run from the Black and Tans, moving from place to place. At one of these legislative meetings he was at, one of their army came to the door at intervals and reported "the enemy has reached such and such a point".

In Casey's play there were harmless explosions representing bombs thrown by the Black and Tans. And real ones were not far off for on Friday Perrin told me that a land mine had been put that morning by armed men who held up the caretaker, in the picture house "Olympia" close to the Abbey. But the fuse had burned out without exploding it.

I have worked incessantly, have re-written the missing part of *Mirandolina*[6] and sent the whole play to be typed. And I recovered old Yeats' letters from W.B.Y. and am getting them typed, and now (Sunday) am going to number the pages of my Memoir in the hope of sending it off from here, I have put off leaving till Tuesday.

Yesterday as I was walking by the National Gallery on my way to lunch at Yeats's house, I came face to face with Stephens. I put out my hand and said "Will you forgive me?" He seemed I thought for a minute to hesitate but then said "Oh, it was my fault". I said "I have been very sorry about it, but I think the fault was neither yours nor mine". He said "I can't tell you how much I have felt it and how sorry I have been", and I said it had been the same with me, and that this meeting made me very happy. He asked me to lunch with him and his wife but I couldn't go, but am going to tea with them today. I am so glad.[7]

16 APRIL. Monday. Very hard work all yesterday numbering and going through pages of the Memoirs hoping to get it off today, but there are still some of J. B. Yeats' letters to be typed, though Robinson very kindly did some pages himself and brought them to me. I was very tired.

Austin Stack's proposal of peace very hopeful.[8] In the evening

I saw in the *Observer* De V.'s "call", but the Irish papers don't publish it. Yeats brought Jackson the young American poet round for me to take to tea at Stephens, and I made him come also, happily as there was no one else, and Y. and Stephens, or rather Stephens and Y. talked all the time, on their philosophies, and that interested the little poet very much. Stephens says America is now the great energy of the world; Russia and Italy also energies though behind her. Ireland an energy also, rather apart. Ireland has kept her energy and individuality in spite of all the immense amount she has exported year by year to America. What America is doing with hers is destroying the folk mind in herself and in Europe, and it is this destruction that has led to the violence that has come upon Europe. France and England have been looking to each other all the while, and are now in decadence.

Everything is aiming at lightning speed, the American shows the whole story of the novel in a few scenes—what will happen to the novelist? Yeats was interested in this idea of increasing swiftness—thought he believes may grow as swift as thought in dreams. It is only the body that keeps it from this swiftness.

Monday very heavy. Saw Munro about our finances, very bad; Directors meeting at Theatre, nil.

Tuesday, 17. Only got *Mirandolina* retyped the night before, 2nd and 3rd Act. 1st Act not till midday, correcting it till time to leave for the station. And got MS of the Memoirs off, or into Perrin's hands to post. A terribly hard week's work, and caught cold today.

Wednesday, 18th in Galway, ill with cold, but much cheered up by a letter A. had from M. saying Richard has come out top of form, got form prize, is being sent up two forms next term; such a joy! But Oh! if Robert could have been here to have that pleasure!

2 MAY. Going to London today. It has been a month of very hard work but the Memoir is now finished all but a few letters of my own; would have been finished yesterday but for entertaining K. Bagot and Mr. Watt, her fiancé.

4 MAY. (1923) RIVER COURT. I arrived the morning of yesterday very tired.

Yeats met me at the Broadstone and came on to Kingstown to see me off. He seemed cheerful but it was a shock to me to hear there had been two executions in Ennis[9] that day, in spite of De Valera's truce being kept. Yeats said the Government might probably have information that these executions had good results (I don't think so) and that anyhow "the young diehards" have strong influence in the Government. MacNeill he says has given up his office to another McNeill, to whom an office was necessary, and sits in his bedroom working at the Brehon Laws. Yeats had, when he heard I was coming up, tried to get the Dail resolution re Lane pictures stirred up, and had fallen back on Darrell Figgis who has put down a resolution in stupid wording but better than no move at all. He says Monsignor Luzio[10] is in an unhappy position. The English Catholics don't like his having been sent, are suspicious that it is preliminary to a Papal Nuncio being established in Ireland, and they don't want that because they like to assume that the English and not the Irish Catholics represent all the Catholic Church in the Empire. The Republicans don't like his having been sent because they suspect an English intrigue. The Government don't want meddlers, having the military situation so well in hand; Cardinal Logue doesn't want a Papal Envoy established because he would be a greater man than himself. Luzio was sent to Logue to introduce him to the most important people in Ireland, and Logue assumed that the Bishops are the most important people and asked no others to meet him. And the papers announce that Luzio is "indisposed" at his hotel and is going back to Rome when he is well enough.

Alton of Trinity had refused to help with the Lane pictures resolution saying his friends were on the other side. And Yeats had said "friendships are always the enemies of justice".

This (River Court) is a beautiful house and looks out on the river. Today I have taken Richard back to Harrow in the Gough's car. He was quite cheery going and seemed quite at home when he arrived. I saw Mr. Kent who was very nice and said how well he had done in work, and that he takes such an interest in it, and is always bright and good humoured and cheerful. And he has got his double remove.

Mr. Kent knew the Gregory prize was given by one of the family, but I don't think he knew of R.'s grandfather's record—Dr. Longley saying "William Gregory was the cleverest boy he ever had under him". And he did not know of Robert entering with first classical scholarship.

I left darling R. quite happy, greeted by the others and quite at home with Mr. Kent. His heart had sunk a little when he came into the Harrow street last January, his first term, but he could laugh at this now.

SUNDAY, 6 MAY. Isle of Wight (Alum Bay). Yesterday I came here to spend a couple of days with Anne and Catherine as Margaret wanted to stay in London, and I was delighted at the chance of seeing the darlings in the funny little cottage, their great excitement being the "Girl Guides" corps which they have joined.

We have been to church, pretty views of the sea, but the brilliant greens and the red houses look violent after the West, even the furze differed in the green from those masses of gold on the brown bogs I passed through in Ireland last Wednesday. Margaret told some political lady who was abusing Ireland the other day "My children just tolerate England, they are just counting the days till they get back to Ireland". And when she was leaving, a lady she didn't know was Irish got up and said "I should like to know your children"! So all the exiles have not gone out in bitterness.

N. Geary writes about books he has been giving to Delhi Legal Council "I am thinking of giving the Ed. Burke also but previously I am reading him through. He objected to the British General Carleton in American war of Independence indenting 'for five gross scalping knives as an issue to Red Indian allies'."

Ascham says: "He that will wryte well in any tongue must follow this council of Aristotle, to speak as the common people do; to think as wise men do". A support for "Kiltartan" if one were needed.

12 MAY. I have had Saturday to Tuesday with the children. They met me at the pier, so bright, not a bit changed, and we had nice days in the little cottage. I had brought Anne Bowman's *Young Nile Voyagers*[10a] and read it to them, a great success. Then Tuesday to Friday at Newbuildings, a sad visit, the house seemed so silent, though I could not wish Wilfrid back in his pain. Dorothy has I think a hard task before her, keeping up the house and what is in her hands on a smaller income and with the illwill of Judith and Anthony. She practically holds the place in trust for him though she has power of appointment within certain limits, and I hope he, now 23, and in East Africa, may be given it over when the right time comes. She gave me the diaries to read, there is a question of when they should be published.[11] I was disappointed, they deal chiefly with the war, and he being away from London and seeing but few friends, gives a résumé of the news in the papers and many conversations with Belloc. So many of these are prophecies that did not come true that Belloc might not like them published—and then he writes his Land and Water articles all that time. It grows in interest towards the end as the news comes from some who have returned from time to time, Nevill Lytton, O. Beauclerk; and as he begins again to read and criticize books. The little bits of gossip, as visits from Margot, are amusing but could not be published in full while some mentioned

in them are still living. And a great deal is taken up with the unhappy quarrel, with Judith over the sale of Crabbet lands, and later of the lawsuit about the stud. Very sad that this last especially should have clouded his last years and upset or deferred the succession, and Anthony, all unoffending, is the one to suffer. The only time I ever gave a strong opinion on any of their affairs was when Wilfrid told me he was going to leave Newbuildings to a Blunt relation. I was indignant that a grandson should be cut out and spoke with some emotion. A little later I heard that he had consented to see Anthony and had liked him, and then I was content and believed all would be right. But he was afraid of Judith's influence on the boy, and left Dorothy as it were in trust for him, and he naturally enough resents this.

There is a great deal in the volume on the evidences of Christianity, he reads the Gospel critically; theological books; is I think anxious to believe but cannot, does not believe in revealed religion or a future life. And so it startled me when Dorothy told me that very near the end he had said "I am broken with pain, you may send for that priest" (an Irish priest who had been coming of late with one excuse or another). And when the priest came he received from him the Sacrament.

I remember long ago, when he had been renouncing Christianity and upholding Mohammedanism W. saying "You will see Wilfrid will die with the wafer in his mouth". And so it has happened.

I found Irish papers waiting for me here, and Yeats has sent some more telling of the debate and resolution on the Lane pictures in the Senate.[12] That will be a good help. And though De Valera's peace terms are not accepted, outrage has not begun again, there must be some hope of settlement.[13]

15 MAY. On Sunday Una and R.P.H. came, and I went back with them to see their house and hear about their jade toad that is to lead to fortune.

Then to see Clara Huth Jackson; she has just learned for certain that she is to have *no* money under Fritz's will, has only the jointure £900 a year. And he had meant to leave her so much, but "the wording" annuls it. Another example of a will drawn up by lawyers going contrary to the wish of the testator. A sad visit to that splendid house where I had received so much kindness.

Yesterday afternoon S. Cockerell came to talk over W.S.B.'s will. His conclusion had been the same as mine about the Diary, except that I think it may have sufficient interest to publish some day, and he is inclined to think not; that it shows so great a falling off in interest and he thinks in power of writing. But I don't agree in that, I think it was matter than failed. He told me something I did not know that had increased, illwill. He had left instructures that Judith was not to be told of his death until Mr. Cockerell was in the house. But he died on Sunday and the telegram did not reach Cockerell till Monday, and he was in Dorsetshire and could not get to Southwater till evening, and there at the station he met Judith and Anthony, furious, for the death had been in the day's papers.

He is not sure the Fitzwilliam trustees would accept charge of the duplicate copy of MS in the "mystery box", for they were unwilling to accept the bequest at all. He had persuaded them to do it on the ground that they would probably all be dead when the time came for opening it, in thirty years.

Cockerell asked me to go on with him to see May Morris.[14] I had never met her and we found her giving a farewell tea party as she is giving up her house, to live in the country. I was glad to meet her, a link with that group I did not know. I told her how Yeats when he first came to Coole so much under her father's influence used to abuse our old mahogany—"a copy of marble" and was all for plain or painted wood. But now he is in Merrion Square he is himself putting in mahogany, "Oh how naughty of him!" she said gently. Emery Walker was there, who Yeats had taken me to see long ago; and old Mr. Rooke at whose house Robert had sometimes spent an evening when at the Slade. I would have liked to thank him but could not risk his misunderstanding or questioning, for he is over eighty. Agnes Goldman came in then, and on here to see the house. It was a pleasant little unexpected hour. Just as I always said of London, its charm is in its possibilities, its unexpectedness.

16 MAY. May Morris came in and likes the house. I am reading De Morgan's life,[15] and it was wonderful seeing her, the heir of the memories of that group of friends. They never quarrelled, she said, and their fun never ebbed. When de Morgan married he wrote to her father "We are *sploce*". She is rather sad at giving up the little house here, but looks forward to work in her garden. I felt that I also had once worked in a little community of friends, now scattered; it gave me a feeling of loneliness.

I got through some of my work of clothing myself and am almost ready to go back to Ireland—the best place for me.

18 MAY. Lord Peel writes that the Cabinet haven't had time yet to consider the Lane pictures "it is however earmarked for discussion, and I will not fail to give it my best attention when the time comes".

The Town Clerk writes from Dublin that I have been made a

member of the Municipal Gallery advisory committee, and I have written thanking him and suggesting, through Reynolds, that they get The Governor-General, Tim Healy, to take up the picture matter with the British Government. Alec Martin thinks Witt is the most obstinate enemy. Poor Alec, one of his children has died and he is very downhearted.

I spent a long time going from shop to shop looking for A.'s luminous paint. And when at last I had found it, in the Building Dept. at Harrods and bought a little box at 3/- I wanted it sent by post. But when I gave the Galway address they said it could not go, as there must be duty paid on it without many formalities, and I had not time for these, and must smuggle it. I wonder what the duty is on a 3/- purchase.

19 MAY. Very cold still. Mrs. Scovell writes from Burren "a tale has reached us that an iceberg is ashore at Aran and three bears have landed, which caused grief to the maid whose home is there."

I lunched with Birrell yesterday. He keeps his interest in Ireland, but doesn't take an Irish paper, and there is nothing or all but nothing in the English papers about us now the outrages have disappeared. He was very much impressed by Glenavy's opinion in the picture debate. He said he had seen the documents and felt certain Hugh had not only intended to leave the pictures to Ireland but believed that he had done so. He says Massingham had to leave the *Nation* because though so good a writer he was not considered a good editor and it was losing money. And Rowntree who had been spending £3000 a year on it "had lost so much, silencing the Press and in other ways since his cocoa was discovered to be made of strychnine, that he can't go on".

We talked of Northcliffe. He says he met his old father not long before his death, lamenting his poverty "What have I ever been good for but to breed children?" and he was afraid his wife would be in want. But each of the sons as he came to riches heaped upon his mother all she could want. She is still living.

I asked him (being just at the end of De Morgan's life) if the novels were still selling. He doesn't know, but thinks they are gone out of fashion. The biographer (Mrs. Stirling) thinks them so much more important than the pots, but Birrell thinks as I do that the pots are more eternal.

I saw poor Innes's watercolours at the Chenil—"The Ash tree at Coole Park" one of them but not very good. (And but a sapling growing from a rock as a specimen of all our fine timber!) And then to the Academy to see Orpen's "Soldier in France", a fine piece of decoration; and Jack Yeats's Pilot, and Lavery's portrait of Cosgrave—quite good. But luckily for the Academician John's Mme. Suggia isn't there,[16] to sweep all their portraits into the rubbish heap.

Having my hair shampooed at Harrods I said "No singeing or cutting, only shampoo"—And then the shampooer said "Will you have a blue rinse?" whatever that may be.

19 MAY. I came down to Ayot by a train an hour too soon, the taxi having found the road clearer than the one to Waterloo did. So I walked about the village, and then G.B.S. came in his little car. He had telephoned in the morning that Charlotte is in bed with a cold, and asked if I was afraid of infection. I said I was not, but of being in the way, and he said I might put that out of my head, so I have come. We went into the church at Hatfield and he showed me the tombs of the Cecils; the great Elizabethan in white marble, a sharply cut refined face; the last Lord in bronze. The sexton came and talked, told us what a great man the last was "it is not yet known how great"; and I had just said to G.B.S. that he would be chiefly remembered by his cession of Heligoland to the Kaiser! The sexton had once spoken to him, at the railway station, had said the train was coming and he had said it was "a minute late" and this is a treasured memory. G.B.S. drove me home, and talked of his *Joan of Arc* play. He has not read Mark Twain, is afraid of being influenced by him. He has read a little of Anatole France and is reading the evidence at the trial, it was published some years ago. He does not idealise her as Mark does, and defends the Church, "it didn't torture her". I think there will be something good about the English soldiers. He tells me that Lawrence[17] who fought in Mesopotamia has been to see him, is an extraordinary man, very small, living as a private in the army having resigned his command, and has written a wonderful book, has had five copies linotyped, and lent him one. "It will be one of the great books of the world. He describes every blade of grass and flower and noxious insect, and all the fighting and the terrible crimes of the Turks and the terrible vengeance he and his men took on them. He has not a religious mission like Gordon but must have a touch of his nature. His brother is a missionary in China, or wants to be one, and his mother has the same desire". He thinks (G.B.S. hears) that all his family will die out because they are all mad. The Government did all they could for him, finally gave him a post in the Colonial Office, but he resigned it and enlisted and for a while it was not known where he was. His comrades knew but would not give him away.

BOOKS TWENTY-FOUR AND TWENTY-FIVE

20 MAY. He showed me in the evening this book, and I read a few sentences and said "It seems as good as Doughty", and G.B.S. said "Lawrence is a great admirer of Doughty".[1] This probably gives him his style.

Then G.B.S. read me the opening of his first act or scene of *Joan of Arc*. A fine and spirited opening, gay and yet getting much of the spiritual side of Joan. I asked about the end, the execution would be too tragic and he thinks so, he thinks of having a final scene of the rehabilitation, the canonisation of a Protestant, which he says is what she was and confessed to being in her examination. He had been working at the play without talking of it, but the other day Drinkwater came to see him and remonstrate with him for having omitted to acknowledge his *Cromwell*[2] which had "A most laudatory dedication to me". And he had said "As you are writing about historical characters I had better warn you that I am writing a play on Joan of Arc".[3] "So next day it was in the papers, and I have had letters from every actress in the Kingdom asking for parts, and a distressed one from a Manager who had commissioned Binyon to write one on Joan. But he does not seem to have begun it". As we were going upstairs he showed me a letter he had written in *Literary Supplement* on "Printed Plays" in which he says "Some writers have a natural gift of writing dialogue and need no training, and the first that come to mind in a literary sense are Molière, Goldsmith, Chesterton and Lady Gregory". Good company to wind up the day with.

Today talking of Frank Harris and his faults "If you ask him to dinner and put him next a cocotte he will talk to her of nothing but Jesus Christ, and if you put him beside a Duchess he will talk to her as no one else would but to a cocotte. Yet he never shows respect to meanness. George Moore on the other hand though his success is a triumph of industry, never does homage to what is highest". It is curious he says that the most indecent writers just now should be three Irishmen, Harris, Moore and Joyce. I think it is reaction from the R. Catholic teaching.

I have just been to church "We have a congregation of fifteen all told"; the clerk said to me as I waited outside. "Where do the country people go? To another church or to chapel"? "No they don't go anywhere. I don't know what they do". I made the sixteenth, and there were a few children. Two clergymen, one taking off and putting on a red cape, reading the lessons in a white gown with thick folded collar and red crossed bands, reading the gospel with his back to the congregation, bowing low to the altar and stretching out his arms; holding the poorbox with both hands over his head. The service was intoned, so we lost the beautiful words of the Liturgy. The sermon, by the other clergyman, advised us not to allow ourselves to forget the presence of Christ in the beauty of the altar (Heavens!) and the music, and said the Church is now coming into its own again there is a stirring, "the people having tried here and there are coming back to God".

G.B.S. says he chose Joan of Arc because of Bernhardt and others having played so many parts turning on sexual attraction he wanted to give Joan as a heroine absolutely without that side. And this he emphasises in the first scene, though keeping her charm.

In all the revision of novels and business letters of these last years he had felt as if his imagination had vanished, that he was "done". And now in the discovery that he writes as well as ever he has grown young again, looks better than for years past, though complaining of aches and pains from sawing wood, which he has taken to for exercise.

I told him of my Memoirs and that I feel unhappy about them. He says if there is nothing ill natured in them or that will cause trouble it will be all right.

I am reading the Lawrence book, it is enthralling, each sentence rich and complete. An Admiral who came to tea told me he had been at Constantinople for a while, and a brother of Emir Feisul who was there each time he saw him asked what news he had of Lawrence. The Admiral thinks he is such another as Nicholson.

Charlotte says Lawrence was a Don at Oxford. He had been taken with the idea of nationality, of each race having its own, and had hesitated whether to take it as his mission to help Arabia or Ireland, but chose the Arabs.

He had come to lunch with the Shaws while (as he still is) a private, but dressed extremely well. And although he said that a couple of weeks ago he had been washing plates for the sergeants' mess, she could hardly believe it because his hands were so well cared. He was charming, but one hears of his thrusting away approaches of friendship with some rudeness. He was disillusioned in Arabia because of Feisul's brother spending and distributing among friends money that was intended for the war.

G.B.S. told me he had given leave to Mrs. Campbell to publish his letters[4] because she had overdrawn £2000 at the Bank and would have been in great trouble for money, and the publishers promised or advanced it for the book chiefly because of these letters. But she had deceived him, saying that Barrie's and Burne Jones's and other letters were to be published also, and that had not been allowed.

21 MAY. We have been to Cambridge; a lovely day and a wonderful drive over the smooth roads, not a stone on them, and through hedges and rows of elms and old fashioned villages. Charlotte is still laid up and couldn't come. Cockerell met us at the Fitzwilliam Museum and showed us its riches—it makes me jealous for the Dublin Gallery, so many donors giving it fine things, and new rooms being built. G.B.S. has given it one of the three John portraits painted at Coole, the Ezekiel* one. Then we had lunch at the Bull, ordered by G.B.S. Mrs. Cockerell there too, and a daughter of De La Mare. There was a good deal of talk about Lawrence and his book. Cockerell says it (the book) is to be kept secret, but G.B.S. says "when Lawrence goes into a secret place it is in the limelight. If he hides in a quarry he puts up red flags all around." Cockerell had first met him on Doughty's business. Doughty had been in a very bad way for money; has a wife and two daughters. Lawrence had said he could get him on the Civil List, knowing Balfour and Lloyd George and the rest. But on the day the last Civil List was announced it contained many names that no one had ever heard of, but not Doughty's. Cockerell had been to see him that day, and found him and his wife looking blankly at the paper. Then friends put their heads together, and knowing he would not take money directly, they made up £400 and offered it to him for the MS of one of his poems to put in the Bodleian, and he accepted it with delight. And at Cambridge Cockerell set to work to collect the same sum, and was within £150 of it when one day a shabby looking Don came in and said he heard there was a subscription on foot. Cockerell nearly said he didn't take guinea subscriptions, but the Don asked how much was wanting, and when he heard it was £150 said "I'll give that". Cockerell thought he might be touched in the head, and went to consult the Head of his College who said it was all right, that he was very generous and liked doing things like that. And then Lawrence did succeed in moving the Government and the Civil List pension was

granted from the time of the appearance of the last list.

Doughty had been at Cambridge as an undergraduate and was remembered as refusing to read anything more modern than the Elizabethans, Hakluyt and the like. That accounts for his style, and Lawrence has evidently founded his upon it. Then I asked how G.B.S. had met Lawrence, and Cockerell said it was through him. Lawrence admired his plays immensely, and one day Cockerell asked him to come and see him, but he refused absolutely. Then Cockerell said he was just going to get a picture from 10, Adelphi Terrace and would want help to get it from the wall, and that G.B.S. would be in the country—was going that day—so he consented to come. But G.B.S. hadn't left so early as expected but was there, and they made friends at once. Lawrence has been offered £7000 for leave to publish the book but has refused. He lives on his private's pay, though he could have got £10,000 from Parliament had he consented to ask for it. He, Lawrence, says none of his family ought to marry, they should die out, for they are all mad.

Last night I asked if I might read a play to G.B.S. (F.S.'s). L.R. had written a note on it "I rather like this and think it might play amusingly, but I've read so many bad plays in the last three days that my judgement may be warped") I thought it hopelessly bad but without saying anything asked leave to read it. At the end G.B.S. burst out "Piffle from the Sandymount sea front!" I showed him L.R.'s note and he wrote under it "Lock Lennox up at once. He has G.P.I. (General Paralysis of the Insane) the thing is manifest piffle"! So I need give no opinion at all. A great relief.

I took Cherry Garrard's book up to bed[5]. G.B.S. advised me to begin on the "Winter Journey", and I did, and could not leave off till I came to its end at ten minutes to one. A wonderful story of heroic endeavour. The book has had fine reviews, but Lady Scott is indignant that Cherry, who when I met her at Lamer she had talked of as "The little cabin-boy", should have criticised anything Scott did. The real mistake he made was in taking five men instead of four on the last journey. Cherry is doing nothing more than looking after his property. And he has bought the Epstein Christ. But he has quarrelled with all his neighbours, and doesn't like his former tenants. Perhaps his energy may awaken again to some fine work.

I hope Curzon won't be made Prime Minister just as Labour is to consider the pictures! (I had written to Ramsay McDonald and had a kind answer).

23 MAY. Curzon not Premier. Yet perhaps if he had been,

this gratification of an ambition might have made him more gracious towards our Gallery. I am pleased to see Baldwin is an Harrovian. I finished Cherry's book at midnight, and read much of Lawrence during the day, so my mind is filled with thoughts of heroism, greater in both cases than what it attained.

24 MAY. I read all the morning at Ayot, skimming through Lawrence, not following the military and political part very closely, but his wonderful descriptions and what told of his own personality—"I had but one craving all my life for the power of self expression in imaginative form, but had been too indolent and weak-willed ever to acquire technique".

He had a great triumph at the end in setting up the Arab Government at Damascus, and then withdrew. And this book will live.

G.B.S. just before I left read me a new scene he had written in the morning, the relief of Orleans in a scene between Joan and Dunois and a boy. "The wind" long waited for comes and is shewn to the audience by the waving of the pennon. I said if I had been writing it for Kiltartan I should have made the little boy sneeze.

He motored me to Hatfield, after a very pleasant four days. This house looked lonely, and I am ready for home, if this governess question could be settled.

25 MAY. Yeats came yesterday morning and we had a long talk. He has still a guard in his house but thinks things are going well. There has been an attempt made to get National Gallery, Municipal Gallery, Hibernian Academy and all the art collections put under one head—and this to be through the influence of priests. But he thinks it was discovered in time to be stopped. Lord Granard had promised to help about the Lane pictures, and I have written to T. P. O'Connor and Lady Leslie on the matter.

I am pleased at getting (besides a cheque) a list of my plays performed in many different places of U.S.A. *Grania* has been given at Washington; *The Dragon* there and at other places. *Spreading* leads with thirty nine. If I had had more faith I need not have given the Memoir for publication.

27 MAY. The night before last I had a shock, finding a hard lump under my left breast . . . I tried to get a name of a doctor that I might not be in suspense all Sunday. But the telephone had gone out of order so at last I went to Una P[ope] H[ennessy] who sent me to a Dr. Barcroft. He did not think it malignant but sent me to a surgeon, Ward. He also said it was not malignant but might become so unless looked to, said it was local inflammation "not from rheumatism but what rheumatism comes from". He

ordered belladonna plasters and said I must see a doctor again in six weeks "make no mistake about that". I told him I was going to Ireland and if an operation was necessary would have it done there. It has been a shake to me, and those hours when I thought an operation might be immediately necessary were very bad. I think I have no dread at all of death, but I don't want to be cut up and become a nuisance.

I had tea on Friday with Ricketts and Shannon in their new house by the Regents Park; their beautiful belongings not yet arranged. They have I think a happy life, living with and creating beauty.

4 JUNE. In a Nursing Home, 96, Lr. Leeson Street. A bad last week. Monday trying to find Gogarty; Tuesday finding him and making appointment for Wednesday;—"Innocent but may become malignant, or in any case fixed in the tissues and a long anxiety to you. Get it out"! Thursday good bye to Anne and Cat, and a glimpse of Margaret, and off to Euston, Gogarty in the train and kind. Friday arrived Hotel Russell, had a sleep, and to 82 Merrion Square. 3.30 Slattery—"Better have it out, and take the whole breast out" another shock! Evening Nursing Home, dreadful preparations. Saturday morning ditto from 6 o'c—they refused me a cup of tea, in spite of Slattery's permission, but "Would you like to see a priest before the operation?" 11 o'c "Theatre" and scaffold. No chloroform, local anaesthetics. I was able to keep a face of courage and ask Gogarty about his feelings when being kidnapped—some pain and at the last I fainted. A bad afternoon, but ever since exhilarated by being "on the hither side and not in the far side" of the trouble. The nurses kind; Gogarty rushing in now and again like a breeze. Yeats so good with me through the bad days.

He says about the Churches and Psychic research, it is strange they should be bent upon destroying the evidence for the immortality of the soul. Someone had said "Well the (Catholic) Church has walked the plank"! and he said "And the English Church is treading the Boards"!

There was an explosion in Dublin on Sunday night, and some firing a few nights before, but no harm done. Yeats says De Valera is being looked for, the Government had a hint a few days ago as to his whereabouts but it led to nothing. A nun was suspected of being De V. in disguise, but it was found she had but a profile very like his, and the same mark across the nose from spectacles. I think they would make a mistake in arresting him, prison with its traditional glory would bring some romance about him again. Yeats says there are known to be men, unconnected with Government, who have sworn to take his life to avenge Michael Collins. It was this knowledge that made it impossible for Government to give him a safe conduct to meet Douglas when the negotiations were going on.

Willie had occasion to write to the Governor-General on picture business the other day, and not knowing him personally began the letter in proper form to his Excellency. But the answer began "My dear Boy, come and see me whenever you like in 'the bee loud glade'", and was signed "Tim Healy".

Today W.B.Y. has a letter from Miss Harrison making "a last appeal" to him to come and see her (about the codicil) "for the sake of those nearest and dearest to you come", or some such words. I thought it dangerous from a lunatic as she is, and made him show it to her brother, who with much reluctance has promised to see her about it, says he has not seen her for months and that whenever he has any discussion with her he "wants to bash her head". Robinson says she told him straight and plain that I had forged the codicil. Very self denying of me to put in no bequest to myself.

L.R. had not received my letter re the Hugh Lane book and Murray, and he and Yeats have been in to talk of that and of the Theatre, where creditors are pressing for payment. I urge going to the Government at once for a subsidy.

5 JUNE. L.R. has seen Hanna who will be glad to take the Hugh Lane surplus copies. I am so glad they will be in Ireland after all.

Reading the Greville Memoirs.[6] I like Burke when Adair asked him a question about the wild parts of Ireland—"Sir you are a knave and a blockhead. There are NO wild parts of Ireland"! I wish his spirit could walk through the Carlton now.

Yeats in the evening, tired after Senate.

6 JUNE. Gogarty this morning just back from London, a little anxious about what danger amnesty may bring some secret society men and others.

There was firing in the street last night which disturbed me, about ten shots. But no one thinks it meant anything.

31 JUNE. My doctor, talking of Free State soldiers he had attended said he liked Tommies better. When the F.S. were asked if they would like to be moved to another hospital they said they would, it would be a change. The Tommies would have said they would stay with their doctor. (Triumph of our social habit!) But he believes our army will turn out well.

Yeats came in, had lunched at Gogarty's, the President there (who brought O'Malley T.D.) and Lady Fingall. She thinks social reconstruction possible; said Sir George Robinson is coming back to live in Dublin. O'Malley, a rough diamond, put his napkin under his chin and told stories of his adventures with the Black and Tans. He was the first man "on his keeping" at that time. But the President was a little grave, felt responsible for O'Malley and was anxious. Yeats walked with him when they left and Cosgrave asked what he can say if, should he press for the Lane pictures, he is asked where they are to be put. I think National Gallery will be the best answer, though we may yet offer them on loan to Manchester. And I sent Yeats on at once to find out from Stephens if N.G. will receive them. (Yes, Stephens says Langton Douglas is ready not only to store but to exhibit at once the pictures whenever we get them) G.Y. says Lady Fingall invited Cosgrave to Killeen on Sunday and will ask people to meet him, people he ought to know.

Yeats told me of his cinema speech in the Senate.[7] And that McKean had said later to a friend ("a fellow Senator I'm afraid") "Did they notice anything"? "I had a few jars in me"! Yeats remembers having heard some story about McKean's grandfather and the King—"and he stole a clock", and Yeats had got it into his head it was the King's father, and though astonished had felt sure that if the Prince Consort had stolen anything it would have been a clock.

Yeats has been in to tell me about the row at the National Gallery as he heard it from Stephens. Bodkin has been attacking L. Douglas, wanting to get him out of office, and Douglas wrote to him the other day telling or reminding him that he and Mr. Hogg are no longer "Governors", their time having lapsed and there being no one in the present state of things with power to reappoint them. However they came to the meeting and Douglas foolishly asked them to elect a Chairman, D. O'Brien, instead of insisting on his own right to preside at any meeting of the Board. And with D.O'B. in the Chair they passed another vote of censure on him! He has gone to the Solicitor General to know if he has not grounds for an action against Bodkin for slander. He mismanaged things, but it is said "When there is a row Douglas is just like a big bumble bee"!

Yeats is to see Cosgrave tomorrow about all this scheme of uniting the art collections and libraries under one head and will propose as alternatives Robinson, Stephens, and George O'Brien.

Still reading Greville—"perfect tranquillity prevails universally (except of course in Ireland)" February 1835. This or words with the same meaning seem so often to come in!

SATURDAY, 9 JUNE. I have moved to 82 Merrion Square, Slattery having taken out the stitches and given me leave, and I may use my arm. So the first terrible week, and the week of convalescence, marred by the tremendous noise of trams and motors outside, and helped by much kindness from Yeats and George and Gogarty, are over—thank God!

Yeats had been to Cosgrave in the morning, had first talked of the Lane pictures and told him they could be lodged and shown in the National Gallery. But Cosgrave was a little doubtful and said "We may have to let out the prisoners. The Republicans who have been fighting won't want to go on with it but the prisoners may". He seemed to think they might burn the National Gallery.

This afternoon Gogarty took Yeats to call on the Governor General. The Lodge is in better order now than one heard of a while ago; a quite imposing butler at the door, and they were taken to the study where Tim offered them tea and whiskey but they refused both. He promised to take up the matter of the pictures on his next visit to London which will be in a fortnight. He says Curzon is still the obstacle. Yeats had told Cosgrave (and I'm sorry he did) S. Purser's story of the Trustees being prepared to yield if we would let them keep the Eva Gonzales, and Cosgrave said "Oh of course we'd give them a present of one if they wanted it"! I begged Y. in talking to Healy to press the simple thing, the making the codicil legal.

X. was gloomy as to Ireland, says they had it from America that Larkin is to make a peace move; and when that has been done and the elections are over, the Republicans are to say they had not been won by fair play, and take to assassination. He attributes a great deal to Bolshevism, says it is in one way or other spreading through the world. He has a very bad opinion of De Valera, says the government had a chance of shooting him the other day and didn't because it would seem mean while the American money is still in dispute. "But what would a million dollars matter compared with getting rid of him". He believes him to have been jealous of Michael Collins and to have for that reason sent him to sign the Treaty that he might turn on him later. Oh these patriots! Yeats says the bitterness has begun in the North, by Mitchell.

Yeats says Tim Healy's portrait, not a bad one, now hangs amongst those of the Lords Lieutenant of the past.

SUNDAY, 10 JUNE. Such a good night in quiet and fine linen! yet more tired than yesterday, the excitement of escaping from the Home being over.

I wrote a letter about the Scovells' anxiety, for Yeats to forward to Hegarty.

O. in the afternoon, hears the first four to be shot when the assassination policy come in are Cosgrave, O'Higgins, Healy and Mulcahy.

Yeats says when X. and X. were talking of De Valera, X. said "The C.I.D. being forbidden to shoot them when they come across them is so bad for their morale". I say the Republicans may say the same of the present ban on shooting being bad for their men's morale.

The qualifying of the oath is in abeyance at present, because of the Diehard Government in England, and there will be greater difficulty in raising the loan, should it be taken up.

12 JUNE. Said goodbye to Dr. Slattery yesterday, and in the afternoon Yeats took me for a little walk, and we met Stephens who brought us into the locked up National Gallery to see Edward Martyn's pictures he has given to it. I used to ask him for the best three or four for the Municipal Gallery, and these will probably be lent to it. Stephens read me a fine translation of what must be a fine poem "The Ghost".[8] I made him read it to Yeats later, when he and a solicitor came in to tea to talk about the row at the National Gallery, when Bodkin and Hogg passed a vote of censure on Langton Douglas, who had objected to their coming to the meeting as their time as Governors had lapsed. L.D. has consulted his solicitor who says they had no right to come in, and that the resolution is illegal; while Bodkin says his solicitor is of opinion that L.D. can be given seven years' penal servitude for having torn the page containing the resolution out of the minute book. Stephens however as peacemaker has stuck in the offending page again. Some say Bodkin knows nothing about art, but someone said with awe "I'm told Tommy Bodkin can tell who a picture was painted by, and it under three inches of dust". Yeats' plan of an art committee is at the same time embarrassed and enlivened by this dispute.

Dr. Coffey and young Esmond came in to see Yeats last night. They say the elections will be in July; say Cosgrave may be President again but there is a party for O'Higgins who is, however, very unpopular; and one for Mulcahy.

I met Frank today. He says they have been able to let all the Roxborough land that has been useless to them for over a year, to the very halldoor, for £1000. He doesn't think the fifteen years purchase offered landlords bad; thinks "The cat" should be given to Bank robbers instead of shooting them, it was the cat that restored order in Belfast; believes it is from his own party De

Valera is hiding, says some of them are ready to shoot him.

13 JUNE. Yeats says he gets on well in the Senate because being a poet he can feel the emotion in the mind of the others, as Colonel Moore can't. Reynolds came with cuttings &c and I made out a letter to the Governor-General which he has taken to have typed.

J. O'Neill told Yeats in the hall as he was leaving, and Y. came up delighted to tell me, that there will be a row about the £30,000 that had been paid by England and now must be paid by Ireland to Trinity College. They find that half the sum had been absorbed by the eight senior Fellows, while the Professors are wretchedly paid; and will insist on a reform in this.

15 JUNE. Yesterday I stayed in, expecting Robinson who had said he would come but didn't. I was afraid of missing him because Abbey affairs have not yet been settled. I finished reading through the translation of the *Lives of Saints*[9] very poor and trivial, very late when all the additions made by the Church had been given time to overlay the old native traditions; full of cruelties, the work of translation misapplied industry, I think, with the great mass of poems said to be still untranslated.

I made up my "dossier" (Lane pictures) for Tim Healy, but must get to a shop to have the parcel made up and posted.

Yeats went up to write but came down excited by finding that Einstein's theory brings in the spirals that are the foundation of his own philosophy. Einstein has done away with materialism, he says, and that his theory is banned from the Soviet schools in Russia because it could upset the proletariat. I can only follow very dimly all this. But I keep to my fifth element—of spirits—and would live in it if I may. I asked him what I ask myself sometimes, if we made God or he made us. For it seems that if the jellyfish's mind could grow to Plato's mind, that mind might well create the Divine. But he says that very question was debated before Plato's time, and it was decided rightly that what is in us of God comes from Him, the Fire that animates all. Mystery of Mysteries! But the Divine is in us, around us, that at least is certain.

Mrs. Green,[10] came in. Says the discontent of the Pressmen (who have left Dail and Senate in a body and will give no reports) is due chiefly to their not being allowed into the tea rooms, and to the draughtiness of their place in the room. She complains of the hard narrow seats in the Senate and the dullness of the speeches.

Mrs. Green said yesterday there would be a troublesome time before the elections. And Yeats when I told him said yes, Cosgrave and another Minister had advised him not to have his pictures back yet awhile. They are rather afraid the Habeas Corpus trial may be in favour of the prisoners if it can be proved there is "not a state of war" in the country, and that they must be released. And it is known they have made plans for taking up arms again.

15TH. Robinson came in. Abbey valuation not ready, but I signed our letter to the Government asking for help. Hogan[11] came to lunch, looks very young. I didn't think I had ever met him, but he said he had been at the Workhouse that day some years ago when I spoke against amalgamation. He says the Republicans were bad fighters or would have beaten the Government. They had an immense supply of arms, more than they could use, but they never put up a real fight but turned their energy to destruction. I asked how he had been treated during his nine months internment at Ballykinlar "very well" he said "though we used to make complaints. But the prisoners now are better off, can read or work in their cell. We were crowded together". I said I had never heard of him in connection with the Nationalists before his internment. He said "I had never even joined any branch of Sinn Fein. But in the camp we all talked and stirred each other up and came out rebels. We were not very ready for actual fighting though, after the long internment."

He had sent for all Maupassant's works while there and read them through there. He says De Valera had intended to accept the Treaty and a very short time before it, "told the Bishop of ? in my presence he could not insist on fiscal autonomy. But fear of Brugha and jealousy of Collins worked in him". He praises Collins very much, his patience with De Valera, his deference to A. Griffith, his management of men, his success at the London Conference. He has seen the shorthand reports, and Collins spoke throughout with perfect naturalness as if among his own people. "No one else could have got so much". He is not anxious to press for the Boundary Commission thinks Ulster is sure eventually to come in.

They cannot release the prisoners, they have found plans made for renewing the war when they come out; they have not given up their arms.

Arson (it has begun now in the Waterford[12] strike) must be stopped. He said to Yeats "What do you think of the cat"? Yeats to whom I had told what F. said answered "I think it should only be used as an alternative to the death penalty". I told him of the sympathy felt for Murphy,[13] that boy shot for the Athenry Bank robbery. He said these boys were the tools of others—robbers—"it is the well-to-do, the rich farmers who are the robbers—and some of them near to Coole". But I would not mention or ask any name.

I finished reading Rossetti's letters.[14] I said to Yeats "It was old Stillman who introduced him to morphia" and he said "Yes, and Hall Caine very nearly saved him, substituting plain water for it, and by suggestion he did not know the difference and it had the same effect until a maid unluckily told him what had been done."

16 JUNE. Packing for the journey. The Independent has a paragraph saying the new gallery at the Tate is now to be begun, "promised by Sir J. Duveen to the British Nation as a thanksgiving for peace". And they tried to persuade us it had been offered to secure Hugh's pictures.

17 JUNE. Home yesterday, Yeats with me. A quiet journey, and all here looks well and peaceful. All has been quiet, the only trouble that Athenry robbery and the execution of young Murphy—only 23. One says the gang were Republicans. Another says they were a land gang, getting money to stock land they were about to seize from Lord Ashtown and wherever they could get it. One of the three, a Dooley from Granagh has not yet been taken. M. says a young fellow came here about ten days ago, looking starved, asked for food. She brought him out bread and butter and milk, and had some coppers in her hand to give him but saw his clothes were good; and he asked for nothing but when he had eaten went away by the yard. She had heard since a description of X. and thinks it was he. A terrible fate, wandering in fear of death.

19 JUNE. Yeats has just left. He talked much of his philosophy—and how it comes to him.

There is trouble over a bog at Lough Cutra.

20TH. Tim here. He says Murphy and the other were "put down in a hole with all their clothes on them and their boots, and not a coffin to keep the clay from them. The Black and Tans did nothing so bad as that". But I reminded him of the Loughnane boys.

22 JUNE. I wrote again this morning to Ministry of Munitions re return of firearms.

A letter from Tim Healy yesterday, will help about the pictures. I am writing to Yeats to keep him up to the mark.

Easily tired, haven't been farther than the garden, but do a little watering there, the young seedlings in want of rain. My mind is turning again towards a Passion Play, but to do it I must be, as Sven Hedin says, a Marionette—moved by invisible hands.

Yeats was rather pleased at my "Fifth Element" recurred to it. And I have felt very peaceful and "without malice" since I came home (I am typing this in July 1924. I can still say I am "Gan mailís" but it is perhaps less a spiritual feeling than my gratitude and the easing of my burden through Healy's and Carson's help, so that I hope the pictures may be gained without bitterness, indeed had used that in my prayers this morning.)

27 JUNE. The children, Anne and Catherine arrived yesterday, shouting! Such a joy to see them back so happy and unchanged, wild with excitement, riding Pud and Tommy and exploring the woods. It makes up for last summer's loneliness, having kept their home for them.

Yeats writes "The Governor-General whom I saw at the Belloc lunch said that a most urgent letter had been sent to the English Government about the pictures but that Curzon was still the enemy; and he was talking of what he could do with Curzon through Carson when we were interrupted. I have asked to see him that we might consider the matter further".

I am idle—but thinking and even making notes for a Passion Play.

29 JUNE. A Holy-day, Peter and Paul, very restful, the children still happy out of doors, have found a swallow's nest with little ones beginning to fly, and a yellow wagtail sitting on her eggs.

I wrote to Reynolds about adding a typed supplement to the pamphlet for Ministers if the Cabinet discussion comes on. And I went on making notes for the passion Play, more definite now. Marian left for a fortnight's holiday, her first for two years. Fahy from Kilbecanty came to ask for sand for the rebuilding of his house, it had been twice burned down, once I think by the Black and Tans. (I am told one burning was after the Ballyturn ambush). And I have some recollection of his brother the Gaelic teacher being a wanted man in the Rising. I promised him some if it is to be had, for much had been recklessly given away by old Mike when he was in charge.

Later some girls and a brother came, Fords of Castletown and Healy, asking to see the garden and I took them to it, and the children came and we gathered flowers for them. Anne and Cat so very happy still, and I am so happy, but very tired at times, and the wound aches (so it does now July 1924). (And now May 1928!)

1 JULY. We have been to church, very empty! But nearer to God it seems to me than the incense and processions at Hammersmith. And I like the Commandments according to

Christ being read instead of those of Moses. "In these two commandments are all the Law and the Prophets".

Carson, in an angry speech at the Mansion House on behalf of the Irish "exiled loyalists" bitterly reproaches himself for ever having told them to trust England, and wishes well, though rather grudgingly to the Free State. I have so often said these years back that the people's hatred of England had come into existence through love of Ireland, and that some day our class would come to love of Ireland through its betrayal by England.

9 JULY. A peaceful time, save for the anxiety about the pictures. Yeats sends a letter from T. Healy. I have just answered it, saying I think the House of Lords dangerous, Curzon being there, and death or illness having removed some of our supporters there, as Lords Plymouth and Ribblesdale. We should have I think better support in the Commons.

A letter saying the Director of the Melbourne Conservatoire has written music for the *Travelling Man*, made an opera of it, wants to publish it. I am glad.

Working at the Passion Play, getting a scenario and getting some life into it. But all my morning letter writing leaves me tired and I can't do very much at a time.

16 JULY. A peaceable time here, the children happy and lively.

Outside not so good. There is a eulogium on Curzon in the *Nation*[15] (no Massingham there now) which makes me feel he has more influence than ever. And Robinson writes about our offer of the Theatre to Government and Cosgrave's objection to do anything to help us, probably from economy. I think it may be necessary, this swing of the pendulum towards unimaginative construction after the recklessness of idealism run wild. The Republicans would have supported a theatre, though they might probably have wrecked it by putting their own people in.

Expenses very heavy since I came back—plumber, harness, Insurance, (house and workmen) painting, garden, besides household expenses. I grieve to think of my poor body having cost some £60. But Slattery writes that the examination proves there is *nothing* malignant. Such a relief.

And whether for good or bad, Watt writes that the Editor of the *Sunday Sun* has *lost* my MSS (*Seventy Years*). I hope it has not been stolen and chopped up for use. Otherwise I am glad of the delay, a relief.

Working at the Passion Play, I began a rough dialogue scenario yesterday.

18 JULY, 1923. Marian, back from her fortnight in Limerick says "They are all Republicans there", and a bad time is expected this winter. But that the prisoners are very angry with De Valera, and some of them say they will shoot him when they get out. "Mugs for us in the gaol and he drinking his tea out of a teacup".

26 JULY. Yeats wrote, 17th "When I was at Viceregal Lodge the upshot of talk was to wait a month or so before doing anything about the pictures to let Curzon's spleen at not being Premier cool. This was advice from a man from the Colonial Office. Then Healy proposes to go over with me".

G. Yeats came yesterday with the children while Ballylee is being made ready. De Valera's announcement[16] was in the papers two days ago that the Republicans will not continue the war, but will give themselves up to the material improvement of the country &c. Then yesterday he had another announcement saying he would stand for Clare. George says the papers have suppressed news of an immense meeting held by Miss McSwiney at Cork where it was decided to carry on the war. George saw De Valera walking about in Dublin a few days ago. The Government have given orders he is not to be arrested. She brought good news that two London Managers want to bring the Abbey plays to London. And that Hutchesson Poe is in favour of having Alec Martin as Director of the National Gallery, and has seen him in London.

28 JULY. Two young Prendergasts were found cutting young trees in Shanwalla and said their father told them I had given leave. I was afraid I should have to prosecute for they had been troublesome this while back. But I wrote to their father and had an apology.

6 AUGUST. Jack Yeats and his wife have been here a week. Hearing he was a Republican I have been trying to get at his point of view, which seems not far from my own, though he would not reason at first, said "I want a Republic because I would like it". I asked him today if the attack on the Four Courts which the Republicans say began the war could have been avoided. He says "No, because they were taking motors &c. As the Government was, there was nothing else to do. The Government has done very little it was not forced to do it if it was to govern at all. But the executions were inexcusable. None of the members of the Government who were responsible can stay in this country for the future. Those executions were against all that the songs of Ireland had taught all these years, all the ideas that had been looked up to". I said the Republic will come when the Colonies

demand that for themselves. But he doesn't think "that is the right way for it to come". But he would not fight for one and thinks the Government have done and worked well, but that the initial fault was accepting the Treaty. I said I am sometimes sorry they did so, for we see now that England would have been very unwilling to fight. But that, as I heard, Michael Collins had before accepting it visited all his outposts and found they were not strong enough to hold out. And the horrors of the Black and Tans might have been continued and intensified. Indeed there is so much to be said on both sides that I can feel no enmity against either.

Richard and the chicks have been very happy through the week, playing about with balls, with Pud and Tommy, picking mushrooms, bathing. He is not changed by Harrow.

16 AUGUST. All are gone. I think all were happy here, they, Yeats, and his children.

This morning a rumour that De Valera was arrested at Ennis. And then Paddy Cahel coming down with some money for trees he had bought from Margaret told me he had gone to the Ennis meeting yesterday, and De Valera had spoken for about five minutes when the Free State soldiers came in an armed lorry and made their way to the platform, firing some shots as they came, and took him. He went quietly. There were he thinks ten thousand there. There were a few hurt or wounded.[17] It is just as Yeats said of the English Government in 1916 "helping the prisoners to make their own ballads" arresting him then, when he had been walking about in Dublin and could have been taken easily enough there or elsewhere. It has been said since then that he had always a bodyguard and there would have been bloodshed.

I am working at my play, just today beginning rewriting the second Act. It began "Oh is it true that he is taken"! but I have been putting the little song first.

I am sorry De V. was not given at least time to state his case. He began by speaking against violence, and the killing of brother by brother. I feel more than ever a Republican "without malice".[18]

17 AUGUST. Peter who was always down on De Valera thinks the arrest a great mistake, and "there will be Holy murder in the country". He hears there were many children injured in the rush caused by the firing.

I did a good bit of work I think, Joel trying to raise a riot . . .

6.30 As I was working again at my play George Yeats appeared bringing a telegram to W.B.Y. "Official and private.

Lane pictures will be returned to Dublin very soon. Bracken" (His new London friend).

Oh what joy! I had never been so low about them, Healy's speech as reported in the *Independent* had seemed feeble. And the new Tate addition is being given paragraphs in the papers which say "Sir Hugh Lane had bequeathed his pictures as a nucleus"; and I could think of nothing to do. All little worries vanish away. (May 7, 1928—Alas! they are still kept from us in London).

20 AUGUST. Margaret on Saturday for the night, Gaynor being too drunk to motor her on, and it was pleasant having her and we had more talk together than in company.

Yeats yesterday afternoon and stayed to dine. He thinks the Government were right to arrest De V. I think they were wrong without at least letting him speak, and finding if there was any basis of peace in the speech. Yeats says the Ministers especially Cosgrave and Higgins have a deadly hatred of him. There is no basis of peace in that. He is disappointed in Cosgrave of whom he has seen most—"our minds have never met". Brennan of the Education Department told him when he asked if the Abbey's taxes could be remitted for a year that it was impossible without starving some other branch of education, that in the next two or three years there must either be the most drastic economy or a paper currency of our own. I said, and Yeats agreed, that if we cannot carry on the Abbey we should let it for a few years to a Film Company and save the money to open again. But I am not without hope that if the London tour comes off we may make money enough to carry on for a while, and perhaps pay our way. For we never could have paid it but for tours, English and American, and the English tours were only cut off by the war, the other by Robinson's catastrophe of running to wrong places on our last tour.

Yeats read me his long philosophical poem, a sort of introduction to or comment on the book.[19]

23 AUGUST. Monday, 21st, Catherine's birthday, to Burren in Guy's motor, showery but fine between, and Burren looked lovely, I hadn't been there for two years. The birthday a great success, little ten-year old delighted with the portrait of "Tommy" by Jack Yeats, and Margaret and all admired it also, and all presents were acceptable, and the opening of Godmother's hamper a great excitement. I went in to see old Tierney, who thinks there never will be peace in the country again; and old Lee who says he doesn't want to vote for either De Valera or the Government and will stay at home "if they will let

me". The Scovells think all Clare will be Republican.

Willy here yesterday. I say the fault of the Government is this hatred of the Republicans they show in their speeches. He says it is justified, or at least excused—by the information they have had from America that it is to be said in case of a Republican defeat that the elections were not carried out fairly, and that then four of them, Cosgrave, O'Higgins and two others are to be assassinated. But with the Republicans saying the prisoners are flogged or tortured they have probably the same hatred. And so, I said, they work on two parallel lines and will never meet, and I think, if they had left De Valera alone as long as he is at all inclined to stop the killings, there would have been a possible chance for the lines to come together.

25 AUGUST. The only election circular I have had is from a Labour candidate and begins: "You are hardworking men and women earning your bread by the sweat of your brow . . . as a rule you work longer hours than the man or woman who earns a daily wage". More truth in this than he knows!

G. Yeats, just back from a day in Dublin came in yesterday. She heard but doesn't know if it is true, that an arrangement has been made with the North. That they will join with the South, but keeping a Parliament for local matters. And will be in return allowed to keep the disputed counties.

27 AUGUST. Polling day. I have decided not to vote, I think not from indolence but because keeping out of this election leaves me free to join those Republicans "without malice" I hope to see organised. And it is my quarrel with the Government that they did not allow De Valera to make that speech declaring his policy, I think it may probably have been on those lines and the foundation of peace. If all should join to ask for the abolition of that insincere oath it could hardly be refused. And if Ulster is coming in there is little or nothing to quarrel over.

I am typing *The Story brought by Brigit*, but near the end of the first act my typewriter struck work again!

Father O'K. from Kilbecanty and a Father Hehir and Miss Power came to see the place, and I brought them in to lunch. Father O'K. a strong Republican. I gave him my views about Gan molais League, and read what I had written in 1919 about Dominion Home Rule. He said when he was leaving "I think if you had voted it would have been for the Republicans". I said "No, because I have no surety they will cease doing violence". He is afraid of the country growing apathetic if we wait for the Colonies to become Republics. But we agreed that the abolition of the oath would probably bring both sides together. And who wants it?

29 AUGUST. J.D. thinks there has been a large Republican vote, because "so many young men and girls came down from the hillsides" (like my Joel!).

Fagan writes asking if he may use my *Mirandolina*[20] for his Oxford Theatre. "It is so full of life and charm and so infinitely better than the wooden one beautifully published by Clifford Bax". But he wants to put back the Dejanira scene, and to call the play "Mine Hostess".[21] I am agreeing reluctantly to the scene but refusing to change the name as Putnam is publishing the play under that name and as "my chief desire in translating or indeed writing a play is to get it into a spoken language, and I don't think 'Mine Hostess' belongs to any language I have heard".

30 AUGUST. P., when I told him of De Valera's immense majority[22] said "With the people going on the way they are, it's no wonder the weather to be the way it is".

2 SEPTEMBER. Republican successes yesterday up to 37. And even in May when I spoke of their probable gains and their strength, Yeats (founding his opinion on Government news) said "De Valera won't have more than six" so confidently that I did not ask if he meant votes or members! I still think it best this strength of Republican feeling has to be acknowledged, it may be the foundation of some compromise—yesterday I thought "friendliness" but a Sinn Fein manifesto was published saying the new members (it looks as if they mean to go into the Dail) will vote against "the murder Government" on *every* question. My mind, and hand still on my play. I keep wondering what Christ would do were he here now, and it all seems to go back to "love worketh no ill to his neighbour" and the forgiveness of your brother's trespasses.

I motored to Burren with Guy, bringing provisions for the chicks, and found them all so well and happy. A great joy!

Old Jordan smelling of whiskey, says he was at Ennistymon for the Election—"Not a drop given by anyone, but to pay for it yourself. The poorest election ever was, not like the old time at all; and Mr. Kally (a publican) said the same thing".

6 SEPTEMBER. Irene Sampson told Margaret that the funerals in Dublin had been constant last winter, sometimes six in a day going through the streets many of them of Republicans—they knew this by only women following these.

I have written a new verse for the end of "The Old Woman remembers":[23]

But who forgives shall be forgiven;
It's likely in the Shining Land
Before that Company of Heaven
From Cathal's hand and Michael's hand
The barren shadow-weapons fall,
The bitter battle angers cease;
So may God grant to them and all
The blessing of his lasting peace.!

Edward Martyn[24] had been ill for some time and on 8 September, I wrote to A.W. "On the way back from Galway we got to Tillyra about 6.30. The chauffeur had never been there before and instead of stopping at the hall door drove a little past it, and there, in the bow window of the library I saw Edward sitting. I thought he would turn or look round at the noise but he stayed quite immovable, like a stuffed figure, it was quite uncanny. I rang the bell, and Dolan the butler appeared, said he was "only pretty well", but showed me into the drawingroom, and came back to say Edward would like to see me. I went in; he did not turn his head, gazed before him. I touched his hands (one could not shake them—all crippled, Dolan says he has to be fed) and spoke to him. He slowly turned his eyes but apparently without recognition. I went on talking without response till I asked if he had any pain and he whispered "No—thank God". I didn't know if he knew me, but talked a little, and presently he whispered "How is Robert?" I said "He is well, as all are in God's hands. He has gone before me and before you". Then I said "My little grandson Richard is well", and he said with difficulty and in a whisper "I am very glad of that". Then I came away, there was no use staying. I had seen a man (his nurse) behind the screen when I came in, but he went away . . . Dolan had tea ready but I could not have touched anything, it seems such a house of death. Poor Edward every moment was picking at the rug over his knees. I thought the best thing to do was to write to Lady Hemphill, as I had promised to write when I saw her in Dublin some time ago, and I have done so, telling of Edward's state, and that he has only servants there and "the doctor who attended him has lately been dismissed and another called in". It was a very sad visit.

(That was the last time I saw Edward Martyn, and I grieve for him.)

Lady Gough and Guy and Margaret have been here these last days. I am copying our third Act of *Brigit*.

14 SEPTEMBER. To Burren for Anne's birthday, on Tuesday, before its time, because of a Carnegie meeting on the 13th. All well there. On Wednesday I came to Dublin (82 Merrion Square).

Last evening Yeats and I were at Gogarty's. He says Cosgrave is sure to resign, had wanted to about six weeks ago and consulted him, suffers from overwork and insomnia. But the success of his visits to Bobbio and Geneva may have set him up again, and today flags are up all through the streets in honour of his arrival this evening. The Governor-General has been giving some dinners, a good many of his relations there, and the irreverent call the Viceregal Lodge "Uncle Tim's Cabin". Yeats had sent me another letter from Bracken "The Lane pictures will be returned very soon. The Duke of Devonshire's secretary has conveyed this information to Sir Edwin Lutyens".

15 SEPTEMBER. Cosgrave's triumphal procession yesterday evening.[25] We had a distant view from the nursery window and heard the bands. Whether joining the League of Nations was a wise move or not it is hard to say. I rather think not. Yeats would have liked it discussed in the Senate, but they found the Government was already bound to it.

16 SEPTEMBER. Yeats saw Cruise O'Brien who said a great many of the Republicans want to take the oath "under protest" and have succeeded in getting a letter to De Valera asking leave to do it. But they have not been able to get an answer. He says the Government don't want them to come into the Dail.

The newspaper headlines are "Wonderful welcome to the President"—"Aeroplanes escort ship. Military salute him on arrival"!

Teignmouth Shore[26] told me he had been in the crowd (an immense crowd lining the streets) but the carriage with Cosgrave passed by while he was looking for it, and there was very faint cheering. W.B.Y. finished his poem on Leda[27]—showed me the reproduction of the carving on which it is founded. And Jack Y. showed me his two fine paintings, "The Wave" and "Glasnevin" (Harry Boland's funeral) very fine indeed and touching. Jack thinks the men responsible for the executions cannot stay in the Government or even in the country. But I told him how there had been as great a bitterness between the North and South in U.S.A., and they had come together. W.B.Y. says the leaders in gaol all mean to fight again if they get out, and some one told me the same of the young men, Seaghan Gonne one of them.

17 SEPTEMBER. An afternoon with Lady Ardilaun at St. Annes. She will give help to the Abbey if we need it. She is a

lonely figure in her wealth; childless and feeling the old life shattered around her. Macroom Castle, her childhood home burned, and a desecration she feels more, the Free State soldiers in it have put a roof over a part "So I have not even my ruins". She laments for Ashford also, now a Barrack,[28] and for the loss of Society and "those nice young officers who used to write their names in our book"; and she speaks with violent despair over Government and its opponents—"Our class is gone, and who is there to replace it?" Yet she has stood her ground, taken a house in Dublin for the winter and brings friends to the Abbey on Saturday afternoons and has given several concerts, or musical afternoons. She is "grande dame" all through, and her welcome touched me, she took my hands and kissed me. Her lovely garden is, she says, the one thing that keeps her there. When she spoke with despair of the country I said it was from outside our help must come, a spiritual influence to do away with rancour, and she said "Oh yes, there must be forgiveness. Monks must go through the country and preach". Today an Anglican brother, Father Fitzgerald has been here and wants to found a community for the brotherhood to which he belongs. Yeats told him of Father Stephen Brown who has at his own expense founded a library of Catholic theology in Westmoreland St.; thinks they might help each other. Yeats talked of his long belief that the reign of democracy is over for the present, and in reaction there will be violent government from above, as now in Russia, and is beginning here. It is the thought of this force coming into the world that he is expressing in his Leda poem, not yet quite complete. He sat up till 3 o'c this morning working over it, and read it to me as complete at midday, and then half an hour later I heard him at it again.

8 SEPTEMBER. Yesterday afternoon I read *The Story brought by Brigit*[29] to Yeats and L. Robinson. To my great relief they both listened absorbed, and were even enthusiastic. Yeats said to L.R. later he thought it the best thing I had ever done. Such a relief. L.R. wants to do it at the Abbey, but I am doubtful—will have it printed first anyhow.

Dragon last night rather disappointing and a poor audience. Sally not at home in the part, and in a dreadful modern evening dress! Miss Crowe rather feeble. Ups and downs!

Today I have been reading with delight Figgis' *Return of the Hero*[30] and at the Abbey again. I gave my new verse of "The Old Woman Remembers" to Sally. She likes it and I do hope it may be a little paving stone on the road to peace.

I went in to see A.E. He believes De Valera was arrested to

save him from some who had sworn to kill him to avenge Collins' death; and to save the Government from being accused of doing it.

24 SEPTEMBER. On Wednesday 19 I came home, by early train. I was alone in my carriage and made up a connecting verse of the "Old Woman". Curious I should have begun it coming home in the train in the week of the Treaty two years ago and now finished it there.

BOOK TWENTY-SIX

24 SEPTEMBER, 1923. Richard and Margaret and the Chicks came back on Thursday, and on Saturday Catherine and I went to see darling Richard off from Galway, always so bright, and has some of his father's little courteous ways.

Now Anne and Catherine and I are alone. The holidays passed very happily, and Margaret begins to take more interest in Coole. Very worried over Income tax papers, no longer having Harris's help, and I'm anxious not to cheat, or to make blunders against myself.

29 SEPTEMBER. Yesterday I went to Galway to see the Income Tax Collector. John drove me in the dogcart. A fine day and all went well. A.E. had told me the other day that he had had the good luck of discovering a wonderful writer on economics, a man in Galway called Kiernan.[1] And this I found was my Tax gatherer! Quite young, and pleased when I told him of the compliment, and took the burden off me by preparing return and appeal, but I don't know yet what I shall have to pay. I gave him complete list of my income from books and plays. Alas their proceeds having been already taxed in the United States is no help, but the reverse.

Today Captain Duggan from Gort Barracks and a Sergeant came, by Mr. Johnson's advice to consult me about a library they want to establish for their men. I gave them the Carnegie circular, and some books I had looked out for them, *Don Quixote, Cuchulain, Huckleberry Finn, The Privateers Man, Martin Chuzzlewit, A Tale of Two Cities, The Lady of the Barge.* And they chose or took from a little heap *Tales from a Jury Room*, and Carlyle's *French Revolution* and *Sea Wolves of the Mediterranean.* Also *Hugh Lane's Life*—Captain Duggan had already read it, and had read all Dickens and a good deal of Mark Twain, and he pounced on the *French Revolution.* He had been brought up at Scariff; has a pleasant intelligent face. I spoke of a possible peace and he said "the best of the Republicans are with us. There is no difference between us except that they are more in a hurry than we are". "Passion and Patience", I said. And I feel more than ever that Republicans "without malice" would take in the best through all the country. But I read him a sentence from Mrs. Jayne's[2] letter that had just come, about "the revolutionary form of radicalism that is spreading among the masses. It seems strange that anyone should be dissatisfied with a Republic like ours". He said there is certainly more liberty here than in America and was, even under English rule.

I had been too tired to sleep last night and had to be down early to have my letters ready for John going to market to buy oats for the fowl. But I had a pleasant quiet day, typing *Brigit*, and reading *Tom and the Crocodiles* to the children, and gathering all the last of the apples, and working with Peter in the flower border; and now I have Flaubert and George Sand's letters to read,[3] when the children's gramaphone is silent.

13 OCTOBER. I have worked very hard over *The Story brought by Brigit*, typing, I hope finally. Today I have corrected proofs of *Mirandolina*. The Chicks' lessons and my letters keep me busy.

Amy Shawe Taylor was here arranging for her auction. She was indignant on Sunday that the King was not prayed for, and wouldn't listen to the explanation that the Archdeacon had industriously prayed for him and Royal Family every Sunday but this one, and let their names drop out because, for Amy's benefit, he had read a lesson as well as Epistle and Gospel, which he had not done for a long time. She says that she had succeeded in having "God save the King" put on at Ardrahan in the war time, but on its first Sunday everyone sat through it, even the police, who when she remonstrated said they didn't know they were to stand, they had never heard that tune before!

John Fahy says there have been seizures of cattle for rates in these last days "And that is through the Republicans, for they always said there would be no rates when they came in power, and so there were many paid none last year, and the two years are come upon them now". The grumbling is now at the size of the army and the high pay of soldiers "but I wouldn't say but there'll be trouble yet. The Republicans are very headstrong".

26 OCTOBER. It has been a hardworking time. I finished typing *Brigit* and sent it off to Putnam, and then found I had typed the last two Acts, three copies, twice over! I have not the least recollection of this, I had probably done them when the typewriter broke down, and then when Richard came home and set it right I must have begun again at a new copy. Anyhow I have set to work to make a new copy of the First Act, so have a good supply of typed copies, but none probably good enough for the printing, with stage directions &c. Then the Chicks' lessons,

and reading to them after lunch and after tea, and an endless correspondence. And now Amy S[haw] T[aylor] for her auction, and Mrs. Scovell. And slight headache all these last days.

In my quiet evenings I read Byron's correspondence with Lady Melbourne with great distaste, and won't get the second volume.[4] Also Flaubert and George Sand correspondence. She charming all through leading I think a happier life, not paying much attention to her writing, though throwing off novels &c, but taken up with home and family, and the little granddaughter Aurore. He a tremendous worker, digging and delving and giving himself entirely to the mastery of his material and of style looking on it as an end, and cut away from life, his only human qualities his affection for G.S. and for his mother.

Some of Flaubert's sentences are best: "Our ignorance of history makes us slander our own times. Men have always been like this. Several years of quiet deceived us. That is all . . . One must wipe out that mistake (of the amelioration of manners) and think of oneself no more highly than they did in the time of Pericles or of Shakespeare, atrocious epochs in which fine things were done."

"Every man as I think has a right to *one* voice, his own, but he is not the equal of his neighbour, who may be worth a hundred times more. In an industrial enterprise each holder votes according to the value of his contribution. It ought to be so in the Government of a Nation. I am worth fully twenty electors of Croisset. Money, mind, and even race ought to be reckoned, in short every resource. But up to the present I only see one—Numbers!

"What a fine thing is Censorship! Axiom! All Governments curse literature; power does not like another power".

. . . "You see I do well to spare you my letters—there is nothing so imbecile as the whiners".

Yesterday I read Lady Henry Somerset's *Life*,[5] a hard one, the careless, dominating, neglectful, worrying, beautiful mother, the unhappy marriage. Then the devotion to "Causes", barren enough it seems. But then at the last the wonderful work to reclaim the wretched drunken women, for Christ's sake. A fine end, the triumphant end of a tragedy, as all tragedies should end.

Disorder breaking out here and there and A. begins to write of raids again.

After Amy S.T.'s auction yesterday Joyce had four soldiers to escort him and his money back to Galway. Poor C.T. furniture scattered, chiefly to shopkeepers, the only class who have any money.

Huntington writes "I read your Passion Play last night, and I feel indeed that it is a beautiful and precious work. It has the inevitable quality, and it seems to depend, as religion should, upon the heart rather than upon the mind. There is the wonderful story just as it is known to children and simple people, and there are no clever new theories to upset our cherished conceptions. I am glad that you left Judas where you found him and resisted the modern mania for explaining and justifying him". A relief!

And in the *Irish Statesman* L. Robinson writes in an article on the Comic Muse "We are too 'genteel' to admire the merely comic. I remember seeing Lady Gregory's *Jackdaw* long ago, and dismissing it with the arrogance of a twenty-year-old as 'only a farce'. I know better now, and envy every line of it".[6]

31 OCTOBER. Yeats writes "Bracken has come and gone. Curzon said to him 'I did not want to give up those pictures but I find that I must'. Curzon then told him that the Commission would decide he thought that they were to be given back on perpetual loan, as the difficulties of bringing in a Bill were too great. I brought him over to the President and got him to repeat his story. President said he would consult the law officers, or rather I asked him to do so and he agreed. If the loan is accepted we must see to it that the loan is truly perpetual".

I have written Yeats that if we get the pictures to this side of course we will never let them go back. But it is an ungracious way of giving them up after all the eight years they have kept them from us.

1 NOVEMBER. I have sold the rabbits to Bernard Cunningham (who was in old days brought before me as a poacher!) He has been very steady and hardworking since his release from gaol.

EVENING. Near 8 o'c when the children had been roasting chestnuts and I was reading *The Castaways*[7] to them in the library, Marian came up looking rather frightened, and said there were men at the door wanting to see me, would not give their names. I went down and opened the hall door. There were three young men, I could only see one, the spokesman, clearly, the light falling on him, but I didn't recognise him, may have seen him before, but I have no gift for remembering faces. He asked if I had sold the rabbits to Cunningham. I. "Yes". He. "What money did he give?" I. "That is between him and me." He. "Did not Murty O'Loughlin get the rabbits for twenty years?" I. "For a good many years certainly." He. "Why didn't he get them now?" I. "He did not ask for them either this year or last year. I had no offer from him or anyone last year." He. "He should have them." I. "He did not ask for them. He has his old age pension now, I don't suppose he wanted them." He. "He could not take them last year because there was no law or order in the country. There will be trouble if Cunningham gets them." I. "Do you mean that you will cause trouble?" Another. "We are here for the sake of quietness." 1st. "It is likely Cunningham will not be allowed to have them. There will be trouble." I. "I suppose you mean by that you will cause trouble but I hope you will think again before you do anything that will break the law of God." He. "You must take back the agreement." I. "That would be a dishonourable thing to do. I will not do what is dishonourable."

Then he harped on Murty's twenty years, and I said I had no reason to believe he wanted them. And I begged them again to keep the peace, to follow the law of Christ "Do unto others as you would they should do unto you". He. "Do you know Cunningham used to take your rabbits?" I. "Yes, he was brought before me once or twice, or came to ask forgiveness." He. "Do you know that he was in gaol?" I. "Yes. It was I who got him out." He. "You did! He was convicted!" I. "Yes, but he was young and foolish, he had been long enough in gaol, others had led him on. And since he came back I have heard nothing but good of him."

Then the speaker put his hand in his pocket, fumbled, and brought out a cigarette which he tipsily offered to another. I laughed and said "I thought it might have been a revolver." The other said "Oh no", and I said Good night, the spokesman saying as he turned to go "There will be trouble and the responsibility will be on you". I only remembered afterwards that Murty could not have taken up the business without losing his pension. But it makes me sad and anxious.

I came back and read to the children, and they knew nothing of it. They were young men, and Marian thinks as I do that the one who spoke had been drinking.

The children are watching the stars. Anne has twice seen falling stars. Ellen tells them that if they can see seven stars at the same time, for seven nights one after another, they will have whatever they wish.

I began today typing my old journals, chiefly about the fight for the pictures.

6 NOVEMBER. No trouble here, but John talks of robberies about Ballyvaughan. A man with a load of potatoes and cabbages worth £7 had his load taken on the road—"a poor man

with a houseful of little children".

9 NOVEMBER, 1923. Yesterday to Dublin, 82 Merrion Square. Yeats lecturing "on novels" at Trinity. He says this morning, about the hungerstrikers, that the Government are prepared to let men die.[8] Gogarty told him they are anxious to let the prisoners out, except 1000, who are dangerous. I asked "Danger of a rebellion?". He thinks of assassination.

10 NOVEMBER. At the Carnegie meeting yesterday there was a renewed request for help for the Catholic Book repository, Westmoreland Street. The Provost, not able to come, wrote against it, on the ground that Protestant societies wanting books of controversy might make the same request. Father Finlay refused to say anything for or against. Mr. McDonell (very anti-church) was against it. I spoke for it, Yeats having said in the morning that they have a very fine collection of books, philosophy, modern thought, which might be valuable to our Carnegie students to whom they propose making them free. But the meeting was lukewarm, Smith Gordon proposed a grant of £100 instead of the £500 asked, and finally it was shelved until next meeting.

Dinner with L.R. at the Metropole; Yeats and I, Mrs. Green, Tom Esmonde[9] who talked most of the time, amusingly enough, giving an account of the Imperial Conference (where Ireland was placed beneath India and beneath Newfoundland). His criticisms were chiefly of D.F. who smoked a cigarette when no one else did, and treated all the business with carelessness and ignorance. The King at the reception, where he had given his hand woodenly to the other representatives, came trotting across the grass to shake hands warmly with the Irish, and said "Cosgrave ought to be here". He had said to John MacNeill, hearing there had been delay in arresting De Valera "a great pity the whole batch of them were not kept locked up in 1916 and there would never have been all this trouble"—forgetting that MacNeill had been one of those locked up! He is anxious for an invitation to Ireland, but Queen Mary still hates us.

We went on to the Abbey to see *John Bull*. There had been some talk about the hunger strike, Esmond saying the Government would not yield. And this is Yeats' view. I had some talk with him after we came home, the first time I had seen him alone, and again this morning. He says the Government cannot give in. That if they had let Miss McSwiney die when she began it this new hunger strike would not have begun, but they had a sentimental feeling for her for her brother's sake. We talked a long time this morning. I had a bad night and thought over it a long time, and had come to a determination of writing to the papers, asking that the crime or accusation against these four hundred men remaining on strike might be told out, that we might know if consenting to their suicide is in accordance with the conscience of Christian nations and the law of God. I meant to go and consult A.E. about this. But Yeats is violently against any protest says it is necessary to the stability of Government to hold out; says they cannot publish the accusations, because many are on suspicion, or as they think certainty, but they have not evidence that can be given. They have however evidence against Aitken, his own handwriting, threatening the editor of the *Freeman* with death if he did not give up his paper. And he, or another, is known to have signed death sentences. I ask if that might not come under an amnesty at the conclusion of the war, for the Government themselves signed death sentences during it. But he says no, and he says the Government cannot publish the real reason for the detention of this thousand, that they themselves are in danger of being assassinated by some among them. I asked if they could not on their side try to get rid of the oath; that would do away with the real cause of trouble, the keeping of Republicans out of the Dail. He says they cannot in the present state of English feeling it would be useless to ask for it, and besides we may probably want English help in getting the loan. And the Senate can make no move in the matter, indeed Senate and Dail and Government seem as helpless as the prisoners, and the war of bitter words goes on. He says there is a split in the Government, two parties, and this nearly broke it up a while ago. There have been serious army scandals. One of the worst the case of a General commanding in Kerry, who had two girls, Unionists, daughters of a doctor, brought out of their house in their nightdresses and he and others lashed them with their belts. Kevin O'Higgins to his credit demanded the exposure and dismissal of this man. But X. and Y. would not allow it, hope to reform the army by degrees and without the scandal being made public. But in consequence of this one, all Kerry has gone republican. All so sad and unsatisfactory and I think humiliating.

As to the Lane pictures, Bracken told him a Commission has been sitting (names unknown) and have decided they must be given back, but this is not yet public. And their suggestion, or the suggestion made to them has been "perpetual loan". Yeats thinks they probably have not even gone into the evidence, but that "Imperial interests" demand the return and Eddie Marsh has been ordered to write a report in favour of it.

11 NOVEMBER. I waited in for Robinson and had a satisfactory talk over the Theatre. We are to get Tulloch of Craig Gardners to take over our business conscience and attend to the accounts once a month, we giving the auditing to his firm and paying him so much per annum. Robinson wishes to give up management and agrees to Dolan;[10] the resentment of the Company was apparently an invention of McG.'s. So I feel at last that the anxiety about Abbey finance will be off my mind, and that we shall have the expert advice we had lost with Harris.

I went to *John Bull* matinée, the acting very good indeed; audience small, the Republican order against amusements accountable; and we shall hardly cover the week's expenses.

Then on to Jack Yeats; found him with McGreevy and a silent man who I later found was Tuohy the artist. Then L.R. came in, said he wanted a word with me, and we left together. He said "Can we not do anything about the hunger-strikers? Write a letter perhaps". Strange, for I had not spoken to him of my own restless night or my talk with Yeats. So we walked and planned and at last went into the Arts Club and wrote a letter, he the body, I the last sentence—that we thought might do. We thought Stephens and Jack Yeats might join in signing it. He called in Cruise O'Brien from another room to ask if the *Independent* would put it in. He thought so; made one or two slight alterations, thinking it showed a slight prepossession against the Government; then I came back to Merrion Square.

Later L.R. telephoned that Jack Yeats had refused to sign "he is much too red to do so", and asked if we should still send it on with our own names and Stephens', who had agreed. I said "Yes." It may perhaps bring letters or suggestions from others and possibly save some lives. Then I told Yeats what I had done and proposed leaving this house for the hotel, as he might disapprove. He would not allow that, and after talking for a while thought perhaps we had done right. Of course one won't have any gratitude from either side. But I slept better.

13 NOVEMBER. Our letter, L.R.'s and mine, in *Independent* and *Irish Times* this morning with no comment:

> Sir: Are the Government and the Republican party playing a game for prestige and power with human lives as counters? Does each side consider the game to be worth the stakes? We (and we are sure thousands of other Irish men and women agree with us) believe that from this contest no victory can come to either party but that the only certain loser will be Ireland herself.

Sooner or later one side or the other must give way for it is inconceivable that obstinate pride will allow hundreds of our fellow-countrymen to die. To save—not the Free State or the Republic—but the fair fame of Ireland we plead that both sides should give way now, before life has been sacrificed.

We ask the Republican Cabinet to order the hunger strike to be abandoned on condition that the Government gives an undertaking to put on trial immediately the men now on hunger-strike. If the Government refuse to do this we ask them to tell us with what crimes these men are charged. We need assurance from both sides that the deaths of these men are in accordance with the conscience of Christian nations and the Divine law.

Yesterday afternoon I went to Bushy Park Road to see Molly Childers. I had not seen her since just after the signing of the Treaty, when she had been so violent. It was sad coming to the house where I had not been since Erskine's execution, they had been so happy and proud in their possession of it, after the little Chelsea flat. She looked well and pretty and calmer than before; began by saying she has no animosities now. I told her I had written a letter she would probably object to, but it was with a good purpose. She said at once she objected to the demand to the Government to try these prisoners "They would not accept this". I said it was very unlikely the Government would offer it (did not tell what Yeats has said as to that) but that it was necessary to make some proposal that might lead to bridge-building—but she was vexed. But then she grew quiet and talked of the hardships in gaol, declared the strike had not been organised but came from within, and says it would not be possible to call it off, they are determined to go on to death. She spoke a good deal of Ernest O'Malley,[11] he had written her a letter saying he was quite resolved and quite happy. She is very anxious, and much more gentle and asked if I knew Lady Arnott, she has so much influence and might help. She asked me to write to one of the prisoners, or of Sinn Fein—says it has given up hatreds and is under new management. I asked what would happen in the future, and she said "There will be two Governments, the existing one and one formed by the quarter or third of a nation that is not satisfied with it." I said that would be all right if the Republicans could come into the Dail, and have an alternative Government, but I supposed the oath was the stumbling block. She said yes, they will never take that. She believes England will never give it up." Erskine always said it would be impossible for England to do so, it would knock out the foundation of her relations with the Colonies. But it might be dropped here. Many are in favour of that, many in the Senate even, and then there would be questions in Parliament after a while, but probably nothing done to enforce it." (This is what Yeats had said Jameson had thought possible some months ago but not now, because of the Diehards in England and because we want backing for the loan). She gave me a photograph of Erskine. Bobby then came in, her boy Erskine is at school in England.

I went then to consult Mrs. Green. She is sympathetic, but says she knows *very* strong pressure has been put on the Government to yield, but in vain. They are afraid of being assassinated. What keeps them safe now is the knowledge that they would retaliate on those in prison, as they did on Rory O'Connor and Mellows, (and of that vengeance and retaliation there seems no possible end)! She thought a petition might be possible. I said if there were names in it that would carry weight in England, it might. I believe the Government would yield more readily to English opinion that to ours. I told Yeats all this when I came in but he was not very comforting.

This morning I went to see Lady Arnott and gave her Mrs. Childers' message, or words. She was touched and said she would do what she could to help, but that the *Irish Times* has no influence with the Government because it has not always been friendly to them. I spoke of my hope of getting English opinion round, and she agreed; and that these men who are not giving in are at least brave men. She, herself English, does feel the heroic element in the strikers who are giving their lives for an idea. So I went away rather comforted.

Then writing to Chief Commissioner of Police for a permit for Richard and Guy and Hugo to bring their guns to Ireland for the holidays.

Then to see A.E., he of course sympathetic but rather in despair of the Government. (Mrs. Green said "That poor little Cosgrave has been so scolded and warned by his colleagues he is a mass of nerves"). He asked how I liked what he had written in the *Irish Statesman*. I said I very much liked his article on "The Squandering of Irish Sentiment",[12] but that now I think he has said enough about the Government view and the faults on both sides, and ought, as I had written in my letter, to write with "the conscience of Christian nations and the Divine law" in his mind, for he has influence in England and ought to put the plea for release on the highest ground, and he agreed to this. Then we spoke of the abolition of the oath, but he says Douglas thinks it impossible. But he will get Douglas to write an article on it in the next Statesman, and that may draw out some possible solution.[13]

11.30. Just back from the Gaelic Plays, the first performance at the Abbey a great success, stalls full, pit full, gallery rather weak, but 115 season tickets sold during the evening, and they will take the Abbey for seven Mondays instead of four. *Shadow of the Glen*, the only one I saw through, went very well, the girl charming. It is sad Synge could not have seen it in its Gaelic speech.

I was introduced to General Beaslai, whose play was to come on next. I was sorry Craoibhin was not there to see this latest success, for the first Gaelic play ever given in Dublin was his *Casad-an-tSugain*.

Robinson came in rather low. Jack Yeats had been violent over the letter, said only a Britisher would sign it, and someone he had met said it would be a cruel thing to bring any of those men up for trial. But I was assured there was no chance of that. Mrs. Green scoffed at the idea of De Valera being tried (Mrs. Childers had said there is great danger of it and of his execution). She says they are keeping him shut up lest his own party should kill him! I said it does seem as if they were making a Queen Bee of him, waxing up his cell.

16 NOVEMBER. On Tuesday morning G. Yeats said at breakfast "Miss MacSwiney has answered your letter in all the papers", and I was rather miserable expecting some hard words. But it was amiable. Someone had said to L.R. it was a "hard letter" and Miss O'Brien had written him something of the kind.[14]

Yeats says De Valera is being guarded by officers on account of the large bribes that are being offered for his release—or escape.

I had a hard morning, telling Munro we were taking the Abbey audit from him as Tulloch of Craig and Gardners has consented to look after our business.

Poor M. much upset, offers to do our business as well as audit, doesn't want to lose us, "had been speaking to Lord Granard about the Abbey only yesterday". I said I thought he would have been glad to get rid of us, more trouble than profit. But no, he will go every *week* through our accounts if we will take him as business adviser. So to the Abbey and L.R. much put out, because he had offered the post to Tulloch, who makes no offer of withdrawing. Then to Yeats, who thinks Munro should have it. I said I think so, by right, but as Robinson feels he can work better with Tulloch and will have to do business at the Abbey, I so much away and with so little grasp of finance, and Yeats too much taken up with writing and other things to attend to, expediency says, have Tulloch. Then Robinson came and suggested leaving the audit with Munro, giving business to Tulloch, who agreed to this by telephone, and I wrote it to Munro, and that was settled. *The Round Table*[15] in the evening and *Apartments*,[16] Sally splendid in both.

On Monday night A.E. and General MacManus were with Yeats, I looked in but didn't stay. Yeats said they had talked of the prisoners. MacManus said they were not on hunger strike, were being fed. And that the stories of ill treatment are not true—gave instances, thinks it "likely only half a dozen men will die". Dreadful I think, even if that half dozen were not of the bravest. It is the abolition or altering of the oath that would save all and make peace possible, and an alternative Government. On Wednesday before leaving I went in to see A.E. and say good-bye. He has written some paragraphs for his *Statesman*[17] says there is a murder gang on both sides, and that the Government have executed or killed over 90 men since the split. I don't know how many the Republicans have killed.

As to the Lane pictures, Yeats had a letter from Lutyens:

13 Mansfield St.
11 November, 1923.

My dear Yeats,

Yes, I stayed with Curzon and spoke to him about Lane's pictures. He said the Trustees under the will could not as Trustees give Ireland the pictures, but they could and are prepared to lend them to Ireland when her affairs seem settled and that they could be properly housed, and that they would (I think he said "in all probability") never ask for them back again, which is more than probable! Whether it is a propitious moment now I am not politician enough to form an opinion. What I should advise you to do is to write to Eddie Marsh who is Devonshire's Secretary at the Colonial Office and ask him. But from what E. Marsh and Curzon said, the Government have undoubtedly decided to allow the pictures to go to Ireland.

E. LUTYENS

I went to the Gallery to tell Reynolds how things are going. He showed me Miss Harrison's cracked letter. Then to settle Abbey business with Robinson and buy some things for the children.

A.E. and Yeats agree (and give instances) that it is impossible to believe anything said about the prisoners by Mme. Gonne.

Seaghan has been to see A.E., looking very well, but A.E. thinks likely to get into mischief again. To Galway for the night of 14th. And to see Kiernan about Income Tax in the morning.

I thought, I don't know why—"What we have to do is not to try to get to Heaven but to bring Heaven about us", and this thought has been with me ever since, with a sort of radiance. I thought also reading some strange sentences at the end of *Vivian Grey*[18] (that began as if written by Mr. Worldly Wiseman) that if there is in us all some atom of the Divine flame, that must be imperishable—must unite again sooner or later with that flame. And what does it matter if the atom keeps its individuality for a while after death from the world or goes back to the Divine soul?

A telegram came from Yeats telling me he has been awarded the Nobel Prize.[19] I am proud and glad of this triumph for I believed in him always and was glad he "never made a poorer song that he might have a heavier purse". In these twenty-six years our friendship has never been broken.

A nice letter today from Sally Allgood.

21 NOVEMBER. A busy week at home, letters to be answered. And the typed copy of *Brigit* (I am sending it off to Huntington today) kept me tied in the afternoons. The children came back very full of their exploits at the sea, had found an eel "tied in a knot, it was very hard to undo", and a metal goblet, they imagine from a German submarine; and they saw lobsters feeding and caught crabs. Here they are riding again, have put up bars in the hobble field.

Bernard Cunningham has been here this morning, he has not been meddled with on our land, but a few nights ago armed men (he knows them but did not give their names nor did I ask) came and put a revolver to his forehead and made him go on his knees and promise not to trap on the land where Cahel had given him leave. He made his promise, and it is now being trapped by Tom McLoughlin. We agreed in regrets for the Volunteers and their law, the most effective we have ever had.

A.E. writes in the *Irish Statesman* about the prisoners.[20] But the Government show no sign of giving in, their heart is hardened and they will not let them go.

22 NOVEMBER. Cold weather has come, ice inside my windows last night when I went to bed. Anne has succeeded in seeing seven stars on seven successive nights, and according to Ellen is now to get her heart's desire.

I have written in answer to the New Jersey Students who asked for a letter, giving quotations as to the life, while yet on earth, in Heaven.

The papers did not come till this morning, and tell of the first death among the hunger strikers, Barry.[21] A terrible responsibility on those who encouraged them and those who will not concede anything to their weakness.

23 NOVEMBER. I have had another account of the Cunningham matter. The three men, X., Y., Z. "he thinks, but they had white bands over their faces, fired two shots and ordered him to kneel and promise he would not trap on that land any more. He made a rush from them at first, and came on T. O'L. who had run behind the butt of a tree". He refused to kneel for any of them, but they made him promise, standing, pointing their revolvers at his head. They made no objection to his trapping on our land, indeed told him there was a rabbit in one of his traps "there below".

24 NOVEMBER. Last evening, cuttings having come, I read what Yeats said of my plays, and still better of the applause. (Lady Gregory . . . who knew nothing about Theatres wrote masterpieces. Any of her compact speeches, analysed sentence by sentence was a masterpiece).[22] And then, finding an old *New Republic* of August, I read a pleasant word of *Cuchulain*—that sometimes seems to be forgotten in the noticing of my work— ". . . One must still go to Lady Gregory's books to find the flavour at its sharpest, the Celtic face at its bleakest, the crafty speech at its wittiest, and the description of women, metal-work, fabrics and hounds at its most sumptuous". And it came at a good moment as I was tired after a visitation of Mrs. B. and M.—1.20 to 4.15.

The papers today say the hunger strike is over, thank God! A defeat for those who supported it, but if the Government will now show magnanimity it may lead towards peace. And if the Loan, now offered, can be subscribed in Ireland, there will be more hope of getting rid of that stumbling block the oath.

The children say that when the plum pudding was being made for their Christmas in London they were told that if they stirred it they would have a wish granted. And they both did so, and their wish was that they might soon come back to Ireland.

25 NOVEMBER, SUNDAY. A hard frost still and we cannot go to church, the hill up Crow Lane dangerous, some horses fell there yesterday. So we have been reading psalms and a chapter of St. John's epistle; and the *Pilgrim's Progress*, the children painting birds from memory as I read this. It is long since there has been such a hard frost, the lake frozen.

The other evening the children gave a little performance in the library for the maids, recitations in costume, the *Woman of*

Three Cows, and little *White Lily*, and then dancing their jig and reel. A great success.

28 NOVEMBER. Yesterday very wet, but brightened by a notice in the *Independent* of *Bubbles* at Belfast, saying it was a success. And a long letter from John Quinn. And the children were glad to hear he is sending off two boxes of apples.

I am told that on Sunday there was a table outside the chapel door, H. and K. "who should know better" and another collecting "for the prisoners and its likely it is for a dance between this and Xmas."

1 DECEMBER. Mrs. Cooney's letter of apology a relief. I don't want to have to prosecute though her sons have been seen more than once cutting even in Shanwalla, but not by anyone authorised to stop them until this week, when they had cut the large limb of a beech in Kincorda. I am going to send her a load of firing as she is poor.

Some nice words in an article by T. P. O'Connor about the Nobel prize. "It is impossible to mention Mr. Yeats without adding something of what he and Ireland owe to the unselfish, devoted and unconquerable woman who has helped him and Ireland towards the great literary renaissance of modern days".

4 DECEMBER. I have been reading the last four *Sinn Fein* numbers, looking for some ground of meeting, but they were barren of all but anger with the Government and bitterness against Collins especially among those who accepted the Treaty. And Mulcahy is held personally responsible for the death of some prisoner. I am sorry, I wish the wound could be healed. Yet one is touched by the portraits and letters given, of boys, Cassidy, Fisher, Gaffney, Twohig, executed a year ago, 17 November, 1922. And of others executed 30 November, 1922. They look so young, and the letters to their mothers go to one's heart— "I send home the mouth organ to you for Paddy"; "Dear Mother, do not worry over me as I am proud to die for Ireland". "Do not be angry or bear me any malice or hatred". Erskine Childers' letter and portrait also. "Died 24 November 1922". "I have been told that I am to be shot tomorrow at seven". And all for that wretched oath; "Gessler's cap"—the Moslem as I wrote a few days ago to John Quinn. I think it will have to be altered before we have peace.

Birrell writes: "I am glad the Loan has been floated and the Hunger Strikers defeated . . . As for the 6800 Prisoners still *untried* and the Arms still *undelivered* what is to be done with them? One thing is clear now that the 'British Tyranny' has been got rid of—Irishmen love autocracy and don't care a Tinker's curse for all that parade of Liberty we Sassanachs love to exhibit.

"A Mussolini is your fate, but are we any better off with our foolish Baldwin and our vulgar Lloyd George"?

7 DECEMBER. Yesterday I took the children to a party at Ballyturin, very merry for them. But I heard of Edward Martyn's death, it had taken place that morning. The doctor told Mr. Bagot a tumour had been taken from his head on Saturday, Dr. McGuinness had come from Dublin for the operation and he lost a good deal of blood. Father O'Kelly said he had after the operation recognised Father Carr, which he had not done for some time. I asked about the funeral. He said Father Carr told him also he had bequeathed his body to Dublin doctors "in the interests of science", so it may probably be in Dublin. Though he had been too ill to see of late and I had not been able to go and see him before that because of the broken bridge and my difficulty about rough roads, I feel a loneliness now he is gone. He was from the beginning of my life here at Coole a good neighbour; he was always grateful for my husband's interest in him. He had gone to see Edward at Oxford to advise him not to build that large addition to his old castle, until at least his own taste and opinion were formed; and though the forces were too strong, his mother and her surroundings, he often regretted that he had not the strength of mind to take that advice. He was very kind to Robert, giving him his first real gun and letting him and his friends shoot Tillyra in the holidays. And then, when Yeats' summers, and the theatre project began, he was constantly here, walking over and staying to dine. It was George Moore who broke that work together, putting his own name to the *Bending of the Bough*, rewritten by him and Yeats but on Edward's foundation. And Edward had been weak about the *Countess Cathleen*, and took a wrong turning I think in withdrawing his support from our Theatre. Of late I was told he felt his support of Sinn Fein in its beginning had been wrong, it was on his conscience. And yet he hated, with a real hatred, England. I always felt there were two natures in him, the old blood of the Martyns and the blood of the Smiths. The country people believed him to be a descendant of Oliver Cromwell, perhaps that was why they never warmed to him, (nor did he to them). It was old Mrs. Quirk who told me Cromwell had "stopped at Tillyra for a while when there was a Mrs. Martyn in the house, and the master of the house not in it. And ever since, there has been an Oliver in the family". I don't think Edward ever heard this, but he was proud of the deed giving permission from Cromwell to leave Tillyra unmolested that

used to hang in his study.

In the evening, alone, I read in the *New Republic*, Wells' last chapter on Sanderson of Oundle[23] and it stirred me. His theory of what a school should be and what he had made one, seems to be akin to our dream, made to some extent a reality in the Abbey. All working to *create*, a fine drama, fine acting, a theatre giving opportunity to every talent in it. "And at the end we too, (Wells & Sanderson) shared the belief that latent in men and perceptible in men is a greater mankind, great enough to make every effort to realise it fully worth while, and to make the whole business of living worth while".

"The Kingdom of God is within you". Christ has said everything first.

11 DECEMBER. Rather worried because having sold out £1000 Tasmanian to put in our new Loan, it closed before my application can have got in. I oughtn't to take part in money matters at all. But this I thought was for the country's sake.

Poor Edward. His body has been taken to Dublin to be dissected, by direction of his will. He directed the Dr. should visit it each day till removal to make sure he was really dead. But if he meant by giving it to the School of Medicine to perhaps save some other sufferer from what he has gone through (no doctor seeming to know what was wrong or be able to help him) it was a fine thing to do. There is a nice notice of him in *The Times*, better than he would have gained by following his family's wishes and settling down to marry and entertain the County.

The *Literary Supplement* has an article on Tchekov[24] and quotes him "One would need to be a God to decide which are the failures and which the successes in life". And writing of his work it says "Where the discord is at extremity and the tangle most obviously beyond all solution this side the grave, to that point he turns and lo! the harmony is there". "He, who preached nothing deliberately, in reality preached no less than this: a reconciliation here and now achieved by an understanding not from the mind but from the soul, or, more truly, from a reborn soul". It says also of what we feel when we listen to Tchekov: "it would be not impossible not inhuman, not stupid, but simply strange not to forgive . . . If we were truly conscious of some fundamental harmony, if we steadily knew that everything had a meaning, then forgiveness and unforgivingness would have none, for they have meaning only in a world which is ignorant of its own".

12 DECEMBER. Forgiveness! Father O'Kelly, a Republican, has been here to lunch and spent the afternoon and we talked of

this—of the possibility of these two parties in Ireland coming together. I asked what hope and he said "just what you said yourself, the only hope is in the oath being so altered that the Republicans can come into the Dail". He thinks there are probably conversations going on with De Valera about this. Yet he thinks De Valera may when released be set aside in favour of some less restrained leader. I asked if any released prisoners had come back to Kilbecanty. He says several. That some, most of them, say they were not badly treated, but others complain. One especially who he is certain is speaking the truth says that he, being imprisoned at the Curragh, was sent with others to build a fence round their camp. He refused, said he would not work at what was to prevent other prisoners from a chance of escape. One of the soldiers, as he continued to refuse, took a pick and beat him on the legs with the handle till they were badly bruised. Then another came, took a bayonet and prodded the bruised legs half a dozen times till blood was streaming. Then he was beaten with a rifle. Then shut up with handcuffs put on that were too small for him so that the wrists swelled and he was in great pain. At last he was taken to hospital and stayed there for some time but never had a change of linen. Then he went on hunger strike and now has been released. He is now lame. I asked if he was very bitter. He said "No he is a gentle young fellow, he had committed no crime, was just 'on the run'". But that there are others who are very bitter. And the great mistake of the Government was the execution of the men in prison, Mellows and the others; that will not be forgiven. He is anxious, is afraid of reprisals, and that the arms in the country are a danger, will perhaps be used in armed raids. He agrees with me that employment now would be the best hope, and the Dail hereafter. But he thinks the Government have great courage, one must admire them for that, though it is said now that their reason for keeping so many prisoners in is fear for their personal safety, they keep them as hostages (just what I had been told in Dublin).

He believes Sean Hayes was killed by the Irish Republican Brotherhood of America, says Colohan and Devoy have been trying to upset De Valera, who they quarrelled with when he was out there; and that Hayes was on his way to the Government Offices to give some information he had received about them when he was shot. Harry Boland he says was certainly killed by them (the I.R.B.) because he knew too much about them. I said if that be so, might not Free State and Republican unite as against them, it might bring them together, and this he thinks a possibility.

He wants books and I lent him the numbers of *London Mercury* with chapters of Trembling of the Veil, and Yeats' poems, and Lionel Johnson's *Essays*,[25] and Bailey's *Slaves of the War Zone*.[26]

I am reading *Cuchulain* to the children after lunch, and we have finished *The Ocean Waifs*[27] for evening, and begun *The Boy Voyagers*.[28]

A loss on the last Abbey week of £52, sad for Dolan, beginning his management—*Building Fund*, and Fitzmaurice's *Carmodys*.[29]

Tim, coming to take a look at the garden and criticising Madden's work thinks it is wonderful we have got on so long without trouble, and says whether in praise or dispraise "But your ladyship gave the hand to good and bad"! I told Father O'K. one should no more be angry with Government or Republicans than with different sections of one's own mind, tilting to good or bad on one or the other side, in many questions besides this.

14 DECEMBER. A wet afternoon. I have been reading longer than usual to the children—*Cuchulain*—the Fight with Ferdiad, so like the fight of all this last year and not less sad:— "We used to be practising together we used to go to every battle together because of our bravery that was equal. You were my heart companion, you were my people, you were my family; I never found one that was dearer".

14 DECEMBER. Application for Loan too late, or anyhow not getting it. I am sorry to have worried myself with unnecessary business, but meant well.

Sinn Fein last evening gives a letter of Griffith's, February 1918, his declaration as to the old sovereignty of Ireland "one of the Five Ancient and Sovereign Nations of the World . . . (Council of Constance, 1414–18) . . . has never lost her sovereign status" . . . A strong document, and seemed as I read it to justify the Republican resistance. But later I thought it shows also how impossible he must have found its recognition by England, how strong the forces against us, before he accepted the terms of the Treaty. Yet it should help at least an understanding of the Republicans' principle, their Creed.

18 DECEMBER. Richard and the others very happy together. Old Niland at the door, regretting his second marriage. His wife he says has £100 a year between the old age pension and the "bloodmoney" for her son that was killed in the war, and gives him nothing "There's no loyalty in her, but there was nature in me and in my breed and in my seven generations before me. You

don't know your comrade till you'll see them. But the first wife I had, she'd divide a halfpenny with me. And she died on the best side of the year between the two Christmases". He is out of tune now with this generation and says "They'll sooner be backbiting than to tell a funny story". He had wine and barmbrack, and ten shillings for Christmas and I sent the car to take him back to Gort for he is getting lame.

A letter in *The Times* quotes a new "logic" of Christ from an Armenian document— "He who is near me is near the fire; and he who is far from me is far from life".

21 DECEMBER. Yesterday's paper told of E. Martyn's funeral. "He had directed in his will that his body like those of many of the friendless poor should be placed at the service of the Cecilia Street School of Surgery, and when it had served its purpose there should be interred in the common grave which holds the unclaimed workhouse dead". The poor body was taken to Glasnevin in the workhouse van with six other bodies being buried by the Union. His coffin the same as theirs. A Mass celebrated in the cemetery Chapel for him and the nameless six who were to share his grave; the "Benedictus" sung when they were lowered into the earth by the Choir he had endowed; this was the only ceremonial.

22 DECEMBER. When I asked old Niland if he knew anything of poor old Cracked Mary, he said she had died about nine months ago, at Cork. I asked why she had gone so far and he said "She wasn't right in her head, and the boys used to be picking at her, and she went away to Cork. She had once been a barmaid there". A tragic ending to the poor thing's life, but in keeping with the wild imaginings of her mind.

24 DECEMBER. Almost all the prisoners from this neighbourhood have been released and are said to be looking well. O. says "I was sitting behind the two Fords at Mass and the one that had been working at home was thin but the other had a big poll of flesh on him, and a red jaw".

28 DECEMBER. Christmas through in peace, the children very gay and happy. Guy stayed here, and the Xmas tree went off well.

Iseult wrote thanking me for my cheque for the prisoners "Mrs. Despard will be very grateful for this help, there are so many needs to meet and so little we can do. We had hoped that all the prisoners would be out for Xmas, but there are still many in, and it was a sad sight on Xmas Eve to see a great number of them at the station being transferred from Newbridge to Kilmainham. The most difficult cases that have to be dealt with are the Six

Counties men; already over ten of them who were released from the camp have been re-arrested in the North and one of them is under sentence of death, so they have to be kept here at all costs, but it is so difficult to find work for everybody".

30 DECEMBER. Margaret has been laid up with a cold, and I keeping up with one, but the chicks keep going.

1 JANUARY, 1924. All well thank God, to begin the year. Margaret at Lough Cutra, and Richard and Anne there today, Catherine and I here. I saw in the paper yesterday evening that *The Old Woman Remembers*[30] is to be given by Sara Allgood at the Abbey. I hope it may help even a little towards a "lasting peace".

Santayana says: "The art of life is to keep step with the celestial orchestra that beats the measure of our career and gives the cue for our exits and our entrances".

5 JANUARY. Richard has shot his first woodcocks, one at Lough Cutra, two here. We had Guy and Bagot, Anne also shooting a pheasant and some rabbits. Yesterday I went out with them to the woods but the rain had made the cover too damp for birds to stay there. The woods so lovely, and a great joy to see Richard have his first shooting party there. Marian said she had been here also for Robert's first.

8 JANUARY. Richard's birthday party passed quietly and pleasantly on Sunday. And yesterday we had the few neighbours we could collect, and he shot with Guy in the morning, and we ended with a fine bonfire. A lovely day, but today wet and stormy again.

10 JANUARY. They are all away at Lough Cutra for two nights (Catherine for one) and I am alone. I went out to see branches cut from a beech that were shading young trees. And I have done some correcting of typed diaries.

12 JANUARY. They came back yesterday afternoon in high spirits, Anne had only shot a rabbit, but Richard seven rabbits and a snipe. Then Anne got hold of Mike and the gun and went off to the woods. I heard three shots, and she came back very proud with her bag, a woodcock and a pheasant. And this morning she and Richard went skirting the lake and he brought down two woodcocks and a pheasant. Mike says one of the woodcocks fell to "as good a shot as ever was made by Mr. Bagot"! Margaret pleased, and I feel the holidays have been a success, and that I am justified, and rewarded for holding on here.

On the other hand, F. having chosen a gun in Dublin for me, I sent for the necessary permit to purchase from the Head of Civic Guard, and had a verbal order that they could not give it, "had orders". Yet "there isn't a shop in Gort that hasn't one—every schemer carrying his gun". So I am writing to the friendly Asst. Commissioner in Dublin, Mr. Barrett. (13 August 1924. have but just today, after many efforts received permission to have a gun!).

16 JANUARY. Margaret has left. We got through some land business on the last day or two. She asked me to London saying "All is quite safe here now". I am glad of that admission, and indeed the holidays have been very free from trouble, and peaceful. I have done no work but some typing of diaries—the part today about the split on the Treaty, bringing back old hopes and disappointments.

Yeats writes proposing to have the "Old Woman Remembers" published as a Cuala Broadside, says "it sounded like a fine thing"; thinks Jack may illustrate it.

19 JANUARY. And the *Irish Statesman*[31] yesterday had a nice word about it "A finely conceived poem in distinguished verse where is narrated the story of seven hundred years of the sorrows of Ireland. The emotion rises to intensity in the last verse, where a passionate appeal for union and peace is made to all who love Ireland, however diversely their love may have manifested itself".

That pleases me for it recognises the desire for peace and union that is indeed its aim.

The little *Sinn Fein* paper always saddens me, it is peevish—snarling; it may be because those who would take a more magnanimous and constructive line are still in gaol.

Yesterday the children left. I motored with them to Galway and saw them into the train. We had not time to go and see "Godmother", but she had come to the station, was on the platform in her bath chair, laden with fruit and cakes and picture papers for the darlings' journey. (And that is the last time they ever saw her, who had been such a fountain of kindness and love and generosity to them all through their little lives. 13 August, 1924).

I returned alone to a very silent house, but I am thankful the holidays passed off so well, the best I think they have had, Richard and Anne enjoying the shooting, that these last years had not been possible. He shot a wild duck and a pigeon on his last day, to vary his woodcocks, rabbits and pheasants. And that helps him to care for the woods and for home. And we have had no trouble this time; no "young fellows at the door".

20 JANUARY. A.E. in a review of Lunacharski's[32] plays quotes a speech put into the mouth of Mephisto, speaking to the

autocrat of the city— "The great of this world strike with a mighty hammer on the hearts of mankind, but a force meets a resistance equal to itself, as your esteemed Florentine teaches. So in a way the old man (the rebel) is your own reflection, as it were a distorted plebeian portrait of you. I really do not know should I have his head struck off? *Such beings are in themselves deathless, being reflexes*. If in the end all the heads of the Rebels are to fall, there would have to be a beheading of authority. Authority strikes off the head of its own shadow, and then wonders that it grows again". But I hope our executions are at an end.

Church today. This house very silent without the voices of the children.

21 JANUARY. I see in a letter of Ramsay MacDonald given in *The Times*: "Labour does not belong to a certain circle. I hope it never will, but will create for itself a circle where dignity and self respect will be the atmosphere. Labour will always be a poor social imitator, but it might become a good social creator".

I hope our new rulers, legislators, officers, may in this way find and make their own dignity.

Old R. has died of some inward malady. I kept employing him as our mower though against opposition, after his son's misdemeanour. That son is now in the Civic Guard, though it is said "It must be a hungry army that took him".

23 JANUARY. This day six years ago Robert died from us. Richard nine then, Anne six, Catherine four. Thank God they are safe and well.

Yesterday I typed and wrote a new Lane picture statement for use with the new Government.

24 JANUARY. Mrs. Bagot brought me back yesterday the books I had lent Fr. O'K. There is an auction being held at his house. He applied to be moved to England, and as an answer he has been reduced to the rank of curate and sent to Ennistymon, whether as a punishment for wanting to leave or for his republican feeling, or merely for convenience, I don't know.

I had letters from the three darling children, and have written to them and sent Richard cakes.

25TH. Have written to R. MacDonald about the pictures, enclosing my statement. (Copy of letter in book).

Also to Barrett about the gun for Mike Dooley. Frank writes "After being sent from post to pillar I got a permit to purchase a gun. It seems that the authorities have barred the sale of single barrel guns in the mistaken idea that they could be more easily turned into rifles than two barrelled ones . . . So far so good, but now the question arises as to how I am to send it to you. A permit has to be obtained in your name to get the gun forwarded to Coole, I have written asking to have it sent to barracks in Galway where you can call for it".

GALWAY. 29 JANUARY. I have been to see Kiernan, and Kenny editor of *Tribune* about Carnegie Library. And have promised Kenny to write something for his Patrick's Day number, that is to be for "praises" of Connacht.

Yesterday I worked at the third act of *Shanwalla*, having found some old criticisms of it by Yeats and L.R.

31 JANUARY. About Carnegie. Yesterday morning Father Hynes the Registrar of the University came to see me, said he had seen the Sligo Library and found the books were not dangerous to the faith, and was all for having one in Galway. He said the Prospect Infirmary will soon be closed, and many of the offices now in the Courthouse will be moved there and that will leave room in the Courthouse for storage of books. He asked me to see Mr. F. connected with the Co. Council, and Dr. Walsh, a great power on it.

So in the evening Mr. F. came, but would not give any attention to what Father Hynes had said. Says he is a "playboy, its all nonsense about our offices being moved". But remembering his poem on Ossian (sent to me in MSS) and noticing by his talk that he was shallow and pretentious I suggested his getting some institution here to have some of the books on loan, and try if they were appreciated. He said he has thought of Galway subscribing for ten sets to be sent out to other towns of the County. But I thought one set of 200 for Galway itself would be enough to begin with. He said the Chamber of Commerce would be suitable, and he would suggest that its Secretary should write. Dr. Walsh writes that he has to go to Dublin today but will see me on Saturday evening. And I wrote this to L.R. asking for more information as to what we can offer to induce them to strike a rate now we don't give buildings, by return post. And then remembered he would be busy with his first *Observer* article on drama, that is to appear on Sunday, and wrote to McGreevy also. Robinson writes to my great relief that Tulloch has gone through our Abbey accounts and says we have no need to be anxious.

Kiernan in this evening; says several students from the University had been fighting for the Republic and imprisoned, but when let out have gone back to their studies, don't seem inclined to fight again. He thinks there is little or no Republicanism in Galway, but a good deal in the country. And that he did not join the Chamber of Commerce, because the club that amalgamated with it was a good deal given to drink. So I said the Carnegie must lay in a stock of Temperance tracts. Working at "Connacht and the Poets" for the Tribune article.

1 FEBRUARY. Nice letters this morning from the chicks. And Miss Elder wants to put in *Spreading the News* for her village drama Society. In the Post office as I telegraphed the answer I met Tomas Concannon, once Gaelic League organiser. He says the enthusiasm for Irish has died away among the young men since the fighting; says there is a great deal of republicanism here, and he does not think there will be any peace until De Valera is released, and the oath done away with. Republicans will then he says go into the Dail. There is a strong feeling against the snappiness of the Government answers, and he agrees with me that there is the same fault in *Sinn Fein*, says it is badly edited. I said "too many women on it" and he laughed and said "My wife says the same thing".

3 FEBRUARY. Yesterday evening Dr. Walsh came in. He spoke of the beauty of the Coole woods and the walk by the lake. He had been at Gort for a while he says, as assistant to Dr. Moran, and his great pleasure had been to walk out there. I had not much to tell him about the Carnegie scheme, McGreevy not having answered the questions I sent, but he says the Court House will, as Father Hynes said, be left with several vacant rooms next summer, and that he agrees with me that it would be best to borrow a few hundred books now, to see if they were used. I mentioned Plato's *Republic* as one of the books I had put on the "Nation Building" list, and he says there is an old clerk in his office reading it now. He said how much more attractive in its dialogue form it is than a treatise would have been; and I said we have the love of dialogue here to build on, the delight in those long arguments in Irish, as of Ossian and Patrick, and Raftery and Death.

We spoke of politics, he with some fire of the ungraciousness of the Government speakers, Cosgrave, O'Higgins, Hogan, that kept up ill feeling; and I told him of the even greater ungraciousness of *Sinn Fein*. I had just been reading this week's number. He has been talking to many of the released prisoners, says they do not say much, but feel much bitterness. He himself takes no side in politics but has a great many republican friends, and (like me) feels that the argument is on their side for the resistance of the Treaty, though practical wisdom would have been to take it on account. He says the Republicans would have swept the country but for their policy of destruction which put the farmers against them. He thinks it likely at the next election they may do so. I asked if the dropping of the oath would bring them into the Dail.

He believes it would, and that this is the only hope of reconcilement; and that were they in power they would become conservative. Some would stay out probably, men like Mellows, who he knew well, and whose one idea of serving the cause was to go out and shoot somebody. He knows many people in Clare who voted republican at the last election because of De Valera's arrest. It had been promised the election would be free, and that was a breach of the promise.

4 FEBRUARY, COOLE. Girvin motored me back today, taking on the way, or out of the way, some villages, Closhea, Logarna, between Kinvara and Duras; good thatched houses, some slated; peeps of sea and mountain. A boy, slowly ploughing, said "These last years the country is turned to a wilderness". But they all seemed to be at work.

Here all looked well, and is well, except that on Thursday night the two large doors that M. had bought at Miss Moran's auction and that were in the barn were taken away—very large doors, but no trace of wheels. And that same night six men had broken into the old Diveney's house at Ballinamantane and searched it but had found no money. They had come to the door and one of the old brothers was going to open the door, as demanded, "but the other said whatever happened he'd stop in his own house". Then the door was broken open, four men came in (two more were outside) with bandaged faces. They searched the whole house, upsetting beds, dresser, everything, but found nothing, the old men kept no money there. They are making no complaint to the Civic Guard.

It is said the Republican released prisoners are in groups together, and the Civic Guard Sergeant who had been here about my gun (which has arrived) had said there is no work in the country and not much money, and it is hard to know what they can do, "And they wearing brown boots".

A note from P.M.'s Secretary this morning, the P.M. desired him "to thank you for your letter and good wishes and to say that he will look into the matter which you write about". So then I wrote to Cosgrave, who is over in London on the Boundary question, asking him to take it up with P.M. and Thomas (This might really be the last letter!)

5TH. But I see that he had left before my letter could have arrived I am writing to tell Yeats. Yeats has sent me *Plays and Controversies* today.[33]

9TH. O'Hegarty wrote yesterday that he will show my letter to Cosgrave and is "sure he will give the matter his earnest attention". And this morning taking up *The Times* before looking at my letters, I see the Tate announcement about the Courtauld gift,[34] and that the Manet "will hang in company with the *Eva Gonzales* and *Fête aux Tuileries*". And the leading article on it mentions "*Hugh Lane's Gift*" as if there had been no question about it! I had just time to write to Yeats. But this stirs up the old bitterness again and brings to mind W.'s proverb, "It is hard to get butter out of a dog's mouth".

I have been working hard at the little article for the *Tribune*,[35] it has given me more trouble than I expected, but I must make it as good as in me lies. I must go and type it now.

SUNDAY, 10 FEBRUARY. Wet morning and no church. I corrected the Connacht article and have done with it, my head rather tired. Reading *Anna Karenina* for a night novel. I had forgotten how fine it is.

14 FEBRUARY. Rather a languid week, no news or answer from Yeats about the Lane pictures, and I feel so helpless. Yesterday I got out *Seventy Years* thinking to arrange some articles from it. But when it comes to the point I dislike the idea so strongly of having just the gossip, the "folklore" printed without the redeeming part of my life, and without what I think will make a fine book, the later history of the country, that I will put it away again; though if money is necessary before the year is out I must face it. I will go on now typing the later diaries, they ought to be copied anyhow.

Reading *Marie Bashkirtcheff*,[36] and feeling it much finer than when it was a sudden fashion. I've worried over Income Tax this morning till my head aches, and wrote a letter to kind young Kiernan to enclose, and lost it, and searched, and only after post had gone found it under my writing table. All for the best probably.

Haven't got leave to use a gun yet. A Civic Guard Sergeant called two days ago but I was having the raspberries pruned, and Marian sent him to the flower garden where he couldn't find me. He refuses to give a licence to my Keeper "as he doesn't know him personally". "And all the youngsters of Crow Lane walking about with gun in hand."

16 FEBRUARY. Still writing letters about the pictures. But I am cheered by Alec Martin having been made a Governor of our National Gallery. A great help to its future and its new Director. He has written me a nice letter.

Copying Diaries rather sad, the breaking out of war after the Treaty. And the present "peace" is not a joyful one, too much ill-will.

Still reading *Marie Bashkirtcheff*, sad and brilliant. I think part of the trouble with her was the want of a country; brought up away from her own, Russia; having enthusiasm for Nice and Paris and Rome in turn, but no close link of habit or duty with any, leaves her as it were without a foundation; all the success she hopes for is for herself. Last night I was reading the 1878–9 chapters, just at that time I was spending my winters at Cannes with poor Richard, my poor brother. I had few even of acquaintances, was tied to the invalid; no gaiety of any sort. Yet my memory of that time is not unhappy, I was learning Italian, reading what books I could get hold of; an exile, but with Roxborough to return to at each winter's end. And I had religion and the poor (that flower seller at Cannes sent for me, alone of her customers when she was in distress and near her death). I must have had some belief in a future life, a full one, on this earth, for I don't think I ever fretted or flagged.

18 FEBRUARY. Poor Marie; she was in love with her own beauty and genius, and no wonder. Now she is at the Art School. I keep thinking of Yeats' lines:

> Some burn damp faggots; others will consume
> All the combustible matter in one room.[37]

Her only tenderness seems to have been for the old grandfather.

20 FEBRUARY. A nice letter from kind young Kiernan making the application for Income tax relief easy for me. A foggy morning, typing; and then out with Mike cutting away rubbish. I've written to L.R. to try and get news about the Lane pictures.

22 FEBRUARY. The plumber, mending the pump, said how quiet Gort is now, the trouble over. And I, feeling that though the Republicans are beaten they are not won, said I hoped good feeling would come and now the fight is over they will all shake hands, and he said "That's right". But later, typing my diaries of 1922, the shooting of that Connemara lad, and of the others at his funeral, I felt more doubtful of a swift forgiveness in the face of such bitter memories. The Dublin executions were more conspicuous, but it is the countryside that remembers. Then again I felt more hopeful as I looked through last week's *Sinn Fein*, it contains less violence, a little less, against the Government, and for the first time proposes some constitutional work, lectures and essays, on citizenship and economics as well as history. And there is an Irish translation by P. de Brun (this is Father Brown), of Shelley's Ode to the West Wind, very close to the original, rhymed and in the same metre: "The years have left a heavy weight on the tired poet who is like the wind, proud, unbound".

Indeed I think "Beside a pumice isle in Baiae's bay" is better as "Le síor-suantraige cois Napoli sa cuan, Connac se suid ar crit fa la-se-tuinn Seana-caisleain is tuis an saogail neambuain—"

23 FEBRUARY. This morning I am told "There has been another raid on those two old Diveneys. Men came at 9 o'c last night the same way as before. They put John out, but Pat wouldn't move out of the house. They took two flitches of bacon and a big crock of butter, it is known the Diveneys always had good butter. They looked for money but there is none kept in the house. It might have been only for robbery they came, or it might be because of that old dispute (about land and a will). Anyway the two old brothers have left the house now and gone to stop in James Noone's at Kiltartan. Two carts they had this morning bringing away their beds and chairs and whatever they had. The Civic Guards were not going near them or to look after them. They would have stopped in the house its likely if they thought they had protection".

Last night in the library the firelight, the lamplight, shining on the rich bindings of that wall of books; and this evening, by the lake, so silent and beautiful, Cranagh so peaceful—"the tilled familiar land"; and later as I went upstairs and looked from my window at the sunset behind the blue range of hills, I felt so grateful, as I have often done of late, to my husband who brought me to this house and home.

SUNDAY. 24 FEBRUARY. Poor Archdeacon very shaky now, made several mistakes in reading the service. He says his sight is failing.

I have been reading the *Travelling Man*, that the children are going to see given in a church in London—that is something new. And Belfast girls, "The Rose Patrol, 2nd Belfast Girls Guide Company" write for leave to give *Spreading the News* "in aid of Patrol Funds", and I am giving leave with some misgiving, not knowing who they are going to "patrol" against, but think it wiser not to ask. And *Sinn Fein* says: "I think Claremorris is going to give *Rising of the Moon*"; And the critic of the Gaelic plays at the Abbey calls for *The White Cockade* in Irish. So I am glad (though feeless!) to see my work hold its place in the life of the country.

The Priest at Kiltartan today preached about the raid on the old Diveneys had only heard of it through the papers—the first raid, had not heard of the new one when so much was stolen. But he spoke with some vigour and told his people it was in their hands now to prevent such acts "and not to be afraid of one another".

26 FEBRUARY. Not a word from Yeats or L.R. about the pictures.

Rita Daly here, said there had been a letter from the Republican Leader (I suppose O'Ruitleis) saying the late robberies must not be attributed to Republicans; their orders are against them. I am glad, for I had been disappointed, seeing no word about them in *Sinn Fein*. She said town and country people had attended the funeral of O'Halloran, the soldier shot by bank robbers.[38] But between going "the longest good road" to the grave at Shanaglish, and a mistake about the motors that were to bring back the soldiers who came with the body, they had to walk about twenty miles and were very foot-sore when they came back to Gort, the soles dropping off their boots.

P. back at work after the winter, says Gort is quiet; he is very angry about the robbing of the old Diveneys "quiet men knocking out a way of living". He agrees that these robberies are not now republican, lays them on ex-English army men, who were in "that war that has the world destroyed". "It was no stranger that robbed the Diveneys. They had their wool sold that day, four packs of it, and it was thought the price of it would be in the house, but they did not bring it there."

Independent says: "The Vicar of St. Paul's Covent Garden . . . said that *The Travelling Man*, a mystic play by Lady Gregory, was produced during the ordinary afternoon service on Sunday, and it attracted a gathering four times as large as the ordinary Sunday congregation. Even the galleries were full".

27 FEBRUARY. A letter from Robinson which I opened with hope there would be good news about the pictures, but he only says "Yeats had got Fitzgerald to speak to the President, who had the matter in mind. Said he'd perhaps write to the President if there was no news within the next couple of days and I'll keep at him. I also think I'll be getting Desmond Fitzgerald to lunch and sounding him about it". (Every link making the chain weaker). So I did what I ought to have done at first, wrote to the Governor-General, with *Times* article (the new Manet hanging next the *Eva Gonzales* &c) and asked him to get McNeill, our High Commissioner in London to see Thomas, the Minister for the Colonies and press for the return of the pictures.

Madden here pruning. He was interested to hear of the *Sinn Fein* lecture plan, may give one himself.

28 FEBRUARY. I have finished *Marie Bashkirtcheff*; a terrible moving tragedy, all the beauty, genius, so rapidly burned up. And the loss of her singing voice, and then the deafness. I had some recollection of my husband not having liked the book, and

found in his 1889 diary a note on it, very indignant at the egotism, selfishness, jealousy which indeed are there. But "to know all is to forgive all" and there must have been some instinct from the first that she had but a few short years from which to squeeze life's juice. And she had courage. She only once, I think, speaks of the journal as perhaps containing what she was trying for in art, something of value, worth while. Her lifelong desire to be "célèbré" came too late but it came. This is the nineteenth edition, 1914.

1 MARCH. Talking of the raid on the old Diveney's the Civic Guard were blamed, but I said "it is the neighbours who should join to get rid of these thieves now. They are no Republicans. "Oh they are not—but what can you say, with all the revolvers and guns that are going about you'd have one at your head". And that is likely enough.

Rather over tired last night, typing and standing out seeing rubbish cleared away in the garden, and then continued typing 7 to 9. And the night was stormy and cold, and this morning the ground was covered with snow. No post when I came down, but Mike Lally arrived with it later, could not get his bicycle through the snow and had to walk. And it brought such a good answer from the Governor-General "Dear Lady Gregory, I have yours re the Lane pictures, I very strongly urged their return upon the late Government, and shall go to London next week and make even stronger representations to the new Government . . . T. M. Healy"

So my hopes are very high, and perhaps my letter of thanks and confidence to him (quoting "So much one man can do, Who does both act and know") may really be the last on that matter!

Marie Bashkirtcheff, writing of Rome in 1878 "les grandes fortunes morcelées . . . les princes de Rome transformés en des très petits gens couvert d'un grand nom comme d'un vieux manteau de thêatres pour couvrir leurs misères". But some of our more—or less—"grands noms" have gone away altogether, and some have stayed to make the best of things as they are in the country.

2 MARCH. Sunday. There was more snow last night, and wind, but today is lovely. I have been out in the garden, all transfigured and beautiful, the snow in heaps on the boughs of fir and laurel and even on every slender twig of beech and shrubs, the sky a soft blue, the sun shining as it has not done all the winter, it was almost Italy in the garden; the ilex, and the cypress-like Irish yews. I basked in the sun as I walked up and down. All the morning (church impossible) I had "holystoned the deck" numbering

the pages of all I have typed, and putting the MS in portfolios. And it is sad to discover I had never corrected Miss Cuffey's typing, and there are many mistakes, and some pages missing.

Last evening I read a three act play of Murrays,[39] rather heavy and machine made, but good enough to put on.

4 MARCH. My wedding day forty-four years ago.

Snow just now, but turning to sleet.

They say J. Hayes who had been in gaol for a while as an Irregular has gone to Canada. The first of our Kiltartan people I have heard of going there. But some have been disappointed about U.S.A. the number filled.

I got through a good deal of typing and correcting. And (evening) as I was feeling rather sad, in the 1919 part, the beginning of our land trouble and the firing at F. Quinn, and thinking I must not let it see the light, I was told that last Saturday a party of men attacked Houston at Lough Cutra,[40] dragged him off his bicycle, gave him a beating. "His jaw is shattered" and he has gone to Dublin. Dreadfully sad, and I am afraid the children will hear of it. It is not known whether it was on account of a field he had taken, or of a man fined £2 and costs at the Sessions the other day. Houston had found him with two rabbits he had snared and had him up. Madden told me last week that this man had come to see Hugo (home for a few days' deer shooting) saying he was poor and asking to be let off some of the fine, but he had refused. All the soldiers have been taken away from Gort.

5 MARCH. I felt very downhearted last night, that violence going on, we need the teaching of Christ again and his example, so blurred it seems now. Today old Niland comes for firing, tells me there were seven men who attacked Houston. One, as I thought, was the man who had been fined. He has been arrested.

Poor old Padraig, his pension has been cut down this week, (or so he said) a shilling from his wife's, a shilling from his. After his glass of wine his indignation rose. "The English will be back again, and this beggarly Government put out, and I'll be glad of it. If I was a scholar to write to the English papers I would put them out". He is certain the English will be back again. I said No, but he is confident, "It is in Columcille's prophecy. There was a Lord one time was with O'Brien at Dromoland and O'Brien promised him whatever he would ask, and he said 'Give me the house of Dromoland and the lands'. So he agreed to that. But then he said he had some request to make, and the Lord said he would give it, and he said 'Give me the house and the land of Dromoland back again', and he had to give it. That will be the way with the English. They gave up Ireland but they have their two eyes fixed on it till they will get it back again".

8 MARCH. Dublin. Yesterday I came up by early train. At Athenry there were about fifteen soldiers, fully equipped, tin plates, knapsacks. I asked Daly where they were bound for, but he said they were to be "demobbed". At Athlone eight or nine young men tumbled in, with little trunks and boxes. One who sat next me was from Mayo, a nice freshfaced boy. They were going he said to Manchester, had got a message that there was work for them there, but did not know what it would be. Another who got in was a young lad, ghastly, looking as if in the last stages of consumption, coughing, spitting, speechless. I meant to change into another carriage, for I had to sit with my eyes shut. But at Mullingar I got out my tea bottle and gave him hot tea that revived him wonderfully, and a clean handkerchief. And then I stayed. He had come from Castlebar was going to a sanatorium near Dublin, "was doing no good at home". Poor lad. It cannot save him. I waited with him at Broadstone till a pleasant looking messenger from the Sanatorium came and took him in a cab. Then to 82 Merrion Square, opened my basket in the hall and had my tea and sandwich. Then to the Bagot St. Hospital to see Houston. He looked better than I expected for he was walking about, though his broken jaw was bandaged, and the wounds on his face had been stitched and had plaster over them. He says he was driving home from church when eight men got over the wall inside Lough Cutra and ordered him to stop, firing a shot over his head. They asked what he meant by having D. fined for three rabbits. He said it was his duty, and they asked if he would pay the fine as he was poor. He refused. "And then I remember nothing until I heard them say 'Shove him into the trap', and I was put into it and drove home, half dazed. They must have struck a blow from behind that broke the jaw and stunned me". He did not tell me, as his brother told J. that these men had first while he was at church, raided his house and taken away 83 cartridges, left from the deer shoot. A very sad and horrible thing, so many coming against one man.

In the evening to the Abbey with W.B.Y. *Juno and the Paycock*[41] a long queue at the door, the theatre crowded, many turned away, so it will be run on next week. A wonderful and terrible play of futility, of irony, humour, tragedy. When I went round to the greenroom I saw O'Casey and had a little talk with him. He is very happy. I asked him to come to tea after the next day matinée as I had brought up a barmbrack for the players, but he said "No I can't come, I'll be at work till the afternoon, and I'm working with cement, and that takes such a long time to get off". "But after that?" "Then I have to cook my dinner. I have but one room and I cook for myself since my mother died." He is of course happy at the great success of the play and I said "You must feel now that we were right in not putting on that first one you sent in *The Crimson in the Tricolour*. I was inclined to put it on because some of it was so good and I thought you might learn by seeing it on the stage, though some was very poor, but Mr. Yeats was firm". He said "You were right not to put it on. I can't read it myself now. But I will tell you that was a bitter disappointment for I not only thought at the time it was the best thing I had written, but I thought that no one in the world had ever written anything so fine". Then he said "You had it typed for me, and I don't know how you could have read it as I sent it in with the bad writing and the poor paper. But at that time it was hard for me to afford even the paper it was written on". And he said "I owe a great deal to you and Mr. Yeats and Mr. Robinson, but to you above all. You gave me encouragement. And it was you who said to me upstairs in the office—I could show you the very spot where you stood—'Mr. O'Casey, your gift is characterisation'. And so I threw over my theories and worked at characters, and this is the result."

Yeats hadn't seen the play before, and thought it very fine, reminding him of Tolstoi. He said when he talked of that imperfect first play "Casey was bad in writing of the vices of the rich which he knows nothing about, but he thoroughly understands the vices of the poor". But that full house, the packed pit and gallery, the fine play, the call of the mother for the putting away of hatred—"give us Thine own eternal love!" made me say to Yeats "This is one of the evenings at the Abbey that makes me glad to have been born".

9 MARCH. I took cakes to the Abbey and after the performance gave tea in the greenroom. An American, Mr. Jewell, had come to see *Juno*, is writing for U.S.A. magazines, so I asked him to tea, and having only the Company themselves was glad of an outsider. They were a little constrained, but I suggested their singing to show what they can do, as in the play they had to turn their songs into a part of the comedy. So Dolan, Will Shields, Nolan, sang. Then Sara Allgood, very charming—"I know who I love" and "Oh, had I wist"! And by that time Yeats had arrived, and he had to read them one or two scraps of verse in his book of plays, there being no volume of his poems there. And then with prompting he repeated "Wandering Angus". So my barmbrack was the centre of a House of Melody.

I came back there for the evening performance—such a

queue! and so many had to be turned away, but we are running on next week and I hope they will come then. Casey was with me watching them and being persuaded to come and meet the Americans on Yeats' Monday evening. Miss Bushell came to ask if she might sell my stall there was such a demand and I said yes, certainly. Then Jack Yeats and his wife came, could get no seat; so we went round to the stage door and when the orchestra stopped we went down and took their chairs. When the mother whose son has been killed—"Leader of an ambush where my neighbour's Free State soldier son was killed" cries out "Mother of Jesus put away from us this murderous hatred and give us thine own eternal love" I whispered to Casey "that is the prayer we must all use, it is the only thing that will save us, the teaching of Christ". He said "Of humanity". But what would that be without the Divine atom?

The Observer critic (Griffith) had come over from London for the night. Such a good moment for him to see the Abbey!

This morning's paper tells of the revolt of the Officers.[42]

10 MARCH. I found Houston going on well at the Hospital, brought him some books. He says the Bank clerks from Gort were poaching all the winter, and he would have prosecuted them had there been a Court. Unluckily when the Court came it was on a poor man his hand fell.

I had tea with Douglas Hyde, he has kept quite out of politics and just does his University work. In the evening L.R. and Mr. Griffith came in, he very enthusiastic about the "Paycock", play and acting "superb".

Someone from *The Irish Times* had been gloomy over the revolt of the Officers, but this morning's news seems to show it has not had much sympathy.

11 MARCH. No more news of "the mutiny" yesterday, and by the papers it doesn't look serious, though the President and other Ministers have given up their intention of dining on Wednesday at "the Round Table", a dinner club formed by their wives.

I had heard nothing said about my *Story brought by Brigit*[43] since I had read it to Yeats and L.R., but Yeats asked on Sunday when it was to be put in rehearsal, said it must certainly be put on, and before the end of Lent. So I went to consult L.R. and he is for putting it on the week before Holy Week. We tried to think out cast, but could not fill it, I am anxious to read it to the Company before deciding anything, to see how they like it. Yeats says they are getting Sara Allgood here for their entertainment for the Drama League to recite "The Old Woman Remembers", which he thinks very fine. After this my pride was cast down, for he gave me the typed article on his visit to Sweden in which he describes me as "An old woman sinking into the infirmities of age"—(not even fighting against them!). However L.R. agreed with me that this description would send down my market value, and be considered to mean I had gone silly, so he has consented to take it out, but confesses he had already sent a copy to the Dail, and will have to write about it and may not be in time.

We made £87 profit on last week's bill, and Casey will get over £15.

He came last night, Yeats' "Monday", also A.E. and Mr. Jewell and A. Duncan; and Gogarty dropped in late. It is supposed to be for men only, and might be better so. Anyhow the talk was rather "scattered", the mutiny, Hashish, whether Darrell Figgis did or did not write "the Return of the Hero".[44] Casey, sheltering by me, interested me most. Yeats explained that the long debates and delay of the Fishery Bill in the Senate had all been caused by the incompetence of the Minister for Fisheries, who had given wrong statistics. Casey asked if he had been dismissed, and could not understand why not, when a labourer found incompetent would be turned out of his job. Someone said he had given good service before the Treaty, and he, Casey, said "Nothing can be done until this Government is out and we have a Government with no one in it that has ever fired a gun. We can abuse them then". They say the occupation of the four Courts, the real beginning of trouble was the result of a quarrel about the appointment of a Chief of Staff. No one can see how Republicans can join a Government, or rather come into the Dail until the watering of the oath. He believes if they ever do form a Government, they will be found just as quiet as the others. And here as in the country the conviction seems to be that nothing towards a reconciliation can come until this Government is out, between the memory of the executions and the harshness of their speeches.

When Gogarty came in he did not find a congenial audience and talk flagged. I got him to talk of his escape from his kidnappers by plunging into the Liffey, for Jewell's benefit—a little "story" for him. When the others were talking of Hashish, Casey told me he had been all but shot in the Rising. He had taken no part in it, but a shot had been fired from some house he was in or near, and the soldiers had dragged him out and were actually raising their rifles to fire at him—"I felt in a daze, just from instinct I said a prayer, was certain death was there. But someone fired a shot that just missed their Captain, and they ran to see where it came from, and I ran for my life through the fields and escaped". He thinks the Rising was "a terrible mistake and we lost such fine men. We should have won freedom by degrees with them. And Parnell's death was a great misfortune, he would have got Home Rule, that would have been a step".

He is studying pictures now, has bought some books but knows so little about painting he wishes lectures could be given, "And if the employers cared for us workers they would sometimes arrange for an afternoon at the Galleries, or an evening at the Abbey for their men".

It was an interesting evening, I enjoyed hearing different views after what Yeats calls in another part of his article "the laborious solitary life".[45] He is very kind, and would ask politicians and officers to meet me but thinks I don't care to meet them, and that is true enough. It is the creators that I like best to meet.

EVENING. Today I went into the National Gallery to see Stephens; the men there so civil and kind, remembering Hugh. Stephens is still working at the epic tales, says he can find nothing of worth that I have not used. He is now beginning on another tale, not in my Saga, and finds the difference not having my clear outline to work on. He also is astonished by the power of Casey's play. And Yeats (in spite of my "sinking" had told him the *Brigit* is the finest thing I have done—"a great play".) I worked all the morning on *Brigit* putting in a verse to be sung before the curtain goes up and giving more words to Sara Allgood. L.R. took me to dine with him at the Metropole, and on to the Abbey not so full as on Friday and Saturday, but Perrin said £30 in the house, and we began with £19 last week. And I signed a cheque of over £17 for Casey. The evening papers give Mulcahy's statement telling that some resignations from the army have taken place here and there, about twenty in Dublin, and there are threats that many officers will resign "if the terms contained in the Government letter are carried out, and set themselves up in arms against the Government".[46] And that he is only anxious about Co. Cork.

There was an immense meeting in College Green as I passed in the tram coming back late, in support of the Anti-Treaty candidate.

12 MARCH. Lewis Hind writes an article on Hugh Lane in the *Independent*, claiming the "Lane gift now hanging in the Tate Gallery". I am writing a protest, I think it is a challenge.

Yeats and George dined at the Glenavys'[47] last night, some Ministers there left early to have a consultation about the Army trouble. But it doesn't seem so serious, and the Republicans don't open their arms to the discontented officers. I dined with L.R. at the Metropole, and Joe Devlin,[48] who I had never met, came from another table "for the pleasure of shaking hands" with me.

I wrote an answer to Hind for the *Independent*.[49] G. Yeats came in saying she had been told there was a split in the Cabinet and that we might be without a Government by 4 o'c.

But later Yeats came in from the debate in the Dail, and told that the Officers who mutinied have written an apology or explanation that they only wanted their grievances looked into; so that is hopeful for peace.

13 MARCH. I had not gone out yesterday, having a cold and saving myself for reading *Brigit* to the players in the evening. And at 4.30 a telegram came from Galway "Mistress very ill. Can you come".[50]

It was too late for afternoon train and I got a girl from the Industries room to telephone to the Broadstone to ask when the next would leave, and the answer was at 7 o'c. So I packed my things, and then George came in and was kind, and then Willie. He sat with me and talked of Richet's book.[51] I had just been reading the chapter on "Premonitions of Death" when the telegram came. He believes fully in that invisible force, or mind, higher than our own, moving and influencing us. Then he took me to the train and saw me off, and I got to Galway not too tired at 11. I found A. drowsy and did not rouse her to say I had come. Presently she grew more restless and her breathing more difficult, and this continued through the night, increasing. I sent the maids to bed and, with the Nurse, stayed in the room, lying down but not sleeping except for one hour before the maids went up, on the study sofa. It was very painful listening, but at last at 6.30 she suddenly grew quiet and slept peacefully. And by 7 o'c we knew she had passed away.

14 MARCH. I wrote so many letters yesterday, trying to remember all who would be hurt at not having one. Wyndham Waithman came in and was very kind, taking all the business of the burial from me. Then about 2 o'c I lay down on my bed and slept till 7. I was quite tired out.

My last letter to her is returned to me, and her last word to me has come, written to me to Dublin saying that she had suffered pain and the Doctor had ordered some remedy. Maggie brought me a little box she had arranged for the children, a card for each, Anne's with three shillings arranged as a shamrock and Catherines six sixpences arranged as two, with their names and "for St. Patrick's Day, 1924". I am sending them on, the last of so many gifts from her hand.

The Governor-General writes asking me to lunch or dine at

the Viceregal Lodge, but saying "The London people are so full of the Boundary Question that there is very little hope of getting them to tackle another thorny question till that is settled". Another delay.

15 MARCH. My birthday, and the day of my sister's funeral. A telegram later from London "Anne and Catherine in bed with measles and high temperature". It makes me anxious.

Some lines quoted in the *Literary Supplement* from Katherine Tynan seem to apply to A.'s quiet passing from this house so near the harbour:

Some morning I shall rise from sleep
When all the house is still and dark.
I shall steal down and find my ship
By the dim quayside and embark.

To no strange country shall I come
But to mine own delightful land,
With Love to bid me welcome home
And Love to lead me by the hand.

We shall not hear the ticking clock,
Nor the swift rustle of Time's wings,
Nor dread the sharp dividing stroke,
Being come now to immortal things.

With all those wonders to admire,
And the heart's hunger satisfied,
Given at the last the heart's desire,
We shall forget we ever died.

There are many to welcome her there, our Mother, the elder generation. My love has been rather with the younger ones, John and Hugh; and my own child.

17 MARCH. Yesterday I went to church, Mr. Ormsby preached on the trial before Pilate. It interested me, his view of Pilate's character much like mine, though he does not give importance to the dream.

Wyndham called and took me to see the grave, covered with wreaths. It is a beautiful burying place, lying high, the sun shining on it, on the silver sea. The Burren hills beyond, and to the north-west the hills of Connemara. I told him I wish to be buried there should I die at Coole. And to have an open motor to bring me here, not a hearse.

He told me that Mr. Ormsby had been a Colonel in the army, and in the war he had been almost killed in a motor smash and while lying in hospital he "saw Jesus come to his bedside" and since then has given his life to Him.

He drove me back by the sea, and when I asked what a great new shed we passed was he said that after the war a large sum of money was voted to the Claddagh fishermen because they had taken service so readily. It was proposed that they, the Claddagh people, should be asked what they would think the best way of laying out the money. But the Government said No, and chose for them a number of steam trawlers, some of which he showed me lying rotting in the docks. They had been of no use, too expensive, and less serviceable than the sailing trawlers which the fishermen had desired.

Jack Yeats wrote me: "I am glad that we were able to see your sister last summer; there was about her a pleasantness and wisdom which will always come before me when I think of Galway".

Today, St. Patrick's, a holiday, no post and no telegram to tell me how the children are. I went through boxes of papers trying to get to business. I think the children will have £100 a year each, but annuity and jointure ceasing take more than half the income. Sad work looking through old letters and journals. I must try for energy to destroy mine.

Archdeacon Derry called. He says Hall the sawyer once at Coole is in hospital for cancer. Lady Ardilaun had sent money to help him but he may want more. I said he had not asked me for any, and the Archdeacon said "He said to me 'I would go on my knees round Galway for Lady Gregory, I would go on my knees to Coole for her, but I would not ask her for anything, she did so much for me. She stood by me when every one else turned their back on me' ".

18 MARCH. A telegram from Margaret "Children very gay I will probably cross Saturday" cheered me up. Also a nice letter from her.

Wyndham came in. I told him when he spoke again of Mr. Ormsby that I did not think the Union Jack should be kept raised over the memorial Cross in St. Nicolas. Our church in Galway is such a fine old church and Mr. Berry has written of its antiquity in the St. Patrick's day supplement of *The Tribune*, that it is likely R. Catholics may be coming in to look at it, and that flag means to them the Black and Tans and the dominance they have been fighting against. He rather agreed, and in talking of the Treaty said the Colonel then commanding here, who he knew very well, had told him that if it did not pass the country would be put under military government, with wire compartments "You yourself would be segregated in Galway", and that they were determined to carry out a thorough conquest. He supposes

Michael Collins knew that, as no doubt he did.

21 MARCH. Headache has knocked me down, but business must be got through.

One afternoon I sat for a while on the quays; a calm sea and a boat being pushed out, its unpainted mast golden in its reflection in the silver sea; the only sound the voices, speaking in Irish, of the two men pulling at the ropes. I think they were from Aran, they wore the white flannel jackets and home woven loose trousers, and it seemed they might have been two of the disciples upon the Lake of Genneseret.

Many letters to answer; and papers to go through, and useless rubbish to be cleared away. A warning to me to get rid of mine. (That is what I am trying to do this February, 1930—alone at Coole).

THURSDAY. 27 MARCH. A week of business. Margaret came on Friday evening to Tuesday and had troublesome work with Bank books and securities. We motored to Coole & back on Sunday, all peaceful there.

Yesterday the Probate valuers all day, Sarsfield and De Groet. Marian has come to help to get the house in order and I am tired of turning out cupboards and deciding about furniture and seeing people on such business.

Reading *Colin-Maillard,*[52] its subject a poor Irish boy as seen through French eyes, as a stranger in London, very good as a study of emotions though a Catholic boy would never have been moved by the Salvation army; would have thought it a display of tom-toms and thanked the Saints for keeping him from harm.

Robinson writes today that the Company have read *Brigit*—"they were all greatly impressed by it and I think it will be liked. I think your play better every time I read it". He says also "I saw George Shields[53] in Antrim, he had just been reading "The Old Woman Remembers" and said 'It's the greatest thing Lady Gregory has done'. I wish you knew him, he is very nice and so gentle and patient though almost entirely confined to a little room. He said 'If you get a State Theatre make me doorman, I wouldn't want much salary' ".

I had been rather sad about "Old Woman" it looks so dreadful in A.E.'s paper with zig-zag lines; and the one or two corrections I had intended, unmade.[54]

COOLE, 6 APRIL. Hard days in Galway, business sad enough, dismantling the house, taking some things away that will be useful here; then getting the rooms in order again for people to see them.

Then to Dublin, thinking to see last rehearsal of *Brigit.* But when I got there I found the production had been put off to Holy Week, it could not be ready. I was vexed at first, but don't think my time was wasted as I decided on dresses from our own wardrobe, only four Roman soldiers' suits to be hired, and I saw rehearsals of the first and second acts. Both seemed to go well, but I had to make some slight alterations. And I heard of a Trinity College lad Lyle Donoughy [sic][55] who might fill the great part, and decided on him as he has a voice with some beauty in it and an impassive face that gives a sort of remote dignity. All the players very nice and pleased with the play and believe it will be liked. So I have come back here for a week with Yeats, who had "a longing for Coole", and I'll go back next Saturday for the real last rehearsals.

Yeats is writing his essay on the lecture given at Stockholm for U.S.A.

Wilde said "To succeed you should talk to every man as if he bored you and to every woman as if you loved her". W.B.Y. told me this apropos of *Vivian Grey*[56] which I am reading to him.

9 APRIL. He says Tim Healy said to V. Asquith "When Dillon and Redmond have to talk to Joe Devlin they both blush pink because he is so coarse"!

15 APRIL. Quiet days at Coole, and then last Saturday by early train to Galway, my last look at the house. Yeats missed the connection at Athenry and came on too and that was a help. It was sad seeing rough men piling up and ticketing the little ornaments, the furniture. And that visit led to trouble for me, for Sinclair, the Dublin dealer was there and I spoke to him and he was interested in the Velasquez though not admitting its authenticity. I told him my reserve was £100 and he said he would not give more than £50. That was all. But yesterday, Monday, when I was at the Abbey he telephoned asking what I would take, and I foolishly, not wishing to waste my time (at rehearsal) said I would call and see him when I passed his shop later. And there he made his offer of £100. I did not refuse it but said I must ask leave of Joyce the auctioneer.

He made some objections but I said I did not think I could withdraw a picture without consulting him. Then he proposed my consulting Keller on the telephone. I told Keller of the offer and said I did not think I could accept it without asking Joyce, that I would like to do the right thing. He answered that it would be perfectly right, that one could withdraw anything from a sale. So having referred it to him I had no further excuse and consented & Sinclair at once gave me a cheque (£5 extra for Joyce which I had said he should have) and receipt for me to sign, and he wrote a wire for Joyce in my name "Please withdraw Velasquez from sale".

When I came in to my lodging after 5 o'c I found a telegram "Impossible withdraw picture would be liable for damages, Joyce". I thought the damages might be against him from dealers who might come, and was much disturbed, wrote hastily to tell him how the thing had happened and rushed off to Sinclair to try if by any means I could withdraw. But his shop was shut. Then to Keller, but he had left the Office and the clerk said one could not reach him on the telephone, he was on the way home. So I could but come back, very miserable, feeling as I still feel I had been very foolish to see Sinclair at all and to give in. I had told Yeats of having sold the picture and he thought it right. And then I had to tell him of the wire, and he was sympathetic and still thought I had acted "logically" asking and taking Keller's advice. And it was not covetousness that led me to it, it was dislike of hauling the picture over to London, giving Alec Martin the trouble of selling it (he had advised me to put a reserve of £100 and if not sold at that he would try to get it into a big sale). And I knew it did not look so well in Galway as the photograph I had sent him from the Moyne catalogue. It was Sinclair who drew my attention to this. But I had a bad night of remorse, though lightened by thinking now it is I myself who am "liable for damages" and not others. A warning never to meddle with money business at all. I had a lesson on that when trying to invest in the Free State loan.

I dined with Yeats at U.A. Club, with Stephens and McGreevy;[57] pleasant talk enough, but this worry gnawing at me.

Meanwhile, I had my rehearsals of *Brigit*, two on Sunday; some disappointments, the Egyptian nurse inadequate, and the little songs I had given Sally spoiled by musical twists and turns, not her old simple style. She is looking for a prize at the Feis. Yesterday again I rehearsed, and hope for the best.

This morning a Directors' meeting at the Abbey, with Tulloch; question of the Bank getting a mortgage on the Abbey buildings.

In the afternoon I went to see Joseph O'Neill of the Education Department to try if there is a possibility of getting a grant for the Abbey from the Government. He says No, they have no money, he cannot get one for the teaching of Irish by Irish speakers which is a part of their policy. But he said I had better see Blythe, and that it was sometimes possible to get a little money saved here and there, he still hopes for some for his Irish teaching by lessening the advertising in two languages in the paper.

16 APRIL. *Brigit* last night, a beautiful performance and received with reverence by the audience; no coughing or laughing, good applause at the end. I was near Jack Yeats, he liked it all through; the Christ especially pleased him, and the last Act. He came with me to the greenroom between second and third Acts. The players seemed content, W.B.Y. a little discontented, lack of the apron, which L.R. had put on and the players had remonstrated against, they said because it made them miss their cues, but he says because it is shaky (which it certainly is) to walk on. The Craig screens made a fine background, and the yew branches I had brought from Coole were strewn. The actors made a beautiful picture in various groups. All but the soldiers' dress we had got out of the wardrobe, rummaging through layers from old plays. It seemed wonderful how smoothly all went and easily, and I felt well content and at peace. I had hidden from the audience but when I thought all had gone I found L.R. in the hall, he came holding out his hands and saying "Thank you, thank you" with real emotion, and said how beautiful he thought it. Then McGreevy spoke in the same way, he had been crying through the last Act.

All liked the Christ, so young, fairhaired, with great dignity and speaking his few lines so well. All this swept Sinclair and Joyce, all that dreadful business from my mind. I hope it may not return!

17 APRIL. Yesterday to the Abbey for small corrections, all the actors in good heart. Then buying Easter eggs for the Chicks, and fish for the maids at home; and to see Keller. No news of the auction. At 4.30 the meeting of the Advisory Board of the Municipal Gallery, the first I had attended. I had brought a statement of what I had done of late with copy of Lutyens' letter about Curzon's change of front. Only Atkinson, Reynolds and Mr. Briscoe[58] there. He talked without ceasing, would hardly listen to my statement, kept saying "We are getting the pictures, great things are being done", and I didn't know if he was vapouring. But when I had read in my letter to the Prime Minister that I was willing to agree to a loan of the pictures if we could not get the Bill passed, though the Bill would be much better and would prevent confusion between the National Gallery and the Municipal, Briscoe became violent and said "They are the property of the Corporation. The Corporation will never let the National Gallery get a hold of them". Then he said the Corporation were about to call on the British Government to return them, and that the London Irish are preparing to march on the Tate Gallery

with placards "Give us back the stolen pictures". I felt this spirited action was much more heartening than Cosgrave and Tim Healy's lukewarmness. And so Yeats thought when I told him.

The evening performance of *Brigit* very fine. A.E. was near me and thought it "most moving and beautiful". He and Lord Monteagle and Norman and his wife came to my barmbrack tea in the green room and congratulated the actors. Lord M. told me that Will Shields would not accept compliments but passed them on to me—"it was all done for me". Douglas Hyde I only saw at the end. He said "I like it twenty times better than anything you have ever done". So I am content. Someone said a priest at Westland Row had advised his congregation to come to it.

This morning I went to see Fanny Trench in old Lady Anne's house, that furniture also being prepared for sale. She had liked the play very much, said the people near her in the stalls were crying and that "it is a wonderful thing for you to leave after you". One doesn't often have praise from one's relations.

Then to lunch with Yeats, and he had an answer from E. Marsh saying "The time is a good one" to move about the pictures, and suggests Cosgrave writing a personal letter to Thomas to re-open the question; so Yeats wrote to Cosgrave while I was there. Y. hears Republicanism is increasing in the South and will return more members at the next election.

Alec Martin wrote about the sale of the Velasquez "I think you have done wisely". A relief.

I took notes for an appeal to the Carnegie Trustees for help for the Abbey Theatre to Robinson and dictated them, and he will draw up a letter.

I sat with A.E. for a while. He thinks that the Republicans, De Valera at least and any not convicted of brutal crime, should be released, chiefly "because the Republicans have now no policy save that of attacking the Free State authorities and their leaders would have to formulate one". He tells again of the book he is trying to write *The Avatars* and is glad to hear Socialists are reading his *Interpreters* trying to find the Divine idea behind the practical one in every movement.

He read me a poem by Donaghy (my "Christ") and spoke of another writer, O'Flaherty,[59] as having much talent. He says there are many of these young men with that, but that they seem to lack a purpose, to lack intensity.

Yeats spoke again of the action of soul on soul; and that evil cannot be driven out except by the exercise of this universal soul. I said that might be the idea of the more intelligent nuns in a convent, the saving of others, of the wicked, by their virtue. But he says that virtue is as if isolated and not of the same force.

18 APRIL. GOOD FRIDAY. A small audience at the Abbey, but appreciative. Keller and his wife there. He was very much interested in the trial scene the change of jurisdiction &c, said it threw a new light on the whole story—and on Ireland. He thought the whole thing very beautiful. Swift MacNeill[60] who introduced himself to me spoke of the beauty of the language, and his wife was weeping. All taken reverently as before.

19 APRIL. Frank yesterday morning, and a family talk. I went to the Hydes to ask Craoibhin to come to the play again and meet the actors. Only Mrs. Hyde was there but she promised they would come. As I left she said "He will like to come, I know you are his friend, and there are some who are not", and tears came to her eyes. I told her I had missed no opportunity of pressing his claim to the Senate. She says he would never ask for it and very likely would not accept it, having so much work to do, but that though he says nothing he feels deeply not having been asked to be on it. I had pressed it on Joseph O'Neill on Tuesday, I asked why Craoibhin had been left out. He said no one had pushed for it, and thinks also he is suffering from Miss O'Farrelly's unpopularity, she is his assistant and very aggressive, and he agreed that his being left out was very wrong.[61] So in the evening, having dined with Yeats at the U.A. Club I pressed him again. He looks on Hyde as part of the "Gaelic group" already strong enough in the Senate and not of much use. But I said it was as a representative of literature he should be put on, of the intellectual side. His history of Irish Literature places him there, and his *Love Songs of Connacht*. Paris has published his folk tales in Irish with a French translation. His name is honoured there and in America, and even for the dignity of the Senate he should be on it. And Yeats was I think convinced.

20 APRIL. EASTER SUNDAY. A very small matinée yesterday, but the actors were pleased by a photographer coming, and were grouped for and by him. Small also in the evening, but appreciative. The Hydes came round to tea in the greenroom, Yeats said "I told you I would give no opinion until I had seen it a second time. Now I am sure it is a good play. I like it". But he abuses the staging and production. Madame Gonne said "They are saying you have written a Republican play", and Miss MacArdle had asked for the script that she might write on it. Perrin was in the hall waiting as I left and said "I thought you might *like to know* that the loss on the week was £72"! Dreadful; but the two days off, Monday and Good Friday account for a good part of this.

I lay awake, happy on the whole at the way it had gone,

though today Yeats has been again abusing poor Dolan's production, which I don't think was bad.

21 APRIL. EASTER MONDAY. Service at St. Anne's. Lunch at Hyde's. Called at Cancer Hospital but Hall was out. Evening dancing and singing performance by children for poor children's clothing fund at the Abbey, I saw a little of it. With Y. at 9 o'c to Gogartys, he and Mrs. G. alone. Yeats had been to an afternoon party at Mr. Douglas's to meet the Australian Premier, had met Cosgrave who had not received his letter about the Lane pictures but promised to write to the Colonial Office on the matter at once. He had been in the train and had walked from the station with Mulcahy, but says "I think I shock those people, they don't respond". He had told Mulcahy of someone having reproved Monseigneur Vaughan for living in such luxury, unlike the life of Christ, and Vaughan had said "It would be presumptuous of me to put myself on a level with my Maker". "And a shadow passed over Mulcahy's face".

21 APRIL. EVENING. I went to see poor Hall at the Cancer Hospital. He looks much worse and I could hardly understand what he said. I gave him £6.6 to pay three more weeks, he has only enough money for four. On my way there a nursemaid was rough with a child, poor little thing. And as I came back from the Municipal Gallery newsboys were shouting and carrying a bill—"Young man shot dead". The Gallery itself comforting, so much of Hugh. One always forgets how many beautiful pictures he has given there.

Young Donaghy in to tea; is writing a play on Deirdre, I'm afraid it has a poor chance of being acted, after Yeats's and Synge's and A.E.'s. He is working very hard for his exams and teaches mathematics every day at Blackrock. A nice young fellow, he deserves success.

BOOK TWENTY-SEVEN

THURSDAY, 24 APRIL, 1924. COOLE. Yesterday I came home, my mind at rest about *Brigit.* (And Joyce had written an amiable letter about the sale and withdrawal of the picture.) The actors were all so nice and friendly it was like old times in the green-room. *John Bull* went very well, all the points taken as well as ever in spite of change in politics, though the English valet, Hodson, was more applauded than anyone in his outburst against London landlords. I don't quite know why. I had a busy last day seeing Hall's doctor who thinks it possible he may be cured; and Fanny Trench, and Abbey business, and to get Catherine's Pageant of Nature bound, and meeting my upholsterer to get materials, and having my pearls strung, and fetching my things left from last visit at Yeats' house, and dined with Yeats at Clery's restaurant. He had seen Cosgrave on Sunday at an afternoon party and C. had promised to take up the picture question. I had to meet a reporter from the *Daily Express* at the Abbey about the pictures at 7.30, and though Yeats had rather scolded me for accepting the appointment, he came before it was over and gave a little interview himself. I have been writing to Kiernan, at the Irish Office about them today.

Up very early yesterday and came by early train. No Galway to visit now—and I had so many bits of news that would have amused A.

All peaceful here, and the rain (it was hail at Athenry) welcomed. "We have a nice drop of rain" said the porter to John as he put up the luggage. Now I have three months before me with but little hope of seeing the darlings.

SUNDAY, 27 APRIL. Trying in these days through confusion to get rid of confusion, putting things of A.'s into their right places, and dreading further earthquakes when the upholsterer comes tomorrow. But yesterday afternoon Peter and I planted out the little phloxes and delphiniums and other plants, (8 Sept. Alas, but one of my 24 phloxes still living; wet and slugs the probable cause.) And I got through the sifting and arrangement of books and feel more hopeful.

The papers say the Boundary Conference has broken up. No

agreement.[1]

I think I went through my wealthy days with simplicity; now I must go through these straitened days with dignity.

A notice of *Brigit* in the *Irish Statesman* by "Y.O.". (A.E.)[2] pleases me: "there is no doubt that the audience which listened to Lady Gregory's Passion Play was deeply moved. I think they were moved because the spiritual tragedy told in language which was new made a new appeal to the heart. Lady Gregory, certainly with the greatest reverence, has made the characters in her Passion play talk in an Irish dialect. The characters themselves seem Irish . . . Because the characters are so realised for us, almost made contemporary, the ancient tragedy suddenly becomes intensely real to us and we feel as if it had been told to us for the first rather than the thousandth time".

28 APRIL. The Boundary question an anxiety, Dublin had seemed quiet though Yeats had heard there would be "some firing—but of no importance" on the Monday evening, and made me promise to have someone with me going home from the Abbey after the play. So Perrin came in the tram, but it was not until I had gone to bed that I heard a few shots. I had noticed in the afternoon a group of armed soldiers on the roof of the Government buildings, anxious I think to be seen.

The last *Sinn Fein* has a very vivid account of Liam Mellows and his escape after the Rising.[3] He was in the mountains near Tulla while the police were searching for him at Kinvara. He did go through hardships, and that Galway Rising was hopeless from the first, Dr. Walsh who had seen much of him and liked him said to me speaking of him "his one idea was to go out and shoot somebody", and this seems not far from the truth. But he was brave and took all with a cheerful courage, and it may be that his prayer this tells of at Moyode was the cause of the extraordinary stupidities of the Government forces, as told us at the time by Vere [Gregory].

Last evening read Lady Dorothy's *Memoirs*, taking me back yet farther to the London life and old acquaintances. I met Bernal Osborne but once that I remember (he died in 1881), at some private view, the Grosvenor I think, as we came in. He was going out and stopped W. and said "How wise you have been Gregory to keep clear of Royalties as you have done. I have just come from Sandringham and have been sent in to dinner the last three nights with Miss Knoyls"! (W. had after a polite interval taken his name off both the Turf and the Marlborough Clubs which the Prince had on his own initiative put him up for and to which he had been elected. He liked and admired the Prince for his intelligence and tact, but disliked his set and surroundings). Lady Dorothy tells of B.O. requiring a butt; and I remember Escott telling me that he had come once as holiday tutor to Hugh (the late Lord) Gough. And that Bernal Osborne had been there for a house party and had caused him actual anguish, making a butt of him, a shy young stranger, at meal times. The Duchess of St. Albans' sweetness and wholehearted good nature must have come from a swing of the pendulum, "the antithesis" according to Yeats' theory.

An account in the paper today of Oliver Gogarty offering his two swans to the Liffey, and illustration shows Cosgrave and Yeats supporting him. They told me the Governor General had been invited but had written in refusing "If they were pleasing birds such as ducks I might think of it, but swans I understand are callous towards their young".[4]

30 APRIL. A quiet day, house and garden being got into order, though I am a little troubled by a telegram from Frank who had asked me to come over and see him at Roxborough "Don't come today. Some unpleasantness probably". He had hoped all was going well there.

The Government, the papers say, is determined to go on with the Boundary Commission.

Reading *Anna Karenina*[5] last evening. In a very good chapter (part 3, Chapter 1) the thought strikes Konstantin that his brother's "faculty of working for the public good was possibly . . . lack of vital force, of what is called heart, of that impulse which drives a man to choose some one out of the innumerable paths of life, and to care only for that one".

Yesterday I had Joyce's accounts of the auction, much better than I expected; he sends cheque £550, and I have Sinclair's £105 as well; something to put by for the darlings.

I had said to Yeats in Dublin that day I was so troubled about the sale of the picture to Sinclair that the auction and the first production of *Brigit* came on the same day and that if only one was to succeed I hoped it might be the play. And now I think both did, for a cutting comes from the *Observer* with L.R.'s most generous praise. It has warmed my heart. And I have had also today and yesterday letters from my little Catherine, and these also have brought warmth to my heart.

SUNDAY, 4 MAY. Quiet days, Bligh doing his upholstery well, a nice young fellow. And Peter is interested in the flower garden as well as the vegetables, and we have found a much longed for needlewoman in Briget Mulloo at our very gate, and the house is getting into order, the Dominic St. things finding their places.

But today I am told M. Quinn has turned our horses and cattle out of the field he has not rented or used since October and for which he has not paid last year's rent. And Frank has asked me to come and meet him at Roxborough where he was to be last Tuesday that I might see its ruins. But he wired in the morning putting me off "there may be unpleasantness". And I hear today the sheep have been driven off the land taken a year ago by Loughrea people, the people near by wanting it.

5 MAY. Today's paper says "200 sheep and lambs driven off by 100 men to their owners' door".

No, Malachi Quinn did not meddle with our horses. John met him today with Raftery and he denied it, yet still has a grievance about the land.

But they persuaded him, or think they did so, to pay his eighteen months' rent, and then try again to buy. They wanted him to come to me but he was "shamed and shy" to come, having [been] "so rough" before.

A hive of industry now; Madden at the vines, Bligh at the upholstery, Connolly doing carpentry, Brigit Mulloo sewing, and then our own 4 men. Poor Grandmama! her pocket will be very light. But French sent £13 for April, three of the plays have been broadcasted and *The Jester* has been put on for a performance at Liverpool.

EVENING. Danny Shaughnessy came, through the rain, with a present of some trout he had caught.

Then John to say Malachi Quinn had come with a note for me. It was written today. "Dear Lady Gregory, I have lodged today £40 to Mrs. Gregory's credit at the Gort National Bank for Rent due. I am taking over the grazing again for this year until such time as the matter is finally arranged. Yours respectfully, Malachi Quinn". John says that he means to put off our stock and put on his own, and asked me to see him. I sent for him and told him he was doing wrong in this, that he should try to come to an agreement about the purchase of the land, that he was putting himself in the wrong by taking this violent measure without having even asked if he might rent it. But he was obstinate "I must have it, I cannot do without it. It is my land I will not wait. Mr. Shields the solicitor says I am in the right. He is Hogan's partner. Mrs. Gregory asked £1500 for it, no one would pay that". I said he should write to her or make a new offer, and reminded him that last year she had consented to let him keep it until October as a convenience at his request and he had made no offer since then. But he would not give in to waiting. "I'll do as I say, I cannot do without it" and he got up and went. I told him I hoped the night and prayer might lead him to a better mind. But he was defiant. (John had told me that in the argument in Gort Raftery had said "Women are women and men are men". I suppose as an excuse for me!)

Rather a heartbreak when we had seemed at peace.

He said also something about "what happened at Roxborough" (the driving off of stock) and said "They will get the land".

6 MAY. I am distressed by Malachi's behaviour, I believe he was urged by his father-in-law, Gilligan, as he did not seem to know of our horses having been driven off and the wall built up. I have sent Margaret his letter and written to her and told her I can do nothing further and I suggest her getting Frank to take up the matter.

Yeats has come, thinks the Boundary question will draggle on, Cosgrave would wait to let things settle themselves but for the Republicans as Craig probably would but for the Orangemen. "O'Higgins said the other day in our house 'it is a question between having murders on the boundary or murders through the whole country'." He is more excited about the army investigation and all that is coming out. O'H. had said also "we have officers who think it is a finer thing to blow off the lock with a revolver than to turn the handle of the door". J. O'Neill told him of an officer being examined; the examiners report on his arithmetic was "He can add up but he cannot subtract". But I called out "That is just what I can and can't do", and Yeats confesses it is not far from his own case also.

I have been in the woods, lovely with bluebells and the new foliage of larch.

8 MAY. I have at last got the Abbey statement off with application for help from the Carnegie Fund. L.R. didn't have it ready before I left Dublin, and Yeats brought it here but forgot which Trustee he had talked with at the Savile and who had promised help. Luckily I remembered it was Sir W. McCormick and with great efforts got the enclosing letter written and addressed and sent to Perrin to forward, if he has a duplicate copy, and if not to make one and to send me one for H. Plunkett.

I still urge the release of De Valera and the political prisoners, but Yeats thinks they will be kept in for a long time, probably till the ammunition dumps are all discovered.

Mr. Johnson here, says a good many of the farmers who put money in the Free State loan are taking it out again. It is at 92 now, but I am less inclined to invest in it now the children have inherited A's money, so much of it is in Irish railways.

9 MAY. Malachi still weighing on my mind. I have asked John if Peter Green his relative might not bring him to make an offer of purchase that would be a possible basis. There seems to be but £200 between his first offer and what Margaret would take.

Yeats described to me a poem that Ezra Pound has written, without rhyme or subject, "in spirals", the very latest and most advanced school.[6] I said it sounded like a cat running after its tail, and he says it is, rather.

I read him this morning a long and dishonest article on the Boundary question in *The Times*.[7] They want to break the Treaty that our Government, whatever its faults, have done their very best to keep. Lloyd George says nothing. Yeats says he (L.G.) said to A.E. in Black and Tan times "I know the English forces have done disgraceful things in Ireland of late, but I'm not going to say so in public".

11 MAY. Yeats says the friends or people we see in dreams are not real—not the real image of our friends. But I think that image is sometimes as clear as reality. I dreamt of G.B.S. the other night, his Norfolk jacket, his beard, though this perhaps a little darker in colour but not more than in shadow.

Yesterday we went to Ballylee but could not get in, someone had tampered with the lock; a great disappointment to W.B.Y.

Raftery and John had seen Malachi in Gort and had talked and argued with him and Peter Green. Malachi now saying "let there be *six* men on each side", a sort of tug of war. But what seems to come out clear is that he has not enough money to buy, and that P. Green would advance it and probably look forward to the land falling eventually into his hands as is probable enough, poor Malachi having had losses, and is being pushed on by him to make his claim—"must have the callows".

I have again pressed on Y. the release of De Valera and other leaders. Now that McGrath is forming a "National Party" avowedly for separation, but by constitutional means, it seems a time when extremists must join it or take up arms again, and nothing can be formed on a good foundation while the leaders are shut up. But Yeats thinks it will not be done yet awhile, says they (the Government) are probably fearing assassination themselves and also fearing De V. may be assassinated, and they blamed. Yet he cannot be shut up for ever.

12 MAY. Yeats working very hard at his philosophy. I asked if it had any ancestor. He says no, possibly Palamedes, but it is in fact new.

13 MAY. This morning at breakfast he said he had solved

something yesterday that makes it easier. He has separate statements but is trying to get them into a synthesis—it is all right if he accepts what comes, but if he begins to think it all goes wrong. I said Moses must have had "the devil of a job" getting the ten commandments fixed in stone. He says Yes, that is just it. He remembers Synge saying "It is the duty of the father of a family to bring up his children as well as is compatible with a certain amount of virtue; and it is the duty of a writer to get as much form as is possible into his work compatible with a certain amount of beauty".

An annoying article in *The Times* on the Boundary question wanting "terms of reference fixed by Government to allay the suspicions of Ulster" which of course would raise the suspicions of the South. He wonders why Ulster objects so much to losing counties, I say they are afraid of their Parliament being left in mid air, seven devils dancing on the top of a needle.

He says Christ himself went to the multitudes but the next Christ's message will be brought—sent—to them. And that His teaching was sympathy with the sorrowful, but the next, perhaps in eighty years, will teach sympathy with the people's joys.

A letter from Chicago asks for a message for a group of girls who are organising a "Girls Week". I sent them that of the Greeks that I keep in a little pocket of my purse putting down as the most desirable of the virtues "Temperance, Justice, Courage, Nobility and Truth". Yeats suggests a Japanese one, rather spun out and I don't like it so much except that it ends with "unfailing courtesy to all". But I think "nobility" covers that.

Rita Daly and her sister for the afternoon. I took them to the woods to see the acres of bluebells. Anne's first letter from school cheery though she says "there are a lot of bluebells out here but so far we have only seen them in vases at breakfast"—not "the heavens upbreaking through the earth" as they are here.

Typing more or less of the old diaries every day—1923 now, the pictures as usual; and the floggings that I stopped.

14 MAY. Talking again of the book, Yeats said "My work is not exposition but suggestion".

15 MAY. Yeats has left today, having some Committee meeting, Arts Federation, in Dublin, but won't do anything about the Lane pictures, except ask Cosgrave if he should see him what he has done. He got through the codifying of the MS he brought down and has covered paper with mysterious signs. It was a nice peaceful week and like old times, he at his work and I at mine, though that is only typing at present and trying to get the serenity of order into house and lands. We talked a little this morning

about the new "National" party. If I were a politician I would join it, and I hope the best of the Republicans may do so, if they can make up their mind to take the oath as we do the Creed, saying we "believe in the resurrection of the body", which we don't, because it is difficult and inexpedient to explain our reservations. Yeats says the oath is framed so as to really mean nothing except loyalty to the Irish Constitution. But I think Gessler's cap would have been equally an offence made of cobweb as of leather. A comforting letter of Dunraven's in the *Times* (though not on the front page) tearing all the arguments against the Commission to flitters.

I have written to Sir Horace with a copy of our application to the Carnegie for an Abbey grant, asking him to support it.

I gave Rita Daly a copy of *Hugh Lane* and she writes the Archdeacon had said "Nothing has come into the house which will give me so much pleasure as this book"; and she herself had read it till 2 a.m.

And T.C. Murray writes about *Brigit* "It was moving and beautiful and its construction was supremely well done". I like appreciation from a fellow dramatist.

My bed-reading *Anna Karenina* still. It is wonderful, the searchlight being thrown on every group, every soul. Yeats doesn't like it because of the end, thinks it insincere. I have taken out *Resurrection*[8] now. I'll feel justified reading it by daylight for it is in French and I should keep that up for the Chicks. Yeats liked our *Vivian Grey*[9] evenings but we hadn't time quite to finish it. He has been delighted by finding in his Encyclopaedia that Dizzy describing his own early experience of trying to found a Review as akin to Vivian's audacity, must have founded his pompous Marquis on the Murray of the day.

I have been planting my Gladioli, and new chrysanthemums, and yesterday plunging through the depths of the wood to find dead or fallen larch for Donohoe's avenue paling to save us from another gate.

Yeats insisted I should use the fountain pen he had given me long ago, and I'm doing so, my fingers covered with ink.

16 MAY. Yesterday's paper says twelve young men had been arrested for the Roxborough cattle driving and taken to Galway gaol, bail refused.[10]

Last night I wondered if those who do not believe in the Divinity of Christ may not have in the denial a yet more exalted belief, that man himself may reach to the Divine height.

17 MAY. I thought of this again last night, reading my Irish testament "Ar na Aithne gur ab ó Dia tainig sé agus gur cum Dia

do bi se ag dul—" "knowing that he was come from God and it was to God He was returning"— may we not believe that of the spirit that dwells in us for a while?

I am still trying to get to the serenity of order and not leave too much untidiness for those who inherit. Now going through the years of Letts Diaries of W.'s—little more than engagements and letters written or received: the movements from Colombo to Kandy and to his dear Anarahapura. His wife's death . . . The Prince of Wales' visit; the visits to India, to Australia; his resignation, his return. London welcoming him; dinners at the Garrick, the Athenaeum; dining with the Duchess of Cleveland, Lady Molesworth, Lady Marian Alford, Lord and Lady Somers, Lord Northbrook, the Roseberys, the Prince and Princess of Wales, with Lady Waldegrave, to meet the Prince; with Lady Ashburton, with Lord Carnarvon, Anthony Trollope. At Mr. Ralli's to meet Sarah Bernhardt; at the Duke of Wellington's. Breakfast also with the Duke of Wellington, with Goschen, with Gladstone. To stay also at Strawberry Hill at Bestwood, at Lord Somers'. In Ireland with the Marlboroughs at the Viceregal Lodge; at Cannes in the springtime dining with the Duke of Vallambrosa, with the Duke of St. Albans on his yacht. And there is an entry, there at Cannes, 10 April, 1878 "To Vallauris with R. Persse". Only my brother's name given not mine. I have still in my room here a terra cotta head of Dante given to me that day at Vallauris.

Some of those friends showed me much kindness; all but all of them have passed away.

19 MAY. Housekeeping and some garden work, and then when post came in a letter from Kiernan, he had not yet had the pamphlet or my letter but writes "I have spoken to Mr. McNeill about the Lane pictures. He will do everything possible . . . I am writing to the Minister for External affairs to see if he can give information. Before approaching the Colonial Office it would be well to have all the facts. If Senator Yeats or any of your personal friends who have the pictures at heart are likely soon to be in London perhaps you will ask them to call on the High Commissioner here. I am certain that this is the quickest channel through which to approach Mr. Thomas. Some information as to previous activities is what Mr. McNeill requires and he will move at once". So I set to work to find a copy—make copies of—my letters to the P.M. and Freeman's Smith's letter &c, and have got through that. Then more of those old diaries—'80, '81, awaking many memories—my marriage—Robert's birth. 1 only left of us three. But thank God for the three darling

grandchildren.

18 MAY. Sunday. Yesterday afternoon young Kiernan's letter in answer to mine about the pictures. "I have spoken to Mr. McNeill about them. He will do everything possible. Would you tell me when the latest activities took place and what department in Dublin had the negotiations in hand . . . Some information as to previous activities is what Mr. McNeill requires and he will then move at once". So neither Healy nor Cosgrave can have mentioned the matter at all.

So I set to work at once to type again copies of my letter to R. Mac Donald with full account. And then it came into my head that I ought to have a fresh clear statement of the whole case published in the *Irish Statesman*.[11] So this morning after breakfast I set to work, and coming from church just at lunch time I set to work again about 2 o'c and worked till 5.30, made an article or letter, and an enclosing letter to A.E. and my head is tired and aches a little.

19 MAY. This morning also typing and correcting and filling up my letters and sent them off to A.E. and Kiernan, a *Life* of Hugh to McNeill the High Commissioner. And going through drawers of W.'s writing table, taking out old account books &c better destroyed now. Typing on also my own diaries, an endless reel. A heavy day, rain threatened, oppressive.

20 MAY. Robert's birthday.

A letter from Yeats saying Cosgrave had sent his secretary to tell him "Cosgrave has been in correspondence with Thomas about the pictures, Curzon (who seems to be backsliding) says there are legal difficulties in the way of a loan and in any case does not want to lose all; and Thomas is 'exploring the question' of legislation. Curtis asks for pamphlets. Can you send me a copy of that new evidence that I may get it typed and added to pamphlet . . ."

And I am so thankful to have all that typed and ready to send him; and so glad to have made out that new, and I do think convincing, statement I sent to Russell, well worth the strain of looking for dates &c and the bad night I had, over tired so that little worries seized hold of me. Anxious now lest W.B.Y. should think my article indiscreet, or A.E. not have room for it.

Cheery letters too from Anne and Catherine, but they want a squirrel caught and tamed for a school friend, and I can't bear to disappoint them but it doesn't seem very practicable. Mike climbing a tree to rob the nest to begin with. And there are enough prisoners in the country already.

Second post brought a letter at last from Margaret, chiefly

about buying Yellow House for George Gough. As to Malachi she says "I will write to Uncle Frank but I handed over Coole as much to have no dealings about it with any of the country people as for any other reason".

I have been to Gort about Yellow House, and I have bought a bicycle new, £7.7., for messages to Gort now Black Pony is such a danger. The second hand bicycle was disapproved by Johnny and as I had had to refuse to let him a field I had to restore him to good humour.

21 MAY. I drove into Gort to see Miss Quinn about the Yellow House. She wants to sell it, would give it over at once, for what she had bought it for, £375. But M. had heard it was £275 and had said George wouldn't give more than £350 so I sent a wire and today have had a reply "George accepts price all of us delighted and grateful for your speedy action". So I have my uses after all.

This morning a letter from A.E. The article came too late for this week but he'll put it in and comment on it next week "You may rely upon me to do the best I can". Just as well. He may have more to comment on then. My mind was so darkened last night thinking of this new "backsliding" of Curzon (prompted I am sure by Witt) that I had to take out at random a volume of the *Noble Greeks and Romans*, and read the comparison between Alcibiades and Coriolanus—he praised for his "temperance and cleane handes from taking of bribes and money" and Alcibiades, taking a lower place, yet even he after they had banished him "would not yet suffer the captains of the Athenians to run into great errours of, neither would he see them cast away by following ill counsell which they take, neither would he forsake them in any daunger they put themselves into".

I have asked Mike about squirrels. He says this is about the time the young are born, he was coming over from Inchy one time "and Nolan's dog began to bark at a tree, and we poked with sticks at a big ivy bush that was in it, and there was a squirrel's nest and three or four of the young ones fell down". But he doesn't think one could be tamed because "they are very cross, and try to bite you if they are caught in a trap".

Still going through W's notebooks. All or almost all of these mentioned entertainers or entertained have passed away. I seem to be the only one left. Perhaps it is this picture business that keeps me living. I must hold on to that.

Young B., running down the Ministry today, says "they know nothing about Art". I said I heard President Cosgrave had bought some fine mahogany furniture. But he says "He made a great row about the price. And it wasn't real old but imitation, I know the fellow that got the job of making it".

I wrote to Ramsay MacDonald about the pictures and sent him Hugh's *Life*. Sent a copy also to Mr. Thomas, the Colonial Secretary. And wrote to A.E.

22 MAY. The morning began well. Sir Horace will help with the Carnegie. French sent a U.S.A. cheque, £58 odd, chiefly *Dragon* and *Spreading* (which I had been afraid was going out of fashion). But I worked my hand tired typing. And just as I was happily beginning to plant sunflowers with Peter, Mr. Johnson called and when I got back to the garden a box of my new dahlias had vanished!

But there has been a debate in the Dail on the release of the prisoners that gives hope. The Government—Cosgrave—speaking without rancour and saying that if De Valera will give the order to surrender arms he may come out tomorrow.

Reynolds sends me a letter from the Editor of the *Burlington*, who wants to reopen the picture controversy, giving both sides. But I hope that may not be necessary, these controversies in public increase ill feeling on both sides.

Nevill Geary writes about some books, Parliamentary Debates, he is presenting to some Institution in India "Edmund Burke objected to the British General Carleton in the American War of Independence indenting for '5 gross scalping knives as an issue to Red Indian Allies".

23 MAY. My dahlias are all right, or all of them that Peter didn't plant in mistake for sunflowers under my own supervision!

A very letter-writing day. To Keller and some army officers about our missing guns. To Reynolds suggesting and writing some non-committal sentences for the *Burlington* editor. To Horace Plunkett about the Abbey request for Carnegie. To the Civic Guard Commandant about permit for a gun. And others to Dorothy Carleton and Perrin. Then afternoon post brought one from Yeats enclosing one from L. Curtis, Colonial Office, who tells of Curzon's letter about the loan, in which he eats his words to Lutyens and others and declares it impossible. I am rather glad for it leaves a legalising Bill the only solution. And one from Kiernan also keen to help, and from McNeill saying he will give it.

I then looked for and typed copies of Sir R. Duke's ruling in a will case, that pencilled alterations signed but unwitnessed (evidently) were valid,.because they showed the wishes of the testator, and sent Kiernan a copy, and one to A.E. for his comments. This with a little gardening was my day. My brain feels rather frittered.

24 MAY. Last night I went through the last of W.'s Diary Note books. 1891 to the beginning of 1892. Very hard to go through, very sad, the last of those sheltered years. The summer at Coole was tranquil, one or two friends to stay now and then; the friendliness of the people had lived through the Land League days. The London winters brought him more of the companionship of equals. I see the names at one of those Grillion dinners in the winter of '91—Sir Alfred Lyall, Mr. Lecky, Lord Morley, Lord Norton, Sir Redvers Buller, Mr. Gladstone, F. Leveson Gower, Lord Cranbrook, Sir Robert Herbert. At another Sir John Lubbock, Lord Derby, Sir R. Meade, Lord Kimberley, Lord Fortescue, Sir M. Grant Duff, Sir James Paget, Lord Justice Bowen. Again, the Archbishop of Canterbury, Lord Herschell, Lord Northbrook, Lord Arthur Russell, J. Chamberlain, Lord Harrowby. Little dinners at home also. At one Mr. Merriman and Sir Hercules Robinson from the Cape, Froude, G. Shaw Lefevre, Edward Martyn (a link between old and new) Lady Dorothy Nevill. Again, Sir Horace and Lady Rumbold from the Hague, Lady Reay, our hostess at Bombay, Nevill Geary, Sir Frederick Haines, G.W.E. Russell, F. Leverson Gower, Lord Justice Bowen. There must have been good talk that evening at our round table.

Then an entry that made me wince with pain as I came upon it "April 25. Mr. Rawnsley, Waterloo, 2.20"—Robert's first journey to school. We were to have dined at Sir F. Geary's that night, but I remember I could not go, I made excuse of the Opera and sat at the back of Lady Osborne's box, where my tear stained face could not be seen. (But in September "To London with Robert" gives me a happier memory, for it began a new interest. W. was very proud of his boy doing so well at school.)

Then in November of that year, 1891, another entry that was to be often repeated "Dr. Maclagan, 11.30", that kind and gifted doctor who was with us at the end.

And in one of the last pages of that year "Shot at Coole 16 and 18 December 47 Woodcocks; 22 woodcocks; 32 pheasants; and a list of the friends to whom we had sent game, not only to the old London friends, Lady Dorothy of course and Thomson Hankey and the rest, but to the incumbents of the two parishes where I worked with his goodwill, St. George the Martyr and St. Stephen's Southwark.

There are but few entries in those first pages of 1892. On 3

February I wrote in pencil "sudden illness". And on 6 March "before daybreak all was over. He passed away in his sleep".

24 MAY. 1924. This morning a letter from A.E. "I was round with Mr. Desmond Fitzgerald yesterday about some other business and I asked him whether the getting back the pictures was not in his department. He told me there was a motion down for a Cabinet meeting this week in regard to them, and that Cosgrave had written to Thomas. I urged him to get McNeill to do what he could in London and to send him all the information and he promised that he would. I think myself James McNeill, who is a charming fellow, is a little sleepy but told Desmond Fitzgerald he had better write to him every week to know what he is doing about it". Then by afternoon post one from Kiernan—"the matter is now in Mr. McNeill's hands, and (immediate) if you will send me two dozen of the pamphlets a definite move will be made. The copies of the pamphlet are required by the Colonial Office". Too late for today's post, but just as well as I must type copies, two dozen, of the additional evidence to put with the pamphlet (though I think Yeats must have sent on those I sent him by this time). And I am glad to have work to do and strength to do it, now that I am alone.

L.R. has sent me a charming picture handkerchief from Valencia for my collection.

26 MAY. Yesterday, Sunday, church; and I went through the papers &c in the writing table, W.'s and R.'s in my room. Today sent off pamphlets to the High Commissioner's Office. The Colonial Secretary, Mr. Thomas, writes thanking me for the *Life* and saying "You have my sympathy in your wishes about the bequest, but it is a very difficult matter to deal with". That is not cheering, and I have just looked at the list of the present Trustees of London N.G. sent me by Reynolds, and it is sad the well-wishers, Brownlow, Pembroke, gone (and Lord Ribblesdale) and less gracious ones in their place.

I have been planting antirrhinums in the porch boxes, and in the children's gardens, with dahlias and hollyhocks. 8 o'c now. I have finished the day as I began, writing endless letters.

28 MAY. Yesterday also letter writing. Kiernan wanting more documents. And planting more sunflowers, those "holy terrors" as Peter calls the snails having destroyed several. Very tired last night, having typed copies of my interview with Macpherson, and Trustees' letters &c. And this I have been continuing today, but having to break off and go out now and then.

But a letter from the Prime Minister thanking me for the *Life* and my letter but saying "I am sorry to say that I have not had five minutes in which to consider the question of the Hugh Lane pictures; but probably Mr. Thomas will be bringing the matter up as a Government business if Mr. Cosgrave has officially approached him". This typed, but after his signature he has written with his own hand "I am always glad to hear of or from you", (and made three inkblots that look nice and unofficial).

That, and a note from Bank of England saying my present balance (having invested proceeds of Auction) is £621.9.9. had cheered me. Coole is safe for another year anyhow.

29 MAY. A holy day. No holiday to me, for I worked the whole morning at picture statements or notes, going through Curzon's changes of face &c. Settled bill with Bligh. All this upholstery has cost something over £50 not much to show, but seven armchairs and my sofa made good as new, and the sofa in playroom very nice,-was useless before, also the three little Dresden chairs have new covers, and the brougham straps have been repaired. All this doing away with untidiness. My pleasantest moment was giving Johnny Hehir leave to use the bicycle on Sundays and holidays, his face lighted up "I'll have it now—I'll go to the country to see my friends".

A wire from Yeats saying they will expect me on Saturday. I have gone through the last (but not the first) of A's diaries, very sad those last entries. On the 12th March in shaky writing "Dr. O'Malley called", that is the last but on a later page, (15th March) she had written "Augusta's birthday".

30 MAY. The *Irish Statesman* has come, has my short statement, good I think, I could not see a word too much. A.E. unluckily weakened it by his comment, mistakenly thinking that Hugh had *spoken* to us, artists and all who now support our claim. But he gives Hugh's words to him on one of the last Dublin days and that is good, and he quoted what I had sent him about Sir H. Duke.

Yeats has sent his new volume of essays, and I have been cutting the pages, recognising page after page, but had forgotten the splendid passage of Blake on the building of Jerusalem "what is immortality but the things relating to the spirit which lives immortally".

And I had not seen and am glad of the little note about Robert's painting.[12]

1 JUNE. The mail car was held up at Kilcolgan "on the morning of the Holy Day" and all parcels taken—"All the world is taken" Mrs. Mitchell said, and there is great indignation. For this was not a robbery of Bank money or of luxuries for "big houses" for these have all vanished (though I received a piece of brown

paper marked "registered fragile" and addressed to me but don't know what it was) but there were many parcels for the "country houses", blouses &c for girls getting their bits of finery for the summer. So there is just a hope they may detect and denounce the robbers though as usual I am told "its best say nothing whatever is known".

A quiet journey to Dublin, being Saturday I had a carriage to myself, and Yeats met me with a taxi, George was dining out so we had the evening to talk of the Lane pictures. I read him my document and notes and he thinks I must go to London and approved of my plan or hope. It is to show the sequence of events, and Curzon's "backsliding" to the authorities, first Curtis at the Colonial Office. And if a Bill is impracticable (and I have doubts of its getting through the Lords) then to demand to be told the findings of the private Commission that sat under the last Government, and if that is not to be had to demand, what Macpherson suggested, a sworn enquiry. I also hope to avoid the rancour of a Press controversy. And I read him extracts from Lord Plymouth and Lord Brownlow's letters, so fair, simple and righteous a statement—the Trustees have not power to give them up, the Government if it thinks right must bring in a Bill to restore them. We as Trustees will accept the Bill—Even Curzon might give in to take the formula of such honoured Trustees and thus honour their memory.

Kiernan writes that McNeill would like to move carefully, thoroughly preparing his steps in advance and thinks of consulting Lord Haldane.

3 JUNE. A meeting, the annual, of Directors at the Abbey this morning. We have for the first time mortgaged the building to clear off our overdrafts. But business has improved in these last months and we are hopeful for next season. But we can't do anything towards painting or doing up except to have some of the chairs mended. And Colonel Moore told Yeats the Government who refuses us a penny on the score of poverty are going to give the Gaelic Theatre £1500 a year!

Juno and the Paycock, taken to Cork as the players' private speculation, made a little money. But the Manager had insisted on their taking out "everything that made any reference to religion" including the Mother's beautiful prayer "Take away these murderous hatreds and give us thine own eternal love"; and also would not allow it to be confessed the girl had been seduced. So Dolan had to arrange (between two performances) that the young man should marry her but should desert her later because she had not brought the expected fortune. Cork they say is for the Government but hates the Civic Guard—"You could argue with the old police but these chaps whip you off and won't let you say a word". And the papers give the new Bishop of Clonfert, Duignin's opening address. He says he is and was a Republican, laments the methods used in 1918 were not carried on and declares the Republican party will be in power before long. But he says he is a democrat and will obey the people's will and advises persuasion without violence—my "Gan molais" policy.

At the Municipal gallery yesterday Reynolds showed me the Burlington sent him by the editor with an article "neither cold nor hot". He gives a "diary" of the enemies' cause evidently supplied by them; weak. Duveen made no *promise* of a gallery until June 1916, a year after Hugh's death when they must either have told him or hidden from him our claim and the terms of the codicil. Also it says, 4 March, 1914 "Mr. MacColl saw Lord Curzon who expressed his approval and talked of the possibility of securing the collection for the Modern Foreign Gallery which Mr. MacColl had proposed at the Committee". But when I saw Lord Curzon in May, just after Hugh's death and the discovery of the codicil, he said nothing and apparently knew nothing of this, saying "It would be very hard if poor Lane's own last wishes could not be carried out. And some of my colleagues would be very glad to get rid of the pictures".

I went then to the National Gallery to try and find by what formula the Trustees had kept the 41 pictures for the N.G. that Hugh had directed to be sold; and Stephens found in the records the resolution of 7th June 1916 "proposed by the Rt. Hon. W.F. Bailey, seconded by the Rt. Hon. A. Waldren and passed unanimously: That the 41 pictures recommended by the Director and enumerated in Schedule A should be excluded from the sale of Sir Hugh Lane's effects in order that they may be taken over by the Governors of the National Gallery of Ireland". The clause directing the French pictures to be sold if no gallery is provided within five years could no doubt be dealt with in the same way.

This evening W.B.Y. met Mrs. Green who told him the names of three candidates recommended for the Clonfert Bishopric had been sent to Rome. One had nine votes, one six, one two. It was the man with two—Duignan—who was appointed. There is great indignation and they are trying to find out what Republican influence was used.[13]

I read *Vivian Grey* this evening and then we talked, Yeats on the old subject of the transformation in England—"Up to Dryden's time it was a feminine race with a masculine literature, then it became a masculine race with a feminine literature".

We differ about De Valera, I think it a great mistake to keep him a prisoner through the Tailteann games "making his own ballad", a romance to foreign visitors. He thinks this right, that as they didn't release him sooner they ought not to do so now.

O'Higgins used to drink too much, now takes nothing. Lady Glenavy asked him at dinner if he never took wine and he said "No, I think there is a certain amount of liquor a man should consume in a lifetime, and I have consumed my share".

5 JUNE. THURSDAY. On Tuesday I felt that the Governor General might now be a help and wrote asking if I might see him either yesterday afternoon or any time today. There was no answer when I set out for the Carnegie meeting so I thought there was no chance of an appointment till next day, The Carnegie meeting was a short one, nothing much except discussion as to what Bishop to ask to take the Archbishop of Tuam's place. After it I went into the Municipal Gallery, asking Dermod O'Brien to come with me to decide about accepting a picture by Conor (Belfast) offered by some Belfast young men. We spoke about the Lane pictures, D. O'B. had sat next Mr. Heseltine (the friendly Trustee) at a dinner in London the other day, and he had spoken of returning them "but we would like to keep one for a memento, the Eva Gonzales"!! D.O'B. said he would block that. I asked him as he was going on to the meeting of N.G. Trustees to look into the question of the pictures having to be sold "if a gallery is not forthcoming in five years, the money to be applied to the purposes of my will", and he wrote down the particulars

5 JUNE. THURSDAY. L.R. came to say the Governor General had telephoned asking me to lunch, would send his car for me, so I ran back to Merrion Square to meet it, and was whirled off to the Viceregal Lodge where I had never been since Lord Aberdeen had sent for me all across Ireland to try and insist on our giving up the intention of putting on *Blanco Posnet*. All looked very spick and span, the flowers in the garden on to which the drawing-room opens lovely; chintzes &c very fresh, several smart footmen. The Governor General came in and I opened my "Dossier" and read him the memo, of Curzon saying to Sir E. Lutyens and Bracken that he found he must give the pictures up, and his last week's refusal to hear of it. He looked grave, said "that is very different to what he said to me". He does not believe the Government ever had that private Commission, thinks they said they had to force Curzon. He thinks a sworn enquiry would be useless. He has been seeing Lionel Curtis about the matter; he is quite friendly and had proposed a "judicial investigation" "two friendly Judges, one Scotch, and if they recommend it, bringing

in a Bill".

Lunch was announced before I had finished and his daughter, Mrs. Sullivan, came in and we three had lunch, excellent clear soup, I didn't take much else, and pleasant talk about Ceylon, and sad about the Black and Tan regime, he questioning me. After lunch he proposed a walk in the garden but I said I had not finished with my dossier, and we went to his study. He took the *Burlington* article to read, said it was very unfair, the way things were put, as "wrote the codicil leaving it unattested" as if he had done that on purpose. But then a card was sent in and I got up to go. He advised my seeing Carson in London, getting him to bring in a Bill in the Lords, and to see Lionel Curtis. I asked if he would not come over himself and help me. He said yes he would, looked in his diary and found he can't come over before 19th; will meet me there on the 20th. So I said good bye, very well pleased and he sent me back in his car which left me at the door of the Senate, my first visit there, to hear Yeats speak on the Irish manuscripts.[14] The Reconstruction Bill was being discussed for some time and was difficult to understand. At last the MS subject came on. Yeats gave his speech very well and was listened to for the most part very attentively. Then Mrs. Green spoke at great length very slowly and gave some irrelevant matter. Then Sir T. Esmonde, and then old Sigerson—bringing out his words very slowly, and all he said quite wide of the mark, favouring the printing of the Ordnance Reports which were not in question at all. I thought there should be a Bill to stop irrelevant or over long speeches.

When I came back I was first given a disagreeable letter from the editor of the *Burlington Magazine* to the Editor of the *Irish Statesman*, very cross over my article and A.E.'s comments. Then George said Miss Purser had come to say there had been a discussion at the Board of the N.G. on the necessity of selling the pictures if a gallery was not forthcoming, and that Bodkin had declared that if the codicil was proved the pictures would under this clause revert to the London N.G. (I don't know how he makes this out); and that they had proposed that if a Bill is passed a clause should be added making the five years start from the period of its being passed. Bodkin had offered to come round and prove this to me, but I said we must have Lord Glenavy's opinion which would be respected in England, and Yeats agreed. But it is now 12.30 and so far all efforts to get Glenavy on the telephone have failed. I sent to the Gallery for a copy of the will and have that ready.

And going to meet Casey at the Abbey last evening, I found he had accepted my invitation to Coole and wants to come on Saturday for a week. So I have to go back to receive him and go to London a week later to meet Tim Healy.[15] Today Kiernan writes saying McNeill is trying to get support from as many members of the Cabinet as possible and "a visit from you would certainly be of immense good in clearing the way". Margaret writes saying she can put me up, that is a comfort.

10TH THURSDAY EVENING. I spent the whole day waiting while Glenavy was being searched for by telephone by members of his family; was afraid to go out lest I should miss a message; just as well for I had not slept and was rather in pieces. But at 8 o'c he telephoned saying that he could see me at his house to-night or meet me in Dublin tomorrow. So I chose the immediate meeting, so glad to get it over, and the Y.'s ordered a taxi and I went in comfort to his villa, very flowery and leafy. He listened to all. I read him the present state of the case, Curzon's "gran rifiuto"—and then told him of this new attack, that the pictures if given to us would have to be sold. He said at once there should be a clause put in the Bill enabling us to keep them unsold, that it is the only way out. And he said it should be put on the ground of the London Trustees having kept the pictures from us all these nine years—how could we build a gallery for what we had not—(as I suggested why buy a cradle till we know the baby is coming). And that the five years should date from the time when we obtained them. I asked him to put this in writing and he will do so and let me have it tomorrow. He thinks as I have always done that we should get Macpherson's Bill and use it. He rather scoffed at Tim and Curtis's idea of a Judicial Commission, though then he said perhaps MacDonald, who he knows well, would let him be one of the two judges to enquire. He was rather shocked at the N.G. having kept those forty-one pictures and is glad they didn't ask his opinion beforehand. So I go to bed tired but comforted.

7 JUNE. Yesterday I saw Dolan about various Theatre matters; and Reynolds who found for me the judgement of Judge Dodd about the National Gallery being able to keep some of the pictures "in kind in lieu of specie" from the Lindsey House collection. And then Lord Glenavy's letter came, rather diffuse but giving his opinion strongly enough. "No sane Municipality or Public Body would have incurred the risk of providing a Gallery so long as their claim to the pictures was in dispute. Again to take an extreme case, had the building of such a Gallery been rendered impossible during these eight years owing to the existence throughout of a strike or lock out in the building trade, could or

would the condition with any semblance of fairness have been insisted on. Yet in truth this is a fair representation of the conditions which prevailed here, to any such enterprise its undertaking was impossible. The fullest effect in substance would and could in my opinion be given to the real meaning of Lane's codicil if by any Act of Parliament or arrangement designed to give effect to it, a condition was attached that a Gallery must be provided within five years from the date of such act or arrangement".

So I left Dublin last evening with a lighter heart, feeling the big men are now in the fight.

I slept at Athenry Hotel (the illness of the last days continuing) and this morning came on home with Casey, who came by morning train. He is writing a new short play, *Penelope's Lovers*[16] founded on the existence of a widow in the milkshop where he buys his eggs, who has three elderly admirers always hanging about, and who was once held up and robbed by a gunman. He is down on the present boasting by men who were never in the fight and who talk now of their deeds and all of whom boast of having been present at the murders on Bloody Sunday.[17] He thinks women are braver than men.

8 JUNE. He grieves for his Mother. She was 89, died in 1919. He had lived all his life with her, the others of her children had died or gone away. "She had a strong sense of humour, could always see the humourous side of human life. I did everything for her, she did not like to have anyone else about her. I had written a little story. Maunsel promised me £15 for it, and after it was published I wanted the money and went three times for it but could never get it. Then when my mother was so ill I had to go again to press for it, and I did get it, but when I came back she was gone.

"I made arrangements for the funeral, but when the day came the undertaker said that if I did not pay at once he would take it back again and there would be no funeral. It had to be put off until I could get change for the cheque. I thought I should have to go to the Bank, but I went to the Rector and he cashed it. I felt the treatment of the undertaker very bitterly, he was a Labour man, I a Labour man, and I had helped him and worked in that movement, worked for them all, and that is how I was treated.

"We formed at one time a workers' union, we were to carry on work ourselves without employers, we were to earn big money. George Russell gave £50 towards it. We did well for a week or two, there was one of us worked from 8 o'c in the morning till 7 o'c at night. But after a little work fell off; one would read the papers and not work more than a couple of hours. I saw it was a hopeless business. I had done my best to help. I have helped strikers and revolution according to what were then my lights. I was a Socialist then".

Now his desire and hope is rather to lead the workers into a better life, in interest in reading, in drama especially. The Abbey Theatre has done so much he has a great belief in Drama.

His eyesight has always been weak, a sort of film over the eyes. A doctor advised him not to read but he said "Then I should be ignorant" and he refused an operation because there was a thousandth chance he might go blind and so remain ignorant. He had been sent to a National school as a child for a few months but learned little more than his letters. Then one day when he was fourteen he listened to his brother and a friend as they talked of William of Orange, trying to make out the date of the Battle of the Boyne" and I thought to myself, Why cannot I tell them that?".

I determined to learn to read. There were a lot of old Primers lying about and I learned from them, and then I went through a grammar and learned the rules. The first book I ever read was Merle D'Aubigny's *History of the Reformation*." (I said here I had never heard that mentioned since I was a child. There was a copy then at Roxborough). "It was hard to understand, at least the long notes were. And many of them were in German, I thought of learning German to read them. But the second book I read was harder still, Locke on the Human Understanding. But when I got a few pennies together I would buy a book here and there from the stalls, Dickens because he was cheap, and some of the Waverley novels. But one day for a shilling I bought the Globe edition of Shakespeare, and that began a new life. I read it over and over and learned a great deal of it by heart".

I am reading him now *The Dynasts*.[18] He is tremendously struck with it.

I have been asking him about Mellows, for through all that wonderful story of his escape I could not find that he was an ordinary Nationalist. He says he was not, but a militant proletarian, a Communist, as was another O'C who was executed with him. It was said at the time it was for this reason they were sent to their death, the Government being more afraid of Labour than of rebellion, and that Rory O'Connor was only thrown in to screen that. But this he does not believe.

9 JUNE. I copied Glenavy's letter yesterday and sent copies to McNeill and to Lord G. himself to look over and say if we might publish it. And there were a great many other letters to write,

and I finished reading the first volume of *Dynasts* to Casey yesterday and have begun the second today. It seems even finer than when I read it before, those listening Spirits weighing all, and below them the confusion and waste of war. Casey had hoped Labour would have stopped the great war, and believes in the future it will have power to prevent wars.

He likes Larkin,[19] tells how he knows all the workmen personally and tried to improve life for them. He had bought an open place for them to use, to come to on Sundays and have games and see the flowers, saying to one man "Where is your wife, So and so—Cooking the dinner? Well now, can't you do without a hot dinner for once in a way on a Sunday and bring her here and push the pram yourself". In some religious procession the priests were saying "Hail to Thee St. Patrick", and the workers drowned it with "Hail to thee Jim Larkin"!

He is very happy walking in the woods, and dipping into the books in the library.

10 JUNE. Letters and typing Lane picture business, and correcting proofs of *Brigit*, and reading the *Dynasts*. I have been trying to get into the workers Utopia. Communism he says the workers Utopia would be, with one strong leader or organiser or organised Council that would be the chief power or only power in the country. But the way to that would be revolution he says, and the seduction of the army, and bloodshed "and there would not be much left to organise after that".

Larkin is the only man he believes in; has intellect and love for his fellows. I talked of possible lectures at the Abbey but he says "The pictures" are too strong a rival. But Larkin had lectures once at Liberty Hall, one on botany.

Kiernan wrote (6th) "when President Cosgrave was in London last week he rushed away, handing a paper to Mr. McNeill for Lionel Curtis, saying 'It relates to the Lane pictures'. Unfortunately he was in a great hurry and Mr. McNeill had not opportunity of having a talk about the matter with him".

11 JUNE. Glenavy returns copy of his letter with alterations and a paragraph added (very good) and leave to publish, so I've been copying it again and sending to *The Irish Statesman* for next week.

12 JUNE. Writing a note for *I. Statesman*, and sending off Richard's cricket bat. Mrs. Warren arrived. Casey a little shy with her at first but wakened up to tell us how he had always been sent to Sunday school and how he had been given a prize *Alone in Zulu Land*. He was delighted thinking it was a book of

adventure but it was only about a missionary and the converts he made among the Zulus. Another time he was given *Little Crowns and how to win them*, and these two gave him a turn against books. Ugly painted Bible texts were also given, and the ugliness of them drove him for a while to admiration of the Virgin in the Chapels.

18 JUNE. 17, CHEYNE WALK. A good journey on the whole. Casey with me to Dublin and Yeats met me at Broadstone: and a calm crossing, and by mistake I was put in a 1st instead of 3rd class carriage, and never knew till Crewe was reached, and then the guard let me stay there, and I had one side to myself and got some sleep.

This house charming and tranquil and Margaret kind. Yesterday I could but lie still. Kiernan wrote that McNeill had seen Lionel Curtis who "is sympathetic but suggests trying for a Bill introduced by a private member, preferably 'proposed by a Unionist Member, seconded by a Liberal or Vice Versa', thinks it would be unwise to approach the Cabinet at once its time being so fully occupied". I went later to York House, Office of the Saorstat and saw both. McNeill has been working at Trevelyan, had promised to lend him Hugh Lane's *Life*, but then wouldn't because of my autograph in it, and Kiernan had to send his own copy. McNeill rather vague still and has had but vague promises.

Later I went to Christies and saw Alec Martin. I asked how it is the enemy are stiffening, which he says they are, even Collins Baker who had been friendly. He says "they think they have got round Ramsay MacDonald, he was at their National Art Collections dinner and has been talking on art. They have been filling Tatlock with arguments, it was he who wrote *The Telegraph* article; they want a controversy in the papers, say their case has never been stated!" I feel very downhearted. McNeill asked if I would go to the Royal Garden Party. I said No, and he said his wife would not go. He agrees that the oath should be done away with. And he is very strong for the release of De Valera. He says they are not sending in many names for the Royal Party "My people don't want to go and those that want to go wouldn't ask for invitations through me". He has sent on Margaret's and Mrs. Warren's names.

19 JUNE. L.R. took me to an amusing play *The Mask and the Face*, an Italian version of *Playboy*. But a troubled night, the pictures farther away than ever.

Darling Richard came to tea, up from Harrow for dentist and doctor—that gland—But so merry and bright and grown so much it was a delight to see him, and he made me learn to "listen in" and we were having tea and strawberries together when Lady Gough came in and outstayed him.

5 o'c. Just now the High Commissioner's Office has rung up to say "Lord Beaverbrook wants to know the Governor General's address"! I could only say he has promised to see me here tomorrow.

A quiet afternoon sitting in the little garden reading that terrible document "Resurrection".

20TH. 11 o'c. No call yet from the Governor-General. And G.B.S.'s Secretary rang up saying they wanted me to lunch, but I couldn't accept. Too bad. They are going away and I shan't see them at all. Waiting, waiting.

12 o'c. "Mr. Tim Healy on the telephone", or his secretary. "Is trying to arrange an interview with Lord Carson and will let you know later". So we are getting on. He has materialised.

Last evening my eyes getting a little tired as I read Resurrection in the dusk, about 9 o'c I tried listening in. First some Irish songs I did not know (or like). Then an "Irish poem" recited . . . "I like a bit of cabbage with a bit of pickled pork—And to get a hot potato cake I'd walk from here to Cork" &c with an assurance "I'm real Irish". Then a musical piece by the London Orchestra. Not getting much out of that I looked in the evening paper to see what was next, and it was a doctor speaking "on the uses of preventive medicine". So I turned on the light and went back contentedly to Resurrection.

M. and I had just finished lunch when Governor-General rang up to say he had arranged the interview with Lord Carson for 4.30 on Monday. So I might have lunched with the Shaws. However I ran off to the Town Hall and took a bus and found them. He was just going off to Constable to sign some of his books—was going to send me one but I begged for it at once that I might read it before the play (though he didn't want me to do so) and he found a copy upstairs and gave it to me and wrote my name. And gave me also stalls for the performance. Charlotte told me he had "put in my sneeze" (that I had suggested at Ayot), I was quite pleased. They are off in the morning, I shan't see them again. I told him of the picture trouble. He says he has no influence with R. MacDonald but thinks the enemy won't influence him. He is suspicious of influence. He, G.B.S., doesn't know anyone he could influence except Sydney Webb. The visit did me good, got me back a little self confidence or respect!

SUNDAY. 22 JUNE. To Chelsea Old Church today, where I used to go with Hugh (and where we had that sad memorial service). I have been feeling very anxious about carrying out his charge but felt more at peace there, and the psalms were comforting—"He hath broken the gates of brass and shattered the bolts of iron"—But waiting on other people takes the heart out of me.

Yesterday I took a document, Curzon's letters in the first year, to Irish Office to be typed. Then as shops were shut and I wasn't in a mood for visiting, and saw the *Farmer's Wife*[19a] was being played at the Court Theatre I went in, and the Manager gave me a stall and sent me tea and was very kind. The play gave great amusement. I felt rather a revenant, my box where I had received good company, the stage where my plays had had triumphs—I could see Ellen Terry standing up, clapping and the audience calling for me after *Rising of the Moon* . . .

Reading *St. Joan*[20] and its prelude, a very fine piece of work even for him.

TUESDAY. 24 JUNE. Yesterday such a good day! First, Margaret had brought such a good report of Richard from Harrow, had seen Mrs. Vassall who said all would be easy about his tonic &c and that "he has the brains of ten".

Then at 4 o'c Governor-General came for me and took me to 5 Eaton Place. I was a little saddened as we drove there, for after all my pamphlets and book and letters he said he heard Hugh had not *signed* the codicil! However Lord Carson was splendid, is going to take up the matter in the House of Lords, to propose a Committee of Enquiry. He said he must have two men in particular to support him and that T. Healy must write to them both as they were friends of his—Arthur Balfour and the Duke of Devonshire. And both these are, or were, already friendly. And he asked me to come and coach him tomorrow, Wednesday, when he won't be at the House of Lords. He said to T.H. "I am taking this up because of my admiration of the way Lady Gregory has stuck to it and fought it, never giving in". So I felt comforted for many disappointments. I stayed and talked a little with him and Lady Carson, we found some relationship. He said "I have plenty of Galway blood". I said "you should come over there". He said "The police won't allow it, they have detectives after me now". I said "But if you get us the pictures we shall all be cheering for you", and told him what he did not know, that his portrait thrown on a screen at the time he had first defied England had been cheered in Cork.

Today I have been at the Irish Office, having "Supplementary evidence" typed for pamphlets I am sending Governor-General to enclose with his letters to members of the House of Lords.

Last night *St. Joan*. Wonderful and beautiful; but terrible in parts.

27 JUNE. On Wednesday I went to 5, Eaton Place, coming into Lord Carson's study as the clock struck 12, and took credit for punctuality (though this exactitude was due to an argument with the taxi driver as to his address—he right and I wrong). We went straight into documents, he had but a shadowy memory of the matter and said when he had gone into it that it would be a difficult one. But he said there was no doubt as to Hugh's intention the codicil should be carried out, was relieved I think to find the evidence so strong. He is not certain as to procedure, will write to consult Governor-General, thinks he will probably ask for a Committee of enquiry, to lead to a Bill; scoffed at the enemy's "evidence", Diary in Burlington &c. He asked if I thought Lord Glenavy would come over and support him with a speech, he would carry weight, representing the Senate. (McNeill on hearing this didn't think Carson would have made such an approach). I said I felt sure he would. I had rather a shock when he said "Did Hugh Lane paint all the pictures himself or only some of them"?!!! I am to collect as many Lords as possible for the Debate, I said I would send Yeats over to get Lady Cunard to do this, (but I won't come unless absolutely necessary.) I came away very happy and content.

Today Governor-General writes that I ought to see Lionel Curtis.

Yesterday I went to meet Richard at the dentist's and take him to tea. That was another happiness, the darling! so bright, and when we parted and he went off in a taxi he waved his hand as far as I could see him.

Last night I went to Mrs. McNeill's "at home", a gathering, chiefly Irish, quite pleasant though I was tired and left early.

28 JUNE. Yesterday rather a blank, arranging to see T.P. O'Connor—he proposed this morning. I asked for Monday because of going to see the Chicks. Then later he put Monday off. I went to Irish Office to arrange to see Curtis as Governor-General wished, but he was not at his office.

Lady Lyttleton had expected to go to Dublin "for the unveiling of Gladstone's statue" which she says is in existence. I thought it had been refused. I don't think it likely it will be put up now Parnell is coming up in retrospect as he seems to be.

SUNDAY, 29 JUNE. Yesterday I went to Folkestone to see the darlings at school, a surprise visit and they were so glad and hugged me and laughed and dragged me off to see their room and their gardens and then with two of their friends we went to the town and had tea &c and they went back loaded with baskets of strawberries. A great joy. I am tired today, and when I came from church I lay down on the sofa to rest before going upstairs and fell asleep for an hour or more. I don't know when I have done that before.

4 JULY. Home again. Slept at Athenry, arriving there at 10.30 last night, and the weather so cold I had to ask for a hot jar and pile on blankets, having slept with only a sheet over me in London. At Gort a wire from Margaret "Richard goes to 50 Weymouth St. tomorrow, will wire Saturday evening". So I suppose that troublesome gland is to be removed. Poor darling. I hope he is not suffering today at the prospect as I was thirteen months ago.

Cold here too and a shower as we came down the avenue. Among my letters one registered, containing Miss Harrison's statement, but so rambling and meaningless I wonder Curtis should have taken it seriously. She speaks of having in May (after Hugh's death) "had an account of a very different will" but doesn't say from whom, and hints that the address of the Cheyne Walk servants who witnessed Hugh's "alleged" will was stolen from her desk.

(I forgot to write of my visit to Lionel Curtis at the Colonial Office He was rather dry and official, and after a few questions produced this statement from Miss Harrison and said it might influence the Commissioners. I laughed and told him of her insanity but he seemed uncertain. He said he had decided to appoint three men who had never heard of the case and were not interested in pictures to take evidence and say whether a Bill should be introduced to legalise the codicil. He was much pleased to hear of Lord Carson's support and intention, and said he would communicate with him, and of course Carson was equally pleased at finding support read to drop into his hand.)

Here at Coole John tells me Micho Dooley has been released, probably mistaken for a political prisoner. He and others were met at Limerick by Miss MacSwiney and entertained and had "a great night at a hotel". Stanford lately released, has been with two others presiding over an arbitration Court, a case between Henderson who had bought a field from Houston and some man (Cusack?) who wants it, and who gets it and is to pay back Henderson his money. There had been a disturbance a night or two before the Court about this, some shots fired and some men taken to gaol. Marian, coming from a visit to Kilcolgan saw a large crowd of men at Druimhasna, at 10 o'c P.M. but didn't know what they had gathered for. She says there are placards up protesting against the proposed election of "A great doctor" in

Dr. Sandys place because he had been employed by the British at Tintown camp. J. D. has a complaint against Bridget Molloy who he found "with her sweetheart, a man that never had a father or mother" in the garden on Sunday. Words were exchanged and the "sweetheart" coming back from races a day or two later the worse for drink searched for John that he might put a knife in him. Rather a plunge into a troubled pond. I am reading "Harbottle" and his questionings. The most hopeful answer yet is "it isn't a toss up between God and the Devil, it's a toss up between Man that once was and Man that is to be". If we are going upward these little stones on the hillside don't matter.

5 JULY. Writing letters and getting things straight all the morning and now must remember the last days in London.

On Sunday, 29 June I went to see Alec Martin at his home, 37 Vicarage Road, East Sheen. A little house for the five children, a very happy family and home, though he is not very well. He is not rich but gets a chance in Christies business and sells something now and then; for a Whistler he had bought for £20 he got £500. He told us, and his children listened with eyes opening very wide, of one Christmas Eve when his mother had bought meat and nuts and other things for their Christmas dinner, and hurrying home to get things ready had left him to carry the parcel. It was a large one and he put it over his shoulder but it grew heavier and heavier, and as he came to Sloane Square the paper broke and the nuts began falling out, and when he had stopped and picked them up he could not get it up again and stood looking at it and cried. Then a man asked what the trouble was and told him to go home and tell his mother and he would mind the parcel until he came back. So he ran on home, but his mother looked grave and came with him. And when they got to the place, just outside Peter Jones' shop, there was neither man nor parcel. "And we had no dinner that Christmas Day". Such a sad memory of treachery to carry through life! He is giving a painting of Cheyne Walk to the Dublin National Gallery, in memory of Hugh.

On Monday, 30 June, I went round to see A. Birrell who had been away, and tell him the present state of the picture matter. He was less sympathetic than of old—"No wonder there is hesitation in giving them back to you when you don't protect your Museum with its gold ornaments from fire". I said we would take good care of the pictures but he said "Oh, it is just your careless Irish way". Glenavy's name also roused him to disparagement "a troublesome chap I found him. Oh yes, I daresay he's all right now".

However he abused Lord Curzon comfortingly, says he is "quite mad, is spending a heap of money, and he hates spending money, on Kedleston, employing Lutyens there on a house he will have to leave to a man that he hates, Lady Curzon not having given him the expected heir . . ."

Very hot, and I had lunch at a Bakery close to Downing Street that I might go there quietly, and was punctual to the hour fixed by L. Curtis.

He came in, very official, his back well to the light, my face to it; listened for a minute or two then said interrupting me "I am very glad you have come. There is a new development. Do you know anything of a Miss Harrison?" I laughed and said what I knew of her, her desire to marry Hugh, his avoidance of her; her delusion coming some time after his death that he had made a will in her favour. Her demand that both Yeats and I should come before President Cosgrave to hear her statement; her threatening letter to Yeats "and those nearest to him" if he refused. Her saying in a Dublin drawing-room that Ruth Shine had forged the will and I had forged the codicil; her later assertion that Hugh "was to have married me that summer". And I said that I had been told in Dublin of her growing madness. He listened without change of countenance and said "It is a very important matter. She has written to the Prime Minister". And he went on to say truly enough that should a Committee or Commission sitting on the matter and this statement be brought in, there might probably be some one man who would take it seriously or be puzzled by it and might break up the meeting. I said I could get evidence sent him from Dublin of her irresponsibility, that I know all the Dublin papers had refused to print this statement of hers, giving her no credence. He seemed relieved when I told him Lord Carson was taking up the case, said he would see him. But as he was leaving he said his idea was to get three men who had never heard of the case, were quite ignorant of it, to go through the evidence and we should be bound by their opinion. As he was getting up to show me out I didn't answer. He said amiably as he came down one flight of stairs with me "I want to get it through as I like to remove causes of friction". Amiable, very official, not interested I think in what Hugh's intention was. But Alec Martin, though saying he would rather keep the pictures for London, was very strong about that.

On Tuesday, 1 July T. P. O'Connor telephoned that he could see me at quarter to two, so I went to him and had a pleasant and satisfactory talk of an hour. He was very glad to know of Carson's interest, offered to join him in a deputation to the

Prime Minister "If Carson and I who have been fighting for so many years walk in together he can hardly refuse anything". However rather to my relief he said then he would go alone to Ramsay MacDonald, thought he could do as much alone. I told him Carson wanted the support of as many Peers as possible, he is afraid of a scanty or languid assembly and I said "You are up to your neck in the Peerage and could bring them in". He said he would do his best and believed he could influence a good many "Buckmaster—perhaps Birkenhead". I interrupted to say he (Birkenhead) might be inclined towards us if he knew Michael Collins had taken up the matter in his last visit to London—; and he went on with a list and was quite anxious to begin to work at once, but I said it would be better to wait till procedure and date had been settled between Healy and Curtis and Carson, and am to let him know. He asked me questions then about Irish politics. "Has Cosgrave any intellect? He was brought to see me by some wild fellow". I said as usual it was wonderful that he and his Ministers had been able to do so much all things considered. "Would they take in Dillon and Devlin"? I said I didn't know about Devlin but I was sure they would not have Dillon, "they don't like him", which seemed to surprise him, and he said "they are running down the party that brought them to success". He said he would never do anything now in Irish politics but will devote himself to having the education of Irish Catholic children in England improved, will try to get money for this purpose from America. I thought his Privy Councillorship had agreed with him, he looked in better health than when I had last seen him. I was quite sorry when I had to go, to lunch with Guy and Margaret at the Berkeley.

Then Harrow, Speech Day; sad in memories, happy in hope. Richard looking so bright and cheery. We had tea in the Vassal's garden, and then heard the songs. Back to London, and Mrs. Scott already there waiting to take me on to the P.E.N. dinner (I think I'm writing like Harbottle)[21] I dressed very quickly and we got to Gatti's in good time and I was introduced to many writers, there were 175 altogether, rather bewildering. But at dinner I was beside Galsworthy, the Chairman, to my joy, and had on my other side Nevinson who I hadn't seen since the night he spent at Coole in the Black and Tan time. So it was a pleasant dinner. Nevinson said when I spoke of the pictures "Charles Trevelyan told me he was taking them up" so James McNeill's loan to him of Hugh's *Life* was not in vain. I told him I had liked his article "Farewell to America" I had read in the *Nation*.[22] He was sad and said it has been printed as a little book and 150,000 copies sold but he has never had anything at all on the sales. Many Americans have said to him "We do like that little book so much" and he says "Yes, but please give me a halfpenny". He, also, asked if Cosgrave has any intelligence. I think Birrell was the third who did so.

Galsworthy also had been at Harrow speeches. He spoke of Ibsen, asked if I thought he had any permanent value. I said I didn't think his plays would last but that he had taught other dramatists something. He doubted this, I said his plays seem like our stone-balanced Galway walls, if you take out a stone the rest fall—if you take out the rope at the beginning of an Ibsen play there is nothing for the hero to be hanged with at the end, and that we learned so much at least. But he wouldn't give him credit even for that, I should have liked more talk with him, but a Swedish lady on his other side had to be attended to. We got on Tolstoi for a little and brought her in. Then a hammer-stroke, and he got up and made a little speech saying "Lady Gregory—*is* Lady Gregory—that is the best thing I can say".

"I wonder if she remembers that I changed the name of a play—now a *Bit of Love*—from the *Full Moon* because she had already written a play with that name" (I did indeed remember his kindness) "I have often got into scrapes about the firmament, have had letters telling me that Mars and Venus cannot appear on the same evening in June, or at whatever date I have placed them. But in one thing I have made no mistake, in hailing Lady Gregory as a very bright star that has risen and who in my opinion will never set!" (applause). And then he and Nevinson asked me to say just a few words, and I did. And then more introductions and at 10.30 I slipped away, tired but happy.

The next day, Wednesday, 2 July, I did shopping and paid my last visit to the High Commissioner's Office, and left by evening train. Read Harbottle for a while, then about midnight couldn't assimilate any more of his speculations, and to my great joy found in my basket—had forgotten having put it there—*Trent's Last Case*. (Only finished it last night, a very good detective story).[23]

Arrived Dublin about 8 o'c and drove to 82 Merrion Square, only a maid up but I went in and had a bath and changed and was ready for breakfast when Willie came down, rather absent, wanted to see how his speech against railway tickets printed in Irish had been reported and was going to the Senate again to speak on the danger of fire to the Museum.[24] But he walked up to talk of the proposed paper Iseult and H. Steuart and some other young people are to publish. The first number was sent back by the printer who said he would not print such blasphemy, had objected chiefly to a story by Robinson who brings in the Blessed Virgin.[25] Willie repeated the manifesto they or he composed, one sentence is "All Bishops are atheists"; and the Catholic Bishops' pastorals are criticised. I was grave and said I was afraid his connection with it would injure the Abbey (already attacks on its influence are being made). I thought that an offensive sentence, he defended himself, says they are atheists, he had once had a conversation with one who had confessed that the Jews had not believed in the immortality of the soul. But I had made him uneasy; when George appeared he told her I had objected. He means to write for every number; however I daresay there won't be many. Then I told what I had done about the pictures but they seemed to have faded from his mind.

I had written to Governor-General saying I would be in Dublin and would like to see him, and as an early answer didn't come George rang up the V.R. Lodge, and the Secretary said he would not be down until 1 o'c and no letters were to be brought to him but she would give him mine as soon as he was visible. So at a little after 1 o'c a message came that he would like to see me at 3. Pouring rain, but I got a taxi and went to the Lodge. Preparations going on for a dinner to the R.C. Archbishop that evening. He had not asked me to lunch because his wife had decided to come down, and being paralysed she does not like to meet strangers. He was very interested in my news, thought I had "done wonders", delighted about T.P.'s promised help and quite excited about Curtis and Miss Harrison thought he ought to be assured she is cracked (he himself had never heard of her before). I said I wanted some other than myself to see her or enquire about her and tell Curtis the whole story, as I might be supposed to have my own end in view and he agreed, though he said one would know she was not sane by the effort to upset a will when there is no other to replace it and neither she nor Dublin to be the gainer. He is going to London on Tuesday and will see Carson and settle procedure. He was very kind, offered to send me back, lamented not having thought of sending for me (so did I, taxi fifteen shillings). "Will you have a cup of tea"? "No thank you, it is rather early". "Or a glass of wine?" "No thank you, I very seldom take wine". "Well I could give you a very good glass of port". Then he took me to see some of his furniture and some pictures, and I said how hard it was our young school of artists having been deprived during nine years of the great French pictures that Hugh had intended them to profit by, and he seemed much struck by this point of view.

G.Y. said we had got our Ambassador at Washington by a threat that without this we would not sign the Lausanne treaty, indeed there had been proposals here that we should sign a separate treaty with Turkey! But it was objected that perhaps Turkey would not accept it.

Back to 82 and played with the children, and when Willie came back from the Senate he waked up about Miss Harrison and wrote to ask Judge Creed Meredith to see him about it and if possible to see her.

He took me to Broadstone. I slept at Athenry and came home Friday morning, yesterday, 3 July.

BOOK TWENTY-EIGHT

6 JULY, 1924. SUNDAY. Cold wet days. The McLoughlin girls came for flowers for the chapel yesterday and we were weather-bound for a long time in the vinery. Today Mr. Trotter at church, I am afraid the poor Archdeacon will never be there again. He was here before I came in 1880.

A telegram told of Richard's well being after that little operation but I'm afraid he and the chicks will miss the Eton and Harrow match. (29 September. That operation was much more severe than I had imagined but thank God he is well and strong now after the holidays).

Mr. Trotter had I think seen something in the English papers about the reservation of the Sacrament, for he preached against the doctrine of Transubstantiation to Mr. Johnson, the Daly family, Mitchells and two or three Lough Cutra employees, who all by nature already look on it as a Popish "Superstitious vanity".

7 JULY. Cold and rain. Mrs. Prendergast a poor widow came to ask my help in getting a pension, her husband having been first a policeman, then a soldier. And Healy from Cranagh came to ask my "influence" to get the Land Court or Department to mend the road to his house.

John Rourke was at Kiltartan chapel yesterday, dressed in black, has joined some religious order. When the police were disbanded he had come back from Belfast to his home but was told he "couldn't stop there". Another lad, a Ford, younger than he has also gone into a monastery.

A letter from Margaret telling me of Richard. I am so thankful it is over, and he will enjoy the recovery.

8 JULY. A wire "Richard Going on very well; listening in". His own-made wireless, the darling.

P. says a poor woman in Gort was robbed of £6 yesterday. They were all out and the window was broken in and the money taken from her box and some clothes of others in the house. "Are the Civic Guard doing nothing"? "They are no good. And what can they do when they get no information? The people afraid to tell; they might be robbed themselves or murdered".

Yeats writes Creed Meredith sent him to Kennedy the Chief Justice re Miss Harrison's cracked letter, and Kennedy said the President was the proper person to write the letter, because "It is too serious a thing to doubt the word of a President, whatever the British felt inclined to".

I don't think I wrote down that when I spoke to Birrell about the oath and that someone had said "it will never be given up", he said "Never is a very foolish word to apply to anything concerning Ireland".

9 JULY. Margaret writes of poor Richard, he has had restless nights, and I was anxious. But this afternoon came a wire from Guy asking for address of official who supplied us with cartridges last year and saying "Richard doing well and cracking jokes" so I feel comforted.

French sends £29 from U.S.A., *W..*, *Spreading, Rising*, wonderful how they keep their audience. And *Dragon* brought in £4.4. from Savannah, Ga.

THURSDAY. 10 JULY. Such a good letter this morning from Governor-General enclosing Carson's. The Colonial Office is to set up a small Committee to go into the Lane case, and Carson is to put a question in the House. I have written to them both and to Yeats and Curtis and to T. P. O'Connor. I do feel we are now on the road to success. I've written to ask Carson when he wants his Peers.

J. says the case for compensation for burning of Roxborough was on in Galway yesterday, but Johnny Quin, (coachman) and the steward who were to have been witnesses had been kidnapped. The Judge very angry and gave a decision for £14,000.[1]

Our old tenants had a case there also, about timber, Regan Fahey and Hanlon against the rest, saying they cut more than their share. They on the other hand ask why the £200 paid by McDonough for timber was not applied to paying off the debt to the Bank but used or squandered "not so much as a gap to be raised without gallons of porter and tins of meat".

Reading Froude's *Caesar* (The war in Gaul)[2] and then *War and Peace*, and ten years ago I would have said "What a Mercy such terror and cruelty can never be in the world again". But now it seems as if the world will never be free of it, that the Millenium must be in "another place".

11 JULY. Another letter from Governor-General. "Today I called at the Colonial Office and ascertained the names of the Committee which the Government proposes to set up. It consists of one member of each party in the House of Commons, and the Terms of Reference will be whether it was Sir Hugh

Lane's intention that the pictures should go to Dublin and if so would it be proper that a bill giving effect to this intention should be passed by Parliament . . ." He made a suggestion that instead of a Bill making the codicil legal the case of the Gold Ornaments should be followed, and the pictures vested in the Crown who would give them to Ireland. He ends "At any rate we are beginning to see some streaks of dawn after a delay of eight years".

And a letter from Mr. Harold Speakman. He called late a few evenings ago from Gort, is travelling through Ireland with a donkey and cart; has come from Cork and is going on to Galway, Connemara and the North. Is painting also to illustrate the book he is writing,[3] and wants to get "at the heart of the people". A nice young fellow. He asks me for a name for his donkey. "She is a friendly little creature, ears forward most of the time, is several years older than the tinker who sold her to me told me, and seems to know the rules of the road almost better than I, for in America we travel to the right instead of the left. She has never lain down in harness, and would work I am sure to the last ounce of her strength".

I have suggested "Grania" who "walked all Ireland" and so far as I know only once lost her temper.

The mail car was robbed last night near Tillyra, the letters sent on but all parcels kept.

Timber stealing at Lough Cutra, a quantity of young ash cut and being carted away, but a Civic Guard inspector was driving past and got reinforcements and all fled.

12 JULY. Writing those endless letters all the morning. I have come to the end of *Caesar*. W. was justified saying in his note he was "a great gentleman". I would like our Government and our Republican leaders to read him now, and learn greatly to forgive.

Three parcels this morning, my new corsets from London, supply of chocolate for the holidays, ginger biscuits (my support of late) came safely—what a loss to the raiders of yesterday!

14 JULY. A quiet Sunday yesterday. But fifteen soldiers have been sent to Gort, it is not known whether this is because of the timber cutting at Lough Cutra or the quarrel about land there, leading to a new "Arbitration Court" at Gort, or some disputes over land at Castle Daly.

15 JULY. Today rain falling, and I having sent my letters by Mike Lally and being tired with getting lumber room into order I did not send to Gort, said we would do without letters and papers for once in a way. And later, taking up the *Times* of Monday I saw notice of business in the House of Lords—"Lord Carson

desires to know the intentions of the Government as to restoring the French pictures of the late Sir Hugh Lane to Dublin". And today's *Independent* would have had the answer! and I can't send now, the sun beginning to shine after a wet morning so that I think the hay can be turned.

G. Yeats came for the night, getting Ballylee ready for the children. I asked her about L.R.'s story which the Dublin printers refused to print in the Stuarts new paper *Tomorrow*. She says the Talbot Press had already refused to print it in his book of short stories; then he sent it to the *Nation* which refused it because it was indecent and dealt with rape. Now he writes indignantly to the *Irish Statesman* and says "My friends who have started *Tomorrow* believe in the immortality of the soul . . . the purpose of this paper is the overthrow of the unbelievers . . . the question is the gravely serious one of the freedom to believe".[4] But it is not belief the printers and the *Nation* objected to but his way of supporting it. I said it would be hardly necessary to display the immortality of the body as an argument for the immortality of the soul. She, though she didn't support me when I told him so—is sorry Willie is writing for them, says everyone will recognise the manifesto as his though he doesn't believe they will, and that he has given them his Leda poem[5] and a fine thing among his other poems in the Cuala book,[6] but is, now it is known it goes into *Tomorrow*, being spoken of as something horribly indecent. However she says he was feeling dull in Dublin and it has given him a great deal of amusement. He writes today he must come back from London without seeing Curtis "as I am called back to vote against Government on the Museum question".[7] G.Y. says Cosgrave is opposing the effort to move the kitchen &c and stop smoking in the Museum. And also that he is supporting to O'Higgins' great indignation, the drink interest.

Yeats in his note to me says "I saw *St. Joan*[8] last night and liked all the ecclesiastical part, thought it even noble, but hated Joan and the actress. Shaw is a dialectician and his genius leaves him when he leaves dialectics. I thought Joan half Cockney slut and half nonconformist preacher. To speak with God and have neither simplicity nor dignity is incredible". I don't agree with him at all. The Spirit was speaking through a country girl, not with her.

Such a nice letter from Catherine yesterday.

16 JULY. This morning *The Times* with an abridgment (evidently) of Lord Carson's speech and a spiteful little article professing impartiality but not keeping to it. The *Independent* gives a fuller column of his speech, very excellent, he has made full use

of the evidence I gave him. But I felt over excited and terrified now the battle is coming and wondered how I should get through the days and nights. So it was a relief when by midday post Yeats' letter came saying he had seen Curtis and that a full statement will have to be written out for Cosgrave to send in, and he suggests my coming up for this. But I am still more terrified by Curtis having said "I do not know what the result will be but you will get a *final* decision". So I will go up tomorrow morning, and have already been working at a statement.

21 JULY. 82 MERRION SQUARE. I came up Thursday morning for this. Was going to the Russell but Yeats met me at the train, made me come here, happily for I can do the work so much better than from an hotel. I had wired him from Athenry to make an appointment with Governor General, and at 3 o'c we went to the V.R. Lodge. Healy kind, but said we must have Counsel, suggested Sir C. Russell. I asked if the Government would pay necessary expenses. He could give no answer except that of course they ought to do so. He is cross with Cosgrave who did not come to his dinner to the Archbishop, or to an important dinner at the Shelbourne where he was expected, so would not write to him but said we should see Duggan, ex-Minister, who has a very good head. He took us to his Office where the telephones are, one out of order but he sat at the other for a very long time trying to get Duggan and entertaining us meanwhile with ancedotes of Isaac Butt. Then at last he said we had better go to the Government offices and he would tell Duggan when he got on to him to expect us.

At Government buildings (Merrion Street) Duggan was said to be at the other side. The Dail part. We walked through the endless passages and enquired for him. He was not to be found. Then we saw Desmond Fitzgerald who undertook to find him, but after a long search came back to say he had been told in his office he was "with the President and Senator Yeats and Lady Gregory"! John McNeill came and talked for a while, and we sat and waited till at last Mr. Duggan came, and took us through many passages to an empty committee room. He seemed very quick and clear headed. When we asked for Counsel to take up the case he asked what the value of the pictures is, as the President might have to defend expenditure on them in the Dail, and Yeats said he would write to Ricketts (and did so in the evening). Duggan promised to see the President and let us know the result next (Friday) morning.

W. heard nothing from Duggan on Friday, and having spent the morning waiting, and my head too tired to work up the case, I spent the afternoon in the newspaper vaults of the National Library, looking for our enemies' letters, the statement of their case when in the autumn of 1916 our fight began. I found MacColl's in the *Observer*, two letters, and one of Aitken's in the *Morning Post*, but was just about to ask for *The Times* to try if there would be one of Witt's there when 5 o'c came, closing time, and I was turned out.

On Saturday nothing from Duggan. So I spent my day making out our case, going through all old documents that I had brought, and did not get out at all.

Sunday also I spent:—now making up our opponents' case, from their letters and the "Diary" in *Burlington* Magazine. It does seem weak but one doesn't know how lawyers may twist it.

And I had a letter from Carson: "It is evident from the speech of Lord Crawford that there will be a considerable amount of effort made before the tribunal to make a case Sir Hugh Lane did not intend to leave the pictures to Dublin. I am afraid it will be necessary to put the matter into some competent hand to collect and deal with all the evidence you have and to sift the evidence that will be brought forward by your opponents"—And not a word from Duggan.

But late, as we were at dinner, Gogarty came in; had been all the afternoon with Cosgrave, receiving Ranji Singh with salutes &c. and was to meet him again at dinner. So I appealed to him and he promised to speak to and get an answer from Cosgrave. I went out for a little after 8 o'c to get air.

This, Monday morning, Yeats rang up Duggan—"not arrived yet". But after 11 o'c we tried again, and he answered; said Cosgrave had referred the matter of Counsel to the Minister of Finance, and that they hope to have an answer from him today. So I must sit and wait. However a telegram came from Ricketts "Approximate value of pictures well over £100,000". So I have written to Duggan as this may give them more respect for the case, and Yeats has left my letter at Government Buildings. But I have need of patience.

The day I came up the papers I got at Mullingar told of the release of De Valera and Stack and others. That is a good thing done.

And in the evening late, sitting with Willie, I took up the *Irish Times* and saw a letter in it from "W. W. West", saying that he, a cousin of Hugh's had been told by him on Saturday, 5 April, 1915, very explicitly that he was giving his pictures back to Dublin.[9] West had said to him "You are the most forgiving man I ever met". So I wrote to ask him to come and see me, and he came on Saturday, and is to make a statutory declaration—another brick for the building up of our case.

I wrote to Mr. Strickland asking if he remembered going to look for papers—a possible will in Hugh's desk, and if the desk was locked. But I have an ungracious answer—his animosity and jealousy still unquenched.

6.30. No answer—I had written to Cosgrave—and none from Duggan. I stayed in all day, wouldn't go to lunch with the Gogartys for fear of being called—or in the hope of it.

Then after 4 o'c George proposed trying to see Duggan and took a letter saying I would myself pay the lawyers to make their preliminary examination of the case if there was difficulty about this, (I'm hoping to be repaid later) if the Government would recommend someone they would employ to go on with it. She took this across, saw Duggan who said the President had only just then gone to consult the Minister of Finance, and that he thinks it is the High Commissioner in London who should provide the lawyer. I am distracted and don't want to go over because of the children at the end of the week, but might go for a day if necessary. However there being nothing more to do this evening I went out, to Pims about blinds for the childrens' rooms. This day of enforced idleness has been worse than Thursday's journey. Friday in Library vaults, Saturday and Sunday working the entire day through the papers. Nothing from Government offices today, but a note from Cosgrave to Yeats, written yesterday, 21st, enclosing one from Thomas, the Colonial Secretary telling him (Cosgrave) of the appointment of the Committee dated 10th July. (This Cosgrave acknowledged 17th July). It gives the terms of reference. Whether in their opinion:

1. Sir Hugh Lane when he signed the codicil of the 3rd February 1915 thought that he was making a legal disposition.

2. If so, whether it is proper that in view of the international character of the matter at issue, the legal defect in the codicil should be remedied by legislation.

I must go home tomorrow. I wired to High Commissioner asking information and have answer "The Committee will sit tomorrow to arrange procedure".

I worked with a typist this morning who had brought in her machine to work for W.B.Y. Weak in spelling and not expert, but got through some.

25 JULY. ATHENRY HOTEL. On Wednesday 23rd things began to move.

I went on with my typing and felt disconsolate, for I had telephoned,—or G.Y. had—asking if I could see Glenavy, but the answer was (through Lady G.) "He has not a minute free today". So I could but work on. But later, Dolan at the Government offices having been rung up, said Ignatius Rice of the Corporation (its lawyer) wanted to see me (G.Y. says he is known as Salacious Rice) and I settled to go to him at the City Hall at 3 o'c. Then Lord Glenavy rang up, said he could see me at 2 o'c at the University Club. So I went there taking my case, happily in pretty good order, in spite of the typist having made many blunders, and twice put the carbon paper wrong side up—so these sheets had to be done again.

Glenavy went through "Opponents' case", the letters I had copied in the National Library &c. I said "I want you to put yourself in their place and make the case against me". He put his finger on a passage in Aitken's letter, read it and said "That is their strong point. Counsel will make a great deal of that. And remember you will have the best Counsel in London against you", and made some comments. I was terrified, gave up all for lost. Then he spoke of Counsel; he recommended Herbert Wilson or Sam Brown.[10] I knew Brown has a great reputation in the Senate and said so, and he said if Brown took it up he would help him to work up the case. Then he spoke quite cheerfully, said the terms of reference were very much in our favour; so I felt better, though sorry I had asked him to put the enemy's case so forcibly! Then to the City Hall, took a cab, but the Cabby took me past St. Patricks and at a jog trot and back again, and I was fifteen minutes late. But Mr. Rice was kind, doesn't know much—or anything—of the case and wanted information. I told him the chief points. Then I asked what Counsel he would have, and he said he thought Sergeant Sullivan would be good, I told him presently that Glenavy had mentioned Brown and had offered to go through the evidence with him should he take it up. So after a little he said "Well, Brown is a good man, and Lord Glenavy's help would be good. I think we might have him". And Mr. O'Dwyer who we met going out assented to this.

When I went back to Merrion Square Yeats was pleased about this, and went over to the Senate and brought Mr. Brown back to see me—an elderly quiet man, I liked him and he gave me an impression of power. I showed him the passage in Aitken's letter Glenavy had thought their strongest argument and he said "If that is the best they can do, I don't think their case can be a strong one". I gave him Hugh's *Life*. He said he would if possible as to time, undertake the case; and when he went downstairs he told Yeats he would not take any fee. So I wrote this to the Law Agent, Ig. Rice. All this gave me new courage, though without those days of preparation there would have been nothing ready, Mr. Rice didn't know the rudiments of the case.

He came next day; asked to go through it with me. I had just, after a hard morning's work, with and without typist, got two sets ready, sent one to McNeill who had asked for it, and gave the other to him. Mr. West sent in his affadavit and Russell brought in his. Then I packed and went out, a cup of tea and bread and butter my lunch—to do a little necessary shopping. But first I went up to Stephens' room in the National Gallery and asked him to take me to the Director's Office where I had last seen Hugh. The desk, or writing table, is just where it was, next the window, it was from there Hugh had written to me. And as I sat in his chair I thought how impossible is the presumption that he did not believe the codicil to be legal. For it was in one of those drawers he had put it, it is there it was found. And if in that last week when he had said to so many that he had decided Dublin should have the pictures, would he not, had he intentionally left it unwitnessed, have called a witness in? Or if, as the opponents say, he meant to give London the collection, would he not have destroyed it and left the will to be carried out? It is impossible to believe he had in the first weeks of April forgotten the document he had written so fully and with such care in the first week of February.

A telegram came from Kiernan "Committee adjourned until September". I thought I would rather have had it over, and my sanity restored, but it is a relief not having to go across.

So I took the evening train and slept at Athenry and on to Coole Friday morning 25th. It was a tiring anxious week.

Yeats was working at an article on the compulsory teaching of Gaelic[11] and we talked sometimes of that, I inclining to think that the acquiring of a second language does so much towards awakening a child's general intelligence and understanding of grammar, that it would probably be as helpful in education as almost anything. He agreed, but we both agreed that if its compulsory teaching would help to keep out Ulster it should not be made compulsory.

It is this fear of keeping Ulster unwilling to come in that makes him anxious to upset the abolition of divorce the Dail is inclined for.

De Valera's release was announced in the papers the day I went up, and Stack's and others.[12] I am so glad. There did not seem to be much excitement and he has made no important speech yet. A letter from Kiernan was in the post for me, re procedure. He thinks they will not employ Counsel; and so best.

When I arrived home I was told there had been a great seizure of trespasser's stock at Roxborough, the road to Gort full of cattle, and the barrack yards. Soon after I arrived a Civic Guard motor drove up with Inspector Courtney from Loughrea. He came to ask for Frank's address; said he had been given orders to drive the stock off Roxborough and had driven it all off, not knowing that a part of the estate is Castleboy. And now the legitimate graziers are demanding their cattle back, and he wants information from Frank, I took the opportunity of asking if I might at last get a permit for my Keeper to use the gun I was allowed to buy; and he promises it for "Lady Gregory and any she employs".

26 JULY. Today the darlings came home, so bright and gay, though Richard a little pulled down, and so glad to be at *home*. Alec Martin writes "How splendidly your efforts have been crowned, for you alone have borne all the heat and burden, and I pray that we shall soon see Hugh's wishes carried out".

SUNDAY, 27 JULY. To church with the children. Mr. Trotter, who prayed for "all the Royal Family" left out by the Archdeacon in favour of the Provisional Government. Also the prayer "For fair weather". I had not heard it for a long time—"O Almighty Lord God who for the sin of man didst once drown all the world except eight persons".

30 JULY. A great blow yesterday. A cable from New York "John Quinn died this morning"—(from Curtin his chief clerk).[13] I had written him a long letter on Sunday telling him of the legal opinion in the picture case, sending him Lord Carson's speech that I knew would interest him. America will seem very distant now without that warm ready sympathy and interest. The children will miss their Christmas apples. So my day and night have been sad and I am heavy hearted.

Yesterday the Johnson children with mother and aunt, and Mrs. Scovell from Burren came for fruit. I said nothing of my sorrow.

Today a good letter from Lord Carson "I shall be available at any time if it is found that I can be of any use", and gives me his summer address.

And by second post Ig. Rice writes enclosing the same statement from the Colonial Office, about the Committee procedure that I have had, and saying "Senator Brown will himself prepare a statement of the Corporation case and suggests that you should be one of the persons, if not the only person, to present the case orally before the Committee on September 5th".

And Freeman Smith sends me his sworn statement and says "I

shall be most happy to further support you by giving evidence before the Committee if desired".

31 JULY. Richard's report *very* good.—Vassall summing up "An excellent term. I hear nothing but good of him from all his masters and genuine sympathy with him on his illness". He is keeping up a good name at Harrow.

Corly the Piper here; says Douglas Hyde is looking very ill. He "hears the King of Spain is in Mr. Berridy's house in Connemara." (Ranji Singh—but in the folk tales any magnificence is apt to be ascribed to a Spanish royalty). Is glad Lord Dudley is married—"It is better for him in every way and more decent" . . . Tells what a hard time he (Lord D.) had in Connemara when the railways were up and "he had no way to get food but a poor way, and was three weeks without eating beef" "It was Lord Dudley opened the gaols when he came to Ireland and that was a good thing to do". He hears De Valera was in Loughrea but there was no reception. I have been sent a cutting from a U.S.A. paper telling of Mrs. Gardner's death. Another friend gone. A very noble woman.[14]

2 AUGUST. Sunshine today after much rain. No post, but papers came to Gort and tell the strike in Dublin has begun, all electricity cut off.[15] That, and anxiety about the Boundary question will damp the Tailteann games, and I'm afraid the Abbey can't open.

Reading *Ariel*, and getting for the first time a clear (and I think unforgettable from its wit) impression of Shelley's life.[16] He seems to have been "astray in the world" from his birth. But what gifts he brought and left to it!

War and Peace still kept for bedtime, the history now almost more absorbing than the people—Borodino and the entry to Moscow. It helps to put the picture matter out of my head at night. I wish it could do so altogether, for there is no more to be done. (January 1930. "No more!" And this very month began with Cosgrave's meeting at Gort offices!)

4 AUGUST. I read last night in the Irish Testament the verse "Jesus knowing . . . that he came from God and went to God" . . . Is there not some atom of the Divine flame in each of us also that has come from above and will return to its place"?

A rainy morning, the children rather tired after the excitement of Margaret's one night here, and were out late last night taking the dogs to hunt rabbits. And Marian X because Taddy had got into the room she had made ready for Guy and slept in the bed and dragged the sheets about. And no post as it is a Bank holiday.

Catherine has been typing "Nature Studies" herself. She wrote all the flower parts from memory while recovering from measles in London, has made a cover for it and written a preface but says "I don't suppose it will be published unless it gets to be very good".

6 AUGUST. The darling children have left today for Burren.

9 AUGUST. I have felt the loneliness, but am glad they are at the sea; the weather here has changed to summer, they are better there. But while the floods continued this house with its contents made the best Noah's Ark.

I go on typing my diaries without joy. Today I think of a possible play, a short one, and have rummaged for old notes. Among them I find one written in May 1918—not about plays but:

"What has been expelled from my life?

"Interest in politics except as they affect Ireland.

"I think any sort of personal ambition. I have done some good work that the children may be proud of—Robert was. I would be glad to do more because it is rather sad giving up creating—but not I think for praise. I have had enough.

"Since Robert's death I do not covet money. I wished to leave him better off. I think the children will have enough for freedom from anxiety. I should like a little more to spend on woods and keep garden better, but if the sale of books &c goes on I shall have that. Desire for society went with Hugh's death, it could never be so pleasant as those Lindsey House visits.

"I passionately wish for the children's love and their happiness. For the return of Hugh's pictures. For the Government of Ireland in the hands of Ireland; for the rebuilding to begin.

"For the increased worthiness of the Abbey until we hand it over.

"With all the anguish of Robert's death I have lost my one great fear of losing his affection. Now there is nothing that could hurt me so much to dread".

(Now I am typing this, 13 January, 1925, seven years all but ten days since his death I have little to add. The children have just been clustering round me, making out a cross word puzzle from Punch. I have kept their home for them. But I want or need money more than I did, all that expense falling on me, rates, taxes, labour, house—but thank God with the help of my plays and books I have kept going so far. A little anxious about this year, and wondering if I might lecture in England). (21 January 1930. Yes I have kept the home all this time, and without, thank God, doing less worthy work).

I have found also a note from Tagore's *Home and the*

World[17]—"I am willing", he said, "to serve my country, but my worship I reserve for Right, which is greater than my country. To worship my country as a God is to bring a curse upon it".

The Clare County Council have decided, by one vote not to present an address of welcome to De Valera on his visit to Ennis next week.

10 AUGUST. Yesterday a man, half blind, and a woman, came to the door asking alms to help them on their journey to Sligo. He said he had been working in Colonel Campbell's garden there, had gone to Dublin for an operation on his eyes which had failed, and was walking back to Sligo with his wife. They had come by Ennis and Crusheen, going on to Galway, said they had been misdirected. An improbable story that they should have gone so far astray, but they looked honest and certainly very poor, and I have given them tea and £1 to help them on their way.

Very tired myself today and missing the darlings' shouts and laughter. I read Tolstoi's *First Distiller*[19] last night, it might be put into Irish for the Gaelic Theatre with good effect.

11 AUGUST. Yesterday, Sunday, church as usual (Mr. Trotter). But after lunch Raftery came about altering the entrance gate, and I helped to gather currants for his children (and he told me that wild boy Cooney has gone to Australia, the first I have heard of going so far). And then just as I had settled myself on the sofa to read I heard a shout, and there was Richard, with Margaret and George Gough, from Burren, and we went out for fruit and had tea, and I felt more in the scheme of things, even as a Swiss Family Robinson wreck, to be visited. Richard had dreamed that there was a spring tide at Burren, and it had come up as far as the house, and Grandmama was sitting at the door and the waves had dashed over her. Someone had said that was a sign of some great good fortune coming to me, the dashing of the waves, and so they believe it will be the return of the Lane pictures!

And then reading *Sinn Fein*, I found among its bitter, barren columns an article by Frank Gallagher[19] on the individual, calling for individual examples among Republicans, of "a clearer, more just, more spiritual life . . . Our whole hope and inspiration from the past is based upon what individuals have done and have inspired others to do".

12 AUGUST. Yesterday all the Archdeacon's party spent the afternoon, and Anne and Michael Yeats, he very bright and can now say his alphabet though as to conversation he only says Yes and No. And again a sudden shout, and there were Richard, Anne and Catherine in G. Gough's motor, Richard driving it.

They stayed a couple of hours and lighted up my afternoon. Irene Howard also here.

14 AUGUST. Yesterday fine, we finished saving the hay in the tillage field and began turning it over in sawpit field what had been cut the day before. But last night and this morning very wet. I puzzled over income tax, but kind Kiernan has made it as clear as may be. Reading Tolstoi's plays, *Living Corpse*[20] a poor one, but I liked a sentence because it said in other words what I had so often said. "You know we love people for the good we do them and dislike them for the harm we do them" (so "If your enemy hunger feed him; if he thirst give him drink" does away with our hatred as well as his hunger). And at night, reading *War and Peace* (very stingy of it now, being in the last volume and not knowing what I can find to come after it and take its place.) I read of Pierre who had sought for God "straining his eyes in looking at a great distance" . . . and now found "what his old nurse had used long long before to say, that God was here, there and everywhere".

"Knowing that he came from God and went to God". . . . I thought again of the atom of Divine life in us all. And that it should be an absorbing business here to look for, to recognise, that hidden flame in all those around us—searching for it as the children in their "treasure hunts", so overlaid as it may be, in them as in oneself.

Keller wrote yesterday that our guns have at last been found, even Robert's, given by his tenants when he came of age. I had written many letters about them in these last two years, and had almost given up hope especially as I had been told (by Rita Daly—a warning against rumour) that this particular gun had been sold by a drunken soldier to a Gort shopkeeper, in whose hands (recognised by the inscription) Dr. Sandys for one had seen it!

15 AUGUST. Our poor hay! A deluge this afternoon, the morning fairly good and the three Johns had offered to come and turn it over after Mass (Lady Day in harvest). De Valera's meeting may have been over before the heavy rain—the maids had seen "the world of motors" going towards Ennis as they came from Mass.

A book from H. Speakman, *Hilltops of Galilee*[21] with a nice letter.

I gathered up all the fallen fruit for the children just in time, and have been making an ornament or decoration for Catherine's birthday cake, a cat sitting at a piano. And good G. Yeats writes that she has got the two bicycles and is bringing them to Dublin tomorrow, a great relief. I am so anxious about these summer birthdays, the first without poor Godmother's wonderful hampers.

L.R. writes "Mrs. Yeats is going to Ballylee tomorrow and will tell you of the last ten days and how the Swedish Minister lay awake all night because the *Workhouse Ward* excited him so much . . . Compton Mackenzie acted Broadbent to perfection and everyone loved him. We ought to be able to pay off a bit more of our Abbey debt this quarter".

Old Niland here, had overslept himself and been late for his old age pension this week, must wait till next—"How was it you slept so long?" "I do be wakeful in the night time. I have a bad covering. And it does be full of fleas, and they give me no rest". I gave him five shillings. His pension has not been reduced because he is over the age. He hears there were nine thousand at De Valera's Ennis meeting,[22] there were motors going through Gort all the night. And that "De Valera said he was going to break the Treaty and fight the English and it's likely he'll be getting another twelve months in gaol". By the newspaper report he said he was back in 1916, 1918, 1921, and that if three *million* men will join him all will be won.

Speakman's *Hilltops in Galilee* has much beauty. I read about half last night. He tried to get back to the simplicity of Christ's teaching among those sacred places, so overlaid with additions, accretions, through the centuries . . . "He told them to love their neighbours—the Gentiles—even as themselves. That was beyond the pale! Yes, with those poignant words that seemed so utterly visionary and unpractical, he broke down the old barriers and with his vision illuminated the world's vision".

9 AUGUST. McGreevy wrote about the Tailteann[23] "There was a great night at the Abbey on Friday. There was a red carpet outside, which excited Colum so much. And the Persian Prince, and the Papal ladies and the Marquis MacSwiney and Mr. Healy's nice Colonel O'Reilly who looked after them well. Fair haired, Freestater and all as he is he looked the most Irish thing imaginable".

G. Yeats, here yesterday, says all went off well (and about £3000 was made on the games) except that Gogarty's "distinguished visitors" and McSwiney's Papal ones didn't amalgamate, there was some friction between him and the Marquis. And the Dutch Minister having gone off by himself to explore, returned late to the Viceregal Lodge and finding the gate closed preceeded to break the lock, and a sentry rushed out and would have fired at him but just in time recognised some mark on his hat. And at the Viceregal dinner party the Yeats were at, the Governor General suddenly stood up when they were in the middle of dessert-raspberries and cream—and proposed "The King!" However all stood up, including John McCormack who had said before he would not do so. And a dignitary of the Church stood up after that and said a very long grace, in the middle of which the Band outside struck up Annie Laurie, but he went on with it, and Lady Lavery giggled. Colonel O'Reilly was invaluable, and at a lunch at the Shelbourne finding the visitors had come with ordinary hats, and were due at some function afterwards, he went off, in a motor and brought their top hats. Yeats has gone to London to get Ricketts (in Shannon's name) to design robes for the Judges. Chief Justice Kennedy was so taken with the idea that he persuaded Cosgrave to allow this.

20 AUGUST. Quiet days. The hay turned for half the day and soaked again at nightfall.

Tuam Co. Council Chairman said, accepting a resolution of congratulation that it was the last political resolution he would accept. And Galway Co. Council Chairman rejecting the same resolution said he would never again accept one. That will save much loss of time and increase of acrimony, these resolutions ran their round as in *The Image* "I tell you there's not a Board or a Boardroom west of the Shannon but will have a comrade cry put out between this and the Feast of Pentecost"!

22 AUGUST. Burren yesterday, Catherine's birthday. I packed up all the little presents I had got together, and we tried to put the bicycles for Anne and Cat on the waggonette, but they didn't seem safe, and I had to send for Geoghagan's lorry. Then Guy came and brought me down, and the three darlings shouted their welcome, little eleven years old running to meet us and ride back on the step of the motor. The cake was first unpacked, the top sponge, the lower part chocolate, iced and decorated with crystalized cherries and marrons glacés, and my decoration, a Cat playing the piano, on the top. Richard liked his knife, the best the Stores could produce, and though it was sad having for the first time a birthday without Godmother's hamper, they seemed satisfied. Catherine rather surprised when I said there was another present and I asked Anne if she would mind having her birthday present now instead of next month. So we went in procession to the coach house, and the two little ones went in—a moment of puzzled silence—a moment of unbelief—and then shouts "BYCYCLES!" "Oh! Oh Grandmama!" and soon they were out and mounted and careering along the roads. This morning before breakfast they had been to Murty-Clough—they have

found wings—there is no limit to the flights they look to. I am a little sad because it will be a long time (should I live) before I can find anything that will give them so much delight. Richard is rejoicing in their joy.

Yesterday morning (in all my packing) a letter from Senator Brown, some questions to answer, but he says "the case seems to me unanswerable".

And one from the Law Agent of the Corporation (Rice) asking me if I am prepared to be at the Colonial Office at 10.15 on 15 September. The quarter of an hour earlier makes me wince it is like a dentist's appointment. The house and garden here are improved, sea and air a delight. This house was a very happy purchase.

21 AUGUST. There was a capture of poteen brought from Connemara the other day. One of the Civic Guard thought there was something going on. Two of the boat's men had gone away over the mountain, it was afterwards known each had carried a keg (they get 17/6 a gallon for it). He got into the boat, "they had a hard fight, they hit at one another and the Connemara man knocked him in the boat and jumped out and cut the rope and pushed out the boat to sea. But the Guard took out his baton and knocked a hole in the bottom that it sank and he was up to his neck and shoulders in the sea". But others of the Guard came then and found more poteen "it used to be good in the old time, made from barley, and oats, but now they make it with bluestone and methylated spirits".

MONDAY. 25 AUGUST. Yesterday I grew anxious about letters, and George Gough, motoring to Lough Cutra bought me home. I found one from City Hall Law Agent, asking me to try and get Glenavy to come over to the Committee enquiry. I hesitated, remembering Kiernan's letter "The Committee is not one of legal experts. They regard themselves as three ordinary intelligent men, and are not disposed to have legal people arguing before them". Between this, and not having seen the statement, I made up my mind to go to Dublin today for one night and go through it with Senator Brown, and consult him about Glenavy. But when I came down in the morning, ready for but dreading the journey, I found a letter from him, very confident, giving his chief point that "No matter what Lane's general attitude of mind as to the ultimate destination of the pictures was when he was discussing the matter with Aitken and McColl, his *particular* intention, when he signed the codicil was that if he did not live to return, the pictures should go to Dublin".

He also presses for Glenavy to be asked, and I bethought me

that it would be natural for him to appear, because Lord Carson had quoted in the House of Lords his assertion in the Senate that the arguments in our favour were "overwhelming", and he should give his reasons for this opinion. So I have written to him, to Ignatius Rice and to Brown.

The poor hay in sawpit field, cut a fortnight ago tomorrow lies, turned over every day and soaked for some part of the twenty-four hours. Yesterday, Sunday afternoon I found John and Mike turning it, very good of them. But through this day there has been no rain and J. says "if the great God gives us a fine night we'll be able to talk to it tomorrow". But clouds are hanging over us now.

A review of Tagore's *Letters*[24] in the *Irish Statesman* quotes: "the complete man must never be sacrificed to the patriotic man"—"beware of organisation my friend. They say organisation is necessary to give a thing its permanence, but it may be the permanence of a tombstone". He would not advise the patriotic Indian students to leave their schools and colleges to show disapproval of English rule . . . "the anarchy of a mere emptiness tempts me. I am frightened at an abstraction which is ready to ignore living reality . . . I wish I were the little creature Jack whose one mission is to kill the giant abstraction which is claiming the sacrifice of individuals all over the world under highly painted marks of illusion". A.E. says "our spiritual, intellectual and economic life, all that is necessary to our humanity and its fulness, has been ravaged by those who have set abstraction above humanity". And indeed De Valera's speech at the immense Ennis meeting may have been in his mind when he writes of those who ". . . wish for the triumph of some logical abstraction which is arid to the heart because it demands the subjection to it of or exile of all the spiritual immortality whose interblending makes rich our lives". Yet such Republicans as F. Gallagher would not shut out the immortals, and who can say for certain which road may lead to the city of our dream?

27 AUGUST. Burren. Yesterday I came back here for a couple of days, Guy bringing me. Old Niland came again, and had 5/- the week before, but he looked so tired I sent for bread and butter and a couple of glasses of port and put half a crown in my pocket and promised him some firing *before* he told me a little story: "There was a poor woman had nothing in the house, nothing for herself and her children, and she went to ask charity from four women that were in rich houses. And she came back empty and when she was sitting in the house and had nothing to give the children there was a man came in and he asked her what ailed

her. And when she told him he said 'Go open that chest you have in the room'. And she said there was nothing in it. But when she opened it she found it was full of every sort of thing. And the man said 'From this day you will never be in want, but as to those four women that refused you, before a twelve-month they will come begging to your door', And so they did before the twelve-month was over. But as to her, she had full and plenty from that out, and she had three daughters in America that helped her. For the man who came to tell her that was an angel from God".

A fine day here; Margaret and Guy and Richard—he driving—have motored off to Cork. Anne and Catherine still happy with their bicycles. Clouds over the hills towards Coole. Old Lee thinks there may be rain there "but the showers we get here are scattered and there's no water in them".

All looks peaceful, the Tierneys bringing in their hay, the Civic Guard playing handball against their little barrack wall.

29 AUGUST. Today, rain; rain, yesterday. I have read more of Sologub's[25] stories,—death of a child, her mother's madness; an unhappy childhood, the madness of a mother and son; a boy humiliated at school. And then Gorkt—story of a crime; of the disgrace and suicide of a woman; darkness without light. I wonder if the horrors Russia has been under have in part been created by these "makers" of clouds, of discord, of cruelty, instead of the hope, the insight of the "music-makers"

But we with our dreaming and singing
Ceaseless and sorrowless we
The glory about us clinging
Of the glorious future we see.

Tolstoi gave the horror but he showed also the resurrection, the power of the soul to throw off the darkness.

Then taking up the *Literary Supplement*, a review of "The Grand Inquisitor of Russia's Letters",[26] I see that had Constantine replaced Nicolas in a gentler revolution, reforms might have come without Bolshevism—"as with a few changed words in the Treaty we might have escaped Civil war."

Mr. S. writes from Donegal that he believes the Free State borderers will want to join the six counties, "from what he hears in railway trains".

SUNDAY, 31 AUGUST, COOLE. I came back on Friday evening in rain and with a cold. I found Senator Brown's "Statement", and read it next morning. Good I think, but one bad mistake, that Hugh had written his codicil "a few days before he left for America" instead of two months. I wired to Rice to correct it.

One or two other mistakes, and a letter from Yeats saying that Duncan's affadavit not having arrived may lose us the case, forgetting I think that it was his neglect to forward Duncan's letter to me that caused the delay. This morning my cold too bad for church, I have been going through evidence again to see where I can strengthen it. And making a "decoration" for Anne's cake, (of her on her bicycle, riding—"from 12 to 13", the two dogs beside her) And Richard suddenly appeared, the darling—and Margaret, on their way from the Southern tour to Burren.

A part of the hay, eight trams—put up, but not all. J. says "the day is well enough but it's the night and the break of day that have us destroyed". Apples all safe, but "next week we'll have the moon we can't depend on" (the September moon).

2 SEPTEMBER. Yesterday Anne's birthday (in advance for 13th) was kept, Guy took me to Burren. Mr. Scovell brought his notes about lobster fisheries and I went through them with him and have been typing them today for the *Irish Statesman*.[27]

Also today a long letter from Curtin about John Quinn's death (and Richard's trust fund). A telegram from Alec Martin, in answer to my letter fixing the dates of Hugh leaving Dublin and London. Also a telegram from Euston "Hotel fully booked". I've wired to Yeats to get me a room.

We drove into a covey of partridge on the way from Burren, they scurried off into a field through the loose wall.

3 SEPTEMBER. About to set out for London.

4 SEPTEMBER. A good journey but expensive, Perrin by mistake having taken a return 1st Class ticket, it is the journey to London by night that needs some comfort, not the return. Belgravia Hotel, rain and mud. Yeats and Mr. Doyle of the Corporation, and Ruth came at 3 o'c and we went through the case. Rather a shock to hear our enemies are not to be examined till October, so there will be no decision till then. And who knows what Government may then be in office? (Typing this 23 January, 1925, the decision has been made, but we have no news of it yet, a long, long waiting.)

We got pretty well through our little conference, though Yeats is urgent to keep exactly to the terms of reference, whether Hugh when he signed the codicil thought it was a legal document. However he gave in that I might be allowed to clear Hugh from the accusation of double dealing by telling of his renewed annoyance with the English Trustees, and the day,—two years—before the London gallery "actively pursued" was promised; and Mr. Duncan's statement that he had since he came back to Dublin "felt keenly the gap left in his collection". But of course the chief point is that he made the codicil at the same time that he tried to insure his life to pay off debts, in preparation for his death, and it is of no great moment what he might have done had he lived. He would certainly have given that collection to Dublin, but might have given the new collection he had spoken of to London.

SUNDAY 7 SEPTEMBER. On Friday we met at the Colonial Office, I first, Yeats last, as I had prophesied. We had to wait a bit while the Committee had their own talk. Then I was called in. They did not stick to the terms of reference, went all through the case, his intentions and disappointments. They were all kind, the Chairman, Wilson charming in manner and appearance. They kept me for just an hour. I think I said all I wanted to say. They then said they would call in Ruth; would have allowed me to stay but I thought it better to go. I asked them to let Mr. Bird's messenger, who had come with the original codicil to show it and go, as he would be wanted at the office, and they agreed but did not seem interested, said they had seen the photograph. They did not keep Ruth long, asked her chiefly about the will and the handwriting, and her having charge of all at Lindsey House. Then Yeats, and while he was there Ruth was sent for again, that was to talk about his having made preparation for death at the time he wrote it. As Ruth and Yeats were coming out there was a burst of laughter Yeats having said that if it would make it easier to get back the pictures "I daresay we could raise a riot". They sent to ask as we were going, if I had any last word to say, but I only called out "I hope for good news".

We all felt that they were sympathetic and believed in his "having believed it to be a legal document". But they are a little anxious about upsetting a legal document for an unwitnessed one—"very unusual". Ruth went to meet some friend at Wembley, and Yeats took me to lunch at Gatti's.

We were tired and he said he would lie down and have a sleep for the afternoon, but I went to the High Commissioner's Office, got his typist to type a letter to Lord Carson telling of the Committee, and sent him Senator Browne's statement. Then I went through my Income Tax papers with Kiernan. Then, on the way back, I went in at Albemarle to see C.E. Lawrence, who I had missed seeing last time I was in London. He came tumbling down the stairs in his old eager way, but at once attacked me "I have read your book". "What book?" "Your memoirs". "Where did you see them?", "Watt sent them here, to Huxley the Cornhill Editor". "But I told him I would not publish here". "The Cornhill won't take a set of articles unless Murray gets the book, I don't like it. It is too long. And I was pained by the hatred of England you show in it". "I don't think I do". "Yes you do. You hate England. It hurt me. You are a figure of peace. You brought me and others to love of Ireland. It is a disappointment". I felt so sorry, and I don't think there is hatred. I must look through it and see. I told him I had to show how the change came or grew, or rather the strengthening of my national feeling. But he was sad and made me so.

Then back to the Hotel, and wrote to Senator Browne, enclosing copy of my letter to Carson. And to Alec Martin, thanking him for letters he had sent. And then I took my luggage, ready packed and set out for Euston.

8 SEPTEMBER. A very tiring journey, the steamer over full, but at last I got a berth. And at Kingstown we had to wait on the platform two hours for the Broadstone train. I had happily kept my suit case with me and sat on it for a while—no benches. Train to Athenry very crowded also, but I got home at last. The journey and hotel (two guineas for the one night) cost £13. I had put the picture business out of my head, I hoped for good and all. Indeed I was too tired to think. I lay down at 2 o'c after a light tea-lunch and awoke at 5! And I fell asleep at once when I went to bed at 10. But in the night I awoke—the "tiger-claw" gnawing, the memory of what the Committee had said about the providing of a Gallery, and I thought and thought. And yesterday, too wet for church, I began writing on that matter to Rice and Senator Brown and Yeats and Glenavy, asking the Corporation to pass a clear resolution about a new Gallery, and the National Gallery to make a formal offer of housing the pictures. I see now that the postponement made by Curzon is all in our favour, will give us time to set this matter right. Then to Mr. West for a statement of what Hugh said to him about his health . . . I really think now I have done all that can be done, and that these may be the last letters! (31 May, 1928 Just written. Just written [words illegible] 31 January 1930. This month began with Cosgrave's meeting).

Alice Burke and her husband appeared, from Limerick and had tea and I gave them grapes for the children. Our final hay cut, and yesterday and today a downpour!

A.E. writes he is putting in Mr. Scovell's letter next week. "I hope you will come back with Lane's pictures in your pocket. Anyhow you have imagined so often having them that if thought has any effect it ought to work out just as much as the imagination of your woman in *The Jackdaw*".

Mr. Burke said yesterday that De Valera's release has reawakened Republican ideas; that a film representing a Viceregal garden party with Tim Healy receiving guests had been hissed the other day.

Yeats took me to *The Great Adventure*[28] in London. Very amusing and well acted. "God save the King" was being played as we went out and he said "They say the name Jehovah is made from some musical piece—I wonder if it was that tune!"

9 SEPTEMBER. J.D. told me that William Farrell has gone back to America "and he cried tears down at the corner, at Kiltartan bridge when he said goodbye to John Rourke, and John Rourke was crying along with him. The two of them worked here at Coole together so many years, and it is well they loved poor Mr. Robert, and William says there was never a gentleman had such good words spoken of him as he had in the American papers. Himself and Jim, his brother when they heard of his death went and got drunk for two days or three. But William never took a drop over there these last years. But last month when he was in Galway with his sister he went wild and drank away hundreds (of dollars). John Rourke has joined the Christian Brothers, he came home now to see his sister that is back from America. But he got no welcome since he was in the Belfast police, and he doesn't go much out of the house. But himself and William were very sorry parting with one another that morning, and the two of them cried".

14 SEPTEMBER. The children came back yesterday safe and well, happy, tearing round the garden and exploring their cupboards.

But it was a bright moonlit night, the brightest yet, and Saturday, and I was uneasy, yet the men being late bringing things back from Burren I did nothing, except pick a basket of the best apples. And this morning John comes to tell me the garden has been robbed, all but all of the ripe apples taken. I am hoping against hope that the children will not know, but fear they must.

Nothing to be done about the apples. I cannot bring those unarmed Civic Guard into danger. The priests have long lost influence, though Father Finlay takes up a good deal of yesterday's *Independent* in a fiery attack on the divorce bill to be brought up next session—wants divorce made impossible except in the case of nullity or (as in Marquis MacSwiney's case) by special dispensation of the Pope.

No answer from Yeats or City Hall to the letters written a week ago. Two from Senator Browne, who mistakes what I said about the Corporation resolution.

19 SEPTEMBER. I wrote two days ago to Yeats and Rice

asking if they were doing anything about resolutions for the Commission. No answer yet. Margaret and Richard left, he much the better for his holiday, Anne and C. with me, and Muriel Sampson.

A moving and terrible play from Upton Sinclair—*Singing Jailbirds*[29]. I am thankful the mass of our political prisoners have been released.

It is a terrible picture of the wrong done by man to man.

The children went out fishing on the lake yesterday evening, caught nothing but it was a lovely evening and they enjoyed it. This morning Anne came in to say she had been down by the lake and had seen and watched for a long time three little foxes playing together on a rock. Rotter caught a rabbit yesterday, his first kill after many chases.

20 SEPTEMBER. A letter by afternoon post from Ignatius Rice. He at the City Hall and Yeats at the National Gallery will get the resolutions I proposed carried. A relief.

21 SEPTEMBER. A terrible storm last night, it began late and I gave the children the hymn for those at sea to read aloud instead of saying one before they went to bed. The bell tree close to the house has been blown down, and a silver fir across the avenue so we can't get to church. But no damage done to garden, and I think not much to the woods.

23 SEPTEMBER. 82 Merrion Square. Yesterday morning I put up grapes for Sara Allgood and Casey and Irene's children, and the chicks, with provisions for their journey. We motored to Galway a round about way, the bridge at Kilcolgan being mended—a road I had never been on, wide-stretching plains and of a sudden Cruachmaa came in sight, very blue, a real hill of the Sidhe. It vanished as suddenly, as our road dipped.

A good journey to Dublin, no crowd. We had tea in our carriage. Then Goodbye to the darlings. Rain had fallen all day, and someone had said as we drew near Dublin "there will be no wind tonight". But this morning's paper tells of a bad gale in the Channel, it must have risen suddenly. I am glad I did not know of it, and hope the darlings slept.

I went straight from the Broadstone to the Abbey, had some tea in the office there through first act of *Paul Twyning*;[30] saw the 2nd, a good audience and much laughter. Casey came to the Office between acts, looking very spruce, has given up work for the present and is thinking out a play. Here, (Merrion Square) I found Yeats entertaining Russell, Gogarty, Stephens, Phibbs[31]—(George away for the night). I didn't stay long with them. They had begun to talk of poets,

A.E. repeating his parodies on Stephens and Starkey[32] Yeats says they went on discussing contemporary poets "Gogarty acknowledging none except myself, and Russell I suspect not acknowledging Gogarty".

Yeats says the Stuart's little paper *Tomorrow* caused a great sensation, it was rumoured that Government intended to suppress it. He went to see Blythe who said Cosgrave had really thought of doing so, not because of anything said in it, but because Hartmann, a German who is anti-church has written saying L. Robinson's idea of the foundation of Christianity in his story is probably the right one, and C. is afraid Robinson is a disciple of Hartmann's and is trying to pervert the nation. However the next number is to contain an article in favour of giving over the Cathedrals now in Protestant hands to the Catholics, and that will puzzle them.

24 SEPTEMBER. I read a part of *Singing Jailbirds* to Casey in the Abbey office. At the first scene he said "Rather melodramatic" which it is. But then he was very much impressed, thinks it a "terrible play". He has an idea of a Labour play himself, says it came to him when looking at my *Brigit* the idea of one man giving himself for the people. He has been afraid to go and see Larkin "because I love the man and am afraid he would bring me into the movement. And I do not believe it will succeed on his present lines, but through art and culture and the people of culture". He says Larkin's brother Peter was for five years in an Australian gaol, on the evidence of having explosives found in his pocket; and it was proved later that these had been put there by emissaries of the Australian Government. Larkin had seen *Juno* at the Abbey, and had said it was a very fine play.

Yeats came with me in the evening to see *Paul Twyning*; wonderful acting by Dolan and Fitzgerald.

At the Carnegie meeting our Abbey appeal was passed to be sent in to Head Quarters. Best was anxious we should add a list of all the published work written for it by the dramatists "who have enriched English literature".

I read Dan Breen's *Fight for Irish Freedom*[33] till midnight, and was awake most of the night, so excited by it. This evening I have finished it. Very vivid, terrible because of the end, the almost bare statement of the beginning of the civil war where "brother by his brother died". A vivid bit of Irish history for the future. I told Yeats and he agrees that the story of the Black and Tans should be collected now from house to house while the witnesses and sufferers are still living, that we may have a protective document when the British denounce us as they may probably do very soon if there is any fighting over the Boundary.

Yeats hears Republicanism has gone down in these last months because of want of a programme, of constructive policy. Mme. Markievicz had complained to Russell of this.

At Gogarty's last night O'Duffy[34] told Yeats and the rest that the English are supplying Ulster with armoured cars and munitions and men, who have encamped where they can shell Clones and other places. O'Duffy is anxious because though the Government are altogether against fighting, the Republicans may make raids over the border and then there will be fighting. It is the Republicans' hope that this will lead to the Free State having to get into the fight. Yeats, going on to Gogarty's after our talk, had proposed that an official history of the war should be written, and suggested that Mulcahy, now idle, should write it. Gogarty took up the idea with enthusiasm and said he would go at once to the Government to propose it.

26 SEPTEMBER. Yesterday morning to the Abbey, going through business with Perrin and Dolan, and desiring that a list of proposed plays should be submitted to me, as had been done all these years until now. L.R. in the afternoon and we talked of this; a good deal of rubbish has been put on for next weeks, *Suburban Grove*,[35] *Insurance Money*,[36] and a foreign play I had never seen or read.[37] I said some more solid work must be taken up. *Playboy*, which he consented to; *Androcles*, consented to. And then for, I think, the first time proposing a play of my own, I said *The Image* could be given a very fine performance now, and the actors had several times asked for it. L.R. agreed, approved. But Yeats refused consent, says it has an act too much and is slow in action. Rather a shock to me, my chief play, and one made much of in London and elsewhere. He proposed *Damer's Gold* and *Shanwalla* but I will not have them, feel too sore. L.R. agreeing with me gave in to Yeats, who as a concession said the receipts of *Image* might be looked at to see how it compared with the takings of other plays in old days. And what of the losses on his plays, even outside the staging, that did not fall on the Theatre or him, but on me.

27 SEPTEMBER. SATURDAY. ATHENRY HOTEL. On Thursday evening Yeats and I went see the *Merchant of Venice* at the Father Matthew Hall, I was glad I brought him as it was a fine achievement, good speaking, quiet actors, a very good Lancelot Gobbo, and a Shylock as fine as I ever wish to see (and I have seen Moskewitch and many earlier ones), very tragic, a sort of beauty in his very spite, the anguish of a disinherited race. There was a full house, many looked poor, there were children, one

little boy shouting with delight at Gobbo's buffoonery. A Friar speaking between the Acts gave the dates of the performances, three times next week, and hoped many children would come to the matinée. He spoke with gratitude of Frank Fay (and we were giving him the credit, but yesterday L.R., when Yeats spoke of this, was indignant, says it is a long established company and that F. Fay only produced this play). The Friar came to greet us after the play, and when I spoke of the Shylock he called for "Jack" and introduced him, a young fellow of no striking appearance, his name Stephenson, a printer in Dollards. (May 1928, now one of our best actors at the Abbey). A good evening.

Yesterday the *Irish Times* told of the passing of the Corporation's resolution about the pictures.[38] I went to see Rice at the City Hall and begged him to send this on to the Committee in London at once, as the papers say Curzon is back and this should be in before his examination. I went also to the Abbey, told Dolan we had decided to have *Playboy*—"very glad"; *Androcles*—not so well pleased, a big cast an expensive play and didn't go so well the second time as the first. I asked if he had any others to propose. He said "*The Image*—a good many people have been asking for it and the players want it; we have been making out a cast". He proposes Miss Allgood in the old woman's part, Miss Delany in her old one. I said it had been proposed but Mr. Yeats was against it. He said Mr. Robinson was for it. But I said I would not myself ask for it again, and left it there. But I feel a little comforted.

Perrin told me of the Drama League using our costumes, properties and stage for rehearsals without any payment. And as there was a meeting of the League at 82 I told Yeats and Robinson of this, and also that it is not fair taking all our best actors for the D.L. plays, not leaving them time to get up fresh, or old work of our own, so that we fall back on used up plays, such as have been arranged for this autumn. I said that Yeats for domestic reasons couldn't stand up against the League, but I left it to L.R. to do so.

Lady Ardilaun asked me to her party at St. Annes, I should have liked to see her garden again, but was afraid of being late for the train, so played with the children and came on here by the evening train. I saw a rehearsal in the morning of Casey's *Nannie's Night Out*,[39] very ironical and amusing, but too short to be of much use, and I couldn't quite enjoy poor Sally rolling about "drunk and disorderly". I hope he will make a big play again, perhaps his Labour one.

28 SEPTEMBER. MONDAY. I slept at Athenry, astonished as I

got out of the train to see the starry sky after the weeks and months of cloud. Saturday also fine and all but two trams of hay got up, these "to be finished on Monday" but alas yesterday heavy rain began and has lasted almost ever since Church very trying, the two Trotters, the father preaching at great length, and such rubbish; the congregation hardly if at all over a dozen. The real hallowing of the day was later when I read in *Brothers Karamazov* "The Russian Monk" the old priest Zozzinovs story, the summing up of his Gospel "Life is paradise, and we are all in paradise but we won't see it. If we could, we should have heaven on earth the next day". "In truth we are each responsible to all for all; it is only that men don't know this. If they knew it the world would be a paradise at once" . . . "Equality is to be found only in the spiritual dignity of man" (and he believes it is in Russia this will first be understood). And he preaches love beyond all—"Love all God's creation, the whole and every grain of sand in it. Love every leaf, every ray of God's light. Love the animals, love the beauty, love everything. If you love everything you will perceive the divine mystery in things". And it happened that earlier in the day I had read in the *New Republic*[40] "The Promethean challenge to religion" that had come to the same conclusion—the stealing of the fire was "a challenge directed against Zeus as the embodiment of unreasoning authority . . . But in Christianity the teaching of Christ is that love to the uttermost limit is the supreme concern of human living . . . the old God of power died and the new God of love was born. Jehovah had been redeemed by Christ".

I can forgive the apple stealers, and feel quite affectionate towards some lads who broke into the vinery, took the sourest of the grapes (threw some away after tasting them) and left the watering can they had borrowed to carry away their booty in Peter's garden that he might bring it back. But I cannot feel anything but hostility to old X. in the pulpit, tho' I daresay he may have given up those habits of which I was told.

In French's U.S.A. account there is £8.8.0 for *The Jester*, I am glad it is being put on.

SATURDAY. 4 OCTOBER. A quiet week, the hay finished two days ago, but now being brought in, so garden must still wait, but we have brought in what apples and grapes there are. My visitors yesterday a poor man who had walked from near Kinvara on crutches, and Mrs. Shaughnessy whose husband has lately died, wanting a paling for her haystack; and Gillane's children for apples. Glad to be able to supply them all. Kathie arrived today.

The National Gallery resolution has been passed.[41] I can think of nothing more to do about the pictures, but am anxious. October brings the enemy's examination.

Working at *Kiltartan History book*, to enlarge it.

8 OCTOBER. Peter says "The world is turned to be very bad and there's a great many it would be no pity if they'd die". But I hope they won't have to go and fight in the North.

Typing bits for *Kiltartan History*; just now about Titus "he let no man or woman go downhearted from him, and he would write and dictate to you at the one time". A good summing up of a life of kindliness and industry.

8 OCTOBER. Yesterday I drove with Kathie to Roxborough, took a motor. We went the lower road by Balinabucky, our old tenants' houses there much improved, flowers in the windows, gates to yards. I was glad to see it. I don't know if they are better off by purchase, or by money made during the war.

Roxborough land, outside the wall, is sold, but there is not much change yet, two or three staring houses, some hay but no tillage. The house, the ruin is very sad, just the walls standing, blackened, and all the long yards silent, all the many buildings, dairy, laundry, cowhouses, coach houses, stables, kennels, smithy, sawmill and carpenter's workshops empty, some of the roofs falling in. I am afraid the house will never be built up. Yet the road by the deerpark and the avenue most beautiful, river and hills and the trees in their autumn foliage. All silent that had been so full of life and stir in my childhood, and never deserted until now. The garden in grass and weeds, but some phloxes that Kathie had planted not yet choked, and I am bringing them here, a great enrichment to my borders.

The first attack, she says, was at night, guns fired, windows broken and a few men, disguised, came in and demanded guns and were given some. Then a little later a larger party, at night, this time with a complete list of the guns in the house. These had been hidden under the floor, but Arthur had to disclose their hiding place as they knew of them. They said there was a revolver also, but he could not remember anything about it and they went. Kathie and Dudley had hidden it in a secret drawer of the study table without Arthur's knowledge. After this they threw it and some hidden cartridges into the river.

Then one morning she was called down and found the hall full of armed men. Arthur was in the dining-room, puzzled by a long typed paper saying he must give up the estate. He thought at first it was from the Free State Government, but it was from the Irregulars. They told him he must leave and give up the estate to them, they would manage it for the future. Lennard was civil, but another in command rough, it was he who would not let her take away some piece of glass or china.

When these men were forced by Government pressure to leave, the pillaging began. She thinks the house was burned by one small gang "a bad gang" that had been the first to come for the guns.

The steward's wife said, what I had thought, that if Arthur had gone back when the Irregulars left it would have been all right. She said "he might have asked a couple of them to stop and help him". I wonder what their answer would have been. It would have been worth trying.

Today Anne's letter says "Isn't it lovely Richard being in the Upper Fifth". Very good, especially as last term had been so broken by his doctors.

11 OCTOBER. Kathie left. Yeats and George arrived yesterday. He expects to finish his philosophy book this month and will feel a free man then. He has been reading over the *Wanderings of Usheen*,[42] which he used to look down on, he used to be vexed when A.E. begged him to write another poem "like *Usheen*", but now he is very much struck by it, the unconquerable old man.

After he wrote it came the M.G. influence and the love poems; then the folk influence, now the philosophy; and he hopes to settle to poems again.

The Government defeat and the dissolution make me anxious about the pictures, Curzon having put off his examination till the 5th there will be no chance of a Bill being even promised by the Government; and if the Tories come in they will not be friendly.

Cosgrave has been forced to break his written promise to the mutinous soldiers to admit them to the Government. And there is danger that if the Commission in Ulster is already prejudiced, leaning to the Ulster side, McNeill may resign from it. Yeats wishes someone would write a history showing how Ireland has always been sacrificed to English party convenience.

13 OCTOBER. Catherine's letter from school makes me a little anxious, there seems to be something wrong, her fainting and having a temperature, and she writes to Marian that her eyes give trouble and she may have to wear glasses. This overshadows minor worries—about Kennedy's auction of trees, and Putnam and French writing about F's name not having been put in *Brigit* for amateur rights. Yeats and George just come back much pleased with Ballylee, such a lovely day to see it.

17 OCTOBER. They left yesterday. She had been twice at

Ballylee. He was working at his philosophy, its last weeks, and was a good deal absorbed in it, but much amused when I told him of having Burke object to the item of five gross of scalping knives supplied to the Indians during the American war. Says he will make a speech on the Boundary question on purpose to use it. The last day or two he was very happy rewriting his old poems—has got rid of "my pigeon" from the Cradle song,[43] and other "bad words" especially in "The Green Branch". I read him in the evenings the *Arrow of Gold*[44] but it seems a little cloudy for that, I liked it better when I read it alone, it seems written in a whisper, as does some of Henry James. For myself I have finished the wonderful *Brothers Karamanzov*, and am in the *Insulted and Injured*,[45] very inferior so far.

17TH. A letter calling a meeting of the Carnegie Committee "to consider what action should be taken in consequence of a letter of resignation from Father Finlay calling attention to a publication by the Secretary". This is L.R.'s story of the girl imagining herself another Madonna. I haven't seen it or the paper (*Tomorrow*) and think both unnecessary and mischievous, and had told Yeats so "Setting fire to your neighbour's house to roast your own pig". I had thought of the Abbey only, but now it is the Carnegie as well, and may probably interfere with its work, and for no purpose that I can see but to fill the Stuart's idleness. And Margaret writes a short note saying Catherine has "marked astigmatism". I'm writing to Dr. Foley to know what that is, poor darling.

18 OCTOBER. Reading *The Times*, or what part of it was not on the election campaign, at breakfast, I saw in the report of the Congregational Union debate, first that "*St. Joan* is the most religious play for a generation, and far more deeply moving than many services" and that pleased me. And then of "a small country church where Lady Gregory's plays and the dramatic pieces of Tolstoi had been found a positive help in religious work". Perhaps I may do another play after all. I wish I could get that idea I am trying to live in "instead of striving to get to Heaven striving to bring Heaven about us on earth" into dramatic shape. (That was the origin of *Dave*. May 1928)[46]

An "urgent and important" second call to the special Carnegie meeting disturbs me, I'm afraid I must not shirk it.

Last night, looking through my folklore. I came on a copybook of the 80's with a few extracts, a poem by C. Rossetti; The Picket of the Potomac; a bit of prose from Matthew Arnold comparing *The Times* proprietors to Hezekiah's Mayor of the Palace, Shebna "not a word is alleged against Shebna's character, but like *The Times*, Shebna is the organ of the governing class, the friend and upholder of the established fact, and Isaiah is their mortal enemy". A bit from Renan about his vanished faith, that has not ceased to govern his life "Apres qu'Orphée, ayant perdu son idéal eut étè mis en pièces par les Ménades, sa lyre ne savait toujours dire que 'Eurydice! Eurydice!'". From A'Kempis "Four things which bring much peace"; and from the Gospel "Behold, I am among you as one that serveth".

Then in my first solitary year Lowell's

"Trust me 'tis something to be cast
Face to face with oneself at last" and on.

And then John Morley[47] on Byron—I have not seen it quoted in this Byron year—ending "only he stands aright who from his little point of present possession ever meditates on the far reaching lines which pass through his point from one interminable star-light distance to another . . . it is only when a man subordinates this absorption in individual sufference and joy to the thought that his life is a trust for humanity that he is sure of making it any other than 'rain fallen on the sand'". And, with my little history book in my mind, I thought, is not my life in trust for my country? (If the pictures come back I shall feel I have fulfilled my trust. But no news yet and I am terribly anxious.)

I don't think Morley's sentence on Byron has been quoted in the argument that came up lately about Westminster Abbey. "Though he may have no place in our own Minster he assuredly belongs to the band of far-shining men of whom Pericles declared the whole world to be the tomb".

22 OCTOBER. Dublin. Came here yesterday by early train for the "urgent and important" Carnegie meeting. Yeats met me at Broadstone and took me to 82 M.Sq. I went in to 84 after a little to see A.E. about the meeting. We had had a visit from Father Finlay in the morning, who told him of having sent in his letter of resignation to the Carnegie Committee because of the article published by the Secretary L.R. in *Tomorrow*—"could not continue association with him". Dermod O'Brien had also been in and told him L.R. intended anyhow to resign in June, doesn't find enough time for his own work, so they inclined to think he might solve the matter by resigning now. A.E. hated the story, and also one in the same number about black men and white women written (not in her own name) by Mrs. C., the wife of a Professor in Trinity.[48] A.E. is unwilling to face "a fight with two churches", for the Provost, by Father Finlay's account

is as indignant with the story as he is. A.E. wouldn't object to the fight if it was on a good ground, but doesn't feel we should fight on this. I came back and told Yeats. He was furious at the idea of letting L.R. resign. And G.Y. said he had only intended it vaguely hadn't decided even for June. Then McGreevy[49] came in, said he has no intention at all of resigning. He and Yeats went in to see A.E. and had rather a row. Yeats came back excited and said he had said too much.

I went to the Abbey, saw a part of the play, and went round and saw the actors, in good spirits. This morning to A.E. again, and with him to the Carnegie meeting. The Provost read Father Finlay's letter and said he had obtained a copy of *Tomorrow*, thought that story very offensive, also Yeats' Leda—"so unlike his early poems". Also another story in the same number "one must speak plainly—it is about the intercourse of white women with black men". He had written to Dunfermline calling attention to L.R.'s story, and Colonel Mitchell had answered they would take no action until they knew what view the Dublin Committee took of it. Then there was discussion. He asked us all in turn to give an opinion. When it came to me I said we all had the Carnegie scheme at heart and must do anything possible to keep it up—"but I do not think it a possible thing to dismiss the Secretary who has helped our work for over nine years so well, and that with a slur on his character". The Provost said "There is no question of dismissing him", crossly, and would give no hint of what action should be taken beyond asking Father Finlay to reconsider his decision. We all agreed to that, but feeling sure he would not. Mr. O'Donnell was L.R.'s chief champion. He said "I was brought up in County Kerry, among Catholics, I am a Catholic, an Irish speaker. I never knew a protestant until I was grown up and came to Dublin. My sisters are pious Catholics, I read them that story and they thought it a beautiful story, could see no harm in it. There is no doubt an obsession with that idea among many Irish country girls, I have three times heard a priest preach against it". The Provost listened with suspicious toleration and some surprise. After endless talk a resolution was proposed by the Provost asking Father F., to reconsider his intention of resigning and saying "we consider the article unfortunate and deplorable". I asked this to be amended to "the publication of the article", saying that was all that concerned us, we had nothing to do with what our Secretary writes, but objected to an article that might give offence being published. He would not at first alter it, put it to the vote, and it was passed by one vote, but he consented to put an amendment making the alteration. A.E., who had approved of the alteration, now could not make up his mind which side to take, and the Provost said it was not necessary for him to vote, and he didn't. But then the numbers were equal, and after a little A.E. voted for the amendment. (He could not make up his mind, all hung on him, then he seemed confused and asked what the amendment was. I said (quoting the Provost) "the milder form", and then he said "I am for the milder form"). The Provost very cross, spoke again against the paper, and "especially that horrible story about the blacks". I said "that is said to have come from Trinity". "Impossible" he said. Someone whispered to him it was a Professor's wife. He looked at the paper and said triumphantly "There is no such name among our professors". "It is signed in her maiden name" said someone. He jumped up and went away evidently intending to have the writer's blood. But she is said to have gone away with Liam O'Flaherty,[50] so he will find only the unoffending husband, who is writing a history of ancient Ireland. I kept them from cursing the article itself, because I fancy the Provost means to ask for L.R.'s resignation at the next meeting, perhaps threatening his own, and I didn't want to let the meeting commit itself against the story. Cosgrave had been prepared to prosecute the paper but sent it on to O'Higgins, minister of Justice, and he refused saying "the prosecution would merely represent the moral attitude of a certain people and place and time". Very good.

Very tired after all this, had some tea (it was 2o'c when I returned) and stayed in. Willie much delighted with the account but wished he had been there; he would have begun by an attack on the Provost for having written to Dunfermline before consulting the Dublin Committee.

23 OCTOBER. A sleepless night, worried by the echoes of that meeting. Yeats says the proper thing would have been to attack the Provost on the demerit of the article, and also that it was quite out of order to put the resolution before the amendment. He would have made a row had he been there.

At the Abbey again last night. Dan Breen had been there the night before, in the stalls, and I never knew and would have liked so much to meet him. Mulcahy says everything in the book is absolutely true. They say De Blacam put it in form.[51]

I had a little talk with Larchet in the Office, he thinks De Valera is losing influence through not having a policy, and that he wants to be arrested in the North. Then I had a talk with Casey, his eyes very bad, is having slight operations, very painful, every few days, can read very little, but can write a little and has begun a new play *The Plough and the Stars*.[52] He has enough money to last five months, had been once or twice to a Labour Agency for the unemployment relief, but had to stand so long in the crowd his patience gave out. He says Jim Larkin has won Dublin, beaten the Transport Workers, but thinks nothing much can be done in Dublin for the next twenty years. (End of Book 28)

As I left the theatre with Perrin the street was rather crowded and we saw a girl being brought along by two policemen, one on each side. Her hair was flying and she looked young and defiant, was singing—the very song "Nannie" sings in Casey's *Nannie's Night Out*—"Mother of mine". A tragic sight, the reality of what had been put on the stage.

Lennox R. came in for a few minutes, said "You made a splendid fight". I said I had done very little, the resolution was not good. I had only stuck to the "publication "of the story, not the story itself being denounced. But he said "O'Donnell[53] says you were wonderful and that none of the men were any good at all. He is full of admiration of you".

BOOK TWENTY-NINE

I said "I think the Provost will resign if he can't get you dismissed" and he said "Yes, he told Smith Gordon as he went out that if Father Finlay resigns he will do so". He thinks we should then make the Head of Maynooth chairman. It would be very good having a Catholic I think, this being a Catholic country; we could get his point of view.

I went to Clontarf to see Lady Ardilaun and her garden, was to have been there at 4 o'c but his visit delayed me. We went straight to the garden even now a wonderful display of flowers, dahlias chiefly, and roses. I said she ought to ask the players to see it, they would enjoy it so much, and she said Yes, she will next summer if she lives, and give a party for them. She finds solace in kindness, showed me in a glasshouse a quantity of geraniums in pots that are grown for poor women of the tenement houses who come to tea sometimes. She gives them each a pot to take away. A party of them come next week, and on another afternoon there comes one of the patients from the Incurable hospital, she has engaged a cinema for each day, Charlie Chaplin and some others they will like. And I found from what her cousin said she had just given a wireless to their rector's wife who has almost lost her sight, that she may have something to cheer her evenings. I stayed so long, talking of the Abbey at tea, Lady A. so interested in all the players, that it was dark when I left and I missed my way on the paths and after wandering for some time had to come back and ask for a guide, and the butler gave me his pantry boy. And I just missed two trams and didn't get to the pillar till 7 o'c and knew dinner was to be at a punctual 7 as G.Y. was going to a Drama League party, so I rushed to the Abbey and telephoned from there that I would stay and see the beginning of the play and would have dinner out (at the Abbey Hotel, excellent bread and butter and cocoa, bill sixpence and no tip possible the proprietor himself as I believe serving it). I went to the Green room and saw Barry Fitzgerald just returned from Paris. He suggests my putting the *Bourgeois Gentilhomme* into English for the Abbey. Then they went down to the stage and I stayed and talked again with Casey, who comes there for company in the evenings.

He talked again of Larkin, had found about twenty people in his office asking him for help on this or that. I asked if he had the same feeling for him as before, and he said "Yes, I love him he is so human. There was a man came in who with another had made false returns and kept some of the money his employers should have had. Jim said 'You were quite wrong in what you did, but I will help you, you are a comrade'. He will pay a lawyer to defend him. Then a poor woman who with four children had been getting twelve shillings a week from the unemployment dole, but one was at the same time earning nine shillings, and she had not told of this and they found out and stopped the dole 'And how can I support my four children on less than twenty-one shillings?' Jim will help her too, but he told her she was wrong."

Then back to W.B.Y. He had after his speech in the Senate on the Boundary[1] question suffered acute pain and had gone to Dr. Moorhead who had some time ago said he had blood pressure and now says it is much worse and that he must give up lecturing, and writing and public speaking for a while, and not eat meat and must take exercise. This was a shock to him though he is glad to think of going abroad as that will be in December or January. He must, though, finish his philosophy book, about a fortnight's work on it, to get it off his mind; and George has proposed his going to her people at Bournemouth where there is sun and he would have "golf and detective stories". But he said he would like to come to Coole first for two or three weeks and get through his writing. So he is to come next week.

He excites himself in Dublin, had been writing a letter to L.R. advising him not to resign but to demand "the liberty of the artist as claimed by Flaubert, Tolstoi and Anatole France"—not very wise linking himself with three heretics—and they were not paid secretaries of an educational Board.

24 OCTOBER. I got an introduction from Sir Philip Hanson to the Private Secretary of the Minister for Public Works and went to see him about Raftery who wants an appointment as Inspector of Buildings, I had already been sent from post to pillar and this time found that only men with an engineering degree can be appointed and that in no case can a builder be appointed, which they might have let me know at once. Then to say good bye to A.E.; he is rather low, thinks the Maynooth president may refuse (if both Father Finlay and the Provost resign) to come on the Board and then what are we to do? I said we must then lay the case before Dunfermline. We agreed that the Provost is no use, except in checking accounts, is even discouraging. For the first time I made a suggestion at the Board it was that "Nation-

building" books should be put on the list. Trevelyan's *American Republic; Life of Alexander Hamilton,*[2] Trevelyan's *Making of Italy*[3] and others For, I said, I think there is a passion for history even outside Irish history, in our people. And A.E. supported me. (He later found an old farmer in the South reading with intense interest the *Making of Italy*, who said "It is Ireland over again"). But the Provost said there was no interest in history, and he doubted there was in any books at all. In Kilkenny there was a library when he was there and the people only read newspapers. A.E. says the Provost talked great nonsense at the old Conference and was snubbed by an Ulsterman, Barry, for a proposal to separate Excise and Customs—give one to each side of the Border! A.E. hates Robinson's story so much he doesn't fight with a good heart. So do I now I have read it, but it is so mild compared to the novels and tales being written that it seems straining out a gnat to make so much bother over it. He thinks of writing it is absurd to protest against books or plays or films while the slums are left as they are, where children in the one family room witness births and every function of nature. He says it is Catholics who produce indecency, as Joyce and Moore, whereas Protestants like Shaw are so correct. I said it is nonsense their protesting against books while they give those confessional catechisms to young girls and boys, teaching them things we Protestants in our youth never knew.

In Nassau St. in the afternoon I lingered while the soldiers marched by with a band, a crowd following. A young man whose face I knew spoke to me, he was Paddy from the Abbey, one of the stage hands; said he has just been reading *Poets and Dreamers* and likes it so much, especially the Raftery part, and Herb Healing. I asked where he had got it as it is out of print; he said in the University Library.

I had a letter from Donaghy, and finding Yeats alone and in a placid mood last night I read it to him.[4] He said "It is a remarkable letter. He has thought and he expresses his thought well." Then I gave him the three poems to read and he thought them good; the rhythm imperfect, but that could be easily remedied. Quite a comforting opinion, I shall have something good to write to Donaghy.

I left last night and slept at Athenry. A fair there and several cattle men got out into my carriage. The newspapers had just come and one said "De Valera has been arrested", and another grunted.[5] Then one said to his neighbour "De Valera was arrested", and the other didn't reply but joined in a talk about cattle and said he never books his pigs. All well here but rain again. I had in Dublin a letter from the Colonial office saying the Lane Picture Committee will have another meeting in November. So that suspense is not at an end.

Casey says Sinn Fein is afraid of the National party (Magrath and the officers who mutined). They are 20,000 strong and have been dictating to the Government, ordering dismissal of officials, and one he hears has been dismissed. But Yeats belittles this, and also republican strength, thinks the Government will have exactly the same majority it kept at the last election.

28 OCTOBER. The weather turning to rain, but the days pass quickly. Sunday church, and wrote to Donaghy of W.B.Y's opinion, and some other letters. And then boys from Crow Lane came for apples, and luckily there were still some on the orchard trees and they were happy filling every pocket. Yesterday letters till after 12 o'c, and then typing bits, the last I think, for the *History Book*. Then it being wet, I got the two Johns to bring in and sort the apples in the hampers. Then more typing, and fine enough to get out towards dusk. The Conyngham girl came with a letter for me to send on about the promises of the C.D.B. to help them for roofing; she came to the garden and got some remaining apples, and I went to the woods for moss to plant my little hyacinths in. (Those planted that or next day are in bloom now. 16 February.) Tea at 6, and then I searched for and found at last *Le Bourgeois Gentilhomme*, the 1732 edition, and read it through, and think it will go very well translated and abridged. Tired then, read a bit of R. MacDonald's new edition of *Socialism*[6] trying to get at the soul of it; and then *The Possessed* for a bit, and to bed with a detective story brought by W.B.Y., *The Million Dollar Suit case*.[7]

This morning answering Kenneth Reddin's letter, and writing to Girvin about Cunningham, and to the children, with sweet herbs and the first violets; and composing menus for Yeats as he is forbidden meat (except white) and meat soups, and doesn't want fattening food either.

I found a novel from kind Harold Speakman from New York, it looks good *This above all*;[8] and I see he was in the only American regiment that went to the Italian front. He may not have been far from Robert.

30 OCTOBER. Yeats arrived last evening; is correcting his poems, making alterations in old ones this morning. I have typed out Bell Branch,[9] much improved. He says he would not have ventured when he wrote it to put in such names as Munster or Connemara, had not power and skill enough to set them, I say what he has now is the power born of belief in his own power. "Quite true". Yet he had used Sligo names then, that had set a

fashion, now rather overdone I think; for the young poets hitch a poor verse to a couple of hard names to give it a sort of solidity. Yeats has advised the Stuarts to appeal to the Pope as to the morality of L.R.'s story. I have just written to G.Y. thanking her for having "given me harbourage last week in that storm in a chalice. Willie wants to stir it up again but I wish he would let *To-Morrow* take care for the things of itself". He says he is sending it his amended Cradle Song[10] for its next number. I say it is time for a baby to appear after all the preliminary preparations. He hears the Provost, returning furious to Trinity, got the wrong Professor and the wrong Professor's wife "On the carpet". Horace Plunkett is vexed that he doesn't write for the *Irish Statesman*, but "he doesn't know the trouble it gives me to write an article of that sort. I remember his writing to Dunsany in the same way, and Dunsany answered 'the spade said to the rake, Why don't you dig'".

All this does not ease my mind of the weight that fell on it yesterday when Margaret's letter told of Richard not being able to see the Bulls-eye on the target, and of taking him to an oculist who says it is short sight beginning, that it will get worse, that he must wear glasses at work and at play. Poor darling, it breaks my heart, and I dreamt of him last night as a little baby on my knees; and another troubled dream. He and Catharine, so sound and flawless, and now wearing glasses.

A terrible storm awoke me this morning, and just now has come the loudest thunder clap I have ever heard, and Yeats, in the library, says the loudest he has ever heard.

L.R. writes "reading a book about the Russian Theatre the other day I noticed in the programme of one of the State Theatres '*When we change places, Gregory*'. This must be the *Rising of the Moon*. Did you know about it? Did they send you millions of roubles?" No I hadn't heard of it.

31 OCTOBER. Reading plays to Yeats, last night that Tailtean prize one, (Y. frantic, wants to know the names of the Judges—can only remember Fagan, says no actor was ever able to judge a play) and a Black and Tan one, no good. This morning Carnegie refusal to give any help to the Abbey, a blow. But James McNeill's message gives me hope that our own Government may help us. And Yeats "putting off what he has to say about *The Image*" and looking gloomy. But I have looked up the London newscuttings about it and have their praises, better even than I remembered them, ready to read him. Dividing apples for Holly Eve.

1 NOVEMBER. Yeats talking after breakfast of his work says

things went wrong yesterday, are clear today—" I believe there are emanations that communicate with me, giving knowledge now, but sometimes sent by the beings that exist somewhere outside us, to seek knowledge. In séances they give foolish answers because of want of knowledge; they are sent as questioners". "I can almost tell what the reviewers of my philosophy in the *Times Supplement* will say, 'it is obscure', but after all Blake and Jacob Boehme and others (now accepted) were once considered difficult and this also may have something in it though it is a pity, &c &c."

Apple dividing yesterday, Hallow Eve, workmen first, servants, many children, Christy Griffin, Raftery—there were some happily for all.

When I said last evening "I must write to Robinson about the list of plays," Y. said "*The Image* is rubbish, it (he denied this later) will cause a drop but as you and Lennox want it you may put it on". I told him I was getting work finally into order and must see it to know if it is really for the rubbish heap, or if I could amend it before I die. I read him an excited letter from Sally, crying out at being given the old woman (a far better) part instead of Mrs. Coppinger[11]—"this last insult"! But Yeats waked up then, said he might like it better with that change; I think is preparing to come round. But of course I am anxious and I can't go to look after next week's rehearsals because of having him here.

2 NOVEMBER. "They're bad because they don't know they're good . . . They'll find out that they are good and they'll all become good every one of them". (*The Possessed*).

All last week working in new bits to the *Kiltartan History Book* . . . as: "But as to where Tir-nan-Og is, it is in every place, all about us". That is Jacob Boehme's teaching:—"He Christ, is in the world, and the world standeth in Heaven and Heaven in the world and are in one another as Day and Night". And "The Kingdom of Heaven in within you".

The papers full of the elections. I am sorry, very sorry Ramsay MacDonald's support failed.[12] He is a good man.

Terribly anxious now we are in November—"early in November" the Committee will decide about the pictures. I think a defeat would kill me—or at least "bring down all the years upon me".

3 NOVEMBER. Yeats talking of his work and of the consciousness outside ourselves from which knowledge comes, and which he believes will lead to another revelation, perhaps not for another two hundred years, he thinks will not be so spiritual, so

outside the world as Christ. I say perhaps more like Buddha and he says "yes, that is the antitithesis 'they' use—Christ and Buddha". He had been interested in psychic things when about 17, but was frightened and the "influences" as it were seizing him and gave it up. Then later Mme. Markievicz, then unmarried took him to a séance in London and then he found he need not fear them. But he did not take up the exploration again "until I read your book". That is the folklore I was collecting from the people.

4 NOVEMBER. Afternoon post yesterday brought Kiernan's letter, saying he had heard "a disquieting rumour" that the decision of the Committee was against us, and had then, at the Colonial Office heard the Commission have not made up their mind and have "summoned another witness"—I am afraid not on our side or we should have heard. This is "disquieting" indeed, though I had suffered so much these last few days, an oppression that seemed to foretell disaster (as on the day of Hugh's death) that it was almost a relief to hear there had not been a final refusal. Yeats puzzled also as they had seemed to accept our case fully when we were examined. He thinks it may be the responsibility of advising a Bill they shrink from. I begin to think of possible action if they do reject us, anyhow to ask for publication of the evidence.

And today L.R. sends me the Provost's letter resigning from the Carnegie Board. I answered him, and Yeats said L.R. should show my letter to Colonel Mitchell. He withdraws, or rather denies ever having said *The Image* was "rubbish". But these anxieties and that trouble about Darling R. and Catherine's eyesight have made these weeks bad ones for me.

Hard frost last night, the dahlias blackened. I had cut the last of the blooms yesterday foreseeing this. The bronze and golden leaves of the beech trees above the wall are the chief beauty now, a background for the ilex and yews.

7 NOVEMBER. Yesterday, opening the *Literary Supplement*[13] I found a notice of "Modern Plays" with such a good notice of *Brigit*, I am so glad, especially as the Kiltartan dialect gets its bit of praise. Perhaps my stars are taking a better turn. "That 'Kiltartan' which she has now developed and refined till she can make it do anything, from being richly comic to being as it is in this Passion play, strange like poetry and useful like plain speech". . . . And as to the rebel dreams ". . . she can forgo all tragic strain and laboured grandeur in the consciousness that the reality—the actuality, one might even call it, of her theme will bring its own profundity and majesty".

Reading *Phineas Finn* to Yeats in the evenings, we had his first effort to speak in Parliament (that Birrell had said was so wonderfullly written by a man who had never himself been an M.P.). I asked Yeats how his speaking had begun, and he said he had become used to it in the little theosophical societies he belonged to. But his best lesson had been from Mme. Blavatsky. He had (like Phineas) prepared a speech with great care; had then written it out and read it to the assembly. It was received in dead silence and he felt that not a word of it had been understood. Mme. Blavatsky had called him over, said "Give me the manuscript. Now you go back and say your say about it". He did so with the greatest success.

When we read about Mr. Kennedy keeping Lady Laura in such order, not allowing her to see anyone or to read a novel on Sundays, I said "What ought she to have done?" and he said "What Jack said Masefield ought to do come home drunk and dance a sailors' hornpipe on the table".

9 NOVEMBER. Sunday. Too wet for church. Yeats with a bad cold, I have a lesser one. He has rewritten or altered some of his stories and poems in these last weeks, and written some of his philosophy. I had suggested some softening or enriching of the old Abbot's words in the Crucifixion of the Outcast.[14] He did not think at first it could be done, but has now made the alteration and is pleased. He says the last time he ever saw Wilde was at the Avenue Theatre and he had said "That story of yours, the Crucifixion is wonderful – stupendous".

I have worked hard at the *Kiltartan History Book*, and today have translated a part of Raftery's Talk with the Bush to put in. I will put in Patrick Sarsfield also from *Poets and Dreamers*, to lift the folk lore, give it more poetry and beauty.

10 NOVEMBER. Yeats, looking at the *Golden Age* Kathie had given me for the children says he once met Kenneth Grahame coming out of Henley's office and asked Henley "Have you been correcting his style?" and Henley said "Oh, no", seemed satisfied. But he had asked because he was told Henley had corrected the style of one of Henry James's early stories and that H.J.'s screams had filled the office and the paper had come to a sudden end.

11 NOVEMBER. Talking of novels he said Jane Austen and Richardson had written only of the upper classes, "Dickens changed all that". Then came Thackeray, half and half, and Trollope half and half. Then Henry James who went back to fine culture of fine characters "there can be no good literature without praise".

Lady Londonderry has written to him, the letter came today, asking where she can get "an authentic portrait of Cuchulain" as she wants to put up a statue of him in her garden! A letter from an Australian also, enthusiastic about his speech at the Tailteann banquet. He says he prepared it very carefully, though knowing he would speak less well, with less fire, but to get a good Press report. Tim Healy spoke afterwards and after that said to him "It is a hard thing to have to make the first speech. I have never done it in my life in Parliament or elsewhere. My plan has been to wait and attack the fellow who spoke first"!

11 NOVEMBER. Blythe is to see me on Monday, 17th. I would go up on Saturday with Yeats but hear the Bishop is to preach at Gort and must help to fill out our skeleton congregation. Have engaged rooms at 19, Adelaide Road. Yeats, a picture of health and in high spirits came here as I told him, looking like his father's portrait in the early poems and now looks like the portrait by Mancini. We are still reading *Phineas Finn.* He says Yorke Powell once said at his father's house "I've had a letter asking me to recommend a private secretary. I would have suggested Willie, but I know he has no enthusiasm for spelling". But now secretaries have their typists, so even that qualification is not needed. He has rewritten "The Sorrow of Love"[15] to his great delight, and made it very fine. Says you can't write well without self-control, and he had not that when it was first written.

I have nearly done with *Kiltartan History Book*, am adding some bits from Braadar and O'Rahilly to lift the prose. Now trying to add some ballads in English. But these are very poor in comparison.

14 NOVEMBER. I've been writing out clearly a couple of Yeats' much corrected Cuchulain and the Waves,[16] for the printers. And he has consented to save Cuchulain's life from the waves. His death in battle is much better known through my Cuchulain than when the poem was written.

Last evening the *Times Supplement* had come and I read him a review of Herbert Trench's poems.[17] which roused him to indignation. "That's all nonsense. What they want is technique. Trench can't write. If he could have been with us at the Rhymers' Club long ago he might have done something. That reviewer praises Hardy as a poet, they all do that when they know nothing about poetry; they like Hardy because he has not technique, they feel he is still a novelist. That man talks nonsense about Shelley. Very little of Shelley will last for say 400 years. I know, for I was reading him the other day. There are about twenty pages of exquisite beauty that will live for ever. Keats has a larger proportion, he has better technique, but there is very little that will live, say of Tennyson about the same, twenty pages. Browning? I think there will be about the same of them all. He applauds Whitman; he likes a preacher, he picks him out because he is all preacher. I remember my father telling me Keats was a better poet than Shelley. I didn't believe him then but I know what he meant now, though I care more for Shelley. But these critics ought to think more of the writing. They have given up God, they shouldn't give up perfection."

Well, he practises what he preaches; is working over these old poems as if for a competition in eternity.

15 NOVEMBER. A Polish novelist has been given this year's Nobel prize.[18] Yeats thinks there is more cultivation in the small European nations than among us—a novelist there is a fully equipped man. I say they can cross the boundary in other countries, we are cut off between England and America. And he says both are commercial countries. Some foreign writer he was talking to about novelists said "The English require so much money". I wondered how few of the English aristocracy are doing fine work in literature, the Peels for instance, brilliant at school; Willy in politics, George but editing his grandfather's letters. He says brilliancy at school is against success in literature. Some examiner had said to him "Our examinations are not a help to education but an ordeal". They strengthen the will rather than develop the mind". "I looked on my school when I was sent there as a dreadful anarchistic interruption. Education is another man's road".

21 NOVEMBER. 19, ADELAIDE ROAD. I came up by early train on Monday, 17th, went straight to Tulloch and through figures with him. Our loss on the Abbey in the last ten years is £4000, the drop beginning in war time, 1915. We recovered in 1918, then fell again in the civil war. But we have paid off all debts now by the sale of our securities and have lodged £500 in the Bank. I was to see Blythe at 3.30, but coming there found he had been sent for to Cork where they are having "a strenuous time" at the election. Then to Yeats, not so well as at Coole. I went very tired to bed, not much sleep, cold and over tired.

On Thursday 18th to the Abbey, they were rehearsing *The Image*. It seems to be going smoothly the players like it. *Juno* had not done so well as before during last week. The Drama League performance had to be put off last Monday through Miss Crowe's illness, and Dolan complains that although the Drama League knew this at 4 o'c, the people who arrived were kept waiting outside the Theatre till 8, and then sent away in very bad humour, and that they don't distinguish between Drama League performances and ours, and lay the blame on us. Dolan furious at this, and at having "all the mess" of the D.L. performance left to him to clear away. George Yeats on the other hand had said they would give up having the Abbey players in future they give too much trouble, so a separation would probably be best, even Perrin complaining of the trouble given by these performances.

A letter from Kiernan saying the Lane Committee is again delayed by the Chairman's illness, almost a relief, but fearing bad news every day.

Then on Wednesday the Carnegie meeting. I had dreaded it, but it was easy in the end. A.E. in the chair and he read the Provost's letter of resignation (giving no reason) and wrote, or induced L.R. to write, an answer begging him to reconsider it. And that put off further trouble until the next meeting, two or three months hence. L.R. read Father Finlay's letter giving his reasons for resigning. I thought it an astounding one, have asked for a copy. I wanted to send someone perhaps Smith Gordon, with the resolution, to the Provost, to explain to him that the paper which caused all the mischief—*To-Morrow* is now practically extinct, as it is going to become a Republican paper, and thus cuts off Yeats and L.R. and other "intellectuals" from it, and it from theology. But there was no enthusiasm for coaxing the Provost. Smith Gordon refused to go and said anyhow the Provost would never rejoin after Finlay's letter. For he had said to him after the last meeting that "When a clergyman of a Christian Church took the view Father Finlay had done he felt he must go with him, and see eye to eye with him". I said "If the Provost intends to see eye to eye with the Catholic church he is not a Protestant". They all burst out laughing and agreed, but S. Gordon said he had not actually used the words eye to eye, but only equivalent ones. Wilkinson the Cork Librarian said it didn't matter whether we had clerics on the Board or not, "the people want the books and will have them". He showed me the figures for Cork, but I cried out at so much fiction, because they can always buy that in the little cheap editions and do so, and I said I didn't see why we supply for instance Ethel Dell. He said St. J. Ervine had lectured in Cork lately and had called out against Ethel Dell.[19] A good deal of history is read, and I believe that should head the list if we reduced the mass of worthless novels.

Yeats had been to his doctor who says blood pressure is only down by ten. He is going to London now, and Devonshire, and

London again, no Italy till April. Yesterday I found him excited because he had been having a discussion with Bryan Cooper who has some plan for organizing ex-service men and who said "we must get the support of the Catholic Church", whereas Yeats thinks that Protestants have been too amiable and weak towards that Church and have so helped to increase the troubles of the country.

Young Donaghy came to see me, very hopeful and joyous and looking well, has written an essay, hoping for a prize, on the suppression of Monasteries by Henry VIII, and has nearly finished his Deirdre play. A nice young fellow. The elections results. S. Dublin and N. Mayo were called out, both defeats for the Government. I said "The Republicans have now got the enthusiasm of the young, but the Government have not got the enthusiasm of the old" and Yeats agreed, but says the Dublin candidate, Cosgrave's man, is a publican no one cared for or took any interest in.

Yesterday, 20th I saw Blythe at 11 o'c. He was very encouraging, had spoken to the executive Council about helping the Abbey and they incline to it. I told him our need, our actors underpaid, our actor Manager getting only £6—7 a week; our building so shaky and wanting repair etc.—as in Carnegie appeal). He asked how much we want to keep going, and I asked for £1000 a year, and £1000 down for repairs. He will go into figures with Tulloch.

SATURDAY, 22 [NOVEMBER]; To Abbey yesterday; told Dolan and Perrin about Blythe. Both pleased. Both complaining of Drama League. I went to say goodbye to Yeats who is off to England and he walked back with me. I worked hard at *Bourgeois Gentilhomme*, till bedtime. Another bad night, Abbey and Drama League the chief worry.

23 NOVEMBER. I worked at the *Bourgeois* most of yesterday, just going to the Abbey through the rain for a part of first act of *Retrievers*,[20] a thin play, but Sally wonderfully fine as the half-witted old servant. I had brought up a barmbrack, and ordered tea and bought cakes and had tea in the greenroom between the first and second acts. I had not invited any outsiders, weather too bad, and feared it would be a flat entertainment, but it was very pleasant. Morgan had come to see the play and I asked him round; he is sad at seeing the *Image* coming on, and he not in his old part of Hosty but was very much pleased because lately someone had told him of *Our Irish Theatre* of which he had never heard, and he bought it and found his own name—where Roosevelt introduces the players to his daughter—"This is Mr.

Morgan" &c. Larchet also came round in what *he* calls "the interval" when the second act began, and I talked to him and Sally about the *Bourgeois*. I proposed making a feature of the songs, having French airs to them, and at the last, as we can't have the apotheosis of old Jordain, as Coquelin did, bursting into triumphant music, the Marseillaise (I now think *Marlbrook se'n va t'en guerre* would be better). Larchet likes the idea and will help us, and I lay awake in the night thinking of it—making Jourdain say "Then if I'm not a Turk I'm still a good French citizen—Give us a good marching tune!" And I think of putting Sally and all the players who can sing on the stage as musicians in the first act, just wearing some of our heroic cloaks over their dress, and little paper half masks from Christmas crackers, that they may sing. I began putting words to "O Richard O mon roi"! "Alas my king and lord: Now all abandon thee: In the wide world no song is heard: Save mine to hold your memory."

And I had said at the theatre that Cleonte and Civiel should come on wearing ordinary cheap masks—of Turk and Merchant (we can touch them up) and Cleonte can take his off for a moment as he reveals himself to Lucile, and drop it again, and they thought that good. Then I had sat with Sally and the girls and Gorman and Casey through the second act and told them bits of folklore; they liked best Queen Elizabeth, and the little St. Patrick story of the soul parting from the body. A very pleasant restful hour.

I had finished before going to the Theatre the last chapter of *The Possessed*, very fine, that whole chapter of poor Stepanovitch's last wandering very touching, and then the ironical sentences "Je vous aimais toute ma vie" and Mme. Varvara's terrible whisper. "And when you were getting yourself up for Dasha you sprinkled yourself with scent!" And before that comes the meaning of the book, of the parable. "You see that's exactly like Russia, those devils that come out of the sick man and enter into the swine . . . all the devils great and small have multiplied in that great invalid, our beloved Russia, in the course of ages and ages and they will beg of themselves to enter into swine and indeed they may have entered into them already! They are we . . . and we shall cast ourselves down, possessed and raving, from the rocks into the sea, and we shall all be drowned, and a good thing too, that is all we are fit for. But the sick man will be healed and will 'sit at the feet of Jesus'".

A part of the prophecy seems to have come true in Russia—and perhaps elsewhere.

I bought some ballads in a little shop. The woman there spoke of the sadness of these years, "little boys you used to be selling marbles to, the best of them shot or thrown into prison". She did not seem hopeful.

Miss Fitz Henry writes about the lecture "I think you won the heart of every girl in the Hall" . . . F. Gallagher's Prison Diary in *Sinn Fein*[21] tells of making a stage with tables "twenty or thirty tiny prison tables placed together to form a platform. Blankets formed the curtain. The play was of course *The Workhouse Ward*, Cock Treacy, with an amazing wig of mattress filling being a Michael McInerney[22] beyond everything even Lady Gregory thought of".

MONDAY, 24 NOVEMBER. To Abbey rehearsal yesterday, 12 to 3. They all worked so hard at *Image*, and it won't be the players' fault if it doesn't succeed. Tea with Lady Ardilaun, pleasant being in the bright flower-filled house.

She lamented the change in London, the Royal garden parties—"You and I remember what they used to be, and now—! One of the Labour Ministers came in a tweed coat and the King himself spoke to him; said he could not say anything to his guests as to what they wore, but he could and would to his Ministers".

Then back here, and Casey for the evening. He is working at his play about Easter week, and he hopes it may be ready for Easter. It may not be popular, giving the human not the heroic side, the reverse of the battlefield. He told me of a woman whose son had been killed and who he had heard shouting curses on Connolly.

He is on Larkin's side in this Worker's Union dispute,[23] because he says he has intellectual uprightness and the leaders on the other side are not much good. He thinks if the Republicans get their daily paper (he hears they are buying the *Freeman*) it will force them to develop a policy. And if they have more victories they must he thinks come into the Dail and make some agreement with Cosgrave to demand the abolition or weakening of the oath. He is rather anxious about the military party "the five mutineers", the Tobin group;[24] they have a good deal of support, they would try to establish a military dictatorship. He doesn't believe they would do so, yet there are people he knows, shopkeepers, who won't have their houses painted because of the unrest and uncertainty. Cosgrave he hears when he had his pub in ———— Street was "a clean publican", wouldn't let his customers get drunk, or spend too much of their wages and was respected for that. I showed him my political ballads and asked him to get me any he came across and he said "I will send you one I wrote myself, 'The Grand Old Dame Britannia' ".[25] But that is one I have, and had read to Yeats the other day, saying it was though fine hardly simple enough for my book, and he had said I should put it in "it had literary quality".

25 NOVEMBER. *The Image* last night,[26] a small Monday audience but appreciative. It was beautifully acted. S.A. held the audience, even when the kitten Seaghan had brought escaped from her in the last act and walked down to the footlights, Donaghy was with me, liked the first and last acts best, especially the last, and I was glad as it was the one Yeats had been down on (but I still think he had forgotten the whole thing). I myself had almost forgotten the play, found it rich, harmonious, strange in its simplicity. L.R.'s witty little "Crabbed Youth and Age" very lively after it and a good contrast.

26 NOVEMBER. A wet yesterday, worked nearly all day at *Bourgeois Gentilhomme*. *Image* in the evening; pouring rain, small audience, Robinson and G. Y. there. A beautiful performance.

27 NOVEMBER. Casey came to tea yesterday. He has been reading his *Crimson in the Tricolour*[27] again and sees no merit at all in it. But he had eight years ago determined to have a play put on at the Abbey, and stuck to it till success came. He had bought my *Irish Theatre* and had read in it that if a play showed any sign of promise we write a personal note, but if hopeless send only a printed form. Though so disappointed when *Crimson in the Tricolour* had come back he was cheered "when he had had time to recover from his first shock" by finding a note from L.R. And also L.R. had enclosed him my detailed criticism on the various characters &c (he had been pleased by the note on the Mayor's wife. "She is a jewel"), and this showed the rejection had not been made in a hurry.

He brought me the *Irish Rosary*[28] with an article, "The Squinting Windows School" attacking *To-Morrow* and the *Irish Statesman*, with a hit at the Abbey Theatre. But he says it is very little read. I noticed the great number of advertisements but he says these are sent by influence of the Church.

Six of my Trinity Hall girls at the Abbey on my invitation. I had Donaghy and L.R. to meet them and gave them tea in the hall. A pouring night, small audience, beautiful performance, Sally applauded at each exit.

29 NOVEMBER. Pouring wet evenings, very small audience but the players wonderful, say they love their parts "and the beautiful rhythm". Rather a troublesome ten minutes with L.R. He had told Perrin to suggest Arthur Shields getting a higher salary which he has asked for . . . I looked at the list, he gets £4,

the same as McCormick and Miss Delany, both far more valuable and doing far better work; his brother so very fine only £2.10, Dolan only £3 for his acting (besides acting as Manager). Impossible! And then L.R. came in and I said so. He said "Shields can't live on £4". I said that did not bear on the question, one could not put him above far finer workers—McCormick stage manager as well as actor. He was cross and went away in a huff. (McC. gets 15/- extra for s.m.) He ought rather to find some other work for Shields to do, as Nolan, who comes when we want him.

Jack Yeats and Casey and Donaghy to tea. Casey still very anxious about the military group, says they have 20,000 men, armed. But I cannot think they will use arms, they would have no popular support. They talked of the schoolchildren being taught Irish. S.O'C. says it is nonsense, they are forced to learn it and the teachers forced to teach it though knowing it imperfectly, just the numbers and the Lord's Prayer, little more than that. He himself had worked at learning it with enthusiasm some years ago and mastered it completely, the spoken language, before he even read a line. Jack is learning it now at a class but hasn't got on very far.

Some good sentences in the *Irish Statesman* by A.E. We want "the quality of mind we find in Bishop Berkeley, in Bernard Shaw and in many others who had that aristocracy of mind which probes truth for itself".

And on Russell "There is no doubt that a nation let alone with no outside enemies will bring its own social order into harmony with what is natural and humane in the character of its people".

30 NOVEMBER. Yesterday wet. Worked at *Bourgeois* and wrote letters. Then to Abbey matinée, good stalls; the play went well. Lady Ardilaun had a party there and took me back to tea at 42 Stephens Green, a pleasant change, the house full of beautiful flowers. And it was like a change of plays at the Abbey, from my intercourse with what I may call progressives, Jack and the others last night, and the actors in the greenroom, all living in a world that is alive, and these in a decaying one. A sort of *ancien régime* party, a lament for banished society. Mrs. Plunkett, the Bishop's wife talked of the burned houses "and if they rebuild them they will be burned again. And if they are not burned who will want to live in them with no society? And all we are paying in postage! And the posts so slow in coming. . . ." Lady A. herself very good and bright, loving our theatre and gathering what scraps of surviving friends she can yet angry with the people—"all bad". But in practice she is kind and if she lived in

the country I am sure would help them. She says there is no chance of any young men of our class getting employment in the future. Some relative of hers had given up a foreign appointment and come back, and knows languages and is very well fitted to be a consul or foreign representative. But he could get nothing from the Government and one of the questions asked was "What did you do in the war?—The war against England?" But an old gentleman whose name I forget (I think Stoney) was louder in his regrets; had been to the Castle, now occupied by lawyers, on some business, and recalled with grief the nights when the ball-room was filled with company. "If you gave a dance then you had only to send a note to the Barracks asking forty or fifty or whatever number of officers you wanted. Now who is there for our daughters to dance with?" (true enough that). "And the Govenor General gets £37,000 a year and what is there to show for it? The Cadogans had only £20,000 and entertained so splendidly". I said I had only been once to the V.R. Lodge in those days, to see Lord Aberdeen about *Blanco Posnet*. "Oh Aberdeen, he wasn't much. But the Cadogans![29] Now the town is peopled with ghosts, it is sad to see the empty houses as you walk about Fitzwilliam Square. The Arnotts' the only house that exists in Merrion Square!"

1 DECEMBER. Yesterday pleasant. Anne and Michael in the morning, staying and playing for a while. Frank later and family talk. Then Donaghy. I had read the 1st and 2nd Acts of his play during the day, and was glad to find it a fine thing in thought and conception though a little stiff in language and wanting some links put in. But whether there is any chance of a Deirdre play ever being acted again I don't know, our Abbey being now so much given to popular work and the Drama League to foreign. I talked it over with him, he has real grit, and intellect. Then we went to a performance by the Father Matthew Hall company at the Abbey of the *Passing of the Third Floor Back*.[30] I was critical at first, the acting seeming feeble after ours on that stage, and when the "passer by" came on, an unimposing figure with a mannerism, putting his head on one side as he talks, I thought Forbes Robertson was needed to make the play effective. But as it went on it gripped, and the Passer (Corrigan) grew in intensity, and the meaning seized one. A fine Sunday sermon, though the presentation of the best self rather knocks out the foundation of the play I had been brooding over, the discovery of the best in each by believing in it—my "Woman who was a great fool".

3 DECEMBER. Home again, found all peaceful though drenched, the fields along the railway like lakes.

7 DECEMBER. Bad weather but got a little done in the garden. And indoors I have worked hard at *Bourgeois Gentilhomme*, have just finished the translation and begun typing it.

No news of the pictures yet. I am anxious.

Looking through my accounts also I am anxious, so much had to be spent this year, the usual rates, taxes, labour, wages. And over £20 extra to Raftery for altering the wall at gate and doing up stable and house eaves. Then the upholstery and carpets and painting for the house, shabbiness too apparent; and the chicks' two bicycles and the yard one. And the two visits to London about the pictures. And only £69 came in, wool, cattle, rabbits! And incoming from publishers and plays £30 short of last year so far. I may have to get out the memoir but hate the idea.

Congregation of eleven at church today.

16 DECEMBER. I've been working very hard at *Bourgeois Gentilhomme*, but today finished and put it up to send to Dublin tomorrow. The typing troublesome and I moved my Remington down to the fire in breakfastroom, the translating itself pleasant enough, the joy of finding the right word. Dances will have to be cut out for our stage but I think it will go well.

On Saturday a letter from Kiernan saying the Commissioners were to hold their deferred meeting yesterday, Monday. So I have been and am in a new anxiety, not seeing how they could give it against us, but puzzled as to what new evidence they can be taking. Margaret wrote that Anne and Catherine might be here tomorrow, I hope so, the darlings.

There has been a letter from Dr. Gilmartin, Ap. of Tuam to the *Independent* saying he had some time ago resigned from the Carnegie Committee "and in view of recent developments am glad I did so", and hoping any Catholic who may still be connected with the organization will be careful as to what books are chosen. And L.R. in a lecture on the drama desired the abolition of critics "an insult to the intelligence of the audience"; and "Jacques"[31] very indignant responds in the *Independent* and says among other things "The sin of Sodom is not a fitting subject for plays" (there has been no allusion to that on our stage). So he will I'm afraid renew his enmity just after Dr. Lombard Murphy had been amiable to me about softening towards the Abbey.

I have finished *The Idiot*. Very fine. His suffering made up for in part by those flashes of vision just before unconsciousness—"What if it is disease" he thinks—"what does it matter that it is an abnormal intensity if the result, if the moment of sensation, remembered and analysed afterwards in health, turns out to be the acme of harmony and beauty, and gives a feeling, unknown and undivined till then, of completeness, of proportion, of reconciliation, and of ecstatic devotional merging in the highest synthesis of life"?

It is as it were a spark from that flash that comes, even to me, sometimes, but very seldom. And again, though he gives it as quoted from an Old Believer. "He who has no roots beneath him has no God"—"the man who has renounced his fatherland has renounced his God". And he has a dream that "reveal to the Russian the 'world' of Russia, let him find the gold, the treasure hidden from him in the earth! Show him the whole of humanity, rising again and renewed by Russian thought alone, by the Russian God and Christ". It was happy for him to die before the Russian earthquake, its volcano, sent up its loud and redhot rubble. We are better off in Ireland. Though today's paper says the new English Government will cancel the registration of the Treaty with the League of Nations. That will make the Republicans rejoice and injure the Government. But if England behaves badly about this and the Boundary we may all unite against her, and perhaps harmony may come though a louder discord. Now I have begun reading *The House of the Dead*.

20 DECEMBER. Casey writes "The *Playboy* is going well; it seems as if, at last, we had decided to call him comrade". There is no opposition at all this time.

Anne and C. came back on Wednesday, just as ever, so bright and cheery delighted to be home, riding Pud and Tommy, gathering primroses and periwinkles and buttercups still flowering in the woods.

I have sent off the *Bourgeois*. A relief.

22 DECEMBER. Storm and rain, but Guy told us at church yesterday he is motoring to Athenry to fetch Margaret and Richard, it may be calmer then. Mr. Trotter read instead of a sermon a paper on peace by the Bishop of Winchester. I, not realizing at first it was not his own was startled when I heard him speak of "that wonderful play *St. Joan* by Bernard Shaw".

W. F. Barrett in the *Times* today, writing on telepathy says "there is strong presumption of the existence in our personality of an immaterial entity, a soul or transcendental self, which is not limited to the confines of our body or conditioned by matter, time or space. Here and now this self lies below the threshold of consciousness and apparently comes into touch, and can interfuse with other souls, whilst our conscious lives emerge like peaks from a dense mist, a mist that comes and hides the vast plain which unites all sentient beings with one another and with the universal".[32]

4 o'c Post just brought a letter from Colonel Mitchell saying they are breaking up Carnegie Committee "as it is no longer representative" because of the resignations. The best thing they could do I think.

26 DECEMBER. And L.R. writes "I have been awfully busy and worried. The Carnegie situation has resolved itself into the suspension of the Committee and my dismissal. It's a complete victory for the obscurantists but only a temporary one I think, as even within the last ten days the county Councils of Clare, Cork and Monaghan have passed resolutions asking for county schemes, so the work will go on. I am awfully sorry that all your work at that horrible meeting in October has resulted only in this. I blame cowardly people like D.O'Brien who were for placating the Church at any price—as Tom O'Donnell says 'the most priest-ridden people in Ireland are the ex-Unionists'". He says also "I love your Molière, I think that with a really sparkling production it might be a big popular success . . . I do sincerely congratulate you on your achievement".

Christmas over, Guy and Olive here for it. The children happy. Richard shot a woodcock today, and Guy has given Anne a gun. The wrenboys, four sets, here today. They still sing Kevin Barry rather than any other song. In the afternoon I was called down to see "more wrenboys"—they were the three children dressed up and doing their little performance extraordinarily well and funnily—"Kevin Barry" and the concertina and dancing; and the two dogs, at first distant, recognised and jumped on them and barked. The servants were looking on in ecstasy.

27 DECEMBER. Richard's report good—Upper Fifth Form—"Satisfactory and consistent worker". (But "Latin weak prose wild") French "maintaining a very satisfactory level of intelligent work, Trials 3rd. Good". Science "A promising boy—done some excellent work especially in Physics. Trials 1st. v.g.". Engineering, "Quite satisfactory, rather slow". House Master "A quite satisfactory term, though he must work hard at Latin or he will jeopardise his certificate". (Robert would have grounded the darling child as well in Latin as his father did him. But I am glad his mind goes exploring for itself as he missed that influence).

28 DECEMBER. Our first snow today.

The *Leader* of 20th sent me by Casey has an attack on A.E. as being influenced by Plotinus—"this man called to Rome to rekindle the dying fires of a monstrous creed that had outraged both heaven and earth. The lectures . . . are simply the last and greatest polemic ever made for the sustainment of False Gods and the false uses of human life". But yesterday's *Independent* has a sonnet praising not only McKenna the translator but Plotinus himself! They can hardly have known of the *Leader* article. I have been looking again into Inge on his "Philosophy"—"Mysticism above all other types of human thought is nearly the same always and everywhere" . . . treats him as "the last of the great Greek philosophers as indeed he was" and says "A thinker may be in advance of his contemporaries but not of his age. The great man gives voice to the deepest thoughts of his own epoch". I looked at the bits I had copied out—one comes ever nearer me as age advances—"use your body as a musician uses his lyre: when it is worn out you can still sing without accompaniment". And I found a note I had myself written after reading Inge—"I feel that neo-Platonism was a straining up towards God; Christianity the descent of God to man". And last evening, opening the last Literary Supplement I found an article on Donne.[33] "It is not remarkable that Donne should have moved over from the Neo-Platonists to the Christians because of his realization of the significance of Christ—St. Augustine said of them 'only the Word made flesh, that found I not among them'. Similarly Donne says that it is useless to believe that Plato can teach us to believe in God, for in him though we certainly find a God we find no Christ".

30 DECEMBER. A nice letter from Molly Childers and one from Yeats. He is better and liked Sidmouth but says "I like Coole best".

Coen here to collect rates. I paid my £71 and he says there will be the same due in August. I hope I may be able to go on.

31 DECEMBER. Writing to Bank of England to sell out £845. The money received by me under A's will (sale of house and furniture &c). This I give to the children to help pay legacy duty on what she left them, as well as not taking my own legacy of £486 (in all with expenses off £1135).

1 JANUARY, 1925. Alone, but happy the children are in new surroundings at Lough Cutra this stormy wet day. My own thoughts last night sad, John Quinn's kind presence in America gone; and Arabella's love for the children and her interest in all that concerns us, and her Christmas and birthday hampers and parcels. Then Hugh's pictures still in enemy hands, a long trial of patience and a long anxiety, and the fear of having to renew the fight under this anti-Irish Government.

But in spite of sadness I must not grumble at the past year, the children are so well; and so bright and simple and happy—(Richard "Oh! a week has gone!" last Monday). But they are only here now for Christmas and whatever bits of the summer holidays they are not at Burren—that makes my life more lonely, and to them less necessary. And M's discontent makes me wonder sometimes "is it worthwhile?" And money, though only £7 under last year's earnings makes me anxious—rates, income tax on land, labour, and those outside repairs before the household expenses begin. I'm afraid I must try to publish the memoir which I've grown cowardly about. But the home once broken up could never be restored. As long as the children are happy here I must go on.

My work last year *Brigit*. And lately the Molière translation;[34] and I've made the additions to the *Kiltartan History*. But none of these mean money "worth while". I had a bad night, all these things in my head. But I have turned to my copybooks. Traherne says "We should be all Life and Mettle and Vigour and Love to everything, and that would poise us". And I had written there a year ago. "One day last week I thought how we had been always told to try and get to Heaven; but should we not rather have been told to strive to live there, to bring it about us now".

2 JANUARY. Such a storm yesterday, I never got out, it is seldom that happens; and didn't send to Gort. But the *Independent* came in the evening, and I see in it that the Lane Committee are to sit on the 8th to consider their report, and that when it is sent in the Government will decide whether it is to be published. So the week after next I should know.

Another stormy night and morning.

A cheerful cheque, £19.6.5. from French, *Jester* played at Kingston and *Golden Apple* at Roundwood—and the usual comedies.

3 JANUARY. Some discords in the house but I am writing out bits from "Neo-Platonists"—Plotinus—to try and see past these clouds to the clear beyond. I've been sending my brother Edward a haunch of the venison Guy brought me, remembering his account of having gone to help our Vereker cousins to shoot the deer there before Lord Gort left and before the place had come into Gough hands.

6 JANUARY. Darling Richard's birthday, his 16th. Thank God he has come safe so far. He looked so happy last night, the drawing-room lighted up, the card table near the fire, he and Anne and Catherine, Margaret, Olive, Mrs. Scovell, Guy. I, sitting near them could see Robert's shadowy portrait on the wall and I felt he would approve. But what a birthday it would have been could he have been here—that is the heartbreak.

I gave Richard today my husband's little revolver to practise with at marks and he is pleased.

8 JANUARY. The birthday went so happily, no outside guests to be had, yet we never had a merrier evening. The bonfire lighted well, and Richard and Anne raced after each other with lighted wisps gigantic fireflies tearing about. And they all dressed up for dinner, had ransacked the camphor chests. I was but "A Spanish grandmother" with high comb and mantle and diamonds and Margaret hadn't time to dress at all when she had costumed the others. Mrs. Scovell came down in a "Du Maurier", and I was sitting with her in the drawing-room when "Miss Persse of Roxboro" was announced and a young lady came in with ringlets, with my old Paris purple brocade (worn as I see in a photograph at Fanny Trench's wedding and she is a grandmother!) and a fan; a very sweet thoughtful face and gentle manner. I was puzzled for a minute and only when the profile was turned I knew it was Richard! The gentle manner continued till towards the end of dinner when he suddenly seized and ate an apple in schoolboy fashion. Then a very tall officer in scarlet—Olive! and a cornet in ditto Anne—and a drummer in the little uniform Mrs. Chatteris had given Anne and that now fits Catherine. Guy had a Highland costume, also from the camphor boxes; and swords were in all directions. We had the maids up after dinner to see them, and Mrs. Scovell played and they danced, Guy a sword dance. Richard said it was the pleasantest birthday he had ever had. (They had gone to the woods for a bit for woodcock) and Guy thought it the pleasantest birthday he had ever known. So they have been happy indoors and out, Richard bringing in a woodcock this morning and Anne a rabbit. But now Margaret has a cold and is in bed.

12 JANUARY. Yesterday, Sunday, so very few in church, only four in the sittings, Guy opposite in his gallery, Rita and George Daly and the Mitchells, Richard with me (the other chicks had colds). Daphne and Mr. Newbold here; Guy to lunch and take them back to Lough Cutra for the night. Margaret and Olive went also. I read *Dr. Doolittle* to the chicks and got them to bed earlier than usual. Today they are on the lake with their guns.

13TH. I stopped writing there, for the wind was rising and I felt a little uneasy about the darlings. Then Margaret came back and said I ought not to have let them go. I went down to the lake and watched and watched, dusk coming on but no sign of them. Then I thought they might have landed farther down, because of the wind, and be walking back through the woods. And once I saw the sheep in the hobble field running, and thought they must hear them coming, but could see or hear nothing. I walked up and down but because of the flood could not get outside the wood to see along the lake, and I had begun to feel terribly anxious when suddenly the boat appeared round the trees and the little troop landed in high spirits, having been on an island where they shot three woodcock, Richard two, Anne one. There were goat on the island, McLoughlins, and the whole adventure delighted them. What happier day could a schoolboy have had than this, going out in his own boat to such wild sport? It comforted me for many anxieties and troubles of the year.

14 JANUARY. But alas yesterday after a very stormy night, the boat had disappeared, Mike thinks the wire had been cut not broken. He [and] John searched yesterday and again this morning, and Mike has gone up the river now, but "No tale or tidings of it". I am very sad, the disappointment just as the chicks had been so delighted with it. And that, and these Gort lads with their dogs and guns, is a breach in our peace. I hope they will not know it was taken—if it was.

15 JANUARY. No sign of the boat, it is sad, and such a lovely day. Happily they are playing on the squash tennis court in the barn, I had to tell them it was gone and that perhaps lads on the other side may be using it. Mike wants to go to the Civic Guard, but I have more hope in our own people.

Tea at Lough Cutra yesterday. Read plays for the Abbey, one of F. H. O'Donnell the best he has written,[35] and one by a new writer I think good. That is encouraging.

16 JANUARY. A good beginning of the day. Mike at the door to say the boat has been found, just across the river, near Raheen, upside down and wedged between two rocks, so it was the storm that was guilty. Such a relief! And such a joy the children can have it. And also, Tom O'L. and McN. helped to get it out and bring it back, and this may be the beginning of a better feeling towards and from them. I have written to the two Gort young preachers, and hope that matter also may be got through without war.

I began last evening reading Zola's *Débacle*,[36] extraordinarily vivid the beginning, the soldiers coming from Paris shouting hopes of getting "A Berlin"!, of sending 400,000 men right through Germany to separate north from south; to win such victories as would make Austria and Italy come to their side. And then the sudden news of disaster, of Weissenberg, of Woerth, then Sedan: the beginning of the retreat to France.

I remember so well that news coming in the papers and the pleasure with which it was greeted; that good industrious Protestant Germany beating those vain bombastic infidel French. And

I cannot feel sure it might not have been better for the world if they had beaten them again in this last war.

18 JANUARY. No, I suppose military domination could have been worse even than this break up of countries and communities. We may be over the worst.

The chicks and Margaret have gone to Church, I was glad of a Sunday morning at home; read *Sutra Nipata*.[37] "The study of worthless writings" is one of the sins Buddha tells us to avoid.

19 JANUARY. The chicks out in the boat yesterday, Anne shot a woodcock. Dalys to lunch. Tired . . .

20 JANUARY. They, Richard and Anne, M. Geoghagan, with Mike and John to beat, are off to Inchy in the boat with sandwiches, for the day.

Reading a little poem of A.E.'s *Exiles*[38] made me think of a possible play. And a nice letter from H. Speakman this morning about *Brigit* gives me more courage.

Written to by M. Henri Corbière for my "Maxim of Life" I wrote my old thought, "it is my desire to live by law and love. Law the serenity of order; love the joy of self-sacrifice".

H. Speakman said in his letter ". . . If tears still came to my eyes at the third reading of your play, it was not at Daniel crying 'Crucify him' nor at his going out with the nails, but at the lad *Joel* crying 'Crucify him'! Haven't I walked Ireland with a donkey cart"?

Anne laid up with a cold, I don't know if she can leave tomorrow.

A. Birrell writes: "Your woodcocks came on my 75th birthday and as they were the only Present I received on that melancholy occasion they were all the more welcome and Tony and I have already devoured them. Time was when I was in the receipt of many such gifts, but now, owing I suppose to Death Duties and supertax, you are the sole survivor of my Territorial Acquaintances who once sent me Game! Many many thanks! I might send you in return some *Crabs* and *Lobsters*, but just now they are not to be had".

I like to think I in Ireland am still a "Territorial Acquaintance" sending gifts while England has failed.

23 JANUARY. The seventh anniversary of Robert's death.

Margaret left with Richard and Catherine but left Anne, a cold not allowing her to travel, and she is delighted to have a little more time here. Poor little Catherine came down in her school uniform, looking so nice, but went off for a farewell ride, and a bullock rushing from a hedge frightened Pud who threw her and galloped off home. Johnny Hehir caught him and went in search of her, she was not hurt but her dress and even her hair was caked with mud. It seemed impossible she could travel in that costume, or take it, but Marian plunged it into hot water and washed it and it dried just in time for her to put on again, though very subdued, poor little thing, and indeed she had a narrow escape, having fallen on her back. I comforted her with little gifts. They have loved their holiday and want to come back instead of going to Isle of Wight or Etretat, so I feel my struggle to keep on the place has not been in vain. Houston came for Richard's gun, but he shot a woodcock in the garden before that. I asked if he expected a remove this term; he said no. He is as high as he can be in the school without a special examination. He has been so boyish and simple, like Robert, though science appeals to him, not literature, and his *Weekly Wireless* was his chief study. I think of Walt Whitman in *Brooklyn Ferry*[39]— ". . . play the old role, the role that is great or small according as we make it"— And I read in his preface . . . "the great poet—he is no arguer, he is judgement. He judges not as the judge judges, but as the sun falling around a helpless thing".

Still reading that Terrible Downfall—the abominations of Sedan. These new inventions of poison gas, destroying a community swiftly, may be better than the cruelty of sending out those boys and men to be maimed and slaughtered, to suffer agony, they know not for what.

24 JANUARY. Poor A's birthday. Her first away from us.

A wet day and so dark the advertised eclipse of the sun was hardly to be noticed.[40] Anne and I alone, her cold heavy still. I began reading her the *Last of the Mohicans*,[41] her first introduction to the Leatherstocking tales, she is delighted with it so far. That and some typing and tidying up after the holidays have pretty well filled the day.

27 JANUARY. Anne now at Pathfinder, consoled for a wet day with very little outing.

I finished last night that most powerful and terrible *Débacle*, the Commune tragedy explaining something of our own, the war lust awakened and then turned against their own government and army. It would be a good book for the Carnegie. Galway has sent me a list of proposed additions with request to mark any I object to. The more solid books are perhaps dull but unobjectionable. There is an immense list of fiction, almost all by authors—novelists—I don't even know the names of, it looks like a surplus sale. I have written saying this, and that (as I told Wilkinson the Cork Librarian) I think we give too much fiction, it is the only thing in the way of books that can be had easily and for very little, at shops and railway stalls. It is finer work we want, only the best novels, and plenty of history, plenty of travel and of biography, my own first choice in any new bookshelf I come across in a house.

The best poems of 1924 came today, my "Old Woman" in it, which Anne made me read her.

A letter from Casey today, he has dined "with J. Larkin and a Communist organiser and we spoke among other things of Hugh Lane. Jim told us of a dinner he had with Sir Hugh in America, and talked of the various artists represented in the Hugh Lane gift to our city. He mentioned that he remained quiet about the matter for fear his championship would have the effect of hardening the hearts of those anxious to retain them. He has asked me to write to ask you to permit him to play the *Rising of the Moon* in the Queen's Theatre on Sunday next. The Union is holding a concert there and Jim would like to show the work of an Abbey playwright to many who have never been inside the Abbey Theatre". I am giving leave—my heart goes out more to workers than to idlers.

29 JANUARY. W. Whitman finds hope for all even "the old man who has lived without purpose and feels it with bitterness worse than gall".

I am trying to get some form into that idea for a play, the belief in good awakening good.

The Bagots spent yesterday here, Bagot and Anne went to the woods and each shot a woodcock. Mrs. B. stayed in and talked of Molly's engagement. Another storm last night, and this morning wet and stormy. I didn't send for post, did cross word puzzles with Anne till post time. Now doing a little typing and getting down some ideas for the play.

Lough Cutra workshop broken into the night before last and the tools all stolen.

DUBLIN, 3 FEBRUARY. RUSSELL HOTEL. A rather tiring journey up; but Anne was happy with *The Prairie* and Crossword puzzles and our picnic lunch at Athenry. We went straight to the Abbey and saw *Cathleen ni Houlihan* and *Mineral Workers*, Anne quite pleased and laughed at the jokes in M.W. and clapped, and I took her round to see Sara Allgood in her dressing-room, who sang a little song about three little fairies for her. And then we saw Sean O'Casey in the Greenroom and he sang a little song in Irish for her, and she gave Sally her woodcock, the last she had shot.

On Sunday 1 February, we went to St. Patrick's looked at the monuments and listened to the music and said our prayers. After lunch into the Municipal Gallery, Anne's first visit there, and she saw the portrait of Hugh, and of John Shawe-Taylor, and Mancini's of me, and Epstein's bust, and Robert's picture *The Lake*. In the evening I took her to Kingstown, not sure if I should have to cross with her myself, but we met her escort, and I got back by 10 o'c very tired but my mind at rest. It is a rest being a few days away from home, the holidays bring much thought for housekeeping, and then I had been anxious about Anne's journey. She herself very sweet bright and joyous. Yesterday, Monday, I went to the Abbey, I was dissatisfied with the plays arranged for the next weeks, poor revivals or revivals of poor plays. We have been losing money nearly every week, Dolan says because of the strike of billposters and that it doesn't matter what we put on just now. But I say if we have to lose money we must keep self respect and keep up good work, and I got L.R. to come there and we decided to drop *The Man Who Missed the Tide*, and *Young Man from Rathmines*, and to hurry on *John Bull* for next week, and put the *The Playboy* this month, and to put Casey's *Kathleen Listens In*[42] on with *Heart's Desire* and Miss McArdle's *Old Man*[43] instead of *Rathmines Young Man*.

I had kept him waiting, because seeing the film *America* was on close by, and being full of Alexander Hamilton and Washington from re-reading *The Conqueror*,[44] I wanted to see it, and went in at 1.30 never dreaming it would last longer than my 3 o'c appointment with L.R. But it lasted till quarter to four, and I was jammed in the middle of a bench and couldn't get out and so kept him waiting. But he had waited for me, and I sent for tea and bread and butter having had nothing since breakfast, and when we had talked our business and he said he was going to London tomorrow I asked if he thought I could get some lectures, my courage having risen since my success with the Trinity Hall girls, and my Income Tax and rates on Coole frightening me. He was very nice and will consult an agent. I am happier for having made the effort even if it fails.

The *America* film[45] was wonderful, the historic part, though a love story running through was rather tedious. No wonder it is banned in England, and no wonder *Sinn Fein* had advised its readers to go and see it, for England isn't spared, the persuading of the Indians to take part against the Americans; English officers "disguising themselves as Indians that they may the better vent their cruelty on the prisoners". And there was cheering whenever the English armies were seen running away. Yet enough was given of the horror of war to make Republicans know what might have to be met should the English come back.

The end shows the triumph of the Colonists, their pride in a new nationhood, in their flag. Yet before a century had passed (1780–1861) the Civil war had broken out and they were killing one another as we the other day, and as the French Communists after the Franco-Prussian war.

Casey came to tea with me. He says Jim Larkin has gained the day, has conquered the Transport Union, has 30,000 men enrolled. He has not joined the Republicans but has advised them to vote Republican, because the workers must be against all Governments. The priests will be yet more against him, because he is going to have a celebration in honour of Lenin. "Why does he honour him?" "Because he had done so much for the workers. Jim has been in Russia, to Moscow, and to the Ukraine. He says the workers there are treated better than anywhere else. They get little or nothing in money, or pay, but everyone is secure of food, one good meal a day, soup. The doctors say that is best for health, only one good meal and biscuits or something of the sort for other meals. The children are well fed and looked after. It is the spirit more than the body that is thought of, there are small theatres everywhere, the workmen run them themselves. It is not true they banish Christianity, the churches are open except when there is not enough of a congregation for them to be kept up. Christianity is not encouraged but it is allowed." Larkin had seen a good deal of Hugh Lane in America and had dined with him, and rails against the stupidity of the Corporation in refusing his terms.

I, now reading *Alton Locke*,[46] asked Casey if such horrors are now possible among workers. He says that though children are not employed here so young (though they are in America) the conditions are terrible, in some cases, ceaseless working to keep body and soul together. And the housing here is terrible, 20,000 families in Dublin living each in one room. The only solution seems to be running cheap trains out of the city and building there, he believes there is a large acreage belonging to the Corporation that might be built on.

Evening to the Abbey to see Drama League in Benavente's *School for Princesses*, bad acting for the most part now they don't have our actors (except Miss Delany and A. S. who was *very* bad). A witty play, or play of witty dialogue, rather stiffly translated. Stalls nearly full of Drama League subscribers. I came away before the last act, read it here this morning.

4 FEBRUARY. Yesterday rather troublesome. Sally Allgood came to see me. Her new agreement cuts her salary, taking off a percentage on takings over £100 and cutting her £10 in half any

week she is not playing. She came chiefly to complain that she is now left without work this and next week. Her old part in *Country Dressmaker* is taken by Miss Craig, but that she doesn't seem to mind, but the little part she liked in *An Imaginary Conversation*[47] is given to a quite new girl. Next week her part Nora—in *John Bull* has been given to Miss Craig. D. had not told me this and I sent for him between acts of *Dressmaker* last evening. He said Sally wasn't good as Nora, and that she would want rehearsing and take too much of his time, and that Miss Craig "has a husband and children to support". I was vexed but had to give in as he is manager. He says "Sally is no draw" (among his friends). Anyhow it gave me a bad night, troubled. I feel that both she and the theatre are being wronged.

Casey lent me *Catholic Bulletin* with its article on L.R., stupid and vulgar, but I'm glad they realise what the result of that action of the priests and Provost has been. "What a dignified and happy status for Irish County Councils and Urban Councils to be in, during the year 1925 in a 'Free Ireland', if you please, under the absolutist control of this 'united Kingdom Trust' whose make-up nobody appears to know, but who meet at Dunfermline, North Britain" ("Und das hat mit ihre singen Provost and Priest gethan").

5 FEBRUARY. Frank came yesterday to help me with the Income Tax on Coole but said I had better go to a professional, Z., I've been to him today. F. when I told him X. the Galway Income Tax man seemed rather cracked, said he drinks. And that is my opinion of the other Bourke, who had only arrived at his office at midday, hadn't looked at his letters, was very flushed and there was an odour of spirits in the office, so at each end Alcohol is King! However he wrote me a list of questions about stock, &c and anyhow I cannot do this work myself, my brain refuses to act.

Donaghy came to tea, frank and bright and fresh. Then O'Rourke to ask leave to play *Rising of the Moon* for a week, which I gave at half price. Then Casey with his *Kathleen listens in*. We went through it to try and sharpen it up a bit and rise at the close. I talked again of Lenin and the Russian workers, wanting to know what force controls them, who is real Sovereign. He says the Red Army. But thinks this and all depend upon the Soviets, the people's will.

At the Abbey I had a little talk with Larchet. He had been musical adviser to Mulcahy while he was in power and says he did wonders. Amongst other things it was he who brought over Colonel Brase. They had tried in France, thinking it would give them a man more in sympathy with us, but the French were too busy with their own affairs so they went on to Berlin and found Brase, who had been in the Kaizer's employ, over his orchestra, and who was hoping to get to America. They brought him here; with pay and house &c he has over £1000 a year, and has done wonders. There are other musical schemes, and Larchet hopes Mulcahy will come into power again to carry them out. Says he often comes to the Abbey. Acting in *Country Dressmaker* very good. Audience but small.

Today, 5th, after my interview on Income Tax I went (in pouring rain) to see the Yeats children; found Michael alone in the nursery, glad to see me, pulled out a chair and said "Will you sit down". Then to A.E., he and Miss Mitchell eating their lunch. He is cheery, has written nearly enough poems for a little book, says the *Statesman* has a good circulation among farmers as well as intellectuals; but isn't hopeful of any great improvement just now, men's minds being still entangled in politics. But there is a report on the electrifying of the Shannon being written in simple language that he thinks may stir the imagination of the people. He finds the Republicans quite barren now of ideas, nothing but hate. We are both delighted at Craoibhin being in the Senate at last.

6 FEBRUARY. I came by evening train to Athenry, but there the Hotel porter came to say all the rooms were full for the fair so I had to go on to Galway, slept well in my expensive bed and got home today by midday. All well and the garden being dug. The country still very flooded.

Pictures from *Daily Mirror* of *Travelling Man* being acted in St. Paul's Covent Garden.

And a Revd. Mr. Elliot writes to ask leave for performances of *Brigit* in his Edinburgh parish—"the whole production to be a devotion of the Passion".

7 FEBRUARY. A letter from Catherine this morning "isn't it lovely coming home for the holidays". I have sent them spring flowers today, anemones, rioes, grape hyacinth, crocus, scilla, lauristinus, narcissus, all outdoor, as well as Christmas roses, tunica and wallflower. A lovely day.

Oxford University Irish Society asks me to lecture—"address them" between 5 February and 6 March. (But I cannot accept).

10 FEBRUARY. Sunday wet and stormy, I couldn't go to church but had, and needed, a real day of rest, on the sofa for most of the morning. But yesterday and today I have worked my poor head very hard at the Income Tax and rates accounts for Bourke, I hope he will take this burden off in future.

Labour, £232.13.11. Rates £123.5.2. Income Tax (and over £100 demanded now on last year) £80.0.9. (£436). Receipts for the year, cattle, wool, rabbits, £64.13. Then servants, food, hospitality, clothes, presents, journeys, the poor, the Chicks' holidays &c &c &c. My own regular income £500 and what I earn. Last year £467, but I am anxious.

Kiernan writes the report of the Commission has only now gone to the Colonial Secretary—Amery! Greenwood's brother-in-law.

12 FEBRUARY. Madden here yesterday, we went through seed list and I corrected, then and today, typed sheets of diary, and covered marmalade. Kathie and Dudley come tomorrow. Finished *The Conqueror* with less interest than I had begun it, the barrenness of party politics coming in even in that new Republic—and its angers and jealousies.

13 FEBRUARY. Dudley and Kathie came today, poor boy a sad "homecoming" for him, the house of Roxborough burned the land all but all sold; his father suffering, I am afraid doomed. I am glad to have this roof to bring him under, and the woods. They have gone, he and Mike and Kathie out with a gun.

S.O'C. sends me his *Two Plays*[48] today. "In earnest appreciation of her kind good counsel when the author was struggling towards dramatic expression."

15 FEBRUARY. Yesterday's paper told of the Government's new Treason Bill.[49] It sounds very tyranical and likely to fill the gaols with protesters and isn't likely to help the Government in the elections.

16 FEBRUARY. Dudley and Kathie went over to Roxborough yesterday, sad for him poor boy, his first sight of the ruined home and the deserted yards. The wood beside the avenue had been cut down by "forty men with eighty carts while I was in Galway one day" the Steward's account. Castleboy also denuded of trees. They have gone to shoot on the mountain today.

They spend the evenings (while Kathie knits) at Crossword puzzles, I sometimes help—found "roscid" for dewy in Johnson last night for them and find it amusing though I quoted from G. Murray's version of *The Frogs*,[50] ". . . Then never . . . make one of the row of fools. Who gabble away at ease. Letting art and music free . . . Or to sit in a gloomy herd. A scraping of word on word. All idle and all absurd.—That is the fate of fools!"

19 FEBRUARY. Yesterday a scattered day, Sally Allgood's request to go away for twelve weeks, if we promise to have her back, and having answered this, "Of course want you back if circumstances permit" and advising her to accept the offer, think-

ing it would lighten our expenses and give a chance to other players to be tried, the papers came and said someone is starting "A new Irish Theatre in London" with Abbey players in it.[51] Sinclair Miss O'Neill, &c. So I've had to do a good deal of writing today, to Sally and Perrin and Robinson, because that might, if we keep our best, give us engagements. Then the Bagots to lunch and tea. Bagot and Dudley went across to shoot at Inchy after lunch, saw nine cock, fired at eight, brought back one. Dudley shot one but too close, blew it to fragments. Madden was here also, and his boy, pruning the fruit trees. This morning Kathie and Dudley packing or getting John to pack their Roxborough spoils and sending them to station. I am reading the *Bacchae*, not so fine as the *Hippolytus*[52] I've just read. G. Murray's beautiful translation.

20 FEBRUARY. Yes, it is as fine as *Hippolytus* but more terrible, even horrible in parts, and that disturbed the memory of it.

Dudley and Kathie left this morning. He says now he would like to keep Roxborough, the possible two hundred acres and the house. Has plans for draining the bog and fattening cattle to utilise the sheds and buildings. But his mother wouldn't come to look after it, there seems to be no one to do so, and if left derelict he would find all a ruin on his return.

21 FEBRUARY. The Government after a good deal of opposition got their treason bill through the Dail, only I think by promising to drop some of the clauses later if necessary—"Swallow it whole but you can throw up the most indigestible bits bye and bye". An undignified proceeding I think.

And Sally writes it is not the new Irish Theatre that wants her but *Pollyanna*; she didn't know about the new Theatre or would have explained in her telegram.

A snow shower this morning and now a lovely day. I go on typing diaries to save others in the future from trying to decipher them.

22 FEBRUARY. Yesterday a big parcel from Hatchard contained G. Wyndham's *Letters*, a present from Guy, very kind of him.

Later, John coming from Gort said Madden who he met there had brought "no good news" from Lough Cutra. Clarke the steward and all Hugo's work-men, about nine, have had notice to leave. Guy had alluded to this in his letter with the book. I asked if there would be trouble, and J. thinks there will—they feel bitter because they hear a good deal of land has been sold to the Land Commission and have had no offer of any. They had written once or twice, some time ago, to Hugo asking that in case of sale they, as workmen, might have some, but hear nothing of this and don't know if he has forgotten it. I said I would be writing to Captain Guy and would mention this to him, and J. thought that would be a great help.

23 FEBRUARY. Writing to Hogan today about the upkeep of the avenue, asking him when taking over the land bordering it from tenants to arrange some scheme, perhaps getting them to contribute to a contractor, to keep it passable.

24 FEBRUARY. John showed me a letter the owners of the land bought from us and that they hope will be taken over by Hogan's Land Commission have received, saying that if they take it the Commission must have "a free hand"—which appears to mean that they can re-divide it. And the inspector who came had been heard to say that Hehir and Mike ought to have more, because of their large families. So there is great uneasiness. I said they should consult a lawyer before signing.

Such a nice letter from M. today.—"Remember *always* that however unpleasant I may wax I couldn't possibly get on at all without you, so *please* hold on to life for ages and ages. I'm sure you can if you will. You can always do everything." But I sent her a letter from Edward, on the verge of 87 and giving a list of his infirmities and said, reading that, she could not wish me to grow so old.

NOTES

Contractions for the names of newspapers referred to in the Notes

T. *The Times*, London
I.T. *The Irish Times*, Dublin
N.Y.T. The *New York Times*
T.L.S. *Times* Literary Supplement, London
I.I: *Irish Independent*, Dublin
C.E. *Cork Examiner*
C.T. *Connacht Tribune*, Galway
I.H. *The Irish Homestead*, Dublin
I.S. *The Irish Statesman*, Dublin

All dates given are for the year of the entry if no year date is given. Cross references in the Notes are given thus: See 19:21, meaning Book 19, note 21.

NOTES

FOREWORD

1 Lady Gregory, *Seventy Years* (Gerrards Cross 1974, New York 1976), pp. 16–17.
2 Wilfrid Scawen Blunt, *The Land War in Ireland* (London 1912), p. 443.
3 Lady Gregory, 'Eothen and the Athenaeum Club', in *Blackwoods Magazine*, December 1895, p. 800.
4 Lady Gregory, *The Kiltartan Poetry Book* (Cuala Press, Dundrum 1918), p. i.
5 Lady Gregory, *Seventy Years*, pp. 12–13.
6 Lady Gregory, *Coole* (Cuala Press, Dublin 1931), pp. 2–3.
7 William Gregory, *Mr. Gregory's Letter-Box, 1813–1830*, ed. Lady Gregory (London 1898), pp. 48, 206.
8 Lady Gregory, *Kiltartan Poetry Book*, pp. i–ii.
9 *Ibid.*, p. i.
10 *Ibid.*, p. ii.
11 *Ibid.*, p. vi.
12 *Ibid.*, p. v.
13 *Ibid.*, p. v.
14 Lady Gregory, *Our Irish Theatre* (New York 1913), p. 4.
15 *Lady Gregory's Journals 1916–1930*, ed. Lennox Robinson (New York 1947), p. 338.
16 *Kiltartan Poetry Book*, p. v.
17 *Ibid.*, pp. v–vi.
18 *Lady Gregory's Journals 1916–1930*, pp. 338–339.
19 *Ibid.*, p. 28.
20 Lady Gregory, 'Ireland Real and Ideal', in *Nineteenth Century*, November 1898, pp. 770–774.
21 W. B. Yeats, 'Dramatis Personae' in *Autobiographies* (London 1955), p. 398.
22 See Anne Gregory's *Me & Nu: Childhood at Coole* (Gerrards Cross 1970) for her memories of this period.
23 For further details, see James White's introduction to Lady Gregory's *Sir Hugh Lane: His Life and Legacy* (Gerrards Cross, New York 1973).

BOOK ONE
10 October–23 December 1916.

1 George Nathaniel Curzon, Marquess Curzon of Kedleston (1859–1925). At this time he was a member of the inner War Cabinet. He married as his second wife, Grace Duggan, daughter of J. M. Hinds, and widow of A. Duggan of Buenos Aires.
2 Sir (Henry) Paul Harvey (1869–1948) had been a friend of Lady Gregory since his school days. He married Ethel Frances, daughter of Col. Edward Persse, in 1896, created K.C.M.G. 1911, compiled and edited *The Oxford Companion to English Literature* (1932) and *Oxford*

Companion to Classical Literature (1937). He had a distinguished career in the Foreign Office and War Office.

3 John Redmond (1856–1918), Irish politician. Leader of the Irish party after the fall of Parnell, but his influence declined after the 1916 Rising.

4 Sir William Montague Orpen (1878–1931), Dublin born painter. He spent two years in World War I in France as an official war artist.

5 George William Russell (1867–1935), used the letters A.E. as his pen name. He was a mystic, poet, artist, visionary, economist, and editor of *The Irish Homestead* (1904–1923) and its successor *The Irish Statesman* (1923–1930).

6 Sir Horace Curzon Plunkett (1854–1932), Irish statesman and agricultural reformer. An ardent exponent of farm co-operatives, he was founder of the Irish Agricultural Organisation Society (I.A.O.S.), which employed A.E. for much of his life.

7 The Rt. Hon. Augustine Birrell (1850–1933), Chief Secretary of Ireland 1907–1916.

8 Robert Baldwin Ross (1869–1918), Additional Trustee of the National Gallery, London.

9 Robert Clutton-Brock (1868–1924), art critic on the staff of *The Times* from 1908.

10 H. G. Wells, *Mr. Britling Sees it Through* (London 1916).

11 Herbert Henry Asquith, 1st Earl of Oxford and Asquith (1852–1928), was Prime Minister at this time, but resigned under pressure on 5 December 1916, and was succeeded by David Lloyd George.

12 The Easter Rising of 1916, suppressed by the British. The execution of the leaders of this rebellion did more to create support for the Irish nationalist cause than any other British action. Yeats's poem "Easter 1916" records the poet's reaction to the event.

13 George Atherton Aitken (1860–1917), Assist. Secretary at the Home Office.

14 John Dillon (1851–1927), Irish politician, became chairman of the Irish Nationalist party in 1918.

15 John Quinn (1870–1924), the New York lawyer and long time friend of Lady Gregory wrote a defence of Sir Roger Casement in the *New York Times* Magazine Section, under the title "Roger Casement, Martyr" (13 August 1916). In this he recalled that Casement was an Irishman by birth, and not therefore a traitor to England.

16 Edward Henry Carson, later Baron Carson (1854–1935), Ulster leader. He became First Lord of the Admiralty under Lloyd George.

17 J. L. Garvin, Editor of *The Observer* 1904–1914.

18 *The Irish Times* (1 November 1916, p. 4) reported that the Dublin Corporation had asked the Trustees of the National Gallery, London, for the return of the Lane Pictures.

19 J. Augustus Keogh became the producer of the Abbey Theatre in 1916. He produced *John Bull's Other Island* for the Abbey and it had its first performance there 25 September 1916. Other Shaw plays were produced in the following months: *Widowers' Houses, Arms and the Man, Man and Superman.*

20 Her Royal Highness Princess Louise Margaret Alexandra Victoria Agnes, Duchess of Connaught and Strathearn (1861–1917), 3rd daughter of H.R.H. Prince Frederick Charles of Prussia, and wife of Prince Arthur, 3rd son of Queen Victoria.

21 *Visions and Beliefs in the West of Ireland*, collected and arranged by Lady

Gregory, with two essays and notes by W. B. Yeats (London & New York, 1920, 2nd edition, Gerrards Cross, and New York, 1970).

22 *The Works of Geoffrey Chaucer*, ed. F. S. Ellis. This book, set in Chaucer type, was the most important book produced by William Morris's Kelmscott Press. There were more than eighty woodcuts by Sir Edward Burne-Jones, and it was published in 1896.

23 G. B. Shaw's "The Emperor and the Little Girl", written for the Vestiaire Marie-José, a Belgian war charity for children, first appeared in the *N.Y. Tribune* on 22 October 1916. It was later collected in his *Short Stories, Scraps & Shavings* (London 1932).

24 Sir Oliver Joseph Lodge, *Raymond, or Life after Death*, with examples of the evidence for survival of memory and affection after death (London 1916).

25 Published in 1918 as *The Sweeps of Ninety-Eight*, in *A Poem and Two Plays*.

26 Wilfrid Scawen Blunt (1840–1922), poet and protagonist of Indian, Egyptian and Irish nationalism, was a close friend of Lady Gregory from the time they met in Egypt, just after her marriage until his death. She wrote a foreword for his *My Diaries* (2 vols. 1919, 1920). The first edition did not have her foreword.

27 Lady Margaret Sackville's volume *The Pageant and other Poems* (London, 1916). The poems were reprinted in part from *The Nation*, *Everyman*, *The Sphere*, *Forum* and *The Times*.

28 Joseph Hilary Pierre Belloc (1870–1953), known as Hilaire Belloc, English writer. He was a close friend of Blunt.

29 George Wyndham (1863–1913), statesman and man of letters, was Chief Secretary for Ireland 1900–1905, and famous for his Land Act. His letters were published in 1915, *Letters of George Wyndham 1877–1913*.

30 Alfred Charles William Harmsworth, Viscount Northcliffe (1865–1922), newspaper magnate. With his brother Viscount Rothermere, he acquired the *Evening News*, and himself founded the *Daily Mail* and *Daily Mirror*, and in 1908 acquired control of *The Times*.

31 Thoor Ballylee, or Ballylee Castle, stands a few miles out of Gort near the Loughrea road. It was once part of the Gregory estates, and was a ruin when Yeats acquired it. It is now run as a tourist centre by the Western Regional Tourism Organisation.

32 Sir John Lavery (1856–1941), British painter.

33 See 1:11.

34 The case for the return to Dublin of Sir Hugh Lane's French pictures (as laid out in his unwitnessed codicil), giving some of the evidence of Dublin's right to them, was contained in a letter from Lady Gregory to *The Times*, which was published 6 December 1916. A letter from W. B. Yeats was published on 28 December.

35 Thomas Power O'Connor (1848–1929), Irish journalist, nationalist, and M.P. from 1880 to the end of his life.

36 Lady Gregory's play *The Golden Apple* (London & New York 1916), was not performed at the Abbey until 6 January 1920.

37 Published in *The Observer* 24 December 1916, together with a letter from W. B. Yeats.

38 *Duty*, a comedy in 1 act by Seumas O'Brien, was first produced at the Abbey 16 December 1913.

39 Sarah Purser (1848–1943), Irish portrait painter, was the first woman member of the Royal Hibernian Academy.

40 Oliver St. John Gogarty (1878–1957), Irish author, wit and surgeon, the prototype of Buck Mulligan in James Joyce's *Ulysses*, was a Senator of the Irish Free State 1922–1936.

BOOK TWO
27 January–28 October 1918

1 *Report of a Public Meeting Held at the Mansion House on the 29th of January, 1918*. Both W. B. Yeats and Jack B. Yeats attended with Lady Gregory. John Quinn cabled his support "on behalf large number Irish Americans".
2 *Sable and Gold*, a play in 3 acts by Maurice Dalton, was first produced at the Abbey 16 September 1918.
3 Kilteragh, Plunkett's mansion in Foxrock, Co. Dublin, was destroyed during the civil war. It was first blown up, and the following night gutted by fire. See 21:22. Amongst its treasures were murals by A.E. which were considered to be his masterpiece: these were of course totally destroyed.
4 Sir Robert Woods (1865–1938), was an eminent doctor, a professor at Dublin University and one of its Members of Parliament 1918–1922.
5 Anthony Trollope, *Castle Richmond*, 3 vols. (London 1860, with introduction by Algar Thorold, New York 1860).
6 *Spreading the News*, one of Lady Gregory's most successful plays, was first produced 27 December 1904.
7 Fred O'Donovan, a leading Abbey actor for several years.
8 *The Grabber*, a play in 3 acts by Edward F. Barrrett, was first produced at the Abbey 12 November 1918. Lady Gregory was well-known as a play doctor.

BOOK THREE
3 February–21 April 1919

1 Yeats's play *On Baile's Strand* was first produced at the Abbey 27 December 1904. It and *Spreading the News* formed the programme for the opening night of the Abbey Theatre.
2 *The Jester*, a play in 3 acts, written at the request of "a little schoolboy [her grandson, Richard] to write a play that could be acted at school". It started out on the lines of *The Discontented Children*, in which the children of the squire and the gamekeeper change places. The character Manannan (the Jester) was derived from aspects of Bernard Shaw. Some of the phrases were borrowed from A.E.'s *The Candle of Vision*. (Coole Edition, VII, 379). See 21:8.
3 *Mixed Marriage*, a play in 4 acts by St. John Ervine, was first produced at the Abbey 30 March 1911.
4 Eithne Magee had acted at the Abbey Theatre as early as 1909. She returned to play in Lady Gregory's *The Dragon* in 1919.
5 *Phineas Finn, the Irish Member*, by Anthony Trollope, with 20 ills. by J. E. Millais, 2 vols. (London 1869).
6 Henry Brook Adams, *The Education of Henry Adams: an Autobiography*, ed. Henry Cabot Lodge (London and Cambridge, Mass. 1919).
7 Helena Moloney was briefly with the Abbey in 1913. Her first role on her return in 1919 seems to have been in *The Rebellion in Ballycullen* by Brinsley MacNamara on 11 March.

8 Lord Russell wrote to Lord Palmerston on 17 September 1862 that Britain ought to recognise the Southern states and to concentrate British troops in Canada. He asked for a Cabinet meeting in the next weeks to decide the issue. Russell wished to support the South "with a view to breaking up the Union" (p. 153ff.). Lord Granville was opposed, but he listened. W. E. Gladstone, who was then Chancellor of the Exchequer, approved recognition, in a letter to Palmerston. Henry Adams, *The Education of Henry Adams.*

9 John Morley, Viscount Morley of Blackburn (1838–1923), writer and politician, was Chief Secretary of Ireland, 1886–1895, Secretary of State for India 1905–1910, and was General Editor of the "English Men of Letters" series.

10 After the death of Lady Anne Blunt, the Trustees for the grandchildren sued Blunt for the valuable Newbuilding Stud. Blunt lost the suit, but was allowed to keep six mares. The rest of the stud went to Crabbet, where it continued for many years. Edith Finch, *Wilfrid Scawen Blunt* (London 1938), p. 362.

11 Stephen Lucius Gwynn, *The Life of the Rt. Hon. Sir Charles Dilke*, completed and edited by Gertrude M. Tuckwell (London 1917).

12 In August 1885, Mr. Donald Crawford filed a petition for divorce against his wife on grounds of alleged adultery with Sir Charles Dilke (1843–1911). Crawford obtained the divorce on the strength of his wife's confession, and though Dilke protested his innocence the rest of his life, he was forced to admit that her mother had been his mistress.

13 Leon Gambetta (1838–1883), French politician. A devoted republican, he had been Prime Minister from November 1881 to January 1882.

14 Lillah McCarthy (1875–1960), English actress and theatre manager. In April 1919 she took over the management of the Kingsway Theatre, and opened with *Judith*, a 3 act play by Arnold Bennett.

15 Otto Eduard Leopold, Prince von Bismarck, *New Chapters of Bismarck's Autobiography* (London 1921).

16 *The Future of Islam* (London 1882).

17 Blunt, in *Later Sonnets*, wrote a number in which the first letter of each line spells out the name of the person about whom the poem is written.

18 John Masefield (1878–1967) became Poet Laureate in 1930 after the death of Robert Bridges.

19 Dorothy Carleton was Blunt's adopted niece. Miss Lawrence was his nurse.

20 Lennox Robinson (1886–1958), Irish dramatist and director of the Abbey Theatre.

21 Maureen Delany a leading actress at the Abbey.

22 William G. Fay formed and acted in the first Irish company at the Abbey. He and his brother Frank left as a result of a disagreement with the Abbey directors in 1908.

23 Robert, Lady Gregory's only child, was shot down by accident on 23 January 1918 while on air patrol in N. Italy. Before the War he had designed sets for a number of Abbey productions, including *Deirdre* (1906) by W. B. Yeats and Lady Gregory's *Dervorgilla* (1907).

24 J. O. P. Bland and E. Backhouse, *China under the Empress Dowager*, being the history of the life and times of Tzu Hsi (London and Philadelphia 1910).

25 H. G. Wells, *Joan and Peter: the Story of an Education* (London 1918).

26 Alex Waugh, *The Loom of Youth*, with a preface by T. Secombe (London 1917).

27 John Henry Foley (1818–1874), Irish sculptor, of among other works, the statues of Burke and Goldsmith in front of Trinity College, Dublin, and that of O'Connell in O'Connell Street.

28 Stephen Lucius Gwynn (1864–1950), author and Irish nationalist, was M.P. for Galway 1906–1918, during the time that John Redmond was titular head of the Irish party.

29 Fridtjof Nansen (1861–1930), Norwegian Arctic explorer, scientist, statesman and humanitarian, received the Nobel Peace Prize in 1922.

30 Lady Gregory's *Gods and Fighting Men* (London and New York 1904).

31 *The Image*, a comedy in 3 acts, was first produced at the Abbey 11 November 1909. Joseph Holloway was at the first night, and thought it "talk, talk, talk", leading nowhere, and wrote that the play was not applauded. However, after the second performance, he thought it the cleverest long play Lady Gregory had so far written. The entry for 13 January 1910 records that when George Moore was asked what he thought of the play, he replied, "A bog slide!" See Holloway's *A Dublin Play-Goer's Impressions*, a manuscript diary in the National Library of Ireland. Lady Gregory herself was not quite satisfied with the play, writing "I think I have not quite failed, yet it is also not what I set out to do." Coole Edition VI, 297.

32 Ibsen's *Brand*, trans. by F. E. Garrett (London 1915).

33 John Drinkwater's *Abraham Lincoln*, with William T. Rea in the title role, opened at the Lyric Opera House 19 February 1919. It was put on at the Lyceum Theatre in August 1921.

34 Thomas James Cobden Sanderson (1840–1922), bookbinder and printer, and, with Emery Walker, founder of the Doves Press.

35 William Morris (1834–1896), English artist, writer, printer and founder of the Kelmscott Press.

36 Sir Edward Burne-Jones (1833–1896), English painter and decorator, and a life-long friend of Morris.

37 Charles Edward Lawrence (1870–1940), *Mrs. Bent* (London 1918).

38 Countess Constance Markievicz (1868–1927), née Gore-Booth, Irish militant, sentenced to death for her part in the 1916 Easter Rising, reprieved, and finally released in June 1917. She was re-arrested 26 September 1919 and released from Cork Gaol early November 1919. Anne Marreco, *The Rebel Countess* (Philadelphia 1967), pp. 258–9.

39 "Great-Heart", in *The Definitive Edition of Rudyard Kipling's Verse* (London 1940), pp. 577–8.

40 *The Mineral Workers*, a comedy in 3 acts by William Boyle was first produced at the Abbey 20 October 1906. It was a favourite with the Abbey audiences, but not the management.

41 Shaw wrote this play for the Abbey at the request of W. B. Yeats, who liked it very much but realised that it was beyond the capabilities of the still inexperienced Abbey actors, especially the part of Broadbent. It was first produced at the Court Theatre 1 November 1904, and only put on at the Abbey 25 September 1916, with J. M. Kerrigan playing Broadbent.

42 James Stephens (1880–1950), Irish author, was Registrar of the National Gallery of Ireland 1915–1924.

43 Thomas Bodkin (1887–1961) succeeded Sir Hugh Lane as Director of the National Gallery of Ireland. He resigned in 1935 to become the first director of the Baker Institute of Fine Arts at the University of Birmingham, retiring in 1953.

44 See 1:5.

45 Pierce McCann, a member of Dail Eireann, died in Gloucester Gaol 6 March 1919, apparently of influenza. D. MacArdle, *The Irish Republic* (Dublin 1951), p. 283.

46 Cruise O'Brien, with Lionel Smith-Gordon, the author of a number of books on co-operation.

46a Possibly *Young Ireland* by Charles Gavan Duffy (London 1880, revised 1896).

47 Sir John Pentland Mahaffy (1839–1919), Provost of Trinity College, Dublin, at that time.

48 Lady Ardilaun (1850–1925), née Lady Olivia Charlotte White, d. of the 3rd Earl of Bantry, the wife of Sir Arthur Edward Guinness, 2nd Baronet and 1st (and last) Baron Ardilaun of Ashford, Co. Galway (1840–1915), was a patroness of the Abbey Theatre.

49 The artist John Singer Sargent (1856–1952) undertook to paint a portrait for the benefit of the Red Cross if it could find someone to give £10,000 to it. On hearing this, just before he left for the U.S.A., Sir Hugh Lane offered to donate this sum. He was returning from this visit on the *Lusitania* when it was torpedoed, and he was drowned. Under the terms of his Will, the unpainted portrait became the property of the National Gallery of Ireland. It paid the £10,000 and commissioned Sargent to paint the portrait of President Woodrow Wilson. See James White's foreword to *Sir Hugh Lane: His Life and Legacy* by Lady Gregory, (Gerrards Cross and New York 1973), Coole Edition X, 14–15.

50 *Rebellion in Ballycullen*, a play in 3 acts by Brinsley MacNamara was first produced at the Abbey 11 March 1919. See following note.

51 Maud Gonne MacBride (1866–1953), Anglo-Irish revolutionary, married Captain John MacBride in 1903. W. B. Yeats repeatedly proposed marriage without success both before the marriage and after MacBride's execution. She inspired *Rebellion in Ballycullen*.

52 Sir William Gregory, her husband, who had died in 1892.

53 "In Memory of Major Robert Gregory" by W. B. Yeats.

54 Joseph Holloway records that Lady Gregory spoke her lines clearly – each word sharp-cut and distinct, and getting the atmosphere all right, without undue effort or over-emphasis, but there seemed to him a lack of enthusiasm at the back of her words and nothing more. Her delivery of the final speech was spoken, not chanted as it is usually done. She looked the part and acted it well. Entry for Friday 21 March 1919, p. 435.

55 *The Dragon*, a wonder play in 3 acts by Lady Gregory was first produced at the Abbey 21 April 1919, with Barry Fitzgerald and Maureen Delaney in the leading roles. Lennox Robinson in his *Ireland's Abbey Theatre* (London 1951) wrote that a new Gregory had appeared, writing three wonder plays, set "halfway between Clare-Galway and Fairyland . . . These are plays for children of all ages from seven to seventy . . ." (pp. 119–120).

56 Either Mrs. Elizabeth Gaskell's *Life of Charlott Brontë* (New York 1857) or that by Augustine Birrell (London 1887).

BOOK FOUR
21 April–23 July 1919

1 Jack B. Yeats (1871–1951) brother of W. B. Yeats, and probably the only

Irish artist of world stature. He married Mary Cottenham White (known as "Cottie") in 1898.

2 John Dillon (1851–1927), Irish nationalist politician who, with John Redmond, was leader of the anti-Parnell faction in the Irish party.

3 Timothy Michael Healy (1855–1933), Irish political leader and first Governor-General of the Irish Free State (1922–1928), was at first a supporter of Parnell, later an opponent, but was a constant thorn in the sides of Dillon and T. P. O'Connor, whom he accused of subservience to English liberalism after the defeat of the Home Rule Bill.

4 Dr. Douglas Hyde (1860–1949), Anglo-Irish poet and translator, as well known by his pseudonym "An Craoibhin Aoibhinn" (the sweet little branch); was founder of the Gaelic League, and first President of Ireland, being the parties' agreed candidate, holding the office for the seven year period of tenure, 1938–45.

5 William R. Inge, Dean of St. Pauls, *The Philosophy of Plotinus* (London 1918).

6 Roxborough, Lady Gregory's family home, as a Persse, about ten miles from Gort, off the Loughrea road.

7 "If I were Four and Twenty" in *The Irish Statesman*, 23, 30 August 1919. Later published in volume form by the Cuala Press, September 1940.

BOOK FIVE
1 August–7 November 1919

1 Edward Martyn (1859–1924), Irish nationalist, author of *The Heather Field*, *Maeve* and other plays, covered the costs of the Irish Literary Theatre for its first productions; founded the Palestrina Choir in Dublin, and features much in George Moore's *Hail and Farewell*. Tillyra Castle is close to Coole Park.

2 *Aristotle's Bellows*, a Wonder Play in 3 acts was first produced at the Abbey 17 March 1921. Lady Gregory wrote that she had begun the play in 1919, but had put off completing it to write *Hugh Lane's Life & Achievement*, and when she had returned to it later, found that she had written more of the scenario than she had imagined. Coole Edition VII, 393.

3 (George) Gilbert (Aimé) Murray (1866–1957), Euripides's *Hippolitus* and *Bacchae*, Aristophanes's *Frogs*, With an Appendix on *The Lost Plays of Euripides*, and an Introduction on *The Significance of the Bacchae in Athenian History* (London 1902).

4 Harris was the Abbey's business agent.

5 *Hugh Lane's Life & Achievement, with some Account of the Dublin Galleries* (London 1921).

6 *A Night at an Inn*, a play in 1 act by Lord Dunsany was first produced at the Abbey 1 September 1919.

7 *John Bull's Other Island*. Edgar Gerson played Broadbent for this performance, and he was, according to Holloway, "rather tame and colourless". See Holloway's *Diary*, July–September 1919, p. 433, and also Book 1, notes 19, 41, above.

8 *The Saint*, a play in 2 scenes by Desmond Fitzgerald, was first produced at the Abbey 2 September 1919.

9 Among the disputed Lane pictures were Renoir's magnificent "Les

Parapluies" and two Manets: "Le Concert aux Tuileries" and "Portrait of Mlle. Eva Gonzales".

10 Professor Joseph Vendryes (1875–1960), French linguist, was undoubtedly in Ireland researching for his *Grammaire du Vieil Irlaindais* (1921).

11 Arthur Edward Weigall, *The Life and Times of Cleopatra, Queen of Egypt* (Edinburgh 1914).

12 Dame Una Pope-Hennessy (d. 1949) née Birch, wife of Major General Ladislaus Pope-Hennessy, was an old and dear friend of Lady Gregory.

13 See 1:6.

14 Martin Wood's biography of Hugh Lane had been twice rejected as unsatisfactory, and Lady Gregory undertook to do it.

15 Erskine Childers (1870–1922) author and Irish nationalist, married Mary Alden Osgood (known as Molly, though Lady Gregory often wrote Milly), of Boston. The gun-running had been in the boat *Asgard* to Howth in 1914.

16 The Hon. Mary Spring Rice, d. of Lord Monteagle, was involved in the Howth Gun Running.

17 Darrell Figgis (1882–1925), Irish author and historian.

18 Clive Bell's article "Renoir" in *The New Republic*, 10 September 1919 (pp. 173–5) mentioned "Les Parapluies" and states that when it was hung in the National Gallery in London, "some hundred English artists and amateaurs" sent Renoir a testimony of their admiration.

19 A strike of steelworkers in America began on 19 September 1919. At the start, 50,000 men came out, but by the 24th, this figure had risen to 300,000, and there were instances of disorder (*N.Y.T.* September 1919).

20 Joseph Biggar (1828–1890), the Irish M.P. who started the obstruction policy in the House of Commons in 1874.

21 Sir Edwin Landseer Lutyens (1869–1944), the noted English architect who designed the proposed gallery to house the Lane pictures for both the St. Stephen's Green and Bridge sites, both of which were rejected by the Dublin Corporation because Lutyens was not Irish.

22 This Preface became an essay entitled "The People's Theatre: A Letter to Lady Gregory", first published in *The Irish Statesman* 29 November, 6 December 1919. The reference to "you and I and Synge" is to be found at the beginning of Part VI of the letter. W. B. Yeats, *Explorations* (London and New York 1962), p. 254.

23 Sir Gerald Festus Kelly (1879–1972), painter, was President of the Royal Academy 1949–1954.

24 Alexander Bell Filson Young (1876–1938), Irish writer on motoring, legal cases, mastersingers, historical matters and of novels.

25 Clara Huth Jackson, wife of the Rt. Hon. Frederick Huth Jackson, P.C., and daughter of Lady Gregory's old friend Sir Mountstuart Elphinstone Grant Duff.

26 Francis John Stephens Hopwood, 1st Baron Southborough (1860–1947), civil servant, made the proposal in a letter to *The Times*, which in an editorial, commented that there was "no one who could more ably and impartially play such a part" (30 October 1919). Erskine Childers endorsed the idea of a conference, but suggested it should be an official one, with accredited representatives from both sides, suggesting Arthur Griffith for Ireland, de Valera being in America (*T.* 1 November). The proposal was rejected by the Irish.

27 Arthur Griffith (1872–1922), Irish statesman, founder of Sinn Fein, was a journalist and propagandist for the Irish cause. After the Anglo-Irish

Treaty, de Valera resigned as President of the Executive Council of Dail Eireann, and offered himself for re-election, but was defeated by two votes. A provisional government pending the General Election scheduled for June was set up under the leadership of Griffith, who was elected to de Valera's old position.

28 Sir Edgar Vincent (1857–1941), 16th Baronet, was created Baron D'Abernon in 1914, and Viscount in 1926. He was a Trustee of the National and Tate Galleries 1909–1935.

BOOK SIX
9 November–21 December 1919

1 *Irish Impressions* (London 1919). Shaw's review, showing that Chesterton really did not know Ireland, yet pretended he did, appeared in *The Irish Statesman* 22 November 1919, entitled "How Ireland Impressed Mr. Chesterton". Among the things that needed correction was Chesterton's belief that the statue of William III in College Green was of St. George.

2 Shaw's *Plays: Pleasant and Unpleasant*, 2 vols. (London 1898).

3 11 November 1919, the first anniversary of the Armistice was celebrated, at the King's suggestion, by two minutes' silence at 11.00 a.m.

4 Apsley Cherry-Garrard (1886–1959), an Arctic explorer and friend of Shaw.

5 When Blunt was informed of Morris's death, he wrote "He is the most wonderful man I have ever known, unique in this, that he had no thought for anything or any person, including himself, but only for the work he had in hand . . . I suppose he had a real affection for Burne Jones . . . I have seen him tender to his daughter Jenny . . . and with his wife . . .". *My Diaries* (London 1932), p. 240.

6 Although Morris considered *Pilgrims Progress*, among other works, for the Kelmscott Press, he did not live to execute it. *A Note by William Morris*, together with a short description of the Press by S. C. Cockerell (London 1898), p. 65.

7 William Morris, *The Story of Sigurd the Volsung, and the Fall of the Niblungs* (London 1877).

8 Sir Henry Morton Stanley and his wife Dorothy, née Tennant.

9 Sir George Otto Trevelyan (1838–1928), 2nd Baronet, Historian, statesman and man of letters.

10 William Ralph Inge, Dean of St. Paul's, *Outspoken Essays* (London 1919).

11 Captain Rt. Hon. Charles Curtis Craig (1869–1960), was at this time Conservative M.P. for S. Antrim.

12 John Drinkwater (1882–1937), poet, actor and playwright.

13 Anne, wife of Sir Richmond Thackeray Ritchie, and elder d. of W. M. Thackeray, the author, died in 1919.

14 Sir Edmond William Gosse (1849–1928), poet and man of letters.

15 Laurence Binyon (1869–1943), poet and art historian, Deputy Keeper in charge of Oriental Prints and Drawings 1913–1932, Keeper of Prints and Drawings 1932–1933.

16 May Sinclair (d. 1946), novelist, poet and author of books on the Brontës.

17 Sir William Newenham Montague Orpen (1878–1931), Irish painter, was an official war artist, with the rank of major. He attended the Versailles Peace Conference and recorded this in a number of works,

principally "The Hall of Mirrors".

18 Lady Gregory, *A Book of Saints and Wonders* (Dun Emer Press 1906, enlarged London and New York 1907).

19 Percy Wyndham Lewis (1884–1957), artist, novelist and critic, was a leader of the Vorticist movement, and with Ezra Pound edited *Blast*, the Review of the Great English Vortex (19–14–15).

20 See 1:7.

21 Either the Rt. Hon. Thomas Wallace Russell (1841–1920), M.P. and active in the passing of the 1896 Land Act, or more likely, "Tony" Watts Russell, a contemporary of Robert Gregory at Harrow School, and a visitor to Coole, who died in 1923.

22 Fergus Hume, *The Millionaire Mystery* (New York and London 1901).

23 Alan Duncan was an actor at the Abbey for a time.

24 *Androcles and the Lion*, a play in 2 acts and a Prologue by G. B. Shaw, had its first Abbey production on 4 November 1918.

25 Sir Horace Plunkett in a speech to the National Liberal Club protested against the substitution of militarism for statesmanship in dealing with Ireland. He called for a firm offer of "the fullest measure of self-government consistent with the necessities of the common defences of the United Kingdom". He also suggested that the question of Ulster could only be settled by a "democratically elected assembly of the whole of Ireland". *T.* 30 October 1919. See 1:6.

26 Many members of Dail Eireann were arrested on 11 November (the Dail having been suppressed on 10 September), and more on 25 November, when Sinn Fein, the Volunteers and the Gaelic League were suppressed. On 12 December, more members were arrested and deported to English gaols. MacArdle, *The Irish Republic*, pp. 308–17, 320.

27 Oliver St. John Gogarty married Martha Duane of Rossdhu, Moyard, Co. Galway, in 1907. See 1:40.

28 *The Bogie Men*, a comedy in 1 act by Lady Gregory was first produced at the Royal Court Theatre on 4 July 1912 by the Abbey Theatre company.

29 *The Man Who Missed the Tide*, a play in 3 acts by W. F. Casey, was first produced on 13 February 1908, with Arthur Sinclair, Fred O'Donovan, J. M. Kerrigan, Sara Allgood and Maire O'Neill.

30 A two car shooting party was ambushed at Shassymore Cross by about twenty men. The Hon. Edward O'Brien (brother of 15th Baron Inchiquin) and Lady O'Brien were hit by pellets around the head and shoulders. MacNamara was shot in the head and both arms, and two other members of the party were hit. *I.T.* 5 December 1919.

31 The Kilfenore Police Barracks were attacked on 8 December. H. V. MacNamara's house was also fired on. *I.T.* 9 December.

32 Sir William Henry Mahon (1856–1926) 5th Bart. lived at Castlegar, Ahascragh, Co. Galway.

33 *The Rising of the Moon* was first produced at the Abbey on 9 March 1907. It is one of Lady Gregory's most successful plays. After the 1916 Rising, the police refused to provide uniforms for the play as they had done previously, as they said the play was too realistic.

BOOK SEVEN
8 January–8 April 1920

1 *The Golden Apple*, a play in 3 acts by Lady Gregory was first performed

at the Abbey 6 January 1920. The Saturday matinee performance for children was a great success, and they were delighted. Holloway, January 1920, p. 52.

2 Susan Langstaff Mitchell was a long time assistant to A.E. on *The Irish Homestead* and *The Irish Statesman*.

3 "Michael" in *Collected Poems* (London 1926), pp. 358–369.

4 Maybe the spelling is incorrect, but I have not been able to trace Col. Hutcheson.

5 Iseult Gonne (1895–1954) was the daughter of Maude Gonne and the French Boulangist deputy Lucien Millevoye, editor of *La Patrie*. Yeats proposed to her after he had once again been turned down by Maud Gonne, in 1917, but she also rejected him.

6 See 1:39.

7 Sir Thomas Henry Grattan Esmonde (1862–1935) 11th Bart., M.P. 1885–1918, and Irish Free State Senator 1922–1935, writer of travel books.

8 Frank Shawe-Taylor was shot 3 March 1920. MacArdle p. 348.

9 *The Player Queen*, a play in 2 scenes by W. B. Yeats was first performed at the Abbey 9 December 1919. Yeats had worked on the play at various times over the previous ten years. In a letter to Lady Gregory at this time, he said how satisfied he was with the play's reception.

10 Epstein's "Risen Christ" received a great deal of criticism when it was exhibited at the Leinster Galleries.

11 *Pygmalion* had been revived at the Aldwych Theatre on 10 February 1920. Mrs. Patrick Campbell played Eliza Doolittle.

12 Thomas MacCurtin, the Lord Mayor of Cork and a prominent Sinn Feiner, was killed at his home by four men who shot him twice at point blank range in the doorway of his bedroom. *T*. 22 March 1920. See also MacArdle, pp. 333–4.

13 *The Jester* has never been produced professionally. See 3:2. *The Dragon*. See 3:55.

14 Mrs. Humphrey Ward died 24 March 1920.

14a Sir Frank Cavendish Lascelles (1841–1920), diplomat, Ambassador to Berlin 1895–1908.

15 Charles M. Doughty, *Travels in Arabia Deserta* (Cambridge 1888). It is notable for its style in which Chaucerian and Elizabethan English is mixed with Arabic. Republished 1920, 1921, 1926. See 24 & 25:1.

16 Charles M. Doughty, *Mansoul, or the Riddle of the World* (London 1920).

17 Thomas Lister, 4th (and last) Baron Ribblesdale (1854–1925), was a Trustee of the National Gallery, London.

18 Lord Osborne de Vere Beauclerk (1874–1964) became 12th Duke of St. Albans in 1934.

19 Henry Charles Keith Petty-Fitzmaurice, 5th Marquess of Lansdowne, 6th Earl of Kerry (1845–1927), English statesman, was Secretary of State for Foreign Affairs 1900–1905.

BOOK EIGHT
8 April–12 June 1920

1 At this time over 150 prisoners were on hunger strike, some for over a

week, and relatives were advising the prison authorities of the weak state of many prisoners. In spite of appeals, the Lord Lieutenant refused to intervene. *I.T.* 12 April. On 13 April a general strike in their support went into effect all over Ireland, which by now was in turmoil. *I.T.* 14 April. On the 14th, the prisoners were paroled, and the strike terminated. All those in need of treatment were transferred to various hospitals. *I.T.* 15 April.

2 Lennox Robinson's *The Whiteheaded Boy* was produced at the Ambassador Theatre 23 September 1920, with Sara Allgood, Maire O'Neill and Arthur Sinclair. *T.* 28 September.

3 *The Life of Man*, a play in 5 acts by Leonid Andreyev (1871–1917), trans. by C. J. Hogarth (London 1915). Lady Gregory is in error as to the author.

4 *The Black Maskers*, published with *The Sabine Women* and *The Life of Man*, trans. from the Russian by C. Meader and F. Newton Scott, with intro. by V. V. Brusyanin (London 1915).

5 See 8:4.

6 *The Lost Leader*, a play in 3 acts by Lennox Robinson was first produced at the Abbey 19 February 1918.

7 Mrs. Martin was for many years the cleaning woman at the Abbey.

8 See 1:15.

9 Eamon de Valera (1882–1974), Irish political leader, was one of the leaders of the 1916 Easter Rising, but was saved from execution because of his nationality. His political career only ended when he became the third President of Ireland in 1959, a position he held for two seven year terms.

10 Colonel Maurice Moore, George Moore's brother.

11 Arthur Griffith died of a cerebral haemorrhage 12 August 1922, apparently from overwork. See 5:27.

12 James McNeill (1869–1938) was Governor-General of the Irish Free State from 1928 until dismissed 3 October 1932.

13 Michael Collins (1890–1922), Irish political leader, who was a signatory of the Peace Treaty with England, which he considered to be his death warrant. He commanded the army of the Provisional Government, and was killed in an ambush 22 August 1922, ten days after the death of Griffith. See 9:6.

14 Cathal Brugha (1874–1922), Irish revolutionary, was wounded during the Easter Rising and was shot at the end of the fighting for the Four Courts, by Government forces as he was coming out of the Hamman Hotel, and died two days later on 5 July.

15 R. Nesbitt Keller, Lady Gregory's solicitor, of the firm Whitney, Moore & Keller.

16 Robert Gregory, Sir Hugh Lane and John Shawe-Taylor.

17 See 1:21.

18 Vicente Blasco Ibáñez, *Arène Sanglantes*, traduit par G. Hérelle (Paris 1923) from *Sangre y Arena* (Madrid), trs. as *Blood and Sand* by Mrs. W. A. Gillespie (London 1913).

19 Arthur Young (1741–1820), English writer on agriculture and social economy. The quotation is from his *Tour of Ireland* (1780).

20 *The Good-Natur'd Man*, a comedy in 5 acts by Oliver Goldsmith, was produced at the Abbey 27 April 1920.

21 Geoffrey Henry Browne (Browne-Guthrie) 3rd Baron Oranmore and Browne (1861–1927), was appointed a member of the Congested Districts Board in 1919.

22 See Frank Persse's letter to Lady Gregory pp. 155–156.

23 *Damer's Gold*, a comedy in 2 acts by Lady Gregory was first produced at the Abbey 21 November 1912, with Sara Allgood, J. M. Kerrigan and Arthur Sinclair. Kerrigan had evidently returned to the Abbey for this production.
24 *Hyacinth Halvey*, a 1 act comedy, was first produced at the Abbey 19 February 1906. It was a great favourite of the audiences.
25 *In the Shadow of the Glen*, a play in 1 act by J. M. Synge was first produced at the Molesworth Hall, Dublin, 8 October 1903.
26 *A Minute's Wait*, a comedy in 1 act by Martin J. McHugh, was first produced at the Abbey 27 August 1914.
27 De Valera held a great number of vast meetings in New York and other cities after his arrival in America in June 1919. MacArdle, p. 310.
28 George Moore, in extracts from *Hail & Farewell* which appeared in the *English Review* in 1914, accused Lady Gregory of being a "souper" (i.e. a Protestant who tried to get conversions through gifts of soup etc. during famine years). After protests, these passages were removed from the book. Both Yeats and Hugh Lane were very angry with Moore over this, and Moore himself remained bitter over it. Lady Gregory denied that she had ever been a souper, but said that one of her sisters was. See *Seventy Years* (Gerrards Cross 1974, New York 1976), Coole Edition XIII, 15–17.
29 Mr. & Mrs. Jayne were friends of Lady Gregory for many years. Whenever she was in Philadelphia, she would stay at their home, 1824 De Lancey Place.
30 *Aristotle's Bellows*, a wonder play in 3 acts was first produced at the Abbey 17 March 1921. See 10:3.

BOOK NINE
15 June–14 November 1920

1 *Du côté de chez Swann*, the first volume of Marcel Proust's *A la Recherche du Temps Perdu*.
2 Brigadier General Lucas and two other officers were captured in the early hours of the morning in Cork. A large number of men "armed to the teeth" burst into the officers' hut and arrested them "in the name of the Irish Republic". Col. Danford, attempting to escape, was wounded, and the other colonel was released to look after him. *I.T.* 28 July 1920. When General Lucas was not found the next day, the town of Fermoy was looted by about 400 of the military. *I.T.* 29 July.
3 Lady Dudley, née Rachel Gurney, the wife of William Humble Ward, 2nd Earl of Dudley, was a lady of great beauty and talent, and greatly influenced him in turning to public service. He was Lord Lieutenant of Ireland 1902–1905, a period of great social success.
4 Henrik Ibsen's *The Enemy of the People* had influenced Martyn's playwriting.
5 See 5: 27.
6 Michael Collins was a growing influence in Ireland during the summer of 1919. He was Minister of Finance in the Dail. Director of Organisation in the I.R.A. and Director of Intelligence. He was also a member of the Supreme Council of the I.R.B. See 8:13.
7 *Crossed Souls* was not produced at the Abbey.
8 The air "Shule Aroon" is sung by Celia at the beginning of Act I and Act

II of *Aristotle's Bellows*. A song to the air of "The Bells of Shandon" occurs twice in Act I.

9 Terence McSwiney, Lord Mayor of Cork, had been on hunger strike in Brixton Prison for about a month at this time. By 23 October he was delirious and unable to recognise his relatives. He died on the 25th on the seventy-fourth day of his hunger strike. *C.E.* 27 October 1920. A fellow hunger striker, Joseph Murray, aged seventeen, died on the same day. There was a huge funeral in Cork on 31 October. MacArdle, pp. 391–392.

10 There were so many cases of police being ambushed at this time that only large raids were reported in the press, and there were few enquiries about police reprisals.

11 The Ballyvaughan Barracks were attacked by a large party and burned on 20 September 1920. *I.T.* 22 September.

12 Lady Gregory got her way, for the first edition of *Hugh Lane's Life and Achievement* contained reproductions of both. "La Toilette" by Puvis de Chavannes and "Les Parapluies" by Renoir. Other pictures reproduced in the book were Rembrandt's "Lady with Gloves", Romney's "Mrs. Edward Taylor", Goya's "A Spanish Girl (La Moue)", "Portrait of a Gentleman" by Strozzi and Titian's "Portrait of Baldassare Castiglione".

13 "Mr. Dooley on the Olympic Games" by Finely Peter Dunne, appeared in the *American Magazine* N.Y., Vol. 68, October 1909, pp. 539–540.

14 *Hugh Lane's Life and Achievement* did not contain a preface by Douglas; instead it had "L'Art de Donner un Musée" by Arsène Alexandre, from *Le Figaro*, 20 March 1908.

15 Maria Edgeworth's *Waste Not Want Not, and Other Tales* (London 1862), and *Mrs Wiggs of the Cabbage Patch*, a dramatisation by Anne Flexner of the novel by Alice Hogan Rice (New York 1924).

16 The text of the articles that Lady Gregory sent to *The Nation* will be published in the first volume of *The Shorter Writings of Lady Gregory*, Coole Edition XVI.

17 George M. Trevelyan's *Garibaldi's Defence of the Roman Republic 1848–49* (London 1907).

18 This line is spoken by Mary Cahel at the end of Lady Gregory's *The Gaol Gate*.

19 George M. Trevelyan's *Garibaldi and the Thousand* (London 1909).

20 Maria Edgeworth's *Rosamund* (London 1821).

BOOK TEN
15 November 1920–14 January 1921

1 Henry James (1843–1916), American novelist and friend of Lady Gregory. *The Letters of Henry James*, selected and edited by Percy Lubbock, 2 vols. (London 1920).

2 William James (1842–1910), philosopher and psychologist, elder brother of Henry James.

3 *Aristotle's Bellows* was first produced at the Abbey 17 March 1921, when it was a great success. The players and Lady Gregory were called to the stage. Maureen Delany was delightfully funny. Lady Gregory thought "it was wonderfully well played and Miss Delany sang delightfully." Jack B. Yeats and one of his sisters were in the stalls. Holloway, January—March 1921, vol. 1, pp. 566–567.

4 A limited rail strike was on in Ireland; engineers refused to move trains that contained Black and Tans or armed soldiers. The strike spread until both trainmen and dockers refused to handle munitions. MacArdle, p. 347.
5 On Sunday morning at 9.00 o'clock, armed men entered houses and hotels where officers resided and shot twelve of them. Two auxiliary officers were also shot. *I.T.* 22 November 1920.
6 Yeats's poem to Robert Gregory was probably his "Reprisals". It was not published in *The Times*, and had its first publication in *Rann* Autumn 1948. It appears in the *Variorum Poems* p. 791.
7 The Postscript was included, pp. 271–273.
8 A number of fires were started by incendiaries in Cork on Saturday and Sunday, 27–28 November, causing extensive damage estimated at over £100,000. *I.T.* 29 November. After this, the Black and Tans celebrated the burning by wearing a bit of burned cork in their caps.
9 The Aran Islands were occupied by a party from a destroyer on 23 December. One islander was shot dead when he refused to halt. Fifty lancers occupied the main island, Inishmore. *I.T.* 24 December 1920.
10 The Wren Boys would sing the traditional song from house to house on St. Stephen's Day, 26 December. The song begins "The wren, the wren, the king of all birds . . .". "The Soldier's Song" by Peadar Kearney, composed in 1907, later became the Irish National Anthem.

BOOK ELEVEN
15 January–20 March 1921

1 Sir Alfred Lyall, *Tennyson* (London 1902). See 40:67.
2 Alexander William Kinglake, *Eothen, or Traces of Travel Brought Home from the East* (London 1844), *The Invasion of the Crimea*, 8 vols (London 1863–1887).
3 Celbridge Abbey, Celbridge, Co. Kildare.
4 Anton Chekov, *The Witch*, a drama in 4 acts was produced for the Dublin Drama League by H. Wien-Jemisen. Holloway, January-March 1921, vol. 2. p. 430.
5 *The Revolutionist*, a play in 5 acts by Terence MacSwiney was first produced at the Abbey 24 February 1921. Lady Gregory told Holloway that she had come up for the play, having arrived the night before. She had originally seen the play in London with Lillah MacCarthy. Among those at the Dublin performance were Lennox Robinson and Sarah Purser. Holloway *ibid.* p. 440. He also noted (p. 452) that the Abbey was packed for the evening performance.
6 Jack B. Yeats's exhibition at 7 St. Stephen's Green took place 19 February to 4 March. Among other large paintings singled out for praise were "The Dark Man", "The Ballina Car", and "A Dusty Lane in Kerry".
7 The Home Rule Agreement—The Treaty—was finally signed in London on 6 December 1921 at 2.30 a.m. It was a draft of Articles of Agreement which had to be submitted to the British Parliament for ratification. MacArdle, p. 590.
8 "To a Friend whose Work has Come to Nothing" first appeared in *Poetry*, May 1914. Lady Gregory reproduced it in *Hugh Lane's Life and Achievement*, stating that Yeats wrote it for Lane (though she corrected this in

her personal copy, in readiness for the next edition) and this was echoed by Thomas Bodkin (who still did not know the truth) in his *Hugh Lane and his Pictures* (Dublin 1958).

9 At one stage Robert Langton Douglas was to have written a foreword to Lady Gregory's book, but later he was more enemy than friend. See Book 9 Note 14.

10 In a review of *Hugh Lane's Life and Achievement*, A.E. wrote "nobody who reads Lady Gregory's book, with the evidence she brings, can doubt any longer that the pictures which hang in the National Gallery in London are as much stolen Irish property, as property taken by the Black and Tans who were dismissed by General Crozier; and there is far less excuse for the theft of the pictures, because it was done deliberately by English gentlemen and was not the actions of rowdy persons of low character out for a day's jollification at the expense of the Irish nation." *I.H.* 5 March 1921. Brig. General F.P. Crozier, Commandant of the Auxiliary Cadets in Ireland, resigned because of the Police Chiefs' veto of his dismissal of twenty-six cadets for looting early in 1921. See his letter to *The Times* 3 March 1921.

11 The Rt. Hon. James Ian MacPherson, 1st Baron Strathcarron (1880–1937), was Chief Secretary for Ireland 1918–1920. Created a baronet in 1933, and baron in 1936.

12 *The Times Literary Supplement* reviewed *Hugh Lane's Life and Achievement* on 10 March 1921, p. 156, and said that the book was worth reading. "Lady Gregory puts the case of Dublin as strongly as she can, and it cannot be met with silence."

12a *The Irish Times* of 14 March had an editorial praising Lady Gregory's book and pressing for the return of the pictures. From Lady Gregory's reference, it was probably wholly or partly written by Lennox Robinson.

13 Six men were shot in Cork for revolutionary activities. *T.* 1 March 1921, and there was also a threat to shoot four (all aged nineteen) who were in prison in Dublin. A.E. wrote that if the executions were carried out, "the soul of Ireland will grow as far apart from the possibility of friendship with Great Britain as earth is from the Pole Star." *The Times* quoted part of the letter on 13 March. Six men were hanged in Mountjoy Prison on 14 March, in pairs at 6.00, 7.00 and 8.00 a.m. All appeals were refused.

14 Probably Patrick Moran, who apparently had nothing to do with the crime of which he was charged. The Dun Laoghaire branch of the Rail Union asked their M.P. to intercede for mercy "in view of the overwhelming evidence of [his] innocence . . . advanced at his trial . . .". *I.I.* 13 March 1921.

14a Probably J. S. Starkey, the real name of Seumas O'Sullivan.

15 Dermot O'Brien, Irish art historian.

16 *Bedmates*, a comedy in 1 act by George Shiels was first produced at the Abbey 6 January 1921.

17 In the 24 March issue of *The Times Literary Supplement*, there were two letters on the Lane controversy, signed "X" and "Art Lover".

18 Both W. B. Yeats and A.E. had letters in the 31 March issue of the *T.L.S.* refuting the claim made by "X" that Lane was bound by promises to give the pictures to London.

19 MacColl's article in *XIXth Century* (January 1921), entitled "Spanish Painters" was on pp. 80–89.

20 Lennox Robinson said that the Abbey would stay open as long as possible under the 9.00 p.m. curfew. *I.I.* 5 March 1921.

BOOK TWELVE
20 March–24 April 1921

1 Sir Robert Woods (1865–1938), Irish surgeon and M.P. for Dublin University.
2 Lady Gregory had a letter published in *The Times* (23 March 1921) which proposed a settlement of the Irish Question: full dominion status, with no tax payable to England, "with no insistence on our army or navy", which she thought would be accepted.
3 W. Y. Yeats's letter in the 31 March issue of the *T.L.S.* was entitled "Sir Hugh Lane and the National Gallery".
4 Mayor Clancy and ex-Mayor O'Callaghan were shot on the morning of 7 March by men who wore motor goggles, false moustaches and had their caps pulled down. Both men's wives were injured in trying to save their husbands. No reasons were given for the killings. *I.I.* 8 March 1921.
5 *The Times Literary Supplement* of 31 April 1921.
6 (Gyles) Lytton Strachey, *Queen Victoria* (London 1921).

BOOK THIRTEEN
24 April–30 May 1921

1 The Rt. Hon. Frederick Huth Jackson (1863–1921) P.C., Director of the Bank of England.
2 "Thoughts upon the present state of the world", in *Seven Poems and a Fragment* (Cuala Press 1922).
3 Sir Claude Phillips (?–1924), art critic, barrister, Keeper of the Wallace Collection 1897–1911.
4 Sir Francesco Paolo Tosti (1846–1916), Italian composer and teacher of singing. He had settled in London in 1876 and became teacher of singing to the Royal Family in 1880.
5 Probably Dr. Thomas Kirkpatrick Monro (1865–1958).
6 See 13:1.
7 G.B. Shaw's *Heartbreak House* ran from 15 December 1920 to 9 February 1921 at the Garrick Theatre in New York, and was first performed in England later in the year.
8 *Back to Methuselah* was first produced in New York in 1922, and in England the following year.
9 G. B. Shaw, *Collected Works* (London 1930–1950).
10 Thomas Bewick (1753–1828), engraver, left his collection in Newcastle upon Tyne, and upon his death were sold by his executors and acquired by Julia Boyd. *Bewick Gleanings*, ed with Notes by Julia Boyd (Newcastle upon Tyne 1886). Bewick died at his home in Gateshead.
11 G. B. Shaw, *Love Among the Artists* (Chicago 1900).
12 Lucy Phillimore, née Fitzpatrick, married Robert Charles Phillimore (1871–1919) eldest son of Sir Walter George Frank Phillimore, 1st Baron Phillimore (1845–1929), cr. 1918. After her husband's death she was not treated well by his family. Her home was Kendalls Hall, Radlett, Herts.
13 Shaw had reviewed *Guy Domville* in the *Saturday Review* 12 January 1895; the review was reprinted in the 1961 (London) edition of the work pp. 205–209.
14 Shaw's mother, née Lucinda E. Gurley (1830–1913) appeared in opera in

Dublin. She married in 1852 and toured with the Carl Rosa Opera Company in 1881.

15 District Inspector Blake, Captain Cornwallis, Lieut. W. Creery and Mrs. Blake were shot dead on 16 May when leaving a tennis party at Ballyturn House. Margaret Gregory was the sole survivor. *I.I.* 17 May 1921.

16 Wilfrid Scawen Blunt, *My Diaries*, 2 vols. (New York 1921).

17 The Hon. Neville Stephen Lytton, later 3rd Earl of Lytton (1879–1951), the 4th son of the 1st Earl.

18 Vernon Lee (pseud. of Violet Paget), *Satan, the Waster* (London 1920).

19 'Clemence Dane', *A Bill of Divorcement*, a play in 3 acts was produced at St. Martin's Theatre, London.

20 Sir Mountstuart Elphinstone Grant Duff (1829–1906) published a series of volumes extracted from his diaries (London 1897–1905). A number of stories by Lady Gregory are quoted in them. The closest quotation to fit this story appears in the entry for 14 January 1901. "I sat between Mr. John Murray and Mr. Augustine Birrell, near enough to speak also to Lord Justice Collins and Mr. Basil Champneys." The sting in the tail of the story was that Sir Alfred Lyall was also a member of the Literary Society, and the story could so easily have been true.

BOOK FOURTEEN
1 June–11 July 1921

1 Correctly, "I have found you an argument, but I am not obliged to find you understanding" from Boswell's *Life of Johnson* (1784).

2 Edmund Bernard Fitzalan-Howard, 1st Viscount Fitz Alan of Derwent (1855–1947), politician and at this time Viceroy (i.e. Lord Lieutenant) of Ireland. In his speech in Belfast he said he hoped for peace in Ireland and he felt it might be soon "a time of happiness and prosperity for Ireland". *T.* 8 June 1921.

3 In order to conduct negotiations about the future of Ireland, a truce was agreed. It came into force at noon 11 July. *Annual Register* p. 75.

4 Alfred A. Knopf, Blunt's American publisher.

5 Elizabeth Mary Margaret Plunkett, née Burke (1859–1944), wife of the 11th Earl of Fingall.

6 Cecil Frederick Macready (1862–1946) was at this time Commander-in-Chief of the British forces in Ireland.

BOOK FIFTEEN
13 July–5 November 1921

1 Dermod O'Brien (1865–1945), Irish artist, President of the Royal Hibernian Academy since 1910.

2 Michael J. Dolan, Will Shields and Eric Gorman were all Abbey actors.

3 Meredith's *Vittoria* (London 1889), *Sandra Belloni* (London 1889) was also published under the title *Emilia in England.*

4 Plunkett House, 84 Merrion Square, named after Sir Horace Plunkett, founder of the I.A.O.S. whose headquarters the house is. A.E. had his offices there.

5 T. W. Lyster (1855–1922), Librarian of the National Library of Ireland.

6 Mary Cholmondeley, *Diana Tempest* (London 1913).

7 *The Image and Other Plays* (London and New York 1922) contained *The*

Image, *Hanrahan's Oath*, *Shanwalla* and *The Wrens*.

8 *Three Wonder Plays* (London and New York 1923) contained *The Dragon*, *Aristotle's Bellows* and *The Jester*.

9 "I wish death and life".

10 M. D. Haviland, *Lives of the Fur Folk* (London 1910).

11 *Little Essays*, drawn from the Writings of G. Santayana, by Logan Pearsall Smith (London 1920).

12 Ivan S. Turgenieff (Turgenev), *Virgin Soil* (London 1878), *On the Eve: A Tale* (New York 1875).

13 On 22 July 1921 it was announced that Lloyd George and de Valera found no basis for a formal conference. *Annual Register* p. 75.

14 London and Great Western Railway.

15 Mme. i.e. Countess Constance Markievicz was released from Mountjoy Prison at 3.00p.m. on Sunday 24 July 1921.

16 *The Independent*'s hopeful tone was out of touch with events. The following month on 18 August, *The Irish Times* stated that de Valera would not accept the peace terms.

17 Turgenieff's *Fathers and Children* (London 1867).

18 Arthur Young, *Tour of Ireland* (1780). See 8:19.

19 The Dail met on 16 August. The following day de Valera turned down Lloyd George's terms. *I.I.*, *I.T.* 18 August.

20 Lloyd George said that Britain had gone as far as it could, and "prolongation of the present state of affairs is dangerous". *I.I.* 27 August.

21 *The Old Woman Remembers* was performed at the Abbey on 31 December 1923 by Sara Allgood. It was published in *The New Republic* (20 February 1924), p. 339 and in *The Irish Statesman* (22 March 1924) pp. 40–41.

22 Robert Barton T.D. was imprisoned by the British in January 1920, sentenced to three years' penal servitude for a seditious speech, but released in July 1921.

23 Michael Butler Yeats has been President of the Irish Senate and more recently vice-president of the E.E.C. Parliament in Brussels.

24 Lloyd George telegraphed de Valera that he would not meet him as a representative of a sovereign state, but as "the chosen leader of the great majority in Southern Ireland".

25 Susan L. Mitchell, *George Moore* (Dublin 1916).

26 *Bricriu's Feast* by Eimar O'Duffy, a dramatisation of the 4th chapter of *Cuchulain of Muirthemne*, was presumably privately performed as there is no record of a public one. At this distance in time, it is not clear what the play had to do with Plunkett's poetry.

27 Count George Noble Plunkett, *Arrows* (Dublin 1921). In a review of the book in the *Irish Independent*, Peter McBrien wrote that at its best moments, Plunkett's poetry ranked as high as that of Yeats, Dora Sigerson Shorter and Francis Ledwidge. *I.I.* 19 September.

28 A reference to her play *Hanrahan's Oath*.

29 *A Serious Thing*, a play in 1 act by Gideon Ousley (pseud. of O.St.J. Gogarty) was first produced at the Abbey 19 August 1919.

30 De Valera wired Lloyd George (in Irish and English) that a delegation would meet in London on 11 October. *I.I.* 1 October.

31 The Dail intervened in the Railway Strike, an agreement was reached with the shopmen, and the strike settled. *I.I.* 1 October.

32 James Larkin, the Irish Labour leader was arrested in New York 8 November 1919, charged with criminal anarchy. He was gaoled, tried and

sentenced to a term "not less than five years and not more than ten years", and was not released until 1923 when he was let out by Governor Al Smith, who branded the trial "an infringement of political discussion". P. M. Fox, *Jim Larkin* (New York 1957), pp. 134–35. See also 27:19, 29:23.

33 A fracas arose outside a Galway dance hall where a dance in aid of the Republican Dependents' Fund was being held. Some shots were fired and Lt. Soveham, who was passing in a motor car, was shot dead. *I.I.* 4 October.

34 Joseph Holloway was, over the years, at odds with the Abbey management about both plays and players.

35 J. M. Kerrigan had acted with the Abbey 1907–1916.

36 Richard James Mulcahy (1886–1971) Minister of Defence in the Dail 1922, and C. in C. of the Free State Forces 1922–23, succeeding Michael Collins. He was President of Fine Gael 1944–1960.

37 Yeats's poem "Easter 1916".

38 A.E. published a number of pamphlets on Ireland's struggle for independence, including *Thoughts for a Convention* (1917) and *Ireland and the Empire at the Court of Conscience* (1921).

39 Either Anne Bowman, *The Young Exiles*, or The Wild Tribes of the North (London 1890), or Stephanie de Saint Aubin, Comtesse de Genlis (1747–1830), *The Young Exiles* (Dublin 1799).

40 On 19 October the Pope telegraphed Lloyd George "We rejoice at the resumption of the Anglo-Irish negotiations . . ." and he prayed that they would bring "to an end the age-long dissention".

41 De Valera telegraphed Pope Benedict XV on 20 October saying that the people of Ireland appreciated the Pope's help, but that the trouble was between Ireland and Britain, and occurred because "the rulers of Britain have sought to impose their will upon Ireland, and by brutal force have endeavoured to rob her people of the liberty which is their natural right and their ancient heritage".

42 *Four Plays for Dancers* (London and New York 1921). Wade's *Bibliography* nos. 129, 130.

43 It may have been for the Cuala Press edition of *Seven Poems and a Fragment* (1922), in which it appeared, though it was also published in the September 1921 issue of *The Dial*, and the November 1921 issue of *The London Mercury*.

44 *Insurance Money*, a comedy in 3 acts by George Shiels was first produced at the Abbey 13 December 1921.

45 Sean O'Casey's first play *The Crimson in the Tricolour* was rejected by the Abbey, though Lady Gregory encouraged him to submit another. The text of this play no longer exists, though Lady Gregory's report on it does.

"The Crimson in the Tricolour—(a very good name)

"This a puzzling play—extremely interesting—Mrs. Budrose is a jewel, & her husband a good setting for her—I don't see any plot in it, unless the Labour unrest culminating in the turning off of the lights at the meeting may be considered one. It is the expression of ideas that makes it interesting (besides feeling that the writer has something in him) & no doubt the point of interest for Dublin audiences. But we could not put it on while the Revolution is still unaccomplished—it might hasten the Labour attack on Sinn Fein, which ought to be kept back till the fight with England is over, & the new Government has had time to show what it can do.

"I think Eileen's rather disagreeable flirtation with O'Regan shd. be cut—their first entrance—or rather exit (or both) seems to be leading to something that doesn't come. In Act II a good deal of O'Regan & Nora shd be cut.

"In Act III almost all the O'Malley and Eileen part shd. be cut. The end is I think good, the entry of the Workmen, & Fagan & Tim Tracy.

"I feel that there is no personal interest worth developing, but that with as much as possible of those barren parts cut, we might find a possible play of ideas in it.

"I suggest that (with the author's leave) it shd. be worth typing the play at theatre's expense—with or without those parts—For it is impossible to go through it again—or show it—or have a reading of it—while in handwriting. A.G.'

See p. 512.

45a "Marcus Crassus, whose father had borne the office of censor, and had been honoured with a triumph, was brought up in a small house with his two brothers. These married while their parents were living, and they all ate at the same table. But he had a love of money . . ."

46 *The Courting of Mary Doyle*, a comedy in 3 acts by Edward McNulty was first produced at the Abbey 8 November 1921.

47 *The Yellow Bittern*, a play in 1 act by Daniel Corkery was first produced at the Abbey 4 May 1920.

BOOK SIXTEEN
14 November 1921–8 January 1922

1 Lionel Smith-Gordon, Irish economist.

2 *The Times* of 29 November 1921 carried a report that the Anglican Synod in Sydney had voted to make the Church of England in Australia free from any affiliation with the Church of England.

3 During this time, there was a great deal of activity in London. On 1 December new proposals were made, and Barton, the Sinn Fein Minister of Economics and Finance, immediately left for Dublin. *I.T.* 2 December. The matter was discussed with de Valera who had come up to Dublin from the West, and the Delegates and Secretaires returned to London. MacArdle, pp. 577–581.

4 The Rt. Hon Frederick Huth Jackson died 3 December.

5 See 11:7.

6 De Valera wrote that he could not recommend the Treaty. "The terms of this agreement are in violent conflict with the wishes of the majority of this Nation." He then suggested that the differences be resolved by constitutional means. *I.T.* 9 December.

7 *Crabbed Youth and Age* by Lennox Robinson was first produced at the Abbey 14 November 1922.

8 *Psalm* 104, vs. 16 and *Psalm* 105 vss. 26–36. Authorised (King James) Version.

9 The essential breach was over the oath. Both de Valera and Austin Stack urged rejection over this point. *I.T.* 20 December.

10 Sara Allgood played Mrs. Rainey in *Mixed Marriage* at the Everyman Theatre.

11 Dail Eireann adjourned on Thursday 22 December for the Christmas recess, to meet again on 3 January. *I.T.* 23 December.

12 The Dail, by a vote of 64 to 57 votes, voted to accept the Treaty on 7 Jan-

uary 1922, and de Valera resigned as President of the Dail. MacArdle, pp. 641–2.

BOOK SEVENTEEN
11 January–1 April 1922

1 *Aftermath*, a play in 3 acts by T. C. Murray, was first produced at the Abbey 10 January 1922.
2 Griffith was elected President of the Dail, and de Valera and his 56 supporters walked out. *I.T.* 11 January 1922.
3 John Joseph Reynolds was Director of the Municipal Gallery of Modern Art, Dublin 1922–1935.
4 Griffith, in a very spirited defence of his role as President, said "I am doing what I am doing . . . because I believe it is absolutely my duty to my country." He also said that he wished de Valera had not resigned, and that he were still President, but since he had, Griffith would take up the burden of responsibility. *I.I.* 11 January.
5 Frank Gallagher (1893–1962), Irish patriot. He spent ten days on hunger strike from 5 April 1920 in Mountjoy Prison; this was the first of four, the longest of which lasted forty-seven days. The record of that was published in his *Days of Fear* (London 1928, New York 1929), and it was a book that moved Lady Gregory greatly. She reviewed it for *The New Republic* and *The Nation* and re-read it a number of times.
6 Probably Harold Adrian Milne Barbour (1874–1938) who was for twenty years a voluntary worker in the Co-operative Organisation of Farmers, a Senator for N. Ireland in 1921, and nineteen years a member of Antrim County Council.
7 A French translation of this poem appeared in Simone Tery's *L'Ile des Bardes* (Paris 1925) but it does not appear to have been published in English until 1973, when the text was given in an article by Weldon Thornton in *Eire-Ireland* VIII (Fall 1973) pp. 26–28. Entitled "A.E.'s 'Ideal Poems: J[ame]s St[ephen]s'", Prof. Thornton's text comes from a ms. written by A.E. in a copy of *Secret Springs of Dublin Song* (Dublin 1918), in the Rare Book Room of the University of North Carolina at Chapel Hill.

Ideal Poems
J——s St——s

Hi God! Get off that throne
You've had your turn & turn about
'S fair play you know. Give me that crown
That cushion too. Be off! hiss cat! get out!

Get off to Hell now! There's a job
I left there, just a quid a week!
You take it and the twenty bob
All I was worth you thought—such cheek!

Now his sour face is gone. All's clear!
Come to me pretty—what'-your-names!
Just tuck your wings up. That's my dear
Sit on my knees and call me James!

Geo. W. Russell

8 Mary Caroline, Lady Fitz Alan, wife of 1st Viscount Fitz Alan, who

was the first Roman Catholic Lord Lieutenant of Ireland. See 14:2.

9 John F. Larchet (1885–1967), Irish organist and composer, who conducted the Abbey Theatre orchestra for many years.

10 Miss Mary MacSwiney, sister of Terence MacSwiney, a T.D. (member of the Dail), and a supporter of de Valera.

11 Prisoners who were gaoled for political crimes committed prior to the truce were granted amnesty. Many in Irish gaols were set free on 12 January; those in English prisons were to be set free, beginning on the 13th. *I.I.* 13 January 1922.

12 Shaw spoke amusingly at the Seventh Annual Lecture on Molière, supporting a vote of thanks for Maurice Donnat's speech. *T.*, 19, 20 January.

13 Shaw wrote a long preface on prisons for Sidney and Beatrice Webb's *English Prisons and Local Government* (London 1922).

14 See 12:6.

15 "Ruskin's Politics", a lecture delivered at the Ruskin Centenary Exhibition, held at the Royal Academy, 21 November 1919. For the text, see *Shaw: Platform and Pulpit*, ed. Dan H. Laurence (London 1962), pp. 130–144.

16 The riots following the Prince's reception left one dead and scores injured. Motor cars were stoned, and the Wellington Theatre, showing films of the Prince's tour, was half wrecked. *T.* 16 January.

17 John Poyntz Spencer, 5th Earl Spencer (1835–1910), Lord Lieutenant and Viceroy of Ireland 1869–1874, 1882–1885.

18 James Hamilton, 2nd Duke of Abercorn (1838–1913), Irish Unionist and Ulster supporter of Carson.

19 Mahdi—one who will arise at the end of the world as leader of the Faithful of Islam, Arabic 'he who is guided aright'. Mohammed Ahmed claimed to be the Mahdi in 1882, and called upon the people of the Sudan to expel the Egyptians. He conquered the Sudan, with the fall of Khartoum and the death of General Gordon in 1885, and died soon after. His tomb at Omdurman became a place of pilgrimage.

20 In the Craig-Collins Agreement, the Goverments of Southern and Northern Ireland agreed that questions of Irish interest would be settled by Irishmen without English interference. *I.T.* 23 January.

21 Lennox Robinson denied a report that Sara Allgood was about to take control of the Abbey, and that Lady Gregory was about to hand it over to the Free State Government. *I.T.* 25 January.

22 For a fuller account, see *Sir William Gregory, An Autobiography*, edited by Lady Gregory (London 1894), pp. 243–44.

BOOK EIGHTEEN
4 April–22 May 1922

1 Under the heading, "Dictatorship the Aim", the *Freeman's Journal* stated that at Sunday's (26 March) meeting, a resolution was passed favouring the declaration of a dictatorship and the suppression of all "pretended Governments in Ireland until such time as an election without threat of war from Britain can be held . . .". (29 March.) On 30th and 31st, the *Journal* was only a handbill. The issue of the 30th stated that close to 100 men broke every machine with sledge hammers, doused the premises with petrol and set it on fire.

2 The I.R.A. claimed that the raid was because of "statements made therein

calculated to cause disaffection and indiscipline in the ranks of the Irish Republican Army". *I.T.* 31 March.

3 George Sand (pseud. of Armandine Aurore Lucile Dupin, Baronne Dudevant), *Consuelo.* Lady Gregory may have had any one of a number of translations.

4 De Valera was asked whether he would support the Treaty if the people voted for it. He replied that if England removed the threat of force and "immediate and terrible war", and the people voted for the Free State, he would never raise the question of the Republic again. *I.I.* 13 April.

5 Sir Sidney Colvin (1845–1927), an authority on Keats.

6 Elah, King of Israel, son of Ba asha, after a reign of two years, was slain by Zimri, commander of half his chariots, during a drinking bout. 1 *Kings* XVI, vss. 9–10.

7 *The Drapier Letters,* a play in 1 act by Arthur Power, was first produced at the Abbey 22 August 1927. *Kathleen's Seamless Coat* was not performed at the Abbey.

8 A peace conference was convened on 13 April by the Archbishop of Dublin, The Most Rev. Dr. Byrne, and the Lord Mayor of Dublin, Mr. L. O'Neill. It was attended by Arthur Griffith, Michael Collins, de Valera and Cathal Brugha. It was adjourned of the 15th without reaching any agreement except to meet again on the 20th. *I.T.* 15 April.

9 Rory O'Connor, Chief of the Volunteer Executive, said that the seizure did not constitute a political act: he needed accommodation for his men. *I.T.* 15 April.

10 The Irish Agricultural Organisation Society, the driving force behind the co-operative movements in Ireland.

11 Desmond Fitzgerald (d. 1947), Minister for External Affairs in the Free State Government and Minister for Defence until 1932.

12 Patrick J. Hogan, Minister for Agriculture in the Free State Government 1922.

13 Kevin O'Higgins (1892–1927), Minister for Justice in the Free State Government until his assassination in 1927. He was also Vice President of the Executive Council, and its most brilliant member.

14 Professor Robert Mitchell Henry, author of *The Evolution of Sinn Fein* (Dublin 1920).

15 Michael Sweeney was being brought back from a court martial by uniformed IRA men. Accounts differ about what happened. According to the Volunteers, Sweeney could hardly walk because of war wounds, but he was shot in cold blood when he stood up in a lorry while passing College Green. *I.I.* 13 April. The inquest found that he had been shot accidentally. He was buried on Monday 16 April. *I.I.* 17 April.

16 Field Marshal Sir Henry Wilson (1864–1922) made a number of inflamatory speeches in N. Ireland in May 1922, and was assassinated on 22 June by members of Sinn Fein.

17 See 26:48.

18 Sir Ivor Churchill Guest, 1st Viscount Wimborne (1873–1939), politician, Lord Lieutenant of Ireland 1915–1918.

19 General Sir John Maxwell, C. in C. of the British Forces, ordered the execution of the leaders of the 1916 Rising.

20 Cathal Brugha had been Minister for Defence up to 1922. See Book 8, Note 14.

21 Harry Boland supported de Valera during the Civil War. He was helping to reorganise the Republican Army in Leinster, when he was shot and killed.

22 With the imminence of the ratification of the Treaty with England, the Unionist North intensified the pressure on the Catholic Republicans. The Dail Eireann Publicity Department issued the following figures for the Belfast troubles for the period 21 July 1920 to 4 June 1922: 423 killed, 1,750 wounded, 3,150 driven from work, 20,500 driven from areas where Catholics were in a minority to major Catholic ones, or from the North to the South. *I.I.* 5 June. The following day, the *Independent* reported that an area a half mile square had been ordered cleared of Catholics or they would be bombed out, and on the 8th it reported that the Belfast Catholic Protection Committee had stated that 20,000 people were homeless in Belfast. There were continuing reports of the arrival of large numbers of Northern refugees in the South.

23 Seven Protestants were murdered in Cork, 26–28 April 1922, apparently as reprisals for those murdered in Belfast. Two of the Protestants were over eighty years old. *N.Y.T.* 29 April.

24 The *Connacht Tribune* of 6 May stated that Roxborough was to be used to house Belfast refugees.

25 The home of the Rev. P. Bradshaw, Rector of Kilchriest, Loughrea, was raided and jewellery, bicycles and clothing taken. *C.T.* 6 May.

26 A truce was signed on Thursday 4 May to last until 8 May, to allow "representatives of both sections of the army an immediate opportunity of discovering a basis for army unification". *I.T.* 5 May.

27 George W. Russell, *Ireland, Past and Future, Being a Paper read to the Sociological Society on 21st February 1922.*

28 *The Book of Common Prayer*. St. John the Baptist's day in the Church calendar is 24 June.

29 Correctly "so we may also in heart and mind thither ascend . . ."

30 Theodore Spicer Simson (1871–1959), painter and creator of a series of portrait medallions, including Yeats, Lady Gregory, A.E., James Stephens, James Joyce, Douglas Hyde and St. John Ervine.

31 Michael Collins and de Valera reached an agreement on Saturday 20 May to form a coalition panel, each party to keep its present strength in the Dail. *I.T.* 22 May.

32 The last lines of "Year that Trembled and Reel'd beneath Me", in the Drum Taps section in *Leaves of Grass*, in *Collected Poems* (London 1975) p. 333.

33 Several stately residences in the North were burned over the weekend of 20–21 May, including Shane Castle, Oldcourt Castle, Crebilly House, as well as railway stations and shops. Fourteen people were murdered in Belfast over the same weekend. *I.T.* 22 May.

BOOK NINETEEN
23 May–6 August 1922

1 "Sir Frederic Burton". Ch. VIII of *Seventy Years* (Gerrards Cross 1974, New York 1976).

2 Epstein's bust of Lady Gregory was in the Hugh Lane Gallery of Modern Art (formerly the Municipal Gallery) in Dublin for many years but is at present in the National Gallery of Ireland.

3 Lord Dunkellin was one of Sir William Gregory's closest friends.

4 "Sir Henry Layard". Ch. IX of *Seventy Years*.

5 "Sir Alfred Lyall". Ch. XI of *Seventy Years*.

6 The 16 February 1924 issue of the *Connacht Tribune* reported that a man was fined £2 for killing rabbits on the land of Viscount Gough. On Sunday 2 March, Robert Houston, Lord Gough's gamekeeper, was brutally beaten up just outside Lough Cutra Castle by ten or twelve masked men. *C.T.* 8 March.

7 Fighting had been going on in Belfast between Catholics and Protestants for some time, with guns and bombs in daily use, mainly against Catholics, who were being killed almost every day. *I.T.* May passim.

8 Yeats's first honorary degree was from Queen's University, Belfast, in July 1922.

9 The Kildare Street Club was occupied by the Irregulars on Monday 1 May, and was supposed to be evacuated on 2 May, on the orders of the Regulars who had surrounded it. *I.T.* 2 May. The following day, that paper reported that the Club was still occupied.

10 Constance Markievicz was defeated in the St. Patrick's, later called the Dublin South constituency, coming bottom of the poll. She regained it in August 1923. Liam Mellows had been contesting Galway. *I.T.* 20 June.

11 *Brand*, by Henrik Ibsen, was written in the summer of 1865 in Rome.

12 "Meditations in Time of Civil War", I, "Ancestral Houses", *Collected Poems*, p. 225.

13 Branches of the Bank of Ireland were raided on 1 and 2 May. The total sum taken was over £50,000. *I.T.* 2,3 May.

14 Government forces launched an attack against Republican forces in the Four Courts, Fowler Hall and other Republican strongholds in the city on 28 June. Fourteen people were killed and thirty wounded in the first encounter. *I.I.* 29 June. The Four Courts were entered on Thursday (29) evening. On the 30th the Irregular surrendered unconditionally. About 170 prisoners were taken, including Rory O'Connor and Liam Mellows. The Public Records Office in the Four Courts was totally destroyed with its priceless archives, and bindings. *I.T.* 1 July.

15 Rory O'Connor had occupied the Four Courts and the Four Courts Hotel on Friday 14 April and began to fortify them. *I.T.* 17 April.

16 There was fighting in Limerick at the Railway Station and other parts of the city, and the Republican forces were forced to surrender.

17 The last of the Irregular strongholds in Dublin fell to Government troops on Wednesday 5 July. Half of O'Connell Street was burned. De Valera and Barton escaped. *I.I.* 6 July.

18 The barracks at Gort, Ardrahan, Kilcolgan, Oranmore, Renmore and Eglinton were burned by the Irregulars before they left Co. Galway. *C.T.* 22 July.

19 "Meditations in Time of Civil War", II, "My House", *Collected Poems*, p. 226.

20 George Santayana, *Soliloquies in England*, and *Later Soliloquies* (New York 1922).

21 Countess Markievicz was not wounded.

22 George Sand, *The Countess of Rudolstadt:* being a sequel to *Consuelo* (London n.d.).

23 See 8:14.

24 "Meditations in Time of Civil War", VI, "The Stare's Nest by My Window", *Collected Poems*, pp. 230–31.

25 On Saturday 15 July, as a funeral procession was passing the bridge, escorted by Free State troops, it was ambushed. One boy was shot dead and two others wounded.

26 "Meditations in Time of Civil War", VII, "I See Phantoms of Hatred and of the Heart's Fullness and of the Coming Emptiness", *Collected Poems*, pp. 231–32.
27 William Ernest Henley (1849–1903), poet, critic, and dramatist, and with Yeats a member of the Rhymers' Club.
28 Government troops began entering Limerick and Waterford on Thursday 20 July, and were shelling the barracks. *I.T.* 21 July. On the following day, Government troops forced the Irregulars to retreat South from Limerick, Watford and Castlerea. *I.T.* 22 July.
29 Leslie Edmunds, an Inspector for the Congested Districts Board in the West of Ireland was shot dead during an ambush by Irregular troops on 25 July in Ballybait, a few miles from Galway, while driving to Galway from Dublin. Neither of the two other people in the car was injured. *I.T.* 27 July.
30 Cork had been occupied by the Irregulars for several weeks, but it was virtually cut off from the rest of Ireland. There had been no effort by Government troops to enter the city as they were cleaning up outlying districts. *I.T.* July passim.
31 There were many reports in *The Irish Times* of General C. G. Bruce's Himalayan expedition, and a summary of the rigours of those mountains in the 24 July issue.

BOOK TWENTY
7 August–2 December 1922

1 Charles Edward Lawrence, *Mr. Ambrose* (London 1922).
2 Troops were landed at Youghal, Passage West and Union Hall on 9 August, and the fall of Cork was expected hourly. *I.T.* 10 August.
3 At 10 a.m. on Saturday 12 August, Arthur Griffith suffered a cerebral haemorrhage and died within minutes. He had been ill, but not seriously with an attack of tonsilitis for about a fortnight, and had been in his office regularly. *I.T.*, 14 August. MacArdle, p. 777.
4 Yeats only brought the Civil War into "Meditations in Time of Civil War" in the fifth section "The Road at My Door". He finished the poem in 1923.
5 Irregular troops were captured at Revendale, near Dundalk and thirteen were captured in the Dundalk area over the weekend. *I.T.* 21 August.
6 Griffith was buried in Glasnevin Cemetery after a massive funeral procession from the Pro-Cathedral, on 16 August. All businesses were closed until the conclusion of the ceremonies. *I.T.* 17 August.
7 This poem "Mourn—And Then Onward!" had first been published in *United Ireland* in 1891, and in *The Irish Weekly Independent* in 1893. The *Irish Independent* printed it in full on 18 August.
8 Michael Collins was killed in an ambush near Bandon on 22 August. The lines continued:

No darkness in the hour; no loss of comrades will daunt you at it.
Ireland! the Army serves—strengthened by its sorrow.

9 On the eve of his return to England, Shaw gave an interview to *The Irish Times* on the situation in Ireland (21 August). Lady Gregory quotes from this interview.
10 The original Irish version "Miss Eire" was published in P. H. Pearse's *Scríbinní* (Dublin 1919), p. 211.
10a (W.B.Y.) in Yeats's handwriting.

11 John Morley, *Rousseau*, 2 vols. (London 1873).

12 The postal strike began on 11 September, and there was no postal, telegraph or telephone service in Southern Ireland. *I.T.* 12 September.

13 Wilfrid Scawen Blunt (1840–1922) died on Sunday 10 September at Shipley, near Horsham.

14 Lady Gregory's *Damer's Gold*, a comedy in 2 acts, was revived at the Abbey on 12 September 1922, with Barry Fitzgerald playing the lead, with Nolan, Dolan and Christine Heyden. Holloway July–September 1922, vol. 2. pp. 470–471. It was first performed at the Abbey 21 November 1912.

15 W. T. Cosgrave's opening speech traced the history of the negotiators in London. Regarding peace prospects he said, "This nation will not submit to an armed minority making war upon it. We insist upon the people's rights. We are the custodian of these rights, and we shall not hesitate to protect them." *I.T.* 12 September.

16 Mulcahy (Minister for Defence) stated that the way to peace was through the Constitution; that the Army should be responsible to the National Government, and that the Government should have control of arms. He called army units of the Irregulars "misled". *I.T.* 13 September.

17 *Freedom*, a small mimeographed publication, appeared during August, September and October. The statement mentioned here appeared in the 13 September issue.

18 The conditions on the two prison ships, S.S. *Avonia* and *Lady Wicklow*, were reputedly filthy. Many of the prisoners were on hunger strike. *Freedom*, 9 September.

19 See 7:3.

20 There were numerous ambushes in Cork. One unit of the Republican army was ambushed four times in one day. *I.T.* 18 September.

21 Hilaire Belloc, *The French Revolution* (New York 1911) had originally appeared in England in 1901 under the title *Robespierre*.

22 Lord Granville Leveson-Gower, 1st Earl Granville (1773–1846), *Private Correspondence*, ed. by his daughter-in-law, Castalia, Countess Granville, 2 vols. (London 1917). Lord Granville's principal correspondent was Henrietta, Countess of Bessborough.

23 An obituary of the Rev. George Youngman, who called himself a mystic, appeared in *The Times*, 21 September 1922.

24 The postal strike ended at midnight 28 September. *I.T.* 29 September.

25 Dr. MacCartan gave notice that he proposed a truce by the Dail to last fourteen days, and a delegation appointed by the Government to meet the representatives of the opposition. The proposal was opposed by the Government, Major General McKeon, and members of the Dail, and was not passed. *I.T.* 29 September.

26 On 3 October the Government offered a conditional amnesty to all those in armed opposition to them if they would deliver their arms, ammunition etc. to the National Forces before 15 October. The offer was not accepted. MacArdle, p. 804.

27 James Ritchie, *The Influence of Man on Animal Life in Scotland: A Study in Faunal Evolution* (Cambridge 1920).

28 Lloyd George resigned on Thursday 19 October 1922. He was succeeded by Andrew Bonar Law. *I.T.* 20 October.

29 *The Round Table*, a comic tragedy in 3 acts by Lennox Robinson, was first produced at the Abbey 31 January 1922.

30 At the quarterly meeting of the Dublin City Council, a number of women,

including Maud Gonne MacBride, called attention to the deplorable condition of the prisoners, some 6,000 to 7,000, many in Dublin. There was a great deal of uproar from the deputation until the City Council agreed to investigate conditions. *I.T.* 10 November. Troops had to fire in the air to disperse demonstrators in front of Mountjoy Prison and in Sackville Street. Maud Gonne MacBride, among others, addressed the crowd. *I.T.* 9 November.

31 Irregulars attacked Wellington Barracks with machine guns on 11 November. Three soldiers were killed.

32 Erskine Childers was captured at the home of his cousin Robert Barton (it was also his childhood home—the Bartons looked after the young Childers family), Glendalough House, Annamoe, Co. Wicklow, on 10 November. He was court-martialed on 17 November.

33 Possibly "Blood and the Moon", *Collected Poems* (London 1950), p. 267.

34 Mrs. Gene Stratton-Porter, *Freckles* (New York 1917?). There were several editions of this popular novel, published in London and New York.

35 *The Times* Literary Supplement reviewed *The Image and Other Plays* (London and New York 1922) on 14 November.

36 Four young men were executed for having been found in Dublin streets with revolvers in their possession. They were Peter Cassidy, John Gaffney, James Fisher and Richard Twohig. *I.T.* 18 November. Childers himself thought that the Government had shot them to prepare the public for his own execution, which he knew was to come. Kevin O'Higgins was an implacable enemy, always referring to Childers as "the Englishman".

37 Childers was shot at dawn in Beggar's Bush Barracks on Friday 24 November, while an appeal was yet to be heard. Before he was executed, he shook hands with each member of the firing squad.

38 Charles A'Court Repington, *Vestigia* (London 1919).

39 See 17:10.

40 *Paul Twining*, a comedy in 3 acts by George Shiels, was first produced at the Abbey 3 October 1922.

BOOK TWENTY-ONE

2 December 1922–14 February 1923

1 *Arms and the Man*, an Anti-Romantic Comedy by G. B. Shaw, was first produced at the Abbey 16 October 1916.

2 See 4:3.

3 Jacob Boehme, *Dialogues on the Supersensual Life*, Tr. William Law and others, (New York n.d.), p. 9. Select Sentences no. 24.

4 Erskine Childers's last statement was published in *The Irish Times* 27 November, but this section was not included.

5 On Thursday 7 December two members of the Dail, Brig. Sean Hales and Padraic O'Maille were shot as they came out of the Ormond Hotel. Hales died and O'Maille was severely wounded. On Friday morning four men were executed in reprisal: Rory O'Connor, Liam Mellows, Joseph McKelvey and Richard Barrett. They had been in prison for five months since their surrender in the Four Courts. Some members of the Government, notably Gavan Duffy, bitterly censored this act. *I.T.* 9 December.

6 On 9 December the Irregulars burned the homes of a number of Free State officials, J. Walsh the Postmaster-General, Sean McGarry the Military Governor of the Maryboro Convict Prison, and of Michael

McDunphy, Assistant Secretary to the Government. McGarry's wife and two children were slightly burned.

7 See 15:8.

8 See 3:2. The borrowed phrase was "I felt at times as one raised from the dead, made virginal and pure, who renews exquisite intimacies with the divine companions, with Earth, Water, Air, and Fire."

9 James Douglas (1887–1954), member of the Irish Senate 1922–1936, 1938–1943, 1944–1954.

10 A.E., *The Avatars* (London 1933).

11 Russell's letter appeared in *The Irish Times*, 29 December 1922. He called for an end of hostilities by the Republicans, claiming they could do so without dishonour. He stated that violence only begat violence. Moreover, A.E. wrote, those fighting now had nothing constructive to leave, as had Pearse, Connolly or Childers.

12 See 15:8.

13 The play she was referring to is *The Jester*, not *The Dragon*, which had been produced in 1919. There is only one prince in the latter play, but a number in the former.

14 John Quinn sent a barrel of apples to Lady Gregory every Christmas.

15 The original poem starting "Who would true valour see" is in the second part of *Pilgrim's Progress*, Ch. 11, where it is spoken by Valour.

16 Gogarty wrote that he was taken on the night of 12 January by three gunmen. Later, when he thought he was about to be shot, he escaped by leaping into the River Liffey after he had thrown his coat over the man guarding him. *It Isn't That Time of Year at All* (London 1954), pp. 208–213. *The Irish Times* of 15 January had substantially the same story. See 27:4.

17 William T. Cosgrave's house, Beech Park, Templeogue, Co. Dublin, was destroyed by fire on 14 January. Only the barns and stables survived. *T.* 15 January.

18 Parnell's supporters wore an ivy leaf. See James Joyce, *Portrait of the Artist*, Ch. 1.

19 A.E.'s notice of *Three Wonder Plays* appeared in *The Irish Homestead* on 13 January, pp. 18–20. He noticed the symbolism and wisdom that the three plays contained, and this brought about his comment given in the text.

20 The grave of Lady Gregory's son, Robert.

21 Palmerstown, the home of the Earl of Mayo, who was a Senator, was gutted by fire on the night of 30 January, apparently as a reprisal for the execution of six men at the Curragh. He was given time to remove some valuables before the house was set on fire. *I.T.* 31 January.

22 Sir Horace Plunkett's home, Kilteragh was blown up by a mine on the night of 30 January. Although much of the house was damaged, few of the valuable possessions—pictures and books among them—were touched. *I.T.* 31 January. On 31 January the house and contents were destroyed by fire. *I.T.* 1 February.

23 Senator John Bagwell, who was also Manager of the Great Northern Railway, was kidnapped on 30 January. The Government issued a statement that if the Senator was not released unharmed in 48 hours, punitive action would be taken "against several associates in this conspiracy". *I.T.* 31 January. However the Senator escaped through a window while his guards were at breakfast on the morning of 1 February. *I.T.* 2 February.

24 The ex-I.R.A. men formed an association whose "sole aim is to secure

peace". *I.T.* 4 January 1923.

25 *The Irish Times* of 4 February stated that rumours of peace were reported, mainly from the South, but that no one seemed able to speak for all the anti-Treaty forces.

26 The Limerick prisoners wanted to have four men paroled, to present proposals for peace to the leaders of the Irregulars. While they were on parole, there should be no executions and for their part, the prisoners would try to stop outrages. *I.T.* 9 February.

27 Liam Deasy, the Deputy Chief of Staff of the Irregulars who was under sentence of death, signed a statement calling for the unconditional surrender of all arms and men, and called on other leaders of the Irregulars to do likewise. *I.T.* 9 February.

28 Liam Lynch, officially on behalf of the Republican (i.e. anti-Treaty) Government and Army Command, replied to the Government's offer to co-operate with Deasy's appeal, that it "cannot be considered". *I.T.* 10 February.

BOOK TWENTY-TWO
17 February–2 March 1923

1 Gene Stratton Porter, *The Girl of the Limberlost* (London and New York 1909).

2 Thomas Johnson, leader of the Labour Party in the Dail from 1922 until his defeat in the 1927 election, Secretary of the Irish Labour Party and the Trade Union Congress.

3 Eoin MacNeill (1867–1945) Gaelic scholar, one of the founders of the Gaelic League, Professor of Early History at University College, Dublin, one of the leaders of the Volunteers, had tried to call off the Easter Rising. He was Speaker of Dail Eireann 1921–1922, Minister of Education 1922–1926, author of *Early Irish Laws and Institutions* (Dublin 1935) and many other works. See F. X. Martin's bibliography in *The Scholar Revolutionary* ed. Martin & Byrne (Shannon 1973).

4 *Duanaire Finn, The Book of the Lays of Finn*, Irish text with translation and notes by Eoin MacNeill (London 1908).

5 On 17 February the mail train from Galway to Dublin was wrecked by armed men at Streamstown. The signals were reversed and the passengers taken off; the train was then rammed into a freight train wrecked at the same spot. *N.Y.T.* 18 February.

6 The Gogartys' home, Renvyle House, Connemara, was burned to the ground. *C.T.* 24 February.

7 Armed men destroyed the Sligo station of the Midland and Great Western Railway, using petrol and explosives, on 11 January. Seven locomotives and two passenger trains were wrecked. Damage was put at £80,000. *N.Y.T.* 12 January.

8 Joseph O'Neill (1886–1953), Irish author, became Permanent Secretary to the Dept. of Education in 1923.

9 Kenneth S. Reddin (1895–1967), author and playwright, had been appointed Justice of the District Court in 1922, a remarkable appointment for a man of twenty seven. He remained on the bench for over thirty seven years.

10 A.E., *The Interpreters* (London 1922).

11 The home of Alec MacCabe, representative for Co. Sligo, in Ranelagh,

Dublin, was blown up by six armed men on the night of 18 February. *I.T.* 19 February.

12 *Julius Caesar* was produced at the Abbey 7 November 1922.

13 "Memorial Verses" in *Poetical Works of Matthew Arnold* (London 1913), p. 289.

14 Seven members of the staff of the Income Tax Office were severely burned during a raid by more than twelve armed men, who set it on fire. *I.T.* 22 February.

15 "War in Irish Folklore" was published in the *Manchester Guardian* Commercial Supplement, 10 May 1923.

16 Bessborough House was burned to the ground by armed men on the morning of 24 February. Damage was estimated at £30,000. *T.* 24 February.

BOOK TWENTY-THREE
12 March–19 May 1923

1 Robinson incurred the wrath of Miss A. E. Horniman over his decision to keep the Abbey open on the day King Edward VII died. She immediately stopped her subsidy to the Abbey, an action that involved lengthy negotiations and aggravated tempers on all sides.

2 Liam Lynch was killed when a meeting he was attending with de Valera, Stack and other members of the Irregulars was surprised by Government troops on Crohan West, in the Knockmealdown Mountains. He was critically wounded in the 10 April attack, and died in hospital that night. *I.T.* 11 April.

3 Six men, who had been arrested in February in Co. Galway for having unauthorised guns and ammunition, were executed at Headford on 11 April. *I.T.* 12 April.

4 Maud Gonne MacBride and her daughter Iseult, were apparently arrested on 10 April, for the 16 April issue of *The Irish Times* reported that Mrs. MacBride was in the sixth day of her hunger strike. She was released on Tuesday 24 April.

5 Sean O'Casey's *Shadow of a Gunman* was first produced at the Abbey 12 April 1923. Holloway talked to Lady Gregory after the performance and she told him she thought the play went very well (p. 663). He wrote (p. 659) that Yeats, who sat a few seats away during the play "applauded vigorously the play and author". At the performance on Saturday 12 April, the theatre was so crowded that Lady Gregory and Yeats had to change seats several times, finally ending up in the vestibule on oak benches. Holloway, *Impressions of a Dublin Playgoer*, 1923 Vol. 1.

6 *Mirandolina*, a comedy in 3 acts, translated and adapted from the Italian (*La Locandiera*) of Goldoni by Lady Gregory, was first produced at the Abbey 24 February 1910.

7 Stephens had taken exception to a passage in *Hugh Lane's Life and Achievement* about the National Gallery of Ireland, in which Lady Gregory in referring to Stephens had written "He said Hugh's death was a great misfortune in his life, for these last four years in the National Gallery that have been so irksome would have been a delight, 'No one has ever showed me a picture, he would have showed them to me.' But by ill chance he had never met him at all." *Sir Hugh Lane: His Life and Legacy* (Gerrards Cross, New York 1973) Coole Edition X, 182. As a result Stephens wrote that "with pleasure" he relinquished Lady Gregory's acquaintance.

8 Austin Stack was captured 14 April. A memorandum prepared for the signature of the army officers, authorising and calling on the President (i.e. de Valera) to order an immediate cessation of hostilities was found on him and published the next day in the pro-Treaty party press. MacArdle, p. 845. *I.T.* 16 April.

9 Two men were executed 2 May at Ennis, Co. Clare, for taking part in an armed attack on the National Forces, which resulted in the death of one of the men. *I.T.* 3 May.

10 Monsignor Salvatore Luzio, the Papal envoy to Ireland, had been sent on a peace mission by the Pope, arriving in March. While de Valera and other members of the Republican side appreciated his interest and help, the Free State Government were much less appreciative. He had been Professor of Canon Law at Maynooth 1897–1910.

10a Anne Bowman, *Young Nile Voyagers*, illustrated by J. B. Zwecker (London 1868).

11 These further diaries have not yet been published.

12 On 9 May, Yeats moved a motion in the Senate that the Government press the British Government for the return of the Lane pictures. He reviewed the history of the case and the motion was passed unanimously. Coole Edition X, 248–251.

13 De Valera had ordered the end of all aggression, and made a number of peace proposals, which included the thorny one about the oath of allegiance to the King, on 27 April. Hostilities were to cease from noon on 30 April. *I.T.* 28 April.

14 May, William Morris's second daughter (1862–1938).

15 Sophia E. De Morgan, *Threescore Years and Ten* (London 1895), or perhaps her memoir on her husband Augustus De Morgan (1806–1871), published in 1882.

16 Augustus John's portrait of Madame Suggia (ca. 1923) is in the Tate Gallery, London.

17 Thomas Edward Lawrence (1888–1935), *The Seven Pillars of Wisdom* (London 1935), had been written 1919–1920. The copies referred to here were printed by the staff of the *Oxford Times*. Richard Aldington, *Lawrence of Arabia* (London 1969), p. 317. Lawrence had a post in the Middle East Department of the Colonial Office 1921–1922, when he enlisted in the Royal Air Force as J. H. Ross to escape publicity. In 1923 he changed his name to T. E. Shaw, after he was recognised and discharged, but was later re-instated by Stanley Baldwin. He remained in the R.A.F. until 1935.

BOOKS TWENTY-FOUR AND TWENTY-FIVE
20 May–24 September 1923

1 Lawrence wrote an introduction to the 1926 edition of Doughty's *Travels in Arabia Deserta*. See 7:15.

2 John Drinkwater, *Cromwell* (London 1922). The dedication read "To Bernard Shaw, with homage to the Master Dramatist Of His Age, and with the gratitude that is due from every younger writer for the English theatre."

3 *Saint Joan* was first produced 26 March 1924 at the New Theatre, London, with Sybil Thorndyke as Joan.

4 *Bernard Shaw and Mrs. Patrick Campbell: Their Correspondence*, ed.

Alan Dent (London 1952).

5 Apsley Cherry-Garrard, *The Worst Journey in the World. Antarctic 1910–1913*, (Scott's Last Expedition) 2 vols. (London 1922).

6 Charles C. F. Greville, *The Greville Memoirs*, ed. Henry Reeve, 2 vols. (London 1874), 2 vols. (London 1885), 2 vols. (London 1887). These memoirs cover English history 1837–1860.

7 Yeats spoke against the censorship of films; he believed that one ought to "leave the arts, superior or inferior, to the general conscience of mankind". *Senate Speeches of W. B. Yeats*, ed. D. R. Pearce (London 1961), pp. 51–52.

8 "The Ghost", translated from the Irish of "Cú Chonnacht O Cléirigh" by James Stephens, in *Golden Treasury of Irish Verse*, ed. Lennox Robinson (London 1930). The translation was dedicated to Osborn Bergin.

9 Charles Plummer, *Bethada Náen nErenn, Lives of Irish Saints*, Edited from the Original MSS. with Introduction, Translations, Notes, Glossary and Indexes, 2 vols (Oxford 1922).

10 Alice Stopford Green (1847–1929), Irish writer and historian.

11 Patrick J. Hogan (1891–1936), Minister for Agriculture.

12 The Irish transport workers went on strike in Waterford to combat a proposed reduction in wages by farmers. *I.T.* 16 June. On Saturday 16 June hay was burned on two farms. *I.T.* 19 June.

13 M. Murphy and J. O'Rourke were executed by the Government as bank robbers. *N.Y.T.* 31 May.

14 *Dante Gabriel Rossetti, His Family Letters*, 2 Vols. (London 1895).

15 Curzon's personality and drawbacks for the post of Prime Minister were discussed in *The Nation* 26 May p. 266.

16 De Valera's statement: "It is not the intention of the Republican Government to renew the war in the autumn or after the election. The war . . . is finished." They would refuse to admit that the country is partitioned. "If elected in a majority, our policy would be to govern the country on Sinn Fein lines as in 1919 . . .'. MacArdle, pp. 863–864.

17 On 14 August de Valera announced that he would address a meeting at Ennis the following day. He was arrested on the 15th, almost as soon as he began to speak. Soldiers fired volleys into the air and the people stampeded. De Valera was taken peacefully, but twenty people were injured in the action. *I.T.* 16 August.

18 When de Valera stated that he would be standing for Clare, he had said that if he were elected, he would not stay "on the run". *I.T.* 24 July.

19 "The Phases of the Moon", renamed "The Wheel and the Phases of the Moon" when it appeared in *A Vision*, Privately Printed for Subscribers only by T. Werner Laurie. (London 1925). Later editions were much revised.

20 *Mirandolina* (London 1924). See 23:6. *La Locandiera*, the original Italian name becomes *Mirandolina* in Spanish.

21 Clifford Bax's version, *Mine Hostess* (London 1922).

22 In the election de Valera received over 17,000 votes, more than twice the number got by his opponent. MacArdle, p. 865. The Republicans won 44 seats compared to the Government's 63.

23 See 15:21.

24 Edward Martyn's home Tillyra Castle was very close to Coole. They had been friends for over forty years. See 5:1.

25 President Cosgrave received an enormous welcome on his return from Geneva. Planes greeted his arrival in Kingstown (now Dun Laoghaire)

and crowds lined the streets. He addressed a crowd that filled Sackville Street (now O'Connell Street) from the Metropole Hotel. *I.T.* 15 September.

26 Thomas Teignmouth Shore (1841–1911), a Church of England clergyman, writer on C. of E. liturgies, the Bible and on various aspects of Christian belief.

27 "Leda and the Swan", one of Yeats's finest poems.

28 Ashford Castle is now one of the finest hotels in Ireland.

29 *The Story Brought by Brigit*, a passion play in 3 acts by Lady Gregory was first performed at the Abbey 15 April 1924. Lyle Donaghy played the Christ, and Eileen Crowe the Mother. Holloway found the play impressive, reverently performed and received. O'Casey, who sat next to him at the first performance said in answer to Holloway's query "It was almost too impressive for me". There was a large audience, with Lady Gregory, W. B. Yeats and his wife, Jack B. Yeats, Lennox Robinson, Brinsley MacNamara etc. Holloway, April-June 1924, Vol. 1, p. 669. Most of the Dublin artists and writers attended either the first or second nights.

30 Michael Ireland (pseud. of Darrell Figgis), *Return of the Hero* (London 1923).

BOOK TWENTY-SIX
24 September 1923–21 April 1924

1 Thomas J. Kiernan (1897–1967) was Lady Gregory's friend and adviser until her death, first helping her with her tax problems, and later about the Lane pictures. He was one of the Literary Executors in her Will. His last post was Irish Ambassador to the U.S.A.

2 See 8:29.

3 Gustave Flaubert (1821–1880), *Lettres de Gustave Flaubert à George Sand* (Paris 1884).

4 Lord Byron's *Correspondence*, chiefly with Lady Melbourne, Mr. Hobhouse, the Hon. Douglas Kinnaird and P. B. Shelley, 2 Vols. ed. John Murray (London 1922). The letters to Lady Melbourne are in the first volume.

5 Kathleen Fitzpatrick, *Lady Henry Somerset* (London 1923). The life of Lady Isabella Caroline Somerset (1851–1921).

6 Lennox Robinson's "The Comic Muse" appeared in *The Irish Statesman* 27 October.

7 William Wymark Jacobs, *The Castaways* (London 1916).

8 On 1 November *The Irish Times* reported that the Republicans claimed that 5,219 prisoners were on hunger strike. In its 5 November issue it stated that over 2,500 prisoners had been on hunger strike, and that by the previous day, 670 still were. On 10 November about 400 were still refusing food.

9 See 7:7. His son O. T. G. Esmonde was a member of the Dail at this time.

10 Michael J. Dolan took over as producer at the Abbey in 1924. He produced O'Casey's *Juno and the Paycock* 3 March 1924.

11 Earnán O'Malley was Assistant Chief of Staff in 1922.

12 "The Squandering of National Feeling" in *The Irish Statesman* 27 October. In this article, Russell called for the release of the prisoners—the fighting was over, and the people wanted no more of it.

13 Senator James G. Douglas (1887–1954). There was an unsigned article

in *The Irish Statesman*, under "Notes and Comments" commenting on and supporting the letter written by Lennox Robinson and Lady Gregory and also signed by Stephens. This was undoubtedly the article A.E. referred to on p. 323. No article by Senator Douglas seems to have appeared in *The Irish Statesman* on 17 November.

14 Miss Mary MacSwiney's letter stated that the men would not stop the hunger strike if ordered to, and added that any civilised country in the world would release them because of the horrible conditions of the prisons. *I.T.* 13 November.

15 Lennox Robinson's *The Round Table*, a comic tragedy in 3 acts was first produced at the Abbey 31 January 1922.

16 *Apartments*, a comedy in 1 act by Fand O'Grady was first produced at the Abbey 3 September 1923.

17 There was a paragraph in "Notes and Comments" commenting that desperadoes on both sides should be kept in gàol. ". . . there should be no release for men capable of organising political assassination." *I.S.* 17 November.

18 Benjamin Disraeli, 1st Earl of Beaconsfield (1804–1881), *Vivian Grey*. There were many editions of the popular work between 1826 and 1919.

19 Yeats received the Nobel Prize for Literature on 14 November 1923.

20 In the 21 November issue of *The Irish Statesman*, A.E. had a long article in support of Lady Gregory, Robinson and Stephens's letter, pp. 291–292.

21 Denis Barry died in the Curragh Military Hospital on 20 November after thirty four days on hunger strike. *I.T.* 21 November.

22 Yeats made this statement in a lecture "The Irish Dramatic Movement" at the Ritz Cafe, Grafton Street, Dublin, on 16 November. He was applauded when he referred to finding the early actors. *I.T.* 17 November.

23 Frederick William Sanderson (1857–1922). "Great Teacher—Pioneer" in the *New Republic*. H. G. Wells had a number of short articles on Sanderson in it, the last on 21 November.

24 An article in the *T.L.S.* of 22 November on Charles Salomon's French translation of Chekov's re-working of the story of the life of a country woman who lived a mile from his estate, *La Vie* (Paris 1923).

25 Lionel Johnson (1867–1902), *Reviews and Critical Papers* (London 1921).

26 William Frederick Bailey, *Slaves of the War Zone* (London 1916).

27 Mayne Reid (1818–1883), *Ocean Waifs* (London 1900).

28 Anne Bowman, *The Boy Voyagers or Pirates of the East* (London 1875).

29 *'Twixt the Giltinans and the Carmodys*, a play in 1 act by George Fitzmaurice was first produced at the Abbey 8 March 1923.

30 Holloway noted that Sara Allgood did not know all the words at the first performance. She spoke the poem wearing a black dress against a simple curtain. Yeats and Lady Gregory were there on 2 January.

31 "Drama Notes", *I.S.* 19 January 1924, p. 592.

32 "Three Plays of Lunacharski", *I.S.*, 19 January, p. 596.

33 W. B. Yeats, *Plays and Controversies* (London 1923).

34 The Tate Gallery accepted a £50,000 gift from Samuel Courtauld for the purchase of 19th Century French paintings. On 8 February 1924 the Trustees announced that the Trust was in operation and six paintings had been acquired. *T.* 8 February.

35 "Connaught and the Poets" in *Connacht Tribune*, Tourist Supplement, March 1924.

36 Mariya Bashkirtseva, *Journal de Marie Bashkirtseff*, 2 vols (Paris 1887). Lady Gregory mentions that she is reading the 19th edition (1914).
37 "In Memory of Major Robert Gregory". The lines come from St.XI.
38 Halloran, the bank guard, was shot during a robbery at the National Bank in Baltinglass. He died in the Curragh Military Hospital 29 January. *T.* 29,30 January.
39 Probably T. C. Murray's *Autumn Fire*, first produced at the Abbey 8 September 1924.
40 See 19:6.
41 Sean O'Casey's *Juno and the Paycock* was first produced at the Abbey 3 March 1924. The play was a tremendous success, with cries of "author, author . . . filling the air". Holloway p. 388. Of the second performance, he wrote that the theatre was filled "to bulging out point" (p. 398), and reports a comment O'Casey made to him—he was upbraided by a gentleman who told him "that a Theosophite (sic) wouldn't seduce a girl" (p. 400). At subsequent performances, crowds were turned away. Lady Gregory told Holloway that she was astonished at the house. (p. 413).
42 There were mutinies at Templemore and Gormanstown Barracks. Major General Tobin and Col. Dalton were charged with mutiny. Twenty five men of the 36th Infantry Battallion were missing. *I.T.* 10 March. On 10 March, General Eoin O'Duffy was appointed General Officer Commanding the Defence Forces of Saorstat Eireann. *I.T.* 11 March.
43 See 24–25:29. Holloway wrote of Donaghy's performance that he was "meek-mannered, gentle-voiced and sedate".
44 See 24 & 25:30.
45 Yeats wrote in the new version, "and of another's laborious, solitary age . . .". *The Bounty of Sweden* (Cuala Press, Dublin 1925).
46 Forty five army officers resigned; they were mainly stationed in Dublin, but included the second in command in Co. Cork. *I.T.* 12 March. No other serious mutiny seems to have occurred.
47 John Henry Mussen Campbell, 1st Baron Glenavy (1851–1931), Irish lawyer and politician, Lord Chancellor of Ireland 1918–1921, Vice-Chancellor of Dublin University 1919–1931, Cathaoirleach (Chairman) of the Irish Senate 1922–1928. Yeats described him as "handsome, watchful, vigorous, dominating, courteous, he seemed like some figure from an historical painting."
48 Joseph Devlin (1871–1934), Irish politician, leader of the Ulster Catholics, and member of the N. Irish Parliament in Stormont 1921–1933. He was a founder of the Ancient Order of the Hibernians, and was its President until his death.
49 Lewis Hind had a letter in the *Irish Independent* 12 March. Lady Gregory's reply the following day stated that Lane wanted the pictures to go to Dublin.
50 Arabella Waithman, Lady Gregory's sister.
51 Charles Richet, *Traite de Metapsychique* (Paris 1922) trans. Stanley de Barth as *Thirty Years of Psychical Research* (London 1923). The reference is to Ch. VII "Premonitions".
52 Louis Hemon, *Colin-Maillard* (Paris 1924).
53 George Shiels (1886–1949), Ulster dramatist. His first play *Bedmates* was performed at the Abbey in 1921, and he continued to write for the Abbey until 1941. His *The Rugged Path* (1940) had the longest run of any play at the Abbey.
54 See 15:21.

55 John Lyle Donaghy, author of several books of poetry, two of which were privately printed by the Cuala Press, *At Dawn above Aherlow* (1926) and *Into the Light, and other poems* (1934), played the Christ. For some reason Lennox Robinson in his *Ireland's Abbey Theatre, A History 1899–1951* (London 1951) left out both his and Eileen Crowe's names from the cast list. See 24 & 25:29.

56 See 26:18.

57 Thomas McGreevy (1893–1967), Irish poet, author, translator from the French, Director of the National Gallery of Ireland 1950–1967. His name had been put up by Yeats in 1927 at the time that Thomas Bodkin had been appointed.

58 Robert Briscoe (1894–1969) the first Mayor of Dublin who was of the Jewish faith, a member of the I.R.A. 1913–1924, and of Dail Eireann 1927–1965.

59 Liam O'Flaherty (b. 1896), Irish novelist and short story writer.

60 John Gordon Swift MacNeill (1849–1926); M.P. for S. Donegal 1887–1918, Dean of the Faculty of Law at the National University of Ireland from 1912, King's Counsel, politician and author of books exposing Britain's self-interests with regard to Ireland in the laws it passed, etc.

61 When the Irish Senate was formed, some members, such as Yeats, were co-opted to it. Douglas Hyde was at first passed over, though he was elected in 1925. He was not re-elected. He was a co-opted member again in 1937, and was the agreed candidate for 1st President of Ireland a few months later.

BOOK TWENTY-SEVEN
24 April–5 July 1924

1 The Boundary difficulty. An attempt to solve the problem was made in London 2 February, when Cosgrave, Craig and Ramsay MacDonald met in a friendly discussion, but after a single sitting the Conference adjourned. It was resumed 24 April, but in a few hours it was apparent that there was no possibility of a settlement by consent. When a Commission was organised to settle the question, N. Ireland refused to send a representative, and England then ruled that no Commission could be set up without a representative from the North being present. *Annual Register* p. 145.

2 In *The Irish Statesman*'s notice of *The Story Brought by Brigit*, (26 April) p. 207, Y.O. (A.E.) wrote that Lady Gregory had so realised her characters that the play made the tragedy "intensely real".

3 *Sinn Fein*, in its issue of 26 April, carried an unsigned account of Liam Mellows while he was on the run in the West of Ireland.

4 Gogarty had vowed to offer two swans to "good father Liffey" if he reached safety after eluding his captors by jumping into the river. *It Isn't That Time of Year at All* (London 1924) pp. 212–213. See 21:16.

5 Leo Nikolaevich Tolstoi, *Anna Karenina*. Lady Gregory could have had any one of a number of editions.

6 Undoubtedly an early draft of Pound's *Cantos*. Pound brought out *A Draft of XVI Cantos* (Paris 1925).

7 The 7 May issue of *The Irish Times* had an article on the Boundary Question in which it called upon both North and South to co-operate, lest the Commission issue a report that would start fighting between them, and bring the British Army back into Ireland. It urged that both sides drop the

urgency of their claim and work for the economic betterment of both Irelands.

8 L. N. Tolstoi, *Resurrection* (Paris 1900).

9 See 26:18.

10 On Tuesday 14 May, sheep, cattle and horses were driven off grazing lands at Roxborough. A large number of arrests were made. *C.T.* 17 May.

11 Lady Gregory's article "Hugh Lane's Desire" appeared in *The Irish Statesman* 31 May. Russell's comments appeared in "Notes and Comments".

12 W. B. Yeats, *Essays* (London 1924). The passage appears on p. 167 in "Blake and the Imagination". The note on Robert Gregory is at the end of "Ireland and the Arts", p. 257.

13 The Most Rev. John Dignan (?–1953) Bishop of Clonfert 1924–1953.

14 Yeats originally spoke on Irish Manuscripts on 19 April 1923. He introduced a report, written by him and Mrs. Green, urging the Government to set up a programme "for the editing, indexing and publishing of manuscripts in the Irish language now lying in the Royal Irish Academy, Trinity College and elsewhere . . ." (p. 68). That a dictionary of older Irish be compiled. To that end "not less than £5,000 per annum should be devoted to Irish Research" (p. 74). W. B. Yeats, *The Senate Speeches,* ed. D. R. Pearce (London 1961).

15 See 4:3.

16 The play does not appear to have been completed.

17 Bloody Sunday 1920. "On the morning of Sunday November 21st, by a plan concerted with the Dublin Brigade, I.R.A., members of Collins's Counter-Intelligence Service entered the houses occupied by fourteen of these [British Government] agents and shot them dead." General Crozier gave the day its name. MacArdle p. 398. Belfast remembers a 1921 Bloody Sunday—July 10, when the Protestant Covenanters attacked the Catholics in that city with terrible ferocity. See MacArdle, p. 478.

18 Thomas Hardy, *The Dynasts,* 3 vols. (1903, 1906, 1908, as a whole, 1910).

19 James Larkin (1876–1947), Irish labour leader, headed the unions in the great strike of 1913. See 15:32, 29:23.

19a *The Farmer's Wife*, a comedy in 3 acts by Eden Phillpotts, had its 100th performance at the Court Theatre on 6 June 1924.

20 *St. Joan,* with Sybil Thorndyke and Raymond Massey opened at the New Theatre, London, 26 March.

21 Thomas B. Harbottle, a compiler of books of quotations and historical allusions.

22 Henry Woodd Nevinson, *Farewell to America* (New York 1922).

23 Edmund Clerihew Bentley, *Trent's Last Case* (London 1913).

24 On 4 June Yeats asked whether the Museum buildings were properly protected against fire, and on 2 July he spoke against printing signs in Gaelic. *Senate Speeches*, pp. 67–68, 79–80.

25 *Tomorrow*, Vol. 1, No. 1. Robinson's story "The Madonna of Slieve Dun", a short story about the rape of a young girl and her belief that she had been chosen to become the mother of the new Christ, by the Virgin Mary.

BOOK TWENTY-EIGHT
6 July—23 October 1924

1 *The Connacht Tribune*'s 12 July issue reported that Major William A.

Persse received damages of £14,000 for the malicious burning of Roxborough and £2,400 for the looting of furniture. Major Persse's agent Mr. MacKenzie was ambushed and kidnapped on his way to court.

2 James Anthony Froude, *Caesar* (London 1886).

3 Harold Speakman, *Here's Ireland* (London [1926]).

4 The Editor of *Tomorrow* wrote to *The Irish Statesman* on 5 July that the appearance of the paper had been delayed because the printers refused to print Robinson's story. The letter was signed "The Editor" but the index identifies it as Robinson's. The letter actually signed by Robinson appeared on 12 July.

5 Yeats's "Leda and the Swan" appeared on p. 1.

6 W. B. Yeats, *The Cat and the Moon and Certain Poems* (Cuala Press 1924).

7 Yeats proposed that Sir Edwin Lutyens should be asked for his opinion as to whether the museums were sufficiently provided for against fire. Motion was put and agreed to. *Senate Speeches* pp. 85–86.

8 See 27:20.

9 A. W. West's letter appeared in *The Irish Times* 17 July. He said that Lane told him on 3 April 1915 that he had definitely and unequivocally decided to give the pictures to Dublin.

10 Senator Samuel Lombard Brown (d. 1939). Irish lawyer and politician, was a Senator 1923–1925, 1926–1936.

11 Yeats's article "Compulsory Gaelic: a Dialogue" appeared in *The Irish Statesman* 2 August. It was between three characters, Peter (a Senator) Paul (a Deputy) and Timothy (an elderly student).

12 *The Irish Times* of 17 July reported that de Valera, Austin Stack and others had been released the preceding evening from Arbour Hill Detention House.

13 Quinn had been a friend of Lady Gregory's for nearly a quarter of a century. He was an early friend of the Abbey, contributing money, arranging registration of copyrights of plays by producing limited editions, and later arranging tours for the players, as he had earlier done for Yeats and Hyde. See 1:15.

14 Mrs. Gardner died 18 July 1924. Lady Gregory had stayed at her palatial Boston home, Fenway Court, during the Abbey Players' visits to Boston.

15 The Municipal Works strike in Dublin began at 11.00 on 1 August and all electricity was cut off. *T*. 2 August.

16 André Maurois, *Ariel* (Paris 1923), and *Ariel, the Life of Shelley* (London, New York 1924).

17 Sir Rabindranath Tagore, *The Home and the World* (New York 1919).

18 Leo Nikolaevich Tolstoi, *First Distiller,* in *Plays,* trans. Louise and Aylmer Maude (London 1914).

19 Frank Gallagher in his "The Volunteer Spirit" in *Sinn Fein,* (2 August) called for a return to the moral and spiritual values exhibited by the Volunteers of 1917.

20 Tolstoi's *The Living Corpse,* a drama in 6 acts and 12 tableaux, trans. Mrs. E. M. Ewart (New York 1919).

21 Harold Speakman, *Hilltops in Gallilee* (New York 1923).

22 De Valera's Ennis meeting took place on 15 August. He spoke about the need for an independent Irish Republic. After that was achieved, the Irish could choose their own form of government. *I.T.* 16 August.

23 The Tailteann Games, held during Horse Show Week, drew huge crowds

to Dublin. The attendance at the Show was 59,966, the largest in twenty five years. *C.T.* 16 August.

24 Rabindranath Tagore, *Letters from Abroad* (Madras 1924) was reviewed in the 23 August issue of *The Irish Statesman* under the title "Wisdom of the East", pp. 758–759.

25 Fiodor Sologub (pseud. of Fiodor Kuzmich), possibly *Sweet-scented Name* and other fairy stories (New York 1915).

26 "The Grand Inquisitor of Russia" in the *T.L.S.* of 21 August reviewed *K.P. Pobedonostsev and His Correspondents*, 2 vols (Moscow 1924), on p. 507.

27 The notes appeared in a letter to the Editor entitled "Lobster Fisheries on the West Coast" by W. R. Scovell. *I.S.* 13 September, p. 15.

28 Arnold Bennett, *The Great Adventure*, a play of fancy in 4 acts (London 1913).

29 Upton Beal Sinclair, *Singing Jailbirds*, a drama in 4 acts (The author, Long Beach, Calif. [1924]).

30 *Paul Twyning*, a comedy in 3 acts by George Shiels, was first produced at the Abbey 3 October 1922. Barry Fitzgerald played the title role, and Michael J. Dolan, his son.

31 Harvey C. Phibbs, Irish writer.

32 James Sullivan Starkey (1879–1958), who wrote under the pen name Seumas O'Sullivan.

33 Dan Breen, *My Fight for Irish Freedom* (Dublin 1924).

34 Probably Eimar Ultan O'Duffy (b. 1893), playwright and novelist, who had been sent by MacNeill to Belfast in 1916 to prevent the Volunteers from rising there.

35 *The Suburban Grove*, a comedy in 3 acts by W. F. Casey was first produced at the Abbey 1 October 1908.

36 *Insurance Money*, a comedy in 3 acts by George Shiels, was first produced at the Abbey 13 December 1921.

37 Probably *The Kingdom of God*, a play in 3 acts by G. Martinez Sierra, trans. Helen and Harley Granville Barker, that was first produced at the Abbey 29 September 1924.

38 The Corporation's resolution on 25 September, at a special meeting of the commissioners . . . of Dublin promised to provide a gallery or if that is not practicable, to house them in the National Gallery. J. G. Reynold ed. for Dublin Corporation—*Statement of Claim* (Dublin 1932) p. 38.

39 *Nannie's Night Out*, a comedy in 1 act by Sean O'Casey, was first produced at the Abbey 29 September 1924.

40 "The Promethean Challenge to Religion" by William Pepperell Montague in 6 August 1924 issue of *The New Republic*, pp. 289–295.

41 A meeting of the Board of Governors and Guardians of the National Gallery on 1 October confirmed the offer to house the Lane Pictures. Reynolds ed., *Statement of Claim*, p. 38.

42 See 24 & 25:19.

43 Yeats's "A Cradle Song" contained in line 10 "my pigeon, my own;" evidently added by Lady Gregory and eliminated in the revised version. *The Variorum Edition of the Poems of W. B. Yeats*, ed. Allt and Alspach (New York, London 1957), p. 118.

44 Joseph Conrad, *The Arrow of Gold* (London 1919).

45 Feodor M. Dostoevsky, *The Insulted and Injured*, trans. Constance Garnett (New York 1923).

46 Lady Gregory, *Dave* in *Three Last Plays* (London, New York 1928).

47 John Viscount Morley, *Critical Essays* (London 1923), p. 173.
48 "Colour" by Margaret Barrington in *Tomorrow*, No. 1, August 1924. Mrs. C. is the wife of Dr. Edmund Curtis (1881–1943), Professor of Modern History at Dublin University.
49 See 26:57.
50 Holloway noted in his diary that Mrs. Curtis has gone off with Liam O'Flaherty.
51 Aodh de Blacam (1891–1951), Irish author and political writer.
52 *The Plough and the Stars*, a tragedy in 4 acts by Sean O'Casey was first produced at the Abbey 8 February 1926. Holloway wrote that the queue for the opening night extended past Old Abbey Street, and not a quarter of the people got in (p. 281). Gogarty, when he was asked if he liked the play, replied that he did: "It will give the smug-minded something to think about." (p. 292). Objections to the play began to be evident on Tuesday 9 February. About the third night "a sort of moaning sound was to be heard tonight from pit during the Rosie Redmond episodes and when the Volunteers brought in flag to pub" (p. 295). Thursday 11th (p. 297) "... a great protest was made tonight and ended in almost all the second act being played in dumb show and pandemonium afterwards. People spoke (pp. 297–298) from all parts of the house and W. B. Yeats moved out from the stalls ... he tried to get a hearing from the stage but not a word he spoke could be heard." Holloway wrote (p. 299) that a protest was organised by some of the women, Mrs. Sheehy Skeffington, Mrs. Tom Clarke and others ... "to vindicate the womanhood of 1916" and said that some of the players got very rough "to some ladies who got on the stage, and threw two of them into the stalls, one young man thrown from the stage got his side hurt by the piano. The chairs of the orchestra were thrown on the stage ... and some four or five tried to pull down half of drop curtain and another caught hold of one side of the railing (p. 300). Then a man came on and begged the audience to give the actors a hearing, and they did and Mac [F. J. McCormick] said he wished the actors should be treated distinct from the play etc. and his speech met with applause. The play proceeded in fits and starts, with the whole house in a state of excitement. Mrs. Sheehy Skeffington was holding forth during the din in the back of the balcony. The play was summed up by one in the audience as "patriots, prostitutes, poets and poltroons". Holloway continued (p. 302) that the Soldiers' Song was sung during Act II, and that detectives were all over the Abbey after the Thursday row, and police outside.
53 Frank Hugh O'Donnell, Irish dramatist, whose plays *Anti-Christ* and *The Drifters* were performed by the Abbey.

BOOK TWENTY-NINE
23 October 1924–24 February 1925

1 Yeats spoke on the Boundary Question on 17 October, supporting the motion that it would be best served "by an agreed solution of outstanding problems affecting the Irish Free State and Northern Ireland". *Senate Speeches*, p. 86.
2 Sir George Otto Trevelyan (1838–1928), *The American Revolution*, 4 vols. (London 1909). Lady Gregory misquotes the title. It is difficult to

identify which life she means, but it might be Frederick Scott Oliver, *Alexander Hamilton* (New York 1921), which was popular at the time, or Gertrude Atherton, *The Conqueror* (New York 1902), which she much liked.

3 George Macaulay Trevelyan (1876–1962), *Garibaldi and the Making of Italy* (London 1914).

4 The letter was about *The Story Brought by Brigit*, dated 21 October 1924. In it Donaghy discussed his acting and writing. He enclosed three poems, "The Grave at Ballylane Fort", "Skeagh" and "They Made Red Tea at Night". He also discussed progress on his *Deirdre* in a letter to Lady Gregory dated 23 December.

5 De Valera was arrested at Newry, Co. Down, detained over-night and escorted over the Border to the Free State the following day. He entered Ulster again and was again arrested and spent a month in prison in Belfast. MacArdle, p. 878.

6 James Ramsay MacDonald, *Socialism: Critical and Constructive* (London 1924).

7 Alice MacGowan and P. Newberry, *The Million Dollar Suit Case* (New York 1922).

8 Harold Speakman, *This Above All* (Indianapolis [1924]).

9 This was a dedicatory poem, starting "There was a green branch hung with many a bell" at the beginning of *Representative Irish Tales* (New York and London [1891]), compiled, with an introduction and notes by W. B. Yeats', Wade 215.

10 "The Cradle Song" did not appear in *Tomorrow* as it discontinued publication after the second issue.

11 Mrs. Coppinger was a character in Lady Gregory's play *The Image*, which Sara Allgood created in the original production. The old midwife was originally played by Maire O'Neill.

12 James Ramsay MacDonald was defeated in the October 1924 election and resigned on 4 November.

13 "Some Modern Plays" in *T.L.S.*, 6 November.

14 "The Crucifixion of the Outcast" first appeared in the *National Observer*, then in *The Secret Rose*.

15 "The Sorrow of Love" was tightened and intensified by Yeats for his new *Collected Poems*, see *Variorum Poems* pp. 119–20.

16 In the version of "Cuchulain's Fight with the Sea" which appeared in the 1895 edition of his poems, Yeats had Cuchulain die fighting the waves, but in the later editions, he is left fighting.

17 "The Poetry of Herbert Trench", *T.L.S.*, 13 November 1924. All the subsequent poets mentioned by Yeats were mentioned in the review, which is generally unfavourable to Trench's poetry.

18 Vladislav Reymont received the Nobel Prize for Literature for his epic novels *Peasants*, 4 vols. (1904–1909), divided into *Autumn*, *Winter*, *Spring* and *Summer*.

19 Ethel May Dell, popular novelist. She published twenty one novels and collections of short stories between 1915 and 1924.

20 *The Retrievers*, a comedy in 3 acts by George Shiels, was first produced at the Abbey 12 May 1924.

21 "Leaves from a Prison Diary—A Prison Stage" in *Sinn Fein* (22 November), p. 2. The play was accompanied by a concert and step-dancing.

22 Michael McInerney, one of the two main characters in the play.

23 The Irish Transport and General Workers' Union was resisting an

attempt by Larkin to re-assert his leadership in the Irish union movement after his return from the U.S.A. where he had been imprisoned for some years. See 15:32. Initially, he was attempting to organise the dock workers into a new union, the Workers' Union of Ireland. *I.T.* 26 November.

24 Twenty five N.C.O.s and sixteen men were dismissed from the Army in connection with the mutiny in March, and two majors were to show cause why their commissions should not be revoked. *I.T.* 30 December.

25 Sean O'Casey's "The Grand Oul' Dame Britannia' Appeared in Lady Gregory's *Kiltartan History Book* (London 1926), pp. 142–3. It is not ascribed to O'Casey in the book.

26 Holloway observed that Lady Gregory sat in the second row of the stalls with Donaghy; so did O'Casey. Brinsley MacNamara thought the play moved more rapidly than formerly, and said that he had always liked the play. Nov–Dec 1924, Vol. 2, p. 1068. Holloway thought that Sara Allgood got a good deal of pathos out of her new role. When she let the kitten out of her arms it took off towards the audience, but she re-captured it and took it off the stage (p. 1069). Lady Gregory had a chat with Larchet before Act III and expressed her pleasure at his recovery (p. 1070).

27 See 15:45.

28 The November issue of *The Irish Rosary* (pp. 372–374) attacked the Abbey, *Tomorrow* and all Protestant writers as pagan and their writing as "utterly unworthy of a Catholic nation".

29 George Henry Cadogan, 5th Earl (1840–1915), was Lord Lieutenant of Ireland 1895–1902.

30 Jerome K. Jerome's *The Passing of the Third Floor Back* was performed at the Abbey by the Fr. Matthew Hall Company on 1 December.

31 Jacques was a Dublin reviewer who was an early critic of the Abbey.

32 Sir William Barrett, in a long letter to *The Times* (20 December) wrote of his experiences with telepathy in all parts of the world from 1876 to 1924. He was convinced beyond a doubt that telepathy was a rare but natural phenomenon.

33 "Donne, the Divine", in *T.L.S.*, (25 December), pp. 877–878.

34 *The Would-be Gentleman,* an entertainment in 2 acts by Molière, translated and adapted by Lady Gregory, was first produced at the Abbey 4 January 1926.

35 *Anti-Christ,* a commentary in 5 scenes by Frank Hugh O'Donnell, was first produced at the Abbey 17 March 1925.

36 Emile Zola, *La Débacle* (Paris 1892).

37 The Sutra or Sutta Pitaka, containing the sermons or teachings of Buddha, were separated into five Nikayas. The Anguttara Nikaya contains 2,308 Suttas (from Skt. Sutra, a thread) divided into eleven groups of Nipatas. C. Humphreys, *Buddhism* (Harmondsworth, Middx. 1951), pp. 234–235. The edition that Lady Gregory most likely used was that translated by Faunsböll (Oxford 1881).

38 A.E., "Exiles" from *Voices of the Stones* (London 1925), p. 2.

39 Walt Whitman, "Crossing Brooklyn Ferry"; the lines occur at the end of stanza VI.

40 The eclipse of the sun on 24 January aroused a great deal of interest, both in America and Europe. *N.Y.T.* 24,25 January 1925.

41 James Fennimore Cooper, *The Last of the Mohicans*. Lady Gregory might have had one of many editions.

42 *Cathleen Listens In,* a phantasy by Sean O'Casey, was first produced at

the Abbey on 24 February 1925.

43 *The Old Man*, a play in 2 acts by Dorothy MacArdle, was first produced at the Abbey on 24 February. *The Young Man From Rathmines*, a play in 1 act by M. M. Brennan, was first produced at the Abbey on 6 April 1922.

44 Gertrude Atherton (1857–1948), *The Conqueror*, being the . . . story of Alexander Hamilton (New York 1902).

45 D. W. Griffith's film *America* with Lionel Barrymore and Carol Dempster. *Sinn Fein* urged its readers to see it. Maud Gonne MacBride in her article "America . . . in England" the 6 December issue, wrote "no republican can look unmoved as the story unwinds itself", and in his January 31 article "America" Frank Gallagher wrote "May every rebel in Dublin see *America*."

46 Charles Kingsley, *Alton Locke*, tailor and poet, an autobiography (London 1882). There were many editions of this popular novel.

47 Norreys Connell, *An Imaginary Conversation*, a play in 1 act, was first produced at the Abbey 13 May 1909.

48 Sean O'Casey, *Two Plays*, containing *Juno and the Paycock* and *Shadow of a Gunman* (London 1925).

49 The Treasonable Offences Act provided the death sentence or deportation for a wide variety of acts. It was designed to suppress the Republican Movement In Ireland, and was passed on 13 April. MacArdle, p. 882.

50 Aristophanes, *The Frogs*, translated into English rhyming verse by Gilbert Murray. The verse quoted by Lady Gregory occurs in the Chorus at the end of the play, beginning "O blessed are they who possess . . .".

51 New Irish Theatre in London was a company formed by Sara Allgood, Arthur Sinclair and Maire O'Neill to produce Irish plays in England.

52 Euripides, *The Bacchae*, translated into English by Gilbert Murray (London 1904) and his *Hippolytus*, translated into English rhyming verse by Gilbert Murray (London 1904).

INDEX

In order to reduce this index to a manageable length, very minor characters (agricultural labourers at Coole, etc.) have been omitted.

Where two footnotes with the same number appear on one page, the relevant Book numbers are also quoted e.g. 19:6.

Relationships to Lady Gregory are given in brackets after the name.